FIFTEENTH EDITION

Consumer Economics

THE CONSUMER IN OUR SOCIETY

Mel J. Zelenak
UNIVERSITY OF MISSOURI–COLUMBIA

Wendy Reiboldt
CALIFORNIA STATE UNIVERSITY–LONG BEACH

Holcomb Hathaway, Publishers
Scottsdale, Arizona

Library of Congress Cataloging-in-Publication Data

Zelenak, Mel J.
Consumer economics : the consumer in our society / Mel J. Zelenak, Wendy Reiboldt. — 15th ed.
p. cm.
ISBN 978-1-890871-94-9
1. Consumption (Economics) 2. Consumers—United States. 3. Consumer education. 4. Consumer protection—United States. 5. Consumer behavior—United States. I. Reiboldt, Wendy. II. Title.
HB801.Z45 2010
381.30973—dc22

2009025582

Dedication

This text is lovingly dedicated:

To Bonnie McKnight Zelenak, Melchior Charles ("Bubby"), Lindsay ("Pumpkin") Kaitlin Zelenak, and our new family member Rachael Elizabeth Zelenak;

To Massimo Costanza, Reno Costanza and Ambra Costanza, Gail Benton, Jim Benton, Norman Reiboldt, Mary Reiboldt, and Mildred Manring;

And to the memory of Menyhert Zelenak, Helen Moldovan Zelenak, Ruth Greenwood McKnight, and Charles Anthony McKnight.

Holcomb Hathaway, Publishers, Inc.
8700 E. Via de Ventura Blvd., Suite 265
Scottsdale, Arizona 85258
(480) 991-7881
www.hh-pub.com

10 9 8 7 6 5 4 3

ISBN 978-1-890871-94-9

Printed in the United States of America.

Contents

17 CONSUMER LAW 292

STATE AND LOCAL GOVERNMENT EFFORTS TO ASSIST CONSUMERS 304

FEDERAL GOVERNMENT EFFORTS TO ASSIST CONSUMERS 314

Preface

This is a challenging time to publish a book such as this one. As we updated the book, things continued to change, and eventually it was time to stop writing and print the book. As we explain to student readers in Chapter 1, "We cannot see into the future to anticipate long-term (or even short-term) effects [of current challenges]; we cannot predict how economic ups and downs will impact some of the matters we discuss here. Our discussions will presume a stable but ever-changing economic foundation much like the one we've experienced in the past decades. Given the constant ebb and flow of free economies over time, it is our hope that the coming months and years bring resolution to problems and help to strengthen rather than weaken our economy."

Consumerism always will be an integral part of our economy. A healthy adversarial relationship between the buyer and the seller in an economy creates the need for consumerism, consumer economics, and consumer education, whose major purpose is to place the consumer on an equitable basis with the producer and seller. This book shows how the marketplace operates to serve the consumer and how it functions at times to disserve and even defraud the consumer. After finishing the book, readers should have a better understanding of themselves and others as consumers.

Consumer Economics: The Consumer in Our Society, Fifteenth Edition, is not only an introductory text on consumer economics but also a reference book for consumers. Its focus is on how the consumer functions in the marketplace, and it identifies the social, economic, and political forces that shape consumer demands. The book examines how an individual may become a better educated, "mature" consumer citizen—it helps consumers make decisions based on current knowledge within the social setting. Readers studying consumer economics will find myriad applications for their newfound knowledge as they face daily and long-term choices that impact their lives, families, and communities.

The text is written for those who believe that consumer economics is much broader than just personal finance, and that it should be much more than just a "how-to-buy" course. If consumers are to really understand the subject, they need a brief background of our economic system and an understanding of factors influencing their buying decisions. Consumers need to be aware of the pressures of customs, trends, and peer groups and the influence of advertising.

PEDAGOGICAL FEATURES

Consumer Economics: The Consumer in Our Society offers a number of significant features. These include, but are not limited to, the following:

- The text is unique in its emphasis on patterns of consumer behavior—the tugs and pulls that consumers feel, how they respond to external and internal pressures, and how advertisers influence consumer decisions.
- An important chapter, "Consumer Law" (Chapter 17), provides a thorough, understandable introduction to basic legal concerns for consumers. Topics such as contracts, small-claims court, and warranties are included.
- An entire chapter (Chapter 5) is devoted to the topic of fraud, with many examples of how sellers may take advantage of consumers. It also offers advice to consumers on how to protect themselves against fraud.
- Local, state, and federal consumer protection efforts and the agencies that enforce consumer laws are covered in Chapters 18 and 19.
- The feature "There Oughta Be a Law . . ." (near the end of each chapter) allows instructors to discuss important consumer laws with each chapter.
- Each chapter begins with a list of key terms. These are defined in the text margins when first used, and are also included in the book-end Glossary for easy reference.
- Each chapter includes key concepts with accompanying instructional objectives. These allow the students and instructor to determine if the essence of the material is being understood.
- The feature Q & A offers brief capsules of information on a variety of topics. These true/false items are designed to give students a reading break while helping them save time, money, and gain exposure to other resources.
- Each chapter includes case studies and related questions highlighting relevant topics.

- The FYI and TIP features present important statistics and nuggets of information related to micro and macro consumer topics.
- Website addresses and information are provided in the margin for more than 200 of the most important consumer sites, allowing students to explore a variety of sites as they seek consumer information, services, and bargains. A comprehensive list of these sites is also included in Chapter 15.
- Each chapter concludes with a Summary, Items for Review & Discussion, Exploring Personal Values: Projects, and Additional Sources of Information.

Revisions to this new edition reflect changes in consumerism and improvements recommended by those who have used previous editions and others currently teaching consumer economics, consumer education, and personal finance courses at the college level. It is our hope that this textbook will continue to be a valuable and enjoyable learning tool for students living in a new century of consumer challenges.

ACKNOWLEDGMENTS

First of all, appreciation is offered to the more than one hundred thousand students and faculty members who have used previous editions of this text. We welcome comments and suggestions and incorporate them into subsequent editions.

Our sincere thanks to the following individuals, who took time to review and comment on the manuscript. *For this edition:* Sharon A. DeVaney, Purdue University; Zoe Engstrom, California State University–Long Beach; Deborah Haynes, Montana State University; Nancy Kaler, North Dakota State University; Mary Mhango, Marshall University; Teresa Robinson, Middle Tennessee State University; Darby Sewell, Abraham Baldwin Agricultural College; Boo Su, College of the Canyons; Candia Varni, Alan Hancock Community College; and Baomei Zhao, University of Akron. *For prior editions:* Sheran Cramer, University of Nebraska–Omaha; Gloria E. Durr, Stephen F. Austin University; Bonita Farmer, California State Polytechnic University–Pomona; Sheila Mammen, University of Massachusetts; Yvonne Moody, Chadron State College; and Candy Sebert, University of Central Oklahoma. The book is much improved as a result of their efforts.

We recognize with gratitude the late Dr. Stewart M. Lee for giving us the opportunity to be part of the *Consumer Economics: The Consumer in Our Society* tradition and for the complete support Dr. Lee offered Dr. Zelenak throughout the writing of previous editions.

The importance of consumer economics is miniscule when compared to family. On the Zelenak side, thanks are extended to Arthur Zelenak, Arthur Junior. AJ, and Ashley Zelenak; Mark and Christine Zelenak; Helen Zelenak and Robert Jr. and Thomas Cracker, Janet and Eric Zoda; Pam, Alexandra, Corin, Isabella, and Victoria Savelli; and Paul and Sheila McKnight for their support throughout this endeavor. On the Reiboldt side, great appreciation goes to my husband, Massimo Costanza; my children, Reno and Ambra Costanza; and my mother, Gail Benton, for their unending support and encouragement. Most of all, we recognize our immediate family members who make our lives so meaningful and to whom this text is lovingly dedicated.

A Note to Readers

You are about to begin an exciting class. Many of our students tell us that it was the best class they have ever taken. We hope after this semester that you feel the same way!

This text will provide you with a great deal of information and advice. It will serve not only as a textbook, but also as a useful reference book for current and future use. Each bit of information, whether contained in the text discussion or in one of the special features, is designed to be practical and to save the typical consumer money. It is also intended to help you become a better consumer. In all likelihood you will not want to or be able to follow all of the helpful hints. Each of us has different priorities and concerns and not all of us have the time or interest always to look for the "best deal." Our intention is to provide you with down-to-earth tips so that when the time is right you will be prepared to make educated choices and thus save money and other resources.

You will find that this book is full of qualifying remarks such as "generally," "often," and "in most cases." We have attempted to provide concrete, practical advice while still recognizing that truisms aren't "always" true and a consumer won't "always" encounter the ideal savings situation. We are especially conscious of changing times and challenges as we write this fifteenth edition. At the beginning of his presidency, the Obama Administration seems to be taking a pro-consumer posture in marketplace issues such as credit, savings, investments, fraud, banking, and automobiles. It is probably too early to determine how the impact of decisions at the federal level will ultimately impact the consumer, but with the prospects of new laws and regulations being implemented, new consumer agencies being discussed and developed, and "czars" being appointed by President Obama in over a dozen areas of consumer interest, the laissez-faire approach of federal involvement in the marketplace appears to be no longer the modus operandi.

Many experts suggest that we may be at the beginning of the fourth era of the consumer movement, the last of which occurred a half century ago in the 1960s. Yet, it is worth noting that other administrations offered the rhetoric of strong support for consumer advocacy issues but then failed to have the desired impact. Because the economic and political climates have changed dramatically in recent years and because of corporate and consumer excesses in recent years, more government activity both at the federal and state levels is likely. It is too early to determine if these changes will positively or negatively impact consumers and the future of our markets.

We want to note that some of the advice in this text requires that a consumer be assertive in the marketplace. If you feel you need help in this area, consider seeking it from books, a counselor, a workshop, and so on. Learn to take advantage of the rewards that come to those who ask! Remember, too, that it takes effort and time to save money. If you take the time to educate yourself in preparation for a major purchase, such as buying a car, you will find that the effort pays off not just in dollars saved but also in confidence in your ability. You may even find that friends and relatives look to you as a source of information and guidance when they interact in the marketplace. The strategies you learn will apply to numerous situations.

We hope you enjoy reading this textbook and will find it a valuable resource in the future. Please feel free to send an e-mail and let us know what you think of the text and what you would like to have added in future editions. Our addresses are:

Mel J. Zelenak	Wendy Reiboldt
zelenakm@missouri.edu	reiboldt@csulb.edu
The Department of Consumer Economics	The Department of Family and Consumer Sciences
The University of Missouri-Columbia	California State University–Long Beach

Thank you.

Please note: The authors and publisher have made every effort to provide current website addresses in this book. However, because web addresses change constantly, it is inevitable that some of the URLs listed here will change following publication of this book.

PART ONE

Who Are You?

THE CONSUMER IN AMERICA

One set of messages of the society we live in is: Consume. Grow. Do what you want. Amuse yourselves. The very working of this economic system, which has bestowed these unprecedented liberties, most cherished in the form of physical mobility and material prosperity, depends on encouraging people to defy limits.

SUSAN SONTAG, U.S. ESSAYIST

KEY TERMS

collective consumption
competition
consumerism
consumer sovereignty
discretionary income
disposable personal income
grassroots
gross domestic product (GDP)
gross national product (GNP)
household
money
monopolistic competition
national income (NI)
net national product (NNP)
oligopoly
outsourcing
per capita disposable income
personal income
principle of diminishing marginal utility
savings

The following concepts will be developed in this chapter:

1. A free economy does not mean a problem-free economy, as the economic ups and downs of recent years remind us.
2. Consumerism-the consumer's effort to influence the marketplace-must continue to make itself heard regardless of the pressures put upon it.
3. The soundness of our economy is based on a healthy balance between production and consumption.
4. For a variety of reasons, the consumer does not exercise the sovereignty in the marketplace that the classical economic theory espouses.

After having read this chapter, you should be able to accomplish the following objectives:

1. Identify the attitudes of business and of the public toward consumerism.
2. Give at least five indicators of problems within the consumer movement.
3. Explain the relationship between the individual as a producer of goods and services and the individual as a consumer of these same goods and services.
4. Cite several examples supporting the idea that the consumer is not ruler of the marketplace.
5. Identify the rights and the responsibilities of the consumer.

INTRODUCTION

As we complete our work on this edition, the country and world face economic challenges that impact many of the topics you will read about in this book. We cannot see into the future to anticipate long-term (or even short-term) effects; we cannot predict how economic ups and downs will impact some of the matters we discuss here. Our discussions will presume a stable but ever-changing economic foundation much like the one we've experienced in the past decades. Given the constant ebb and flow of free economies over time, it is our hope that the coming months and years bring resolution to problems and help to strengthen rather than weaken our economy.

All of us (even the "experts"!) have a lot to learn in the coming years, and we hope this book stimulates your desire to better understand how

The Consumer in a Free Society

things work in your country and in the world around you. As you read and learn, use that knowledge to guide your actions in a constantly changing and challenging world marketplace.

WE ARE ALL CONSUMERS

Simply by reading this book, you are a consumer. You are also consuming shelter, heat or air conditioning, natural or artificial light, and furniture. You are consuming the clothes you wear and eyeglasses (if you wear them). You might have a marker or pen in hand to highlight certain portions. Or you may have on your desk a sheet of paper and a pencil to make notes as you read.

Like everyone, you are a consumer every moment of your life, night and day. From the moment of conception until after death, the process of consumption continues. Individuals participate actively in the economy from the day they put their first money in a vending machine.

Whereas childhood purchases are the acts of economic novices, the consumer role of college students is more mature and rational. Or is it? College students are certainly susceptible to financial aid frauds, work-at-home scams, and spring break vacation ploys, to name just a few. In addition, many legal endeavors that college students typically engage in (e.g., landlord–tenant relationships, credit card commitments, and cell phone plans) are often fertile grounds for deceptive practices. As a consumer, you have an important role to play in the economy. The way you perform will affect the performance of the economy. Perhaps more important, the habits you develop as a college student will likely continue throughout your lifetime. These habits include behavior related to purchasing, saving, researching product information, and scrutinizing contracts and other offers. It is important to cultivate positive habits and behaviors now so that market interactions across your lifetime will be as positive as possible.

Consuming is more complicated than simply going to a store to buy food or clothing. It encompasses the purchase of housing and the use of services of banks and credit institutions. It includes purchases from public utilities of services such as gas, electricity, telephones, and water. In the years ahead, most present-day college students will buy insurance, medical and dental care, and hospital services. Government estimates indicate that throughout their lifetime they each will pay more than $500,000 in taxes for local, state, and federal government services. Their total individual expenditures will amount to more than $2 million! To spend this money wisely, they must know something about how our economy works.

How the Economy Operates

Household one or more people who occupy a housing unit.

Money something generally accepted as a medium of exchange, a measure of value, or a means of payment.

Savings income not spent.

The United States has approximately 304 million consumers, including more than 111 million families of two or more individuals related by blood, marriage, or adoption living in the same household. **Households** are the basic consuming units in the economy. Family income gives family members the purchasing power with which to buy goods and services to satisfy their needs and wants.

Economists define **money** as a medium of exchange. To consumers, money is something to be spent. Year after year, consumer expenditures constitute about two-thirds of total expenditures in the economy. If family incomes are steady or if they increase, family expenditures will either continue at the same level or increase. If family expenditures increase, the economy will continue to grow and family income will therefore grow.

After all their expenditures, consumers may still have money left. The **savings** rate since 2000 has been hovering around 3 percent of total disposable income. However, in 2008 it dropped below zero.

Economists measure the performance and growth of the economy in terms of the following concepts:

- **Gross national product (GNP):** The total value of goods and services produced by an economy in a given year.
- **Gross domestic product (GDP):** The total value of goods and services produced for consumers within U.S. borders.
- **Net national product (NNP):** The gross national product minus depreciation.
- **National income (NI):** The net national product minus indirect business taxes.
- **Personal income:** The total of wages, rent, interest, dividends, transfer payments, and unincorporated net income.
- **Disposable personal income:** The amount of income left after deducting personal taxes from personal income.
- **Per capita disposable income:** The total disposable personal income divided by current total population figures.
- **Discretionary income:** That portion of disposable income remaining after paying basic necessities.

WWW

www.usa.gov

This website connects the public to all U.S. federal government resources on-line. Individuals can perform such tasks as applying for a student loan, tracking Social Security benefits, or researching a branch of government.

Who Owes What?

The U.S. economy can be described as a debt economy. In 2008, prior to subsequent "bail-out" efforts undertaken by the government—the total U.S. deficit reached $10 trillion. Since the early to mid-1980s, the United States has been identified as the largest debtor nation in the world. Conversely, Japan has been called the biggest creditor nation in the world.

The annual U.S. budget affects the deficit. In 2000 the budget was in surplus, while the estimated budget deficit for 2008 was approximately $450 billion.

All segments of the economy are in debt. The biggest debtors are business, farm enterprises, and government. Total personal debt amounts to well over a trillion dollars. In thinking about the size of the private and public debt, though, we must remember that for every debtor there is a creditor. All of the more than $50 trillion that debtors

Outsourcing: A Negative or Positive Step? CASE STUDY

Corporations across the United States and Europe in virtually every industry now outsource business processes to Mexico, China, the Philippines, India, and other countries, citing greater efficiency and the potential for improved customer service. Companies may refer to this process as "transformational outsourcing," which they say stimulates corporate growth and makes more efficient use of U.S. employees. Outsourcing companies say it is not simply about hiring cheaper labor outside the United States and that efficiency, productivity, quality, and revenue gains are enjoyed when the talents of offshore employees are utilized.

The flip side of this argument is that U.S. workers face job loss when outsourcing occurs. Highly educated technical and service workers in the countries mentioned above typically work for a far lower hourly rate, and may also work harder and longer.

QUESTIONS

1. What is your personal opinion of and experience with outsourcing?
2. Do you believe the overall effect on the U.S. economy is and will be positive or negative?
3. What if anything do you think can be done to protect U.S. jobs while allowing companies to take advantage of outsourcing opportunities?
4. Should there be federal protection related to outsourcing?

owe is owed to other people, organizations, and foreign entities, which count this indebtedness as part of their assets. Some consumer debt has an associated asset, such as a house.

Consumers or Producers?

Engaged in thousands of different kinds of occupations, people in the labor force work on average 40 hours each week producing economic goods and services that, it is assumed, consumers will buy. These workers produce goods and perform services either in connection with the productive process or directly for consumers.

The same citizens who spend 40 or more hours each week in productive activity also are consumers every moment of the 168 hours in each week. While they work, they are consuming clothing, shelter, and food. When their working period ends, their consuming activities become more varied. In addition, people who are not in the labor force are consumers. Economics has to deal with the role of consumers in the economy, not just with the role of producers.

Economic statistics do not include homemakers as a part of the labor force or as gainfully employed, which is a serious defect in economic analysis. Those who manage the basic consuming units are vitally important in the economy. As homemakers, they operate miniature hotels in which they provide food, shelter, and services for members of the family. They make important consumption decisions and influence what is produced. They also pass along specific consumer traits to their children.

If all homemakers were to give up their jobs as homemakers, they would have to be rehired, or others would have to be hired to do the same work. The fact that homemakers do not receive salaries or wages does not alter the fact that they are engaged in productive economic activity and must be included in any study of consumers and the economy. Exhibit 1.1 illustrates a realistic sampling of the costs of replacing a homemaker. The literature refers to this as *replacement cost,* or the value of a homemaker if that person were replaced by other laborers.

> **www.choosetosave.org**
>
> This website is sponsored by a national education program of the nonpartisan Employee Benefits Research Institute (EBRI). The site offers tips and current information about saving and retirement planning.
>
> WWW

In addition to those in the labor force and homemakers, consumers include tens of millions of men, women, and children in the United States who are not engaged in

EXHIBIT 1.1

Estimates of costs to replace a homemaker (replacement cost).

TASK	HOURS PER WEEK	COST PER YEAR
In-home childcare	45	$ 20,922
Housecleaning	7	$ 4,068
Laundry	6	$ 2,527
Yard work	2	$ 1,511
Grocery shopping	3	$ 2,340
Meal preparation	10	$ 4,316
Financial planning and bill paying	2	$ 1,395
Errand running	3.5	$ 1,640
TOTAL	78.5	$ 38,719

productive enterprise. Some of them are older people living on incomes from savings accumulated during their working years. Others are children too young to be employed. Still others are men, women, and children who are incapacitated, homeless, or unemployed, for whom others in the economy must assume the responsibility of providing necessary goods and services.

Who Decides What Shall Be Produced?

Sometimes the most familiar aspects of daily life are the least understood. We go to the grocery store and fully expect to find milk and bread, or visit the hardware store and expect to find tools. We are able to find goods and services in various retail outlets with a high degree of reliability. How do those commodities come to be produced? Why do they happen to be in the stores at the time consumers want them?

FYI: *The vast majority (90 percent) of new businesses fail within the first five years of operation. Most of these failures result from undercapitalization and poor management.*

In the armed forces of the United States, appropriate amounts and types of food, clothing, and shelter are furnished automatically to all military personnel. The system by which this is accomplished is fundamentally different from that by which civilians are supplied with the things they want. The military establishment decides what kind of shelter, food, and clothing shall be provided. Members of the armed forces must accept what they are issued. By contrast, civilian consumers make their own decisions about which goods and services to buy. In both cases, approximately the proper amounts of consumer goods and services are made available. For civilian consumers, they are provided in retail outlets.

Who are the "supply officers" for civilian consumers? Most are self-appointed enterprisers or storekeepers. Many people choose to earn their living by operating retail stores. In the U.S. system of free enterprise, any person who has enough money to start a business can become a retailer.

If the store's owner has judged the market correctly, some of the purchases consumers make in that market area will be made in the individual's store. Soon the storeowner will know approximately what quantities of goods to keep on the shelves every day. These estimates of what customers will purchase daily, weekly, monthly, and yearly are passed on to the wholesale suppliers in the form of orders. The wholesale suppliers in turn pass them on in the form of orders to the processors. Then the processors order the necessary raw materials.

As consumers, we are free to change our minds at any time about what we wish to consume. The retailer may have ordered bread, butter, and milk on the assumption that all her customers will buy the usual amount today. Some customers, however, may cancel out and purchase nothing. That is one of many risks business firms assume.

CONSUMER SOVEREIGNTY

The actions and reactions of consumers often seem irrational or unpredictable. Therefore, economists construct models to analyze consumer behavior. The most widely accepted model is the classical model.

The Classical Economists' Model

In the traditional economic model, the consumer is cast in the role of "ruler." This is the concept of **consumer sovereignty**—the idea that meeting consumers' needs is the primary function of the economy. The job of consumers is to guide the economy so the goods and services they want will be produced. In this model, all consumer decisions are considered valid, even if consumers demand goods and services that are detrimental to themselves or society. The economy operates for the sole purpose of satisfying consumer wants. This model assumes that the production and consumption of goods and services automatically promote consumer welfare, with no exploitation of consumers by producers or misuse of products by consumers.

Consumer sovereignty literally, "the consumer as ruler"; meeting the consumer's need is the only important function of an economy.

In this model of a free economy, the basic purpose—to promote consumer welfare—is accomplished by free persons engaging freely in productive enterprises to produce what consumers want. Exercising their freedom to choose, consumers accept or reject what the market offers at the prices sellers ask. **Competition** is relied upon to assure good quality and full measure at prices equal to or close to the costs of production.

Competition rivalry in buying and selling.

When firms have the power and ability to influence consumer decisions, this is referred to as *producer sovereignty*. For example, if a monopoly exists, consumers have no choice and must buy the goods offered and pay the set price. Some consider persuasive advertising techniques, through which consumers may be manipulated to buy what firms wish to sell, an aspect of producer sovereignty. In reality, although a mixture of consumer and producer sovereignty exists, in a competitive market, consumer sovereignty plays a more important role.

The Institutional Framework

In the classical economy, the mechanism through which consumers' demands are registered is the price system. Free to make their choices, consumers register their decisions in retail stores by purchasing or refusing to purchase the goods and services that are available. If consumers demand more of a specific commodity or service, the price system reflects the increased demand in the form of higher prices. The higher prices encourage retailers to increase their supplies.

The more competition that is present in a specific industry, the greater is the likelihood that the consumer will obtain high-quality goods or services at competitive prices.

FYI

Operating independently in the hope of increasing their profit, business managers watch consumers' reactions as reflected in the price system. If prices go down, the decision makers curtail production. If prices go up, they increase production. The classical model assumes that consumers reach decisions about what to buy or not to buy on the basis of full knowledge of the marketplace and rational choice.

Exhibit 1.2 illustrates the organization and operation of a model economy, with emphasis on consumers' functions. The outer border represents the political and social institutions within which the economy functions. These are government, family, free speech and the right of assembly, public school, church, and free press. Within the framework of political and social institutions, the exhibit shows the framework of the economic system. The key concepts are: free enterprise with a profit motive, right of private property, free competition, and free contract. The profit system is the keystone in the classical model of the economy. Actually, few of the millions of workers in the labor force ever earn profit, because they are employees, not owners, of businesses. Most earn wages. Since all are motivated by a desire to earn more money, the term *money motive* might be more accurate.

EXHIBIT 1.2

The organization and operation of a free economy.

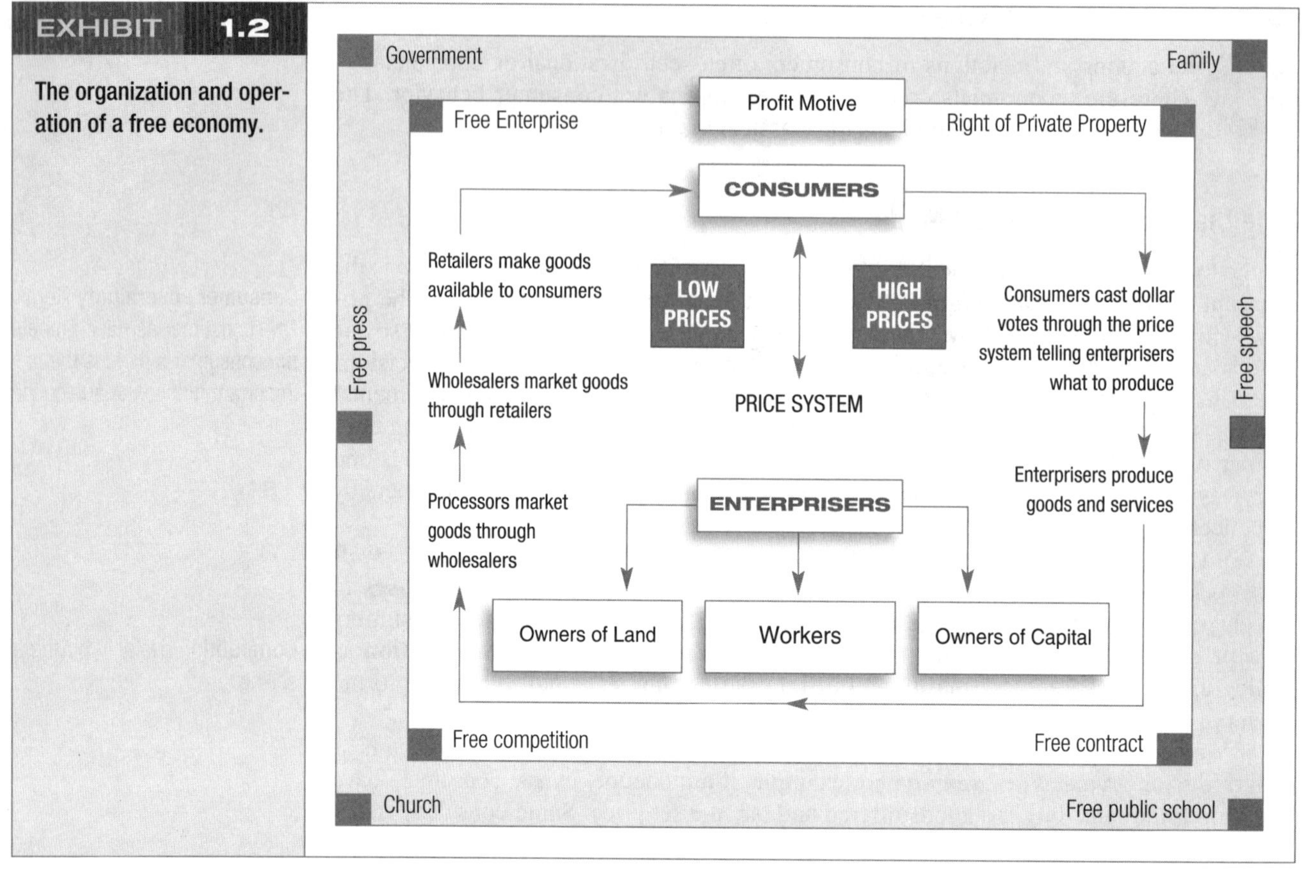

SATISFYING CONSUMER WANTS

What Makes Our Economy Go?

Men, women, and children must have food, clothing, and shelter to satisfy their minimum wants. In addition, they wish to enjoy many other kinds of material goods and many kinds of services. The purpose of the economy is to provide these goods and services. Although providing jobs for workers, profits for business owners, or tax revenue for government are desirable goals, they are incidental to the primary purpose of satisfying consumer wants. To quote the father of our economic system, Adam Smith:

> Consumption is the sole end purpose of all production, and the interest of the producer ought to be attended to only so far as it may be necessary for promoting that of the consumer. The maxim is so perfectly self-evident that it would be absurd to attempt to prove it. But in the mercantile system, the interest of the consumer is almost constantly sacrificed to that of the producer, and it seems to consider production, and not consumption, as the ultimate end and object of all industry and commerce.*

The term *free,* as it is used in describing economic institutions, does not necessarily mean absolutely unfettered. One of the many functions of government is to prevent monopolies and sometimes oligopolies from interfering with others' engagement in free enterprise. Furthermore, "free enterprise" and "free competition" are not synonymous. The United States has a free enterprise system. Because of government involvement and lack of competition in many industries, however, the United States seldom has truly free competition.

* Adam Smith, *An Inquiry into the Nature and Causes of the Wealth of Nations* (New York: Modern Library, 1937), p. 625.

The simplicity of the classical model is appealing. It is also somewhat deceptive because the real world is more complex. For example, does production and consumption of goods and services promote consumer welfare when resource depletion is an issue? What are the trade-offs?

Significant Differences Among Consumers

The literature of economics is filled with misconceptions about the consumer. Although economists try to describe and predict what people do, each consumer is a person first and a statistic second. Each person passes through a life cycle from infancy, through childhood, adolescence, young adulthood, and middle age, to old age. At any given time, the total number of consumers consists of some who are infants, some who are children, some who are teenagers, some who are young adults, some who are middle-aged, and some who are elderly. Obviously, consumers in each of these groups have different needs and interests, and these change as they move through the life cycle.

In the early 2000s, the vast majority of elderly people had adequate financial resources, but because of health problems and other factors, many others lacked enough to live in simple dignity in their last years. In part because of improvements in health care, many elderly people will live longer in retirement, and many will outlive their savings. This reflects the unequal distribution of income among Americans. Many households in this country are relatively affluent, and the economy is geared to these households. Many people, however, live on incomes below the poverty level. Who are the poor? Mostly they are people over age 65, people with disabilities, members of one-parent families, and low-wage and unskilled workers. Often they are recent immigrants who do not speak English and have not completed a high school education.

Many affluent people avoid inheritance taxes on most, if not all, of their estates by using trusts.

FYI

Aside from variance in income, other significant differences among consumers arise out of geographical location, national origin, cultural differences, religious affiliation, occupation, and place of residence, whether rural, urban, or suburban. All these differences affect consumer values, attitudes, choices, and practices.

Collective Consumption

Consumers make many of their economic decisions at the individual or household level. But consumers also make consumption decisions as part of a collective—as voting citizens.

As citizens, consumers may, for example, favor or oppose rent controls in their state or the sale of pornography in their local community. The consumption of military goods and services is an important segment of the economy. Military expenditures since 2000 are high—following the tragic events of September 11, 2001, military spending increased. As of January 2009, the "war on terrorism" is estimated to have cost over $500 billion, and this figure will continue to rise. Decisions to spend hundreds of billions of dollars for defense are made by people as citizens, not as consumers. No individual consumer makes a voluntary military expenditure in the market.

The federal budget is the key instrument in national policy making. Even the most intelligent and effective individual consumer citizen cannot realistically expect to influence budget makers. Public expenditures for schools, libraries, museums, parks, and highways also are made by people as citizens, not as consumers. In contrast to individual, family, or group expenditures, all these expenditures may be described as **collective consumption.**

Collective consumption expenditures for public needs, such as education, highways, and police.

Do Consumers Really Know What They Want?

Some economists hold that the best way to evaluate consumer wants is through the market. (In Chapter 2, we will discuss "wants vs. needs.") They assume that the purpose of production is to produce what consumers want and that consumers' wants are known by their behavior in the market. The first assumption raises this question: Are managers of business firms motivated by a desire to satisfy consumer wants, or are they motivated primarily by a desire to make money? The second assumption is also open to question. Consumer choices in the market may not reflect their "real" or "true" preferences. Consumers select among the options that are available to them. It is possible that none of these options is an exact fit to the consumers' preference. Hence it can be difficult to know what consumers really want.

The supply of goods and services in the world market is vast. Shopping malls, supermarkets, and other retail establishments offer thousands upon thousands of products. Internet shopping or e-commerce allows for virtually unlimited numbers of products to be offered. Of these myriad products, how can consumers know which they want? How can they know which products they need? How can they even know what is available?

Many consumers have had the experience of window-shopping, discovering some new item, and responding, "That's just what I want!" When this happens, consumers find that they want a product that a moment before they did not even know existed. Of course, the discovery of a new product does not always result in a new want, but this does happen often. By contrast, consumers often purchase an item only to discover that it is not wanted or needed.

Many wants are derivative. This means that purchasing one product requires purchasing another product or service in order to enjoy the first. An electric lightbulb is useless without electricity. A gas furnace will yield no heat without gas. An automobile will not travel without gasoline and oil. A DVD player cannot entertain without a DVD.

Can Consumers Determine Quality?

A penny saved is better than a penny earned because a penny saved is tax-free!

FYI

Various studies have indicated that consumers cannot determine quality. They simply do not have the necessary information or perhaps the interest to make the determination. For example, many packaged foods include additives. A food additive is a substance other than a basic food, used by manufacturers to preserve, to aid in processing, or to improve the texture, appearance, or taste of food. Obviously, consumers cannot possibly detect all the additives or their amounts in order to determine a food's quality.

In the United States, the Food and Drug Administration (FDA) employs technically qualified personnel to monitor the use of additives and occurrences of contaminated products. In recent years, product recalls due to the contaminants have included produce, meat, pet food, toothpaste, and others. Recalls for food items are numerous, and the latest food recall information can be found at the USDA's Food Safety and Inspection Service website, www.fsis.usda.gov; for example, in early 2009 this site and others helped consumers search an extensive list of hundreds of products that were produced containing salmonella-contaminated peanut paste.

Consumers are also called upon to evaluate labels and determine how dependable they are. (See Chapters 15 and 16 for more on labeling.) For example, many consider organic food an alternative to foods that may be processed with chemicals or genetically treated. To assist consumers, the USDA has established a *USDA Organic* certification for food claiming to be organic. This certification says that the product is at least 95 percent organic. More information on this program can be found at the adjoining link.

WWW

www.organic.org

This site includes information regarding organic products, including product reviews and a store finder.

Use caution regarding foods labeled "natural." This label merely indicates that the food originates from natural sources; the product may still contain additives such as preservatives and flavor enhancers. Concerned consumers should seek to educate themselves about seller-applied labels.

Consumer desire to purchase drugs manufactured outside the United States concerns the FDA, which is adamant about the safety risks involved with such a practice. According to the FDA, the primary risks include improper use of a drug without a doctor's supervision, expired drugs, contaminated drugs, and counterfeit drugs. The FDA warns that even if a drug is approved outside the United States, standards for approval may be lower than what FDA regulations require.

Making the evaluation of food products more complex is new technology that enables manufacturers to construct synthetic food products from processed materials and chemicals. The number of synthetic food products continues to increase. For example, among dairy products, consumers might not be able to distinguish between synthetic cream and cream obtained from cow's milk. Additionally, unless labels are clearly marked, consumers would not know whether they are buying milk from cows given recombinant bovine growth hormone (rbGH). Consumers who are not well informed may not even know why this is important.

www.shopping.com

The search engine at www.shopping.com allows consumers to comparison shop for items at on-line stores, auctions, and buying groups. If the consumer provides an e-mail a ... umber, Shopping.com will s ... nds a better deal.

Just as consumers cannot determine the quality of food products, they cannot determine the quality of many other products they buy: They cannot measure the tensile strength of thread or rope. They cannot evaluate the fastness of dyes in fabrics they buy, although some labels warn of colors that may run. Consumers cannot differentiate synthetic fabrics. Without accurate labeling, they cannot possibly know the characteristics of gasoline, including the octane rating, nor can they know before making a purchase how an automobile, a television set, or an appliance will perform. Of course, rating services similar to those furnished by the publication *Consumer Reports* can inform consumers about products' performance and past reliability, but this is information that consumers must actively seek out.

TIP Consumers should read and be sure they understand labels, warranties, and other consumer information. The federal government, through disclosure laws, requires manufacturers and retailers to furnish much consumer information. However, unless consumers read and understand these disclosures, they have little value.

Every day, consumers use products and services produced by people they have never met. As the volume and variety of available goods increase, consumers' ability to judge quality decreases. Consumers must depend on the reliability and responsibility of the sellers from whom they purchase goods and services. They must trust those who prepare their food, those who are responsible for the purity of their water, and those who are responsible for the safety of gas and electrical installations. They trust their lives to operators of automobiles, airplanes, trains, and ships. Their daily life is an act of faith. Most sellers keep that faith, but some do not. For this reason, government inspectors work to ensure consumers' safety. Product recalls are implemented when information about violations comes to light.

www.recalls.gov

This site is a "one stop shop" for government recalls. It includes recall notices from the Consumer Product Safety Commission, U.S. Coast Guard, Food and Drug Administration, U.S. Department of Agriculture, U.S. Environmental Protection Agency, and National Highway Transportation Safety Administration (which also offers the site www.safecar.gov).

Can Consumers Be Sure of Safety?

Automobiles, power mowers, and even toys injure and kill consumers. Every year, thousands of people are injured in accidents involving glass doors and windows. Significant numbers are severely burned by defective space heaters and heating stoves. Federal agencies have recalled many products because of safety defects or hazards, but it is also necessary that consumers be informed and alert. Today, with the Internet, it is relatively easy to check on the recall status of products; several websites provide this information. For

www.cpsc.gov

The Consumer Product Safety Commission site offers recall news, the means to report an unsafe product, information about product safety standards, and much more.

example, the Consumer Product Safety Commission allows consumers to sign up online for notification of recalls.

TIP Always read product labels on toys to ascertain for what ages the toy is appropriate. A seemingly harmless toy may have parts that would be harmful if swallowed by a small child. Choke tubes are inexpensive devices that help parents determine whether a toy is too small and could be swallowed by an infant.

Can Consumers Check the Quantity?

Evaluating a product often involves measuring it by weight, volume, or number. Meat is weighed in ounces and pounds. Milk is measured in pints, quarts, and gallons. Eggs are measured by size and by number, usually 12. Services are also measured—by time or piece. A worker may be paid by the hour, by the number of pieces produced, or by the job.

As a marketing strategy, manufacturers sometimes reduce the contents of a product without changing the size of the container. A container that used to hold one pound (16 ounces) of coffee, for example, may now contain only 12 or 13 ounces.

FYI

The classical economic model assumes that, for all transactions, the purchaser is present at the time of measurement and therefore is able and willing to check the accuracy of the measurement. In retail stores today, however, most measurements take place before the purchaser reaches the store. Nearly all meats are packaged, weighed, and priced in advance. When a buyer picks up a package of meat marked "1 lb. 13 oz.," there is no practical way for the buyer to check the accuracy of that statement. When a buyer puts a loaf of bread in a shopping cart, there is no way for her to know whether the weight declared on the label is accurate. When purchasers buy goods in cans or cartons, they have no way of knowing whether the cans or boxes are full or whether the stated net weight is accurate.

Food is not the only area where this is a problem. A growing number of items in retail stores are packaged. Buyers are not permitted to break open a package, and they usually have no way of checking the accuracy of the contents until after they have bought the product.

Government statistics show that a considerable amount of short-counting, short-measuring, and short-weighing goes on. In addition, some short-changing occurs at checkout counters. Because consumers cannot ascertain the accuracy of weighing and measuring devices or supervise their accuracy, local, state, and federal government inspectors do it for them. In the classical model of the economy, competition is supposed to regulate this aspect of trade. In actuality, competition may result in more, rather than less, short-measurement. In addition, the measuring devices are often complicated and expensive and require supervision by trained and skilled inspectors. These factors may limit their use.

Can Consumers Detect Fraud?

The classical economic model makes no allowance for the possibility of fraud. In dealing with merchants, consumers today too often encounter evasions, half-truths, misrepresentations, deceptions, and outright frauds. Chapter 5 deals with this subject.

TIP Purchase fuel with the octane level required for your vehicle, as stated in your owner's manual. Most autos do not require premium gasoline. If yours does, and you notice a "ping" when you accelerate, the gasoline station may be mislabeling lower-octane gas.

Can Consumers Cope with Pricing Practices?

Most consumers assume that a high price guarantees good quality and that a low price is evidence of inferiority. These assumptions give sellers a great advantage, and many sellers make the most of it. Sellers know that few consumers have any idea of the expenses actually incurred in the production process, so they can easily sell inferior products at high prices. This practice can continue because consumers often have no way to compare the quality of competing products. Among competing brands, quality may be quite different with no difference in price.

The concept of fair price is relative, not absolute. To judge the fairness of the price of a product, one must know the cost to produce it. However, it is virtually impossible for consumers to obtain the true cost of production of items. Consumers can protect themselves to an extent by being aware of market pricing practices such as customary prices and loss leaders (discussed in Chapter 8).

TIP The organization Consumers Union tests various products and services. It provides the most reliable product evaluations available to consumers. Before you make any major purchase, consult *Consumer Reports* magazine or browse the website www.consumerreports.org.

Does Competition Control Prices?

The classical model of the economy assumes pure competition. An economy of pure competition is one with so many sellers and so many buyers that no one seller or buyer can control supply, demand, or price. Despite the fact that the U.S. economy consists of millions of buyers and sellers, pure competition does not necessarily result. Instead, many markets are characterized by **oligopoly** and **monopolistic competition.**

Oligopoly a situation in which few sellers control the majority of the supply of a product or service.

Monopolistic competition a situation in which numerous sellers have similar or identical products and services.

Over the long term, prices in an oligopoly usually are higher than prices in a competitive market. Items that are produced and purchased under oligopolistic conditions include, but certainly are not limited to: automobiles, appliances, aluminum, tires, chewing gum, breakfast cereals, lightbulbs, matches, soap, heating oil, natural gas, cigarettes, sporting goods, digital cameras, DVD players, televisions, and soda.

Competition may operate in oligopolistic industries in one of three ways.

1. Foreign competition may affect the industry. When an oligopoly misreads consumer demand, as the automobile oligopoly did, enough consumers can purchase foreign goods, as they did with automobiles, to compel American producers to change and improve their products.
2. Substitute services provide competition. In air transportation, when the federal government deregulated airfares in the late 1970s, competition of substitute services (discount airlines) forced the major airlines to reduce their prices. (In markets where one airline has the bulk of the market, even the discount airlines cannot affect price, however.)
3. The government may intervene and provide competition. In the electric light and power industry, the Tennessee Valley Authority in the 1930s provided competition that forced private companies to reduce their prices.

Economic concentration may well be the number one consumer "rip-off." In concentrated markets, large-scale inefficiencies, price fixing, excess profits, and barriers to entry can occur quite easily and keep prices artificially high. FYI

Does Market Price Measure Subjective Value?

In the classical model, when a consumer pays the asking price for a good or service, the price is assumed to reflect the consumer's subjective value of the good or service. If it does not, the consumer presumably will not make the purchase. However, this assumption is valid only if all consumers have equal purchasing power, are fully informed, and are equally well trained in bargaining abilities. In reality, consumer incomes vary greatly, not many consumers fully understand the operation of the economy, and some sellers adulterate and falsify their products in ways that many buyers are unable to detect. As a result, it is unrealistic to assume that if two buyers pay the same price for a loaf of bread, their subjective valuations of the loaves are identical.

> **TIP** In negotiating, the buyer typically is in a better position than the seller to negotiate. The buyer has something everyone wants (money), whereas the seller often has a product that is available in virtually unlimited supply and that may be desired by a limited number of consumers. Use this knowledge in negotiations, and you will be effective.

Principle of diminishing marginal utility the concept that consuming more of a product or service with a given period will at some point result in diminishing utility. For example, regardless of price, an individual will only consume so many haircuts in a six-month period. Thus, the per-unit power of the product to satisfy a human want decreases.

The **principle of diminishing marginal utility** applies to money, as well as to other goods and services. Families with high incomes generally value each dollar much less than do families whose incomes are below the poverty level. The lower-income families, which tend to value their dollars much more than the higher-income families, place a much higher use-value on bread. If all families had equal purchasing power, the willingness of two purchasers to pay the same price would reflect more closely their subjective evaluation of the bread.

Even if all families were to have equal incomes, the assumption that price is a measure of subjective value would not hold. Clearly, some consumers, as buyers, are much more shrewd than others. They know better how to judge quality and price. They are more skillful at bargaining, a practice from which many consumers shrink. In our highly specialized economy, sellers generally have more savvy and are better informed than consumers. Many of them are good practical psychologists. They know consumer weaknesses, and some sellers exploit those weaknesses. The pricing of goods and services is an art, not a science. Sellers ask for what they hope to get, and they often get it.

THE CONSUMER MOVEMENT: A BRIEF HISTORY

Consumerism a movement whose objective is to ensure that the consumer will pay a fair price for quality goods and services in the marketplace.

In giving a brief overview of the history of the consumer movement, we can note cyclical patterns and similarities among the three eras of **consumerism.** Each period involved a significant safety problem, which, when exposed, angered the general public. Each stage also had the strong support of the U.S. president, and each had a consumer spokesperson who was able to articulate the consumer cause eloquently. Conversely, consumer eras generally have ended because of U.S. involvement in a major international conflict, which was followed by economic prosperity. During economic prosperity, consumerism declines in importance. The consumer movement wanes at these times because of the lack of support for consumer issues by the president and the dearth of creditable consumer spokespersons.

The First Era

The first era of the consumer movement originated in the 1880s with the efforts of Dr. Harvey W. Wiley, generally known as the father of consumerism. Wiley believed that our nation's food buyers needed protection. He served in the federal Department of Agriculture, where his role was to determine the safety of the nation's food supply. He was amazed to find that numerous external ingredients—metals, acorns, and other fillers—were added to practically every food offered to the U.S. consumer. In the late 1880s, he published and circulated his findings to other professionals. This limited exposure had little impact on the total population. During the early 1890s, he decided to change tactics and speak out more publicly. He urged consumers to join a campaign aimed at getting Congress to initiate laws governing our foods.

Dr. Wiley was astonished to find that many special-interest groups termed his ideas "anti-business" and "inflationary"—a charge frequently leveled against consumer activists throughout the history of the movement. Wiley noted that he was not advocating changes in the products, only that correct labeling be provided. Nonetheless, a hostile Congress and an indifferent citizenry ignored his ideas.

He continued his experiments with little publicity. Then, in 1902, he set up a lab and recruited a dozen healthy young individuals who would become his associates. He first fed them unadulterated food for a period of time, observing their weight and physical condition carefully. Then he fed them the same diet with the addition of common food preservatives. His findings noted that preservatives re-administered continuously in small doses created disturbances in appetite, digestion, and general health. The results of the investigation became common knowledge. The nation's newspapers began writing about the accomplishments of Wiley and his "Poison Squad."

As a result of his efforts, the American Medical Association (AMA) began analyzing drugs. Despite many AMA reports concerning improper drug circulation, various business groups continued to assert that the efforts by Wiley and others were anti-business and not in the best interest of America. By the turn of the 20th century, congressional scrutiny was initiated in the food and drug arenas. Several food and drug bills were introduced in Congress, but no laws were passed. Wiley's and others' efforts to protect consumers seemed to have failed. However, as happened again in subsequent eras, a muckraking book alerted the general public to the need for action. The exposè in this era was *The Jungle* (1906), by Upton Sinclair, which revealed unsanitary conditions in meatpacking plants. Sinclair wrote:

> These rats were nuisances, and the packers would put poisoned bread out for them and they would die, and then rats, bread and meat would go into the hoppers together. . . . Men who worked in the tank rooms full of steam . . . fell into the vats; and when they were fished out, there was never enough of them to be worth exhibiting—sometimes they would be overlooked for days, till all but the bones of them had gone out to the world as Durham's Pure Leaf Lard!

This book, along with the efforts of Wiley, the AMA, and others, gave Congress the impetus to pass the Pure Food and Drugs Act of 1906. This was the first federal law in U.S. history enacted specifically to protect consumers. Although the act had many loopholes, the consumer was finally represented at the federal level.

The first court case under the new law was brought to trial in 1908. A product that had been sold since the 1880s (Cuforhedake Brane-Fude) was shown to be worthless. It did not cure headaches, nor did it make consumers of the product more intelligent, as claimed. The assertions made in advertising were false and misleading and in direct violation of the new law. The jury found the defendant guilty as charged. The sentence was a $700 fine and an order to change the labels on the product. The manufacturer of the worthless product had profited in the millions, and he paid only a minimal fine. Similar verdicts have continued throughout the history of consumerism. The result has been that unscrupulous merchants have been willing to take risks with deception because the penalties for their illegal actions usually have been minimal as compared to the profit.

www.consumersinternational.org

Consumers International is a global network that represents and links consumer groups and agencies. It is an independent nonprofit organization that stands up for consumer rights and promotes the consumer movement.

By 1912, business leaders themselves recognized that legislative mandates would be inevitable unless they initiated a self-policing system. This concern led to the establishment of the Better Business Bureau (BBB) to discourage dishonest business practices. Criticisms of the BBB by many advocates then and now assert that the BBB is simply a public relations outlet for local business. The criticism may be generally valid, although many BBBs do seem to promote honest business dealings among their members. The Boston and St. Louis BBBs have historically been considered a notch above the norm in assisting consumers with their problems.

By 1917, the United States was involved in World War I. Concern was transferred from domestic to international issues. Further, the public sentiment was that government was doing all that had to be done to protect consumers. President Calvin Coolidge and the Congress agreed. Postwar prosperity in the United States was historic. Many felt that questioning U.S. industry was unpatriotic. This sentiment continued through the early and mid-1920s. As a result of the war and the prosperity that followed, the first era of the consumer movement ended.

The Second Era

In 1929, two significant events resulted in the emergence of the second era of the consumer movement. The first was that the nation's first consumer-oriented magazine, *Consumer Research,* began publication. Second, and far more significant, the stock market crashed.

People were losing faith in U.S. industry. A few years later, as in 1906, a book aroused public interest in consumerism. *One Million Guinea Pigs,* by F. J. Schlink (cofounder with Colston Warne of Consumers Union), offered numerous illustrations of unscrupulous merchants who tested food and drugs on the public with no government scrutiny. The only law to protect consumers was the Food and Drug Act of 1906, filled with loopholes and ineffective for this new age of merchant fraud. Schlink suggested to consumers that the only way to level the playing field was to "let your voice be heard loud and often."

Women's and labor organizations, whose roles in U.S. life were expanding under the New Deal programs of President Franklin Roosevelt, did, indeed, let their voices be heard. Although these groups were instrumental in the development of many consumer causes during all three eras of the consumer movement, they offered specific impetus during this second era. The General Federation of Women's Clubs inundated Congress with letters endorsing various proposed laws that set severe penalties on manufacturers who defrauded consumers. President Roosevelt's wife, Eleanor, was an outspoken and effective advocate for consumer causes during this second era.

Women and women's groups are instrumental in the development of consumer movements. This was true especially during the second era of the consumer movement.

FYI

President Roosevelt commended the efforts of these groups and supported pending legislation to help remedy consumers' problems. People appointed by Roosevelt proposed that government inspectors be granted broader powers and that stiffer penalties be imposed on all offenders. Business leaders again were enraged. As a result, the debate concerning passage of a new food law was even more bitter than the battle three decades earlier. On one side, virtually every business group claimed that the proposed measures were un-American. On the other side, representatives of various groups made their first concentrated effort on behalf of the "beleaguered consumer."

Although the consumer-related bills had some legislative support, they were summarily defeated. The movement again appeared to be waning. In 1937, however, a "miracle drug" (sulfanilamide) was introduced into the market, and shortly thereafter people who were taking the drug began dying. Investigation revealed that a chemist in Tennessee had added alcohol to the formula, resulting in the deaths of more than 100 people. No law protected consumers. Nothing could be done to the chemist or the company because they were not required to test the drug for safety.

President Roosevelt and many congressional leaders were horrified. Roosevelt called for and Congress passed the Food, Drug, and Cosmetics Act of 1938. The 1938 law amended the 1906 act by allowing inspectors to remove potentially dangerous products from the market while tests were being completed. Cosmetics were included in the law because ingredients in some of the products were disfiguring the faces of those who used them. Consumerists, including Warne and Schlink, began advocating consumer rights in other areas of the market. For the first time, Congress began considering issues other than safety.

By 1940, World War II was imminent, and U.S. citizens turned away from the consumer movement. By 1946, the war was over and the voices of consumer advocates again stressed consumer awareness, but no one was listening. People who were unable to purchase many of their wants during the war years were eager to buy, and buy they did. Competition among various businesses for the consumer dollar was ferocious. Advertising costs surged upward. Businesses hired sociologists and psychologists to determine why consumers purchased as they did.

The Third Era

During the 1940s and early 1950s, the consumer movement received little public support. Then came another book, this one written by Vance Packard. *The Hidden Persuaders* described psychological methods that entrepreneurs use to stimulate sales. Americans detested the idea that these methods were being used on them for corporate profits. Perhaps a greater impact on legislation of this era than Packard's book was the cranberry crop scare of 1959. Cranberries sprayed with certain chemicals were causing cancer in rats. The FDA, a virtually powerless and unknown organization until this time, exploded into the news by terminating all distribution of cranberries.

Consumerists were overtly critical of various segments of the marketplace, and citizens and politicians began to support their efforts. Speaking out for the consumer became popular among politicians.

The 1960s brought the greatest impetus to the third era of the consumer movement. This era lasted nearly 20 years, and more consumer legislation was passed in this era than at any time in the past. This era had many consumer heroes. Some of the more influential were:

- *Rachel Carson.* Her book, *Silent Spring,* offered an exposè of the widespread use of DDT and other chemicals. President Kennedy read her book and as a result took an active interest in environmental and other consumer issues.
- *President John F. Kennedy.* Many historians suggest that his support of consumers through the Consumer Bill of Rights initiated the third era of the consumer movement.
- *Senator Paul Douglas* (Illinois). His support of disclosures to consumers led to passage of Truth-in-Lending legislation.
- *Senator Philip Hart* (Michigan). His interest in fairness in product labeling led to passage of the Fair Packaging and Labeling Act.
- *Senator Estes Kefauver* (Tennessee). This senator was instrumental in exposing problems with highly concentrated industries, most notably the drug industry.
- *Senator Warren Magnuson* (Washington). The senator emphasized the need for safety legislation and also wrote the book *Dark Side of the Marketplace.* This best-seller enumerated the unique problems of poor people in the marketplace.
- *Ralph Nader.* Most people consider him to be the most influential consumer advocate in U.S. history, championing a multitude of consumer causes. He began his career with a book, *Unsafe at Any Speed,* which condemned automobiles and the automobile industry. Nader made unsuccessful bids for the White House in 2000, 2004, and 2008.
- *President Lyndon Johnson.* A supporter of the consumer movement, he introduced and passed more consumer legislation during his presidency than any other president in U.S. history.
- *President Richard Nixon.* Although he resigned from office prematurely, President Nixon was able to sign numerous pieces of consumer legislation into law. He also

President Kennedy read Rachel Carson's exposé, Silent Spring, *and, as a result, took an active interest in environmental and other consumer issues. This interest culminated in his advocacy of a Consumer Bill of Rights (the right to safety, the right to choose, the right to be heard, and the right to information).*

FYI

appointed Virginia Knauer as the first Special Assistant to the President for Consumer Affairs and advocated the fifth consumer right, the right to redress. This became the impetus for development of small claims courts throughout the United States.

- *President Gerald Ford.* He announced the sixth consumer right, the right to consumer education. This was a forerunner to various consumer education programs in public schools and communities.
- *President Jimmy Carter.* Many historians believe that he was a stronger supporter of consumer causes than any other president in U.S. history. He appointed numerous strong consumer advocates who became top officials in his administration. These included:

  Joan Claybrook (National Highway and Safety Administration)

  Michael Pertschuk (Federal Trade Commission)

  Carol Tucker Foreman (Agriculture Department)

  David Pittle (Consumer Product Safety Commission)

  Esther Peterson (Special Assistant to President Carter for Consumer Affairs)

  All these advocates had a profound impact on consumer causes during the Carter years.

Although he was not considered a consumer advocate, Alfred Kahn, a member of the Carter administration, merits special mention. Kahn advocated the demise of his own agency, the Civil Aeronautics Board (CAB). He believed that airfares, which were set by his agency, were too high and that a competitive market was needed. Airline executives criticized Kahn because he was, in effect, eliminating their guaranteed profits. He was successful, and the result is that, in most competitive markets, airfares are lower than they were 20 years ago. This is one example illustrating that when true competition is allowed in the marketplace, the consumer benefits.

Many historians note that, despite the efforts of President Carter and the consumer advocates he appointed, the third era of the consumer movement probably ended with the defeat of the Consumer Protection Agency (CPA) bill, which was strongly supported by President Carter, Ralph Nader, and virtually every consumer advocate in the country. Its purpose was to set up an agency to represent consumers in Congress when laws were being developed that would directly affect consumers. Business and labor unions and other organizations had strong lobbying groups, but consumers had no such representation because their political voice was fragmented. By the late 1970s, however, the country was becoming more conservative, and the general consensus among politicians and the public was that we needed to reduce the bureaucracy in Washington, not add to it. The result was that the Consumer Protection Agency bill was narrowly defeated in the House. The defeat was devastating for Carter and the consumer movement. The third wave of the consumer movement ebbed after the CPA vote, and it terminated with the election of President Ronald Reagan in 1980.

President Reagan and his administration cut most federal programs that were geared to assist consumers. Reagan believed the marketplace is a better protector of consumers than the federal government is, and he had support for that view throughout Congress. Although Presidents George Bush, Bill Clinton, and George W. Bush have supported various consumer causes, a major blow to consumer protection came during Clinton's administration. In 1999, the Office of Consumer Affairs was closed during Clinton's efforts to downsize government and cut "unnecessary" offices.

After the Office of Consumer Affairs was closed, people were concerned that efforts to inform consumers would not continue. Fortunately, a group of representatives from government agencies, nonprofit consumer groups, major corporations, trade associations, educational institutions, and others involved with consumer issues met in 1998 to keep the work alive. The steering committee from that first year included AARP, Consumer Federation of America, the Federal Trade Commission, the National

Association of Attorneys General, the National Association of Consumer Agency Administrators, the National Consumers League, and the U.S. Postal Inspection Service. They launched the first annual National Consumer Protection Week in 1999. Their work has continued to the present day, with an annual National Consumer Protection Week designated each spring, including an annual theme.

While much of the major consumer protection work has been completed, the government continues to have a role in protecting consumers. Laws that address cutting-edge issues, such as telemarketing, technology, and privacy, have been implemented in recent years. And, as always, laws need to be reviewed and adapted, as necessary.

The Fourth Era: Will There Be One?

With booming economic times in the United States in the late 1990s, and record consumer confidence figures, low unemployment, and low inflation, conditions were such that a fourth era of the consumer movement was improbable. However, the economy in the first decade of the new century became a roller-coaster ride, with a decade of ups and downs. Late in the decade, the financial and real estate industries collapsed, the stock market fell, consumer confidence levels eroded, and unemployment rose. How these challenges will affect the consumer movement has yet to be determined, but it appears likely that the Obama administration will push for new legislation concerning consumer issues.

The consumer movement is an economic movement, and thus it will always play a role in the marketplace. The extent of its role is determined by economic and political factors in both the domestic and international arenas. Historically, when the economy is strong, consumers are less interested in consumer issues. Conversely, when the economy is not so strong, consumers pay closer attention to budgeting, "righting" wrongs in the marketplace, and so forth. As we move into the second decade of the 21st century, consumer issues and trends will reflect our changing economy.

According to the federal government, the average dollar bill lasts only 18 months in circulation. Other denominations and their estimated lifespans:

$5	*15 months*
$10	*18 months*
$20	*24 months*
$50	*5 years*
$100	*25 years*

Coins are in active circulation about 25 years.

FYI

THE DUAL ROLE OF CONSUMERS

onsumers are the biggest spenders in the economy. This consumer spending is what propels the economy. If spending is sustained at a high level, the economy operates at a high level.

Consumers both earn and spend in our economy. They are, in fact, both producers and consumers. When consumers are earning and acting as producers, their goal is to get the highest profit possible. When consumers are spending, the reverse is true: They demand the lowest price and the best quality possible. This adversarial relationship is important to understand because it can be a strength of a competitive marketplace.

The flow of money in the economy is illustrated in Exhibit 1.3. Most consumer expenditures are made in retail stores, which in turn spend money to buy supplies from wholesalers. The wholesalers then spend money to buy supplies from processors, and processors spend money to buy from raw material producers. Local, state, and federal governments take a portion of consumers' incomes for the services the governments perform. The remaining amount is saved. Retailers, wholesalers, processors, producers of raw materials, governments, and financial institutions then pay wages, interest, rent, profits, and transfers (such as Social Security payments). The recipients of all these various payments comprise all consumers.

www.consumer-action.org

This organization's purpose is to advance the consumer activist movement of the information age.

Consumer Rights

President John F. Kennedy's Consumer Bill of Rights marked the first time in the history of the nation that a president had considered consumers and their needs for

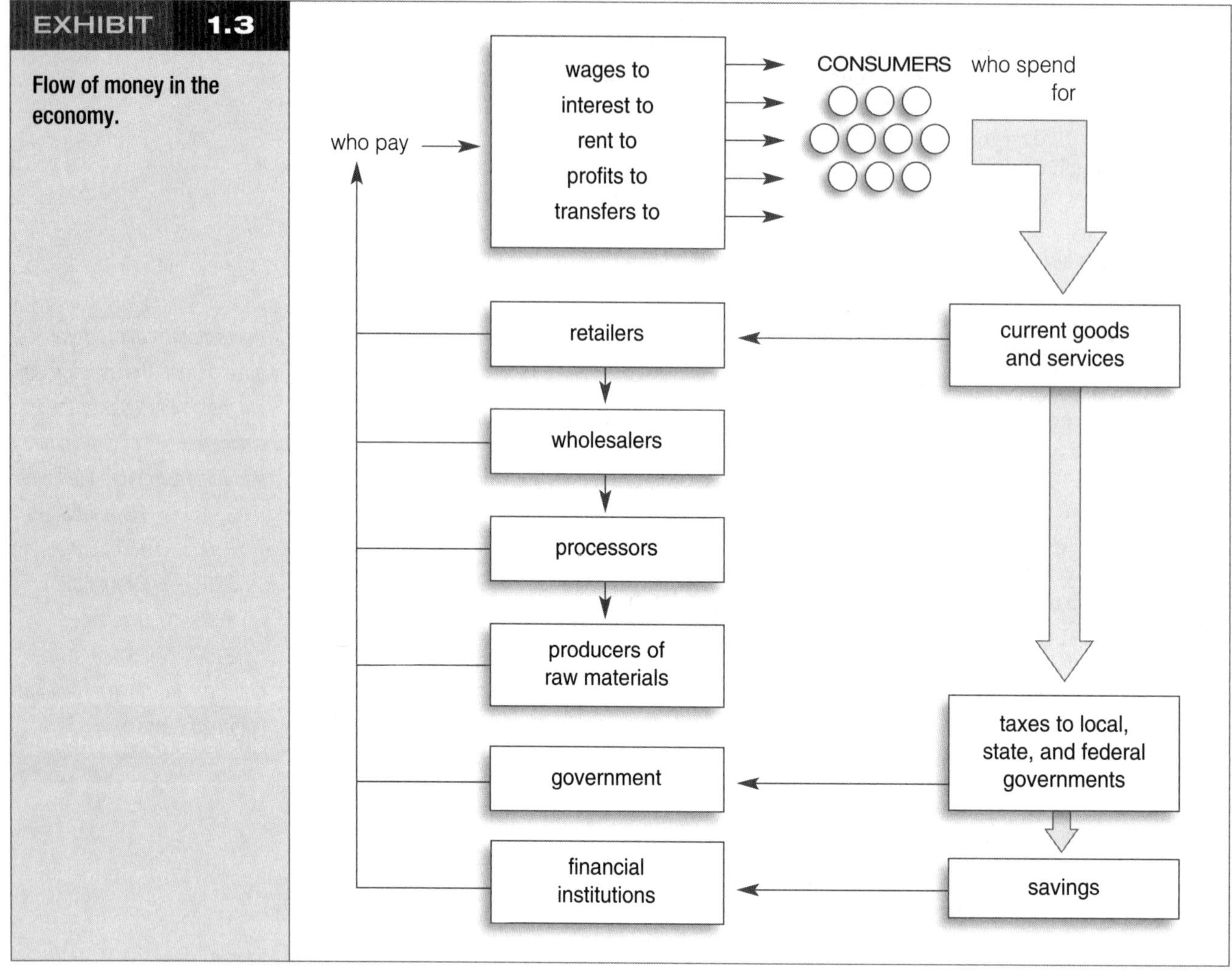

Flow of money in the economy.

protection sufficiently important to submit to Congress a message devoted to their interests. In his message on March 15, 1962, the president listed the following consumer rights:

- *The right to safety:* to be protected against the marketing of goods that are hazardous to health or life
- *The right to be informed:* to be protected against fraudulent, deceitful, or grossly misleading information, advertising, labeling, and other such practices, and to be given the facts needed to make informed choices. This right led to later laws that required disclosure statements. An example of these disclosure laws is Truth-in-Lending.
- *The right to choose:* to be assured, wherever possible, access to a variety of products and services at competitive prices, and in those industries in which competition is not workable and government regulation is substituted, to be assured of satisfactory quality and service at fair prices
- *The right to be heard:* to be assured that consumer interests will receive full and sympathetic consideration in formulating government policy, and fair and expeditious treatment in the government's administrative tribunals

The rights of redress, consumer education, environmental health, and service followed the four Kennedy-developed consumer rights.

Consumer Responsibilities

Where there are rights, there are also responsibilities. A primary responsibility of consumers is to be aware of their role and function in the economy. Anyone can spend money, but responsible consumers know that in spending money, they are engaging in actions that, together with those of other consumers, influence what shall and shall not be produced.

A second responsibility of consumers is to perform their role effectively. This requires training and knowledge as well as good judgment. Consumers have an important job to do and must work at it conscientiously in order to do it well. In the U.S. economy, consumers have an impressive freedom of choice. This freedom is not to be taken lightly or abused, nor should it be abdicated.

The U.S. population makes up about 5 percent of the world's population and uses as much as one-third of the world's resources.

FYI

Responsible consumers have a sense of responsibility to their own nation, to consumers in other nations, and to future generations. Many resources are irreplaceable. This places a responsibility upon the consumer to avoid waste. Consumers now are aware that they have an important responsibility to avoid polluting air, water, and soil.

Consumers have a responsibility to avoid exploitation of those in the labor force who supply goods and services. At the same time, they have a right to buy products and services that have been produced efficiently. This responsibility raises some difficult questions. Should consumers always buy in the cheapest market? What is the responsibility of consumers if goods and services are cheap because people around the world, including children, have been exploited to produce them? At times, some consumer groups and unions who believed workers were being exploited have organized boycotts urging the public not to buy certain products. Ethical practices by business, at both the domestic and international levels, are becoming increasingly important to consumers.

Consumers also have a responsibility to be honest in their dealings. Honest sellers and honest buyers have a mutuality of interests. Both sides of the counter have a responsibility to give and to receive no less and no more than the exact quantity at the agreed price. Consumers have a responsibility to pay their bills. They have a responsibility to call attention to errors that are to their advantage as well as those that are to their disadvantage. A person does not have to be anti-business to be pro-consumer, nor does a person have to be anti-consumer to be pro-business.

In a free society, consumers have the right and the responsibility to protest. They may exercise the protest function individually or in groups. Individual consumers may utilize their protest function by refusing to purchase or by complaining when a product or service is not what it is purported to be. The collective effect of such action may bring about a change. Consumers may exercise their protest function in groups such as consumer cooperatives. If social control is necessary, consumers may exercise their protest function by supporting or opposing proposed legislation.

Herb Weisbaum of MSNBC created the "Ten Commandments for Consumers,"* to which we add our thoughts:

1. **Thou shalt not assume.**

   Ask questions. Problems arise out of misunderstandings. For example, do not assume that you can return that new computer you are buying. If the return policy is not posted, then ask.

2. **Thou shalt get all promises in writing.**

   Verbal promises are worthless when there is a dispute because there is no way to prove what was said.

3. **Thou shalt do thy homework before making a major purchase.**

   The more you know before you head into the store, the more likely you are to get a good deal on the right product. Ask friends, read expert reviews, and use shopping bots to compare prices.

---

* The Ten Commandments of Consumerism by Herb Weisman, www.msnbc.com/id/16991452, Feb. 12, 2007.

4. **Thou shalt not be penny wise and pound foolish.**

   Cheaper is not always better. Sometimes spending more now will save money in the long run. A more expensive washing machine may be of higher quality and thus last longer and be more energy efficient.

5. **Thou shalt not hire a contractor who just shows up at the door.**

   Never hire a contractor without verifying his or her license, checking for complaints filed against them, and obtaining and calling a list of references.

6. **Thou shalt not be pressured into buying.**

   The high pressure, buy now approach is an attempt to keep you from doing any comparison shopping or research. If the price they quote you is no good once you walk out that door, avoid doing business with this company.

7. **Thou shalt not assume a transaction can be undone.**

   The three-day cooling off period does not apply to most purchases. It applies only to sales of $25 or more that take place at your home or away from the company's normal place of business.

8. **Thou shalt not buy a used car without an inspection.**

   A mechanic can spot problems not revealed by a CARFAX report or the dealer. This inspection will cost about $100, but it may save you from purchasing a lemon.

9. **Thou shalt guard all personal information.**

   Keep private information private. Do not give your information out in response to a call or e-mail. Call the company back yourself at the number you know to be legitimate and ask what is going on. Shred documents.

10. **Thou shalt be more skeptical.**

    If it sounds too good to be true, it probably is.

Consumer Democracy

Democracy can be defined broadly as a society in which citizens are continually creating the conditions under which they wish to live and work. The concept of economic democracy implies sharing of control of the economic system by the three groups of people most concerned with its operation: consumers, owners, and workers. Consumer democracy, similarly, implies that consumers participate continually in the economy to decide what goods and services shall be produced. If the goods and services produced promote consumer "illfare" rather than consumer welfare, consumers share the responsibility.

Some consumers fail in their responsibility to make free and intelligent choices. They permit themselves to fall under the influence of habit, custom, fashion, and aggressive selling practices. As a result, their decisions are made for them rather than by them. Other consumers willingly choose to buy and use products that are harmful to their health, such as tobacco products, alcoholic beverages, and illegal drugs. If political democracy is to work, it must be supported by an under-structure of economic democracy. If economic democracy is to work, consumers must intelligently exercise their right to make free choices and must take their responsibilities as consumers seriously.

Consumers and Social Networking Sites

Social networking has exploded in popularity in recent years. Hitwise (an Experian company) estimates that social network sites account for approximately 6.5 percent of all traffic on the Web, and this number is growing. People use social networking sites such as MySpace, Facebook, and Live Journal to stay in touch with friends and families, locate old friends, and make new ones.

The growing popularity of these sites means consumers must be aware of marketing tactics and dangers stemming from site use. When information and photos are posted online, they are available for the whole world to view; consumers may find that future employers and others have access to material posted previously. In addition, online predators may use social networking sites to target and victimize individuals both personally and for monetary gain. Use caution when interacting on these sites.

Social networking sites are used extensively to market companies and products. Such sites offer links to music, advertisements, and movies, and these links can also be placed on a person's personal page. Companies also develop personal pages on these sites for music, movies, artists, and other products that serve as a way to "spread the word." It can be difficult to separate and identify personal from "sponsored" content. The role of social networking sites in the marketplace will continue to evolve, and their impact is likely to continue to grow.

www.hitwise.com

This site's data center tracks activity on social networking sites, and other sites as well. It provides current information on Internet use and related industry trends.

INTERNATIONAL CONSUMER ISSUES

More today than ever before, we exist in a global economy—that is, economic decisions and policies made in one part of the world often have dramatic and substantial impacts on economies and consumers in other parts of the world. One important manifestation of the global economy is the concept of outsourcing. **Outsourcing** is viewed by many as a quick and cost-effective alternative to hiring full-time corporate employees. An employer paying an American employee $32,000 annually (plus other costs and benefits) might pay only $3,000 annually to an employee in India to perform the job. Outsourcing is often thought of only in terms of job loss in the United States, but ideally when a company cuts costs, the company, and thus its employees, benefit. Assuming company profits increase, outsourcing theoretically will lead to job creation in other areas. However, the long-term effects of outsourcing, both in the United States and in other countries, remain to be seen.

Outsourcing paying another company to provide services that a company might otherwise have employed its own staff to perform. Often, the "outside" employees are located overseas (offshoring).

The world feels like a smaller place today than it did a few decades ago, because products and traditions are more easily transferred from one society to another. The resulting world economy is more accessible, more open, more global. As the United States continues to influence other parts of the world, through its military presence, outsourcing, and international marketing and sales, westernization and globalization will continue. Other countries will adopt Western traditions, including clothing, food (e.g., American fast-food establishments across the globe), and so forth.

As a result of our global economy, many new consumer organizations have developed and prospered during the past several decades. Many countries now have consumer groups that are similar to those in the United States. That is, they are **grassroots,** private organizations often representing consumers with respect to specific causes. In a few countries, most notably the United Kingdom and the Scandinavian countries, consumers are represented formally by government entities.

Grassroots generally, local organizations developed to represent specific issues and goals.

World Consumer Rights Day (WCRD) is an annual event whose intent is to exhibit solidarity within the international consumer movement. The first WCRD was observed in 1983. By 1985, the United Nations General Assembly, through the efforts of Consumers International (CI), adopted guidelines for consumer protection throughout the world. Consumers International, formally known as the International Organization of Consumers Unions (IOCU), has become the catalyst behind the international consumer movement.

Consumer organizations throughout the world embrace the "Eight Consumer Rights." To the rights noted by President Kennedy (the right to safety, the right to be informed, the right to choose, and the right to be heard), President Nixon (the right to redress), and President Ford (the right to consumer education), CI members have added the right to satisfaction of basic needs and the right to a healthy environment. The right to satisfaction of basic needs endorses the concept that all consumers must have access to essential goods and services and adequate food, clothing, and shelter, as well as health care, education, public utilities, water, and sanitation. The right to a healthy environment indicates that all consumers must be allowed to live and work in an environment that is nonthreatening to the well-being of present and future generations.

SUMMARY

The United States is home to approximately 304 million persons, all of whom are consumers. The United States has a market economy that exists to satisfy the consumers' need for goods and services. Most Americans are producers as well as consumers. In a perfect competitive market, consumers dictate their production needs. This is called consumer sovereignty. However, in part because of lack of competition in a variety of industries, producers often determine what is to be produced. There are varying views as to whether consumers:

1. know what they want
2. can determine quality of goods and services
3. can determine safety of goods and services
4. can verify quantity of goods
5. can detect fraud
6. readily understand pricing practices
7. have access to the information needed to make wise decisions in the marketplace

Most historians believe that President John F. Kennedy initiated the most recent era of consumerism when he developed the four rights of consumers (safety, information, choice, and to be heard). Along with rights, consumers have responsibilities. These responsibilities include the need to be honest with merchants, to avoid being exploited, and to be aware that buying decisions our society makes will affect (positively or negatively) all other nations.

We are moving toward a one-world economy. The international consumer movement has increased in its importance in recent years.

ITEMS FOR REVIEW & DISCUSSION

1. Explain the basics of how the U.S. economy operates. Does it operate like that of the model economy set forth by economists? How do economists measure the performance and growth of the economy?
2. Explain the concept of consumer sovereignty.
3. Explain the dual role of consumers.
4. Delineate the rights that have been enumerated for consumers. To what extent are these rights being achieved?
5. Explain how competition does or does not control prices.
6. List the responsibilities of consumers.
7. Explain how consumers' stage in the life cycle affects their decisions as consumers.
8. Who really decides what shall be produced? Explain.
9. Do you believe that we are moving toward a one-world economy? Why or why not?
10. What are your views of outsourcing? Do you think it hurts or helps the U.S. economy?
11. Do consumers really know what they want? What influences their decisions? How much influence do you as an individual have on determining what is produced?

Truth-in-Lending

The Truth-in-Lending Act requires creditors to disclose to the consumer in writing certain cost information, such as the annual percentage rate (APR), before consumers enter into credit transactions.

"Only $6 down and $20 a week" is typical of statements that appeared frequently in advertisements prior to passage of the Truth-in-Lending legislation. The problem with statements of that sort was that consumers were not given important information about credit costs, such as the total finance charges or the annual percentage rate (APR).

The original Truth-in-Lending Act became effective on July 1, 1969. Since that time, all other credit laws have been considered amendments to the 1969 act. The law lets consumers who are taking out a loan know exactly what the finance charges are and more readily to compare charges from various credit sources. The law makes it easier to know two of the most important factors about the cost of credit. Both the finance charge and the annual percentage rate must be displayed prominently on the forms and statements a creditor uses to make the required disclosures.

Credit Cards

The Truth-in-Lending Act also protects against unauthorized use of credit cards. If a credit card is lost or stolen, the maximum amount the consumer must pay for charges someone else makes is $50. For the card issuer to hold the consumer liable for even that amount, the unauthorized use must have occurred before the card issuer was notified that the card was lost or stolen. A card issuer also cannot hold a consumer liable for any unauthorized use unless the card issuer has provided

- some means, such as a signature panel or photograph on the card, to identify the user as the person authorized to use the card
- notification of the potential $50 liability
- a form to use in notifying the card issuer of loss or theft of the card

The law also prohibits card issuers from sending a credit card without an application having been initiated.

Advertising

The law regulates the advertising of credit terms. It says that if a business is going to mention one feature of credit in its advertising, such as the amount of the down payment, it must mention all other important terms, such as the number, amount, and period of payments that follow.

Cancellations

Another important provision of the law indicates that if a home is used as security in a credit transaction, the creditor must give written notice to the consumer that he or she may cancel the transaction within three business days. The right of cancellation does not apply to a first mortgage to finance the purchase of a home.

Other Provisions

The law provides criminal penalties for willful violations as well as civil remedies that allow for twice the amount of the finance charge, from a minimum of $100 up to a maximum of $1,000, plus court costs and reasonable attorney's fees.

Truth-in-Lending has been amended several times since it was first developed. Generally, the intent has been to simplify the Act. Recent revisions include determinations that:

- a creditor is a business that extends credit more than 25 times a year
- "layaway" plans are exempted
- borrowing money from an accrued cash value of an insurance policy is exempt
- many informal credit arrangements, such as those with doctors, hospitals, and small merchants, are exempt
- "business investment" loans are exempt
- minimum finance charges must be disclosed only if imposed during the billing cycle
- complete disclosures on home equity mortgages must be offered when the consumer applies for the loan
- complete disclosures on the costs of credit cards must be offered when the consumer applies for the card, and these disclosures must be made in mail and telephone solicitations

Generally, the Federal Trade Commission (FTC) enforces the Truth-in-Lending Act. Violations should be reported to a regional FTC office or to the Federal Trade Commission, Credit Practices Division, Washington, DC 20580.

EXPLORING PERSONAL VALUES: PROJECTS

1. Using your local newspaper as a source for the prices of goods and services, plan a monthly budget for a retired couple living on a fixed income of $2,500 per month.
2. Debate the topic, "Resolved: The consumer never has been and is not now sovereign."
3. Debate the topic, "Resolved: The consumer movement is here to stay."
4. Interview a retailer and ask him how he decides what to buy to stock the shelves or store. If the retailer does not make the decisions, who does?
5. Ask a business executive for her opinion concerning consumer rights.
6. Discuss in class the idea that current college-age consumers will not live as well as their parents. In what ways can you substantiate or refute this assertion?
7. Debate the topic, "Resolved: We are moving toward a one-world economy."
8. What are your views on outsourcing? Do you think it hurts or helps the U.S. economy?

ADDITIONAL SOURCES OF INFORMATION

Brobeck, Stephen, Robert N. Mayer, and Robert O. Herrmann. *Encyclopedia of the Consumer Movement.* Santa Barbara, CA: ABC-CLIO, 1997.

Glickman, Lawrence B. *Consumer Issues in American History: A Reader.* Ithaca, NY: Cornell University Press, 1999.

Rosenblatt, Roger. *Consuming Desires: Consumption, Culture, and the Pursuit of Happiness.* Washington, DC: Island Press, 2005.

Schor, Juliet, and Douglas B. Holt. *The Consumer Society Reader.* New York: New Press, 2000.

Solomon, Michael. *Consumer Behavior.* Upper Saddle River, NJ: Prentice Hall, 2008.

> Consumer wants can have bizarre, frivolous, or even immoral origins, and an admirable case can still be made for a society that seeks to satisfy them. But the case cannot stand if it is the process of satisfying wants that creates the wants.
>
> **JOHN KENNETH GALBRAITH,** U.S. ECONOMIST

KEY TERMS

assimilation
consumer behavior
culture
demand
demand schedule
diminishing utility
elasticity of demand
fiscal policy
harmonious consumption
inelasticity of demand
law of diminishing returns
marginal tax bracket
monetary policy
money income
progressive tax
proportional tax
psychic income
quota
real income
reference group
regressive tax
satiety
tariff
tax expenditures
utility
variety

The following concepts will be developed in this chapter:

1. Happiness is subjective; it means different things to different people.
2. Needs, wants, and demands often are confused, but they invariably have physiological, psychological, sociological, and environmental roots.
3. Seller supply is an important aspect of the demand concept.

After having read this chapter, you should be able to accomplish the following objectives:

1. Explain why achieving perfect happiness is virtually impossible.
2. For the principles of consumption-harmonious consumption, diminishing utility, variety, and satiety-give an illustration of how each is involved in your buying decisions.
3. Give several examples of how your needs, wants, and demands are influenced by physiological, psychological, sociological, and environmental forces.
4. Explain how supply and demand co-exist.
5. Define elastic and inelastic demand and give examples of each.

THE SEARCH FOR HAPPINESS

Each human being is a bundle of physiological, psychological, and social wants. If these wants are satisfied, an individual is more likely to be happy than if they go unsatisfied. We use the qualifying word "likely" because some people fail to find happiness as a result of the satisfaction of wants.

If economic happiness is defined as a state of pleasurable contentment with one's condition in life, we can inquire whether a person best achieves this state by acquiring enough income to satisfy more and more of his unlimited wants or by limiting his wants to those that his income can satisfy. The first method goes hand-in-hand with a materialistic philosophy of life, or the belief that the highest value is material well-being. Those who follow that philosophy claim to find satisfaction in acquiring and consuming ever-increasing amounts of goods and services. Many critics believe that Western civilization in the 21st century is motivated primarily by this materialistic philosophy. The critics contend that we have lost our way and confuse the acquisition of goods and services with the pursuit of real happiness.

The Complexity of Consumer Demand and Seller Supply

In a similar way, people may approach consumer economics from one of two extremes. On the one hand, the emphasis may be on ways of getting the best value for each dollar spent; the overriding consideration in marketplace decisions is to obtain more for less. On the other hand, the emphasis may be on minimizing the importance of money and the material aspects of life, in which case the individual is likely to pay little attention to marketplace decisions and, therefore, to be a careless and wasteful shopper. Neither extreme is an intelligent position to take. A proper balance between the two is a desirable goal.

Do Consumer Wants Have Any Limit?

Traditional economic analysis begins with one basic fact of life: the insatiability of human wants. Consumers' desire for goods and services presumably is capable of indefinite expansion. Most economists accept this as a basic fact so obvious that it requires no demonstration. Consumers today want and expect to have goods and services that were unknown to their ancestors or, if known, were considered luxuries to be enjoyed only by royalty and the very rich. In many respects the modern, middle-income family lives in greater comfort than royalty enjoyed as recently as a century ago. Although the counterculture youth movement of the 1960s seemed to indicate a reaction against a materialistic society, U.S. consumption patterns in the decades since then seem to support the "unlimited wants" theory.

The view that the human race has unlimited material wants is challenged by some. It has been suggested that our wants are in fact limited and, therefore, can be satisfied. Other cultures, particularly non-Western cultures past and present, appear to have found satisfaction with certain levels of consumption. Some economists contend that the unlimited-wants concept has been used falsely as the primary motivator in free-enterprise economics—unlimited wants continuously propelling the economy upward.

Can All Wants Be Satisfied?

Economics has been described as "the dismal science." Perhaps this is because, in response to consumers clamoring for more and more, economists have told them that

Law of diminishing returns a principle holding that, after a given time, increasing use of labor and capital combined with a fixed amount of land will produce progressively smaller yields.

nature is miserly. An example is the **law of diminishing returns.** This is a physical law with far-reaching economic effects.

For years the GNP increased steadily in the United States as the use of energy increased. From the late 1960s to the early 2000s, total energy consumption in the United States more than quadrupled. Compared to a century ago, more than 30 times as much horsepower per person per day is available now.

Since the 1970s, the course of an ever-increasing GNP has reversed itself somewhat, the result not only of energy issues but of other marketplace issues as well. U.S. economic supremacy in the world community continues to be challenged. Coun--tries such as Japan and Germany compete effectively with the United States on a global basis. The attention of the government and the business community is directed in part to making the United States more competitive in the world market. The need for competitive efficiency in producing our products has consequences. Layoffs of workers, closings of plants, increased interest in research to make a better-quality product—these are among the results during the past two decades of attempts to make the United States more competitive.

A force that has offset the tendency toward diminishing returns is the development of new and more effective ways of utilizing scarce resources. Many scientists hold that science and technology have replaced natural resources as a basis for economic growth. It seems we find new methods of producing goods and services when the economic pressure becomes great enough. For example, we are now actively exploring alternative forms of energy to decrease our dependence on oil. In general, however, the supply of goods and services continues to fall far below the volume required to satisfy all current consumer wants at prices all can pay.

WWW

www.simpleliving.net

This website encourages consumers to "learn to do more with less" and stop the endless cycle of "want." Learning to accept less, want less, and potentially save more will be one component of helping to solve the nation's debt crisis.

TIP

If you utilize well water for drinking, it may become contaminated at any time from groundwater contamination. Check well water at least once a year. Many states have an agency that provides water analyses free or at a nominal cost.

Unlimited wants in the face of limited supplies create scarcity. Because humans as producers cannot produce enough to satisfy all our wants as consumers, the question arises as to whose wants shall be satisfied. Scarce products and services are valued according to the expense of producing them. The power of individual consumers to acquire these scarce goods depends on their income and total wealth. The central struggle of economic life is a contest to determine which of the unlimited consumer wants will be satisfied.

Harmonious consumption a principle of consumption referring to the tendency to purchase combinations of things.

Diminishing utility the principle holding that as more of a given product is consumed, per-unit satisfaction of the product declines.

Variety a principle of consumption referring to the desire to accumulate different kinds of goods.

Satiety a principle of consumption concerning the desire to obtain an unlimited amount of goods and services.

FOUR PRINCIPLES OF CONSUMPTION

To understand buying behavior, it is helpful to consider four principles of consumption: harmonious consumption, diminishing utility, variety, and satiety. An example of **harmonious consumption** is the matching of clothes and accompanying accessories. As an example of **diminishing utility,** owning one handheld or laptop computer is pleasurable, but owning two is rather useless. **Variety** indicates that people usually like to own such things as shoes in different colors and styles. Variety often overcomes diminishing utility. **Satiety** suggests that people can come up with unending reasons for buying something new.

These principles almost always are involved, in one way or another, in purchasing decisions. Consumers who recognize the influence of these four principles on their buying decisions will be better able to control their buying habits and, therefore, able to make better use of their money.

NEEDS AND WANTS

Basic consumer needs are limited to the necessities of life. These include enough food to sustain the physical strength necessary to work, and clothing and shelter adequate for the climate. According to current standards, a family of four needs an income of about $25,200 to live at a minimum level, and more than $47,000 to live at a moderate level. Exhibit 2.1 shows the poverty guidelines for U.S. families. Of course, these estimates can vary widely depending on geographic location. In addition to needs, consumers at all income levels have wants. These include comforts and luxuries and may even include what moralists consider to be extravagances. Many consumers can attempt to meet those wants only by taking on a high debt load, often by misusing credit cards.

TIP The additional cost of owning "premium" credit cards often exceeds the benefits. Most consumers should obtain a no-annual-fee, low-interest national credit card. Nonetheless, there may be circumstances in which paying an annual fee is of value. One example is an airline credit card that allows consumers to accumulate miles toward free trips. Another exception might be a student promotional credit card that offers substantial perks. However, even in these exceptional situations, it is always wise to pay the balance each month so that no interest is incurred. Also, consumers should check their credit statements at the end of each month for billing errors.

These differences among needs and wants require further analysis. Consumers are not born with an intuitive sense that enables them always to make choices that will promote their welfare. Nor can they always acquire the wisdom to make those choices well. Many consumers want goods and services that retard rather than promote their well-being. Others want goods and services that are not essential to life itself but are necessary for a more complete, abundant life.

EXHIBIT 2.1

Health and Human Services poverty guidelines, 2008.

PERSONS IN FAMILY OR HOUSEHOLD	48 CONTIGUOUS STATES AND D.C.	ALASKA	HAWAII
1	$10,400	$13,000	$11,960
2	14,000	17,500	16,100
3	17,600	22,000	20,240
4	21,200	26,500	24,380
5	24,800	31,000	28,520
6	28,400	35,500	32,660
7	32,000	40,000	36,800
8	35,600	44,500	40,940
For each additional person, add	3,600	4,500	4,140

Source: Federal Register, vol. 73, no. 15, January 23, 2008, pp. 3971–3972.

The Complexity of Wants

Economists in the past almost completely ignored consumers. It was assumed that the purpose of production was to satisfy consumer wants, but the nature and origin of consumer wants and the factors influencing them were considered to lie largely outside the field of economics. For example, hunger is an observed fact, but what lies behind hunger is biological and, therefore, not included in the field of economics.

Wants have psychological and social as well as physical origins. People living in Asia or Africa often have physical wants different from those of people in the United States because of differences in geography, climate, and social institutions. Yet, basic wants and needs are the same the world over. People get hungry, thirsty, cold, hot, and tired. They like certain sounds, sights, and tastes. A consumer in Africa may satisfy hunger by eating foods that are different from those a consumer in North America eats, but in either place food is necessary to satisfy the biological craving we call hunger.

The demands of individual consumers also reflect differences in personality. In choosing clothing, for example, a person selects specific items not only for protection but also for possible improvement in appearance. Hence, those who wish to understand consumer behavior must know psychology.

Simply put, most people want to gain pleasure and avoid pain. On one level, pleasure is largely sensory, depending on the satisfaction of basic bodily appetites and a state of physical health. On other levels, pleasure also includes aesthetic, moral, and intellectual satisfactions, which are concerned with more than physical sensation.

www.travelocity.com

Consumers who wish to travel should visit www.travelocity.com. Among other features, it enables consumers to purchase airline tickets, car rentals, hotel accommodations, and vacation reservations on-line.

The senses—an aspect of psychology—have significant effects on people's choices of goods and services. Some people, for example, are tone-deaf and have no desire for music. Others are color-blind. Individual differences in the sense of taste result in demand for various kinds of foods. No one can know precisely how a product affects the senses of taste, smell, hearing, or sight of another person. We often assume that all people receive the same sensations, but we cannot be sure. Nor do we have any way of measuring the intensity of satisfaction people feel when consuming a product or service. Hence, this level of motivation is likely to remain somewhat mysterious.

The consumer is a bio-psycho-sociological being influenced by diverse stimuli. Although science knows little about certain areas of influence, such as prenatal influence, we do have significant knowledge about basic biological/physiological, psychological, and sociological influences. This knowledge can help us understand consumer behavior.

Physiological Needs and Wants

Needs lead people to act. The action may be an innate response, or it may be learned. Needs lead to *drives,* which produce tension until the needs are satisfied. A *motive* is the urge to satisfy a need. Abraham Maslow's classic work on the hierarchy of needs is important in this discussion (see Exhibit 2.2). He contends that lower-order needs must be met before higher-order needs. In Maslow's pyramid, physiological needs must be met first, safety needs second, belongingness and love third, esteem fourth, and, finally, self-actualization is reached at the top of the pyramid.

The basic biological needs, which must be met if the body is to survive, include oxygen, water, food, elimination, relief from pain, and protection from heat, cold, and fatigue. Although these needs are determined biologically, the physiological drives are subject to social influences. For example, most people in the United States reject horse meat and insects as food because our society rejects them, whereas consumers in other countries may enjoy these "edibles." Conversely, most people in the United States like pizza, whereas members of some societies consider this food to be unpalatable.

Economically speaking, the action a person takes to meet a need is called *consumer behavior.* Most of the basic biological needs are consumer needs as well because indi-

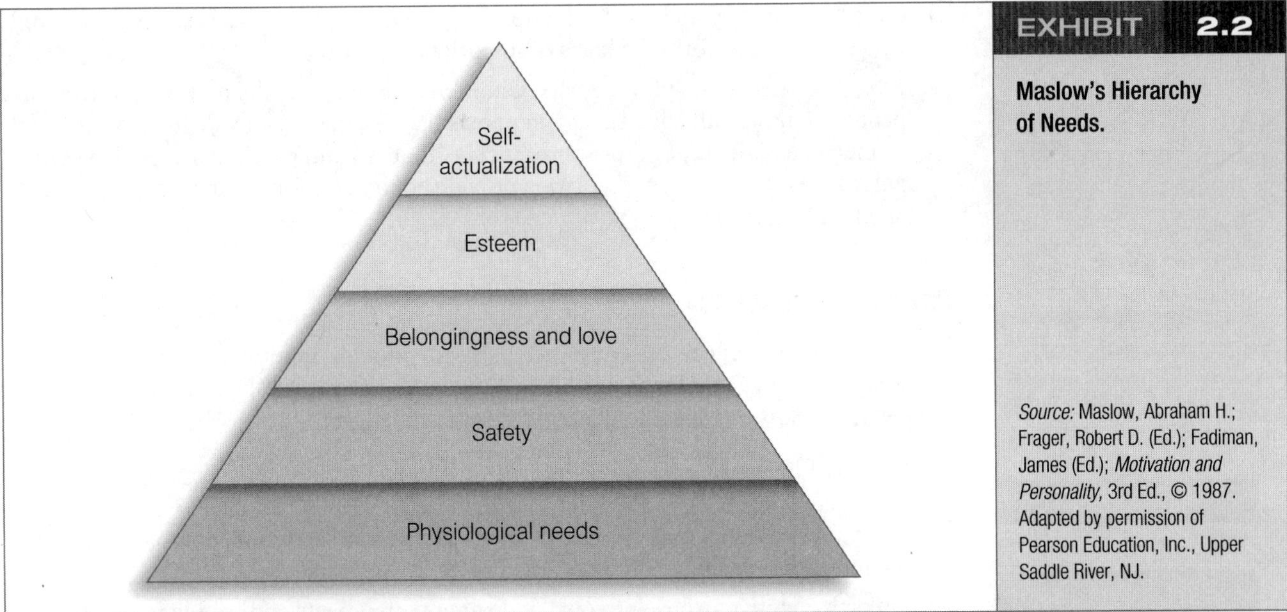

EXHIBIT 2.2

Maslow's Hierarchy of Needs.

Source: Maslow, Abraham H.; Frager, Robert D. (Ed.); Fadiman, James (Ed.); *Motivation and Personality*, 3rd Ed., © 1987. Adapted by permission of Pearson Education, Inc., Upper Saddle River, NJ.

viduals must, or may, be willing to purchase the satisfaction of them. Consumer needs based on biological needs include the following:

1. *Oxygen.* Oxygen is the most basic physiological need. Billions of dollars are spent to purify polluted air in many cities, as we witnessed as China prepared for the 2008 Olympics. "Oxygen bars" in some cities provide a place for consumers to go and inhale high levels of oxygen, presumably for health benefits (increased energy, reduced stress, decrease in headaches). No scientific studies have proven the alleged benefits or risks.
2. *Water.* Water is essential to maintain life. It is such a fundamental need that supplying water is a public enterprise in most communities. In addition, consumers buy bottled water if they live in a dry area, dislike tap water, or require distilled or spring water for some product or process.
3. *Food.* Middle-class and poor families spend a large percentage of their income on food, which is the basis of a major industry stretching from farm to retail store.
4. *Protection from the elements.* People need protection from heat and cold, wind and rain. This leads us to build houses and transportation facilities that are warm in cold weather and cool in hot weather. Consumers also need protection in the form of clothing, which the garment and fashion industries supply.
5. *Health.* The desire to enjoy good health and accommodate poor health is the basis for the medical profession, hospitals, assisted living facilities, and the manufacture of special equipment required in the medical field.
6. *Tactile sensations.* In addition to the fundamental needs for food, water, oxygen, and so on, people want pleasurable tactile sensations. This desire is the basis for products such as lubricants, astringents, and those that provide relief from itching, burning, and roughness, as well as those that satisfy the psychological urge for beauty and fashion.
7. *Sound.* The desire for hearing pleasant sounds is the basis of the music industry, and those whose hearing is defective form a market for the manufacture of hearing aids.
8. *Sight.* The perception of color, which creates reactions that are pleasant or unpleasant, causes consumers to prefer goods of one color over those of another. Sellers have found that by changing the color of a package, sales of a product can be increased by as much as 1,000 percent. Many people have defective vision, and

corrective surgery and the production of eyeglasses, contact lenses, and other products to aid vision form the basis of important industries.

9. *Play.* Humans are playful animals. Children and young adults play instinctively, and people of almost all ages engage in games that require varying degrees of physical or mental activity. Spectator sports such as football and baseball are big business enterprises, and thousands of firms provide equipment for fishing, hunting, skiing, and taking part in sports.

Psychological Wants

Psychological influences on consumer behavior include emotional responses such as fear and anger, love and hate, self-interest, and a desire for prestige or recognition. The three main groups of psychological drives (or motives) are:

1. Organic motives, which depend on internal body conditions.
2. Emergency motives, including those that are aroused when events in the environment require quick and vigorous action. They include escape, combat, efforts to overcome an obstacle, and pursuit.
3. Objective motives, those directed at dealing with objects and people in the environment that do not require immediate action. They include exploration, manipulation, and curiosity.

Organic motives operate in a cycle and subside when satisfied, whereas emergency and objective motives are continuous.

Three important objective motives in consumer behavior are love, extraversion, and creativity. Love of other people and the desire for companionship are basic and universal. Love of a mate results in consumer demand for objects that display this relationship and a wide range of items to be used as gifts and tokens. Love of children leads to the consumption of many goods and services throughout life.

An inborn tendency to extraversion can lead to a wide range of social activities and consumer demands. For some people, this tendency can develop into conspicuous and lavish display for the purpose of attracting attention.

In addition to being social creatures, human beings are creative. We create buildings and transportation facilities, develop new consumer goods, produce paintings and sculptures, compose music, and write books and plays. Publishers of newspapers, magazines, and books; developers of Internet websites; and writers and producers of

CASE STUDY The Gift Card

Gift cards are now among the most popular of gifts. The National Retail Federation estimates Americans spend approximately $26 billion on gift cards each year. The cards are convenient and versatile. One drawback, however, is if there are only a few dollars left on the card, you may be forced to keep spending until you exhaust the value of the card. Retailers are not required to give you back the money, even if it is only a small amount.

A new law in California proposes that retailers must give back cash if the gift card has less than $10 remaining; in addition, retailers cannot charge service fees, impose expiration dates, or deduct value from cards if the cards are not used (unless the card value is less than $5 and has been dormant for two years).

QUESTIONS

1. What do you think the impact of this law will be on retailers? Consumers?
2. Do you agree or disagree with this law?
3. Have you had any experience with gift cards?
4. How do you think this law affects the supply and demand of gift cards?

television programs and films respond to objective consumer wants for information, news, entertainment, and knowledge. The educational system is a response to demand for knowledge, as is the wealth of information on the Internet.

Social Wants

Society is more than a collection of people. It is an organized body of men, women, and children bound together by social customs and institutions. U.S. society is characterized by, among other things, the desire for achievement, which is highly esteemed; the desire for security, which is highly valued; conformity; sociability; an appreciation of leisure, which takes precedence over the preference for hard work; and admiration for youthfulness, which is valued more highly than wisdom and age. The values of U.S. society are largely based on the Puritans and their Reformation of the 1600s. The Puritans' religious beliefs helped mold the idea of a strong work ethic coupled with an underlying conservatism. Certainly much has evolved and changed in the past 400 years, but some of the core religious and economic values of that time remain strong.

In every society, the ideas of the dominant group tend to become institutionalized. The society's institutions then become instruments through which the society guides individual consumption patterns. In other words, within an advanced society are stable groups, such as farmers, labor unions, trade associations, political parties, and families, which have characteristics distinct from those of their individual members. These groups influence the economic wants of their members. Individuals also join temporary groups, such as audiences, crowds, or gangs, which also have characteristics quite different from those of individual members and also may influence members' consumer behavior.

Social and economic institutions change. They may be modified by strong individual leaders or by controlling groups. Occasionally social institutions are uprooted, but even in stable societies the institutions are constantly pruned and trimmed. As a result of relatively gradual change, the social and economic framework of the United States is much different today from what it was a generation ago. An example is child care, which has changed, in part, because of the increased prevalence of two-income families. The "traditional" view of family, where the father works outside the home and the mother stays home to care for the children, has evolved into a view that permits both parents to work outside the home, and child care to be given over either to a willing relative or to a child care provider outside the family.

People are products of the culture of their time and place. Their culture includes the group's attitude toward women and children, toward minority groups, and toward workers, the conditions of work, and labor unions. The culture also includes the group's attitudes concerning food and clothing, education, religion, medical care, and science. In U.S. society, younger members are expected to attend school, to get a job, and to conform to the community pattern of living. Those who deviate from these norms are subject to social pressure to conform. Norms, of course, include many aspects of consumer behavior.

All individuals must find ways to live in the society that surrounds them. One of the strongest guiding forces is the desire for social approval. One way to gain approval is to emulate the actions and choices of other group members. Most people find it easiest to get along with their group by doing as the group does. This is especially true of recently immigrated families, many of whom make special efforts to fit in with their new culture. The adoption of the new culture is commonly referred to as **assimilation.** It often involves the adoption of consumer behaviors found in the new culture.

Assimilation the process whereby an immigrant group gradually adopts the characteristics of the new culture.

Patterns of consumer wants may be consistent for limited periods, but they do change over longer periods. The underlying physiological and psychological bases of wants do not change, but the types of goods and services capable of satisfying wants do change. Consider the ways in which patterns of food, clothing, and shelter consumption in the United States have changed over the last few decades.

THE ROLE OF GROUPS

Culture learned patterns of behavior and symbols passed on in a society from one generation to the next.

Reference group a group that influences an individual's attitudes or behavior.

The **culture** of a society includes a complex set of values, ideas, attitudes, and symbols created by human beings to shape human behavior. In a nation as large as the United States, many cultures may co-exist. Within these frameworks of attitude and behavior patterns, smaller entities, known as **reference groups,** take shape. A reference group may be a group to which an individual belongs, to which she would like to belong, or to which she does not wish to belong. Reference groups are important sources of values, norms, and perspectives.

Characteristics of Groups

Groups may be distinguished by many characteristics, including language, religion, government, art, organizations, and the use of stimulants and sedatives. These characteristics may not be exclusively social (they may have roots in the individuals, too), but they are predominantly social. Group characteristics are summarized as follows:

1. *The ability to communicate thoughts by means of speech, pictures, and writing is a characteristic of every human group.* Every human group has its language. The desire to communicate gives rise to consumer demand for instruments of communication. Examples are books, newspapers, magazines, paintings, prints, recordings, films, and, most recently, communication via the computer.

2. Most societies have or have had a *religion.* Religions recognize a supreme being or mysterious power greater than humans, and they prescribe forms of worship ranging from a tribal sun dance to the elaborate ritual of the Roman Catholic Church. Religious feeling is so strong that millions of consumers deny themselves material pleasures in order to gain the spiritual values of their religion. The money that consumers spend for religion satisfies their desire for outward expression of religious feeling. In many societies, a significant portion of economic life is devoted to creating goods and rendering services to satisfy religious wants.

3. When people live in groups, they need a *government and a means of social control.* The larger a group becomes, the more complex are its interrelationships and the greater is the need for social controls. Approximately a third of the U.S. gross national product is generated by local, state, and federal governments. In addition, the process of governing, either in providing direct, personal services or in other functions, requires the consumption of goods. From consumers' point of view, important functions of government include protecting consumer rights in the areas of safety, choice, information, redress, education, environment, and formulation of government policy.

4 *Recognition and appreciation of beauty* is a group characteristic that finds expression in various forms of visual art, such as drawing, painting, sculpture, and architecture. From the crudely carved or painted stone caves of prehistory to the magnificent modern galleries of art, this group want has motivated a significant portion of economic activity.

5 Most people are *social.* They want to be with other people, and they crave companionship and friendship. In the United States, scores of organizations in every community help to fill this need. Some are open groups, such as political clubs and parent/teacher associations. Other organizations have exclusive or even secret qualities that confer prestige value. Clubs, fraternities, lodges, and sororities generate consumer wants for costumes, insignia, and regalia. The social activities of groups generally result in consumer demand for decorations, gifts, and food.

6. In many societies, the members make use of *stimulants and sedatives.* Some social groups encourage the consumption of intoxicating drinks or narcotics, and others oppose it on health or religious grounds. In industrialized countries, as the pace of life quickens

and society becomes increasingly complex, many people feel the need for stimulants or tranquilizers. In the United States, billions of dollars are spent every year for such products.

www.cspinet.org

The mission of the website for the Center for Science in the Public Interest (CSPI) is to educate policy makers and the public about nutrition and food safety. It promotes food labeling and educates the public on deceptive advertising.

Group Influence

The influence of the group on its members can become clear through an examination of its taboos, concepts of survival, prestige, and group welfare; and its social conventions. In every societal group, some goods or practices are taboo. For example, the group may shun certain foods because of a belief that those foods cause illness or death. For example, some people will not eat mushrooms because of the poisonous species among them. A notion such as this may be handed down from one generation to the next and become a taboo.

Social conventions may arise from group beliefs about survival. In some parts of the world, people customarily remove their shoes before entering the home; not to do so is considered disrespectful, but in fact this custom probably developed out of hygienic concerns. In jungles, some groups build houses on stilts for protection from wildlife. In earthquake areas, houses are made of light, flexible materials that can withstand shock.

All societal groups encourage or discourage certain wants on the basis of the group concept of prestige. Military dress uniforms have had high prestige value in many societies, especially in militaristic societies such as pre–World War II Germany, Italy, and Japan. In most religions, the clergy sets itself apart by special attire, such as the colorful robes of Roman Catholic prelates. Judicial robes are considered to give judges an additional aura of dignity and prestige. The caps and gowns worn at graduation ceremonies contribute to the prestige attached to the educational institution; this tradition started with medieval university students and professors who wished to set themselves apart from "common folk." Thus, the desire for prestige continues today.

It is easy to understand why individuals bow to the wishes of the group. The social tendency of most people is so strong that they will do almost anything to win admission to a group. Still, how can we explain members' acceptance of the group's *ideas?* And why does one group wish to set itself off from another?

Just as individuals try to command others' attention or respect by their actions, so societal groups endeavor to command the admiration, respect, or envy of other groups. Just like individuals, groups inhabit social and economic levels. Within each level are organizations that have varying degrees of prestige. On a university campus, for example, some individuals may consider a certain fraternity or sorority to be the number one "prestige" group. Prestige seekers would like to belong to this type of organization. Prestige, however, is achieved by exclusion, so the "top" groups limit the number of members. Prestige seekers who do not gain membership in the "top" group then must turn to other groups. Rather than join a low-prestige group, some individuals gain prestige by remaining independent.

The group concept of welfare is broader than the group ideas mentioned so far. A group's concept of what constitutes and promotes its welfare may include its attitudes toward education, military strength, religion, artistic achievement, and economic productivity, to mention only a few. Nations and societal groups in some parts of the Middle East, for example, emphasize religion and philosophy in their scale of value, whereas Americans place great importance on producing economic goods and accumulating wealth.

OTHER FORCES INFLUENCING WANTS

Additional factors that influence wants include environmental, socioeconomic, and political influences.

Environmental Influences

The federal government estimates 60 million or more trees are destroyed each year to produce junk mail that is never opened. To remove yourself from mail lists, visit www.directmail.com.

FYI

The environment heavily influences consumers' wants, whether they recognize it or not. Basic wants and necessities are universal, but how they are satisfied is largely determined by the environment in which the consumer lives, including the climate and natural resources available.

Climate

Climate influences economic wants. People who live in frigid zones want fuel to heat their houses and warm clothing to wear. People who live where temperatures get hot want air conditioning for their houses and minimal or lightweight clothing.

Natural resources

Although global trade and improved transportation have lessened the impact of geographical influences on wants and needs, to a certain extent the economic resources available to various groups do limit their means to satisfy these wants. Even though all people need and want food, the kind of food they want is largely determined by what is available. All people need and want shelter. The kind of shelter they want, though, depends partly on the climate and partly on the materials available where they live. Almost all people need and want clothing, but what they wear depends on the climate and on the materials available. People in frigid zones wear furs and thermal underwear. In damp, chilly areas, people prefer warm woolens. In warmer areas, people wear cotton and lightweight synthetic materials.

WWW

www.ers.usda.gov/data

The website for the Economic Research Service at the USDA provides facts and figures on farming, poverty, unemployment, and many other interesting aspects of the U.S. economy.

In addition to wants for life-sustaining essentials, other wants—for luxuries, ornaments, styles of architecture, religious ceremonies, and games—historically were influenced by the materials available. The decorative headdress of the American Indian of the plains is made of feathers; traditional Eskimo ornaments consist of bones, teeth, and tusks of fish, seals, and walrus.

As an economy develops, transportation facilities are expanded, making the resources of other regions available to consumers in a specific area. As a result, the range of consumer wants widens.

Socioeconomic Influences

Socioeconomic issues, such as income and occupation, directly influence consumer wants.

Income

Money income the amount of pay one receives.

Real income the amount of goods and services that one's money income will purchase.

Psychic income the satisfaction gained in consuming the goods and services purchased with one's income. Also refers to income in a form other than monetary, such as power, prestige, job satisfaction, and so forth.

Money income, real income, and **psychic income** are important concepts in economics. The income of members of a society is dependent on the resources available to that society. The United States is a "rich" country, in part because it has an abundance of natural resources within its borders. As a consequence, its gross national product is large and per capita income is high. The higher one's income, the more wants one can satisfy.

Within the United States, the level of family income varies widely by region. In the early 2000s, median household income in the United States was approximately $48,500. (See Exhibit 2.3 for a list of the wealthiest and poorest states.) In addition, household income levels vary over a large range. Many U.S. families have money income of less than $20,000 a year; many others have income in excess of $250,000 a year; in between is the "middle class."

EXHIBIT 2.3

The wealthiest and poorest states.

TOP 10 WEALTHIEST STATES
Here's where the median household income is highest

STATE	INCOME
Maryland	$65,144
New Jersey	$64,470
Connecticut	$63,422
Hawaii	$61,160
Massachusetts	$59,963
New Hampshire	$59,683
Alaska	$59,393
California	$56,645
Virginia	$56,277
Minnesota	$54,023

THE 10 POOREST STATES
The states with the lowest median household income

STATE	INCOME
New Mexico	$40,629
Montana	$40,627
Tennessee	$40,315
Kentucky	$39,372
Louisiana	$39,337
Alabama	$38,783
Oklahoma	$38,770
Arkansas	$36,599
West Virginia	$35,059
Mississippi	$34,473

Source: U.S. Census Bureau, 2006.

Occupation

An important group of wants is determined by the nature of work people do. Many people engage in occupations that require special clothing. Some employers provide uniforms to their employees; other employees must purchase their own. For example, office workers are frequently required to wear suits. Construction workers require durable fabrics, hard hats, and steel-toed boots to protect their bodies. Workers in the health care fields wear loose, washable clothing, often with cute or calming patterns.

The nature of one's occupation gives rise to wants for a wide variety of supplemental equipment and facilities. Traveling sales representatives must have automobiles. Most doctors and dentists must have equipment for diagnosis and treatment, as well as waiting rooms equipped with furniture and reading materials. Members of the clergy, lawyers, and professors usually need office space, equipment, and libraries.

According to the Department of Labor, women earn approximately 77 cents for every dollar a man earns. In comparison, in 1951, women earned 64 cents for every dollar a man earned.

FYI

Political and Governmental Influences

Political influences on consumer wants include the effects of taxes, tariffs, and international trade. Consumers might adjust their wants depending on the advantages or disadvantages associated with a tax or trade issue, for example.

Governments utilize fiscal policy and monetary policy refers to government attempts to influence the economy. The two main instruments of **fiscal policy** are government spending and taxation. **Monetary policy** attempts to stabilize the economy by controlling interest rates and the supply of money. Adjustments in these several factors are used to encourage a lagging economy or to brake a too-active economy. Despite government action, however, recessions do occur, with large numbers of people who are able and willing to work unable to find jobs. Though they may receive unemployment compensation, the amount is less than their normal income, and their freedom of choice consequently is restricted.

Fiscal policy a tool of government to achieve economic goals through its power to tax and spend.

Monetary policy the government's attempt to achieve economic goals by regulating the supply of money and credit through the Federal Reserve System.

Taxes

Taxes are payments to local, state, and federal governments. As population and urbanization increase, society becomes more complex and citizens demand that government agencies provide additional services. As consumers, citizens must pay for these services. A hypothetical family of four, living in their own home, can expect to allocate about a third of their total budget for various taxes. In return for these tax payments, citizens receive a wide range of services, most of which they could not provide for themselves or obtain from private firms. Because the individual cannot spend money paid to government agencies for other goods and services, taxes diminish personal income and reduce the freedom of consumer choice. However, they provide many necessary and desirable services.

Progressive tax a tax that requires a larger fraction of income as income increases.

Proportional tax a tax that requires the same fraction of income from all income levels. Some income taxes at the state level require a specific percentage to be paid by all.

Regressive tax a tax requiring a smaller fraction of income as that income increases. Sales tax is an example of a regressive tax; the tax is measured against what is spent, which for low-income taxpayers is a larger proportion of their income.

Tax expenditures deductions and expenditures that reduce actual taxes due. These also are called tax loopholes.

Marginal tax bracket the percentage of taxes paid on the top dollar's worth of taxable income.

Taxes can be classified as progressive, proportional, or regressive. The U.S. tax system is purported to be **progressive**—that is, based on the principle of ability to pay. Some critics of the system argue that this is not really the case—that if the system were truly progressive, families with higher incomes would pay a higher percentage of their incomes in taxes. For the bulk of American taxpayers, the tax structure is not progressive. For them, progressive taxes such as the federal income tax are counter-balanced by **regressive** taxes such as sales taxes. The result is an overall tax that is approximately **proportional.** Thus, the ratio of tax to income is about the same for members of the various income classes.

Even the progressive federal income tax system is not as progressive as it seems to be. Many citizens believe, incorrectly, that an individual whose salary is in excess of $50,000 must pay 28 percent, or $14,000 in federal taxes, and a person whose income is $500,000 a year must also pay 28 percent, or $140,000. Actually, because of **tax expenditures,** or loopholes, individuals in high-income brackets often pay a small fraction (if any) of their income. When coupled with the **marginal tax bracket,** the result is that many high-income citizens and corporations pay little federal income tax. The concept of marginal tax bracket refers to the fact that even people in high tax brackets pay lower taxes on a portion of their income. An individual in a 28 percent marginal tax bracket pays 28 percent only on the income that is above the cutoff level for that bracket. Dollars earned before reaching the bracket are taxed at lower rates.

Because of these two factors—tax expenditures and marginal tax brackets—and because they encompass the majority of taxpayers, most taxes are collected from middle-income citizens. Various recent tax reform law changes have reduced some inequities; nevertheless, dozens of the largest U.S. corporations and thousands of high-income individuals continue to pay little or no federal income tax. The federal tax system continues to be less than fair for most Americans and is coming under increasing scrutiny.

Tariffs and quotas

Tariff a tax assessed on imported goods.

Quota a limitation placed on the quantity of a product permitted to be imported.

Like taxes, **tariffs** and **quotas** also create inequities in the marketplace. The federal government may levy tariffs to yield revenue or to protect selected industries. For most consumers, the tariff is a concealed tax. The tariff on an import is intended primarily to yield revenue. It operates in the same way that a sales tax does in reducing individual and family income, because the price at retail will be higher to cover the tariff. With quotas, the federal government does not collect any revenue, but again the domestic price of the product is higher than it would have been otherwise because the effect of the quota is to reduce supply and lessen price competition.

Over the years, various U.S. and foreign companies have obtained protection in the form of tariffs and quotas, with the effect of limiting competition from companies in other countries. The textile and automobile industries in the United States are two examples of many that can be cited. Japan has been highly protective of its automobile and television industries and Canada of its lumber industry. The arguments for these protectionist measures include:

1. All governments protect their various industries.
2. Protectionism decreases unemployment.
3. Protectionism helps a troubled national economy.

The counter-argument is that tariffs and quotas, although they have short-term advantages for some members of the society, often have long-term, detrimental effects for the majority, because these measures often inflate prices, reduce competition, and induce other countries to set up similar barriers.

NAFTA

The North American Free Trade Agreement (NAFTA) went into effect in 1994. As of January 1, 2008, the agreement eliminated tariffs among Canada, Mexico, and the United States on most products. Under NAFTA, a tariff reduction schedule was worked out for trade between the United States and Mexico. Key provisions of NAFTA are the elimination of tariffs and the provision that each country will treat the other country's goods, services, and investors the same way it treats its own. Additional provisions include a comprehensive dispute resolution process, accessibility of government procurement contracts, and simplified business travel procedures.

There continue to be mixed opinions as to the benefits of NAFTA to consumers. Some feel that the agreement will dismantle many of the United States' strong consumer and environmental protection laws. Additionally, they contend that foreign countries could challenge various U.S. laws as being unfair and anticompetitive. Many also fear additional job losses in the United States and dismantling of worker protections. Proponents of NAFTA cite the obvious advantage of free trade to consumers—increased competition that will lead to availability of higher-quality goods at competitive prices.

www.citizen.org/trade/nafta

The website for Public Citizen gives information regarding NAFTA. Public Citizen is funded through donations by individuals and does not accept political or corporate funds.

In a 2003 study the Congressional Budget Office reported three main findings on the impact of NAFTA. First, trade with Mexico was growing prior to NAFTA and would have continued to increase regardless of NAFTA. Second, the impact on U.S.–Mexico trade has been small and subsequently impact on the U.S. labor market has been minimal. Last, NAFTA has very slightly increased the GDPs for Canada, Mexico, and the United States. However, NAFTA opponents point out that income inequality has increased because of NAFTA. Wages have not risen in conjunction with labor output.

HOW CONSUMER DEMAND AND SELLER SUPPLY COME TOGETHER

It is clear that consumer needs and wants, from physiological, psychological, social, environmental, socioeconomic, and political perspectives, are complex. How these needs and wants come together in the marketplace as consumer demand is important. How sellers respond by providing supply is another piece of the intricate economic puzzle. The two sides of the market equation, demand and supply, are described here.

Consumer Demand

The concepts of want and demand are significantly different. As discussed earlier in the chapter, wants have psychological, social, and physical origins and include comforts and luxuries. **Demand,** however, is defined as the combination of desire and ability to pay. Economic demand is determined by both income and desire. The fact that differences in desire result in different levels of demand is fairly obvious. The foods that some consumers want do not appeal to others. The art that delights some consumers leaves others puzzled. **Utility** is subjective and consequently is not measurable. Thus, no one can measure how much utility is served for two different people each consuming a pint of milk. It may be equal, or it may be unequal.

Demand the amount of a product or service that buyers will purchase at a specific price.

Utility the power of an economic product or service to satisfy a human want.

Demand schedule a series of amounts of a product or service that buyers will purchase at a series of prices at a given time in a given market.

The **demand schedule** is a chart showing that people will buy larger quantities of a product or service as the price declines. In a given market, consumers might purchase 10,000 quarts of milk if the price is $2.00, compared with 20,000 quarts if the price is $1.50. Usually, sellers know that if they are to sell more goods or services, prices must be lower. At some point, though, even lower prices will not yield additional demand. This is due to the principle of diminishing marginal utility. This principle, introduced in Chapter 1, holds that additional units of a product or service may offer only incremental satisfaction; for example, a consumer may buy an additional quart of milk when prices decrease, but at some point the power of the product or service to satisfy a human want will decrease.

The law of supply and demand states that when a completely free market operates, the quantity supplied will meet the quantity demanded, thus determining the price. But this principle rarely operates in its purest form in real markets, due to other influencing factors.

Inelasticity of demand an insufficient rise in demand for a product or service in relation to a reduction in its price, leading to a decline in total sales revenues.

Elasticity of demand a rise in demand for a product or service in proportion to the reduction in its price, which leads to a rise in total sales revenues.

Consumer responses to price changes are measurable. Elasticity and inelasticity of demand are key economic terms. **Inelasticity of demand** refers to an insufficient rise in demand for a product or service in relation to a reduction in its price, so that a price reduction results in a decline in total sales revenues. The **elasticity of demand** refers to whether people will continue to buy an item if its price decreases. It depends upon the extent to which that product alone can satisfy a want and upon the importance of that product to the standard of living of the group to which it appeals. Sellers determine their pricing policies on the basis of their estimates of the elasticity of demand for their products.

The relationship between price changes and the behavior of buyers is complex. A few consumers have so much money that they do not respond to lower prices, and some consumers, even with limited incomes, have established consuming habits that price increases cannot deter. Consumers often have a notion as to the proper relation between quality and price, looking with suspicion upon a product or service with a low price. In a period of falling prices, a price reduction may not increase sales because consumers will wait for still further price reductions. Conversely, in a period of rising prices, consumers actually may purchase more because they may expect prices to rise still further. For all these reasons, many sellers believe the demand for their products is relatively inelastic. As a result, they follow a policy of maintaining a constant price for nationally advertised, brand-name, or trademarked merchandise. They sell surpluses under another brand name and perhaps in different types of stores, such as discount stores and outlet centers.

As demand for fuel goes down due to rising fuel costs, a domino effect occurs. Cars with poor MPG ratings are worth less, hybrids are more in demand, and public transportation options experience an increase in users (demand).

FYI

A *real increase in demand* occurs when consumers become willing and able to purchase more of a product or service at the same price or the same amount at a higher price. As family incomes increase, the demand for some goods and services increases. In a dynamic economy, new goods and services are offered for sale, and demand for them may represent an increase in demand resulting from a change in desire. Population changes also result in changes in demand, as do changes in the composition of the population. For example, young people with children demand different goods and services than do older people who are retired.

When a consumer/buyer enters a store, his demand represents a composite of many factors, including the influence of marketing efforts by sellers. Consumer demand represents not only physiological and psychological factors but also the influence of sellers, family, religion, school, and other groups.

In a food store, for example, the demand for food in general is translated into demand for specific quantities of specific products at specific prices. Each of the several thousand items in a store has a different demand schedule. The elasticity of demand for food products as a whole is slight in the middle- and upper-income groups, but demand for items such as fruits, vegetables, dairy products, and meat is elastic in the lower-income groups. Demand for coffee, bread, and milk is relatively inelastic, but the store manager knows that, for most of the other items in a food store, consumers will respond to price changes by purchasing more or less. If the store is located in an area where family incomes are low, the manager knows the store must carry low-priced food items, whereas a grocer in a higher-income neighborhood will carry goods that sell at higher prices.

Seller Supply

Professionals who do research on consumers try to understand what makes consumers buy so that sellers can increase their revenues. Prospective buyers want to pick up merchandise, handle it, and inspect it. They are attracted by colorful displays. They can hardly resist new items and reduced prices. Many consumers cannot distinguish between real and apparent price reductions. Therefore, for many products, laws require sellers to display the quantity and price of the contents. However, laws do not require sellers to show differences in quality. Sellers prefer to have buyers depend on brand names as assurances of quality.

Most markets have many buyers (a situation termed multiopsony) and a few sellers (oligopoly). Theoretically, every family within a market area is a potential buyer in each store. In practice, however, this is not true. Some people rarely buy in a chain store. Others nearly always buy from independent store A, even though store B next door is also independent. Because families in an area tend to attach themselves to various stores, pure competition among buyers does not prevail. Those who purchase all their merchandise from one store do not compete with those who buy regularly from another store. Store managers know that some shoppers are unaware of prices elsewhere and take advantage of this fact to price their products higher.

In most market areas, several stores compete with one another in imperfect competition. Each seller has more control over price than would be possible under conditions of perfect competition. As a result, identical merchandise can be bought in all stores, but not at identical prices. Prices vary because sellers sell different services. Even though all stores in a market area may sell the same brands of bread, coffee, and flour, they offer different conditions, such as convenience of location, organization and layout, and reputation for fairness, courtesy, and efficiency. Some stores take orders by telephone, deliver merchandise to the buyer's home, and give credit. These services are expensive and often result in price differences.

WWW

www.ebay.com

Auction website eBay allows collectors, dealers, sellers, small businesses, bargain hunters, and others to trade on-line. Very small items such as baseball cards, to very large items, such as airplanes, can be auctioned on this website.

TIP

Generally, being too loyal to a single merchant can be costly to a consumer. Let the merchant know that you will go elsewhere if better products or services are available elsewhere. The result is that the merchant will continually attempt to earn your business.

Store managers endeavor to convert shoppers to customers. In popular language, *customer* and *buyer* mean the same thing, but the retail trade notes an important difference between the casual shopper and the regular customer. To the extent that a store owner or manager succeeds in establishing a clientele of customers, she achieves a monopoly as far as these customers are concerned. In this situation, the store owner's monopoly is not strong, but it does enable the owner to secure higher prices for the store's goods and services.

When sellers attempt to convert buyers into customers, noneconomic factors are important. People are likely to patronize a store operated by a member of their family or a close friend. If a retailer belongs to a small church or club, members of that group may tend to buy from their fellow member. Reciprocity—companies purchasing from other

There Oughta Be a Law . . .

The Franchise and Business Opportunities Rule

The American dream often includes owning one's own business. Unfortunately, many business opportunities that seem too good to be true turn out to be just that.

For years, business franchises were fraught with swindles. The FTC passed a trade rule in 1978 requiring certain disclosures by franchise and business-opportunity sellers. A disclosure document must be presented to the buyer at least 10 business days before any money is exchanged or legal contract is signed. The document must include:

- the seller's history, background, and financial status
- the cost of starting and maintaining the business
- the buyer's responsibilities to the seller
- the names of suppliers and other services the buyer will have to use
- the names of other people who bought the business
- the conditions under which the agreement can be canceled

The FTC recommends buyers take the following precautions before making a decision to invest in a specific company:

- Compare franchises of the same type.
- Look through the *Franchised Opportunities Handbook;* it lists and describes more than 850 companies by type. Call or write several listed companies and ask for their disclosure documents, then compare offerings.
- Talk to current owners. The disclosure document lists names and addresses of people who currently own and operate franchises or business-opportunity ventures. These people are a vital source of information that the buyer cannot afford to ignore when reaching a decision. Try to call a minimum of 10 owners to find out what is good and not so good about the company.
- Investigate earnings claims. Earnings claims are only estimates. The FTC rule requires companies to explain the facts upon which they base their earnings claims.
- Listen to the sales presentation. If you are told, "Sign today because prices will go up tomorrow," or "Another buyer wants this deal if you don't take it now," slow down—do not speed up—your purchase. A seller with a good offer does not have to use this sort of pressure.
- Obtain the seller's promises in writing. Any important promises obtained from a salesperson should be written into the signed contract.

companies that purchase from them—is a common business practice. For example, a local business may spend a significant amount to purchase travel services from a local agency, even though those same services could have been obtained less expensively on the Internet.

Price surveys have disclosed that no one store has lower prices on all merchandise at all times. An independent store that offers telephone or Internet orders, delivery, and credit service may have lower prices than a cash-and-carry chain store on some items. In times of scarcity, sales at independent stores tend to increase because their store managers favor regular customers by reserving items that are difficult to secure. In such times, consumers are less concerned about prices than they are about availability. During a recession, independent stores are more subject to elasticity of demand than are chain stores because consumers are more price-conscious at that time.

SUMMARY

Economists generally agree that consumers have unlimited wants. Because of limited incomes and limited supplies of goods in the marketplace, however, these wants cannot be totally satisfied. Scholars have attempted to determine why consumers purchase specific goods and services with their limited incomes. The conclusion is that consumers' decision making is based, in part, on the principles of harmonious consumption, diminishing utility, variety, and satiety. Needs and wants that influence consumers can be refined and classified further as biological, psychological, and social. Climate, natural resources, income, occupation, taxes, tariffs, and quotas have effects on the behavior of consumers in the marketplace.

The flow of goods from producer to consumer typically involves the manufacturer, wholesaler, and retailer. The market is where the forces that represent demand (consumer) and supply (retailers) meet.

ITEMS FOR REVIEW & DISCUSSION

1. Define insatiability of human wants.
2. Explain how the principle of diminishing returns affects the way an individual spends money.
3. Explain why the desire for the goods and services that money will buy increases more rapidly than the ability to increase income. How do personal psychological wants affect consuming activities?
4. Discuss Maslow's Hierarchy of Needs.
5. Identify the four principles of consumption and give implications of each.
6. Differentiate among needs, wants, and demand.
7. Define the relationship between reference group and consumer behavior.
8. Name some possible advantages and adverse effects of restrictive tariffs and quotas.
9. What problems may develop within the United States because of disparities in family income within the country and around the world? Discuss the reasons.
10. Major tax reform has occurred in the past few decades (1986, 2001, 2009). What is the potential for reform in the future?
11. Estimate what percentage of your income you pay in local, state, and federal taxes. Now look at your paycheck and determine if your estimates were correct.
12. Distinguish among the terms *demand, desire,* and *utility.* Define elastic and inelastic demands and give examples.
13. What are some of the potential costs and benefits resulting from full implementation of NAFTA?

EXPLORING PERSONAL VALUES: PROJECTS

1. The owners of many professional sports teams operate at a loss and take a substantial tax write-off. Discuss the fairness of this practice in light of the social contribution professional sports make and the less than progressive system of federal income tax.
2. Keep a journal. Write about one of the following:
   a. List the basic goals of your life. Write how these goals affect your purchases.
   b. Describe your culture (or reference group). Also, describe social and peer-group pressures that you encounter. Discuss how your culture or group affects you as a consumer.
   c. Interview your parents, grandparents, and other family members. Describe how their goals and philosophies have influenced you as a consumer.
   d. Identify components of Maslow's Hierarchy of Needs and how they relate to your life as a consumer.
3. Analyze what your needs and wants might be if you had been born (a) into a family whose economic position is much higher than yours is now, and (b) into a family whose economic position is much lower than yours.

4. Describe how the changing occupational opportunities for college graduates may affect your future consumption patterns.
5. Consider this statement from the point of view of a business person, a union member, and an economist: "Tariffs and quotas have long-term detrimental effects for the majority; thus, they must be eliminated."
6. Drawing on the four principles of consumption, write a character sketch of someone who is vastly influenced by one of these principles.
7. Keep a record of all that you consume or purchase for one week. Check your record against the basic biological and security needs. How much of what you used or bought was to satisfy needs? How much was to satisfy wants?
8. Research another country. Diagram the influences of consumer wants in that country.

ADDITIONAL SOURCES OF INFORMATION

Bacon, David. *The Children of NAFTA: Labor Wars on the U.S./Mexico Border.* Berkeley, CA: University of California Press, 2004.

Becker, Gary S., and Kevin M. Murphy. *Social Economics: Market Behavior in a Social Environment.* Cambridge, MA: Belknap Press, 2003.

Fisher, Byron. *The Supply and Demand Paradox: A Treatise on Economics.* Charleston, SC: BookSurge Publishing, 2007.

Gilmore, James H., and B. Joseph Pine II. *Authenticity: What Consumers Really Want.* Boston: Harvard Business School Press, 2007.

Hakim, Peter, and Robert E. Litan. *The Future of North American Integration: Beyond NAFTA.* Washington, DC: Brookings Institution Press, 2002.

MacArthur, John R. *The Selling of "Free Trade": NAFTA, Washington, and the Subversion of American Democracy.* New York: Hill and Wang, 2001.

Maslow, Abraham. *Motivation and Personality.* New York: Harper & Row, 1954.

Mayer, Frederick W. *Interpreting NAFTA.* New York: Columbia University Press, 1998.

Russell, Cheryl. *Best Customers: Demographics of Consumer Demand.* Ithaca, NY: New Strategist Publications, 2006.

Terry, Deborah J., and Michael A. Hogg. *Attitudes, Behavior, and Social Context: The Role of Norms and Group Membership.* Mahwah, NJ: L. Erlbaum Associates, 2000.

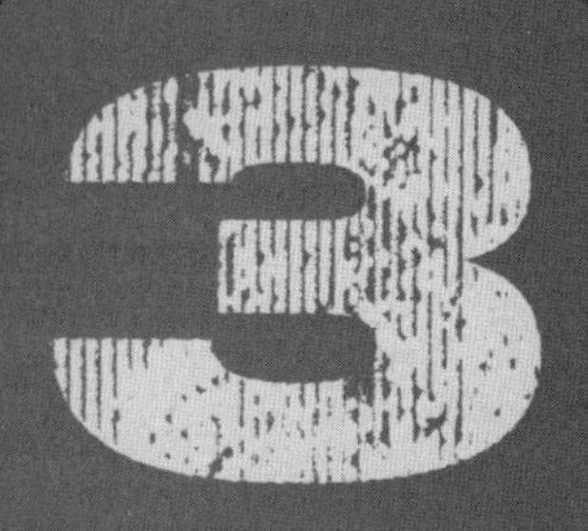

3

> All things should be laid bare so that the buyer may not be in any way ignorant of anything the seller knows.
>
> CICERO

KEY TERMS

consumption
consumption patterns
economic adult
economic minor
ignorant-consumer standard
level of living
material measure
reasonable-consumer standard
standard of living
values

The following concepts will be developed in this chapter:

1. The quality of our life is determined by the goods and services we are able to buy. The question is: Who makes the buying decisions, the buyer or the seller?
2. The American economy is motivated by the profit system.
3. Manufacturers produce many goods that consumers do not need or want.

After having read this chapter, you should be able to accomplish the following objectives:

1. Discuss the effects the lack of consumer education has on the buying public, and list ways in which the seller influences the consumer's buying decisions.
2. Develop a comprehensive list of the strengths and weaknesses of the profit system.
3. Explain the interaction between supply and demand.
4. Explain criticisms of the profit system.

Consumption the use of a good or service.

THE FAMILY AS A CONSUMING AND PRODUCING UNIT

One purpose of productivity in an economy is **consumption.** In a few simple economies, such as in parts of Northern Canada where some Inuit (members of the Eskimo population) cultures are still considered hunting-and-gathering societies, production and consumption occur almost simultaneously, and those who provide the goods use them. Generally, however, with industrialization, the self-sufficient economic unit has changed. The wider array of goods provided in a complex economy requires specialists to produce them. Thus, the family is viewed primarily as a consuming unit; most production takes place in the business sector of the economy. However, it should be noted that "home production" does occur, and many believe that it is becoming a more common phenomenon in the United States. This can be seen through the increased expenditures for raw materials that are used for goods made in the home.

Consumers: Leading and Following

Standards and Levels of Living

Family members serve an important social role of providing labor and also engage in activities aimed at meeting their needs and wants for satisfaction or well-being. To meet their needs and wants, the family purchases, combines, and consumes goods and services within the home. To do so effectively, they need to be educated so they can achieve maximum satisfaction from their purchases. An assumption among some economists is that consumption "just happens." This view obscures the skill and technique necessary for consumers to derive the most value from their income and to combine limited amounts of their time with purchased goods in order to achieve satisfaction.

Individuals' motivations differ when they are performing roles in the labor force and as family members. A fundamental difference is that business life in the United States is based on competition and maximization of profit as measured in dollars, whereas family life is based on cooperation among members and maximization of satisfaction as they share economic goods. The outcome of economic activity within the family also is more nebulous, consisting of subjective measures of satisfaction and utility, which are more difficult to recognize and measure than are dollars.

The lack of a monetary approach is responsible, in part, for the difficulty in measuring satisfaction. Although most people recognize the economic value of services performed in the marketplace, the value of services provided in private life, such as the work of socializing children or of buying wisely, often is not considered.

Concepts that help us to understand economic life in the home include **standard of living** and **values.** The standard of living usually is characterized as a **material measure.** Consumers compare their **level of living** to their desired standard of living. It is this comparison, among other things, that influences the extent to which people are willing to go into debt in an effort to "keep up."

Standard of living the quality or quantity of goods and services aspired to by individuals or societies.

Values individual or collective beliefs or ideas about what is desirable.

Material measure a synonym for standard of living.

Level of living the actual quality and quantity of goods and services experienced by individuals and society.

Family Structure

The family is a timeless and continuing social institution, although it does undergo transformations as people seek to adjust to changing social and economic forces. These

Consumption patterns the extent to which goods and services are used up.

forces affect **consumption patterns** in several ways. For example, many families today have two wage earners, diminishing the time available for one partner to specialize in home activities. This change is partially the result of increasing demands on a family's income, especially as reflected in installment purchases. It also is a result of providing better education for women, who are often prepared for a role in the labor force rather than in homemaking. In addition, more individuals are now living in single-member households, partly because people often are marrying at a later age, partly because one mate outlives the other, and partly because of the high divorce rate. Divorce also alters the structure of families so that one parent must be both wage earner and homemaker. In addition, cultural changes during the past half century have led to a significant number of people choosing to live in households of unrelated individuals organized around some common cause—economic, political, religious, or other. An example is college students sharing an apartment or house for economic reasons.

Accompanying these changing social configurations are changes in the way money is spent. The general trend has been toward the purchase of separate goods, such as cell phones, DVDs, televisions, automobiles, and computers, for each family member. In addition, goods increasingly are purchased at later stages of production, when they are more ready to be consumed. Goods are being packaged and promoted more frequently in amounts and types for individual rather than family use. If the family is to attain a given level of living, these developments require more economic resources.

WHO GUIDES CONSUMERS IN THE MARKET?

Consumption Patterns of Minors

When children are infants, their parents freely supply them with the goods and services they need. As they mature, one of the many things they must learn is how to use money to meet their own needs. In their first six years, most children are dominated by parental influence. Other influences, such as those of religion, school, friends, and advertisers, grow in significance between ages 6 and 18. Might we assume that, as children develop from infancy to maturity, their parents have taught them to spend money wisely? As young people develop the ability to earn money, do they also develop the ability to spend it to their best advantage? The answer depends in large part on the training and education the parents provide. Parents themselves, like their children, may be **economic adults** or **economic minors.**

Economic adult a rational and informed consumer, regardless of age.

Economic minor an irrational and uninformed consumer, regardless of age.

Young children are remarkably alert and observant. They learn by listening to what their parents say and by observing what they do. They develop attitudes concerning money even before they know what money is and how it operates in the economy. If parents are economic adults, they demonstrate to their children how to spend income to promote the welfare of family members. If the parents are economic minors, they perpetuate problems. Their children will likely be swayed easily by advertising and peer-group pressure. They probably will not learn how to do their job as consumers. The result is often misuse of credit and other problems inherent in being an economic minor.

People assume that children somehow grow effortlessly into economic adulthood. The truth is that too many people never become mature consumers. We also tend to assume that as people earn money of their own, they also learn how to spend it wisely. Although neither of these assumptions is valid, public schools in the United States include little, if any, training in how to use income intelligently.

According to various surveys conducted in the past three decades, the vast majority of consumers would like to have consumer education mandated in our public schools.

FYI

The family is the most important institution for educating children to become economic adults. This is where children should learn that money is a valuable tool for reaching goals and that acquiring money is not a goal in itself. If a child has parents who are intelligent consumers, he or she is likely to become a mature consumer. A child reared by parents who are economic minors, however, is not likely to become a good consumer.

Who Guides the Adults?

Sellers of goods and services use advertising and salesmanship in an effort to guide consumer wants to benefit themselves. With the increasing use of technology and with occupational specialization, the use of advertising and salesmanship has intensified. Business firms have found that the economies of production on a large scale demand steady, maximum output. Because they cannot afford to let expensive equipment stand idle while waiting for consumers to buy, they produce goods in anticipation of consumer demand. As output increases, firms cannot afford to let inventories accumulate while they wait for consumers to order goods. Aggressive sellers found that they could increase demand for their products through marketing techniques. Sellers, increasingly skillful in the art of persuasion, now play a significant role in determining consumer choices. On the other hand, consumers have proved to be less capable of guiding producers to provide goods and services of their choice.

> WWW
>
> **www.consumerworld.org**
>
> Consumer World provides product reviews, price comparisons, and information on car buying, mortgage rates, long distance rates, airfares, magazine subscriptions, and other products and services. Consumers can visit this site for up-to-date information.

Neither the family nor the school has prepared consumers adequately for the world in which we live. The main school in which consumers learn is the school of experience. The tuition is high, and attendance does not ensure success. Still, each person faces the fundamental challenge of acquiring the knowledge and developing the inner discipline that underlie real freedom of choice. Occasionally when consumers are unable or unwilling to assume economic adult status, the government steps in with assistance, such as by regulating certain segments of trade.

How Much Guidance?

Local, state, and federal governments have been given the responsibility under law to protect consumers. Government officials have struggled to determine the amount and extent of consumer protection that is necessary. Should their task be to protect only sensible, intelligent consumers who conduct themselves carefully in the marketplace, or should it also be to protect consumers who are uninformed, careless, and wasteful? At times, agencies have acted on behalf of the latter by invoking the **ignorant-consumer standard.** At other times, courts and legislatures have ordered agencies to ignore these people and invoke the **reasonable-consumer standard.**

Ignorant-consumer standard a standard based on the assumption that the law should protect even consumers who are ignorant, careless, and wasteful.

Reasonable-consumer standard a standard based on the assumption that the government should protect consumers but also that consumers have the responsibility to be informed and rational.

> **TIP** At the state level, the agency that typically enforces the state consumer protection law is the Attorney General's Office. At the federal level, the Federal Trade Commission has a similar role. Go to these agencies to lodge complaints and to obtain quality consumer information.

How much guidance do consumers need? Who is to do the guiding? How much government interference should there be between buyers and sellers? These are just a few of the questions that must be asked when determining how the marketplace should serve the consumer and what degree of freedom sellers should have in pursuing their goals.

Putting It All Together

Several concepts that have been discussed fit together (see Exhibit 3.1). They can be placed on a continuum as the exhibit shows.

EXHIBIT 3.1

Continuum of economic concepts.

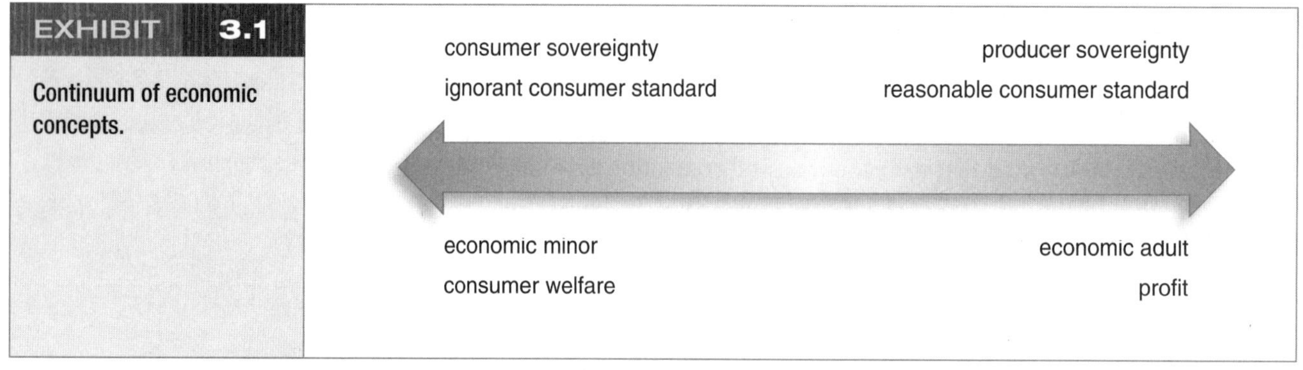

Although the exhibit labels only the extremes of the continuum, in reality, these concepts exist all along the continuum. For example, in reality there is no pure consumer sovereignty, nor is there pure producer sovereignty. However, in some industries, for example in the manufacturing of computers, there may be more producer sovereignty than consumer sovereignty. (That is, consumers are not typically asked their opinions about what types of computers they would like to see produced; producers are the experts and give us what technology allows.) On the continuum, the computer-manufacturing industry would fall toward the right side.

The exhibit also shows how the concepts relate to each other. For example, the ignorant consumer standard is most likely applied to economic minors; conversely, the reasonable consumer standard is applied to economic adults. And, finally, the consumer-sovereignty side is most concerned with consumer welfare, while the producer-sovereignty side is primarily concerned with profit. The latter two concepts are discussed further in the next section.

CASE STUDY Economic Maturity (or Lack Thereof)

The Ortiz family lives in a small rural town in the Midwest. The father, Enrique, is a real estate agent, and the mother, Camilla, works at a credit union. They have two teenage sons, Ryan and Jackson.

In the midst of the real estate boom, Enrique was making so much money he didn't know what to do with it all—as home prices went up his commissions grew. He decided to give his sons a generous allowance for investment purposes: $150 a week. He still had more money than he needed to pay the family's bills, so he bought a sports car and a boat.

Camilla's credit union was doing so much real estate loan business that her salary increased and she received bonuses, as well. Camilla had a strong hunch that her money would be best invested in a rental property and set about acquiring a house in a well-maintained neighborhood down the street. The credit union was happy to extend the credit even though technically the payment put the Ortiz family beyond a safe expenditure threshold.

Ryan and Jackson took a different approach to managing their money. For more than five years, they turned over their allowances to a financial planning consultant, who created a portfolio of stocks and mutual funds that earned a good return. As the real estate market peaked, the boys encouraged their advisor to be conservative with investments, keeping the principal safe.

When the real estate boom subsided, Enrique and Camilla no longer had income to make payments on the car and boat, which were repossessed, or on the rental house, on which the bank foreclosed. Ryan's and Jackson's savings helped to keep the family from bankruptcy.

QUESTIONS

1. Which members of the Ortiz family would you say are economic minors? Which are economic adults?
2. In your opinion, are the credit union and dealerships partially to blame for allowing Mr. and Mrs. Ortiz to over-extend themselves?
3. How is the Ortiz family similar to or different from many families today in the maturity with which its members fulfill their roles as consumers?

THE PROFIT-AND-LOSS STATEMENT: A GUIDE TO SELLERS

If consumers do not guide producers, what does guide producers? How do they decide what and how much to produce? How do they decide upon standards of quality? How do they detect consumer wants and how these change? Answers to these questions are provided by the driving force that motivates modern business: the desire for profit. Business firms guide production according to the standard, "Will it be profitable?"

Profit-and-loss statements provide business managers with objective measures of success. If an established product begins to show less profit, management must consider whether to discontinue its production or to spend more on advertising. For a new product, management tests it in a limited market area to perform market research. If consumers in the test area buy the new product, the business manager interprets that response as evidence of acceptance of the product, its appearance or package, and the price. Management personnel then may decide to sell the product more widely. If, however, consumers in the test area reject the product, consumers in other parts of the nation will not hear about it.

CRITICISMS OF THE PROFIT SYSTEM

The basic assumption of the profit system is that business firms will benefit by offering for sale only those goods and services that consumers want. This assumption, in turn, is predicated on the assumption that consumers know what they want. These two assumptions are not always valid.

Markups in the supermarket industry can range from 5 percent to 20 percent, depending on the item. Markups are typically lower (about 13 percent maximum) for warehouse supermarkets that charge a yearly membership fee.

FYI

Profit over Consumer Welfare

Business firms may be motivated by the desire to serve their customers (the service motive) or by the desire to make a profit, or both. The desire for profit may supersede the service motive. Sometimes business firms realize a profit by performing no service or by performing a disservice. For example, profits are greater in an economy of scarcity than in an economy of abundance. From a business point of view, scarcity results in high prices and, often, in greater profits. From a consumer point of view, however, more wants can be satisfied when there is an abundance of goods and services at low prices. Deliberate restrictions on output by managers of factories or farms can be explained only by the fact that the restrictions allow them to maintain or raise prices by limiting the supply.

Not many firms operate at full capacity. Management sets a profit goal and then sets prices and restricts production to achieve that goal. This strategy was developed during the 19th century, and it seems to be prevalent today. In highly concentrated industries with few producers, the goal of restricting supply can be attained easily. This is one reason that having many sellers in a marketplace is crucial.

Manipulation of Consumer Demand

In addition to restricting production, business firms often try to manipulate consumer demand. They attempt to persuade consumers to buy goods and services that will be profitable to the sellers even though the goods and services may be detrimental or worthless to consumers. This approach leads business firms to spend more and more money on advertising and other efforts to increase sales.

The purpose of persuasive selling efforts is not primarily to help consumers find the goods and services they want but, rather, to induce them to buy specific goods and brands. The result is competitive waste. For example, the dairy industry may urge consumers to drink more milk. If they respond, producers of other products—say, vitamin pills—find their sales diminishing. In turn, they increase their advertising expenditures to urge consumers to purchase their pills. It is small wonder that consumers become bewildered!

Exploitation of Consumers

The desire for profit may be so strong that it leads some sellers to resort to unscrupulous and even fraudulent practices to generate a profit. During the time when consumer economics as a science was in its infancy, retailers had difficulty defrauding consumers because the market was so small. Once a fraud was detected, word got around among consumers, and the fraud could no longer yield profits. Today, with a complex and ever-changing marketplace in the United States and internationally, unscrupulous sellers are less accountable to consumer well-being; it is difficult to identify and to catch them. Some Internet sites, such as Urban Legend and Snopes, allow consumers to check into a potential fraud online before they might be lured in. However, scam artists are still likely to find victims who do not research the "opportunity."

TIP

Beware of artificial list pricing. With this practice, a manufacturer or retailer inflates the list price of a product and immediately marks down the merchandise to a "sale price" to give the impression that the consumer is getting a good deal.

DOES THE ECONOMY PRODUCE WHAT CONSUMERS WANT?

Demand First or Supply First?

In the handicraft economy of 18th-century America, nearly all goods and services were produced after consumers had ordered them; they were "custom made." In today's marketplace, most services and a significant volume of goods are still rendered or produced after buyers have placed their orders (production on demand). Examples include house painting and repair and maintenance work in general. Automobiles may be partially custom made; a prospective buyer may choose the color and accessories from several thousand variations.

All domestic automobile dealers, as well as many foreign automobile dealers, receive an extra profit from the manufacturer for selling a new auto. Called a "holdback," it increases their profit by 1 percent to 3 percent of the MSRP.

FYI

Nevertheless, goods are most often produced in anticipation of demand. Manufacturers and processors cannot realize the economies of large-scale production if they wait for consumers to express their demands in retail markets. To keep large plants operating continuously, manufacturers must estimate and produce what and how much consumers will want. If their estimates are correct, the products will sell and profits will be made. Sellers use advertising to try to increase the desire for their products and create demand for what they have already decided to produce.

Goods that are produced in anticipation of demand include almost all food products, tobacco products, alcoholic beverages, and soft drinks. Many large building projects are carried out by developers who anticipate demand for houses. Transportation by trains, buses, ships, planes, and rental cars is provided in anticipation of demand. Billions of gallons of gasoline are refined and delivered to retail gasoline service stations in anticipation of demand by motorists. Medical and dental care, insurance services, banking, education, hotel and motel services, and the services of restaurants are also made available in anticipation of demand.

The Economy Produces Enough and More

The real problem of production in anticipation of demand is that manufacturers produce many things consumers do not want or need and then may spend millions of dollars to persuade consumers to buy them. This leads to waste, which results when any consideration other than utility determines what is consumed.

The Fair Packaging and Labeling Act and Related Legislation

The Fair Packaging and Labeling Act (FPLA) became law in 1967. The Act states that informed consumers are essential to the fair and efficient functioning of a free-market economy and that food and nonfood packages and their labels should tell consumers clearly what the contents are and help them compare values. The law contains mandatory, discretionary, and voluntary provisions.

Mandatory Labeling Provisions

A primary objective of the Act is to promote uniformity and simplification of labeling. It provides that

- The net quantity of contents shall be stated in a uniform and prominent location on the package.
- The net quantity of contents shall be clearly expressed in ounces and, if applicable, pounds, or, in the case of liquid measures, in the largest whole unit of quarts or pints.
- The net quantity of a serving must be stated if the package bears a representation concerning servings.

Discretionary Labeling Provisions

The Act authorizes the administering agencies to promulgate regulations when necessary to prevent consumer deception or to facilitate value comparisons:

- to determine what size packages may be represented by descriptions such as "small," "medium," and "large"
- to regulate the use of promotions such as "cents off" and "economy size" on any package
- to require the listing of ingredients in the order of decreasing predominance
- to prevent nonfunctional slack fill

Voluntary Packaging Provisions

The Act provides for the voluntary adoption of packaging standards. It authorizes the Secretary of Commerce to call upon manufacturers, packers, and distributors to develop standards whenever it is found that undue proliferation of weights, measures, or quantities impairs the ability of consumers to make value comparisons. If voluntary standards are not adopted, the Secretary of Commerce shall report this fact to Congress together with a legislation recommendation. The Act does not require percentage labeling of ingredients or drained weights of canned fruits and vegetables, which would be useful information for the consumer to have.

Amendment to the Fair Packaging and Labeling Act

The nutritional labeling provisions of the Nutrition Labeling and Education Act (NLEA) became law in 1994. NLEA, the first major change in food labels since 1974, eliminates much of the confusion and deception that permeated supermarket shelves for decades. Health claim provisions were mandated in 1993. The law affects almost all packaged food and is administered by two federal agencies, the Food and Drug Administration (FDA) and the U.S. Department of Agriculture (USDA) for meat and poultry labeling.

NLEA mandates that nutrition labels include information on total calories and calories from total fat and saturated fat, total carbohydrates, dietary fiber, protein, vitamins and minerals, cholesterol, and sodium. In addition, a standard format is required for disclosures of serving sizes, the amount of each nutrient as a percentage of the Daily Value for a 2,000-calorie diet, a notation for reference values of selected nutrients based on 2,000- and 2,500-calorie daily diets, and calorie conversion information.

Related Legislation

The Food Allergen Labeling and Consumer Protection Act of 2004 is an amendment to the Federal Food, Drug, and Cosmetic Act. It requires labeling all food containing an ingredient from any of a group of major allergens, including milk, eggs, fish, crustacean shellfish, tree nuts, peanuts, wheat, and soybeans. This legislation will also allow for the labeling of foods as "gluten-free."

It might be argued that the fact that consumers purchase products and services implies that those are the goods and services the consumers want. In this argument, if consumers did not want the products, they would not buy them. The sellers would incur losses, and these losses would discourage further attempts to market those goods or services. On the other hand, if consumers like what they find in the stores, they will buy them, and sellers will be encouraged to offer more.

Within limits, this picture of what happens in the retail markets is accurate. The real question, however, is not whether consumers buy what they find in the market but, instead, whether business firms are constantly experimenting and testing to discover unknown demands for goods. If competition is really effective, business firms survive only by producing what consumers want and by meeting the standards of quality and price set by the marketplace. This process of experimentation and risk-taking on the part of businesses allows the marketplace to be an effective means of meeting the needs of present-day consumers. Whether businesses actually engage in this kind of experimentation and thus actually fulfill consumers' wants is open to debate.

SUMMARY

The family unit both consumes and produces. Many families produce goods for use in the home. Family configurations have changed, as have the types and amounts of goods produced outside the home, but the family still guides most consumption patterns. Decisions as to which products to produce are made not by consumers but instead by producers, some of whom are overzealous in the manipulation of demand. Other producers engage in more overt and illegal deceptions.

When the marketplace does not function properly, government sometimes intervenes. As we saw beginning in 2008, the extent to which government should become involved, whether to protect consumer interests or for other reasons, is an important issue for a free society to address.

ITEMS FOR REVIEW & DISCUSSION

1. Some people suggest that "home production" (producing goods in the home for family use) is increasing. Discuss some of the possible economic and social effects of this trend on society.
2. Determine which standards your family has used to measure its success. Is consuming a measure of success for you? Do you attempt to keep up with the Joneses?
3. Discuss the statement, "Rich parents do not necessarily choose wisely for their children, and poor parents do not necessarily choose unwisely for their children." Are there benefits to be gained by having families train their children in techniques of being an intelligent consumer?
4. Who guides consumer decision making in the marketplace? Explain your answer.
5. What are the strengths and weaknesses of the profit system as presented in this chapter?
6. Explore the ways in which consumers guide sellers.
7. Describe economic waste and what causes it.
8. "If what is offered can be sold at a profit, it is legitimate. The business owner should not be concerned about any other considerations, moral, ethical, or religious." Discuss the implications of this position.
9. What are the differences in motives between the family and the business world?
10. What is implied by the question, "Does the economy produce what consumers want?"

EXPLORING PERSONAL VALUES: PROJECTS

1. Consumer educators sometimes refer to government breaks given to large corporations as "corporate welfare." Discuss your views on "socialism at the top" (welfare programs for the rich) and "socialism at the bottom" (welfare programs for persons with low income).
2. Some people advocate giving children an allowance. Others believe that even young children should have to perform some service in exchange for any money they receive. Some believe that families adequately teach children how to manage money and consumer issues, while others feel that a consumer economics course should be part of the high school curriculum. Discuss with your friends or classmates the positions you take.
3. In your journal, write a scene or a story with one character who is an economic minor and one who is an economic adult. At the end of your story, comment about the statement, "Resolved: A child reared by parents who are economic minors is not likely to be a good consumer later in life."
4. Discuss with your classmates whether the ignorant-consumer or reasonable-consumer standard should be used. Provide examples to support your opinion.
5. In your family, do some thinking and asking about which member has the greatest influence on buying decisions. Which member has the least? Give examples.
6. With the assistance of your parents or guardians, estimate how much it has cost to maintain you from birth to college.
7. What is your opinion of government financial assistance to ailing companies?
8. Write a paper about how a family's life cycle stage affects and will continue to affect its consumption.
9. Consider: "Each person feels the fundamental challenge of acquiring the knowledge and developing the inner discipline that underlie real freedom of choice." Expand on this proposition.
10. Write a paper on how one company advertises to entice consumers to buy. Using example ads from this company, discuss your opinion of the effectiveness of these ads.

ADDITIONAL SOURCES OF INFORMATION

Cross, Gary S. *An All-Consuming Century: Why Commercialism Won in Modern America.* New York: Columbia University Press, 2002.

De Graaf, John, David Wann, and Thomas H. Naylor. *Affluenza: The All-Consuming Epidemic.* San Francisco: Berrett-Koehler, 2005.

Farrell, James J. *One Nation Under Goods: Malls and the Seductions of American Shopping.* Washington, DC: Smithsonian Institution Press, 2003.

Frank, Robert H. *Microeconomics and Behavior.* Columbus, OH: McGraw-Hill/Irwin, 2006.

Harrington, Lee, and Denise Bielby. *Popular Culture: Production and Consumption (Blackwell Readers in Sociology).* Malden, MA: Wiley-Blackwell, 2000.

Levering, Frank, and Wanda Urbanska. *Simple Living: One Couple's Search for a Better Life.* Winston-Salem, NC: John F. Blair Publisher, 2003.

Mansvelt, Juliana. *Geographies of Consumption.* London: Sage Publications Ltd., 2005.

Milner Jr., Murray. *Freaks, Geeks, and Cool Kids: American Teenagers, Schools, and the Culture of Consumption.* New York: Routledge, 2006.

Osenton, Tom. *The Death of Demand: Finding Growth in a Saturated Global Economy.* Indianapolis, IN: Financial Times Prentice Hall, 2004.

Consumer freedom of choice is the mainspring of our economic system.

COLSTON E. WARNE, COFOUNDER OF CONSUMERS UNION

KEY TERMS

economic freedom
free entry
full information
illth
nealth
negative economic freedom of choice
positive economic freedom of choice
wealth

The following concepts will be developed in this chapter:

1. Because the conditions necessary for freedom of choice are not always present, producers produce and consumers consume nealth and illth—goods and services that have a neutral effect and those that have a negative effect—as well as wealth—goods and services that promote well-being.
2. Some conditions restrict consumers' freedom of choice, and other conditions promote it.

After having read this chapter, you should be able to accomplish the following objectives:

1. State the conditions necessary for freedom of choice in the marketplace.
2. Define and give examples of wealth, nealth, and illth.
3. Name and give examples of conditions that restrict and conditions that promote freedom of choice for the consumer.

THE CONCEPT OF ECONOMIC FREEDOM

Most people agree that producers and consumers in the United States have more freedom than those in any other country. These freedoms are a result of our economic, political, and social institutions and our abundance of natural and human resources. Even in the United States, though, absolute freedom does not exist.

The counterpart of free choice is "free rejection." In a free society, consumers presumably know what they do *not* want as well as what they do want. Freedom of choice encompasses freedom to choose badly. It implies willingness to accept the consequences of bad choices even though those consequences may be unknown or unknowable.

Wealth goods and services that promote the well-being of consumers.

Illth goods and services that harm consumers.

Nealth goods and services that have a neutral effect, neither helping nor harming the consumer.

WEALTH, NEALTH, AND ILLTH

If consumers are to make intelligent choices, they must know that some goods and services promote their well-being, other goods and services have harmful effects, and some goods and services neither promote nor damage their well-being. Traditional economists consider as *wealth* all goods that have a monetary exchange value, whether they help or harm consumers. Consumer economists make a distinction between **wealth, illth,** and **nealth.**

Consumer Freedoms and Restrictions

By what standard can products and services be classified as wealth, nealth, or illth? Does any product or service that anyone wishes to sell and for which there is a willing buyer represent wealth, and should all products and services in this category be legal? If so, prostitution and hard drugs represent wealth and should be legal. Classifying goods and services as to their contribution to the well-being of the human race is both complicated and controversial. Most observers, however, consider some products and services clearly harmful. These represent illth.

If a typical person were to classify products and services, the result might appear like the sampling in Exhibit 4.1. Various levels of government already have made many decisions about goods that are considered illth, by prohibiting or limiting their use. Each individual, though, must decide which products and services to buy or not to buy.

The concept of **economic freedom** implies a standard or standards. The standard applied most commonly is that of *welfare.* The dictionary definition of "welfare" mentions good fortune and prosperity. The implication is that if people have an abundance of economic goods, they will enjoy a state of well-being. One only has to look around to observe that not all people with an abundance of worldly goods consider themselves to be in a state of well-being. Some people with few goods find enjoyment in nonmaterial things. Obviously, the concepts of well-being and happiness are subjective.

Positive economic freedom of choice and **negative economic freedom of choice** are important concepts. Freedom of choice in an economy of relative abundance is different from freedom of choice in an economy of scarcity. Within an economy of abundance are degrees of freedom. The very rich can live in mansions and can own yachts, airplanes, libraries, and art collections. People in very low income groups have the legal right to enjoy such luxuries, but they do not have the economic right because they lack the necessary purchasing power. For them, freedom of choice is a negative right.

Economic freedom consumers' implied right to choose the goods and services they want.

Positive economic freedom of choice the right to consume anything one wishes, along with the purchasing power necessary to implement that right.

Negative economic freedom of choice the lack of purchasing power to implement the right to consume anything an individual wishes.

TIP Generally, mouthwashes are nealth products. Only those that have the American Dental Association endorsement have some medicinal value.

EXHIBIT 4.1

Classification of sample products and services.

WEALTH	NEALTH	ILLTH
education	mouthwash	cocaine
health care	Chia pets	prostitution
shelter	bumper stickers	pornography
clothing		tobacco
food		

CONDITIONS NECESSARY FOR FREEDOM OF CHOICE

Conditions that are needed to have freedom of choice include free entry, full information, some restriction on freedom of choice, and a price system. (Pricing will be discussed in Chapter 8.)

Free Entry

Free entry the freedom to enter or supply; the implied right of any individual to enter a business or profession and to choose or to reject a job.

Full information the implied right of any individual to obtain essential information that allows intelligent choices in the market.

If consumers are to have freedom to choose, other people in the economy must have **free entry.** This right is fundamental in a free-choice, free-enterprise economy.

Full Information

Full information is a second imperative in a free society. Uninformed choice is not really free choice. An educated, informed, rational consumer can and does engage in free choice and free rejection. Economic minors, however, cannot really exercise their freedom to choose. Sellers have a responsibility to tell prospective buyers, through advertising and labeling, the essential information needed to make an intelligent choice.

The most substantive consumer development in recent years has been the continued growth of the Internet. It is evident that the Internet is transforming the way consumers interact with the marketplace. Currently, consumers can pay bills, save and invest at a "virtual bank," and purchase virtually any manufactured product from the convenience and comfort of home. More important, consumers can find thousands of websites that provide free, substantive consumer information heretofore available only through exhaustive study.

www.consumersunion.org

The Consumers Union (CU) website serves the consumer as a nonprofit organization. The CU researches various products and publishes the results in Consumer Reports magazine. Magazine sales are the primary support for this organization.

One caveat that consumers must abide is that information gained via the Internet should be evaluated cautiously. The value and accuracy of the information is only as good as its source. To help consumers in this area, some associations (e.g., the Better Business Bureau) and other reputable organizations rate Internet sites.

RESTRICTIONS ON FREEDOM OF CHOICE

Consumer freedom of choice has natural, economic, governmental, social, and physical and self-imposed restrictions. These restrictions and their effects on society are discussed in the following pages.

Natural Restrictions

The authority of nature restricts and determines consumer choice. Nature can be awesome and also destructive. Earthquakes, tornadoes, and floods kill and injure people and destroy their material possessions. When a disaster takes place, suddenly the supply of goods and services in that area is limited. In cases like these, the remaining goods usually are divided equitably among the survivors, not by means of the price system but instead by rational authoritative control. Freedom of choice is restricted in these emergency situations.

Natural restrictions exist at all times, not just in emergencies. For example, the OPEC oil embargo created an energy crisis in the United States in the 1970s. In more recent years, fuel prices have steadily increased to the point that some consumers, by choice or by necessity, have chosen to modify lifestyles to compensate for the increased cost of living associated with these rising costs. The awareness of natural limitations is leading to private and government efforts to conserve energy, which is likely to affect the availability and prices of some products and thereby affect consumer choices. As we experience increasing concerns about fuel resources, renewable power sources and alternative fuel vehicles will become more appealing.

TIP Natural disasters can have devastating effects on consumers. Having all important documents in an easily accessible, emergency-safe container can help recovery following a disaster. Additionally, copies of these documents could be kept at another location, such as work or a relative's house. Visit www.fema.gov for additional information.

Economic Restrictions

In the U.S. economy, people produce goods and supply services they expect will yield the greatest profit. As discussed earlier, the welfare of consumers is often a secondary rather than a primary motive. As a consequence, considerable quantities of illth and nealth are produced, which reduce the supply of wealth and hence diminish consumer freedom of choice.

Freedom of choice may also be restricted through the composition of the market. A free enterprise economy requires many sellers competing against one another in the marketplace. In many U.S. industries, a few sellers control the majority of the market, with the effect that the industry subeconomy cannot perform as it should. Industries considered to be heavily concentrated include, but are not limited to, aluminum, appliances, rubber tires, electrical supplies, cereals, and soaps.

Bad Credit, No Job — CASE STUDY

Suzanne is excited about finding a new job. She finally has her financial issues managed properly following her recent divorce, and she is ready to go back to work full-time. Suzanne has an interview with a large bank and feels that the interview goes well. She is excited to get a second interview, which also goes well. When she receives the call saying that she hasn't gotten the job, she is surprised. When she investigates their rationale, she discovers that it is customary for that company to examine the credit report of all potential employees. Suzanne vaguely remembers signing permission for them to view her credit report, but she is now furious that this has cost her the job.

The company followed the law (the Fair Credit Reporting Act), obtaining permission before viewing the report. There was no legal wrongdoing.

QUESTIONS

1. How could Suzanne have prevented this from happening?
2. What restrictions did Suzanne face in this example?
3. Do you think it is legitimate for an employer to review the credit reports of potential employees?
4. What do you think an employer is looking for when it reviews credit reports?

Manufacturers of "name brand" products often produce items in the same product line for other name brand and private-label companies. Often the price of the private-label product (or "generic") is much lower than the price of the name brand, even though the two products usually are comparable or identical in quality.

FYI

In general, industry concentration in the United States is becoming more pervasive. The many corporate mergers that have taken place in the past several decades have increased this concentration. At what point does concentration of economic power result in restriction of a free market economy? In recent years, the Federal Trade Commission has stepped in to limit or stop some highly publicized mergers, while allowing others to merge, in the hopes that the economy will operate more freely.

Governmental Restrictions

In a free society, government is the agent and servant of the people. The goal of responsible government is to promote the greatest good for the greatest number of people. Often, the larger the population of a nation and the more complex its economy, the greater is the need for restricting the freedom of some business firms and consumers. For the sake of group welfare, individual consumers are restricted legally in the types of houses they may construct, in the way they may drive their automobiles, in the amount of liquor they may consume before driving, and so on. Analogous restrictions may be placed on business firms. Governmental restrictions can be indirect as well as direct.

Restrictions that result from the country being at war provide clear examples, although peacetime restrictions are common as well. Since the end of World War II, the United States has been involved in numerous wars, including those in Korea, Vietnam, Bosnia, Afghanistan, and Iraq. During these conflicts, although most citizens retained most of their freedoms, certain indirect restrictions were imposed on consumer freedom. For example, strict procedures for security related to airline travel were implemented as a result of the September 11, 2001, attacks and other threats.

TIP

Visit the Transportation Security Administration (TSA) website (www.tsa.gov) for information regarding restrictions before traveling. It is also wise to visit your airline carrier's website for information about your flight and about additional fees (e.g., baggage, paper tickets, oversize items, etc.) that may be incurred.

Social Restrictions

As a member of a group, every individual is restricted in freedom of choice. Group authority is exercised through custom, rules, mores, and laws. Compulsory public education in some form is a prime example of the legal authority that society exercises in the United States. Children are required to go to school or be home schooled; the individual child has little choice. One reason for this requirement is that, economically, one of the major resources of a nation is its people. Education enhances this resource. Conversely, people who cease to be resources and become liabilities are a drag on the economy. For example, drug addicts' excessive consumption of illth may incapacitate them and cause society to have to hospitalize them. To prevent this, society restricts individuals' freedom to choose certain consumer goods—in this case, drugs.

If you have a reservation, a hotel cannot legally deny you a room because it has overbooked. True or false?

False. Unless you have paid in advance, the hotel can legally deny you a room. Your reservation by itself is simply a courtesy. Get a written confirmation from the hotel when you reserve a room. This may assist you if the hotel is overbooked.

Any social group has individuals who cannot or will not abide by the rules and laws of society. In the United States, chronic and serious offenders are jailed, where they lose all freedom of choice. Social restrictions may take the form of group authority, religious restrictions, family restrictions, or discriminatory restrictions.

Group authority

Consumers are often controlled or strongly influenced by those with whom they live in close association. Social approval is extremely important for some people, especially teenagers. Often, teens will dress alike, adopt similar hairstyles, and use the same slang in order to fit in. The desire to dress alike and wear the same hairstyles can limit consumer freedom of choice for young adults. In some cases such conformist behavior is also seen in adults who join clubs or organizations. To show their affiliation, they will purchase clothing or other products that bear a logo, and engage in other group-related activities and expenditures.

Individuals often face restrictions because they do not belong to the majority group. After September 11, 2001, incidences of racial profiling increased, and some groups have been repeatedly singled out.

Religious restrictions

Religious authority has had a major restrictive influence throughout recorded history. In the United States our work ethic, adopted from the Puritans, extols hard work, thrift, and competition. The emphasis on economic competition can create a dilemma: having to be aggressive and competitive while also following religious injunctions to be concerned for the welfare of others. Religious doctrines can dictate what people wear (e.g., head coverings), the foods they eat (e.g., kosher), when they pray (day and time of day), and whom they marry (some religions will not recognize "outsiders").

Family restrictions

The family is the institution that is primarily responsible for socializing children to participate in society as responsible citizens. Families exert great influence over children in their early years, as do other child care providers. Not surprisingly, children learn consumer behaviors primarily by modeling the actions of their parents. Grandparents also may play a role in this process, as many have both time and resources to devote to their grandchildren. From youth through young adulthood, the child is also subjected to group influence through association with other students and friends in the neighborhood (or through online social networking sites), Scouts, 4-H clubs, and other organizations. Consciously and unconsciously, however, the family continues to exercise a strong restrictive influence on the freedom of its members. These restrictions serve to promote individual as well as family welfare. Nevertheless, they reflect family prejudices and in some cases are detrimental rather than beneficial to the individual's welfare.

Discriminatory restrictions

Historically, individuals' freedom to choose consumer goods and services has been limited as a result of discriminatory practices based on social class, gender, marital status, color, religion, sexual preference, disability status, and national origin. The dominant social group has at times attempted to deny others the right to exercise certain freedoms; the pattern has been for people in privileged groups to reserve for themselves what they consider to be the good and choice things of life, while those in underprivileged groups have to content themselves with what is left. Antidiscrimination legislation and evolving attitudes have done much to remedy such attitudes, but discrimination still exists in many forms.

Physical and Self-Imposed Restrictions

Millions of people in the United States have physical disabilities that limit their freedom of economic choice. For example, a child with highly defective eyesight is not likely to take up stamp collecting as a hobby, nor is a child who is tone-deaf likely to purchase a musical instrument.

Equal Credit Opportunity Act

The Equal Credit Opportunity Act prohibits any creditor from denying credit to a consumer on the basis of gender, marital status, color, race, religion, national origin, age, or receipt of public assistance. In the past, women and various minority groups were frequently denied credit privileges. At one time, a woman whose salary was higher than her husband's would have an application for her own credit card rejected simply because she was a female. Lending institutions overtly initiated many other discriminatory practices.

In 1975 Congress enacted the Equal Credit Opportunity Act (ECOA). This law doesn't mean that all consumers who apply for credit will receive it. Creditors still can use factors such as income, expenses, debts, and credit history to judge applicants.

The law protects consumers when dealing with any creditor who regularly extends credit, including banks, small-loan and finance companies, retail and department stores, credit card companies, and credit unions. Anyone participating in the decision to grant credit, such as a real estate broker who arranges financing, is covered by the law. Businesses applying for credit are protected by the law.

Consumers have equal rights in every phase of the credit application process. A creditor may not:

- discourage anyone from applying because of gender, marital status, age, religion, race, or national origin, or because of receipt of public assistance income such as welfare and Social Security
- ask applicants to reveal gender, race, national origin, or religion (a creditor may ask for voluntary disclosure for real estate loans because this information helps federal agencies enforce antidiscrimination laws)
- ask anyone his or her marital status if the application is for a separate, unsecured account (this does not apply in "community property" states)
- ask for information about a spouse unless the spouse is applying jointly or the spouse will be allowed to use the account; or the applicant is relying on the spouse's income or on alimony or child support income from a former spouse
- ask about plans for having or rearing children
- ask about receiving alimony, child support, or separate maintenance payments

When deciding to offer credit, a creditor may not:

- consider gender, marital status, race, national origin, or religion
- consider whether the applicant has a telephone listing (a creditor may consider whether there is a phone in the home)
- consider the race of the people who live in the neighborhood where the applicant wants to buy or improve a house with borrowed money
- consider age, with certain exceptions such as youth (18 years and under) and advanced age (applicants 62 and over unless they are favored)

When evaluating income, a creditor may not:

- refuse to consider reliable public assistance income in the same manner as other income
- discount income because of gender or marital status
- discount or refuse to consider income because it is derived from part-time employment or from pension, annuity, or retirement benefit programs
- refuse to consider consistently received alimony, child support, or separate-maintenance payments

Consumers have the right to:

- have credit in a maiden name or any other legal name
- obtain credit without a cosigner, if they meet the creditor's standards
- keep individual accounts after a change in name or marital status or reaching a certain age or retirement, unless the creditor has evidence that the debtor is unable or unwilling to pay
- know whether an application has been accepted or rejected within 30 days after filing it
- know why an application was rejected
- know the specific reasons an account was closed or the terms of the account were made less favorable (this does not hold if these actions were taken because an account was delinquent or because an account was not used for some time)

If discrimination seems to be present, the consumer should consider:

- complaining to the creditor
- checking with the Attorney General's Office to see if the creditor violated state laws (the state may decide to take the creditor to court)
- bringing a case to federal district court (if successful, the plaintiff can recover actual damages and be awarded a penalty, plus reasonable attorney's fees and court costs)
- joining with others to file a class-action suit up to $500,000 or 5 percent of the creditor's net worth, whichever is less

Violations of the Equal Credit Opportunity Act should be reported to the regional FTC office or the Federal Trade Commission Credit Practices Division, 6th and Pennsylvania, N.W., Washington, DC 20580. To find the most recent contact information, visit www.ftc.gov and select the "Contact Us" icon.

Habit also limits the freedom of many individuals. Habitual patterns of consumption develop in childhood and often persist throughout life. Some habits, such as smoking addiction, may cause demand for a product. However, a habit may also cause negative demand, resulting in refusal to purchase or consume certain goods or services.

CONDITIONS PROMOTING FREEDOM OF CHOICE

Political Freedom

Many governments, past and present, are authoritarian and often despotic. A breakthrough in the progress from political authoritarianism to political freedom happened in North America in the 18th century. A new nation emerged, dedicated to the proposition that all people are created equal and that they have the right to be free. In that climate of political freedom, economic freedom also flourished. People were free to engage in the occupations of their choice. Consumers were free to choose and to consume, in any quantity, anything they could afford. The United States became, and continues to be despite many problems, the nation with the highest degree of personal freedom of choice.

Economic Freedom in a Mixed Economy

The economy that has developed in the United States is best described as mixed. It combines unrestricted private enterprise, regulated private enterprise, and private/public enterprise. The combination works reasonably well to promote freedom of enterprise and freedom of choice. The complexities of economic life leave little room for completely unrestricted private enterprise.

A large segment of the American economy may be described as regulated private enterprise. The term *public utility* describes private firms that are permitted to own and operate companies supplying electricity, gas, cable television, and transportation services. Complete or partial monopolies are permitted in fields such as these because a single firm may provide the service more economically than two or more competing firms could. To protect consumers from monopoly prices, which would restrict their freedom of choice, local, state, and federal government agencies sometimes regulate the quality of the service and the prices consumers pay.

> **www.mapquest.com**
>
> In addition to providing driving directions, mapquest.com also offers traffic reports and useful telephone numbers for travelers.

In a mixed economy, enterprises that are operated by a public agency may be owned by private parties, or, more commonly, an enterprise may be owned by the public but operated by a private firm. Public ownership and operation are much more common in the United States than many people realize. Village, town, city, and county governments own and operate streets, water works, hospitals, and airports. They also own and operate the public schools. They provide fire protection and police protection. Taxes are collected to pay for these services.

State governments provide economic services such as the construction and maintenance of highways, hospitals, and penal and corrective institutions. In some states, they operate employment offices and liquor stores. They protect people and their property through law enforcement; they also provide education, medical care, and public health services.

The federal government is engaged in economic operations ranging from surveillance of the purity of food and drugs to regulation of advertising. It protects citizens' property and lives, protects consumers against fraud by mail, and regulates the sale of stocks and bonds. The federal government operates many businesses. One example is the Government Printing Office.

> **www.gpo.gov**
>
> Since 1860, the Government Printing Office (GPO) has created and disseminated information to the United States. The GPO strives to satisfy the informational needs of Congress, federal agencies, and the public.

SUMMARY

Producers and consumers in the United States have more economic freedom than do people in most other countries. With this economic freedom comes the responsibility to select goods and services that promote consumers' well-being—called wealth. Illth is the term designating goods and services that harm the consumer. Nealth denotes goods and services that have a neutral effect.

Conditions necessary for freedom of choice include free entry, full information, and a price system. Natural restrictions, economic restrictions, governmental restrictions, and social restrictions often inhibit these ideals. Conditions that help promote the ideals include political freedom and economic freedom in a mixed economy.

ITEMS FOR REVIEW & DISCUSSION

1. Identify the conditions necessary for freedom of choice. Is freedom of choice possible in the United States?
2. Differentiate the concepts of wealth, nealth, and illth.
3. State the advantages and disadvantages to consumers and to the economy of having fewer companies manufacture a larger proportion of consumer goods.
4. Explain what a mixed economy is.
5. Identify some of the weaknesses of an economy under authoritarian control.
6. Why do people knowingly continue to buy and use products that contribute to illth?
7. How much income do you think you need to be happy?
8. Can you think of restrictions on your freedom of choice that were not mentioned in this chapter? Have you imposed any of these restrictions yourself?
9. Which is more important to a consumer: freedom of choice or consumer welfare? Explain.

EXPLORING PERSONAL VALUES: PROJECTS

1. Assume that you have the necessary funds to buy any 10 goods or services in any combination you want. List these items, then classify each item as to whether it represents wealth, nealth, or illth. Have several friends or classmates also classify your items as wealth, nealth, or illth. Would you make any changes to your list based on the evaluations by your friends or classmates? Discuss how or why you classify each item as you do. Do you think that, to some extent, wealth, nealth, and illth are subjective in nature?
2. Negative freedom of choice is a condition in which consumers have the right to consume anything they wish but lack the purchasing power to effect that right. Discuss with your classmates the positive aspect of negative freedom of choice (making more intelligent choices; more wealth, less illth; better appreciation of things owned, etc.).
3. In your journal, write a story describing a character who lives under authoritarian control. In your story, take a position on whether authoritarian control is better for consumers than freedom of choice.
4. Give an example of how being a member of a group during your high school years restricted your freedom of choice.
5. Participate in a class debate on the topic, "Resolved: Concentration of economic power is a threat to a market economy."

6. List some economic services the federal government provides.
7. Interview someone who has been discriminated against on the basis of social class, gender, marital status, race, creed, or national origin (someone whose individual freedom to choose consumer goods or services was restricted). Record your impressions of the interview.
8. Write a paper explaining why uninformed choice is not free choice.
9. Visit a facility that is publicly owned (e.g., hospital, airport, school). Critique the service it provides and share your results with the class.
10. Interview someone who lived during a full-scale war (in their country, region, or area) or who survived a natural disaster. Ask how the person dealt with the government restrictions that were imposed. How do you think you would deal with government restrictions?

ADDITIONAL SOURCES OF INFORMATION

Court, Jamie, and Michael Moore. *Corporateering: How Corporate Power Steals Your Personal Freedom . . . and What You Can Do About It.* New York: J.P. Tarcher/Putnam, 2003.

Dowling, John Malcolm, and Yap Chin-Fang. *Modern Developments in Behavioral Economics: Social Science Perspectives on Choice and Decision.* Hackensack, NJ: World Scientific Publishing Company, 2007.

Feldman, Allan M., and Roberto Serrano. *Welfare Economics and Social Choice Theory.* New York: Springer Science, 2006.

Hartmann, Thom. *Unequal Protection: The Rise of Corporate Dominance and the Theft of Human Rights.* Emmaus, PA: Rodale Press, 2004.

Holmes, Kim R., Edwin J. Feulner, Mary Anastasia O'Grady, Anthony B. Kim, and Daniella Markheim. *2008 Index of Economic Freedom.* Washington, DC: Heritage Foundation, 2008.

Palast, Greg. *The Best Democracy Money Can Buy: The Truth About Corporate Cons, Globalization and High-Finance Fraudsters.* New York: Plume, 2003.

Sen, Amartya. *Development as Freedom.* Oxford: Oxford University Press, 2001.

Sowell, Thomas. *Economic Facts & Fallacies.* New York: Basic Books, 2008.

PART TWO

Going to Market

THE CONSUMER AND THE MARKETPLACE

> If a man defrauds you one time, he is a rascal;
> if he does it twice, you are a fool.
>
> AUTHOR UNKNOWN

KEY TERMS

antitrust
bushing
caveat emptor
caveat venditor
deception
double-dipping
fee splitting
fraud
high-balling
incentives
low-balling
packing
pharming
phishing
price-fixing
pyramid franchising scheme
quackery
referral selling
rip-offs
spamming
telemarketing schemes

Deception the perversion of truth, most often—but not necessarily—intentional, that results in a person, having been misled, parting with something of value for something of no or little value.

Fraud the intentional perversion of truth to induce another person to part with something of value.

The following concepts will be developed in this chapter:

1. The legal definition of fraud makes it difficult to prosecute persons who are knowingly perpetrating fraud upon the consuming public.
2. The entire range of human wants presents opportunities for fraud, and unscrupulous sellers are eager to take advantage of them.

After having read this chapter, you should be able to accomplish the following objectives:

1. Explain why fraud is so hard to prove, and offer suggestions for how this weakness in the law might be corrected.
2. List several common types of fraud perpetrated on consumers.
3. Identify several reasons for the persistent practice of fraud.

WHAT IS FRAUD?

In 1776 Adam Smith wrote in his *Wealth of Nations,* "Every man, as long as he does not violate the laws of justice, is left perfectly free to pursue his own interest his own way, and to bring both his industry and capital into competition with those of any man, or order of men." In an economic system organized on the assumption that everyone will seek to promote his or her self-interest by acquiring as much profit as possible, inevitably some people will attempt to secure profit by any possible means, including through deception or fraud. **Deception** and **fraud** are likely outcomes of the untrammeled pursuit of self-interest and profit. Whether profit results from the rendering of a service or a disservice makes no difference to some individuals, as long as they make a profit.

Traditional laissez-faire economic doctrine holds that competition protects consumers from fraud. Consumers are supposed to act as economic persons, meaning that in a given market area, they will shop in all stores, comparing prices, quantity, quality, and service, and make purchases at the stores offering the highest quality and the greatest quantity at the lowest price. If, by any chance, an economic person should be defrauded, theory holds that she will refuse to patronize the same merchant again. The assumed result is that dishonest dealers will be driven out of business and only the honest merchants will survive.

Business executives have said repeatedly that a business cannot continue if it defrauds buyers. Nevertheless, reports of Better Business Bureaus, state consumer protection bureaus, the Federal Trade Commission, the

Fraud

Justice Department, the Food and Drug Administration, and many others provide evidence to the contrary. If fraudulent operators constitute only 1 percent of all business firms, in absolute numbers that equals more than 225,000 firms that prosper by cheating.

In real life, consumers are not economic persons, so competition fails to operate as a completely protective device. All too frequently, **caveat emptor** is the rule. From the abundance of available evidence, this chapter presents a small sampling of practices against which buyers must be on guard. When buyers are on guard and know the avenues to fight fraud, the situation becomes one of **caveat venditor.**

Caveat emptor "Let the buyer beware"—a principle in commerce that makes the buyer responsible for determining quality.

Caveat venditor "Let the seller beware"—a principle in commerce implying that consumers are alert and will not tolerate poor quality.

Deception, Fraud, and "Rip-Offs"

Just what constitutes fraud is a matter of definition. If fraud were defined in law, as it is in the dictionary, as "any artifice by which the right or interest of another person is injured," consumers would have more protection and fraudulent sellers less. Actually, laws and courts have defined fraud so as to restrict it to deliberate deceit. This means that the buyer–plaintiff must prove that the seller intended to deceive, which is difficult to do. As a result, the law protects many fraudulent sellers.

Further, some activities are neither fraudulent nor deceptive, but simply are not in the best interest of consumers. These activities may be deemed consumer **"rip-offs."** It has been suggested, for example, that industry concentration is the biggest consumer rip-off because consumers pay billions of dollars each year over and above what might be charged if the market were truly competitive. Other examples of large-scale rip-offs include various selling methods, government regulations that prevent the normal functioning of a competitive market, income tax loopholes, and many white-collar improprieties.

Rip-offs activities that are not in the best interests of consumers.

Antitrust Laws

Antitrust laws and regulations to protect trade and commerce from unlawful restraints.

Antitrust enforcement is critical in the U.S. marketplace. At the federal level, the Sherman Antitrust Act, as amended, is the law most often used to prosecute violators. States, too, have antitrust laws. In a typical year, fines in the millions of dollars are levied against individuals and corporations guilty of price-fixing. The pursuit of violators often becomes a political issue. In the 1970s, antitrust enforcement was quite apparent under the Carter administration. The political environment in the 1980s resulted in the reversal of government antitrust efforts. The 1990s and 2000s brought renewed interest in this issue with the litigation against Microsoft and Enron, and investigations involving other companies and industries. (And with the failures of companies due to questionable and even fraudulent business practices, the government continues to more aggressively investigate business conduct beyond antitrust violations.)

Price-fixing when businesses conspire to set prices higher than they would be if normal competition were at play.

Punitive actions, such as fines, help to curb **price-fixing.** For consumers and businesses affected adversely by these illegal acts, however, direct-payment settlements may be better remedies.

AREAS OF FRAUD

If something seems too good to be true, it usually is. Stay away from any "deal" that appears to be a certain moneymaker.

FYI

The entire range of human wants presents a plethora of opportunities for fraud. The sale of food and clothing has long been a profitable field for forms of fraud such as adulteration, misbranding, misrepresentation, short-changing, short-measuring, short-weighing, and overpricing. Charlatans also cater to the natural human desire for health, wealth, and beauty. Religion, too, is subject to fraudulent practice. Charity schemes exploit people's generous and humane impulses. Many sellers cater to the irrational hopes and beliefs of people who are credulous and naive.

"Health" for Sale

Every year consumers spend billions of dollars on products for relief from all manner of ailments, mental and physical. When people become ill, they go to doctors for treatment. If they are not satisfied with the outcome, they may turn to patent medicines and quack doctors, who promise wonders. The Food and Drug Administration reports that sick people are so eager to believe in quick, easy, miraculous cure-alls that reputable practitioners have little success in convincing them that a product is worthless or harmful.

Three major kinds of health frauds violate the Federal Food, Drug, and Cosmetic Act:

Quackery a concept named after a duck's noise; making a lot of noise about nothing. For example, blatant self-promotion about a "miracle cure."

1. **Quackery** in the promotion of so-called therapeutic devices
2. Quackery in the marketing of food supplements and so-called health foods
3. False claims for drugs and cosmetics

Many people fall for frauds related to therapeutic devices. For example, some medical devices, such as muscle stimulators, have been approved by the Food and Drug Administration for muscle rehabilitation following an injury. However, the FTC has stated they have no value in building and defining muscle, as some fraudulent ads have claimed.

WWW

www.quackwatch.org

This website is sponsored by a nonprofit corporation whose mission is to inform consumers about health-related frauds, myths, fads, and fallacies.

www.eatright.org

The American Dietetics Association is a recognized expert on nutritional information. The site has a multitude of facts and resources for consumers wanting to learn more about nutrition and proper eating.

Food faddism and nutritional quackery rank as the biggest racket in the health field today. Diet foods and diet programs are multibillion-dollar industries. The FTC scrutinizes diet clubs and diet programs closely because of the prevalence of false claims. Weight-loss centers across the United States have been investigated by the FTC, and wrongdoing has been discovered in many cases. Examples include misleading claims about average weight loss, quoted program pricing that does not include the cost of purchasing the required food, and fake or touched-up before-and-after pictures.

Selling various drugs and cosmetics under false claims yields enormous profits. The counterfeiting of legitimate drugs defrauds consumers, and imitation drugs may endanger health or life. Some counterfeit drugs are produced and marketed under independent labels; others are marketed under counterfeit labels of reputable pharmaceutical firms. Drug-related products also may be sold under false pretenses. Common nonprescription drugs of questionable or even harmful effect include antacids, cold remedies, diet pills, herbal supplements, and many vitamin and mineral supplements.

The FTC and the FDA continue to identify examples of health fraud. Promotion of shark cartilage to treat arthritis, St. John's wort to treat HIV, pills that "shrink tumors," supplements to cure Alzheimer's, and ancient remedies are just a few examples. Consumers should be skeptical about any outrageous claims. FDA-approved clinical trials are ongoing, and consumers should contact the FDA directly for information regarding these trials.

www.worstpills.org

This website, offered by Public Citizen, offers a wide variety of information on health topics such as drug claims, drug safety, medical devices, hospital safety, and insurance issues.

Buying Beauty

Beauty is a multibillion-dollar business based on advertising claims that it can be bought in bottles, jars, or packages. In probably no other field is advertising more extravagant, misleading, and fraudulent. Not only are the claims made for many cosmetics grossly misleading, but the ingredients in some actually may be harmful. Moreover, almost all preparations are overpriced.

Advertising and other forms of marketing are used to bolster an artificial demand. Some cosmetic companies spend up to one-quarter or more of their budget on marketing. Consumers receive products such as cleansing cream and skin lotion in formulas that are fairly standard and commonly available.

Consumers might assume that every firm making cosmetics employs a manufacturing chemist, but some do not. Some so-called manufacturers actually do no manufacturing at all but, instead, hire an independent chemist to do this for them. This means that the only difference between some cosmetics is the container or label. Consumers do not know this unless they have inside information or are guided by a consumer-testing agency.

Consumer protection in the cosmetics industry is difficult. As fast as regulatory agencies catch up with and stop one fraud, another springs up. The concoctions that quacks have peddled include a cosmetic containing chick-embryo extract, purported to regenerate cells and prevent wrinkles and sagging skin; pigskin extract and horse-blood serum as skin rejuvenators; and shark oil claimed to revitalize aging skin.

When a company offers lifetime memberships to consumers, the lifetime of the business and not the lifetime of the consumer is the determining factor. If the company terminates, the lifetime membership usually dies with it.

FYI

Medical and Surgical Frauds

Some presumably reputable professionals perpetrate frauds such as **fee splitting.** In this practice, associated most often with the medical profession, the consumer is referred to another doctor, not knowing that the referring doctor will be paid for doing so. Knowledge of this might make the consumer question the legitimacy of the referral and the professionals involved. Performing unnecessary operations is another major fraud. Appendectomies, tonsillectomies, hysterectomies, and gall bladder removal are often needless operations.

Fee splitting a payment from one professional to another for referring a client. The payment may be in the form of money or "in kind," such as dinner certificates.

Reality television shows chronicling amazing makeovers have stimulated interest in cosmetic surgery and related services. The growing quest to stay and look young has encouraged increased availability of these services and has also increased related medical and surgical fraud. "Experienced, reputable operators" offer to perform a variety of cosmetic enhancements such as chemical peels to "remove" wrinkles, laser treatments to remove skin discolorations, and permanent hair removal or makeup. Enticements of "quick, easy, affordable" methods to improve physical appearance are commonplace. In reality, claims are often overstated, and many practitioners are unqualified. The government receives a multitude of complaints about botched cosmetic surgeries and procedures. Media coverage, complete with graphic pictures of the unsuccessful surgeries, is common. Even with government warnings and media reports, this burgeoning industry has hardly been deterred. Consumers seeking cosmetic enhancement should

The only safe way to lose weight and fat permanently is to reduce caloric intake (especially calories from fats) and to exercise regularly.

FYI

check with their state consumer protection agencies and ask family and friends for recommendations before undergoing procedures. Keep in mind, also, that the long-term consequences of many of these procedures are unknown, as longitudinal studies have not been completed.

Medical and cosmetic quackery has some well-defined characteristics. The FDA suggests that if you answer "yes" to any of the following questions, you are probably dealing with quackery.

- Is the product or service a "secret remedy" or not available from other sources?
- Does the sponsor claim that it is battling a medical profession that does not accept this wonderful discovery?
- Is this "miracle" drug, device, or diet being promoted in a sensational magazine, a questionable website, a faith healer's group, or a crusading organization?
- Does the promoter tout the miracles the product or service has performed for others?
- Is the product or service good for a wide variety of illnesses, real or fancied?

A person who is considering joining a reducing salon, a health spa, or a similar program should watch out for the common abuses that pervade the field. Experts give the following advice:

- Do not be taken in by misleading advertising, high-pressure sales tactics, and emotional appeals.
- Before signing a contract for lessons or a membership, know exactly what you will get and how much it will cost.
- Try to enroll on a pay-as-you-go basis or for only a short period. Then, if you are not satisfied, you have not lost much.
- Until you have investigated the program carefully, ignore "discount," group, or "package" rates and other gimmicks to get you to sign a long-term contract.
- Do not be fooled by before-and-after photos, guarantees of weight loss, or claims of weight reduction by the use of machines or facilities.

TIP Get a second and perhaps a third opinion before consenting to surgery.

Fraud in Selling Automobiles

When buying either a new or a used car, the consumer can be defrauded in many ways. Much automobile advertising is unethical. In addition to bait-and-switch advertising, many sellers of automobiles use a variety of gimmicks. Even though some of these gimmicks are illegal, effective enforcement of the law is difficult, if not impossible.

High-balling a deceptive sales practice whereby the salesperson offers a high trade-in price in order to sell an artificially high-priced product or service.

Low-balling a deceptive sales practice whereby the salesperson offers an unrealistic price for a good or service that will not be honored.

Bushing a deceptive sales practice whereby the salesperson adds unordered products or services to the final price.

1. **High-balling.** A dealer offers a high trade-in but charges high prices for extras on the new car, reducing the advantage to the consumer.
2. **Low-balling.** A new-car buyer might be offered a price just $25 over the factory cost to the dealer, compared with the $200 to $500 the dealer must get to cover operating expenses and profit margin. When the prospect decides to buy, the salesperson then says that he made a mistake in figuring the price and that the car will cost $400 to $500 more. Many times the prospect goes ahead and buys the auto anyway.
3. **Bushing.** A buyer who calls for an ordered car is told that the only way the dealer can obtain the car immediately is by giving the buyer one that has extra options, for which the buyer has to pay extra. Many buyers, though they complain, will pay. Bushing is common, as is the signing of blank orders, although both practices are illegal. Another deception is to overcharge installment buyers for insurance coverage.

4. **Packing.** Sellers tack on extra charges such as dealer prep fees, charges for "extra" items that are standard equipment, and so forth. "Soft" items, such as warranties or paint sealants, and "hard" items, such as stereos and wheels, are other examples of added items. Packing occurs less frequently than in the past, because of more informed consumers, but it still happens.
5. **Double-dipping.** The seller may arrange financing in which three-fourths of the price of a car, for example, may be financed at a bank at a reasonable rate of interest and the remainder financed at a loan company at a high rate of interest. The buyer then finds that she has two payments to make on the car each month.
6. **Incentives.** Sales people push certain items to increase their commission (incentive) for the sale. Estimates are that 40 percent of all car purchasers are talked into buying extended service contracts (maintenance contracts), yet research has shown that most are never used.
7. *Misusing personal credit information.* Some dealerships obtain credit reports without permission. This provides them with valuable information to use in the negotiation process (e.g., your bureau score, current car payment, etc.). Dealers also use this information to encourage the consumer to buy a more expensive car than he needs, wants, or can afford. Obtaining a credit report without permission is a direct violation of federal law.

Packing adding extra charges, such as exorbitant preparation fees, to the price to raise the final price; associated with auto sales.

Double-dipping a legal but questionable sales tactic whereby the buyer, with little or no down payment, acquires two loans—one from a bank at a reasonable interest rate and one from a loan company at a higher interest rate.

Incentives money, bonuses, or special consideration during performance reviews received by dealership personnel for selling additional products such as service contracts.

Prior to passage of the Motor Vehicle Information and Cost Savings (MVICS) Act several decades ago, odometer tampering was a common trade practice. Illegal rollbacks continue, although the practice is not as prevalent as it once was. In addition, in recent years, federal and state laws have been strengthened so now many states are required to issue automobile titles that are resistant to counterfeiting.

Buying a new car does not have to be a negative experience. Many banks, credit unions, and organizations (such as the American Automobile Association) offer fleet discounts that allow you to buy a car with minimal negotiation through your affiliation with the organization. However, if you negotiate on a dealer lot, you may get a better deal (especially at the end of the month or end of the year when the dealer is trying to make quotas). With the Internet, consumers can obtain valuable information, including invoices, dealer comparisons, and new and used car prices, before they proceed in a car purchase. Armed with this information, consumers can better negotiate. In fact, if they so desire, they can even purchase a new car online.

Experts recommend that consumers bargain up from an invoice price rather than down from a sticker price. Invoice prices are readily found on the Internet.

FYI

Similarly, buying a used car does not have to be an off-putting experience. Easy-to-use websites provide used car prices. *Consumer Reports* offers reliability ratings for used cars and identifies the best used-car buys. The website www.carfax.com provides extensive vehicle history reports to help car buyers learn more about the condition of the vehicle in question. To be certain a car is in good working order, ask the owner to let you take the car to a trusted mechanic. Pay the nominal fee to have the mechanic look it over and note any repairs that will need to be made in the near future. Upcoming repairs may be used as a negotiation point.

www.edmunds.com

Edmunds.com provides consumers with unbiased information regarding new and used vehicles.

Automobile Repair Swindlers

Not many automobile owners in the United States understand the technicalities of car operation and repair, and still fewer can or do service their own cars. They have to trust employees of service centers and garages. Sometimes their trust is misplaced. A tourist who has a breakdown away from home is fair game for repair personnel who charge excessive prices, often for work that is not done or not needed and for parts that are not supplied or not needed.

Various studies have found that as much as half of all repairs are either unnecessary or overpriced. The loss to consumers is in the billions of dollars each year. The licensing or registering of automobile repair technicians and repair shops might be a reasonable step for the government to take to lessen the fraud in automobile-repair work and to improve service. In addition, manufacturers should take steps to reduce repair costs by making repairs simpler and replacement of parts less costly.

TIP

If an auto repair bill is more than $50, charge it on a credit card. A federal law allows withholding payment if the repair was not done properly. Certain restrictions do apply. Your credit card statement will disclose additional details.

Some states have passed laws in an attempt to police auto-repair shops. A strong law empowers a bureau within a state agency to license (register) almost every automobile-repair and diagnostic business in that state, except shops that perform only minor maintenance functions and those that repair only trucks and tractors. An annual registration fee paid by the participating shops largely underwrites the cost of running the bureau. The bureau has the power to refuse and revoke licenses, without which a repair shop governed by the law cannot operate in the state.

The American Automobile Association (AAA; www.aaa.com) operates a program that rates auto repair facilities. The Approved Auto Repair Facilities link on the AAA website allows consumers to research facilities in their area that have received positive feedback from consumers.

FYI

The National Institute for Automotive Service Excellence (ASE), an independent, nonprofit organization, was established in an attempt to improve automobile-repair service. It runs a voluntary, nationwide program for testing and certifying the competence of automobile repair technicians. Certifications are issued to repair technicians who pass the tests. Car owners may check to see if the repair technicians working on their cars have this certification. More than 400,000 repair technicians are ASE-certified nationwide.

Several state bureaus of auto repair offer the following tips to avoid fraud in auto repair:

1. Find a shop before you need one.
2. Make sure the shop honors any warranty coverage you might have.
3. Make sure the shop is qualified to do the repairs that are needed.
4. Get a written estimate of repairs costing more than $100; permission is required if the repairs will exceed 10 percent of the estimate or $20 (whichever is greater).
5. Comparison shop by phone; see what shops charge for the repairs.
6. Get a copy of the written invoice when repairs are complete; review it for accuracy.
7. Ask for your old parts to be returned to you upon completion of the work.
8. Keep a copy of all receipts.

TIP

The best way to identify a competent and reliable mechanic is to ask friends for recommendations. If several of your resources give the same name, that mechanic is probably a good choice.

Counterfeited Products

Counterfeit products that violate copyright and/or trademark laws are abundant in the marketplace, especially on the Internet, at fairs, swap meets, and at private parties. Commonly counterfeited items include falsely labeled watches, purses, jeans, and other clothing. This practice, while profitable to the seller, misleads consumers, and it is illegal. Since 1946, the Lanham Act has protected trademarks and their ownership. In 1995, the Federal Trademark Dilution Act expanded the scope of the Lanham Act, providing further protection for famous trademarks and unauthorized use that would "dilute" their credibility. To further combat the problem, the Anticounterfeiting Consumer Protection Act of 1996 increased the penalties for counterfeiting.

Interstate Land Sales

www.fraud.org

The National Fraud Information Center and Internet Fraud Watch provide tips, trends, and reports on a variety of frauds. In addition, they provide both an online complaint form and a toll-free phone number that allow victims of fraud to report the problem.

Each year Americans contract to buy billions of dollars' worth of recreation-oriented land, retirement homesites, development plots, and small tracts of raw acreage. Although many buyers are dealt with ethically and fairly, far too many are defrauded or pressured by salespersons into buying worthless property.

Too often, vacation and retirement sites are sold to eager, out-of-state buyers who have not inspected the property adequately. Many of these frauds occur on the Internet. The ability to pay for lots in small monthly installments tends to make buyers casual about checking on the properties. In a significant number of cases, buyers do not receive what they thought they were buying.

To protect the public in interstate land transactions, Congress has passed various laws requiring people engaged in the interstate sale or leasing of land to register the offering with the U.S. Department of Housing and Urban Development (HUD). Further, nearly every state has a law making certain questionable actions in intrastate land sales illegal.

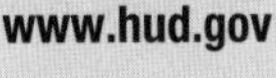

www.hud.gov

The website for the Department of Housing and Urban Development (HUD) provides consumers with unbiased housing and development information.

A person who is contemplating the purchase of land from a land-development organization should obtain the Department of Housing and Urban Development property report from the developer and should read it carefully before signing any papers. HUD judges neither the merits of an offering nor the value of the property, but it does require the developer to spell out in detail information pertaining to the transaction.

Buying land or timeshares for vacationing is a particularly hazardous venture because of the questionable and sometimes outright unscrupulous selling tactics that are common in this arena. Before signing a contract for vacation land, the potential buyer should be able to answer "yes" to the following questions:

- Have you inspected the land and surrounding area personally?
- Have you seen a property report and a map showing the actual or proposed division and dimensions of the lots?
- Have you had the opportunity to examine a public offering statement containing relevant facts about the seller, the land, and your financial obligations?
- Have you been given a written statement about the installation of water and sewage facilities, as well as roads and recreational facilities?
- Has an attorney investigated the status of the seller's title to the land and reviewed the appropriate legal documents?

Timeshares are poor investments. They are generally difficult to resell.

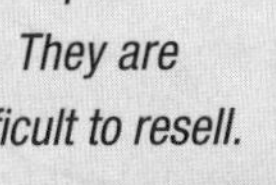

The Federal Trade Commission has power to investigate fraudulent practices in land sales. This agency has investigated hundreds of companies over the years and in a few instances has issued consent orders and required refunds to be offered. Land sales and timeshares, perhaps more than any other kind of sale, should be approached with great caution and skepticism.

Education Frauds

An area in which fraud might not be expected is education. Nevertheless, frauds are perpetrated on consumers of education along with consumers of almost every other kind of product or service. Countless schools offering home-study and vocational programs advertise for students on television, by mail, and via the Internet. This multibillion-dollar industry is not immune to unethical and outright fraudulent practices. "Degree mills," for example, bilk consumers out of millions of dollars each year.

Many home-study programs offered through the mail or via the Internet are developed by fully accredited schools and have realistic requirements, and many

WWW

www.usdoj.gov

The website for the United States Attorney General's Office explains the primary role of the Attorney General, who is the chief administrator for the Department of Justice.

major colleges and universities offer these courses. Some "schools," however, offer credit or degrees to students who do little more than pay a sum of money. Many unaccredited schools sell phony high school diplomas and bachelor's, master's, and doctorate degrees for fees that can amount to thousands of dollars.

Proprietary schools—those established as profit-making operations—present another problem. Many of these schools enroll students in their courses, promising substantive careers in a chosen field. Students are encouraged to borrow thousands of dollars in federally insured loans. Often these students receive inadequate training and are unable to find a job in a related field.

TIP

Your state government may be able to provide information regarding accredited, nonaccredited, and "fraudulent" schools.

Here are some guidelines to follow when choosing a school:

1. Decide in advance exactly what you want to study.
2. Make certain that you know all of the state or local requirements for the field you are pursuing. In some fields, successful completion of courses is not enough; actual work experience in the field also may be required.
3. Do not sign up with the first school you investigate. Research at least three.
4. Try to find out as much as possible about each school on your list:
   a. Carefully look through the school's catalog or brochure.
   b. Check with people who have taken courses at the schools. If you do not know anyone, ask the schools to give you the names of people in your area who have studied with them.
   c. Compare the fees and charges of the schools on your list.
   d. Ask to see an outline of each course and the content of the first lesson, to make sure they are neither too elementary nor too difficult for you.
   e. Check with the U.S. and State Departments of Education.
   f. Check with the Better Business Bureau.
   g. Check with your state Attorney General's Office or your state consumer affairs office.
5. Do not sign a contract with any school until you are certain you understand what you are agreeing to: the total amount of money you will owe, course of study, and provisions for refund if you withdraw. Be sure to get a copy of the signed contract.
6. Do not allow yourself to be pressured into signing a contract. A reputable school will allow you to take time to make your decision.
7. A school that promises you a job upon completing the course is doing so illegally. Do not sign a contract with a school that makes such promises.

In most states, a business license—often costing less than $100—is all that is required to open a business.

FYI

Consumers should be aware that they have certain rights in regard to both home-study and more traditional educational programs. The Federal Trade Commission has issued rules prohibiting false representations of facilities, equipment, job placement, teachers, and the value of certificates and diplomas. Most states give some protection by regulating private trade schools. Finally, the Family Education Rights and Privacy Act allows students and parents (if the student is under age 18) the right to obtain information from a student's file and to correct inaccurate or misleading data. Complaints against colleges and universities may often be lodged with state authorities.

Another type of fraud related to education is scholarship fraud. Such frauds are most commonly perpetrated through fake scholarship organizations and high-pressure financial aid consulting firms. The fraudulent organizations often require a fee for services that are never performed, or they get the student's or parents' credit card or checking account information and make unauthorized charges or debits to their accounts. In addition, consulting firms' representatives may ask for an advance fee, make promises that cannot be met, purport a false success rate, or require that products be purchased before the student is eligible for scholarships.

The FTC oversees this area through its Scholarship Fraud Prevention Program and the College Scholarship Fraud Prevention Act of 2000. The Act provides for penalties, implementation of a nationwide awareness campaign, and yearly reporting of incidences. The Department of Education and the Department of Justice are working with the FTC in this area. Some tips to help students avoid being scammed by scholarship fraud include:

1. Watch for success rates that appear too good to be true.
2. Do not give your credit card or banking information to "hold" an offer.
3. Do not buy products to qualify for a scholarship.
4. Do not pay a fee—most scholarships do not require it.
5. Be wary of claims that this firm has an "exclusive" offer.
6. Be wary of claims that guarantee success or your money is returned.
7. Do not falsify your Free Application for Federal Student Aid (FAFSA) in order to "qualify."

www.studentaid.ed.gov

This website, sponsored by the Department of Education, offers information about federal student aid, as well as general information about other student aid alternatives.

www.nces.ed.gov/globallocator

The National Center for Education Statistics website offers thorough information on schools across the nation. The site offers up-to-date information on tuition, school type, and gender and ethnic breakdown, among other things.

Employment Frauds

Because of stiff competition for jobs, employment agencies, often called "headhunters," have assumed an important role in the lives of many citizens. The following tips may help you in the search for employment:

1. Before you go to an employment agency, look through the help-wanted ads in the newspaper, go online, and visit an employment office. You may be able to find a satisfactory job without the services of an employment agency.
2. If you decide to use an employment agency, comparison-shop. Check the contract obligations and fees at a minimum of three agencies.
3. Before you sign any contract, talk to the job counselor with whom you will be dealing. Try to assess his honesty and sincerity. Does the agency seem genuinely interested in finding you the right job rather than just any job?
4. Make certain that you describe your qualifications and background honestly. Representing yourself in such a way that you are placed in a job for which you are either overqualified or underqualified is unwise.
5. Before signing a contract with an agency, be certain that you understand all of its details, especially the financial obligations. Get a copy of the signed contract.

Many legitimate opportunities are available to consumers who wish to earn money by working at home. This area, however, is plagued by fraudulent practices. Be particularly careful in the following circumstances:

1. When an advertisement promises large profits in a short time period.
2. When an advertisement requires you to pay money to obtain further information. Many swindlers keep the money and never reply.

3. When you cannot obtain the names of people who have been employed in this manner so you can learn of their experiences.
4. When you are required to pay money to buy products that you must resell for a profit. The items sold to you may be of poor quality or have an inflated price.
5. When you are sold instructions and materials for making items at home and the company promises to purchase the finished product if the work is "acceptable" or "up to our standards." The company may reject every item, leaving you with a room full of unsalable products.

Pyramid franchising scheme the granting, on condition that an investment be made, of a license or right to recruit for additional investment one or more persons who also are granted such a license to recruit others.

One investment opportunity in which consumers inevitably lose is the **pyramid franchising scheme.** If you attend an "opportunity meeting" promoted by pyramid franchise sellers, you might hear a pitch something like, "We'll show you how you can earn $500 to $1,000 a month, and for those who are a little more serious, $3,000, $5,000 per month and more."

Initially, promoters engaged in pyramid franchising tell potential investors that there is a product to be sold. Eventually, though, it becomes obvious that the real money comes in recruiting other investors into the scheme.

Why has this type of scheme been made illegal? The answer is that by its very nature, large numbers of consumers must lose money. Suppose, at the beginning, the promoters bring five investors into the scheme. If each of these investors recruits five more people, the total number of individuals allowed to recruit is 25, then 125, and so on. Within 10 steps, there would have to be 9,765,625 investors! Those who get in early are often required by the organization to return the money they received and may also face substantial fines. Those who get in late (most investors) cannot recruit enough new investors to break even. Some recommendations are:

1. Do not invest in any company whose primary profit-making scheme is the recruiting of others.
2. Do not sign any papers of any kind while attending a promotional meeting. Always take time to think over the deal at home, away from the salesperson.

CASE STUDY Biz Op Flop

Promises of a flexible schedule, no risk, good income, and customers already lined up lured Judy, a working mom of two boys, right in. Invest $30,000 for seven vending machines and then make $7000 a month after placing them with customers and servicing them as needed. This Maryland mother saw this business investment as a great opportunity to spend more time with her family while still earning a decent income.

Accent Marketing, an Alabama company, provided a great business plan citing customers already eager to allow placement of the machines. Accent ads appeared in newspapers and on professional websites, and the company even had good standing with the Better Business Bureau. Accent provided referrals for her to call; these contacts all gave favorable testimonies for Accent Marketing and all were completely satisfied. Judy made the decision to invest.

Just before Christmas 2001 the vending machines arrived and out went Judy to place machines with the "eager" customers. All 25 that had been lined up by Accent Marketing turned her down; many were not enthused by her visit. Her $30,000 was gone and she had no takers for her vending machines.

QUESTIONS

1. What are some of the signals, or red flags, to look for in a situation like this?
2. What are some of the emotions or needs, that these scam artists use as leverage to appeal to new clients?
3. Do you think that Judy's culpability is partly to blame or does all the blame belong to the seller of this business opportunity?
4. Frauds sometimes reach their victims through legitimate advertising media. How much responsibility would you say the radio, television stations, newspapers, and websites should have?

3. Do not invest in a product for resale without knowing the territories you are being offered. Before investing, assess the potential for profit.
4. Do not make any major investment without consulting an attorney first.
5. Investigate the legitimacy and complaint records of the company (the FTC and BBB websites are good places to start).

Referral selling is illegal in some states because consumers inevitably lose at it. In some cases, promised refunds are never made. In other cases, refunds are insignificant. In all cases, not only you but many others as well will be referring names to the salesperson. Those referred, in turn, will refer still others. Consequently, any given area is quickly exhausted of possible references. This also has a pyramid effect.

Referral selling an attempt—often illegal—by salespeople to get consumers to buy a product by offering an incentive (usually a refund) for every person the consumer recommends to them.

One area of fraud that requires special mention is magazine sales. Almost every consumer has been solicited at some time by a magazine salesperson, a telemarketer, or an Internet ad. Frequently the salespeople say they are working their way through college, or trying to win a scholarship, or competing for a trip to Europe. These sales pitches have nothing to do with whether the magazine is a good buy. Before signing any contract for magazines, consumers should protect themselves against making an agreement they might regret later. One pitch is that the subscription will cost only pennies a day. Twenty-five cents a day equals $91.25 in a year!

Charity and Religious Frauds

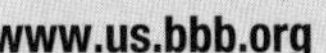

www.us.bbb.org

Consumers who want to donate to a particular charity, but are unsure as to the creditability of that charity, should visit this website, operated by the Better Business Bureau.

People in the United States contribute significant sums of money annually to charitable, philanthropic, and religious causes. Most people are sympathetic and generous. Therefore, dishonest operators can capitalize readily on people's charitable instincts. One popular fraud is to solicit funds after a disaster, for example, a flood, a tsunami, an earthquake, or a terrorist attack. Preying on consumers' emotions is a common ploy of charity con artists.

Outright fraud can be documented in thousands of cases. The solicitors collect large sums of money and simply keep the donations for their own use. More pervasive are the quasi-legitimate solicitation schemes that charge excessive administrative expenses and engage in other questionable fund-raising practices. Administrative costs in excess of 20 percent are questionable. Before you respond to any charitable solicitation, find out what percentage of the money actually goes to benefit those for whom it is collected.

Two national organizations, the Council of Better Business Bureaus and the National Charities Information Bureau, rate major charities. They have developed standards that include disclosure of financial reports, fund-raising practices, and truthfulness of advertising. Even though the law offers consumers some protection against phony charities, individuals must remain vigilant. The following suggestions can help you avoid charity frauds:

1. Do not contribute without having solicitors show identification for themselves and the charity.
2. Do not contribute to a charity you know nothing about.
3. Do not allow yourself to be pressured into making a contribution.
4. Do not feel that you have to make the contribution on the spot; ask for literature about the charity and use this to check on its authenticity.
5. Do not be fooled by names. Often a crooked charity has a most impressive-sounding name, or one that sounds similar to a legitimate organization.
6. Do not succumb merely because of the tear-jerking hard-luck stories solicitors tell. Find out how the charity benefits those for whom it is collecting funds.
7. Do not give cash.
8. Make your check payable to the charity, not an individual person.

9. Check out the charity with a reputable charity rating organization.

The best defense against charity fraud is to have a policy never to give to a solicitor. Locate the charity of your choice and make your donation directly.

Defrauding Older Adults

Older adults are particularly susceptible to fraud. Because they are part of a more trusting generation, they seem to be more willing to trust a person who seems to show real concern for their welfare. Two schemes frequently perpetrated on older persons are the "pigeon drop" and the "bank examiner's scheme." In the pigeon drop scheme, a con artist requires that the "pigeon" put up good-faith money to share the contents of a package "found" filled with money. The package is switched, and the naive consumer is left with a package filled with paper. In the bank examiner's scheme, a con artist poses as a government or bank official. The con artist indicates that the bank believes a teller is withdrawing money illegally from the consumer's account. The consumer is asked to withdraw money from his or her bank account and to give the money to the "examiner," who in turn falsely promises to redeposit the money in the consumer's account. Other common schemes perpetrated on older people involve medical and long-term insurance, Medicare supplements, home repair, and religious fraud.

Because people 55 and older control more than 70 percent of the wealth in the country, and because more older persons are going online, more and more online fraud is being aimed at seniors. Approximately 30 million seniors are now Internet users. Although the most popular way to reach and defraud seniors is still by telephone, this is declining as online scams increase. As with all contacts by strangers, whether through the mail, over the telephone, or via the Internet, seniors need to be on guard.

www.usps.gov

The website for the United States Postal Service (USPS) is useful for such services as finding ZIP codes, calculating postage, changing an address, locating post offices, and tracking packages.

Defrauding Persons with Low Income

Frauds are perpetrated on people at all income levels, but persons with low income are especially susceptible to fraudulent operators and also are least able to afford being defrauded. Many persons with low income are ignorant in the marketplace. Their lack of knowledge creates real hardships for them and makes them easy prey for fraudulent operators. Persons with low income often do not read contracts, and they are less likely to save contracts, sales slips, receipts, and warranties. They tend to place their trust in the merchant, and sometimes that trust is misplaced.

White-Collar Fraud

The sociologist C. Wright Mills once observed, "It is better to take one dime from each of 10 million people at the point of a corporation than $100,000 from each of 10 banks at the point of a gun. It is also safer." Tens of billions of dollars are lost each year through white-collar crime in America. Consumers pay for this form of fraud indirectly because businesses add the cost of it to the prices of goods and services.

Although much white-collar crime consists of employees stealing from their employers, it also includes "respectable" business people stealing from consumers. Illegal price-fixing is one example. Another example came to the public's attention when the FTC forced four department stores to return unclaimed credit balances to their charge customers. According to the FTC, the stores kept millions of dollars in customer funds over a five-year period. The stores wrote off the balances of the accounts when the customers failed to use them or to ask for refunds. Illegal political contributions and the millions of dollars in payoffs and bribes major corporations pay to foreign government officials are additional "costs of doing business" that consumers pay for indirectly in the prices of goods and services.

HOW FRAUDS ARE PERPETRATED

Internet Fraud

Many fraudulent and unethical practices occur on the Internet, yet the federal government currently has little power to assist consumers. Although numerous bills have been introduced in Congress dealing with a plethora of Internet-related issues, little has been accomplished. Direct-damage suits by injured consumers are comparatively uncommon and often are unsuccessful. State and federal laws are inadequate to give consumers the protection they need. In this situation, consumers are the victims of their own weaknesses and the dishonesty of sellers. This area of consumer protection will receive much scrutiny in the immediate future.

With more consumers shopping, banking, and interacting online, the potential for online fraud has increased. The federal government provides practical tips for protection against Internet fraud, securing your computer, and protecting your personal information. Visit www.onguardonline.gov for more information.

FYI

The Department of Justice is trying to combat fraud on the Internet. Operation E-Con and Operation Cyber Sweep combined have revealed more than 214,000 victims with a total estimated loss of over $275 million. Arrests and convictions have been made, but as with most frauds, it is difficult to pinpoint and prosecute the perpetrators.

The National Consumer League's Internet Fraud Watch program offers valuable information to consumers who use the Internet. A majority of frauds that are perpetrated on the Internet are done through websites (95 percent). The majority of complaints (72 percent) involve online auctions; goods are either misrepresented or never delivered. Using a reputable online escrow service can protect consumers. Escrow services, for a fee, hold the payment in an account until the consumer has received the goods and is satisfied that they are as promised. Only after the consumer approves the items does the seller get paid. The consumer should make sure that the escrow service is reputable. One of the more recent frauds is fake online escrow services.

Other activities on the Internet that might lure a consumer into a fraudulent situation are the practices of **spamming, phishing,** and **pharming.** Spamming is a popular technique to "advertise" and reach a large group of people who have not solicited such information. Many Internet providers identify and mark messages as "spam" before they enter the recipient's inbox. Spamming can occur in mass e-mails, instant messaging, newsgroups, and even mobile phone messaging. Phishing is the online solicitation of private or personal information, such as passwords, ID numbers, bank account numbers, and so forth. The phisher may lead the potential victim to a fake, but very professional and convincing website that appears to be legitimate. For example, a phisher may pose as a bank employee who sends the potential victim an e-mail, claiming to need to verify routing and account numbers. The return e-mail address is from the bank, and the link in the e-mail goes to what seems to be the bank's official website. It is difficult for the potential victim to know if the e-mail and website are legitimate. If you find yourself in a situation like this, it is best to contact the company directly. Most, if not all companies, report that they would never seek verification of personal information; they already have such information.

Spamming sending unsolicited electronic messages in bulk.

Phishing obtaining sensitive information about a person by posing online as someone trustworthy with a true need for the information.

Pharming exploitation of a vulnerability in server software that allows a hacker to redirect traffic from that website to another without the user's knowledge.

Pharming (also known as domain spoofing) is the exploitation of a vulnerability in server software that allows a hacker to poison the domain name server (DNS), and redirect traffic from that website to another website (without your knowledge). DNS servers are the machines responsible for resolving internet names into their real addresses—the "signposts" of the Internet. If the website receiving the traffic is a fake website, such as a copy of a bank's website, it can be used to "phish" or steal a computer user's passwords, PIN number, or account numbers. In the past, sites such as Amazon and Google have been victims of this fraud, though no resulting identity theft has been reported. Experts recommend that servers need to offer certificates of authenticity (such as VeriSign) to verify they are who they say.

www.antiphishing.org

The goal of this website is to help stop Internet scams and frauds. It offers a mechanism to report phishing as well as information on related crimes, conferences, and ways to join.

TIP The best way to avoid phishing scams is to go directly to a company's site—do not click there from an email link you receive. Never click on links sent by sources you cannot verify, especially e-mails from supposedly legitimate entities such as your bank, PayPal, and so forth.

The National Consumer League's Internet Fraud Watch offers the following tips to help you avoid being taken by Internet fraud:

The Postal Reorganization Act resolved the problem of unordered merchandise. The law stipulates that persons receiving unordered merchandise by mail may do whatever they want with it, and no payment need be made.

FYI

1. Know who you are dealing with. Do research on the person, company, or seller. Get physical addresses and contact numbers.
2. Look for information about how complaints are handled. See what standards the company meets.
3. Be aware that if a company has no record of complaints, this is still no guarantee of legitimacy.
4. Do not believe promises of easy money.
5. Understand the offer. Make sure you read all the details.
6. Resist high-pressure tactics. Take the time you need to make an informed decision.
7. Think twice before entering contests operated by unfamiliar companies.
8. Be cautious of any unsolicited e-mail. It is best just to delete the e-mail. Sometimes replying to an e-mail, even with a plea to be removed from the list, will let the sender know this is a live e-mail address, and more unwanted messages may appear.
9. Beware of impostors. Find alternative ways to contact companies that are sending you information.
10. Guard your personal information.
11. Beware of "dangerous downloads." Be cautious about viruses. Download only from trusted, legitimate sites.
12. When possible, verify website authenticity through certificates.
13. Pay the safest way. Using a credit card gives you federal protections.

Mail Frauds

The Inspection Service of the U.S. Postal Service estimates that fraudulent mail schemes represent an annual loss to the public in the billions of dollars. In general, the mail is used for the same types of frauds that are perpetrated face to face, by telephone contact, and on the Internet. Major frauds conducted through the mail include chain referral schemes, fake contests, low-price traps, home improvement fraud, debt consolidation fraud, auto insurance fraud, retirement home fraud, missing heir schemes, charity rackets, and business franchise fraud. As a result of the millions of complaints received in a typical year, thousands of individuals are convicted of mail fraud. The Postal Inspection Service processes these complaints and in many cases is able to obtain restitution for the victims and assess fines to flagrant violators.

Chain letters are illegal. True or false?

True. These are scams. The way you receive money from a chain letter is by recruiting others. Recruiting others to participate in these schemes is a felony in most states.

In spite of such vigilance, the fleecing continues year after year. People can help the postal service detect fraud by returning suspicious matter to the local post office or notifying the Postal Inspection Service. Recipients can also write "Forward to Postal Inspector" on suspicious pieces of mail. The mail will then be forwarded to the proper authorities.

Although buying by mail is convenient, it can be far from trouble-free. Often, recipients discover that what they thought they ordered (what they saw in the catalog or newspaper ad) is not what they received. In other instances, refunds are not given despite money-back guarantees. If you shop by mail, these tips may be useful:

1. Comparison-shop to make sure you are getting the best buy. Check local stores as well as other mail-order firms to compare prices.
2. Ask friends about their experiences with the company; find out if it is reliable.
3. If a guarantee is offered, read its provisions before you order (for instance, who pays the postage if you return the merchandise?).
4. Keep a copy of your order.
5. Record the mail-order company's address.
6. Pay by check or money order. Do not send cash through the mail.

The Federal Trade Commission has promulgated a trade regulation allowing consumers the option to cancel most mail-order transactions if the merchandise is not shipped within 30 days.

http://postalinspectors.uspis.gov

The United States Postal Inspection Service's mission is to protect the Postal Service, its employees, and customers from criminal activity. The site includes information about scams that are perpetrated through the mail.

WWW

www.ftc.gov

The website for the Federal Trade Commission (FTC) offers information on how the FTC enforces federal antitrust and consumer-protection laws.

WWW

Telemarketing Schemes

Telemarketing schemes remain popular. These schemes were nonexistent until the early 1980s, but currently telemarketing schemes are considered among the top 10 areas of fraud. Various states and the federal government have developed or are developing laws to restrict fraudulent telemarketing activity.

Telemarketing schemes fraudulent use of the telephone to sell a wide range of products and services.

Variations on telemarketing schemes are too numerous to list. Often they involve "unbelievable" investment opportunities, "free" vacations, or "free" magazines. To take advantage of the "bargain," consumers may be asked to send money or furnish a credit card number or checking account information. The result may be that no product or service is forthcoming, and the unscrupulous merchant keeps the money sent or makes unauthorized charges or debits to the credit card or checking account. Fraudulent solicitors work their schemes for a few weeks at one location and then move on to a new location and work under a different name. The consumer is left with no service or merchandise and an empty wallet. It should go without saying that you should never give your credit card or banking information unless *you* initiated the call and are certain to whom you are speaking.

THE PERSISTENCE OF FRAUD

Fraud is as old as the human race; it changes only in form and amount. Frauds of a generation or a century ago have given way to newer frauds, which probably are no more clever, for few frauds are or have to be clever. Fraud exists because of gullible consumers, greedy sellers, and inadequate laws that are inadequately enforced.

Gullible Consumers and Greedy Sellers

Even well-informed and circumspect consumers lack important information about their purchases. Even when merchandisers represent their wares honestly, few buyers have any way of judging the validity of the prices. Some dealers keep this in mind as they set the retail prices for their merchandise and services.

Not all sellers, of course, are greedy. Nor are all greedy sellers devoid of conscience, but many are. Manufacturers of dangerous products that injure their users may be operating within the limits of law but not within the restrictions of any code of ethics. With the

The CAN-SPAM Act

This Act, officially titled the Controlling the Assault of Non-Solicited Pornography and Marketing Act, took effect on January 1, 2004. The Act attempts to control the sending of bulk commercial e-mail with false or misleading subject lines. Provisions are as follows:

- All commercial e-mail must be identified with a valid postal address and must provide an opt-out procedure for recipients.
- If pornographic content is involved, an appropriate warning label must be provided.
- Violators will be liable for up to $250 per spam e-mail violation; fines cannot total more than $2 million, except in extreme circumstances.
- Violators may also be required to serve up to five years in prison.

One directive related to the Act required the FTC to study the feasibility of a do-not-spam list similar to the Do Not Call Registry. After careful consideration, in June 2004, the FTC determined that this seemingly pro-consumer action to help eliminate unwanted spam was not feasible. They pointed to the fact that such a list could be obtained and used by scammers and therefore would present more problems than solutions for consumers. As a result, while the CAN-SPAM Act remains in place, a do-not-spam list has not been assembled to date.

WWW

www.donotcall.gov

This is the National Do Not Call Registry. On this site you can register your phone numbers, check to see if they are already on the list, file a complaint, and get related information. Note that the extension is ".gov". Both .org and .com versions of "donotcall" exist, and we cannot verify their motives or actions. To be safe, register only with donotcall.gov.

growth of a large, impersonal market, conscienceless producers can ply their trade more easily, not only because detection is more difficult but also because personal relationships with their victims are unnecessary.

Impotent Laws and Poor Enforcement

Consumers need protection from their own ignorance and from the avarice of predatory sellers. To talk about educating consumers adequately is futile. No person can be trained sufficiently in all fields of knowledge of the marketplace to combat the specialized skills of predatory sellers. The best that can be done is to develop a body of more wary consumers. This effort has to be supplemented by law. Consumer ignorance, however, makes enactment and enforcement of legislation difficult.

The challenge of consumer protection through the law is complicated by the fact that many such laws are defective and enforcement authority is divided among local, state, and federal governments. The Internet creates additional problems because many e-commerce schemes are virtually immune from federal, state, or local laws. Even if laws exist that are enforceable, the practical reality is that schemes usually cannot be prosecuted in a timely manner. By the time Internet scam artists are exposed and prosecuted, they are often out of business, having kept the money and moved on to their next scheme.

Effective consumer-protection legislation is lacking not only because uninformed, unorganized consumers fail to demand it but also because well-organized and well-informed groups of business executives oppose it. Moreover, the punitive provisions of laws already on the books are absurdly lenient. Rarely is the perpetrator of a fraud committed to jail, and fines are so small as to be only an additional cost of doing business.

The term "419 scam" refers to the infamous Nigerian (usually) letter claiming that a large sum of money is available to you if you send a small sum of money to them up front. The term is a reference to a section of relevant criminal code in Nigeria. This scam is also called an advance fee fraud and takes many other forms, some more subtle than the Nigerian letter.

FYI

ARE CONSUMERS HELPLESS?

Consumers cannot do much as individuals to combat fraud. To be sure, the better informed they are, the more they can be on guard and avoid becoming victims themselves. Every individual would do well to ask questions and to investigate before signing a contract or making a major purchase. Inquiries can be made at the Better Business Bureau or the local Chamber of Commerce in communities not served by a Better Business Bureau.

A travel club offers free airfare and a week of lodging for two anywhere in the world if you purchase a new membership in the club. You will pay only $350 for this limited offer. This is a gimmick. True or false?

True. In such cases your money will disappear and the trip will never materialize because the company goes out of business.

The Federal Trade Commission and other federal agencies have consumer-complaint offices in Washington, DC, and at regional centers to deal with consumer-fraud problems. The FTC has specific jurisdiction over unfair trade practices in the District of Columbia, but elsewhere it has authority only in cases involving interstate commerce. Attorney generals' offices in all states have established consumer-fraud divisions to render protection to the public. In addition, most states have Departments of Consumer Affairs, and some localities' police departments have fraud or "bunco" divisions.

The consumer who needs to turn to government for help in this area usually is disappointed. The best remedy for fraud is "preventive consumerism": Do not place yourself in the position to be defrauded in the first place. Some general guidelines are worth noting here:

1. Work only with reputable, known companies.
2. Deal with local companies whenever you can.
3. Do not look for "impossible" deals. They almost never exist.
4. Assert yourself; often fraud is effective because the consumer dislikes saying no.
5. Be wary of mail-order companies, telephone solicitors, and Internet offers unless you have clear knowledge that the company is honest.
6. Always have your defenses up. People who suggest that they cannot be defrauded are often the ones most susceptible to fraud.
7. Do not keep quiet because you are ashamed of having been defrauded. Report it! Many schemes work for years because they go unreported and thus are never investigated.

WWW

www.bbb.org

The Better Business Bureaus (BBB) are private, non-for-profit entities that promote ethical relationships between businesses and consumers through assisting voluntary self-regulation, educating consumers and businesses, and promoting excellence in service.

www.staysafe.org

This site provides information about online safety to individuals of all ages and types. It also provides a toolbox to help keep your computer and software safe.

Protection for consumers also comes in the form of computer software. Available and widely used software includes virus protection, spam-blockers, programs that allow parents to monitor and control the websites their children visit, and many more. You can even sign up for e-mail alerts from Homeland Security's U.S. Computer Emergency Readiness Team. Resources such as these should help you feel less vulnerable and more in control, if you take advantage of them.

FRAUDULENT BUYERS

Some consumers perpetrate fraud on the seller. Shoplifting is the most blatant example. Sellers have had to counteract customer fraud by making it more difficult for consumers to be dishonest. For example, the practice of price switching has been stymied by bar codes, and retailers now package small products in large "bubble" packages to make them harder to steal.

"Refund reapers" create another problem for retailers. They purchase an item at a discount and then take it to a store selling it at list price and request a refund, in cash if possible. They state they have no sales slip because the item was a gift. If the store gives them a refund slip instead of cash, they can take the refund slip, buy new merchandise, and then have a confederate return in a few days with the item and the sales slip for a cash refund. Consumers should realize that stores cover losses such as these by charging higher prices.

SUMMARY

Traditional laissez-faire economic doctrine holds that competition protects consumers from fraud. This would be true if consumers were always rational economic persons, but they are not. The result is *caveat emptor*—"let the buyer beware."

Fraud is difficult to prove because the buyer must establish that the seller intended to deceive. Often, state and federal laws and enforcement of those laws are inadequate to give consumers the protection they need.

Major categories of consumer complaints include mail order, automobile sales and repair, home furnishings, remodeling and maintenance, and electronics repair. Other areas prone to fraud include the sale of food, health aids, cosmetics, medicine, and land; education; charity and religion; telephone solicitations; and insurance. The Internet, telemarketing, and mail solicitations are major avenues for fraudulent operators; scams perpetrated door-to-door, though less common now, do still occur. Groups that seem to be most susceptible to fraud are persons with low income and older persons, but anyone can become a victim.

www.planetfeedback.com

Consumers who want to give retail or service providers feedback about their purchases may send it through planetfeedback.com/consumer.

Fraud persists in the marketplace because of gullible consumers, greedy sellers, and impotent laws. Consumers must assume part of the responsibility because they often are ill-informed or act impulsively. Some fraud is perpetrated by consumers on sellers; the cost of this type of fraud is reflected in higher prices that the seller must charge consumers to compensate.

ITEMS FOR REVIEW & DISCUSSION

1. What is fraud? What are some examples? Why do sellers perpetrate fraud against buyers and buyers against sellers?
2. Explain industry concentration and why it is not considered to be a consumer fraud.
3. Explain where and how the practice of fraud fits into the traditional economic theory of the competitive, free-enterprise system.
4. Explain why the government should or should not protect the consumer from fraud.
5. Explain why fraud exists in some areas more than in others.
6. Why do doctors sometimes perform unnecessary medical operations? Give reasons why the health care field is particularly susceptible to fraud.
7. Give the steps to find a reputable repair shop.
8. Give reasons why certain groups are more susceptible to fraud than others.
9. Debate whether honesty is the best policy in business.
10. Telephone solicitations are big business, yet only a small percentage of consumers actually buy the product offered. Why do these companies persist? Can the consumer do anything other than hang up on the caller?
11. Internet fraud is a relatively new, but growing business. What steps can a consumer take to avoid falling victim to this type of fraud?
12. Have you seen college scholarship posters around your campus? Do you think they are legitimate?

EXPLORING PERSONAL VALUES: PROJECTS

1. Respond to the following statements, indicating whether you strongly agree, agree, disagree, or strongly disagree. Discuss and compare your responses with those of your classmates.

a. Although weak, the laws protecting the consumer against fraud are still more than is needed because a free enterprise system should operate on the principle of *caveat emptor.*
b. Most of what is labeled "consumer deception" is really self-deception.
c. If you change your mind about a recent purchase, you are justified in deliberately breaking the item and returning it for a refund.

2. Search for fraudulent or deceptive trade practices, and write to the appropriate governmental agency (probably the FTC) or your congressional representative about them. Alternatively, write a letter to the editor of your local newspaper regarding these trade practices.
3. In your journal, list the times you have felt defrauded. Describe what happened. How did you feel? What did you do? What can you do to reduce the risks of fraud?
4. Interview a number of students to find out if any of them has ever been the victim of a fraudulent scheme. If so, what fraud was involved? Also, ask them what kinds of fraud they know of that consumers have perpetrated on sellers.
5. Interview personnel at your local Better Business Bureau or Chamber of Commerce. What are these organizations doing to combat fraud?
6. Interview several professors and campus administrators regarding the need to "generate student/credit hours" on your campus. Report your findings to the class.
7. Prepare a report on frauds perpetrated on older persons and persons with low income.
8. Interview a local post office representative regarding postal fraud.
9. Ask a government employee or a business person in your community about the ways frauds are perpetrated on consumers.
10. Interview a senior citizen. Ask whether the person receives solicitations, and ask the person to show you his or her mail pile. Talk about fraud aimed at the elderly.
11. Discuss with your family ways to keep safe while using the Internet.

ADDITIONAL SOURCES OF INFORMATION

Abagnale, Frank W. *The Art of the Steal: How to Protect Yourself and Your Business from Fraud, America's #1 Crime.* New York: Broadway Books, 2002.

Busch, Rebecca S. *Healthcare Fraud: Auditing and Detection Guide.* Hoboken, NJ: John Wiley & Sons, 2008.

Davia, Howard R., and Howard Silverston. *Fraud 101: Techniques and Strategies for Detection.* Hoboken, NJ: John Wiley & Sons, 2005.

Garman, E. Thomas. *Rip-Offs and Frauds: How to Avoid and How to Get Away.* Mason, OH: Thomson Custom Publishing, 2004.

Henderson, Les. *Crimes of Persuasion.* Azilda, ON: Coyote Ridge Publishing, 2003.

Kirchheimer, Sid. *Scam-Proof Your Life.* AARP, 2007.

McMillan, Edward J. *Policies and Procedures to Prevent Fraud and Embezzlement: Guidance, Internal Controls, and Investigation.* Hoboken, NJ: John Wiley & Sons, 2006.

Montague, David A. *Fraud Prevention Techniques for Credit Card Fraud.* Victoria, Canada: Trafford Publishing, 2006.

U.S.G.P.O. Elder Fraud and Abuse: New Challenges in the Digital Economy: Hearing Before the Special Committee on Aging, United States Senate, One Hundred Sixth Congress, Second Session, Portland, OR, March 15, 2000. (SuDoc Y 4.AG 4:S.HRG.106-587).

Wells, Joseph, T. *Corporate Fraud Handbook: Prevention and Detection.* Hoboken, NJ: John Wiley & Sons, 2005.

Zack, Gerard M. *Fraud and Abuse in Nonprofit Organizations: A Guide to Prevention and Detection.* Hoboken, NJ: John Wiley & Sons, 2003.

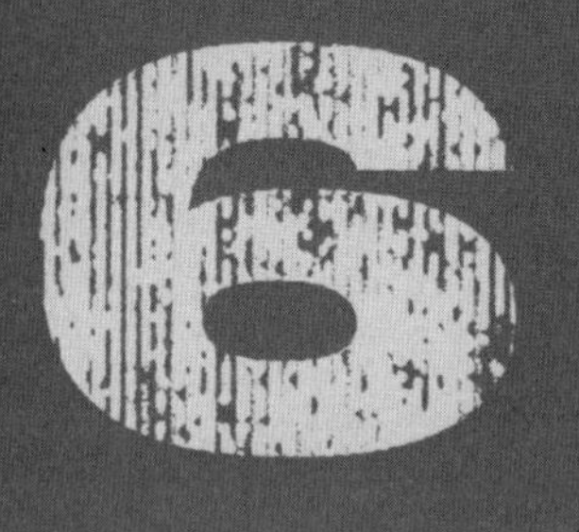

> Everyone wins when consumers know how to deal effectively in the marketplace. Educated consumers are better citizens . . . and make better customers.
>
> **VIRGINIA KNAUER,**
> SPECIAL ASSISTANT FOR CONSUMER AFFAIRS TO FORMER PRESIDENT RONALD REAGAN

KEY TERMS

commission-only financial planner
contingency fee
credence good
custodial care
fee-and-commission financial planner
fee-only financial planner
financial counselor
financial planner
flat-rate book
hourly fee
intermediate care
Medicaid residents
ophthalmologist
optician
optometrist
paralegal
portfolio
private-pay residents
service
skilled nursing care
specific job fee

The following concepts will be developed in this chapter:

1. The costs of services continue to spiral upward in their percentage share of the consumer's buying power.
2. Consumers can improve their position in the purchasing of services by accumulating as much buying knowledge as they can about the services they seek.
3. Careful shoppers of services are much more likely than careless shoppers of services to get the most value for their dollars.

After having read this chapter, you should be able to accomplish the following objectives:

1. Enumerate and evaluate various services offered to consumers.
2. List techniques the informed shopper of services customarily practices.
3. Propose questions to be answered before selecting various service personnel.

The United States has an ever-expanding **service** industry and information economy. Service and information industries consume more dollars and a larger percentage of consumers' incomes in the United States than in any other industrial society. The challenges facing consumers in selecting services are considerable.

Service an offer of intangible assistance to consumers.

Buying services usually involves far more risk than buying products. Once a service is used, it has little or no monetary value, in contrast to a tangible purchase. If a consumer purchases a product such as a digital camera, a market probably exists for that camera. If the consumer decides the purchase was unwise, she may sell it or return it to the store for a refund. If the consumer purchases a service, however, once the accommodation is offered, no resale and little refund potential remains. Further, the purchase of a specific service usually is limited in frequency. A consumer may be responsible for selecting an assisted living facility or a child care center, for example, only once or twice in a lifetime. This generally is not true with the purchase of products. In part because of the infrequency of the purchase, consumers usually have little knowledge of or interest in how to select the service. Finally, many services are available in a limited supply, but the demand may seem limitless.

In the service area, perhaps more than any other, the consumer has to take a proactive rather than a reactive position. Adequate research will help the consumer save money, avoid frustration and anxiety, and avoid injuries that may result from poorly performed services.

Consumer Services

Among the services that seem most difficult to assess and most costly for consumers are automobile services, attorney assistance, child care services, financial-planning aid, health care services, assisted living services, and vision care services. The following pages focus on the issues involved in selecting these services. From the literally hundreds of services that are available, these were selected because of consumers' difficulty in evaluating options, the high dollar value, the health importance of the service, the illegal and unethical practices that are common with the service, or the lack of viable remedies available if poor services are rendered. Much of the understanding of one service area can be applied to services in other areas. For example, a consumer can use many of the suggestions for selecting a physician to selecting a quality real estate salesperson.

In many cases it is hard for consumers to measure the quality of a good or service. Goods and services whose quality is difficult to measure are termed **credence goods.** The services discussed below are good examples of credence goods. For example, suppose a consumer's car is making a "clunk, clunk, clunk" noise. The consumer goes to a car repair shop, and the noise ceases. However, the consumer never really knows for sure if the $1,000 repair bill was warranted to stop the noise. Perhaps a simple adjustment could have solved the problem. Similarly, a consumer who is taking a prescribed medication for pain may not know whether the medicine really stopped the pain, or the pain coincidentally ended at the time when the medication was started. In these situations, the seller (i.e., mechanic or doctor) is the expert in the needs of the consumer. Unfortunately, this imbalance in expertise may encourage the seller to cheat and defraud the consumer.

Credence good a good or service whose quality consumers cannot assess before, during, or even after use.

AUTOMOBILE MECHANIC SERVICES

Attorney general's offices in most states periodically publish a list of the most frequent complaints that consumers register. Invariably, at or near the top of the list are complaints about automobile repairs. Since the 1970s, the manner in which consumers service their vehicles has changed substantially. Engineering advances have complicated the service of vehicles and now necessitate special training on each vehicle. As a result, in many situations, the only option available to the

www.bbbonline.org

www.safeshopping.org

With more services and products being purchased online, it is important for consumers to shop safely. These sites, sponsored by the Better Business Bureau and the American Bar Association, respectively, may aid consumers in making online purchases.

consumer is to return to the dealer for service, which may be more costly than at another type of service center.

When consumers need automobile maintenance and repair, they have various general options available to them. These include the diagnostic center, the independent service center, the new automobile service center, the retail store service center, and the specialty service center. Each has advantages and disadvantages.

The diagnostic center. For a predetermined fee, the diagnostic center will provide a list of repairs and maintenance needed for a specific vehicle. Generally these facilities generate their income from fees for the service; most do not do the actual repairs.

Independent service center. The independent service center is a repair shop that is privately owned and operated by one or several mechanics. The quality of these centers as a group is inconsistent, ranging from outstanding to poor. They often do not provide warranties on the work they perform. Indeed, automobile manufacturers may attempt to void existing warranties if an unauthorized mechanic works on a vehicle that is under warranty. They often do not have a waiting room or convenient pick-up and delivery service.

www.asecert.org

The National Institute for Automotive Service Excellence (ASE) is an independent nonprofit organization that was created in 1972. The ASE website helps to ensure that vehicle and repair service stations are trustworthy and that they provide competent automotive services to consumers.

Car dealership. The car dealership is often the most reliable option. The mechanics usually are well trained, and the work is often warranted. Typically, dealerships feature clean waiting rooms, offer convenient pick-up and delivery service, and accept various forms of payment. However, compared to others in this grouping, repair costs usually are highest with automobile dealerships. Today's car dealerships take full advantage of sales and service records, regularly using these databases to mail customers service reminders, with coupons and other incentives.

www.autobytel.com

Autobytel.com permits consumers to access automotive information, vehicle reviews, manufacturer incentives, and more. Individuals also may purchase an automobile online.

Retail store auto service center. These retail store centers are part of a major retailer. The overall competence of the mechanics is inconsistent, and their expertise usually is limited to simple repairs. These centers provide small waiting areas and accept various forms of payment. Generally, no pick-up and drop-off service is available. Costs of repairs and maintenance are competitive.

TIP Many retail auto service centers advertise specials. Time your maintenance needs so you can take advantage of the discounts.

Specialty service centers. Specialty service centers, which have become quite popular, have expertise in one or two areas, such as tires, mufflers, and oil changes. Generally, their mechanics are limited to specific tasks, although they tend to be highly competent in their specialty area. These centers usually have waiting areas, accept various forms of payment, but offer no drop-off and pickup service. Fees compare favorably with their competition, and they offer "specials" periodically.

Many consumers want to be able to rely on a single auto mechanic for the vast majority of their auto needs. These consumers consider a variety of factors involved in shopping for a mechanic and in following the repair and maintenance processes. The overall selection process should include, but should not be limited to, the following:

1. *Recommendations.* Before selecting a mechanic, ask friends, the Better Business Bureau, relatives, and coworkers for names of mechanics who have given them long-term and fair service.
2. *Competency.* Determine the specific training, practical experience, and certification of the mechanic(s) who may be working on your specific make of automobile. Be skeptical of those who say they are experts on all makes.
3. *Costs.* Ask about cost schedules. Most shops have a statement of charges for repairs. Some charge by the type of repair, others charge an hourly rate, and still others use the **flat-rate book.**
4. *Diagnosis.* If a repair is required, let competent mechanics make the diagnosis based on your statement of the problem. Some consumers decide the car needs some expensive repair when the problem actually is minor. A qualified, honest mechanic will troubleshoot and consider the most cost-effective remedy before proceeding with other, more expensive possibilities.
5. *Work order.* If a repair is required, be certain that a work order is completed, denoting the anticipated work to be performed and an estimate of charges.

www.cars.com

Cars.com is a comprehensive website that offers automobile information. Automotive reviews, model reports, advice, a dealer locator, and information on financing a car purchase can be obtained from this website.

Flat-rate book a publication listing the time a specific re[pair] should take. Mechanics mul[tiply] that time by their hourly wag[e to] determine the total labor cost of the repair.

www.carpoint.com

MSN Carpoint aids consumers in researching, buying, and rating cars. Additionally, automobiles may be purchased online.

ATTORNEY SERVICES

At some point in their lives, most consumers will need the services of an attorney. According to surveys, consumers rate lawyers low as a profession in regard to prestige and trust. Yet lawyers perform valuable and often-needed services. As with most professions, the quality of services ranges from outstanding to poor. The consequences of hiring an incompetent attorney range from emotional stress to the risk of severe legal liability.

When shopping for legal representation, the overall process should include, but not be limited to, the following steps:

1. *Seek recommendations.* Before selecting an attorney, ask friends, relatives, coworkers, local law school professors, and other attorneys for the names of lawyers who have a good reputation and track record in the specific area of your need.
2. *Determine competency.* Determine the specific training and practical experience of the attorney who will be working with your legal problem. Be skeptical of anyone who indicates that he is an expert in all areas of law.
3. *Determine costs.* Find out the fee arrangement. Most attorneys charge fees based on a **contingency fee,** an **hourly fee,** or a **specific job fee.**
4. *Hold a consultation.* Most attorneys provide a free or minimal charge consultation. During the visit, discuss fees and the attorney's experience level with your type of case.
5. *Research costs.* Many attorneys have assistants (who are not attorneys) do the research and other tasks associated with their practice. Be certain that such a person is well qualified to work on your behalf. Some attorneys have **paralegals** perform specified tasks. An attorney may charge a set amount, say $150 an hour, regardless of who performs the service. Thus, a paralegal may research a point of law for your case, and you may be charged $150 per hour, even though the paralegal's salary is much less than the attorney's fee.

Contingency fee a fee determined on a percentage basis; the attorney receives a predetermined portion of the amount of money awarded to the client. If the client receives no award, the attorney also receives no payment for her services. With a contingency agreement, the client still must pay expenses, filing fees, and the like.

Hourly fee a fee based on the actual amount of time expended on the client's case.

Specific job fee a predetermined amount, usually involving a simple legal service (a flat fee).

Paralegal a person trained in law who can legally perform specific tasks under the direction of a practicing attorney. Allowable tasks are diverse and depend upon individual state mandates.

FYI

Many attorneys who are hired on an hourly fee basis charge by minimum fractional increments regardless of the actual amount of time they spend. For example, if a phone call between the attorney and the opposing attorney consumes two minutes, the attorney may charge a minimum increment, perhaps 10 minutes.

TIP

Unless you need only a simple, basic legal service, hire an attorney who has specialized expertise in the area for which you need help. You will be better represented, and the fees may be lower than those of an inexperienced attorney, who will have to expend energies on researching the law at your expense.

CHILD CARE SERVICES

The majority of families now need, or want, two or more incomes. As a result, parents have to consider arranging for child care services and must choose from a great variety of care options. The quality of child care, whether in a home or a center, varies widely, and the better facilities often have a waiting list. As with assisted living facilities, media reports of poor care are noteworthy. Parents searching for child care should consider the following factors, among others:

1. *Licensing and accreditation.* Ask about certification or licensing with the state and accreditations with professional organizations. Each state has different levels of certification. Be sure the person or facility meets your requirements. Ideally, you should choose a provider that exceeds minimum requirements. Note any problems that inspectors have identified during state visitations, the nature and frequency of the problems, and how rapidly they were corrected.
2. *Costs.* Obtain a listing of the total costs, including all services and potential services. Also determine deposits required; costs for full-, part-time, and overtime services; prepayment requirements; cancellation policies; vacation credits allowed; and so on.
3. *Child/adult ratio.* Determine the number of children per full-time adult supervision.
4. *Financial assistance.* Determine if any monetary assistance is available (such as government aid and scholarships).
5. *Health care services.* Ask about health provisions. Inquire about emergency care, administration of medications, certifications (such as CPR), and the like. Also note policies regarding children who become ill and when those children are allowed to return to the center after having communicable illnesses.
6. *Food services.* Ask about the food provided to the children. Review a typical weekly menu for all meals and snacks. Visit during mealtime and note how meals are served and the children's general satisfaction with the food.
7. *Exercise.* Determine the nature (frequency, regularity, and quality) of physical activities.
8. *Safety.* Determine if the home or facility is in full compliance with health regulations, fire codes, and other state and local regulations regarding safety.
9. *Transportation availability.* Note the adequacy of any transport services for getting children to and from home, to and from schools, to special events, and so forth, as specified in the contract.
10. *Ancillary services.* Note any other services offered that may help you in your decision.
11. *Policies and related materials.* Request and review copies of policies, parents' rights handbook, the activities guide, and any other written materials distributed to the children and parents.
12. *Discipline.* Ascertain the discipline orientation of the child care provider and be certain these policies are consistent with your own.
13. *Infant care.* If leaving an infant, determine the timetable for various activities (feeding schedule, frequency of holding the child, etc.).

FYI

The major voluntary accrediting organization for child care centers is the National Association for the Education of Young Children (www.naeyc.org). The National Association of Child Care Resource and Referral Agencies offers child care referral agency information in your community (www.naccrra.net).

The consumer should look for indications of the child care provider's commitment to children. For example, if the playground has limited space and the equipment is poor, these indicate that this aspect of the service is a low priority for this provider.

As you begin your search, ask friends, teachers, parents, health care professionals, and children for recommendations. What are their feelings? What are their complaints?

When you visit providers' facilities, talk with center employees. What are their feelings about the facility? What are their complaints? Visit a center on several days and at different times of the day. This should give you a good basis for making your final selection.

Dependent care expenses may reduce your total taxes due. True or false?

True. Dependent expenses may be deducted pre-tax under certain circumstances. Or, a portion of child care expenses may be used as a tax credit. These are important tax savings devices available to most consumers, yet many consumers do not take advantage of them. Check with the IRS, your employer, and/or your tax accountant for further information.

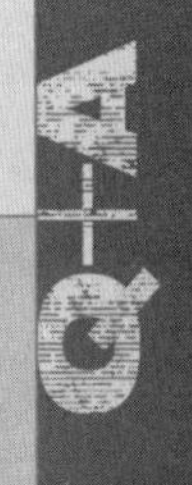

ASSISTED LIVING SERVICES

Exposés involving assisted living facilities are all too common. When considering homes for loved ones, many consumers feel helpless because the supply is limited and the demand substantial. In many parts of the country, a person must be on a waiting list many months before any housing is available. To further complicate the problem, many facilities limit or simply will not take low-income residents; their policy is to accept only **private-pay residents.** Others accept only a limited number of **Medicaid residents.**

Consumers choose from three types of assisted living facilities: **custodial care, intermediate care,** and **skilled nursing care.** Often the family, in consultation with the family physician and other health professionals, will determine which is appropriate. Skilled nursing care is the most expensive of these, and custodial care is the least expensive. Various types of federal, state, and private insurance programs may cover part or all of the costs of care for intermediate and skilled care services. In keeping with federal law, insurance programs that cover the costs of assisted living services have become much easier to understand and compare. A family searching for an assisted living facility should consider, among other factors, the following:

1. *Licensing.* Ask about the facility's certification with the state. All assisted living facilities have to be state licensed. Most states, however, have minimal standards. Ideally, the selected facility should be one that far exceeds the minimums in many, if not all, areas of concern. Note any problems that inspectors have identified during state inspections. If problems occurred, determine their nature and how rapidly they were corrected.
2. *Costs.* Obtain a list of the total costs of the facility, including all services and potential services. Also determine lease requirements, deposits, and the like.
3. *Private-pay or Medicaid availability.* Determine the facility's policy regarding accepting Medicaid or private-pay only. Also find out what happens to a private-pay resident if assets become depleted.
4. *Health care services.* Ask about the level of care provided by physicians, nurses, and other health care workers. Inquire about the use and cost of prescription and nonprescription medications. Observe the residents to see if they appear to be in good health, well fed, and the like.
5. *Food services.* Ask about the food provided to the residents. Review copies of a typical weekly menu for breakfast, lunch, dinner, and snacks. Visit the facility during mealtime, noting how meals are served and the residents' general satisfaction or lack thereof.
6. *Exercise and rehabilitation services.* Determine the nature of any programs available.
7. *Activities program.* Ascertain the frequency, regularity, and quality of organized activities, including any special programs.

Private-pay resident an elderly consumer who does not need government assistance to help pay for assisted living.

Medicaid resident an elderly consumer who qualifies for Medicaid assistance in the assisted living facility because the person's total assets do not exceed state minimums.

Custodial care room and board services but minimal assistance for personal living and health needs.

Intermediate care room and board services and some minimal personal living and health care services.

Skilled nursing care extensive personal living and health care services in addition to room and board.

Many families are installing baby cam monitors in their homes to record and monitor the in-home care their children are receiving from caregivers.

8. *Safety.* Determine if the facility is in full compliance with health codes, fire codes, and other state and local required regulations.
9. *Transportation availability.* Note the adequacy and frequency of city- or facility-owned bus/transport services.
10. *Ancillary services.* Ask about any other services available that may be unique to the facility.
11. *Policies and related materials.* Request and review copies of the facility's policy handbook, residents' rights handbook, activities guide, and other written materials distributed to clients.

The oversight of the adequacy of assisted living facilities typically is the responsibility of a state agency. Many state agencies have substantial supervision and commitment in this area. Unfortunately, many other states lack adequate interest, financial commitment, and support for assisted living supervision. How does your state agency fare?

FYI

A consumer who is considering assisted living services should assess the qualifications of staff members and determine the facility's commitment to each service it provides. For example, if the physical therapy room has limited and antiquated equipment and the staff is unqualified, that service clearly has low priority.

Ask friends, your own health care professionals, and others for recommendations. Talk with a random selection of residents. How do they feel about the facility? What are their complaints? Talk with the employees. How do they feel about the facility? What are their complaints? Visit each facility you are considering on several days and during varying times of the day. Visit all areas in the facility, including sleeping rooms, lunchrooms, and activities rooms. Your observations should reveal if the facility is clean, safe, and pleasant, and whether the overall morale of residents and employees is high or low.

FINANCIAL PLANNING SERVICES

Of the more than half a million people in the United States who identify themselves as financial planners, some are competent, trustworthy, and committed to maximizing their clients' profit potential. Too many, though, are "fast-buck" operators, exploiting consumers who lack the knowledge and interest to oversee their own investments. Further, many planners have expertise in only one area. A financial planner who began as a life insurance agent, for example, may tend to oversell life insurance and annuities. A financial planner who was a stockbroker may prefer to sell specific types of stocks and bonds. The banker who is now a financial planner may be apt to recommend conservative, risk-free investments that generate little or no asset appreciation for the client.

As recent financial downturns have shown, investing and managing money can be a complicated business. The more you know as a consumer, the more qualified you'll be to make informed investment decisions.

TIP

Many financial planners are certified. Those who hold designations such as Registered Financial Consultant (RFC), Certified Financial Planner (CFP), or Chartered Financial Consultant (ChFC) or who are members of the National Association of Personal Financial Advisers are obligated to uphold codes related to ethics, honesty, and conflicts of interests. There is no guarantee that these commitments will be honored. Nonetheless, consumers should look for these designations when they seek a financial planner.

The Internet has transformed the financial-planning industry. Prudent investors who shop the Internet for financial-planning advice can achieve enormous savings. Many very reliable resources are free (e.g., www.morningstar.com, www.vanguard.com). By studying sites like these, investors can gain knowledge without the need of financial-planning services. Even consumers who decide to avail themselves of competent and honest financial planners should prepare by learning basic information about investments, so that they and the financial planner can work together more effectively.

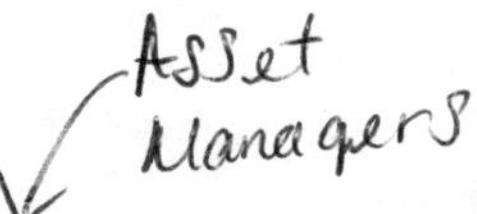

Consumers should be aware that financial planners most often have no real estate training and usually have limited experience in that area. Even financial planners who are fully certified are not required to have any expertise in real estate. Yet many self-made wealthy people have become so by investing in real estate. Consumers who turn to financial planners will probably not be offered real estate investments as an option.

Financial planner a professional whose main objective is to manage clients' assets.

Financial counselor a professional whose main function is to attempt to reduce clients' debt.

The stated objectives of the **financial planner** and the **financial counselor** are substantially different. Financial planners are also called asset managers. They help clients to invest their money and manage other assets. Financial counselors are frequently called debt managers. They assist clients in reducing their debt. Identifying a qualified asset manager is much more difficult than identifying a debt manager.

Portfolio all the securities and related assets an investor owns.

Most consumers do not need the advice of a financial planner because they have a relatively simple investment **portfolio.** Those who want to invest can avoid the need for a planner by spending a few hours each month reading business-oriented financial publications and financial websites such as *Kiplinger's, Money, Consumer Reports,* and *Barron's.* This small expenditure of time should be more than adequate to allow them to determine how they should invest their money. Again, people who seek financial advice should become educated with regard to investment options so that they will be in a position to evaluate the planner's advice.

TIP Regardless of the fee structure of the financial planner you work with, make sure you obtain a written estimate of what services you can expect and for what price. Compare this estimate with others, and select the package of services that best meets your needs at a reasonable cost.

Financial planners are paid in various ways, depending on whether the individual is a commission-only financial planner, a fee-and-commission financial planner, or a fee-only financial planner.

Commission-only financial planner a professional who offers free services to clients and is paid through commissions earned by selling the recommended investments.

The **commission-only financial planner** makes his salary through commissions he earns by selling investment products. For example, if the planner recommends and sells a specific insurance product, he or she will receive a commission from the insurance company. Commission-only planners are likely to direct consumers toward purchasing products that provide the highest commissions, even though these may not be the best options for the client. Therefore, consumers should carefully scrutinize recommendations before following any advice from a commission-only financial planner.

Fee-and-commission financial planner charges the client a fee and also is paid commissions on the investments recommended.

Fee-and-commission financial planners receive both a sales commission from the company that sells the product and a fee from the client. These planners typically charge the client a lower fee than a fee-only planner would charge. Some clients may be unaware that the planner is also receiving commissions, and it's important for clients to educate themselves about where the planner stands to earn money.

Fee-only financial planner a professional who charges the client a fee for recommending an investment plan.

The **fee-only financial planner** receives an hourly wage or a previously negotiated amount from the client. These planners are paid for determining a client's financial net worth and recommending a plan of action based on the client's financial goals. They do not make commissions from the financial products they suggest. All other factors being equal, the fee-only type of financial planner tends to be the least biased and, therefore, the most trustworthy of the various types of planners.

If you decide you would benefit from the services of a financial planner, your inquiries should include, at a minimum, the following:

1. *Credentials.* Many professional organizations offer credentials to planners who meet their professional standards. Determine if the planner has a credential, and find out the type of training and experience necessary to earn that credential.

2. *Training and experience.* In addition to being credentialed, most planners have one or more degrees in a finance-related area. Ascertain the extent of the planner's formal education and practical experience in the field.
3. *Continuing education.* Determine the frequency and type of continuing training the planner pursues. Keeping up with the changes in investments, tax laws, and related areas is imperative.

TIP Be cautious of the free financial seminars that various individuals and companies offer. Some of them offer valuable advice, but frequently the people who offer these seminars promise quick and easy profits on your investment in their services. If it sounds too good to be true, it probably is.

4. *Fees.* Calculate the total cost of the services to be provided. If the planner works on an hourly basis, obtain an estimate of charges after the planner is aware of your financial situation and needs.
5. *Conflict of interest.* Find out if the planner receives commissions from any source.
6. *The financial plan.* A quality planner will develop a complete picture of the client's financial position and discuss long-term and short-term goals, risk (comfort levels), and so on, before making any recommendations.
7. *Interaction.* Ask yourself how you feel about the planner. Do you feel comfortable with the person? Do you sense a personality conflict? Do you think the planner is overbearing?

HEALTH CARE SERVICES

Health care costs in the United States are higher than in any country in the world. One of the most important consumer issues of the past two decades has been how to reduce these costs and make the health care system available to all consumers. Currently, many children and older consumers do not have health insurance coverage. Other consumers have very limited options because HMOs and related health care insurance offerings define the care that is available to the individual.

FYI *More than 47 million people in the United States do not have health insurance, largely because the cost of insurance is unaffordable for them.*

TIP Try to schedule medical appointments at the beginning of the day when the physician's schedule is less likely to be "backed up."

The Federal Trade Commission, in cooperation with the American Association of Retired Persons, publishes a guide to help consumers select health care services. The health care professionals considered in the guide are physicians, pharmacists, dentists, and vision care specialists. The following discussion draws upon advice from that guide.

WWW **www.aarp.org**

A consumer who is 50 years old or over may elect to become a member of the American Association of Retired Persons (AARP), a nonprofit association. The organization's website offers helpful information and benefits to members of this age group.

Finding the health professional who best suits your needs may take time and effort. A good place to start is by asking friends and relatives to recommend the health professional they use. Other sources of referrals are teaching hospitals, medical schools, dental schools, other health professionals, professional societies, and local consumer groups. For information about a specific health professional's education and specialties, call the person's office and ask, or check your library for professional membership directories such as the *American Medical Association Directory.*

After you have collected a list of candidates, call their offices to get information about topics that are particularly important to you. For example, you might ask:

1. How much will services cost, and when are payments due?
2. Can a special payment schedule be arranged to fit my budget?
3. Does the professional accept the type of insurance I carry?
4. Does the professional employ or recommend the use of other health professionals, such as physician's assistants or nurse practitioners?
5. What are the office hours?
6. How does the office respond to emergencies after office hours?
7. Is another professional on call when the doctor is unavailable?
8. At what hospitals does the doctor have admitting privileges?
9. Does the doctor have access to facilities where simple procedures can be done on an outpatient basis?
10. Will the doctor prescribe generic drugs?

Q+A

Health care expenses may be deducted from your paycheck, reducing your reported taxable income. True or false?

True. Health care expenses may be deducted, but only if they meet certain criteria. This allows for a tax savings that many consumers could utilize. Check with the IRS, your employer, and/or your tax accountant for further information.

You can learn the answers to the following questions from a personal visit:

1. Is the service prompt and efficient?
2. Does the professional give a thorough examination?
3. Does the professional make you feel at ease and respond thoughtfully to your questions?
4. Does the professional clearly and simply explain diagnoses, test results, treatments, and prescribed medications?
5. Does the professional suggest ways to keep costs down?
6. Is the office clean and well equipped?

WWW

www.cdc.gov

The website for the Centers for Disease Control and Prevention (CDC) provides information to help consumers make better health decisions. This federal agency fulfills its mission by creating alliances with other health organizations and focusing on preventive measures for better health.

TIP

Before agreeing to any surgical procedure, obtain a second and perhaps a third opinion. Many insurance policies cover the cost of the additional opinions.

Pharmacists

Pharmacists are an excellent, often underutilized, source of information about drugs. Questions to ask when you are selecting a pharmacist are:

TIP

Shop around for generic drugs. The difference in costs for essentially the same drug among various pharmacies is often significant.

1. When appropriate, do you substitute generic equivalents for brand-name drugs?
2. Will you compound special prescriptions for me?

WWW

www.nabp.net

The National Association of Boards of Pharmacy (NABP) sponsors this website offering pharmaceutical information; consumers can confirm which pharmacies are certified and find other relevant information.

3. Where can I get medicines in an emergency?
4. Will your pharmacy deliver medicines when I can't pick them up? Is there a delivery fee?
5. Do you offer discounts? How much?
6. Do you accept all forms of prescription drug insurance?
7. Do you keep patient profiles listing all the medicines each customer has purchased?

Dentists

When looking for a dentist, consumers should consider many factors. Start with the following questions:

1. What are the fees for a routine checkup and cleaning?
2. Does the dentist accept the type of insurance I carry?
3. Does the dentist employ a certified dental hygienist?
4. Is an X-ray absolutely necessary? Is a lead apron or bib provided?
5. How can I prevent dental problems?

For a thorough eye exam, go to an ophthalmologist or optometrist. True or false?

True. Ophthalmologists and optometrists are professionals in the eye care industry, and they will give a thorough eye exam as well as a proper prescription if glasses or contacts are needed.

Vision Care Specialists

Following are some questions to ask when choosing a vision care specialist:

1. How much does your basic eye examination cost, and what does it include?
2. When is payment expected?
3. Do you sell eyeglasses and contact lenses?
4. How much will eyeglasses or contact lenses cost?

CASE STUDY Eyeglass Ruling

Pearle Vision and Pearle VisionCare are one of the nation's largest retailers of eyeglasses. In 2006, a California court ruled that the company was operating illegally, including unlicensed practice of optometry, employing deceptive marketing, and participating in unfair business practices. The company falsely advertised that it provided optometric care, including eye exams and eye care completed by optometrists. They also told customers that optometrists in the retail outlets were independent, when in fact they were not. Optometrists working in the company centers were controlled by and financially subsidized by the company.

QUESTIONS

1. What is your personal opinion of the ruling?
2. Do you have any personal experience with this company or a similar company?
3. Why might it matter whether on-site optometrists operated independently?
4. Do you think past consumers should receive some notification or financial settlement?
5. What do you think should happen to companies who gain from false advertisement and illegal business practices?

Source: California Department of Justice, Office of the Attorney General, June 12, 2006.

The Eyeglass Rule

The Eyeglass Rule, enacted in 1978, requires eye doctors to make available to patients their eyeglass prescriptions, at no extra cost, immediately after an eye exam.

Over one-half of the U.S. population wears eyeglasses or contact lenses. Prior to the 1970s, many consumers did not have the tools and information to make intelligent purchasing decisions for better eye care. An FTC trade-regulation rule, the Eyeglass Rule, provided help.

Before the rule was in place, people who examined eyes often required customers to buy glasses from them. Because the service provider held the results of the eye examination, consumers had few alternatives if they were unhappy with the prices, quality, and selection of eyeglasses offered. The rule requires eye doctors to give patients their prescriptions immediately after an eye exam. They cannot charge extra for doing this. The Eyeglass Rule does not apply to contact lens fittings, only eye examinations.

Previously, some states and professional associations prevented sellers from advertising eyewear and vision services. The rule removes those restrictions. People now can advertise prices of eye exams, glasses, contact lenses, and other eye care products and services. Consumers receive two benefits from this rule:

1. Comparison shopping is possible everywhere. Consumers will quickly know the prices available in their area.
2. Advertising may create more competition among sellers, which may cause retail prices to go down and the level of quality to increase.

Federal law requires that vision care specialists give a copy of the eyeglass prescription to the patient so the patient may shop around for glasses. The law does not apply to contact lens fittings.

FYI

5. Do you charge for follow-up visits to adjust frames or check contact lenses?
6. What is your refund policy for contact lenses?
7. How much do you charge for replacement lenses?
8. Will you give me a complete copy of my contact lens specification and fitting results?

The three types of vision care specialists are the **ophthalmologist,** the **optometrist,** and the **optician.** Ophthalmologists are physicians with a specialty in vision care. They provide the most comprehensive services, including surgery. Optometrists have optometry degrees. Opticians take measurements and issue vision aids based on prescriptions made by ophthalmologists and optometrists.

Ophthalmologist a physician who specializes in diagnosing and treating eye diseases; prescribes drugs, performs examinations and eye surgery; and also may provide eyeglasses and contact lenses.

Optometrist a medical professional who has a doctor of optometry degree in eye care.

Optician a vision specialist who takes measurements and produces vision aids based on prescriptions written by ophthalmologists or optometrists.

SUMMARY

The service industry is an important part of the U.S. marketplace. The costs of services continue to increase in their percentage share of the consumer's buying power.

Because the services offered are intangible and are usually purchased infrequently, and because the supply is limited and demand is often high, services are more difficult to select and evaluate than are products. Consumers can improve their position in purchasing services by accumulating as much knowledge as they can about buying specific services.

Careful shoppers of services are much more likely than careless shoppers to get the most value for their dollar. Prudent consumers shop around for services. One way to compare offerings is to develop a list of questions by which to evaluate service providers.

www.consumerlab.com

ConsumerLab.com performs independent tests of health, wellness, and nutrition products and makes the results available to consumers and health care professionals. It tests such products as vitamins and herbal supplements.

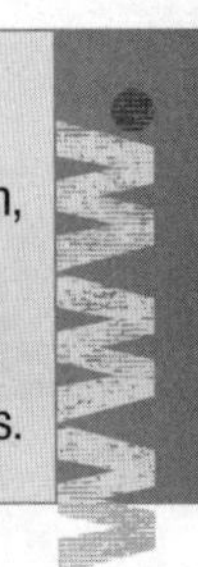

ITEMS FOR REVIEW & DISCUSSION

1. Differentiate shopping for services and shopping for products. Would you classify yourself as a careful or careless shopper of services?
2. Name some fraudulent and unethical practices perpetrated by practitioners in the health care and financial services industry.
3. Describe various ways by which attorneys and financial planners are paid for services they render.
4. Delineate the levels of care available in assisted living facilities.
5. Explain the major differences between financial planners and financial counselors.
6. Why are products offered for sale usually under the jurisdiction of the state Attorney General's Office, whereas services offered for sale often are the responsibility of other agencies?
7. Should the various trade, medical, and related professional associations have more or less control over their members in licensing and censuring? Why?
8. What services require expertise that the typical consumer does not have? Discuss ways in which consumers could assist professionals in these areas with the intent of reducing overall costs or fees.

EXPLORING PERSONAL VALUES: PROJECTS

1. Some individuals would agree with the statement, "Older parents should be cared for by their children," and others would concur with, "Assisted living care should be operated by the federal and state governments and should be readily available and free to all older persons." Is your opinion the same as one of these or somewhere in between? Compare your opinions with those of your classmates, citing reasons for your viewpoint.
2. List the ways you spend your money on services. Then prepare a pie chart that illustrates your spending on services, and answer and complete the following:
   a. Are you satisfied with the percentage of each slice?
   b. Draw a pie chart representing what you consider to be an ideal spending pattern for services purchased.
   c. Project the ways your need for services will change over the next 5 years, 10 years, 20 years, and 40 years, noting how the pie chart will change for you during these periods.
3. In your journal, write down your thoughts about the fact that consumers cannot return services as they can products.
4. Make a list of services you have used or your parents have used during the last few years. What, if any, complaints did you or they have about those services? How did you or they resolve the complaints?
5. Contact three financial planners who are *not* paid on a fee-only basis. Ask each planner if he or she believes that accepting commissions is a conflict of interest. Report your findings to the class. Do you think you will ever need a financial planner or counselor? Why or why not?
6. Contact three pharmacies and ask for the price of a specific brand-name prescription drug and its generic equivalent. Determine how the prices differ among pharmacies and report your findings to the class.
7. Visit a child care or assisted living facility and evaluate it based on the questions in this chapter. Report your findings to the class.

8. For each of the services covered in this chapter, identify the state agency, if any, that has legal authority to oversee that service.
9. Lead a class discussion on why consumers do not seem to evaluate services they buy properly and how best to reduce service needs now and in the future.
10. Interview an automobile mechanic and determine how consumers can decrease their chances of being overcharged for services.

ADDITIONAL SOURCES OF INFORMATION

American Red Cross Staff and American Red Cross Badger Chapter. *Choosing Quality Child Care: How to Be Confident You Make the Right Choice. The American Red Cross Search Guide.* Madison, WI: The American Red Cross, Badger Chapter, 2001.

Barton, Phoebe Lindsey. *Understanding the U.S. Health Services System.* Chicago, IL: Health Administration Press, 2006.

Clarke, John. *Creating Citizen-Consumers: Changing Publics and Changing Public Services.* London: Sage, 2007.

Harms, Thelma, Debby Cryer, and Richard M. Clifford. *Infant/Toddler Environment Rating Scale.* New York: Teachers College Press, 2003.

Lieberman, Trudy. *Consumer Reports Complete Guide to Health Services for Seniors: What Your Family Needs to Know About Finding and Financing, Medicare, Assisted Living, Nursing Homes, Home Care, Adult Day Care.* New York: Three Rivers Press, 2000.

Shomer, Molly. *Insiders Guide to Assisted Living: What You Really Need to Know Before You Sign a Contract.* Dallas, TX: Aeltern Press, 2005.

Sultz, Harry A., and Kristina M. Young. *Health Care USA: Understanding Its Organization and Delivery.* Sudbury, MA: Jones & Bartlett, 2008.

Weisman, Steve. *A Guide to Elder Planning: Everything You Need to Know to Protect Yourself Legally and Financially.* Upper Saddle River, NJ: Financial Times Prentice Hall, 2004.

Wurman, Richard Saul. *Understanding Healthcare.* Newport, RI: TOP, 2004.

> We are nothing but ceremony; ceremony carries us away, and we leave the substance of things; we hang on to the branches and abandon the trunk and body.
>
> **MICHEL DE MONTAIGNE,** FRENCH ESSAYIST

KEY TERMS

affluenza
bequest
built-in obsolescence
ceremony
competitive consumption
conspicuous consumption
cremation
custom
fad
fashion
habit
memorial societies
obsolescence of quality
pecuniary power
planned obsolescence
pre-need contracts
resistance lane
style
taste
trade (or industry) association

The following concepts will be developed in this chapter:

1. Custom exerts an overwhelming influence on consumer choice making.
2. Human beings interact through social and cultural symbols as well as economic self-interest.
3. People make billions of dollars' worth of personal economic decisions based on the customary ceremonies to be followed with regard to burial services, weddings, birthdays, holidays, and similar occasions.
4. Opinion is divided as to the value of conspicuous consumption to an economy.
5. How consumers consume depends on a set of external and internal factors.
6. Various social and economic factors contribute to the influence of consumer wants.

After having read this chapter, you should be able to accomplish the following objectives:

1. Define custom, give several factors responsible for the continuance of customs, and set forth several factors that cause customs to change.
2. Compare and contrast conspicuous and nonconspicuous consumption.
3. Give examples of the ways in which pecuniary power is displayed.
4. Define and give examples of emulation as it relates to consumption.
5. Distinguish among the effects of fashion, fad, style, and custom.
6. Enumerate the factors that encourage or inhibit the development of fashions.
7. Give examples of planned obsolescence and its consequences to individuals and society.

MEANING AND ORIGIN OF CUSTOMS

A **custom** is a long-established action, convention, practice, or usage that regulates the lives of a group of people. A **habit** refers to an individual's pattern of behavior.

Custom the tendency of a group to consume according to a fixed pattern.

Habit the tendency of an individual to consume in a fixed pattern.

Many customs probably had their origin in utility. Once a custom becomes established, however, it may continue to control consumption long after the original justification for it has disappeared. The assertion that a custom originates and endures only because the populace desires it is based on an assumption that people are rational. People are not always rational, though, as amply illustrated in the literature of anthropology, psychology, and sociology.

Customs and Consumption

The power of custom is stronger in consuming activities than in occupational activities. Customary practices do develop in business firms, but in a dynamic economy, competitors compel firms to abandon customary practices that lack utility. Moreover, custom is valued much more highly in consumption than in production. The pioneer or innovator who reflects custom in business is considered smart, whereas the pioneer or innovator who rejects custom in consuming practices is often ridiculed or labeled eccentric.

A group may have both good customs and bad customs. The following discussion is intended to give the reader some basis on which to evaluate customs.

WHY DO CUSTOMS CONTINUE?

Customs continue as a result of inertia, institutionalism, stratification, isolation, and illiteracy.

- *Inertia.* Experimenting with new consumer products or services requires positive action. In business firms, the prospect of monetary gain helps overcome inertia, but for consumers the prospect of greater satisfaction often is too intangible to motivate them to change their habits.
- *Institutionalism.* Social institutions such as the family, government, religion, and school are essentially static, with fixed consuming patterns. If changes occur, they usually come slowly or as a result of a major upheaval or power shift.
- *Stratification.* Economically, there are rich and poor; sociologically, there are dominant and minority groups. People at the top enjoy a more abundant economic life, and they fear that change may weaken their position or displace them. Thus, they have a vested interest in maintaining the status quo.
- *Isolation.* Whether isolation results from physical, political, racial, or linguistic barriers, the results are the same. Isolation perpetuates customs. The interchange of knowledge, on the other hand, constantly challenges accepted customs. This interchange has been accelerated by such things as air travel, imports, and the Internet.
- *Illiteracy.* In societies with high illiteracy rates, customs typically persist, partly because the inability to read or write creates isolation. In societies that are both largely illiterate and physically isolated, customs change even more slowly, if at all.

WHAT CAUSES CUSTOMS TO CHANGE?

Despite their resistance to change, customs can and do change. Communication, transportation, advertising, education, and competition facilitate change.

> *Until the early 1990s, most U.S. rural areas received fewer than 10 radio and television stations. With the advent of satellite technology, many rural satellite dish owners now may receive thousands of radio and television channels from all over the world.*
>
> FYI

- *Communication.* Radio, television, film, and more recently the Internet have surmounted the barriers of space, time, and illiteracy. In the most remote regions today, people can hear and see what is going on around the world and learn about the customs of other societies.
- *Transportation.* In the United States, automobiles, airplanes, trains, and buses have made people mobile. In their travels people see new sights and learn new customs.
- *Advertising.* One of the functions of advertising is to tell people about new products, new services, and new ways to use known products. What advertisers call sales resistance is likely to be resistance caused by custom. In the process of convincing consumers to buy their products, advertisers break down customs and promote change.
- *Education.* Both formal and informal education tend to break down customs. Even though a curriculum itself may be traditional, the educational process promotes literacy, which facilitates change. Students read newspapers, magazines, and books, and have access to computers; these activities expand their horizons and weaken the hold of customs.
- *Competition.* In a free economy, competition among business firms results in new products, new services, and new ways of doing things. A competitive economy is a changing economy, and a changing economy challenges customs.

CEREMONIAL CUSTOMS

Ceremony a formal series of acts prescribed by ritual, protocol, or convention.

A **ceremony** is an elaborate way of satisfying important emotional needs. Each of the primary events in life—birth, coming of age, marriage, and death—is significant for individuals and for society, and societies have developed ceremonial practices to mark them, such as weddings and funerals. These most significant ceremonies are termed *primary ceremonials. Secondary ceremonials* are exemplified by graduation from high school and from college. *Tertiary ceremonials* include acceptance into a religious group, induction into a lodge, and events marking achievements, such as the awarding of an honorary degree.

Practically, ceremonial events could be ignored, but nonetheless consumers continue to spend a great deal of money on ceremony. The reason for this is a matter of interest to psychologists and sociologists. The amount of money spent on ceremonies is of interest to economists. Naturally, sellers of ceremonial supplies and services encourage lavish celebrations.

Funerary Customs

> *A 1964 book entitled* The American Way of Death, *by Jessica Mitford, first exposed the massive abuses perpetrated by the funeral industry on consumers and helped lead to passage of a federal regulation in the 1970s.*
>
> FYI

It has been written, "What man shall live and not see death?" As death is inevitable and universal, so are the ceremonies that mark it. When a person dies, the family usually is responsible for arranging the burial. Often, the method of disposing of the body is prescribed by the family's religion, the community, and other groups.

Practices vary among religions. An Orthodox Jew, for example, is given a starkly simple burial service. The body is not embalmed, there is no viewing at the services, and there are no flowers and no music.

Early Christians adopted equally simple practices. Burial was a communal ceremony. The body was laid out with lights around it and was sprinkled with holy water and incense. A cross was placed on the chest, or the hands were folded on the chest. The body was buried in consecrated ground, with no coffin. White was the mourning color, although mourning was discouraged.

The simplicity of early funerals eventually gave way to pomp and display. In Europe and the Americas, funerals served to acknowledge religious beliefs, affirm the deceased's social status, and provide an opportunity for social interaction.

In present-day society, the business ethic has partially displaced religion's role in the funeral service. Except for a chosen religious reading and the eulogy, which are the clergy's responsibilities, funeral directors are prepared to assume all activities associated with death.

www.nfda.org

The website for the National Funeral Directors Association (NFDA), an organization that represents funeral home directors, helps to promote the quality of the funeral profession.

Burial as a business: Demand

The funeral industry is challenging to categorize. Is it a business or a profession? More than most business firms, funeral directors operate within the limits of religion and custom. The demand is constant, and the supply usually is fixed. There is practically no free entry into the industry, and no free market. Prospective buyers normally are in a state of shock. They usually do not shop around or bargain for lower prices. Prices often are not based on cost, and there is no marginal pricing. In many markets the price is what the traffic will bear.

How do prospective buyers of funeral services make their choices? Few of them have ever given thought to purchasing a funeral service. Confronted with the need, they turn to family and friends.

By planning ahead for a funeral, you can save 50 percent or more. Funeral companies must grant reasonable requests for price quotes and other information by telephone.

FYI

Burial as a business: Supply

As a service rather than a product industry, the funeral business does not have a national market. It consists of a composite of local markets characterized by a monopoly or an oligopoly. In a monopoly one seller controls the supply of a product or service, and in an oligopoly a few sellers control the majority of the supply of a product or service.

Trade associations or **industry associations** dominate some industries. This is the case with the funeral industry, in which associations have created and continue to support a structure of legislative and administrative barriers that maintain artificially high price levels. All facets of the funeral industry are well organized. In addition to national associations of funeral directors are trade associations that represent cemeteries and crematories, manufacturers of burial merchandise such as caskets and burial vaults, manufacturers of monuments and markers, and manufacturers of embalming chemicals.

Trade (or industry) association an organization that has been developed by businesses whose members agree to abide by established standards or practices and codes of ethics.

The trade associations effectively control the funeral industry. They dominate the state boards of funeral directors, which establish the rules for entry. No one may be a funeral director or an embalmer without a license, and members of the regulating agencies typically must be licensed funeral directors or embalmers. Thus, the regulated are also the regulators.

www.funerals.org

The nonprofit group Funeral Consumers Alliance provides information on funerals, death, and dying. An FCA ombudsman is also available to answer consumers' questions.

WWW

Pricing funerals

According to economic theory, an increase in the supply of a product or service when demand remains constant results in lower prices in a free market. Funeral firms, however, do not operate in a free market. As a consequence, prices for funeral services have risen sharply in the United States and do not reflect costs, as they would in more competitive industries.

The pricing of a funeral service represents a combination of cost, custom, and psychology. As a starting point, the price of a funeral includes the costs of a casket, a cemetery plot or crematory, a grave marker or urn, burial clothing, transportation, flowers, music, and other incidentals. The casket often is the key to funeral pricing.

Funeral businesses use custom and psychology to entice buyers to spend more. One popular technique is to arrange the caskets so the prospective buyer sees the highest-

Funerals can cost as little as $5,000 or up to $20,000, depending on the choices made by the family. The cost of cremation alone is between $2,000 and $3,000.

FYI

Resistance lane a high-pressure sales tactic that many funeral directors use to persuade the buyer to purchase a higher-priced funeral.

priced one first. If the buyer objects, he is moved along what is called **resistance lane.** Subtly but effectively, the salesperson suggests that the buyer would not wish to buy a "cheap" casket. In view of his status in the community, and to show devotion to the deceased, the salesman argues, should not the buyer select one of the "nicer" caskets? This play on emotion is usually effective.

One way a funeral director can get a clue to the family's ability to pay is to ask, "How many copies of the death certificate do you need?" Depending on the response, the director knows at once how many insurance policies the family has. If there are many, the director shows the family only the high-priced caskets. The family usually chooses one of these without asking the prices of others.

Many state laws provide that the state board of embalmers and funeral directors shall consist of a specific number of members, most or all of whom must be licensed embalmers or practicing funeral directors in good standing.

FYI

Choices for Consumers

The book *Dealing Creatively with Death: A Manual of Death Education and Simple Burial* tells briefly, but authoritatively, about a variety of choices open to consumers. Its approximately 200 pages tell all one need know about memorial societies, eye banks, temporal bone banks, and the option of bequeathing bodies to medical schools and for research. The manual lists names and addresses of many organizations. People who wish to arrange for a simple burial or an alternative disposition of the remains might benefit from the suggestions in this book.

Memorial societies

Memorial societies cooperative programs providing simple, dignified funerals at low cost.

Memorial societies are nonprofit organizations with the major function of providing simple, dignified funerals at low cost. Memorial societies were formed to promote the dignity, simplicity, and spiritual value of funeral rites and memorial services; to deepen understanding of the religious meaning of death in accordance with the religious, philosophical, and ethical beliefs of each individual; to reduce unjustifiable expenses of funeral services; and to promote the opportunity for every person to predetermine the price of the desired funeral or memorial service.

TIP

If you want to attend a relative's funeral that requires you to fly to the destination, inquire about a bereavement fare. For funerals and other emergencies, many U.S. airlines have special fares requiring no advance purchase. These fares often are reduced 50 percent or more off regular coach fares.

Memorial society services are not as expensive as standard funeral services. The cost of joining a society is minimal; often, only a donation is requested. Members can have the entire funeral for a price that is 20 percent to 50 percent lower than a nonmember rate. This is usually accomplished through contractual agreements between the society and one or several local funeral directors who agree to provide low-cost funerals to society members. Alternatively, the society may have informal agreements with funeral directors or offer quality information regarding funeral purchase and options.

Pre-need contracts

Pre-need contract an agreement between the consumer and the funeral director specifying in advance a price and arrangements for the consumer's own funeral.

Pre-need contracts may benefit some consumers, but they also can be problematic. On the surface, pre-need arrangements seem to be a rational means to spare survivors and reduce costs. Planning before need can also create problems, however. No one knows when, where, or under what circumstances he or she will die. The funeral firm may go out of business, the person's death may occur far away, or the person's feelings about the ceremony may change. These and many other unknowns can complicate the most carefully arranged plans.

Unscrupulous operators have found that pre-need arrangements have a psychological appeal that allows them to readily exploit people. High-pressure sales, pre-need written contracts that do not include services that were verbally promised, and money collected for services that is not deposited as intended are a few examples of fraudulent practices in this industry segment.

Most states have laws requiring that specified amounts of money paid on pre-need contracts be deposited in an escrow account under state supervision. This provides some safeguards for the consumer. However, the full amount seldom has to be placed in escrow. Often a trust arrangement is established whereby the total amount is placed in the trust but the funeral director is entitled to the interest.

www.medicalert.org

The website for the MedicAlert organization explains how, in the event of an emergency, a MedicAlert bracelet can inform medical professionals of vital health information when individuals are unable to speak for themselves. MedicAlert, a nonprofit membership organization, was founded in 1956 to protect and save lives.

WWW

Cremation

Many people choose **cremation** rather than preservation of the body by embalming. Although many individuals, including those who believe in physical resurrection of the body, prefer embalming and burial, the traditional resistance to cremation has subsided dramatically in recent decades. This change in attitude apparently stems from wider acceptance of cremation by many religious groups, as well as the reality that cremations are less costly than other choices. Approximately 28 percent of all deaths in the United States result in cremation, and the practice seems to be gaining popularity.

Cremation the practice of reducing the remains to ashes by intense heat.

To offset the loss of revenue from simple cremation services, funeral directors may try to convince consumers that a funeral service should be the same up to the point of burial or cremation. Funeral directors suggest that a coffin be used, that the coffin be burned (even though metal caskets will not burn), and that ashes be buried or deposited in an urn in a crypt. This renders cremation just as expensive as a customary earth burial.

www.ama-assn.org

The website for the American Medical Association (AMA) provides information regarding the association's strong commitment to standards, ethics, top-quality medical education, medical practice, and advocacy.

WWW

Bodies for research and transplants

A **bequest** often specifies how the body is to be disposed of. Socially concerned people can arrange to serve others after they themselves have died, by donating their remains to a medical school for research or becoming organ donors. The salvaging of organs and tissues from individuals who have died can save lives and restore health and eyesight to the living. Donation for research is another option. In years past, city morgues gave medical schools their unclaimed bodies. Today, our society provides enough money for a decent burial for almost everyone. As a result, not enough bodies are available for research and education. Thousands of bodies are needed each year for the training of future doctors and dentists, and only the escalating practice of bequeathing bodies to medical schools has averted a serious crisis.

Bequest a provision in an individual's will specifying how the deceased's assets should be distributed.

About half a million blind people live in the United States. Approximately 10 percent of them can regain their sight through a corneal transplant.

FYI

In the past, lack of uniformity in state body-donation laws created problems. Most states permitted living persons to bequeath their bodies in advance for medical research. Few, however, permitted donations of corneas. Moreover, state laws differed, and body gifts in one state often were not recognized in another. In an effort to achieve uniformity, the American Medical Association, the American Bar Association, and the National Society for Medical Research jointly sponsored the Uniform Anatomical Gift Act as a model for reform. All states now have passed the Uniform Anatomical Gift Act, so any person of sound mind who is 18 years of age or older is legally able to donate all or part of his body for medical research. (Sale of one's body is illegal, however.) A person wishing to bequeath his or her body to a

www.livingbank.org

The website for the Living Bank organization educates consumers about organ donation. This organization accumulates computerized records of donor data.

WWW

More people have hearing defects than visual impairments, heart disease, or other chronic disabilities. According to the FDA, approximately 40 million people in the United States have some degree of hearing loss, and the number increases every year. The temporal bones of a deceased person may be donated for research. Temporal bone banks are not like nerve or eye banks, where healthy parts are stored and later transplanted to the living; they are ear-research laboratories where defective inner-ear structures can be studied, together with donors' medical and hearing records.

FYI

medical school should make arrangements with the aid of a family physician or by writing directly to the dean of the nearest medical school.

The Living Bank and MedicAlert are two nonprofit corporations organized to help people who wish to donate all or parts of their body for transplantation, therapy, medical research, or anatomical studies. The Living Bank explains the procedures and furnishes a donor card, which is the only legal document required by the Uniform Anatomical Gift Act and similar laws. Each organization emphasizes that removing organs or parts does not disfigure the body, nor does it interfere with funeral or burial arrangements. If a body is donated to a medical school, survivors can arrange a memorial service.

Marriage Customs

Marriage customs center primarily on the engagement and the wedding itself. Each of these events presents the consumer with purchasing choices.

Engagement customs

Modern engagements to be married are vestiges of the practice of signing and sealing formal contracts governing the economic aspects of an approaching marriage. Formerly, the contract was vitally important to the families involved, as well as to the engaged couple. The increasing tendency in the United States, however, is to regard the engagement as a contract between and affecting only the couple to be married. Engagements still do have the binding force of a contract, as demonstrated by the success of some lawsuits for breach of contract when an engagement is broken.

The engagement ring is a survivor of ancient custom. In former days, when most people were illiterate, a person of property sealed a contract by stamping his or her signet ring on soft wax. Consequently, the ring came to be regarded as evidence of a contractual relationship. Betrothed people gave signet and other rings as pledges of faith. By the 19th century, these engagement rings had been replaced by diamond rings—a custom that serves admirably to sustain the diamond market. The vast majority of all engaged women in the United States receive diamond rings.

TIP

Jewelry store salespeople may tell you that purchasing an engagement ring is a sound investment. In reality, cut diamonds are worth only a small fraction of their original retail cost on the open market.

WWW

www.weddings-online.com

Weddings-Online links grooms- and brides-to-be to various wedding-planning resources. Information about services such as cake decorators and tuxedo suppliers, as well as do's and don'ts of wedding planning, is provided on this website.

Wedding customs

Custom usually dictates the type of wedding a couple chooses. In the United States, a couple may be married by a representative of the church or by an official of the state, at a simple or an elaborate ceremony.

During the 1960s, when many young people rebelled against tradition of all kinds, some brides and grooms were married in jeans and did not give rings. Others planned individualistic marriage ceremonies in unusual places with unusual costumes. Some rejected licensing and other marriage procedures entirely and chose to live together without marriage. These nontraditional patterns are the exception, however. Formal weddings have increased in popularity since the late 1960s, when only two-thirds of first marriages were formal. The average cost for a wedding and reception today is approximately $28,000. This does not include the cost of the honeymoon.

Religious Customs

More than half of the people in the United States have some religious affiliation. The great diversity of faiths and denominations is reflected in the various ceremonies and other customs that influence the economic lives of believers. Ceremonial worship ranges from an elaborate Roman Catholic or Orthodox mass with rich vestments, candles, and a choir in a magnificent church building, to a simple Quaker meeting in an unadorned meeting house. Whatever the differences, these ceremonies are all inspired by belief and shaped by tradition.

Religion influences other ceremonial occasions too, including weddings, funerals, christenings, first communions, bar mitzvahs, and bat mitzvahs. Members of churches, synagogues, and mosques spend or contribute large sums of money to purchase the goods and services these religious ceremonies entail.

Religious rites of conduct

Religion affects other aspects of economic choice through the authoritative decrees of some faiths regulating their members' daily conduct. Negative rules may be as economically significant as positive ones. Members of some religions are told what they should and should not wear, what they may and may not eat or drink, and how they may and may not behave. Although these rules most strongly affect the clergy—who may be set apart by ceremonial vestments or other forms of dress—many apply to laypeople as well.

Members of some faiths must abstain from alcoholic beverages, tobacco, tea, coffee, and other caffeinated drinks. Orthodox Jews and Muslims may not eat pork. Until the 1960s, Roman Catholics could not eat meat on Friday, with the consequence that more than 90 percent of the weekly supply of seafood in the United States was sold on Fridays. Until the 1960s, many churches required women to wear head coverings at services. Religious customs clearly have significant influence on consumer choice.

Holiday customs

In the West, December is the month for major religious celebrations each year. In the United States, however, for many families, these celebrations are not what they used to be. Commercialization is increasingly overshadowing the religious aspects of the holiday season, and for many people, the exchange of gifts has become predominant.

To encourage holiday shopping, U.S. retailers traditionally hold sales the Friday following Thanksgiving. This day is known as "Black Friday," for this reason: many retailers operate in the red all year until this popular shopping day. Profits from the big day push them into the "black." The first Monday after Thanksgiving has become known as "Cyber Monday," and is the online equivalent to Black Friday. Retailers offer deep discounts on merchandise and other incentives such as no sales tax and free shipping.

Commercialization has extended to non-Western cultures. In Japan, for example, merchants have adopted the commercial aspects of Christmas, trimming Tokyo department stores with decorations and displaying toys and other gifts. The preservation and extension of the gift-giving custom are based partly on the profit it generates.

> **TIP** Consider delaying major purchases until after the holiday season. By delaying purchases even a few days you may save 50 to 75 percent on specific items.

In the business world, the holiday season means sales. In the months before December, business and trade journals contain news of the holiday trade, which, in the United States, involves billions of dollars annually. Nearly half of the sales of sporting goods, cameras, jewels, and watches are made during the holiday season. For toys and games, the figure is more than 50 percent. In addition, the holiday trade includes millions of dollars spent on gift wrapping and natural and plastic trees.

The holiday season also is a bonanza for the liquor industry. Holiday sales account for about a fourth of total annual liquor sales. An industry spokesperson reported that sales during this period could make or break a company's business for the entire year.

Other Ceremonial Celebrations

Among the occasions celebrated in the United States are Mother's Day, Father's Day, birthdays, baby showers, and graduations. On these and other occasions consumers often give cards and gifts.

Mother's Day/Father's Day

Mother's Day, a comparatively new occasion for celebration, started during the 20th century. A presidential proclamation designated the second Sunday in May as Mother's Day. Before long, business promoters saw the potential for gift giving. A promotional committee was created to persuade sons and daughters to honor their mothers by giving them flowers, telegrams, candy, and sentimental cards. The amount of money spent for Mother's Day gifts now exceeds the amount spent at Easter, partly because the giving has expanded to include grandmothers, aunts, great-aunts, and cousins.

Father's Day also started during the 20th century. The third Sunday in June is designated as Father's Day. Although Father's Day has not become as popular as Mother's Day, it has expanded to include grandfathers, uncles, great-uncles, cousins, and special male role models. Mother's Day and Father's Day are so profitable that promoters have created Grandparents' Day, Mother-in-Law's Day, and other specific holidays.

Birthday celebrations

By custom, people often celebrate the anniversary of their own birth and those of people they know. Regardless of the family's economic status, they often mark the birthday of each member with gifts or a party. All of those invited, whether relatives, neighbors, friends, or others, are expected to bring cards and gifts.

Graduation ceremonies

Certain customs have developed in connection with the graduation of students from high school, college, and sometimes elementary school. In addition to ceremonial programs and speeches, graduation exercises often require academic caps and gowns or other special dress. Giving presents to the graduates has become customary. Formerly these tokens of admiration were simple and inexpensive, but today parents, grandparents, uncles, and aunts often give costlier gifts, such as computers, watches, and cars.

The Phenomenon of Gift Giving

Gift giving is a multibillion-dollar business. Many average-income families spend hundreds of dollars each year on gifts. Gifts are given on many occasions and for many reasons: because it is the expected thing to do, as a means of showing off one's wealth, in return for a gift received, or as a tangible way to show affection for another person.

In giving gifts, the giver has to decide how much to spend as well as how to spend it. The giver may choose something he thinks the other person would like but would hesitate to spend money on, or the giver might buy something he likes himself, hoping the recipient will also like it. Giving money is simpler, but it sometimes gives an impression of coldness and detachment. Consequently, sellers have come to the rescue with the gift card, which is not as practical as money but suggests a more personal touch.

CONSUMPTION

Approximately 5 percent of the world's population lives in the United States, but Americans consume more than 25 percent of the world's resources. The United States is truly a nation of wealth, and truly a nation of **conspicuous consumption.** America has thousands of millionaires, and even average families have two or more cars and two or more television sets. Many Americans own two or more computers, boats, and homes. Can this level of consumption last? Should it last? Is it fair to others in less affluent countries, and indeed to others less fortunate in the United States? These questions became more relevant as we and the rest of the world faced severe economic challenges beginning in 2008.

Conspicuous consumption spending and consuming on a lavish scale.

Pecuniary power monetary and financial well-being.

Affluenza a feeling of unfulfillment that results from efforts to keep up with the rest of society; an epidemic of stress, overwork, waste, and indebtedness caused by consumers' pursuit of the American Dream.

The prime purpose and effect of conspicuous consumption is to demonstrate **pecuniary power.** Historically, such lavish living was possible only among nobility. In an affluent economy, however, large numbers of people are able to exercise pecuniary power, and conspicuous consumption may become an epidemic. The label **affluenza,** a play on words (i.e., affluent and influenza), is sometimes used to refer to this "keeping up" disease.

Competitive Consumption

When people consume because they are comparing themselves with or imitating others, the result is **competitive consumption.** The concept of competitive consumption is expressed in the phrase, "keeping up with the Joneses." Some family spending may be for the purpose of bolstering family pride, striving to equal or excel friends and neighbors in regarding income and expenditures. Automobiles, clothing, jewelry, housing, home furnishings, entertainment, club memberships, and travel are areas of the family budget that invite extravagance because the consumption is visible.

Competitive consumption the irrational desire by consumers to compete with one another to prove financial superiority by spending more.

Emulation is the tendency of people in each socioeconomic class to look to the next higher income group as they set goals for how to live. Should income distribution become more equal, conspicuous consumption would decrease because the pressure of emulation would lessen. More money would be available to spend on consumption that is less conspicuous and for savings. The savings rate in the United States has hit record lows. In many groups, the savings rate is actually negative.

Super Size Me — CASE STUDY

Morgan Spurlock wrote, produced, directed, and stars in *Super Size Me.* This 2004 documentary film focuses on the obesity epidemic in America as aggravated by our fast food eating habits, with the specific goal of demonstrating that McDonald's encourages poor nutrition for its own profit. In 2003, cameras followed Spurlock over a 30-day period. During this time he ate every meal, three meals a day, at McDonald's. His parameters were that he had to try each menu item at least once, and if he was asked if he wanted his order "super sized," he had to say yes. Spurlock also kept his physical activity to a minimum, walking no more than 5,000 steps per day (the number walked by the average American). Over the course of the 30 days, he ate an average of 5,000 calories each day and gained 24.5 pounds, representing a 13 percent increase in his body mass index.

The effects on his mental, physical, and psychological health were monitored by a team of doctors and a registered dietitian. Their observations show that Spurlock exhibited sexual dysfunction and moodiness, as well as liver damage, which doctors say may be irreversible. It took him 14 months to lose the weight he had gained.

QUESTIONS

1. What are your personal observations about this movie and its subject?
2. Do you think this movie accurately reflects current eating habits and customs in American culture?
3. Can you suggest some strategies to break the cycle of obesity in America?
4. What obligations, if any, do you think McDonald's and other fast food chains have to help deal with obesity in America?

Is emulation desirable? The imitative tendency is powerful but in itself is neither good nor bad. Whether emulation is good or bad depends on the form it takes. Whom do consumers copy? And why? The answers to these questions determine whether emulation promotes or detracts from consumer welfare. Emulation can be beneficial if, for example, people imitate good taste, resulting in wider appreciation of the goods and services that contribute to individual and group welfare. If people imitate appreciation of music, art, literature, and drama, their lives will be enriched. If college students emulate the practice of purchasing and reading good books, they will benefit.

Conversely, the practice of emulating may be damaging, if people are imitating poor spending habits. In this case, people will consume goods and services that do not promote their welfare.

WWW

www.affluenza.org

This site, connected to a site for the Center for a New American Dream, discusses issues surrounding affluenza and provides suggestions to conserve resources and counter commercialism.

Consumer Wants

What are consumer wants?

Fashion the accepted manner in which a group of people behave at a given time.

Fad the accepted manner in which a group of people behave for a brief time.

Style a distinctive human expression.

Taste the ability to discern and appreciate that which is appropriate.

Consumer wants are largely driven by custom, which tends to determine what things are bought and done in a broad sense. Specific desires and purchases are often heavily influenced by the "fashion of the times." **Fashion** is an important aspect of most cultures. Makes of automobiles, architectural style of houses, type of house furnishings—actually nearly all consumer goods—may be in or out of fashion. For a good to be in fashion, a majority of a group must accept it. For the individual, conforming to fashion expresses personality, defines status, and announces a role. For the group, it distinguishes occupational groups, identifies peer groups, and singles out prestige groups. A **fad** is a temporary, often short-lived fashion—a practice or interest followed for a time with zeal before passing from favor.

In contrast to fashion and fads is **style.** Styles are ways of acting that may go in or out of fashion. The styles that were in fashion when your parents were in college may be out of fashion now, but they still are styles because they exist as distinctive methods of expression. Styles commonly go through cycles of fashionability. An example is the length of women's hemlines, which has varied as fashions have changed.

Taste is important to fashion. Marketers encourage the view that even though a style may be artistic, good taste forbids its use if it is not in fashion. Conversely, items in fashion may be ugly, but it may be in good taste to use them anyway.

Obsolescence

Planned obsolescence the superficial redesign of a product for sales purposes only.

Built-in obsolescence the deliberate under-engineering of a product to give it an unnecessarily short life span so as to require premature replacement.

Obsolescence of quality a substantial change in the product that actually increases the performance of that product.

Planned obsolescence and **built-in obsolescence** tend to cause waste. The cost of obsolescence in an automobile is in the thousands of dollars per vehicle per year. In fact, many automobiles lose from 20 to 30 percent of their value in the first year. According to economic theory, manufacturers are simply giving the public what it wants when they sell items that are designed to become obsolete. This raises the question as to whether obsolescence is a virtue or a vice.

Planned obsolescence is a trend that has spread to many categories of product. Starting with automobiles, it spread to appliances, houses, hardware, and building materials. In many cases manufacturers simply produce shoddy products that are designed to break or wear out. Planned obsolescence often involves wasteful use of natural and human resources.

Not all obsolescence is negative. **Obsolescence of quality** simply means that products have gotten better. An example is the introduction of digital and high-definition (HD) television. Older models do not approach the picture quality of digital and HD TV.

Obsolescence actually may render a benefit to individuals and families with limited incomes. They might not be able to purchase new automobiles, new appliances, and new furniture. Because obsolescence encourages people who can afford it to replace products before their useful life has expired, it also makes these usable products available to buyers at considerably lower prices than new products. The advent of reliable auction sites on the Internet (e.g., eBay) has made it much easier for consumers to find a wide array of such used items at competitive prices.

The pervasiveness of consumer wants

Consumer wants have no boundaries. They permeate all aspects of society. Consumers' desire for clothing, houses, home furnishings, and automobiles is highlighted here.

Clothing. Although fashion dictates or influences consumer choice among many consumer goods, its power is probably greatest in determining the kind of clothing men and women wear at any given time. The chief difference between fashion in earlier centuries and fashion in the 21st century is the rapidity with which fashions change. In earlier times, fashions often were in vogue for a generation or more.

> **TIP** Before you purchase clothing, read the label to determine if you are willing and able to fulfill the care and maintenance requirements.

Advertisers and merchandisers have helped to make consumers of all ages fashion conscious. In our affluent society, students as a group spend large sums every year on clothing and accessories.

Houses and house furnishings. The current generation of homeowners seeks fashionable, convenient housing to a much greater degree than did previous generations. Such trends as vaulted ceilings, tile floors, multicar garages, and so forth have found their way into even modestly priced new housing. Older homes are being remodeled to incorporate these features.

The furniture and furnishings of a house also reflect the influence of fashion. Even kitchens and bathrooms are now appointed with fashionable accessories and features. Along with very real utilitarian improvements in kitchen and bathroom design and fixtures, builders have learned they can get a higher price for houses appointed with fashionable items. Homeowners are more concerned than ever with style, drama, and luxury. Unfortunately, consumer spending to achieve these results is often excessive.

> **TIP** When selecting the style of a home, keep the resale of the home in mind. Building a home that is typical for your area is probably wise. The base of potential buyers will be maximized.

Automobiles. Car trends come and go with the times. And, as with other fashions, consumers want to be current. As a result of higher gas prices, demand for sport utility vehicles (SUVs) is being replaced by demand for smaller cars and hybrids. Most manufacturers, in addition to creating smaller SUV styles, are introducing hybrid SUVs of all sizes. A focus on hybrids (and eventually on all-electric, hydrogen-cell, or other alternatively powered cars) is likely to continue in response to concerns about the environment, rising gas prices, and dependence on foreign oil. The additional benefit of driving in the carpool lane is also a selling point for hybrids.

What drives consumer wants?

The factors that propel trends in consumer wants include the pursuit of profit, advertising and marketing, communication and transportation, leisure, political freedom, and a philosophy of change.

The Federal Reserve reports that consumers tend to increase spending and decrease saving as their wealth (i.e., income and net worth) increases. This is commonly referred to as the "wealth effect."

FYI

Pursuit of profit. In the production and sale of many products, including clothing, automobiles, and appliances, fashion and obsolescence are devices that many sellers have found profitable. Persuading consumers to discard the old and buy the new results in higher sales volumes and revenues.

Advertising and marketing. Although changes are introduced and spread in a variety of ways, commercial advertising and other marketing techniques are largely responsible. The consumer often has an intense desire to be accepted by the group. If advertisers can convince the consumer that the group requires him to wear clothing in the latest fashion and drive the newest model of an automobile, he will probably attempt to do so.

Communication and transportation. Television, computers, and satellite transmissions have made the spread of trends instantaneous, and air travel has made the world seem smaller. Trends sweep the world in very little time.

Leisure time. When people have leisure time in which to display and use new fashions, those fashions tend to continue and spread. As leisure time expands, travel and other forms of leisure activities increase in importance. These often involve activities and purchases influenced by trends.

Political freedom. Nations in which a caste system prevails cannot present a broad base for trends and fashions as we know it in the West. Some countries further limit the influence of trends with legislation prohibiting certain groups of people to use certain products. Where people are free to choose, their choices often support trends.

A philosophy of change. Product changes thrive in groups that accept change. Custom and tradition, on the other hand, are powerful deterrents to changing consumer wants. In the United States, as the population has shifted from rural to urban areas, the willingness to accept change has increased. Today's philosophy of change encompasses consumer desire to "go green," and all manner of products are changing and evolving as a result.

Who controls consumer wants?

Some sellers seem to believe that, by means of advertising, they can persuade consumers to adopt changes whenever the sellers wish. If this were true, businesses could become successful by creating fashions that favor their products. Fashion and trends, however, are stronger than individual business firms. Some evidence suggests that they are even stronger than trade associations that represent groups of firms and sometimes attempt to influence trends in the interests of their members. Most firms manufacture on a large scale in anticipation of demand. Lacking effective control over consumer wants, they incur considerable risk by doing so. If they anticipate consumer demand incorrectly, the products they produce might be sold only at a loss. Hence, they try to influence as well as predict trends. They often fail.

If the advertisers and marketers who believe they can create and control consumer wants were more knowledgeable of the history of their profession, they would know that it is filled with failures. Advertising and marketing cannot manipulate people to make them buy. Neither can they stop a trend. What advertising can do effectively is to hasten the acceptance of goods. This is an entirely different function. Advertising probably has not seriously altered any fashion trend. Fashions come in without anyone's conscious effort, and they go out despite all efforts to retain them.

Somewhere in the world there are probably individuals or groups with sufficient prestige to influence fashions. Such influence is typically spontaneous, however, rather than planned. Ultimately, consumers as a group have the most control over changes in fashion. Sellers can suggest changes, but consumers determine fashion by accepting or rejecting those suggestions.

Prior to 1945, most consumers considered debt as deplorable. In part because of advertising and marketing techniques that encourage excess spending, being overextended has now become the norm for many U.S. families. This tendency is likely to change in response to recent credit and financial woes; whether changes are modest or drastic remains to be seen.

FYI

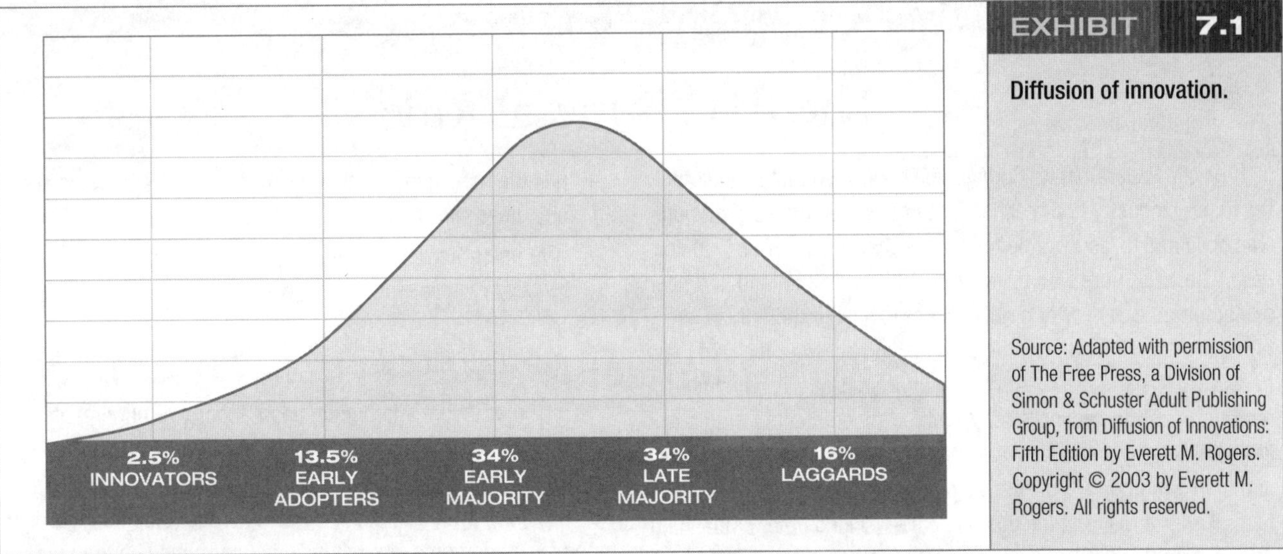

EXHIBIT 7.1

Diffusion of innovation.

Source: Adapted with permission of The Free Press, a Division of Simon & Schuster Adult Publishing Group, from Diffusion of Innovations: Fifth Edition by Everett M. Rogers.

Diffusion of consumer wants

How consumers move through the "cycle of wants" is a topic of great interest to marketers and economists. Everett Rogers's work on the diffusion of innovation, originally published in the early 1960s, is still used today. He identified the following five categories of consumers that relate to how quickly consumers adopt a new product. A bell-shaped diffusion curve, as shown in Exhibit 7.1, illustrates how wants spread.

Of course, how quickly a product is adopted depends on a variety of issues, such as the type of product, the perceived benefits and costs, and promotional efforts on the part of producers.

1. *Innovators are the first to adopt a product.* They are well-informed risk-takers who are willing to try new things.
2. *Early adopters* look to the positive response from innovators before they purchase an item. They are educated opinion leaders who are social and outgoing.
3. The *early majority* is the first large group in the adoption process. They are careful consumers, who avoid risk by relying on recommendations from experienced users.
4. The *late majority* is composed of skeptical consumers. They tend to buy a product only after it has become commonplace in the market.
5. *Laggards* are the last group to adopt a new product. They are very risk averse and avoid change until it becomes necessary (for example, because their old product is no longer available).

SUMMARY

Customs are long-established actions, conventions, practices, and usages that regulate the lives of a group of people. In economic life, customary ways of consuming are transmitted from generation to generation largely through the family by means of example and precept.

Customs are perpetuated because of inertia, institutionalism, stratification, isolation, and illiteracy. Customs change because of communication, transportation, advertising, education, and competition.

Ceremonies are elaborate ways of satisfying important emotional needs. One customary ceremony—arranging for burial of the deceased—is prescribed by religion, community, or other groups. The funeral defies economic analysis. The demand is inelastic, and price competition is practically nonexistent. In part, this is the case because trade associations

The FTC Funeral Rule

In 1984 the Federal Trade Commission concluded that conditions in the funeral industry had reached a point at which the Commission was obligated to issue a rule to regulate the industry. This was necessary because bereaved buyers were susceptible to, and had been subjected to, a variety of practices that exploited their disadvantaged position. In addition, the Commission believed the rule was necessary to halt unfair and deceptive practices; these included restraints on price advertising and other impediments to the market; bait-and-switch tactics (advertising a low-price funeral as bait and then attempting to switch the consumer to a more expensive funeral after arriving at the funeral home); picking up or embalming corpses without the family's permission; requiring people who chose to have the deceased cremated to buy a casket; misrepresenting the legal or public health necessity of embalming or of using caskets or burial vaults; and interfering with the offering of low-cost funerals, direct cremation services, or other modes of disposition, pre-need arrangements, and memorial society activities.

The rule enables consumers to select only those goods and services they want or need and to pay for only those they select. It also helps to eliminate unconscionable practices such as claims that caskets, embalming, and burial vaults are required by law. Violators of the Funeral Rule are subject to penalties of up to $10,000 per violation.

Telephone Price Disclosures

The rule makes it possible for consumers to compare prices among funeral providers by telephone. When a consumer calls a funeral provider and asks about terms, conditions, or prices of funeral goods or services, the funeral provider must:

- indicate that price information is available by telephone
- provide reasonable answers to questions about prices and any other information
- give any other information about prices or offerings that is readily available, and reasonably answer additional questions

General Price List

If a consumer inquires in person about funeral arrangements, the funeral provider must provide a general price list stating the cost of individual funeral items and services offered. The price list also discloses important legal rights and requirements regarding funeral arrangements. It must include information on embalming, cash advance sales (such as newspaper notices or flowers), caskets for cremation, and required purchases.

Embalming Information

The FTC Funeral Rule also requires funeral providers to give consumers information about embalming that can help them decide whether to purchase this service. Under the rule, a funeral provider:

- may not falsely state that embalming is required by law
- must disclose in writing that, except in certain special cases, embalming is *not* required by law
- may not charge a fee for unauthorized embalming unless the embalming is required by state law
- must disclose that consumers have the right to choose a disposition such as direct cremation or immediate burial
- must disclose that certain funeral arrangements, such as a funeral with a viewing, may make embalming a practical necessity and, thus, a required purchase

effectively control the industry and dominate the state boards of funeral directors. The pricing of funeral services represents a combination of cost, custom, and psychology. Consumers do have alternatives to the traditional funeral. These include memorial societies, pre-need contracts, cremation, and donating bodies for research and transplants.

Marriage customs have evolved to include the engagement, engagement ring, engagement party, wedding ceremony, and honeymoon. The trend currently seems to be a return to more traditional marriage customs.

A wide range of customs among religious faiths and denominations is reflected in the diversity of ceremonies and related customs that influence the economic lives of adherents. Religious rules often influence clothing purchases, eating and drinking habits, and the manner in which members participate in ceremonies (for example, weddings, funerals, and holidays).

In the United States, conspicuous consumption occurs in purchases of automobiles, clothing, jewelry, housing, home furnishings, entertainment, and travel. Conspicuous consumption to the extreme is referred to as affluenza. Fashion, fads, styles, and cus-

Cash Advance Sales

Cash advance items are goods or services the funeral provider pays on your behalf. Some examples are flowers, obituary notices, pallbearers, and clergy honoraria. The Funeral Rule requires funeral providers to disclose that they charge a fee for buying cash advance items.

Caskets for Cremation

Some consumers want to select direct cremation, which is cremation of the deceased without a viewing or other ceremony at which the body is present. If a consumer selects direct cremation, the funeral provider must offer either an inexpensive alternative container or an unfinished wood box (a type of casket). Under the Funeral Rule, funeral directors who offer direct cremations:

- may not claim that state or local law requires a casket for direct cremation
- must disclose the right to buy an unfinished wood box or an alternative container for a direct cremation
- must make an unfinished wood box or alternative container available for direct cremation

Required Purchase

Consumers may not be required to purchase unwanted goods or services as a condition of obtaining desired ones, unless state law requires them. The rule provides:

- Consumers have the right to choose only the funeral goods and services they want.
- The funeral provider must disclose this right on the general price list.
- The funeral provider must disclose, on the statement of goods and services selected, the specific law that requires one to purchase any particular item.

Statement of Funeral Goods and Services Selected

The funeral provider must provide an itemized statement with the total cost of the funeral goods and services selected. This statement also must disclose any legal, cemetery, or crematory requirements that compel the purchase of any specific funeral goods or services.

Preservative and Protective Claims

Funeral providers are prohibited from claiming that a specific funeral item, such as a special casket, or service, such as embalming, can indefinitely preserve the body of the deceased in the grave. Information gathered during the FTC's investigation indicates that these claims are not true. The rule also prohibits funeral providers from making claims that funeral goods, such as caskets or vaults, will keep out water, dirt, and other gravesite substances when that is not true. The Funeral Rule is not as strong as its proponents originally hoped. Nevertheless, some disclosure is probably better than no disclosure.

toms affect all consumers. Factors that promote fashions include pursuit of profit, advertising and marketing, transportation and communication, leisure time, political freedom, and a philosophy of change. Consumers move through a cycle of wants that helps explain their adoption of new products.

ITEMS FOR REVIEW & DISCUSSION

1. Distinguish between fashion, fad, style, and taste.
2. Differentiate custom and habit.
3. State several conditions that cause customs to both change and continue.
4. What is conspicuous consumption? What is its purpose? Is it something new? Give reasons why consumers have become conspicuous consumers. How would you go about finding it in your own life?

5. What is affluenza?
6. Set forth the advantages and disadvantages to individuals and society of manufacturers' annually changing models of automobiles and other products.
7. Do you agree that not many consumers are able or willing to disregard group customs? Give some reasons why this might be true.
8. Do you think the power of custom is as strong now as it was in the past? What forces are at work to bring about changes?
9. Do you think emulation is good or bad?
10. What is your opinion of the practice of obsoletism in the automobile industry? Do you think planned obsolescence is good or bad?
11. What are some status symbols on your campus?
12. Briefly describe the five categories of the product adoption process.
13. What are some factors that might influence how quickly a product is adopted?
14. Apply the principles of economic analysis to the funeral industry. Explain what is meant by the statement, "The funeral industry defies economic analysis." Do you think the rendering of funeral services is a business or a profession? Why?
15. List elements that constitute a "decent" burial. What is your attitude toward cremation, memorial societies, and the donating of bodies for transplantation, therapy, medical research, or anatomical studies?
16. State the provisions regulating the funeral industry as developed by the Federal Trade Commission.
17. Give the apparent advantages and disadvantages of cremation.
18. Define pre-need contracts.
19. Explain how religious customs influence consumption patterns.
20. Describe the influence of ceremonial custom on consumer spending patterns.
21. What religious customs do you consider important? Why?
22. If you marry, do you plan to have a big wedding? Why or why not?
23. Discuss the statement, "All ceremonial events could be ignored, but life would be drab and dull without them."

EXPLORING PERSONAL VALUES: PROJECTS

1. Are you currently wearing name-brand shoes or carrying a name-brand purse? Discuss with your classmates some of the implications of the brands you choose to wear and what message you are trying to convey in the way you dress.
2. Assume that current college-age students will not live as well as their parents. Discuss the way in which you would change to cope with the dilemma.
3. Discuss with your fellow students your attitude toward fashion changes. Explain why you feel the way you do.
4. Discuss your thoughts regarding a classless society. Explain why you feel the way you do.
5. List all the gifts you remember receiving in the past year. How many do you value or use?
6. Debate this topic: "Resolved: Our age of affluence is nearing an end."
7. Arrange a class debate on the topic, "Resolved: Planned obsolescence is desirable."
8. "A man is rich in proportion to what he can do without." Do you agree or disagree with Thoreau's statement? Why?
9. Give several examples of how the power of custom is stronger in consuming activities than in occupation activities.

10. What category of product adoption do you fall into? Can you identify other people you know who fit into the other categories?
11. Divide a sheet of paper into four columns with the following headings: *Gift, To Whom Given, Reason for Giving, How I Felt About It.* In the columns, list all the gifts you have given over the past year. What percentage of your gifts were given in connection with a ceremony? Do you feel the same about all the gifts you gave? Are you going to change your gift-giving practices after reading this chapter?
12. Prepare a list of all the services that funeral directors perform. Discuss these with your classmates, giving attention to both economic and noneconomic issues.
13. Interview a funeral director in your college or home area. Ask questions suggested by this chapter. Also, interview five students about their attitudes concerning funeral customs. Summarize your responses and findings in a written report.
14. Some holiday customs were initiated by business people. How do you feel about each holiday?
15. In your journal, write your general reactions to what you read in this chapter.
16. Assume you have the full responsibility for making burial arrangements for a member of your family. Explain in detail what you would do.
17. Survey five males and five females on their attitudes toward small versus large weddings.
18. When faced with a decision to buy a new car, how much would "helping the environment" affect your purchasing decision? What type of car would you choose?

ADDITIONAL SOURCES OF INFORMATION

De Graaf, John, David Wann, Thomas H. Naylor, David Horsey, and Scott Simon. *Affluenza: The All-Consuming Epidemic.* San Francisco: Berrett-Koehler Publishers, 2005.

Diehl, Daniel, and Mark P. Donnelly. *Medieval Celebrations: How to Plan Holidays, Weddings, and Reenactments with Recipes, Customs, Costumes, Decorations, Songs, Dances, and Games.* Mechanicsburg, PA: Stackpole Books, 2001.

Laderman, Gary. *Rest in Peace: A Cultural History of Death and the Funeral Home in Twentieth-Century America.* New York: Oxford University Press, 2005.

Maniates, Michael F., and Ken Conca. *Confronting Consumption.* Cambridge, MA: MIT Press, 2002.

Mill, John Stuart. *Principles of Political Economy.* Amherst, NY: Prometheus Books, 2004.

Mitford, Jennifer. *The American Way of Death Revisited.* New York: Vintage Books, 2000.

Morgan, Ernest and Jennifer Morgan. *Dealing Creatively with Death: A Manual of Death Education and Simple Burial.* Burnsville, NC: Celo Press, 2001.

Otnes, Cele C., and Tina M. Lowrey. *Contemporary Consumption Rituals: A Research Anthology.* Mahwah, NJ: Lawrence Erlbaum Associates, 2003.

Rogers, Everett M. *Diffusion of Innovations.* New York: The Free Press, 2003.

Schiffman, Leon and Leslie Kanuk. *Consumer Behavior.* Upper Saddle River, NJ: Pearson Prentice Hall, 2006.

Schmidt, Leigh Eric. *Consumer Rites: The Buying and Selling of American Holidays.* Princeton, NJ: Princeton University Press, 1997.

Silverstein, Michael and Neil Fiske. *Trading Up: The New American Luxury.* New York: Portfolio, 2003.

Slater, Don. *Consumer Culture and Modernity.* Malden, MA: Blackwell Publishing, 1999.

Urbanska, Wanda and Frank Levering. *Nothing's Too Small to Make a Difference.* Winston-Salem, NC: J. F. Blair, 2004.

Veblen, Thorstein. *Conspicuous Consumption.* New York: Penguin, 2006.

Veblen, Thorstein. *The Theory of the Leisure Class.* New York: Random House, 2001.

> You can fool all the people all the time if the advertising is right and the budget is big enough.
>
> **JOSEPH E. LEVINE,** U.S. FILM PRODUCER AND EXECUTIVE

KEY TERMS

advertising
bait-and-switch
cease-and-desist
consent order
duopoly
exchange transaction
iceberg research
informational advertising
loss-leader pricing
market
marketing
market segmentation
monopolistic competition
objective exchange value
perfect competition
puffery
Television Code
testimonial advertising
unit pricing
variable pricing
word-of-mouth advertising

The following concepts will be developed in this chapter:

1. Advertising influences not only the consumer but also the medium in which the ads appear.
2. Whether advertising creates demand, lowers or raises prices, or improves products through competition is subject to argument.
3. Strong evidence indicates that advertisers are able to manipulate consumer behavior with techniques developed through motivational research.
4. Controlling advertising is a difficult task, whether by the government, the consumer, or the industry itself.

After having read this chapter, you should be able to accomplish the following objectives:

1. Define the term *advertising.*
2. Analyze the statement, "It pays to advertise," and be able to give a rationale for advertising and why it is effective.
3. Enumerate the positive and negative effects of advertising on consumer welfare.
4. List several criticisms of advertising from several sources, including advertisers themselves.
5. Identify, compare, and contrast efforts by the government, the consumer, and business to control advertising.
6. Differentiate between price and value.
7. Identify a number of pricing strategies that sellers use.
8. Identify a number of ways in which alert consumers can apply knowledge of pricing strategies to their advantage.

ADVERTISING AROUND THE CLOCK

From the moment people turn on their radio or television or check the Internet for the morning news until they turn it off at night, they are subjected to repeated exhortations to buy. Newspapers and magazines are filled with ads. Ads pop up on the Internet. Buses

Advertising, Marketing, and Pricing

and subway cars carry advertising. The mail carrier brings direct-advertising messages. The packages on store shelves are designed to sell you whatever is inside, and advertisements appear even on the floors of grocery stores.

Advertising exposure has reached or even passed the point of saturation. So many ads surround us that the intended audience often reacts by blocking them out. Consumers who are in the market for a product or a service tend to pay more attention to ads for that product or service. When consumers have made the purchase or decided against it, they stop paying attention to the ads. This ability to block out the constant bombardment of advertising protects consumers from mental distress, and it creates problems for advertisers, who are trying to reach consumers with their messages.

Advertising and Marketing Defined

Advertising is only one of many **marketing** methods. Among others are personal selling, price policy, premiums, and special-price offerings. The International Chamber of Commerce has defined advertising and its relationship to public relations as:

> a nonpersonal, multiple presentation to the market of goods, services, or commercial ideas by an identified sponsor who pays for the delivery of the message to the carrier (advertising medium); distinguished from publicity, which does not pay the medium and does not necessarily identify the sponsor.

Advertising Expenditures: How Much and Where

U.S. advertisers spend hundreds of billions of dollars annually. The main channels through which advertisers reach consumers are newspapers, television, direct mail, radio, magazines, and the Internet. These six mass media channels account for the vast majority of all advertising expenditures. Currently, television advertising expenditures lead in dollar volume spent; even with print newspapers facing circulation challenges in today's electronic age, newspaper advertising is still a close second.

Advertising any paid form of nonpersonal presentation and promotion of ideas, goods, or services by an identified sponsor.

Marketing the process of moving goods and services from producer to consumer, influencing sales by changing stimulus conditions.

DOES ADVERTISING PAY?

The widely held view promoted by advertising agencies and the media is that it pays to advertise. Those in the advertising business would like sellers to believe that a clear relationship exists between the amount of advertising expenditures and the amount of, or increase in, sales. However, many successful companies seldom, if ever, advertise. Nevertheless, successful advertising campaigns can increase sales from 50 to 800 percent.

Even though Madison Avenue likes to believe that advertising stimulates business growth, the prevailing view among economists is that the effect of advertising on growth is minimal. The fact that businesses spend billions of dollars to advertise their goods and services nevertheless is evidence that, in the minds of business executives, advertising is a necessary expenditure and that the economic benefits of advertising outweigh the economic costs.

WWW

www.iccwbo.org

The website for the International Chamber of Commerce (ICC) promotes international trading and investing.

The success of persuasive advertising is evidence that consumers are not sure what they want. If they were sure, they would express their wants in the marketplace in the form of effective demand. The things they demand would be produced. That is not what happens. With the advent of production on a large scale in anticipation of consumer demand, sellers have been under increasing pressure to create an expanding market to support maximum output and thus reduce the cost of production per unit. Their success in persuading consumers to buy what they have to sell is responsible for the growth of advertising.

BENEFITS OF ADVERTISING

Advertising is potentially beneficial in several ways. It can provide useful information. It announces new products and services of which consumers otherwise would be unaware and suggests new uses for known products. It may stimulate competition through pricing and sales, and, by increasing the amount or volume sold, can allow sellers to reduce their prices.

Informational Ads

Informational advertising a form of advertising that offers useful information about products or services.

Informational advertising includes business and professional announcements such as those found in newspapers. The lawyer's shingle and the doctor's card or nameplate inform consumers where they may obtain legal and medical services. Other types of informative advertising include theater programs, newspaper and magazine notices of auctions and sheriffs' sales, and classified advertisements announcing houses for sale or rent and personal services for hire.

Even advertising that is not technically informational can inform consumers about where they can buy specific goods and services. To a busy consumer who must purchase small amounts of a wide variety of goods, this type of advertising may be genuinely helpful. This value of advertising is limited, however, to consumers' unusual requirements, for consumers know where they can find the things they need from day to day. Even for items that consumers do not buy on a regular basis, they have sources of information other than advertisements. Store directories in large shopping centers and the yellow pages of telephone directories provide this information. Advertisements promoting safety and safe uses of products also are informative and helpful to consumers.

Most informational advertising is done locally. National ads seldom offer quality information.

FYI

Ads Announcing New Products and Services

In the dynamic U.S. economy, business firms are continually developing new goods and services. Unless consumers are aware of new products, they do not constitute a potential market. When innovations such as cell phones, digital cameras, iPods, and hybrid cars came on the market, consumers learned about and purchased them. If consumers had not learned of these new products, the products would have failed.

Word-of-mouth advertising is a valuable resource to consumers, although from the manufacturers' point of view this form of advertising is too slow to develop a market large enough to sustain large-scale production of a product. Therefore, business firms feel justified in spending millions of dollars to tell consumers about new products and to persuade consumers to buy them.

Word-of-mouth advertising a form of advertising in which consumers talk among themselves regarding the merits of products or services.

New Uses for Known Products

Sometimes new uses are discovered—either accidentally or as a result of research or contests among users—for products already on the market. Advertising for a brand of baking soda, for example, might feature new uses for that product. To the extent that advertising actually increases the utility of a product, it is helpful. Consumer wants may be satisfied just as fully by new uses for known products as by new products. This type of advertising also benefits sellers if it increases sales.

Advertising Prices

Advertisers claim they provide a consumer service by telling prospective buyers what prices sellers are asking for their goods and services. National advertising, however, is based most often on emotional persuasion and assertions about quality. Price advertising is found mostly in local newspapers, local radio commercials, and direct-mail ads. At the local level, advertising for special sales typically emphasizes price. Grocery stores advertise weekly sales specials, and other types of stores advertise seasonal sales featuring reduced prices.

TIP Read the fine print in ads. Often the large print makes an extraordinary claim and the small print takes the claim away!

To the extent that price advertising enables consumers to compare prices among competing stores and competing products, it is helpful. When it helps buyers by reducing the time required for comparative shopping, it is genuinely useful.

Stimulating Competition

In a dynamic competitive economy, the rivalry of sellers usually protects consumers from overpricing, short measure, and inferior quality. If one store overcharges, gives short measure, or sells inferior merchandise, buyers presumably will turn to competitors. As personal relationships between sellers and buyers have declined, advertising has become a method of helping buyers find stores whose products are priced fairly, measured accurately, and of good quality.

A company's image or reputation is vital to its competitiveness. A retail store that has a good image converts casual buyers into customers. A manufacturer whose corporate image is good develops brand loyalty. Casual buyers then become steady customers who do not buy competing brands. Advertising is one means by which companies build their image.

At the local level, advertising stimulates competition. If a supermarket advertises a sale price on a loaf of bread for $1.99 and competing stores maintain the regular price of $3.39, the advertising tends to compel price reductions in all competing stores in the area. The extent to which this happens depends on consumer response to the ad.

Apparent competition is not always genuine competition. In many cases a holding company has subsidiary operating companies that produce supposedly competing products. Holding company A may control companies B and C, which produce different

In the advertising industry, word-of-mouth advertising is sometimes called viral marketing. *This refers to the rapid spread of information within social networks, mimicking the quick spread of a virus. Today the term* viral *is also used to refer to the rapid spread of content via the Internet, as in "viral video."*

FYI

brands of coffee. Most consumers are unaware of the relationship between these three companies. Although company A could combine companies B and C to secure the economies of large-scale production, which might be passed on to consumers in lower prices, company A might instead continue separate operations to give consumers the impression that the two companies are competitive. Drinkers of brand B then continue their loyal devotion to the coffee that suits their taste, even though the price per package may be greater and the formula essentially the same as that for brand C.

Often, major manufacturers sell several products that compete with each other. The laundry detergents Tide, Gain, and Cheer are sold by the same manufacturer. The coffees Maxwell House, Yuban, and Sanka are also the products of a single manufacturer. These examples are only a few of many that could be noted.

Advertising may induce consumers to pay prices above those of the competition. Wholesale prices for most products are reasonably related to costs of production, and retail prices are reasonably related to wholesale prices. The prices of many products, however, are considerably higher than the costs of production, and advertising supports those prices. In this sense, advertising sometimes contributes a great deal to the price of products. It may be that when the cost of a product's advertising is divided among all the packages sold of that product, the cost is very small. (Several years ago one manufacturer calculated the advertising cost per package of its aspirin to be only 16/1000 of a cent.) This does not seem to be much to be concerned about. However, if the consumer pays more for an advertised product than he would for an identical unadvertised product, the real cost of the advertising is much more. For example, if buyers pay \$6.99 for a package of aspirin tablets that are advertised nationally when they could buy the identical but unadvertised product at a price of \$3.99, the real cost of advertising to the consumer is \$3.00.

Several U.S. tobacco companies own some of the nation's largest food companies.

FYI

The purpose of much advertising is to sway consumers so they will switch from one brand to another or from one product to another. Mounting evidence, however, shows that this kind of advertising has reached a point of diminishing returns. Consumers are not responding as they did at one time. Advertisers are spending more dollars to maintain the same sales volume. If one firm increases its advertising expenditures, competing firms increase theirs proportionately. The result is that all of them stay in the same place, except that their marketing costs are higher. Almost all leading advertisers admit that advertising budgets are too large and that a small reduction in advertising expenditures would not decrease sales.

The U.S. economy has little real competition when compared to the classical concept of competition, which assumed that there were so many sellers and so many buyers that no one seller or buyer could influence the price of a product. The U.S. economy today is characterized by industries of few sellers—monopolies and oligopolies. Prices are set by business firms, and competitors stress quality rather than price in their advertisements. Through advertising, manufacturers attempt to sell more of their products at the same price, or to sell the same amount as before at a higher price. This sort of competitive advertising is not helpful to consumers, nor is it meant to be. It is intended to strengthen the positions of competitive and oligopolistic firms.

Mass Production, Per-Unit Costs, and Pricing

It has been suggested that advertising results in savings because it makes possible the mass production of goods. The theory is that a large volume lowers the selling cost per unit, creates faster turnover, and enables lower-margin operations. In addition, it is argued that advertising and the larger sales volumes it leads to result in economies in buying materials and in financing. The validity of this argument depends on the validity of the implied underlying assumptions. These are:

1. that advertising is responsible for the increase in sales. This may or may not be true. There is no way of demonstrating that advertising alone causes increased sales. In many instances, sales decline even as advertising expenditures increase.

2. that large firms pass along to consumers economies they achieve through price reductions that offset or more than offset the cost of advertising
3. that barriers to entry by potential competitors are not established
4. that the costs of operating large plants are lower than the costs of operating smaller ones. This is not always true. The argument is valid only if the industry is one in which costs of production per unit decline as production increases.

The validity of this argument as a whole has never been established. Evidence shows that advertising can push up or push down the price of a product. The extent of competition in the marketplace determines which way the price goes. In an oligopolistic market, advertising primarily emphasizes product differentiation and rarely stresses price, so prices are higher. More competitive market situations have more price advertising, and prices are lower.

Something for Nothing?

Consumers are told that advertising reduces the prices of goods and services, reduces the prices for newspapers and magazines, and provides free radio and television programs and Internet sites. It is sometimes asserted that advertising itself is entertainment. Consumer polls have revealed that many consumers enjoy ads even though they may not buy the product advertised.

Radio and network television programs are free in the sense that the audience does not pay for the service beyond purchasing the equipment. The price the audience pays is having to listen to the advertisements and paying higher prices when buying the product whose company paid for the ad. On the other hand, dish networks and cable television are not free, yet consumers are exposed to a wide array of advertising on many channels. Presumably, consumers are willing both to pay for and to tolerate advertising because of the advantages of these technologies.

Online Shopping

The trend that appears to have had the most significant impact on the retail industry in the past several years is online shopping. Internet sales in the early 2000s were estimated at around $130 billion per year; in 2007, this number topped $166 billion. This figure includes business-to-business transactions as well as business-to-consumer purchases. Some futurists predict that shopping malls will become a thing of the past as Internet shopping becomes widely accepted by consumers. In fact, retailers who ignore online shoppers are likely to experience fewer sales and lower profits. As lifestyles change and people become busier, fewer Americans view shopping as a form of recreation. Many consumers are looking for ways to cut shopping time, and Internet buying is one answer.

> **www.adcouncil.org**
>
> The website for the Ad Council organization offers public service messages. It is well known for campaigns such as "Friends Don't Let Friends Drive Drunk" and Smokey Bear's "Only You Can Prevent Wildfires."

Optimism for the future of Internet shopping is fueled by the fact that major retailers are now devoting substantial resources to their Internet shopping sites. Retailers appear to be endorsing this technological innovation because of the prospects of huge sales increases at comparatively lower costs per unit sold.

Online advertising offers companies new opportunities and new challenges. Advertisers may be able to choose sites for which the target market is well-defined by the content of the site; this type of focused promotion can be lucrative to advertisers trying to reach a specific group of people. However, consumers being bombarded by online ads may be overwhelmed and tuned out, and the effectiveness of Internet advertising will be studied in depth in the coming years.

Free Ads for Public Service

The Advertising Council, a private, nonprofit organization supported by business and advertising firms, creates and distributes public service advertisements. Advertisers, advertising agencies, and media groups contribute the money for the operating budget. Thousands of television and radio stations contribute air time, and newspapers, magazines, and billboard companies supply free space. The value of advertising given each year to support campaigns such as forest fire prevention, aid to higher education, and mental health is estimated to be over a billion dollars.

CRITICISMS OF ADVERTISING

Critics of advertising say it often is deceptive; it promotes illth and nealth; it generates dissatisfaction and fear; it fosters waste; it misuses art, science, and language; it encourages unnecessary spending; and it uses questionable testimonials.

Deception in Advertising

In a society that has as much commercial communication as the United States does and with a marketplace in which billions of dollars are spent annually for advertising, some deceitful advertising is bound to exist. The amount of overt deception in advertising is relatively small, but the number of "sins of omission" is large. What an ad states is seldom false, but what it does not state can seriously mislead the consumer. Political campaigns often exemplify the sin of omission, employing half-truths, innuendos, and similar tactics.

Bait-and-switch a tactic in which a product or service is advertised at a low price (bait), but when the consumer offers to buy, the merchant discourages the consumer from buying the product or service advertised and recommends a higher-priced product or service (switch).

Bait-and-switch advertising is illegal. If a product or service is advertised at a low price but a salesperson is unwilling to show it to the customer, the customer should be on guard. Similarly, if the salesperson says the item is sold out and urges the customer to look at another, more expensive item, the customer is a potential victim of the bait-and-switch technique. Another form of this practice is when the salesperson downgrades the advertised product or says the item can be ordered but will take a long time to be delivered. Even though bait-and-switch is illegal, laws against it are difficult to enforce.

"Reduction from list," "manufacturer's suggested retail price," and simply the word "sale" are effective advertising come-ons, but they frequently constitute deceptive advertising. Sometimes the sale price quoted is the same as the typical retail price.

Consumers should be skeptical of ads that include phrases like the following: "warehouse sale," "at or below wholesale," "factory outlet," "direct from the factory," "below our cost." The seller may have inflated the "original" price to give the impression of significant savings. "Going-out-of-business," "freight-damaged," and other types of distress sales sometimes are falsely advertised, leading consumers to believe that quick action is necessary to gain substantial savings. Many states have laws requiring merchants who make these claims to file for bankruptcy or declare the number of days the company will remain in business. Nonetheless, false going-out-of-business sales and similar types of distress sales continue to plague consumers.

Another form of deception is additional charges that are not stated in ads or are stated unclearly. An automobile advertised for $19,999 may seem to be a good buy, until the consumer finds that items such as delivery, dealer preparation, taxes, and licenses are not included in the advertised price. The final price may be several thousand dollars more.

Many of the practices noted above are illegal. Enforcement of the laws, however, is at times minimal or nonexistent.

Promoting Illth and Nealth

Some advertised products are definitely harmful, others potentially harmful, and still others innocuous. The distinctions among wealth, nealth, and illth can be ambiguous and are often subjective. Regarded objectively and based on available evidence, narcotics and hard liquor are illth, or harmful products. Research has concluded that cigarette smoking is hazardous to health; cigarettes are also clearly illth. Yet tobacco companies spend billions of dollars each year in advertising and marketing to promote this unsafe product; according to the Federal Trade Commission (2007), the top five manufacturers alone spent an estimated $13 billion in 2005. Most mouthwashes may be classified as nealth products, because they have essentially no value. Yet, millions of dollars are spent each year on promoting this virtually useless product. Promotions for such illth and nealth products generate billions of dollars of revenue.

If a 40-year-old smoker who spends $4.00 a day on cigarettes invests that money instead, by the time he is 70, he'll accumulate over $43,000, and that's without the benefit of compounding interest. At an interest rate of 5%, the actual income saved could up being over $101,000.

FYI

Promoting Dissatisfaction and Fear

The purpose of much advertising is to make consumers dissatisfied. If sellers can persuade consumers to discard what they have and purchase new clothing, new automobiles, or a new house, the sellers will increase their profit. Sellers may promote the idea of obsoletism, encourage artificial and competitive consuming practices, suggest false standards, and exalt the philosophy of materialism. Consumers, in their pursuit of happiness, may be persuaded that they must have more and newer material things. Many ads play on the average person's fears and insecurities to sell products such as home security systems, cures for baldness, antiperspirants, life insurance, fire insurance, and even plastic surgery.

Missing the Mark

Much of advertising is wasted and ineffective. Advertising agencies and advertisers admit that determining the effectiveness of advertising is difficult, if not impossible. Sometimes the ad itself is ineffective; other times the target audiences are not selected properly.

In attempts to sell magazines, publishers send out millions of pieces of promotional mail annually. If only 2 percent of the recipients respond, the mailing is considered successful. This means that 98 percent of these mail advertisements are wasted. The way advertising campaigns are approved encourages waste. Often they are selected on the basis of personal opinions instead of being subjected to scientific methods to predict their effectiveness. This is the case partly because the success of an advertisement or campaign can be very difficult to measure.

Misuse of Science and Language

Americans are impressed with science. If an advertiser claims that scientists have tested and approved its product, sales probably will increase. The mere assertion that two of three doctors surveyed endorse the advertised product impresses many consumers. For all they know, however, only three doctors may have been questioned. Claims about scientific testing may be similarly misleading. Manufacturers pay chemists and physicists to make tests, and the manufacturers publicize only the portions favorable to their products. This is **iceberg research,** a term implying that a claim is only the tip of the iceberg.

Iceberg research research done on specific products revealing only results that are favorable to the advertiser.

Advertisers also distort the meaning of words. Advertising copywriters often assert that their employer's brand is the best in the world. This is known as **puffery.** Obviously all brands of a product cannot be the best, but in legal challenges, puffery consistently has been ruled a legal means of advertising.

Puffery a claim that is obviously false but is used anyway.

Encouraging Spending

Advertising hails spenders and debtors as necessary to keep the economy going. According to economics theory, the main role of consumers, as a group, is to spend money. Macroeconomists do not care what consumers spend their money for; the important thing is that they spend. This view coincides with sellers' views that the consumer's function is to buy whatever sellers advertise, whether the goods and services are wealth, nealth, or illth, or whether they are or are not needed.

TIP Before making a purchase, ask yourself if this is a need or a want. If it is a want, reconsider the purchase.

During recessions, advertisers tell consumers they have an obligation to spend money to keep the economy going. When consumers spend for the sake of spending, however, they often do so on credit to purchase aggressively advertised nealth or illth. Economic stability and high employment are desirable goals, but consumer well-being is also desirable. Spending for the purchase of wealth will maintain high employment just as effectively as spending for illth.

Questionable Testimonials

Testimonial advertising the endorsement of a product or service by a recognized person, such as a television star.

Testimonial advertising is a questionable practice. Some consumers are impressed by what prominent people say and do. If, for example, popular professional and amateur athletes testify that their success is attributable in part to eating an advertised brand of cereal, then consumers, especially young children and teenagers, might want to purchase that cereal. If a famous football, basketball, or tennis player appears on television endorsing a product, consumers may be persuaded to buy that brand, whether it is shoes, beer, or cosmetics. Athletes are paid a great deal of money to endorse products that they may or may not actually use or believe in.

Concentration of Companies

Advertising in industries that are highly concentrated, such as those that produce cereals, soap, liquor, and cigarettes, creates brand loyalty that deters the entry of new brands. The initial marketing costs required for a newly developed company to compete with established firms in the cereal industry, for example, would be prohibitive. Thus, the potential for companies to enter that industry is remote.

Studies addressing the causal relationship between advertising and industry concentration yield conflicting results. Some indicate that advertising does contribute to

CASE STUDY SmartMouth Fights Back

This mouthwash "prevents bad breath 12 times longer than any other mouthwash"; "no other mouthwash has been clinically proven to provide fresh breath longer than one hour"; "wake up every morning with NO morning breath." These are the advertising claims of SmartMouth mouthwash. The company maintains that these claims are true, due in part to the clinically proven zinc ion technology that the product employs.

SmartMouth is made up of two basic solutions, sodium chlorite (odor eliminator) and zinc chloride (when mixed, generates free zinc ions). The combined solution penetrates plaque, blocking the ability of odor-producing bacteria to activate.

The independent research conducted by the company, research provided by the American Dental Association, and passing results of the cysteine challenge test (a methodology to create severe halitosis) were reviewed. Following the review, the National Advertising Division of the Council of Better Business Bureaus determined that the company's claims were accurate and proven.

QUESTIONS

1. What do you think about the claims made by SmartMouth mouthwash? Do they seem too good to be true?
2. Do you feel confident in NAD's findings?
3. Do you have any personal experience with this product, or a similar product?
4. Do you think there should be more or less protection when it comes to advertising?

Source: NAD News, January 22, 2008.

industry concentration; others conclude that no causal relationship exists. It is clear that advertising in concentrated industries does not increase real competition and may have an adverse effect.

WHO OVERSEES ADVERTISING?

The major networks and most television stations have advertising review committees in an attempt at self-regulation. Major television and cable networks and most on-air and licensed television stations subscribe to the voluntary **Television Code,** written by the National Association of Broadcasters. This code recommends minimum programming and advertising standards.

Television Code a self-regulating system that enumerates specific minimum standards in programming and advertising.

Print publications are less likely to police themselves. For every newspaper and magazine that exercises some control over advertising, scores of others make no such attempt. Because these publications are published for profit, their advertising managers cannot ignore the ability and willingness of deceptive advertisers to pay high prices. For these and other reasons, much objectionable advertising appears in newspapers and magazines.

The Internet is entirely different, with no such self-regulatory group or code under which it operates. It is also different in that most any person with a computer and the appropriate software can create a website and sell advertising. As a result, it has become necessary for the federal government, most notably the Federal Trade Commission, to amend its anti-trust laws to state explicitly that consumer protection laws also apply to the Internet. Furthermore, additional legislation relating only to Internet advertising has been enacted (e.g., the CAN-SPAM Act; see Chapter 5).

Better Business Bureaus

In 1912 responsible sellers throughout the United States organized to control "badvertising" and other objectionable retail selling practices. Better Business Bureaus (BBB) were established in metropolitan areas in the United States and Canada to monitor local ads. Doubtful claims were investigated, and in some cases an investigation was enough to cause advertisers to discontinue an undesirable ad. By means of bulletins, leaflets, radio and television appearances, and speeches to consumer groups, bureau representatives warned consumers to be on guard against fraudulent practices and deceptive ads.

The Better Business Bureau movement was laudable, but its own officials finally admitted it had not been very effective because it lacked unified effort and adequate money. In an effort to revitalize the movement, the Council of Better Business Bureaus was incorporated in 1970 by merger of the Association of Better Business Bureaus and the National Better Business Bureaus. The intent was to have one cohesive operation to deal with national advertising problems and industry self-regulation in a variety of areas. The council, consisting of approximately 120 Better Business Bureaus in the United States and Canada, has its headquarters in metropolitan Washington, DC.

www.bbb.org

The Better Business Bureau offers this "safe shopping" site.

Better Business Bureaus are organizations of business firms. The firms create and finance the bureaus to foster ethical practices and protect consumers from unscrupulous firms. A bureau, therefore, is not a disinterested spectator; it is a group of business firms that renders a service within its scope of interest, financial strength, and concern. Bureaus are neither panaceas nor public-relations ploys. Voluntary membership fees support the programs of each bureau.

In 1971 four associations—the American Advertising Federation, the American Association of Advertising Agencies, the Association of National Advertisers, and the Council of Better Business Bureaus—joined forces to establish the National Advertising Review Board (NARB). NARB works closely with the National Advertising Division (NAD) of the Council of Better Business Bureaus. NAD initially

Children's Advertising Review Unit (CARU) works in conjunction with NARB and NARC. Its mission is focused on advertising directed at or viewed by children under the age of 12. CARU activities include promoting responsible children's advertising, evaluating child-directed advertising and promotional material in all media, protecting children's on-line privacy, and seeking voluntary change in advertising practices that negatively affect children.

FYI

reviews and investigates all complaints, and most matters are settled at this level through negotiations with the advertiser. If NAD is unable to resolve a matter, NAD refers it to NARB, which adjudicates it through a panel consisting of five of its members. Approximately 400 complaints are filed with NAD each year.

If NAD refers a complaint to NARB, the panel members evaluate the complaint. If they consider it valid, they request the advertiser to make appropriate changes. If the advertiser does this and the basis for the complaint is removed, the matter is considered settled. If the advertiser does not cooperate, the chairperson of NARB publicly refers the matter to an appropriate government enforcement agency. All NARB panel reports, whether favorable or unfavorable to an advertiser, are published.

Although this complaint-handling service is not perfect, it does put a business against which an advertising complaint has been filed in an unfavorable public position if it rejects the decision of the NARB panel. In many cases this procedure has brought an end to deceptive advertising faster than would have been possible through the legal processes of the Federal Trade Commission. Neither NAD nor NARB, however, has the legal power of enforcement.

In addition, the council has established nationwide binding-arbitration programs in more than 100 bureaus, to settle disputes between consumers and business firms. The bureaus used nonbinding mediation for many years, but its success was so limited that establishing the binding-arbitration programs became a top priority.

Federal Government Control of Advertising

More than half of all advertising is national in coverage. It involves interstate commerce and thus comes under federal government jurisdiction. Advertising subject to federal controls includes magazines and television and radio broadcasts that cross state lines, as well as Internet advertising. The federal agency with the task of overseeing most national advertising is the Federal Trade Commission.

WWW

www.narcpartners.org

The National Advertising Review Council (NARC) sets the policies for the National Advertising Review Board. Through partnership with several organizations, including the BBB, NARC encourages self-regulation in the advertising industry in an effort to ensure public trust.

The FTC is primarily concerned with preventing false advertising. A false advertisement is one that is misleading in a material respect. Determinations of whether an ad is false take into account not only representations made or suggested but also failure to reveal material facts. Proving that an advertisement is deceptive is often time-consuming and difficult.

The FTC's law enforcement work includes conducting formal litigation against offenders and obtaining compliance with the law through voluntary and cooperative action. The FTC may issue advisory opinions, trade-regulation rules, and guides outlining legal requirements concerning particular business practices.

Consent order an agreement between an enforcement agency and a merchant requiring the merchant to stop a specific action.

Cease-and-desist an order by an enforcement agency requiring the seller to discontinue a specific action that may violate the law.

If the FTC believes the law has been violated, it may attempt to obtain voluntary compliance by entering into a **consent order.** If a consent agreement cannot be reached, the FTC may issue an administrative complaint, or in some circumstances the FTC can go directly to court to obtain an injunction, civil penalties, or consumer redress. If an administrative complaint is issued, a formal proceeding before an administrative law judge ensues, much like a court trial. Evidence is submitted, testimony is heard, and witnesses are examined and cross-examined. If a law violation is found, a **cease-and-desist** order may be issued. Initial decisions by administrative law judges may be appealed to the full commission.

Final decisions issued by the commission may be appealed to the U.S. Court of Appeals and, ultimately, to the U.S. Supreme Court. If the commission's position is upheld, the FTC, in certain circumstances, may seek consumer redress in court. If the company violates an order, the commission may seek civil penalties or an injunction.

Publishers, Internet site managers, radio and television stations, and advertising agencies are exempt from the penalties of the law if they give the FTC the name and address of the firm that caused them to disseminate a violative advertisement.

WHAT CONSUMERS CAN DO

Consumers themselves have several methods of recourse against advertisers.

1. *Reject mailings.* If consumers object to receiving sexually oriented materials through the mail, all they have to do is to go to the post office and ask for Form 2201, on which they indicate their request not to have those materials delivered to them. The mailers then are responsible for removing these consumers' names from their mailing lists.
2. *Demand proof-of-ad claims.* As an individual or a member of a consumer organization, a consumer can write letters to manufacturers and advertising agencies requesting proof to support their advertising claims. Consumers also can register complaints with the National Advertising Division of the Council of Better Business Bureaus (www.bbb.org/advertising.asp).
3. *Fight back.* The Federal Trade Commission recommends the following action concerning deceptive advertising and other related practices:
   - *Shop around before you buy.* No government agency is as effective as purchasers who are willing to shop for what they want and are intelligent enough to judge what quantity and quality they should receive for the price they pay.
   - *If you have a complaint, make it directly to the seller.* The practice you are complaining about might have been a mistake or unintentional. Give the seller a chance to make restitution. If the seller shrugs you off, take your complaint to the Better Business Bureau and to the advertising media.
   - *Take your complaint to your local government.* This is important because most of the things you buy are marketed locally. As a person engaged in intrastate commerce, a local seller is not subject to certain federal laws. Some cities and states have fraud bureaus, some form of consumer counsel, or a consumer protection agency. If you do not have an effective agency, work with other consumers in your city and state to make it effective.
   - *Report deceptive practices by contacting the FTC (www.ftc.org).* The FTC then may investigate, and you may not have to be involved any further. Resources are limited, so the effect of a single complaint is often minimal. If enough consumers have similar complaints, the FTC is more likely to investigate a potential trend.

As long as consumers permit themselves to be influenced by misleading and emotional advertising, it will continue to be profitable for advertisers. When advertisers find that false and misleading advertising no longer sells their product or service, they will advertise truthfully and factually. In the final analysis, consumers, in cooperation with private and public agencies, must exercise control of advertising. Enacting legislation that unscrupulous advertisers cannot circumvent is difficult.

THE MARKETING PROCESS

The marketing process begins as soon as production starts. Production of consumer goods begins with raw materials supplied by the extractive industries, those industries that draw natural resources from the earth for production. Agriculture, for example, is a basic extractive industry that provides food and fiber for consumers. Raw materials are transported to processing and manufacturing plants, where they are converted into finished products for consumer use. The finished products then are transported to wholesalers and finally to retail stores. More than 10 million people are employed to transport, process, finance, store, sell, and deliver the flow of goods that constitutes the marketing process. Exhibit 8.1 illustrates this process.

As productive and marketing processes have become more specialized, the percentage of each food dollar farmers receive has declined steadily. For each dollar consumers spend for food, less than a third now goes to the farmer; the remainder pays for the marketing process.

EXHIBIT 8.1

Flow of goods from producers to consumers.

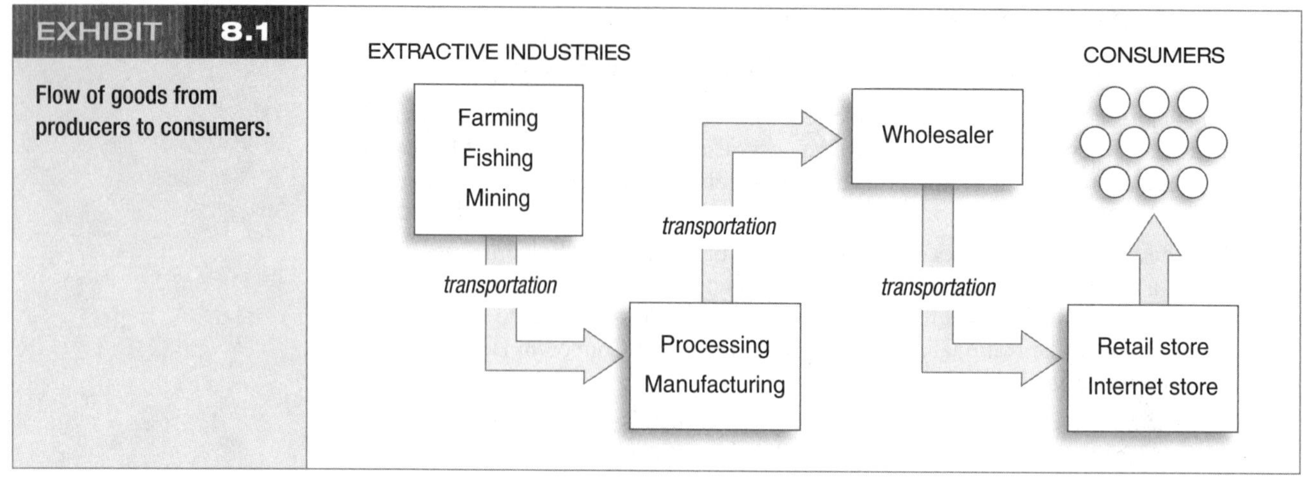

What Is a Market?

Market a place where the individuals representing demand and supply meet.

Exchange transaction a transfer in which the buyer sells money and buys merchandise, and the seller sells merchandise and buys money.

A **market** is a place where buyers and sellers meet regularly, such as a retail store or a commodity exchange. It also may be a place where buyers and sellers meet irregularly, as at an auction or farmer's market. Buyers and sellers do not have to meet in person, although that is more common. Markets are places for **exchange transactions.**

Markets may be Internet based, local, regional, national, or worldwide. The local market is the one most familiar to consumers. A retail store is a market. A geographic region may also be called a market. In this sense, a local market may have several food stores that compete to sell to consumers in the market. The continental United States is typically divided into several regions—New England, the Middle Atlantic States, the Midwest, the Southeast, the Southwest, the Mountain States, and the Pacific Northwest—each of which represents a regional market. The nation as a whole is the market for some types of merchandise. Today's Internet shopping sites serve national and international markets.

The prices of retailers in a market are influenced not only by the actions of competitors in that market but also by the actions of potential competitors in adjoining market areas. If food prices were to rise in one market area by an amount greater than prices in adjoining market areas, consumers might be tempted to buy in one of the other markets. This ability of consumers to buy in various markets limits the degree of price difference among markets. Consumers can shop for many goods in markets nationally or even globally by purchasing from mail-order and on-line stores, often obtaining significant savings.

TIP Mail-order and e-commerce shopping are frequently the most affordable ways to buy, but customer service often is lacking. Consider obtaining your best price through these venues and then asking a local merchant to match that price.

Types of Market Situations

Perfect competition a market situation with so many knowledgeable sellers and so many knowledgeable buyers that the action or inaction of one or a few cannot have any noticeable effect on market price.

Markets vary in the type of competition they offer. These range from perfect competition to a monopoly.

Perfect competition. Perfect competition refers to a situation of rivalry in buying and selling. With the possible exception of a few agricultural industries, perfect competition no longer exists in the United States. It probably never was as common as has been generally supposed, and it seems to be becoming less common. Theoretically, if perfect competition were to exist in U.S. markets, the "invisible hand" of competition would protect consumers from high prices and inferior merchandise. In the real world, many factors, including inordinate market power, imperfect information, and fraud, obviate the theoretical ideal.

Monopolistic competition. **Monopolistic competition** is a type of market in which competition operates imperfectly. The products each seller offers for sale are essentially alike, but they are made to appear different by brand names, distinctive packages, and advertising that represents each product as possessing unique qualities.

Monopolistic competition a market situation in which numerous merchants sell similar or identical products or services.

Retail stores evidence a great deal of monopolistic competition. Each store may have several brands of bread. Each seller has a different name for his product, yet the only distinguishing characteristic may be on the wrappers. The products may be identical in price or quantity and very similar in quality. As a result of advertising, however, many consumers are convinced of significant quality differences. Exercising their freedom to choose, consumers accordingly divide their purchases among the several brands of bread. Sometimes their conviction that the bread they buy is superior is so strong that it amounts to loyalty, giving the seller a monopoly of a specific portion of the market. This type of market situation is common.

Oligopoly. Oligopoly consists of few sellers (usually four or fewer) that control the majority of the supply of a product or service. Because only a few sellers are involved, the action of any one of them is likely to affect the actions of the others. This is the feature that distinguishes oligopoly from pure competition. Products may be homogeneous, but they are more likely to have distinguishing differences. The major oil companies and cell phone companies are clear examples of powerful oligopolies. Oligopolistic industries usually do not compete much in price. Most of the so-called competition takes the form of differentiation through advertising.

Duopoly. **Duopoly** occurs infrequently in the U.S. marketplace. In a duopoly, two branded or trademarked products may be basically identical, but they are differentiated to the extent that the buyer thinks of them as different and distinctive. Two sellers can usually agree on production and price policies. The resulting price is almost certain to be higher than it would be under purely competitive conditions. When it exists, duopoly typically is found in regional or local markets. For example, some smaller communities are serviced by only two regional airlines.

Duopoly a market situation in which two sellers dominate a specific market or industry.

Monopoly. Monopoly is a relatively rare market situation. In this situation, one seller controls the supply of a product or service. When monopoly exists, the one seller has the power to set a price that she thinks will yield the greatest net profit in the long run. Monopoly prices tend to be higher than competitive prices, and the amount of a product or service offered for sale tends to be less. Even though absolute monopoly is rare, monopoly power is not uncommon. Monopolistic power prevails in a market in which several firms have achieved control over the supply of a large part of an industry by means of ownership or by agreement to control supply and fix prices. The Antitrust Division of the U.S. Department of Justice is obligated to protect consumers from monopoly power.

Only a handful of companies actually manufacture major appliances, although these products are marketed under dozens of nameplates.

FYI

THE PRICE SYSTEM

In any economy, decisions must be made about how resources shall be used and how supplies of goods and services shall be divided among consumers. In the United States, most of these decisions are made through the price system. In a competitive economy, the impersonal forces underlying demand and supply are brought to the surface in the market, resulting in prices that balance supply and demand.

Although consumers may not be satisfied with a given price, they at least have the assurance in a competitive economy that a high price usually reflects a shortage of supply and that no one producer has undue influence in determining that price.

The record shows, however, that some sellers continually endeavor to restrict competition. To the extent that they succeed, their prices are arbitrary and are higher than they would be otherwise. As a consequence, some consumers and competitors are priced out of the market. In these situations, the price system is still functioning, but it is controlled rather than free. The more rigid prices become, the less satisfactorily the price system performs its functions.

Traditional Price Theory

Objective exchange value the power of a product or service to command other products or services in return.

Objective exchange value is a central concept of traditional price theory. If a loaf of bread exchanges for a package of oatmeal, the value of the bread is a package of oatmeal, and the value of a package of oatmeal is a loaf of bread. Under a monetary system, the values of bread, oatmeal, and nearly all other goods are measured in terms of money, but the principle remains the same.

Since the days of Adam Smith, most theoretical economists and business executives have insisted that the "consumer is king." Consumers supposedly guide the economic system. They are presumed to be omniscient—fully informed about quantity, quality, and price. Acting on the basis of this knowledge, they express their choices in a completely competitive market. If consumers want more of certain goods or services, the prices of those goods and services rise. Those higher prices induce producers to increase supplies. Conversely, if consumers want less, prices fall and supplies are curtailed. If prices rise in response to increasing demand or decreasing supplies, consumers are discouraged from buying. As prices begin to fall, sellers are warned to curtail output and consumers are encouraged to buy more. This balance of market forces is presumed to result in an equilibrium of supply and price.

Bartering is popular in many parts of the United States. Several national companies exist to coordinate bartering for companies and consumers.

FYI

Traditional price theory holds that demand is the active determining factor of prices in the short run. Price is determined by consumers' willingness to buy. If the supply of bread is limited on any given day, its price is determined by the importance of the last loaf to the buyer whose purchase will clear the market.

If a disaster drastically reduces the supply of an item such as bread, then theoretically, in a free and fiercely competitive market, the price of bread would rise sharply. In practice, sellers rarely raise their prices to take full advantage of an emergency shortage. At times, they even reduce their prices to aid those in need.

Similarly, even during normal times, prices are not available as theory assumes. Store managers usually sell their inventory at the same price as long as it lasts. As new supplies come in, they might raise or lower prices.

Does Price Measure Value?

Traditional price theory assumes that price measures value. The assumption is invalid, however, because of significant differences in the market information available to consumers, as well as in their bargaining ability and their purchasing power. Many consumers are unable to judge the quality of merchandise. They also do not check the quantity, and in many cases doing so is not even feasible. As a result, they may not receive all they pay for.

If price measured value, the highest-priced products would always be of superior value; the least expensive would be the poorest. Consumer Reports *refutes this "axiom" with many of the products it evaluates.*

FYI

Sometimes consumers are actually attracted by higher prices. Those who cannot judge quality may depend on price as an indication. Some believe the old adage that says, "You get what you pay for." People who believe this are likely to be attracted by high prices. If buyers expect to pay high prices, one can hardly expect store managers to disappoint them. Marketing journals are filled with examples where sales increased after prices went up.

Convenience sometimes takes precedence over price. Buyers often choose stores according to the convenience of the location. Store managers know that prospective buyers rarely shop around and buyers often know little or nothing about comparative prices. In many cases, the only limit to a retailer's markup is the retailer's judgment of what the traffic will bear. An impressive amount of evidence shows that the traffic will bear a heavy load.

The One-Price System

In the United States the one-price system prevails in retail food stores and, with some exceptions, predominates in other retail stores as well. Under this system, the retail-store manager is the active participant in setting a price. The usual practice is to charge as much as consumers are willing to pay. This does not mean, however, that retailers can set the price wherever they wish. Considering all the factors of demand, retailers will set their prices at the highest point at which they can move their merchandise. They must recover the cost of the merchandise and the expenses of operating the store. Whatever they can get above those expenses is their net profit.

> **www.unclaimedbaggage.com**
>
> The UnclaimedBaggage website primarily sells the contents of lost luggage. Often these items are offered at substantial discounts.

If a retailer pays $2.00 for an article and estimates it will cost 80¢ to resell it to a consumer-buyer, the minimum price usually will be more than $2.80—more than 40 percent above the price the retailer paid. If the retailer thinks he can get more, the price will be marked still higher. The individual consumer can choose to buy or not to buy. If enough shoppers refuse to buy at the asking price, the seller subsequently may lower the price. This is the way supply and demand is supposed to operate under the one-price plan.

RETAIL PRICING

To set retail prices, sellers refer to strategy and policy to make specific decisions. Strategy deals with location, store size, and store image. A firm's prices are set to achieve broad objectives, some of which may be nonmonetary. Policies involve general choices about the number and frequency of special sales, the types of items to run as specials, the days of the week to run specials, whether to meet competitors' specials, what prices to feature in advertising, and the like. Also, a store manager must decide whether to maintain the level of prices above, below, or similar to that of other stores. He must make specific decisions as to which items to offer in special sales and what price to assign to each item.

The prices that a retailer sets will have an effect on his profit margin. Margins may vary among departments and are usually higher on private brands than on nationally advertised brands. They use specials to attract attention. These vary from season to season and often are developed by the seller's suppliers.

> **TIP** When you purchase virtually any consumer product, consider attempting to negotiate the price. A key to successful negotiation is to put yourself in the seller's position. Because the seller usually has an unlimited supply and limited buyers, logic suggests that the seller should be willing to bargain with the buyer.

Pricing Strategies

After considering the wholesale cost of merchandise and store expenses, the seller can determine retail price of goods to be sold. Various pricing mechanisms the retailer might consider are discussed below. The retailer would likely choose an overall pricing strategy after considering the costs and benefits of each mechanism.

Watching competitors' prices

Regardless of their general markup policy, store managers find that if their prices on specific items are much higher than those of other stores, their merchandise will not sell. Directly and indirectly, competitive store managers watch the prices their competitors are quoting for the same items. They read the advertisements of other stores and might employ shoppers to compare prices in other stores. Sellers usually agree to match lower prices when alert shoppers tell salesclerks they can buy items elsewhere at a lower price. If a prospective buyer is looking at a $295 microwave and tells a salesclerk that he can purchase the microwave for $265 at another store, the manager might alter the price tag and sell the microwave for $265. Many stores advertise and follow the policies "We will not be undersold" or "We will match any competitor's price."

TIP Generally, it is wise to purchase toiletries at discount stores, not at food stores. Discounters usually offer substantial savings.

Suggested prices

Manufacturers, processors, and wholesalers frequently suggest the retail prices that they believe store managers should charge for their products. Sometimes these suppliers exert strong pressure on store managers to conform to suggested retail prices. Other times the "suggested retail price" is set artificially high, and any reduction from this price gives the appearance of substantial savings.

Nationally advertised prices

Nationally advertised prices usually are closely related to suggested prices. Sometimes manufacturers whose products are sold all over the country advertise uniform prices for every region. As a general rule, nationally advertised prices are high enough to assure all retail stores a profit. They may be so high that some store managers decide they can make more sales and more profit by charging less than the advertised price.

Price lines

Market segmentation a marketing practice in which the seller attempts to modify a product so it will appeal to a specified group.

Market segmentation is a significant part of some sellers' strategy. Retail stores commonly maintain variously priced lines of merchandise, perhaps including one line for low-income buyers and another for those in upper-income brackets. Other stores cater exclusively to one of the income groups. Stores that attract shoppers from all income classes have found that price lines aid sales.

Seasonal pricing

When the first shipments of seasonal merchandise reach retail stores, they often are priced considerably higher than the average markup. As the season advances and the supplies of merchandise increase, prices will be reduced. At the height of a season, prices usually are much lower than they were at the beginning. Food store managers adjust the prices of seasonal products to secure substantial profits when supplies are limited and demand is strong and to dispose of surpluses when demand diminishes and supplies are abundant.

Stores that handle fashion merchandise adjust their prices similarly during the fashion season. Sellers of automobiles start the new-car model season by attempting to charge the full, nationally advertised, suggested or sticker price. Then, as the cars become more plentiful, price reduction begins, and toward the end of the model year, bigger discounts follow. At the end of the model year, as the next year's models are being introduced, prices of the old models are discounted sharply to make way for the new ones.

FYI *When a store offers several price lines, the middle-line merchandise usually is the best buy. Typically, the lowest-priced products are inferior to the other lines. The highest-priced products are similar to the middle lines with the addition of unnecessary "frills."*

Clearance pricing

Seasonal pricing and clearance pricing are similar, but the time scale may be much shorter for clearance items. Prices for prepared items and bakery products might change in a single day. Early-morning buyers pay the highest price. By mid-afternoon, if the stock is still large, prices may be reduced. Just before closing time, prices may be reduced drastically for final clearance. If the store can use refrigeration and chemicals to retard spoilage of perishable products, this lessens the pressure to reduce prices.

Not all stores have clearance-pricing policies. Some maintain the original asking price even though it means throwing away or giving away unsold portions. As a general rule, chain store management uses clearance pricing.

Variable pricing

Many large retail stores use variable pricing. **Variable pricing** refers not to changing the prices of items but to merchandise arrangement. Advertised specials are tucked away here and there so the shopper has to hunt for them. The store manager hopes that while shoppers are hunting, they may see and select other items that are selling at full price. Alert shoppers and the store manager both can gain—the shoppers by finding real bargains and the manager by establishing a reputation for reducing prices. The manager might even raise prices on some items to compensate for the discounted ones.

Variable pricing marking down the prices of some items and raising the prices of other items.

Cents-off pricing

Cents-off pricing refers to reducing prices on specific products for a limited time. Sellers like the idea of cents-off pricing because a "50¢ off" sale draws attention to a specific product and package. Also, the retailer can tie in the sale with advertising. This helps to smooth out low seasonal sales periods and to meet competition.

Cents-off pricing was abused in the past to such an extent that the FTC developed a rule requiring merchants to prove that the advertised "cents-off" reduction is actually a reduction from the price normally charged.

TIP Verify the price charged on an advertised special. Some merchants, through oversight or deception, do not change the price in their computers.

Loss-leader pricing

Loss-leader pricing often results in good consumer buys. Loss leaders are items that are priced very low to entice buyers into the store. While shoppers are in the store to purchase the loss leaders, the store hopes they will purchase enough other high-markup items to offset the loss the store takes on the loss leaders. In practice, the term *loss leader* refers to any item priced below normal markup. A loss leader may be priced to recover no more than the cost of the merchandise, or it may even be priced below the cost to the store. Consumers can save money by purchasing loss-leader items and resisting purchases of higher-priced items.

Loss-leader pricing the practice of pricing some products in a store so low that the store makes no profit on these items.

Quantity discounts

Consumers who buy a large quantity of some types of consumer goods may be able to secure lower prices. Large packages are usually, but not always, lower in price per unit than small packages. Two or more items may be offered at prices lower than separate purchases; for example, canned goods may be priced at 99¢ each or two for $1.89. Although quantity sales often result in economies, these may be difficult to calculate. Unit pricing can help the consumer determine savings.

From a consumer's point of view, nothing is a bargain if it is not needed. If a large quantity cannot be stored or used within a reasonable time, the quantity price offers no real advantage. On the other hand, buyers for large families can sometimes realize substantial savings by purchasing large quantities, whether at a "warehouse" store or at a grocery stores that offers bulk or large-quantity products.

Odd-number pricing

Stores commonly quote prices in odd numbers, such as 99¢, $19.95, and $99.95. Retailers are convinced that they improve their results by doing this. When an item is priced at 99¢, shoppers tend to think of it as being about 90¢ rather than $1.00. The 88¢ price has been successful because many shoppers think of that as a discount from a higher price. Even prices, however, would allow shoppers to compare prices more readily and to calculate the unit price of products more easily (price per pound, per hundred, or per unit).

Multiple pricing

Merchants have found that consumers are easily influenced by multiple pricing. For example, a consumer may purchase four oranges advertised at 4/$1.00 instead of one for 25¢, even though he may not have intended to buy four oranges.

Customary prices

As retail-store managers set prices for merchandise, they must keep in mind buyers' notions as to what is fair and customary. Generally, people are willing to pay what they are accustomed to paying. As a result of national advertising of brand merchandise, the tendency is for prices of items to remain stable. If prices have been stable for a long time, customers regard the established price as customary and retailers have difficulty making a change. Although customary prices tend to diminish profits in periods of rising prices, they also tend to increase profits in periods of falling prices.

Consumers likely will accept a drop in price without question but will be critical of price increases above those to which they are accustomed. When prices increase, managers sometimes have to offer explanations. The usual justification for a price increase is an increase in the cost of merchandise or an increase in the expenses of operating the store. As a rule, store managers wait a long time before changing a customary price, except during periods of rapid inflation, when they have little choice.

Manufacturers are also aware of the power of custom. In a period of increasing prices, they are more likely to reduce quantity or quality than to raise the price. For example, for decades, the customary price for a candy bar or a package of chewing gum was stable. As candy manufacturers' costs increased, they varied the weight instead of varying the price until their costs rose so sharply that they had no choice but to raise the price. Gum manufacturers were also forced to raise prices. Now, instead of one customary price for these products, there are various prices based on the weight of the candy bar and the number of sticks in the package of gum.

Manufacturers can maintain a customary price for some time, even after production costs go up, by diluting the quality. One candy bar manufacturer reduced the amount of chocolate in its candy to zero, substituting cheap, artificial chocolate-flavored material and artificial coloring. Unless products are fully labeled, only consumer-financed testing agencies are able to ascertain and report to consumers whether quality has been diluted.

TIP Ask the merchant for a cash discount in lieu of paying with a credit card. When you pay cash, the merchant saves the fee she would have had to pay the credit company. She may be willing to pass on those savings to you.

Store-image pricing

Different stores project different images to prospective buyers. A discount store operating in a warehouse with unshaded lightbulbs projects an image of economy to some people and cheapness to others. At the other extreme, a luxury store presents a decor of carpeted floors, pleasing colors, soft lighting, and elegant furniture. People who patronize those stores expect to pay higher prices, and store managers fulfill their expectations through high markups.

Unit pricing

In retail food prices, **unit pricing** benefits the buyer and enhances the image of stores that adopt it. Comparing prices can be difficult, especially when fractional pricing (e.g., offering three items for $1) and fractional measuring (e.g., contents contain 15.3 ounces) make calculations burdensome. The effect, if not the intent, of fractional pricing and measuring is to confuse buyers into paying more than they think they are paying. In many cases, fractional pricing does not allow shoppers to calculate the price per unit without pencil and paper or a calculator. Unit pricing simplifies comparisons.

Unit pricing stating the price of a given item by the pound, ounce, quart, or other standard measure.

TIP

When comparing different packages of food, use unit pricing rather than total price. The price per ounce, per pound, or per item is the best measure of value. Small-quantity packages sometimes cost less per unit than large "bargain" packages. Choose the best unit price whenever possible.

Unit price labels are posted on the edges of the shelves where packages are displayed. Often these labels show the name of the product, the contents in ounces or other appropriate measures, the price of the item, and the price per unit. Some states have a form of mandatory unit pricing of foods.

Boom-and-recession pricing

In a period of rising prices, if a store manager has purchased a stock of merchandise at low prices, he may be able to mark it up according to the higher prices and thus make more profit. As noted before, consumers are likely to increase their purchases in periods of rising prices if they expect prices to rise still higher. Conversely, in a recession, when prices are declining, consumers may defer purchases in anticipation of still lower prices. In a recession, store managers may have to mark up less or mark down more. If a recession is severe, consumers are likely to shift their purchases to low-margin items.

Pricing: A Science or an Art?

Pricing merchandise requires a combination of art, psychology, expense analysis, guesses, and hunches. Retailers attempt to operate their stores so they can make as much profit as possible. Retailers are not completely informed about all costs, however, nor do they really know much about the way a prospective buyer will react to certain prices. Abundant evidence shows that retailers are motivated by noneconomic as well as economic factors. This is changing somewhat because of the sophistication of computer programs that aid in pricing. Nonetheless, few managers of retail stores engage in theoretical calculation of the optimum level of operation by comparing marginal revenue and marginal costs. Their methods are better than rule-of-thumb, but they are by no means as sophisticated as marginal analysis.

The analysis of retail-store operations seems to justify the conclusion that chain store prices *do* result from careful calculation and a profit-maximizing markup, and that pricing by managers of stores with just a few locations is based increasingly on careful calculation of percentage markup. Pricing in independent stores, however, typically reflects trial-and-error and "guesstimates" at least as much as it reflects rational calculation.

When buyers and sellers meet in a retail store, sellers have an advantage. They are full-time specialists whose primary goal is to make money. Consumers are part-time amateurs, motivated by a variety of forces, one of which may be economic but many of which are noneconomic. Even their goals are mixed. Basically they wish to satisfy their wants and those of their families, but in addition they may be seeking status or prestige.

Amateur, part-time buyers cannot possibly be as well informed as sellers. Why do sales in food stores increase 20 percent when a display shelf is full, compared to a shelf depleted normally by sales? Would a full shelf make any difference to rational buyers? Why does a placard placed at right angles to a shelf increase sales by as much as 150 percent? Why do sales increase by 80 percent when items are raised from floor level to eye level? Why do sales decline 40 percent when items are changed from waist level to floor level? Why do consumers not recognize selective price increases that raise store profits by as much as 20 percent? Are these consumer responses rational?

In light of the many factors entering into the price of a specific item in a retail store, price variations among stores are not surprising. In a price comparison in two stores, the managers of which pay the same prices to wholesalers for their merchandise and use the same percentage markup, prices more likely than not still would be different. One reason is that the two managers might differ in the way they convert general markup into specific prices. This difference may explain why lower prices may sometimes be found in deluxe service stores on merchandise selling at higher prices in chain stores.

Another reason for price differences is that chains generally vary their prices from community to community, depending upon competitive conditions. If a chain is dominant in a local market, its prices may be higher than its prices for identical products in other market areas.

The more shoppers know about pricing, the better able they are to play the game of shrewd buying. Informed shoppers know comparative prices in competing stores and are on the watch for selective price increases. They pass by high-price items displayed next to items on sale. Like merchandisers, informed shoppers, too, have a goal. Theirs is to buy as much merchandise as possible for as little money as possible.

SUMMARY

Advertising can benefit consumers if it is informative, announces new products and services, suggests new uses for known products, reduces prices, or specifies price. Advertising can be detrimental if it reduces or eliminates competition, increases prices, increases production costs, or controls media.

Studies indicate that most U.S. consumers distrust advertising claims but still are influenced by ads. Advertising often is deceptive; it promotes illth and nealth; it emphasizes dissatisfaction and fear; it is wasteful; it misuses science and language; it provides questionable testimonials; and it tends to create concentrated industries.

Although business has attempted to correct the problems, collusion and lack of enforcement powers have hindered these efforts. Nonetheless, the National Advertising Division (NAD) of the Council of Better Business Bureaus has made some progress on behalf of consumers.

The Federal Trade Commission (FTC) is the enforcement agency at the federal level. Specific FTC policies address deceptive advertising, but enforcement is difficult.

Mail-Order Merchandise Rule

Ordering merchandise by mail can be convenient and save consumers time, effort, and money. Sometimes a consumer can buy articles not available in local stores. When merchandise ordered by mail arrives late, or not at all, though, mail-order buying can be a real headache.

The Federal Trade Commission has a rule that gives some rights to consumers who order by mail. The mail-order rule provides that

- The buyer must receive the merchandise when the seller promises it.
- If delivery is not promised within a certain time, the seller must ship the merchandise no later than 30 days after the order comes in.
- If the buyer does not receive the merchandise within 30 days, the order can be canceled.

The seller must notify the buyer if the promised delivery date (or the 30-day limit) cannot be met. The seller also must indicate the new shipping date and offer the consumer the option to cancel the order or agree to the new shipping date. The seller must provide a free way to send back the response. If a prepaid order is canceled, the seller must mail the refund within seven business days.

The rule does not apply to mail-order photo finishing, magazine subscriptions, and other serial deliveries (except for the initial shipment); mail-order seeds and growing plants; COD orders; or credit orders in which the buyer's account is not charged prior to shipment of the merchandise.

Amendment to Mail-Order Merchandise Rule

Telephone ordering is big business. It provides billions of dollars to merchants each year. A variety of deceptive trade practices in the industry caused the FTC to hold hearings and ultimately promulgate the Mail or Telephone Order Merchandise Rule, which became law in March 1994. The rule amended the Mail-Order Merchandise Rule by extending protections of the rule to include merchandise purchased by telephone, computer, fax machine, and similar apparatus.

The rule states that if a company cannot ship merchandise as promised, or within 30 days if no promise is offered, the consumer has the option of canceling the order and receiving a full refund, or of agreeing to a new shipping date. An exception to the 30-day rule is for credit applications that result in sales. These purchases must be concluded within 50 days. The company is obligated to provide a postage-free procedure for the consumer to exercise the option. The rule does not apply to photo finishing, magazine subscriptions (except for the first issue), COD orders, and seed and plant sales.

The FTC suggests that consumers fight deceptive advertising by shopping around, complaining to the seller, and reporting deceptive ads to the appropriate local, state, and federal enforcement agencies.

Markets (where demand and supply meet) may be local, regional, national, or worldwide. Market situations may represent perfect competition, monopolistic competition, oligopoly, duopoly, or monopoly. Most market situations are imperfect, with the result that the seller has inordinate control over price.

The price system is the device by which it is decided how scarce resources shall be used and how limited supplies of goods and services shall be divided among consumers. Traditional price theory assumes that price measures value. Because of differences in bargaining ability, information, and other related factors, however, theory does not always translate to practice.

The seller determines prices of products after considering the wholesale cost of merchandise, store expenses, and pricing strategies. Pricing strategies include competition, suggested and nationally advertised prices, price lines, seasonal pricing, clearance pricing, variable pricing, cents-off pricing, loss-leader pricing, quantity discounts, odd-number pricing, multiple pricing, customary pricing, cash pricing, store-image pricing, unit pricing, and boom-and-recession pricing. The more shoppers know about pricing, the better they will be able to cope in the marketplace.

ITEMS FOR REVIEW & DISCUSSION

1. Analyze this statement: "The advertising industry can control itself through self-regulation."
2. Describe what is involved in the flow of goods from producer to consumer.
3. Explain each of the kinds of market situations discussed.
4. Describe the various influences that advertisers exert on the mass media.
5. Explain how advertising helps consumers by giving them information. From the consumer's point of view, list some advantages and disadvantages of advertising. What ad can you think of that informed you of a new product or service?
6. Describe how advertising stimulates competition and its effect on prices.
7. Name at least five techniques sellers use to take advantage of buyers' ignorance. Do you think it is unethical for an advertiser to disparage the product or service of a competitor? What are some current examples of deceptive ads?
8. Have you or someone you know ever been subjected to bait-and-switch advertising? Describe it. Have you ever switched from one brand of a product to another or from the service of one company to another because of advertising? If so, why? In general, how susceptible are you to the many ads you are exposed to each day? Can you really know?
9. Do you think that advertising promotes values that are too materialistic? Have critics of advertising overstated their case?

EXPLORING PERSONAL VALUES: PROJECTS

1. It has been suggested that the solution to glut is gluttony, that the sale of products produced in anticipation of demand should be aided by the deluge of advertising we see, and that the service this activity provides is a healthy, growing economy. Use these ideas as a basis for discussion with your classmates, examining things such as the morality of advertisers' half-truths and the trade-off between inaccurate advertising and unemployment levels.
2. Collect printed advertisements and notes from radio and television commercials for products and services of industries in which you or members of your family are employed. Ask a classmate to study and criticize the ads and their claims. Defend the advertising against your classmate's criticism.
3. List five things you find most offensive about advertising. Compare and contrast your list with your classmates' lists.
4. Select several advertisements from newspapers and magazines. Decide whether they promote illth, nealth, or wealth, and judge the extent to which they misuse science and language.
5. Discuss the following questions with your classmates. Point out instances in which the classical theory of supply, demand, and price is violated.
   a. Do you believe oil shortages are fabrications of the oil industry?
   b. Have you ever paid more for a product or service than you thought it was worth?
   c. Do you make an effort to shop sales?
   d. Do you believe the U.S. economy has too much monopolistic competition?
   e. Have you ever purchased a product or service you did not need just because it seemed like a bargain?
6. Discuss with your classmates how price determines the distribution of scarce goods. Examine the efficacy of alternatives to the price system.

7. Interview a retailer and ask for the person's views on the effectiveness, truthfulness, and competitive aspects of advertising. Also, ask the retailer about the store's pricing policies and ask why the retailer follows these policies.
8. Interview a group of shoppers and determine if they use and like unit pricing.
9. Write a report on the role of Internet shopping in the United States.
10. Select three ads each from magazines, newspapers, television, and the Internet that you think are helpful to consumers. What standards did you use to decide?

ADDITIONAL SOURCES OF INFORMATION

Cialdini, Robert B. *Influence: Science and Practice.* Boston: Allyn & Bacon, 2001.

Federal Trade Commission. *Cigarette Report for 2004–2005.* April 2007.

Mankiw, N. Gregory. *Principles of Microeconomics.* Mason, OH: Thomson/South-Western, 2006.

Nagle, Thomas T., and Reed K. Holden. *The Strategy and Tactics of Pricing: A Guide to Profitable Decision Making.* Upper Saddle River, NJ: Prentice Hall, 2002.

Reynolds, Thomas J., and Jerry C. Olson. *Understanding Consumer Decision Making: The Means-end Approach to Marketing and Advertising Strategy.* Mahwah, NJ: Lawrence Erlbaum, 2001.

Schumann, David W., and Esther Thorson. *Internet Advertising: Theory and Research.* Mahwah, NJ: Lawrence Erlbaum, 2007.

Sutherland, Max, and Alice K. Sylvester. *Advertising and the Mind of the Consumer: What Works, What Doesn't, and Why.* St. Leonards, Australia: Allen & Unwin, 2001.

Tharpe, Marye C. *Marketing and Consumer Identity in Multicultural America.* Thousand Oaks, CA: Sage Publications, 2001.

Underhill, Paco. *Why We Buy: The Science of Shopping.* New York: Simon & Schuster, 2000.

Zaltman, Gerald. *How Customers Think: Essential Insights into the Mind of the Market.* Boston: Harvard Business School Press, 2003.

> Only within the present century has one species, man, acquired significant power to alter the nature of the world.
>
> **RACHEL CARSON,** AUTHOR

KEY TERMS

acid rain

carbon footprint

chlorofluorocarbons (CFCs)

corporate average fuel economy (CAFE)

global warming

ozone layer

R-value

The following concepts will be developed in this chapter:

1. The United States must consider the impact of waste of natural resources.
2. Federal and state governments are attempting to reduce consumption and waste through a variety of programs.
3. Many environmental groups at the national, state, and local levels are involved in cleaning up the environment.
4. Individual consumers can impact energy use through a variety of energy-saving and conservation techniques.

After having read this chapter, you should be able to accomplish the following objectives:

1. Define and summarize the energy and environmental issues affecting consumers.
2. Cite some energy-saving tips that will help consumers reduce consumption.
3. Name some of the environmental agencies and groups that have a long-term commitment to environmental causes.

HISTORY OF CONCERN WITH THE ENVIRONMENT AND ENERGY

Energy and the environment have been among the most important consumer issues during the past five decades. President John F. Kennedy, who presented to Congress his Consumer Protection and Interest Program (better known as Kennedy's Four Consumer Rights), recognized the importance of the environment and energy, as well as consumer issues in general, after reading *Silent Spring,* by Rachel Carson. Carson described environmental and energy problems that were adversely affecting the United States and the world, cautioning that if these challenges were left unaddressed, severe economic and social problems would in turn develop. Today, almost 50 years later, we recognize that although we may have addressed some concerns, other serious problems still loom.

Most presidents and congressional leaders since the Kennedy administration have advocated improved environmental protections, with varying

Energy and the Environment

degrees of commitment and success. Most state and local governments have instituted recycling requirements and pollution controls. Businesses, too, have developed energy and environmental programs. And consumers, as a group, clearly have grown more concerned about energy and the environment. In the past few years, being "green" has taken on a new meaning, and a growing movement to be environmentally aware is good not only for the environment, but also for consumers' budgets!

In the coming years, efforts by consumers, corporations, and governments around the world will continue to shift processes and priorities with the goal of resolving environmental problems. We will all learn much more about what it means to be "green." We will learn to sort out what helps and what harms, and to distinguish significant efforts from superficial ones.

The following discussion highlights important environmental issues, as well as a few ways in which individual consumers can help conserve energy and make responsible environmental decisions. The focus in this discussion will be less on governmental and corporate efforts than in the past, because policies and practices are evolving daily as the first decade of the new millennium closes.

ENERGY, FUEL, TRANSPORTATION

Since the oil embargoes of the 1970s, the United States and other industrial nations have experienced various energy crises, caused in part by the misuse of resources and in part by political developments in the Middle East. In 2008 and 2009, gas prices at U.S. pumps ranged from below $2 a gallon to almost $5 per gallon. Such drastic fluctuations of gas prices over such a short period caused some calls for regulation and oversight of oil companies and for reduction of U.S. dependence on foreign oil. How such a reduction will best be achieved is a matter of debate; options include further development of new and existing power sources such as wind, solar, and other; use of alternative fuel vehicles; and new and increased drilling for oil in certain reserve areas.

www.doe.gov

The website for the U.S. Department of Energy (DOE) provides information about energy efficiency and renewable energy for consumers.

www.eere.energy.gov

This site provides links to a multitude of websites and on-line documents on the topics of energy efficiency and renewable energy.

For now, the United States and most countries of the world remain dependent on petroleum-based fuels. It appears likely that worldwide consumption of these fuels will continue to increase despite a slight reversal of that trend in 2008 as a result of the worldwide economic crisis. Energy consumption in the United States increases annually at a rate of up to 3 percent, and energy use by developing countries such as India and China is growing at a higher rate. As of this writing, natural gas, solar, electric, hydrogen, and other alternative fuels have yet to be widely pursued as viable options to petroleum. The Obama administration's proposed "New Energy for America Plan" included the following goals:

- Help create new jobs by strategically investing over the next 10 years to catalyze private efforts to build a clean energy future
- Within 10 years, save more oil than the country currently imports from the Middle East and Venezuela combined
- Put one million plug-in hybrid cars that can get up to 150 miles per gallon on the road by 2015; ensure that these cars are built in the United States
- Ensure 10 percent of U.S. electricity comes from renewable sources by 2012, and 25 percent by 2025
- Implement an economy-wide cap-and-trade program to reduce greenhouse gas emissions 80 percent by 2050

Earthday.gov

Earth Day is April 22 each year, and it focuses on accelerating environmental progress throughout the world. This website provides a multitude of information on Earth Day activities as well as other environmental issues.

CAFE (corporate average fuel economy) the average miles per gallon the federal government allows for a specific manufacturer's fleet of automobiles.

More environmentally friendly automobiles are being produced, and consumer demand for them continues to increase. As might be expected, the efforts of car manufacturers are guided to a great degree by legislative demands regarding **CAFE** limits, and consumer interest grows during times of highest gas prices. In general, though, growing acceptance of electric and hybrid vehicles is evidence that consumers and car manufacturers are thinking more about energy and the environment. Unfortunately,

CASE STUDY Energy Nightmares

The line of cars stretches from the gas station pumps into the street and down the block. Vanessa looks at the gas gauge of her Hummer. It quivers as if it is about to expire. She knows she won't make it to the next station.

When she looks up from the gas gauge, the line of cars has somehow lengthened. Are people cutting in front of her? The station looks small and distant. Vanessa feels a wave of panic. She is sure the station will run out of gas before she can get there, or the price will go up so much that she won't be able to buy enough to get to the next station.

And still the line gets longer. Soon the station is enveloped in a distant shadow. Vanessa turns on the radio, hoping to find a little music to calm her nerves, but every station is carrying news—news of world war breaking out. The cause, the newscasters say: oil. Nations are fighting over the distribution of scarce oil supplies. Vanessa feels like screaming.

Then she wakes up. She is not in her Hummer in a never-ending gas station line. She is in her bed. It has just been a bad dream. Everything is all right. Or is it?

QUESTIONS:

1. What events from history and current events invaded Vanessa's dream?
2. Describe the energy policies of the United States and other countries that contribute to the situations Vanessa dreamed about.
3. Do you think Vanessa is naive or realistic in concluding that "everything is all right" regarding energy availability. Why?
4. Do you think policies now being considered and enacted will help prevent the situations Vanessa imagined?

many automobiles still get very poor gas mileage, while still staying within CAFE limits.

Energy expended on transportation could also be conserved by encouraging the use of public transportation and car pooling.

www.epa.gov

The Environmental Protection Agency (EPA) is the federal agency that oversees a wide range of environmental issues.

ENVIRONMENTAL CHALLENGES

The Environmental Defense Fund (EDF), the Consumer Federation of America (CFA), and the Department of Energy (DOE) all provide resolutions related to energy and the environment. One consistent conclusion is the mantra "reduce, reuse, recycle." The following overview and environmental recommendations are drawn from these relevant groups.

In this country and worldwide we face challenging environmental issues, including pollution, **global warming,** and **acid rain.** Many believe that manmade assaults are disrupting the delicate balance of nature. The **ozone layer,** a layer of the atmosphere approximately 20 miles above the earth, screens out harmful radiation from the sun. **Chlorofluorocarbons (CFCs)** are one contributor to reductions in the ozone layer. Deforestation and carbon dioxide emissions are other popularly cited contributors to the decay of the ozone layer. These factors combine to cause the effects of global warming.

Though phase-out has begun in the United States and other countries, chlorofluorocarbons are still widely used in refrigerants, plastic foams, and solvents. They create few problems at the earth's surface but adversely affect the ozone layer. Calculating from 1980, an estimated 4 percent of the ozone layer is being depleted every 10 years. Many nations have agreed to reduce or eliminate CFCs in a wide range of products. The U.S. Environmental Protection Agency (EPA) is working to eliminate the release of CFCs in the environment.

Global warming an increase in the average temperature of the earth's atmosphere (note: the scientific community is debating the true effects, and even the existence of global warming).

Acid rain rain contaminated by various forms of industrial air pollution with toxic chemicals that harm living beings and plant life; more accurately termed acid precipitation.

Ozone layer a thin zone of gas in the upper atmosphere that screens the sun's ultraviolet rays.

Chlorofluorocarbons (CFCs) synthetic chemical substances consisting of chlorine, fluorine, and carbon. They are released by various household appliances and products.

TIP Radon is a dangerous and potentially deadly gas found in many homes and apartments. Kits that detect levels of radon are available in most hardware stores. Once a year, check the radon level in your dwelling.

We must also address the problem of waste accumulation and the contamination of groundwater, rivers, and lakes by bacteria, parasites, and toxic chemicals from sources such as farms, factories, runoff from urban and suburban areas, and leaking underground storage tanks. Disposition of solid waste and durable goods presents an additional environmental challenge. Recycling and composting are crucial. The goal must be to reduce, reuse, and recycle all solid, toxic, and hazardous waste. Programs and standards must be developed to provide incentives for this goal and for the development of markets for recycled products. Recycling containers in homes and businesses are evidence that consumers are pitching in on an individual level. Landfills, incinerators, and similar facilities increase societal costs and must be utilized only as a last resort.

www.carbonfootprint.com

www.carboncounter.org

To measure your **carbon footprint,** go to one of these sites. They will provide you with your carbon footprint number, as well as, ways to decrease your carbon footprint.

Carbon footprint the total amount of greenhouse gases directly and indirectly produced by an entity (e.g., human, corporation, country), usually expressed in equivalent tons of carbon dioxide (CO_2).

TIP Coils on air-conditioning units often get clogged, causing the units to become less efficient and wear out rapidly. Clean these units by simply vacuuming the coils as needed. The energy savings can be as much as 10 percent.

WWW

www.usda.gov

The website for the United States Department of Agriculture (USDA) offers information on land conservation programs.

www.consumerfed.org

The website for the Consumer Federation of America (CFA) informs consumers about issues that affect their daily lives. CFA's membership includes 300 nonprofit organizations.

CONSERVATION AND ENERGY-SAVING MEASURES

Conservation occurs when consumers decrease demands for energy and when they maximize energy efficiency. Conservation measures that have proved to be effective are outlined below.

Automobiles

Hybrid vehicles are fuel-efficient (40 to 70 miles per gallon) because they combine gasoline and electric power. Hybrids never have to be plugged in, they pollute less than typical vehicles, and their road performance equals conventional vehicles. Hybrid cars became available in the early 2000s. In 2005, hybrid SUVs made their way into the mainstream marketplace and continue to grow in acceptance and popularity. To encourage the purchase of hybrids, state and federal governments offer various incentives.

The even more efficient fuel cell vehicles (FCV) hold promise for the not-too-distant future. The U.S. Department of Energy (DOE) is working with manufacturers to develop a car that produces electricity from the chemical reaction between hydrogen and oxygen. These cars are virtually pollution free and are powered by pure hydrogen, the most abundant resource in the universe. Fuel cell systems are targeted to function at 60 percent efficiency sometime in the next decade, according to the DOE Hybrid Energy Program.

Another alternative to the gas-powered automobile is the neighborhood electric vehicle (NEV). Electric cars first appeared in the late 1970s as an alternative with limited emissions. The battery power was not strong, and it was difficult for owners to find a charging station. The technology was not at a sustainable level, and therefore these vehicles did not become popular. For today's consumers who commute short distances and need little cargo space, NEVs may be a plausible alternative. Many communities throughout the United States now have electric charging stations for these quiet and zero-emission vehicles.

Further efforts in the transportation area include the addition of high occupancy vehicle (HOV) lanes on roads. In large cities, these lanes provide quicker commute times. Some cities allow hybrid vehicles and motorcycles (lower emission vehicles) to use the HOV lanes with only one passenger.

Radiation released in 1986 during the accident at the Chernobyl power plant was nearly 100 times the radiation released by the atomic bomb dropped on Hiroshima, Japan.

FYI

TIP Insulate your hot water heater. You will probably receive a 100 percent payback in less than a year!

Housing Insulation

Housing insulation saves money and also increases one's comfort level. Adequate home insulation is based on choosing the proper **R-value.**

R-value the "resistance" measure or the capacity of insulation to resist the flow of heat from a warm room to the cold outside.

R-value measures the effectiveness of the insulation. The higher the R-value, the better the insulation. According to various government sources, using R-value to choose the most effective insulation for your home is simple if you follow the recommended steps.

1. Do research to find out what R-value you need. This varies according to the part of the house you are insulating and the part of the country you live in. Online resources are available, and retail outlets that sell insulation are happy to make recommendations.

TIP Caulk and weatherstrip doors and windows. You will receive a 100 percent payback in less than a year!

2. Decide what kind of insulation to install. Insulation is sold in batts, blankets, loose fill, foam, plastic, and foil.
3. Measure the area you are going to insulate. Check the coverage charts on insulation packages to figure out how much insulation you will need to get the recommended R-value.
4. Shop for the best insulation deal. You can figure out what gives you the R-value you want at the lowest cost by using this simple formula:

   the price of the package ÷ the square feet of insulation needed for the R-value you select ÷ the R-value number you select = the cost of one unit of R-value

The thickness of insulation is virtually meaningless as it relates to efficiency. R-value is the pertinent guide to follow.

TIP Before you purchase or rent a home or an apartment, obtain an energy audit. Most communities offer these audits free or at little cost. Following the suggestions that the audit provides can save you 10 percent to 50 percent or even more on your energy costs.

Recycling

The Environmental Protection Agency (EPA) reports that in the early 1980s, only one curbside recycling program existed in the United States, compared with over 8,000 in 2006. Although recycling has grown in general, recycling of specific materials has grown even more drastically: 52 percent of all paper, 31 percent of all plastic soft drink bottles, 45 percent of all aluminum beer and soft drink cans, 63 percent of all steel packaging, and 67 percent of all major appliances are now recycled. However, there is still progress to be made; only about 33 percent of waste in the United States is recycled, according to the EPA.

At least one-third of the garbage produced in the United States is recyclable, according to estimates.

FYI

Consumer Tips

Consumers can make changes at home, at work, and in the car that can have positive effects on the environment. Many of the following tips can be implemented immediately, whereas others may take more time.

AROUND THE HOUSE

- Recycle grocery bags, or use fabric bags and avoid plastic and paper bags altogether
- Use rechargeable batteries
- Unplug computers when not in use
- Go paperless when paying bills, banking, and so forth
- Opt out of junk mail
- If you must drink bottled water, use a home filter and bring your own in a reusable bottle
- Use compact fluorescent lamp (CFL) lightbulbs
- Avoid using plastic items that can't be rewashed and reused
- Use recycled, organic, and biodegradable products

People should check their air-conditioning and furnace filter once a year. True or false?

False. Filters should be checked more frequently. By changing your filters once a month, you will save $40 to $100 every year on heating and air-conditioning bills. The price for the filter is just a few dollars. Other ways to save money are to arrange furniture so it does not block the airflow and to keep the fan-compartment door closed tightly.

TIP Before you rent, check public records for the average monthly utility costs of the specific rental unit you are considering. Do not accept the owner's or current tenant's estimates. The owner will tend to underestimate the costs; the tenant will tend to overestimate costs.

THE HOME ITSELF

- Caulk and putty leaks in doors and windows
- Keep hot water temperature lower
- Use low flow shower heads
- Use low flow toilets
- Use a programmable thermostat
- Use double- or triple-pane windows
- Install insulation
- Use energy efficient appliances
- Replace filters regularly
- Keep fireplace dampers closed
- Maintain proper seals on appliances
- Wash clothes in cold water

By buying a showerhead that uses 2.4 gallons of water per minute or less, the typical household will save thousands of gallons of water annually. True or false?

True. Most showerheads use between 3 and 8 gallons of water per minute. Replacing them with ones that use only 2.4 gallons per minute should reduce water use substantially.

AT WORK

- Encourage telecommuting
- Encourage your employer to go paperless
- Use programmable lights

IN THE YARD

- Plant trees (for shade and wind protection)
- Do not throw yard waste in the regular trash
- Compost
- Do not over water
- Use a pool cover and heat the pool with solar heat if possible

www.weather.com

The website for the Weather Channel reports current weather information. Users can enter location and destination information to see current weather conditions and forecasts.

WHILE ON VACATION

- Use timers to regulate lights
- Check timer on sprinkler system
- Turn heating or AC off, if possible
- Reuse towels in the hotel
- Do not have sheets changed every day in the hotel

TRANSPORTATION

- Drive less
- Carpool
- Buy hybrid
- Avoid high MPG vehicles
- Stay current with maintenance

Clean Air Acts

In the 1970s, two significant federal laws addressed environmental and energy issues: the Clean Air Acts of 1970 and 1977. These laws established 247 air-quality control regions, each of which was required to develop a plan for air-quality control. The laws required reductions in motor vehicle emissions of carbon monoxide, hydrocarbons, and nitrogen oxides. After 1977, additional federal legislation was delayed. In 1990, however, a significant bill—the Clean Air Act of 1990—was passed.

Provisions of the Law

As a result of the 1990 law, sulfur dioxide emissions from coal-burning plants have been curtailed greatly. Consequently, visibility has improved by as much as 50 percent in some sections of the country.

Major changes continue in how people in the United States drive and maintain automobiles. Some of these changes affect all consumers, and others affect only those in cities with unique air-quality problems. Since 1994, all automobiles have been required to have warning lights indicating if the auto emissions controls are not working properly. Also beginning in 1994, manufacturers of automobiles and light trucks were required to cut nitrous oxides by 60 percent and hydrocarbon emissions from tailpipes by more than 50 percent from previous levels. Gasoline stations are required to have special hoses to capture fumes and vapors that contribute to pollution. Auto pollution–control warranties are extended to 100,000 miles, up from an earlier 50,000-mile requirement. Better maintenance on vehicles has become essential because state inspection programs are much stricter. Finally, the requirement of catalytic converters on motor vehicles is perhaps the single most significant factor in reducing air pollution.

Diesel fuels are cleaner and more efficient than gasoline. Many bus companies and bus manufacturers have switched to clean-burning fuels other than diesel because the controls that eliminate the black substance emitted by diesel vehicles are costly to develop and maintain. Various fleet owners have found it cost-effective to implement different fuel systems.

Some cities have brought about dramatic changes in the ways vehicles are fueled and operated. For example, many cities with winter pollution problems are required to sell gasoline that helps curtail smog problems during the winter months. In other cities, cleaner gasoline is required at all times. Hydrocarbons and toxic ingredients are targeted for significant cuts.

TIP Keep your car tuned up. Not only will your car perform better, but you also will save as much as 10 percent on your fuel bills.

Replace incandescent lightbulbs with compact fluorescent ones. You will receive a 100 percent payback in less than a year!

ENVIRONMENTAL GROUPS

Thousands of environmental groups have been formed, claiming to have the consumer's interest in mind. A sample of those that have established exemplary reputations are listed here.

- Environmental Defense, www.environmentaldefense.org. Its objective is one of oversight, to ensure that environmental laws are being followed and enforced.
- National Audubon Society, www.audubon.org. The society's major interests are to preserve wildlife and to protect the environment.

www.osha.gov

The Occupational Safety and Health Administration (OSHA) approves and monitors job safety and health programs. The OSHA website provides information about individual state programs and the functions of OSHA.

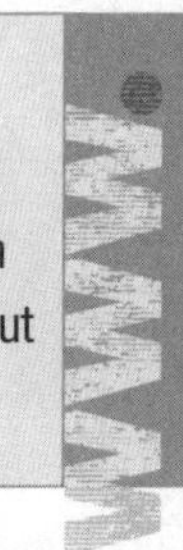

- National Resources Defense Council, www.nrdc.org. NRDC is particularly interested in the enforcement of environmental laws.
- Sierra Club, www.sierraclub.org. Sierra Club has local chapters that often organize grassroots activities involving a multitude of environmental concerns.
- World Wildlife Federation, www.wwf.org. The WWF's objective is to save endangered species and their homes, both of which are essential to the planet's health and survival.

All these organizations offer publications and activities for their members. Most of them have nominal membership fees.

SUMMARY

Few dispute the need for energy conservation and care of the environment. A multitude of programs, both voluntary and mandated, are now in place. Positive changes are needed and will require commitment by individuals, corporations, and government.

Auto manufacturers are working on alternative fuel vehicles to increase mileage and lessen harm to the environment. Hybrids are now commonplace in the market, and hydrogen fuel cell and electric vehicles are also promising.

Consumers can take steps to conserve energy, recycle, and help the environment. Even small efforts can produce big results.

ITEMS FOR REVIEW & DISCUSSION

1. Explain global warming.
2. Describe carbon footprinting and its relevance to this chapter.
3. Identify CAFE standards.
4. Identify two environmental agencies or organizations and their functions.
5. Enumerate various energy alternatives.
6. Explain R-value as it relates to energy conservation.
7. Some people assert that enough energy is currently available to accommodate our needs for the next thousand years. What is your response?
8. What effect does U.S. dependence on foreign oil have on individual consumers and the overall U.S. economy?
9. Name some ways consumers can help the environment.

EXPLORING PERSONAL VALUES: PROJECTS

1. Discuss your attitude toward recycling programs in your community. Do you participate in any of them? Also, discuss your attitude toward environmental and consumer groups. Do these groups have a positive or a negative effect on our economy? Explain why you feel the way you do.
2. Discuss or write about the following: What do you think our world will be like in 25 years? Will it be a better world? What will be the state of natural resources?
3. Discuss your attitude toward energy conservation. Do you practice what you preach? Record and analyze your energy-saving choices for one week.
4. Ask 10 students what part peer pressure and society pressures have played in their use of resources.

5. Research one of the environmental groups mentioned in this chapter. Report your findings to the class.
6. Interview five people about their recycling habits. Share your findings with the class.
7. Choose a country (Germany, for example) and research its recycling/environmental laws. Write a paper comparing that country's laws with U.S. laws.

ADDITIONAL SOURCES OF INFORMATION

Amann, Jennifer Thorne, Alex Wilson, and Katie Ackerly. *Consumer Guide to Home Energy Savings: Save Money, Save the Earth.* Gabriola Island, BC, Canada: New Society Publishers, 2007.

Carson, Rachel. *Silent Spring.* Boston: Houghton Mifflin, 1970.

Chiras, Daniel D., John P. Reganold, and Oliver S. Owen. *Natural Resource Conservation: Management for a Sustainable Future.* Upper Saddle River, NJ: Prentice Hall, 2004.

Consumer Reports. *The Complete Guide to Reducing Energy Costs.* Yonkers, NY: Consumer Reports, 2006.

Durning, Alan. *How Much Is Enough? The Consumer Society and the Future of the Earth.* New York: W.W. Norton, 1992.

Harper, Charles L. *Environment and Society: Human Perspectives on Environmental Issues.* Upper Saddle River, NJ: Pearson Prentice Hall, 2004.

Hollender, Jeffrey, and Stephen Fenichell. *What Matters Most: How a Small Group of Pioneers Is Teaching Social Responsibility to Big Business, and Why Big Business Is Listening.* London: Century, 2006.

McCarthy, Tom. *Auto Mania: Cars, Consumers, and the Environment.* New Haven, CT: Yale University Press, 2007.

Myers, Norman, and Jennifer Kent. *The New Consumers: The Influence of Affluence on the Environment.* Washington, DC: Island Press, 2004.

Schor, Juliet, and Betsy Taylor. *Sustainable Planet: Solutions for the Twenty-First Century.* Boston: Beacon Press, 2003.

Suzuki, David T., and Holly Dressel. *Good News for a Change: How Everyday People Are Helping the Planet.* Berkeley, CA: Greystone Books, 2003.

PART THREE

Money Matters

FINANCIAL ISSUES FACING CONSUMERS

Budgeting: telling your money where to go instead of wondering where it went.

SOURCE UNKNOWN

KEY TERMS

anticipated expenditures
anticipated income
assets
budgeting
consumer life cycle
continuous market
liabilities
liquid assets
money management
net worth
nonliquid assets

The following concepts will be developed in this chapter:

1. Healthy personal finance requires effective money management for changing needs.
2. The key to effective money management is the family or individual budget.
3. One outcome of effective money management is improvement of the family's or individual's net worth through the passing years.

After having read this chapter, you should be able to accomplish the following objectives:

1. Enumerate the stages of the consumer life cycle.
2. Identify problems created by irresponsible money management.
3. Identify benefits that accrue to the family that plans its spending through a budget.
4. Give a number of reasons people do not budget, and offer arguments against these reasons.
5. Enumerate the steps in developing and maintaining a budget.

WISE MONEY MANAGEMENT

Mark Twain professed that "the lack of money is the root of all evil." It is not a secret that money, or more accurately the mismanagement of money, creates problems in families, in friendships, and in business relationships.

Many people seem to have great difficulty managing money. Sound money management is a skill, perhaps an art. Without it, consumers may suffer economic, sociological, and psychological injuries. With it, they may benefit greatly.

Effective **money management** is an essential skill. How a person thinks about money is as important as how a person spends money. The individual's or family's goal in personal money management should be to keep purchases within the limitations of income and to spend resources wisely. A family's or person's living standard and financial stability may be dictated more by spending habits than by the amount of income.

Money management the prudent handling of income and expenditures by an individual or family.

Consumer life cycle stages in the average person's life that present varying sets of conditions affecting the person's needs and ability to meet those needs.

Consumer Life Cycle

Patterns of spending change rather dramatically through the **consumer life cycle** of the individual or family. Although lifestyles are changing, the stages of the life cycle tend to follow this pattern:

Budgeting and Spending

1. Young, single person living alone
2. Young married couple with no children—generally with both earning an income
3. Young married couple with young children
4. Middle-aged married couple with dependent children at home
5. Older married couple with no children living with them or dependent upon them
6. Older married couple, retired
7. Solitary survivor—older single, divorced, or widowed person

Of course, not all individuals and families follow this "traditional" life cycle pattern. Nontraditional life cycle stages include adoption by a single parent, divorce, remarriage, and the loss of a spouse before retirement.

Intelligent budgeting has to consider the significant changes in spending and income patterns as a person moves from one stage of life to another.

Spending According to a Plan

In some ways, a household is like a business firm. Both have income and expenditures. However, the task of purchasing for a household is different from that of purchasing for a business firm. The purchasing agent for a business firm performs one specialized task and buys a range of items limited to those the firm requires. The "purchasing agent" for a household fits buying into other daily tasks, and the range of items to be purchased covers the whole spectrum of human wants.

Traditionally, women were the "buying agents" for items inside the household (e.g., groceries, clothing, and household items), while men were responsible for items outside the household (e.g., insurance, automobiles, and yard work). Depending on the agreed-upon division of labor in the household, today's couples may choose to share the purchasing tasks, or they may choose to delegate all of the tasks to one person. In either case, it is important for whoever does the buying to do so wisely.

Purchasing for a household is an important responsibility. Just as an irresponsible purchasing agent can destroy a business firm, a spendthrift buyer can damage a household. For families one ingredient of living together successfully is cooperation in spending the family income. Family members must work together to make the most of their money. For both individuals and larger households, the planned budget, supplemented with a record of expenditures, is the key to achieving maximum financial well-being.

> **TIP** One good way to compare the way you and a potential partner manage money is to swap credit reports. This will give both of you insight into the other's money management practices, an especially important issue in community property states.

Benefits of a Budget

Budgeting planning for the coordination of income and expenditures.

Budgeting is important for all families, regardless of income. Many families informally plan their expenditures, whether it be casual planning of recurring expenditures or deliberate and organized planning for larger, nonrecurring expenditures. Only a few families, however, prepare a complete budget. Budgeting is the act of putting on paper or computer the total amount of income and a complete plan of spending for a definite period, such as one year. Some advantages of a budget are listed next.

> **TIP** Because financial difficulty is one of the leading causes of divorce, be certain your financial goals and values are compatible with those of the person you are considering marrying. If they are not, recognize that your risk of divorce will be higher.

1. *A budget acts as a guide.* It encourages rational spending and provides direction in meeting goals. It lets you control your money instead of your money controlling you. Remember, as the saying goes, if you don't plan where you are going, you will probably end up someplace else. It is inconceivable that a successful business or government would operate without a budget, so why should consumers?

2. *A budget serves as a report card.* It will tell you if you are living within your means or not. The use of credit cards often masks their users' true ability to pay. Widespread use of credit leads some individuals to believe they can afford most any item. Prior to this common use of credit, it was easy for people to determine if they were living within their means; they had money left over at the "end of the month."

www.mymoney.gov

This federally sponsored site aims at helping consumers better deal with money issues such as budgeting, saving, and investing.

3. *A budget encourages saving*. It includes a mechanism for setting aside money for savings and future investments. Experts recommend saving 10 percent of income, but putting away any fixed amount each month can help you develop the saving habit. Savings and investments become particularly important in later years, when incomes no longer grow or even decline.

4. *A budget provides for emergencies.* Part of savings should go toward the establishment of an emergency fund. This emergency fund should be large enough to pay necessary household expenses for two to three months. This will protect an individual or family in the event of illness, job loss, or another unexpected event.

5. *A budget helps to adjust irregular income to regular expenditures.* The minimum amount of money necessary to maintain the desired standard of living usually remains the same from month to month. However, for some families the amount and timing of

income are irregular or uncertain. A family that receives a regular monthly salary or income has less trouble planning expenditures than a family with intermittent income. Salespeople on commission, business owners dependent on profits, many professionals, and even wage earners cannot be certain of their annual income. A family budget based on past experience will help solve the problem of uncertain income.

> **www.financialplan.about.com**
>
> This excellent website has a wide variety of articles and resources regarding effective money management. Information ranging from budget worksheets to tips to save money to advice on tax planning and mortgages is provided.
>
> WWW

6. *A budget is helpful when disposable personal income increases or decreases.* Disposable personal income is the amount of income left after deducting taxes from personal income. When the economy is booming, a family's income may increase unexpectedly, but it may later fall back again. To increase family expenditures is much easier than to curtail them. Failure to budget may lead a family into a scale of living that it cannot maintain in the lean years that may follow.

7. *Adjustments to increases and decreases in family size are easier to make when a family operates on a budget.* In the first year or two following marriage, the family is apt to consist of only two. They may budget a modest income to include some comforts and a few luxuries. Then children begin to arrive, and family expenses increase. Unless the family income increases proportionately, expenditures must be reallocated. Rearing a child born in 2002 to age 17 is estimated to cost between $169,750 for low-income families and $338,370 for high-income families. These figures are in estimated year 2019 dollars.

As the children establish their own homes, the size of the family reverts to two, and the parents' expenses diminish. Finally, when the wage-earners retire, family income is likely to diminish by as much as 50 percent, and the retired couple must revise the budget again. In all phases of the family life cycle, budgeting facilitates adjustment to change.

Consumers Controlling Their Money, or Vice Versa? CASE STUDY

Jim and Mary Wayman have great difficulty managing their money. They make some money, put a chunk of it in the bank, and the next thing they know, the bank mails them costly little reminders that people should have enough money in their accounts to cover the checks they write. In addition, they carry a credit card balance instead of paying off the full balance each month. Although they do pay more than the "minimum balance due," they nonetheless pay interest each month. Most months, the Waymans spend as much or more than they earn. They do not save and cannot envision accumulating enough wealth to retire.

Of course, not all consumers are this way. Anne and Mike DeLucia, who live in the same neighborhood and make salaries comparable to the Waymans, are consumers who know how to plan and record expenditures, manage money, budget, and spend responsibly. The DeLucias have figured out the consumer life cycle. Their financial planning and preparation are balanced and prudent, and they project they will be able to retire, if they choose, when they are 60 years old.

QUESTIONS

1. What are the important elements of sound money management?
2. Do your own money management habits more closely resemble those of the Waymans or the DeLucias?
3. In addition to overdrafts and distant prospects of retirement, what consequences, financial and nonfinancial, might the Waymans' lack of wise money management bring upon them?
4. What changes in your own money management habits do you need to make to more closely approximate the DeLucias' methods?
5. Why do you think more couples do not discuss money management habits before they decide to marry?

8. *Preparing a budget requires examining family goals and values.* The act of putting anticipated expenditures on paper makes the important ones stand out more sharply than those that are less important. A couple that uses a budget will experience a more successful marriage because a budget is also a communication tool. An agreed-upon budget can provide stability in the family and reduce arguments about money.

9. *A budget can help in allocating discretionary income.* Discretionary income—that portion of disposable income remaining after paying for basic necessities—is uncommitted income that a family can spend as it pleases. Being able to spend extra money on purchases that matter to you is one reward for successful budgeting. When a family has increasing discretionary income, a budget promotes rational planning for spending that money.

10. *A budget is a record keeper.* People commonly discover that within a short time after receiving a paycheck, they cannot recall what they bought with it. If money is spent as planned in the budget, the records will show where every dollar went.

11. *A budget provides peace of mind.* Because you have a handle on your financial situation, you will have better psychological health. You will not have to worry about how to make ends meet.

WWW

www.stretcher.com

Stretcher.com offers a multitude of strategies to "stretch your dollar." Links to a variety of articles, resources, and relevant information provide consumers with valuable money-saving tips.

Why Don't All Families and Individuals Budget?

Considering that budgeting has so many demonstrable advantages, why don't most families have a budget? Perhaps the basic reason is that most U.S. consumers believe the way to raise the family level of living is to increase income. They ignore the possibility of increasing real income, which they can do dramatically if they plan expenditures and buy intelligently. Another reason is the fact that few adult consumers experienced, either through their family or their school, good consuming and budgeting practices. Public schools have offered little consumer education, though there is a current push for more financial education at all levels of secondary education. In some families, children are taught to handle their money intelligently, but in too many families the children are exposed to spendthrift habits. Habits developed in childhood tend to persist in later years. By teaching children the value of money, as well as proper money management, parents can prepare their children to spend wisely. Initiating an allowance, along with a savings account, is one first step in this process. However, teaching by example may be the best of all.

WWW

www.jumpstart.org

The website for the JumpStart Coalition for Personal Financial Literacy is intended to educate K–12 students about financial matters.

The time involved in budgeting may be a deterring factor. Preparing a budget and recording expenditures take time and effort, although online tools make it easier than ever before (see the FYI box at left). Even maintaining a simple system of financial records is too time consuming for many people. Budgeting for an irregular income is even more difficult, though the advantages of preparing and following a budget are likely to be greater.

Some sites offer free services to create and manage your budget. If you like using online tools, this might be the motivation you need to get on track with a budget. Check out the following sites: www.buxfer.com, www.geezeo.com, www.yodlee.com.

You may hear the comment, "There's no point in budgeting our income because it's so small. It takes all we earn just to live." Yet, when people who hold this view are converted to budgeting, they discover that planning and recording expenditures help them use their limited incomes more effectively to increase their real incomes.

Effective budgeting requires the cooperation of all family members. If one of the adults refuses to cooperate, budgeting is not possible. As the children grow older, their cooperation is also necessary. Each family member should have a voice in determining the amount to be spent on each budget item, regardless of whether every member contributes to the family income. Each member of the family also must cooperate in keeping a record of expenditures.

THE ABCS OF FAMILY BUDGETING

The first step in budgeting is to estimate all income as accurately as possible. This may be done weekly, biweekly, or monthly, depending on the payday schedule. The income figure should include the gross income less all deductions withheld from the paycheck, thus indicating what is available for budgeted expenditures. Individuals who do not receive their income from wages or a salary must be particularly careful in estimating income accurately. After recording all income, budgeting for expenditures can begin.

For those who have never seen a budget, it might be helpful to locate a sample budget before getting started. Local extension agents and consumer credit counseling services can provide samples. Review the sample budget and make notes on how the sample can serve as your model.

The Federal Reserve reported that in 2004, electronic payments exceeded check payments for the first time. Consumers are increasingly utilizing technology to make financial transactions.

FYI

STEPS IN BUDGETING

Budgeting entails three steps. The first is to put on paper or computer a weekly or monthly expenditure plan. The second is to keep a record of actual expenditures week by week or month by month. The final step is to compare actual expenditures with **anticipated expenditures.**

Anticipated expenditures the total amount of financial obligations an individual or a family expects to incur within a specified period.

Step 1: Planning a Budget

Start by writing down the major categories of your monthly expenditures. Then assign each one a percentage of your income. The suggested allocations shown in Exhibit 10.1 may be useful to some people. Others may find that keeping a log where they record their actual expenditures is more helpful.

A more detailed budget, with 18 to 20 items, is better. Up to a certain point, the more items, the more accurate and useful the budget will be. Exhibit 10.2 presents a suggested budget form. The items are arranged in approximate order of importance. Your own items and priorities may be different. Seeing how the importance of items compare can help you reallocate or reduce expenditures when necessary. This does not mean that if stricter bud-

Percent	Category
30%	Housing
18%	Transportation
16%	Food
8%	Miscellaneous
5%	Clothing
5%	Medical
5%	Recreation
5%	Utilities
4%	Savings
4%	Debts

EXHIBIT 10.1

Breakdown of typical expenditures as a percent of total budget.

From www.practicalmoneyskills.com.

geting becomes necessary, certain items should be discontinued completely but, rather, that expenditures on some of the essential items might be reduced and less essential items might be cut drastically. If necessary, nonessentials could be eliminated.

> **TIP** Numerous software packages simplify the budgeting process. Consider Quicken from Intuit, Money from Microsoft, or other software programs designed to assist with budgeting.

The next step is to fill in numbers showing the monthly budget. Because situations are different for every individual and family, it is impossible to suggest specifics. Beginning budgeters might use the percentages from Exhibit 10.1 as a guide. You can make adjustments as you gain experience with budgeting. In Exhibit 10.2 the "Monthly Actual Amount" column is for recording the amounts actually spent. At the end of each month, the amount allocated for each account can be compared with the amount actually spent. This will help with planning the next month and finding spending problems. At the end of the year, the monthly sheets provide a summary of the financial record for the year.

> **WWW** **www.practicalmoneyskills.com**
> Numerous prestigious financial organizations endorse and support this website. Valuable information regarding all aspects of money management is available; there is even a special section for college students.

If an expense is incurred more or less often than monthly, convert it to a monthly amount when calculating the monthly budget amount. For instance, an auto insurance expense that is billed every six months would be converted to monthly by dividing the six-month premium by six.

Step 2: Keeping the Records

After planning a budget and putting it into operation, the next step is to keep a record of expenditures. There are many methods for doing this; experiment to find one that works for you. Bills paid by check provide a convenient record on the check ledger. Another method is to use a computer program where you can enter spending data. Simpler record-keeping techniques include the envelope method, where you place cash for monthly expenditures into labeled envelopes, then make payments by cash from the envelopes and record the payments on the envelope. Perhaps an easier method is to keep a notepad in which to record expenditures every day. That data can be transferred into an electronic or online format or into an account-type notebook with budget categories. Still another method is the receipt box method: A box, drawer, or other container is set aside in the house, and all receipts are dropped into it for sorting and recording at the end of a specified time period, say a week. Whatever method is chosen, it is important that it be used consistently.

> **FYI** *Future and present value of money tables are helpful tools in investigating past, present, and future values of money. Consumers can use them to help in budgeting, saving, and investing activities.*

At first, the more detailed the record, the more useful it will be. From time to time, you can refer back to the records to ascertain where money is going. Later, you may find that keeping a detailed record of expenditures is not necessary.

How accurate should the records be? Record-keeping is not bookkeeping. Accounts need not balance to the last penny. Use the budget as a guide to better living. Budgeting and record-keeping are a means to an end, not an end in themselves.

Step 3: Comparing the Records with the Plan

At the end of each month, total the figures in each category and transfer them to the proper column on the budget sheet (Exhibit 10.2). At a glance, you can compare the amount actually spent with the amount budgeted. For example, if the amount spent for food in January was a few dollars more than the amount budgeted, you will know that you need to reduce your spending a little in the future. If excess expenditures show up in several successive months, this tells you that you either need to reallocate budget amounts or monitor and control your spending more carefully.

EXHIBIT 10.2

Basic budget worksheet for personal budgets.

CATEGORY	MONTHLY BUDGET AMOUNT	MONTHLY ACTUAL AMOUNT	DIFFERENCE BETWEEN ACTUAL AND BUDGET
INCOME:			
Wages/Salary			
Bonuses			
Interest Income			
Capital Gains Income			
Dividend Income			
Miscellaneous Income			
INCOME SUBTOTAL			
EXPENSES:			
Mortgage or Rent			
TV/Cable			
Telephone			
Home Repairs/Maintenance			
Car Payments			
Household Utilities			
Auto Repairs/Maintenance/Fees			
Other Transportation (tolls, bus, subway, etc.)			
Child Care			
Auto Insurance			
Homeowners/Renters Insurance			
Computer Expense/Internet			
Entertainment/Recreation			
Groceries			
Toiletries, Household Products			
Clothing			
Eating Out			
Gifts/Donations			
Health Care (medical/dental/ vision, inclu. insurance)			
Hobbies			
Interest Expense (mortgage, credit cards, fees)			
Magazines/Newspapers			
Personal Property Tax			
Pets			
Miscellaneous Expenses			
EXPENSES SUBTOTAL			
NET INCOME (Income Less Expenses)			

Source: Adapted from "Financial Planning" at About.com, http://financialplan.about.com

If you find that your actual expenditures for some categories are less than the amounts budgeted, you can transfer the surplus to one or more other items. If expenditures for one category fall below the amount budgeted every month, you should reallocate your budget and reduce the monthly amount for that category.

Determining Net Worth

Assets the value of owned items, stated in dollars.

Liabilities financial obligations (or debts) for which an individual or family is responsible.

Net worth the difference between total assets and total liabilities for an individual or a family.

Liquid assets resources that can be converted quickly to cash.

Nonliquid assets resources that cannot be converted quickly to cash.

Continuous market a market with sufficient activity that a normal-sized sale can be made at any time without affecting the current market price.

At least once a year you should calculate your **assets** and **liabilities** to determine your overall financial status. Your monthly records will show how much you have saved or invested as well as how much you have spent. A well-managed household, like a well-managed business firm, should show an annually increasing **net worth.** Exhibit 10.3 provides an example of a financial statement. Adopt this form to your own assets and liabilities.

Family assets are classified as **liquid assets** or **nonliquid assets.** Liquid assets include a checking account on which checks may be written or cashed on demand. For withdrawals from savings accounts, a few banking institutions require 30, 60, or 90 days' notice, but most permit depositors to withdraw cash on demand. Corporation stocks listed on one of the major stock exchanges can be converted into cash quickly at current market prices. Life insurance companies usually require advance notice of an insured person's request to borrow against a contract or to cash it in. In practice, however, it is acceptable to list the cash value of insurance contracts as a liquid asset.

Nonliquid assets have no **continuous market.** In a booming market, a house may sell quickly, but in a depressed market a seller may have to wait months before finding a buyer. The same is true of household items, unless they are offered for sale at an auction. Used automobiles have no stable continuous market. They may sell quickly at one time and slowly at another time.

TIP Before purchasing a used car, check the most current monthly NADA Guide from the National Automobile Dealers' Association to determine if the asking price is reasonable. Other excellent sources are www.edmunds.com and www.kbb.com. A reasonable compromise is to split the difference between the "retail price" and the "trade-in price" as listed in the Guide.

Nonliquid assets include annuity contracts, which usually contain a clause denying to the annuitant the right to borrow on the contract or to cash it in before retirement age. The same is true of 401(k) and pension plan funds. Unlisted stocks or bonds are also nonliquid assets because they have no continuous market. In calculating net worth, the bid prices may be used as approximations.

Savings that are invested in undeveloped land or in buildings for income purposes have no continuous market, but their market value can be estimated for purposes of ascertaining net worth. Money you have loaned to others should be listed as a nonliquid asset.

The primary liability of most families is the mortgage on their house. They also may have borrowed money from a bank or from a life insurance contract. Many individuals and families have credit card debt, and many owe money on installment contracts for the purchase of an automobile. All of these are liabilities.

FYI *The vast majority of individuals attending college make their most important economic and social decisions (job, marriage, family decisions) during that time and within five years after leaving college.*

A BUDGET FOR COLLEGE STUDENTS

Families with dependent college students should include the expenditures for the student in the family budget. Each student, in addition, should maintain an individual budget. Loans, grants, financial aid, scholarships, or other support that is being received should be listed as separate budget items. Some grants and most scholarships are forgivable, meaning they do not have to be paid back. Other forms of support, for example student loans, will have to be paid back.

EXHIBIT 10.3

Net worth worksheet.

CATEGORY	CURRENT VALUE
ASSETS:	
Cash in Savings Accounts	
Cash in Checking Accounts	
Certificates of Deposit (CDs)	
Cash on Hand	
Money Market Accounts	
Money Owed to Me (Rent Deposits, etc.)	
Cash Value of Life Insurance	
Savings Bonds (current value)	
Stocks	
Bonds	
Mutual Funds	
Vested Value of Stock Options	
Other Investments	
Individual Retirement Accounts (IRAs)	
Keogh Accounts	
401(k) or 403(b) Accounts	
Other Retirement Plans	
Market Value of Your Home	
Market Value of Other Real Estate	
Blue Book Value of Cars/Trucks	
Boats, Planes, Other Vehicles	
Jewelry	
Collectibles	
Furnishings and Other Personal Property	
Other	
TOTAL ASSETS	
LIABILITIES	
Mortgages	
Car Loans	
Bank Loans	
Student Loans	
Home Equity Loans	
Other Loans	
Credit Card Balances	
Real Estate Taxes Owed	
Income Taxes Owed	
Other Taxes Owed	
Other Debts	
TOTAL LIABILITIES	
NET WORTH (Total Assets Less Total Liabilities)	

www.finaid.org

The website for FinAid, a public service organization, disseminates information about loans, scholarships, and other types of aid to students and educators.

Student budgeting is helpful in several ways. For one thing, it enables students to give an accounting to their parents of money they received and spent. Budgeting also is likely to encourage careful use of money. It helps educate students in rational spending and encourages thoughtful behavior that will be helpful throughout life. For students who are contributing to their own college education, budgeting can help in planning ahead for expenses.

A Sample Budget Form for College Students

The advantages of budgeting are essentially the same for college students as for other individuals and families, and the technique is the same. The only difference is in the accounts. Exhibit 10.4 presents a suggested budget form for college students. Expenses such as tuition, board, room, books, and dues are usually easy to predict. Many colleges provide medical and dental care at a flat rate if the student is not covered by the parents' insurance, and this expense should be included in the budget. All transportation costs, including travel from home to school during breaks, should be figured into the budget.

EXHIBIT 10.4

Budget worksheet for college students.

CATEGORY	MONTHLY BUDGET	MONTHLY ACTUAL	SEMESTER BUDGET	SEMESTER ACTUAL	SCHOOL YEAR BUDGET	SCHOOL YEAR ACTUAL
INCOME:						
From Work						
From Family						
From Loans						
From Scholarships						
From Financial Aid						
Miscellaneous Income						
INCOME SUBTOTAL						
EXPENSES:						
Rent or Room & Board						
Utilities						
Telephone/Cable						
Groceries						
Car/Transportation						
Insurance/Health Care						
Gasoline/Oil						
Entertainment						
Eating Out						
Tuition						
Books						
School Fees						
Computer/Internet						
Miscellaneous Expense						
EXPENSE SUBTOTAL						
NET INCOME (Income Less Expenses)						

Credit Practices Rule

In 1985 the Federal Trade Commission developed the Credit Practices Rule. The rule applies to consumer credit contracts offered by finance companies, retailers (such as auto dealers and furniture and department stores), and credit unions for any personal purpose except to buy real estate. It does not apply to banks or bank credit cards, to thrifts, or to some nonprofit organizations; however, similar rules administered through other governmental oversight agencies do apply to these institutions. The rule does not apply to business credit.

The Credit Practices Rule prohibits creditors from including certain provisions in their consumer credit contracts. Specifically, credit contracts cannot include provisions that:

- require you to agree in advance, should the creditor sue you for nonpayment of a debt, to give up your right to be notified of a court hearing to present your side of the case or to hire an attorney to represent you. (These clauses often were called "confessions of judgment" or "cognovits.")
- require you to give up your state-law protection that allows you to keep certain personal belongings even if you do not pay your debt as agreed. (These clauses were called "waivers of exemption.") State law generally allows you to keep your home, clothing, dishes, and other belongings of a fixed minimum value. When the debt incurred is to purchase an item and that item is used as security for the debt, however, the rule allows a creditor to repossess that item.
- permit you to agree in advance to wage deductions that would pay the creditor directly if you default on the debt, unless you can cancel that permission at any time. (These clauses were called "wage assignments.") Nevertheless, a wage or payroll deduction plan, through which you arrange to repay a loan, is a common payment method and is permissible under the rule.
- require you to use as collateral certain household and uniquely personal items that are of significant value to you but are of little economic value to a creditor. These items include appliances, linens, china, crockery, kitchenware, wedding rings, family photographs, personal papers, the family Bible, and household pets. (These were called "household goods security" clauses.) If you borrowed money to buy any of these household or personal items and use the items as collateral, however, the creditor can repossess the purchased item if you do not repay the loan.

Under the rule, co-signers of a debt must receive certain notices. A co-signer is someone who guarantees to pay a debt if the debtor fails to do so. The rule requires that co-signers be given a notice explaining the responsibility they are undertaking. Under the rule, if you co-sign a debt the co-signer notice must inform you:

- You are being asked to guarantee this debt. Think carefully before you do. If the borrower does not pay the debt, you will have to. Be sure you can afford to pay if you have to, and that you want to accept this responsibility.
- You may have to pay up to the full amount of the debt if the borrower does not pay. You also may have to pay late fees or collection costs, which increase this amount.
- The creditor can collect this debt from you without first trying to collect from the borrower. The creditor can use the same collection methods against you that can be used against the borrower, such as suing you or garnishing your wages. If this debt is ever in default, that fact may become a part of your credit record. (Depending on your state, this provision may not apply. If state law forbids a creditor from collecting from a co-signer without first trying to collect from the primary debtor, this sentence may be crossed out or omitted on your co-signer notice.)
- This notice is not the contract that makes you liable for the debt.

This notice is not required when the co-signer receives benefits from the contract, such as when one person buys goods, takes out a loan, or opens a joint credit card account with another. In these cases the person would be a co-buyer, co-borrower, or co-applicant (co-cardholder) rather than a co-signer. Therefore, the creditor would not be required to provide the notice.

Under the rule, late charges must be assessed in a specified manner. A creditor can charge a late fee if you do not make your loan payment on time. It is illegal under the rule, however, for a creditor to charge you late fees or payments simply because you have not yet paid a late fee you owe. This practice is called "pyramiding late fees." Under the rule, this means that if the borrower does not include the late fee with the next regular payment, the creditor cannot subtract the late fee from the payment and then charge a second late fee because the current payment is insufficient. If you skip one month's payment entirely, however, the creditor can charge late fees on all subsequent payments until you bring your account up to date.

Violations of the Credit Practices Rule are under the purview of the FTC. If you wish to report a violation, contact the Federal Trade Commission, Credit Practices Division, Washington, DC 20580.

Anticipated income the total financial resources an individual or a family expects to obtain within a specified period.

Six specific sources usually contribute to students' **anticipated income.** In addition to allowances from parents, these include income in the form of scholarships, awards, and wages for part- or full-time work. Income from all sources should be included in the budget.

BUDGETING AND INFLATION

The annual rate of inflation can impact a household budget dramatically unless income increases at the same or a faster rate. By being aware of inflation and adjusting your budget accordingly, you can accommodate inflation's effects.

One way for individuals and families to plan for inflation is to use future and present value of money tables.

SUMMARY

Many people have great difficulty managing their money properly. Without sound money management, consumers may suffer economic, sociological, and psychological injuries. One way to reduce this negative potential is to develop a money management plan or budget. Budgeting offers many benefits.

Budgeting entails three basic steps: planning, keeping records, and comparing the records with the plan. Individuals should review their budgets periodically and revise them as necessary. They should also prepare annual financial statements to determine their net worth. By tracking net worth over several years, individuals and families can see their financial progress. A budget plan for college students is similar to a household budget, except that the categories may be different.

www.xe.com/ucc/

World travelers can visit this website to calculate current exchange rates.

ITEMS FOR REVIEW & DISCUSSION

1. Give reasons why personal bankruptcies are so prevalent in the United States.
2. Discuss what is involved in responsible spending. How has your family influenced your money management ideas?
3. Delineate the steps in developing and maintaining a budget.
4. Do you know the income and net worth of your household? Do you think you should?
5. Compare the percentages shown in Exhibit 10.1 for various items in the typical budget for a family of four with the percentages allotted to the same items in your household budget.
6. Discuss the significant differences in budget preparation for a college student and for a household.
7. "Keeping a budget does not increase your income; therefore, there is no point to budgeting." Discuss this assertion.
8. If your income does not increase and inflation continues, what will you do?
9. Do you think that planning and recording expenditures and calculating net worth merit the time and trouble required?
10. Identify several advantages to budgeting and several misconceptions surrounding budgeting.

EXPLORING PERSONAL VALUES: PROJECTS

1. Consider the ways in which you spend your money.
   a. Prepare a pie chart that illustrates the amount you spend on each category. Are you satisfied with the size of each slice? Draw a pie chart representing what

you consider an ideal spending pattern for yourself. Are you willing to make changes in your spending pattern to better represent the ideal?

b. Assume that a drastic reduction in income requires you to realign your spending patterns substantially. List the expenses to be reduced and rank them according to how deeply you will cut them.

2. Ask five students whether they budget and record expenditures and whether they know their net worth. Record their responses in your journal. Also, write how you think using a budget will affect your life (if you do not already do so).
3. List the significant changes in spending patterns that take place as a person moves from one stage of life to the next.
4. Keep a budget for the duration of this course, following the suggestions in this chapter. At the end of the course, outline the advantages and disadvantages you found in maintaining this budget.
5. Take an inventory of your present assets and liabilities. Did anything surprise you?
6. For one week, keep a record of every cent you spend. At the end of the week, evaluate your spending. Were you a responsible spender?
7. Interview members of a family that keeps a budget and another one that does not. Report your findings in class.
8. Interview five people who do not budget. Show them Exhibit 10.2 and tell them what you have learned about budgeting. Record their reactions in your journal.
9. Debate this topic: "Resolved: Budgeting is important for all households, regardless of income."
10. Write a newspaper article about planning and recording expenditures.

ADDITIONAL SOURCES OF INFORMATION

Boyett, Joseph H., and Jimmie J. Boyett. *The Guru Guide to Money Management: The Best Advice from Top Financial Thinkers on Managing Your Money.* Hoboken, NJ: John Wiley & Sons, 2003.

Chatzky, Jean S. *You Don't Have to Be Rich: Comfort, Happiness, and Financial Security on Your Own Terms.* New York: Portfolio, 2003.

Duguay, Dara. *Please Send Money: A Financial Survival Guide for Young Adults on Their Own.* Naperville, IL: Sourcebooks, 2008.

Fowles, Debby. *The Everything Personal Finance in Your 20s & 30s Book: Erase Your Debt, Personalize Your Budget and Plan Now to Secure Your Future.* Avon, MA: Adams Media, 2004.

Knox, Susan. *Financial Basics: Money Management Guide for Students.* Columbus: Ohio State University Press, 2004.

Lawrence, Judy. *The Budget Kit: The Common Cents Money Management Workbook.* New York: Kaplan, 2008.

Orman, Suze. *The Road to Wealth.* New York: Riverhead, 2008.

Paris, James L. *Money Management for Those Who Don't Have Any.* Eugene, OR: Harvest House, 2004.

Ramsey, Dave. *The Financial Peace Planner: A Step-by-Step Guide to Restoring Your Family's Financial Health.* New York: Penguin, 1998.

Ramsey, Dave. *The Total Money Makeover: A Proven Plan for Financial Fitness.* Nashville, TN: Thomas Nelson, 2007.

Sander, Peter J., and Jennifer Basye Sanders. *The Pocket Idiot's Guide to Living on a Budget.* New York: Alpha Books, 2005.

Tyson, Eric. *Personal Finance for Dummies.* Foster City, CA: IDG Books Worldwide, 2006.

11

A good debt is not as good as no debt.

CHINESE PROVERB

KEY TERMS

boom
chattel mortgage
commercial banks
consumer credit
consumer finance companies
credit life insurance
credit unions
debt consolidation
durable goods
FICO score
finance companies
garnishment
identity theft
installment buying
levy
lien
loan origination fee
mechanic's lien
one-sided contract
Rule of 78
third-party debt collectors
usury

The following concepts will be developed in this chapter:

1. Nearly everyone uses consumer credit at one time or another, and credit, as any other product, is "purchased" most intelligently after comparison shopping.
2. Whether or not it is wise to use consumer credit depends upon individual circumstances.
3. Federal and state legislation is necessary to protect the consumer because the seller of credit is more of an expert in the marketplace.
4. Debt taken to the extreme often results in bankruptcy.
5. Opinion is somewhat divided as to the effect of consumer credit on the economy.

After having read this chapter, you should be able to accomplish the following objectives:

1. Trace the historical development of consumer credit.
2. List several legitimate sources of credit, giving an advantage and a disadvantage for each.
3. List the advantages and disadvantages of buying on credit.
4. Identify the services that consumer credit counselors provide.
5. Compare and contrast bankruptcy options.
6. Discuss varying expert opinions regarding the effect of consumer credit on the economy.

THE DEBT SYNDROME

The total amount of debt in the U.S. economy (consumer, business, and government) is in the trillions of dollars. Consumer and federal debt continue to hit all-time highs. According to statistics from the Federal Reserve, the total household debt of the United States in 2007 was $13.3 trillion, up from just over $2 trillion in 2004. Not surprisingly, personal bankruptcies have also reached record levels in recent years. The problem of consumer debt has become almost uncontrollable. The dilemma for many families, businesses, and governments is how to close the gap between earnings on one side and expenses plus repayment of the debt on the other.

Consumer Credit, Debt, and Bankruptcy

The most common family financial problem is overindebtedness. Many consumers are economic minors; like children, they cannot resist the pressure to buy. As a result, some find themselves in a condition of perpetual debt. **Installment buying** is a major factor in consumer debt. Unfortunately, aggressive sales tactics and predatory lending practices, coupled with consumers' willingness to take on too much debt, have led to unprecedented defaults and foreclosures. Evidence now indicates that many cash lenders and installment sellers have failed to check a prospective buyer's total commitments before granting additional credit.

Installment buying arranging to purchase a good or service by paying the debt in specified amounts over a specified period.

Some creditors, such as car dealers, tempt consumers with deals such as "no down payment, only $150 per month." To evaluate such an offer, the consumer must know the rate of interest, the loan period, and the total price to be paid including interest. Although installment sellers are required to provide this information at the time the buyer signs the installment contract, many buyers fail to ask. Too often, credit buyers succumb to sales pressure, and before they realize it they are hopelessly in debt. Credit card companies, requiring only a "minimum payment" each month regardless of the total balance due, also encourage over-indebtedness.

Historical Use of Credit

In colonial America, when money was in short supply, the use of credit for consumption purposes was more common than the use of cash. Much like today, all economic and social groups used credit—the wealthy for convenience, others out of necessity. Losses on bad debts were high; nevertheless, the extensive use of credit arguably had beneficial effects in increasing the productivity of the country.

Prior to the 20th century, cash lending to consumers was done almost entirely by lenders that violated state usury laws. These laws set the maximum interest rate too low to cover the expenses of making small loans. **Usury** was considered immoral if it was "taking advantage of the ignorance or necessitous conditions of the needy borrower." Those guilty of this practice were called loan sharks, a descriptive term still in use.

Usury the lending of money at a rate greater than that allowed by law.

Buying houses on the installment plan by mortgages, where the house serves as security for repayment of the loan, has long been an accepted practice. Other

Durable goods items usually consumed over a period of at least one year.

Chattel mortgage type of debt in which the creditor holds the title to the goods or home purchased until the debt is paid.

Boom a period of rapid business growth.

durable goods are not as widely accepted as security for credit. The **chattel mortgage,** by which goods purchased serve as security for repaying the loan, is a comparatively recent innovation that is frequently used for automobile purchases. Rapid population growth accompanied by development of a large-scale, impersonal market necessitated this new merchandising method. As production of automobiles and appliances exceeded effective demand, the solution was to lend buyers the money with which to purchase them.

Attitudes toward credit have changed since World War II. Consumers are encouraged to buy now and pay later. The word *debtor* is no longer a disparaging term. In a **boom** economy, more consumers are willing to borrow. In recessionary times, consumers typically curtail their borrowing and are more likely to pay cash for products and services they need.

Because the United States had experienced a growth economy for several generations, many consumers took for granted the idea that incomes would continue to increase. The result is that many individuals borrowed heavily, confident that they would be able to repay their loans. Economic and real estate downturns left many consumers unemployed and unable to handle their debts. Such times of recession affect how we as consumers will look at credit and indebtedness in the years to come.

Current Use and Volume of Consumer Credit

Consumer credit the money or purchasing power that lending institutions grant to individuals.

Consumer credit is often misused and abused. Installment debt in recent years has taken more than 20 percent of the take-home pay of the average American, whereas experts consider 15 percent a dangerous level and 10 percent to be a suggested maximum. Consumers would be wise to follow the 20/10 rule: do not borrow more than 20 percent of your net income, and do not accrue debt of more than 10 percent of your monthly income.

Obviously, the availability of credit encourages buying. A buyer does not have to have cash in hand to make a purchase. Consumers are told they can have practically everything they want by paying nothing now or a small amount down and then a small amount each week or month. This significantly affects consumer demand. Extending retail credit has become a popular means by which sellers temporarily expand the market for consumer goods and services.

It is estimated that, on average, consumers now spend $1.22 for every dollar they earn.

FYI

Holiday spending in the United States accounts for a large portion of consumer spending and debt. Reports from Consumer Credit Counseling Services, a nonprofit debt counseling organization, indicate that holiday spending is now at an all-time high. In fact, according to this organization, many consumers have not finished paying off debt from the previous year's holiday when the next one comes around. This is just one example of the heavy use of consumer credit and the accumulation of consumer debt.

Formal Sources of Consumer Credit

Formal sources of consumer credit include credit cards, commercial banks, finance companies, and credit unions.

Credit cards

Credit cards are a commonly used credit source among consumers. They provide consumers with convenience and the ability to avoid carrying large amounts of cash. They are also useful in emergency situations. Unfortunately, the use of this credit is not without cost, to be discussed later in this chapter.

Commercial banks

Commercial banks state or federally licensed organizations that make fairly competitive loans for a variety of consumer goods.

Commercial banks are a major source of consumer credit. Commercial banks commonly have personal loan departments, and these make more than half of all loans for automobile purchases by individuals and more than a third of all other installment credit loans.

Finance companies

Finance companies are another major source of consumer credit. These financial institutions often buy installment credit contracts from retail merchants. When a person buys an automobile on credit, the retailer often sells the contract to a finance company for cash. The finance company then has title to the car and collects the monthly or weekly payments. In case of default, the finance company repossesses the car, hoping to resell it for at least enough money to cover the unpaid balance on the loan. If that amount is not recovered, the finance company will sue the debtor for the balance due plus any other charges incurred.

Finance companies state-licensed institutions that make high-interest installment loans to consumers for a variety of goods.

Q+A

You lose your credit cards, but a Good Samaritan calls to tell you he has found them and will mail them back to you. You should feel relieved. True or false?

False. Report the cards as lost or stolen. This is a gimmick used by some operators, who steal cards and then call with assurances that the cards have been found. This allows them more time to use your cards because you don't report them stolen.

Credit unions

As a source of consumer credit, **credit unions** offer competitive rates to consumers. The credit union concept is based on the principle that the funds necessary to meet any group's credit needs can be found within that group. The credit union makes these funds available to members for loans by pooling them. Credit unions now offer mortgage loans in many communities. All credit unions are insured; the vast majority are federally insured, and the rest are privately insured.

Consumer Finance Companies

Consumer finance companies are also called small-loan companies and personal finance companies. They are regulated under laws established in 1916, when the Russell Sage Foundation cooperated with the National Federation of Remedial Loan Associations to draft a model law regulating interest rates and practices in making small loans. The original maximum loan permitted was $300. Legislative action has increased loan limits in keeping with price and wage increases. Most states permit consumer finance companies to make loans of $2,000 or more. These companies are regulated at the state level.

Credit unions cooperative agencies that consumers organize for the purpose of saving and borrowing at competitive rates.

Consumer finance companies state-licensed firms that make installment cash loans to customers.

TIP

If a bank, a credit union, or a similar institution rejects your application for credit, do not pursue other avenues. These sources are indicating that you should not borrow. Seeking other sources (finance companies, pawn shops, and the like) is a poor decision. Reduce your current debts so you can qualify for better terms.

Other Financial Institutions and Retailers

Other financial institutions and retailers extend credit primarily for personal loans and automobile loans. Many retailers supply credit for the purchase of the retailer's consumer durables.

Of all legal lenders, two credit sources charge the most; they are *payday lenders* and *pawnbrokers*. Their role as a source of loan funds, however, is relatively minor, and the interest rates paid by borrowers are among the highest allowed.

www.paydayloaninfo.org

This site is sponsored by the Consumer Federation of America and provides valuable information about payday loans. Included are information about legalities, a loan calculator, and other helpful tools.

Payday lenders offer a *payday loan* (also called a *paycheck advance* or *payday advance*), a small, fast, short-term loan intended to cover a borrower's expenses until his or her next payday. Legislation regarding payday loans varies widely between different states. Some jurisdictions impose strict usury limits, limiting the annual percentage rate (APR) that payday lenders can charge; some outlaw payday lending entirely; and some have very few restrictions on payday lenders.

Pawnbrokers lend money for goods deposited and charge a rate of interest within the usury laws of the state in which they operate. If the loan is not repaid, the pawnbroker tries to sell the goods to recover the loan. Many states have restrictive laws supervising pawnshops.

THE COST OF BUYING ON CREDIT

"I'll lend you five dollars this week if you pay me six dollars next week." Does this sound like a low rate of interest? The annual rate on this transaction is an astonishing 1,040 percent. If the credit charge were at the rate of 6 percent per year, the interest on this loan for a week would be just a little more than a cent.

Consumer borrowers pay billions of dollars a year for credit, many without fully realizing how much it costs. Often they do not know the various rates and sources of credit, and they do not shop around.

> **www.joinacu.org**
>
> This site can help you discover credit unions to which you may be entitled membership. It includes listings of credit unions for most states.

The market for consumer credit is an oligopoly—it is composed of comparatively few sellers, whose services differ. The product is the same—money—but the competition is imperfect because of differentiation in the services offered. Differences include duration of the loan, type of security required, amount of the loan, and cost of the loan. In addition, state loan laws differ.

Rates differ markedly within competing commercial areas, across the country, and even between lenders of the same type, and of course rates change as economic conditions change. Over the full term of a loan, a consumer could save thousands of dollars by obtaining the lowest rate rather than the highest. It pays to shop around.

Prudent consumers do not restrict their shopping for a loan to one lending agency, one type of agency, or even one city. Potential sources include banks, thrifts, finance companies, credit unions, small-loan companies, pawnbrokers, payday lenders, mortgage companies, department stores, and even Internet loan companies. Each offers distinct advantages and disadvantages for various types of loans.

> **www.bankrate.com**
>
> This website provides calculators for a variety of calculations, including those related to credit cards, auto loans, mortgages, cost of living, and more.

The total cost of borrowing includes all finance charges and fees that have to be paid to obtain the loan or buy the item on credit. To borrowers it often makes no difference if credit costs are considered as interest charges or as service costs. The result is the same: the total credit price is considerably more than the cash price. Exhibit 11.1 illustrates the cost of credit. The entries represent the cost of carrying the loan balance for one year. Check the APR on your credit card or loan statement to see what it is costing you.

The federal Truth-in-Lending Act, passed by Congress in 1968, requires creditors to specify the APR, total finance charges, and other terms of loans they make. This disclosure law allows the borrower to compare credit costs. Nonetheless, many consumers are not aware of the benefits of shopping around and comparing interest rates and credit terms.

Monitoring Personal Credit

Once personal credit is established, it is important to monitor and maintain it. As a result of the Fair and Accurate Credit Transactions Act of 2003, each consumer can obtain a free credit report from each of the three major credit reporting agencies (Equifax, Experian, and TransUnion) on a yearly basis. It is a good practice to check your credit report each year. If you do this at the same time each year, for example a birthday or anniversary date, it will become habit. Credit monitoring services are typically not a good value.

EXHIBIT 11.1

The cost of carrying a loan balance for one year at various interest rates.

	AVERAGE DAILY BALANCE				
APR	**$1,000**	**$2,000**	**$3,000**	**$4,000**	**$5,000**
12.0%	$120	$240	$360	$480	$600
12.5%	125	250	375	500	625
13.0%	130	260	390	520	650
13.5%	135	270	405	540	675
14.0%	140	280	420	560	700
14.5%	145	290	435	580	725
15.0%	150	300	450	600	750
15.5%	155	310	465	620	775
16.0%	160	320	480	640	800
16.5%	165	330	495	660	825
17.0%	170	340	510	680	850
17.5%	175	350	525	700	875
18.0%	180	360	540	720	900

Your credit history is most commonly summarized in your **FICO score.** FICO stands for Fair, Isaac, and Company, the firm that calculates and provides these scores. Other calculations are available, depending on the credit bureau. A person's credit score can vary because the three bureaus have traditionally used differing means of calculating the score. To combat this problem, the three major credit bureaus have implemented VantageScore, designed to simplify the credit risk scoring system and make it more consistent. The system assigns a letter grade from A to F based on a low score of 501 to a high score of 990.

FICO score a score (a number between 300 and 850) that helps lenders predict, based on an individual's credit history, the type of borrower he or she will be.

If you do not have a credit history, it is important to build one. In the eyes of most lenders, having no credit history is almost as bad as having a poor or negative credit history. You can build your credit by doing the following:

1. *Pay your bills on time.* If it is difficult for you to remember when bills are due, set up a system with your bank to pay your bills on-line, or have them automatically paid through your on-line banking system. Of course, this will only work if you know you will always have enough money in your account when the bill payment will be withdrawn.
2. *Order your three major credit reports at least one time each year.* Check them for accuracy. If they are incorrect, make sure you dispute the inaccuracy and document your actions.
3. *Resolve negative issues on your credit report if you are able.* Showing responsibility on a "bad" debt can help restore your credit.
4. *Close out old, inactive, and seldom used accounts.* This will decrease the amount of debt you might be able to incur and improve your credit profile. Verify that your accounts have been closed by following up with the credit bureaus. These accounts should be labeled "closed by consumer."
5. *Keep your balances low and avoid revolving all of them.* This will show ability to pay and responsibility on your part.
6. *Do not accept each time a creditor offers to raise your credit limit.* While it may be tempting, doing so will increase the amount of debt you might incur. Keep your credit limits moderate.

Many banks and credit card companies charge fees from the first day of purchase, without clearly informing consumers of these charges. Also, interest charges often begin on new purchases on the day of the purchase if there is a balance on the account from the previous month.

FYI

7. *When opening a new line of credit, ask if the company reports to the credit bureaus.* You might also ask existing creditors that have positive information to share if they could report that to the credit bureaus. Not all will do so, but it is worth asking.

Q+A

For a small service fee ($25–$50) your tax preparation service will give you an "instant refund" on your taxes, which is a good deal. True or false?

False. This is basically a short-term loan that typically works out to have a very high interest rate. It is not a very good idea.

8. *If you have bad credit or have filed bankruptcy, attempt to reestablish your credit history quickly.* Paying on time, every time, will improve your credit score dramatically. You can do this by obtaining a secured credit card (these require you to put money into an account in advance), use it, and pay it wisely. Opening a savings account, if you do not have one already, will also show an effort on your part.
9. *Avoid inquiring for additional credit.* A flood of "inquiries" on your part will lower your score because it sends up a red flag to creditors. It may indicate that you are having money problems.

The Fair Credit Reporting Act is another piece of legislation that helps to protect consumers. It requires credit bureaus to disclose the contents of a consumer's credit file and to remove inaccurate and obsolete information. In addition, consumers may write an explanatory statement about items that are noted in the file and request the credit bureau to include the statement in the file.

Protecting Personal Credit

Identity theft the use of an individual's personal information, without his or her knowledge, to commit fraud or other crimes.

Identity theft is one of the fastest growing white-collar crimes in the United States. According to the FTC, in 2005 approximately 8 million people fell victim to identity theft. This equates to about 4 percent of the population. Depending on the type of theft, the dollar amount lost by victims varies. The FTC reports the average loss by consumers ranges from $500 to $30,000. Of course, the time spent by a victim to recover from such a theft is not included, and may be as many as 40 hours. The annual cost to the American people is well over $50 billion.

In 2006 the federal government established the President's Task Force on Identity Theft. The main charge of this group is to create a strategic plan to make the federal government's efforts more effective and efficient through three key areas: law enforcement, education, and government safeguards. To date, the task force has created fact sheets and press releases and has released a comprehensive report detailing the optimal strategic plan. Many of the actions proposed in the strategic plan are now in effect, and related agencies have adjusted their practices and their websites accordingly. For example, under the FTC's identity theft section, they have adopted the following mantra: deter, detect, defend. In addition, the site offers several posters, brochures, presentation packages, and so on in a variety of forms and languages.

Although the FTC estimates that the percentages of ID theft victims actually decreased (from 4.6% to 3.7%) based on surveys in 2003 and 2006, the legitimacy of the survey question measuring this figure is somewhat dubious. Continually evolving technology gives criminals new ways to capture consumer information; in addition, it's very difficult for authorities to catch perpetrators. Given these factors, identity theft is likely to be an ongoing problem. Consumers should take precautions to protect themselves from this crime.

Pretexting is the act of acquiring a consumer's personal information under false pretenses. Pretexters may sell personal information to scammers, who use it to obtain credit in the consumer's name or attempt to steal assets. Pretexting is illegal.

FYI

Experts recommend several steps to take to avoid becoming a victim of identity theft. These steps include:

1. Using a cross-cut shredder, shred all items that contain personal information before throwing them in your trash. "Dumpster diving" is a common way for scammers to obtain personal information.
2. Protect your Social Security number. Because employees (of your own employer, of a business you frequent, or with a company where you are applying for a job) are

sources from which scammers obtain personal information, try to avoid disclosing your personal identification information. Do not allow companies or institutions to use your Social Security number as an ID number under any circumstances. When forms ask you for your SSN, question the purpose and provide it only when absolutely necessary.

3. Check the three credit bureaus each year to assure that credit in your name has not been issued without your knowledge. This is an especially critical step if you have suddenly and for the first time been denied credit.
4. Use the Internet with care. Many sites have privacy software, but you should still use caution when transferring sensitive data on-line. Keep your virus protection up to date. Delete any suspicious e-mail without opening it and do *not* open attachments unless you are certain they come from a reliable source.
5. Minimize the amount of information that is "out there" about you. Join the FTC's Do Not Call Registry and opt out of marketing lists from the three credit bureaus, the Direct Marketing Association, and any company with which you do business.
6. Do not keep passwords with your account information. That is, for example, do not write your ATM PIN on your ATM card.
7. Install a mail slot in your door or a locked mailbox so that your mail is not evident to passersby, or rent a mailbox at your post office.
8. When ordering new checks, either pick them up at the bank or, if you order them from another place, ask the printer to require that you sign for them when they arrive.
9. Photocopy all of the personal identification information in your wallet and retain the originals in a safe place.
10. Credit card receipts should no longer show the entire card number, but in any case take receipts with you after you make transactions. Shred and discard them yourself after you have received the statements where they appear.
11. When you mail items that contain your personal information (bills, credit card numbers, etc.), use mailboxes that are closed and secure. It is not safe to leave outgoing mail in a box or slot that is accessible to others.
12. Keep your personal information at home in a secure place. This is especially important for college students who may have roommates they do not know very well.

www.idtheft.gov

www.idtheftcenter.com

For up-to-date information on identity theft, visit these sites. The FTC is the primary federal agency overseeing identity theft. Additional valuable and trustworthy information may be obtained from the Identity Theft Resource Center, a nonprofit organization.

WWW

Synthetic identity theft involves the combination of one person's name with another person's social security number. Even though it never shows up on either person's credit report, it is a creative and effective way for thieves to create a fictional identity.

FYI

Even the most vigilant consumer cannot prevent identity theft, but you can reduce your risk. The best defense is a good offense, and adding as many deterrents as possible will help. Authorities recommend you take the following steps if identity theft occurs:

1. Contact all three credit bureaus. Implement a fraud alert on all credit files.
2. Contact the FTC to file a complaint.
3. File an ID theft affidavit (see the FTC website at www.ftc.gov).
4. File a police report.
5. Contact all credit card companies and your bank. Change all accounts and passwords.

www.annualcreditreport.com

With the passage of Fair and Accurate Credit Transactions Act in 2003, each consumer may now obtain one free credit report from each of the three major credit reporting agencies each year. This website makes it easy to do so. If you need to contact one of the agencies directly, the web addresses are www.equifax.com, www.experian.com, and www.transunion.com. You should make it a habit to check your credit report for accuracy once each year. Avoid credit monitoring services; they are not good values.

WWW

Diligent monitoring of personal financial information can help consumers detect fraud promptly and act quickly. Quick action and thorough reporting can help victims get back on track.

Credit Misuse

For many college students, the allure of easy credit has dire consequences. Credit cards are easy to obtain and easier to use. Credit card companies target college students because these companies recognize that many college students are naive and do not realize the full impact of credit card use and misuse. Suppose, for example, that you purchase a big-screen HD television for $2,500. Also suppose that you are like most credit card holders and you do not pay your credit card charges off each month. Indeed, like many consumers, you make the minimum monthly payments at a current rate of 17 to 18 percent. At this rate, it will take you over 30 years to satisfy this debt. Consumers who incur credit card debt each month carry an average of approximately $8,000. For college students, the average credit card debt is estimated at between $2,000 and $5,000.

Many college students unknowingly and quickly become permanently in debt to credit card companies. Their optimism for a good job and a high income gives many students a false sense of confidence in their ability to pay off debt later. Some college campuses prevent credit card companies from soliciting on campus in an effort to protect students.

THE 5 C'S OF CREDIT

hen deciding whether to offer credit, creditors commonly consider the "5 C's of credit." These criteria are typically used in business sector lending but are also important for consumers to understand.

1. *Character.* Personal and business conduct and leadership give a lender insight regarding your ability to handle credit. Trustworthiness, educational background, references, and experience are all factors that contribute to character.
2. *Capacity.* Borrowing history and track record of repayment are considerations in this factor. Ability to handle and repay more debt, including liquidity, provides predictions about repayment success.
3. *Capital.* Lenders consider the amount of money already invested. In business ventures, personal capital investment shows a higher level of commitment, including a higher level of assumed personal risk. However, do not be too risky. Having too much credit available, obtaining additional credit cards, or looking into obtaining a loan may result in a rate hike.
4. *Conditions.* Lenders weigh current economic and market conditions, as well as the intended purpose of the loan. In a business situation, how the money will be used provides evidence to the lender of potential payoff and realistic ability to repay.
5. *Collateral.* This may be the biggest element in a decision to grant credit. Items of worth, such as real estate, equipment, and other real property, offer security to lenders. If the loan is not repaid, this collateral can be seized, sold, and credited toward the loan payment.

Lenders consider all five C's of credit, but they give each factor different weight. One particularly weak area can make the lender cautious, and one very strong area can gain the lender's confidence.

PROS AND CONS OF CONSUMER CREDIT

he advantages and disadvantages of using credit are discussed in the following pages.

Advantages of Using Credit

Using credit has several benefits.

It encourages better future financial planning. Buying on credit forces consumers to work payments into their budgeting. Doing so may help them set up a more accurate plan for the future.

TIP

Credit card companies offer vastly different terms. Some offer rates of less than 5 percent; others charge 20 percent or more if you typically do not pay off your balance within the grace period. Shop for low-interest cards if you are incapable of paying the debt in full each month. Also be aware of additional fees, (over limit fees, late fees, etc.) when you comparison shop among credit card choices.

Buyers can enjoy goods while paying for them. Installment credit allows people with small incomes to purchase relatively high-priced, durable goods. When they are able to purchase on credit, consumers can enjoy a higher standard of living. The alternative is to save first and pay cash at the time of purchase. Some advise that the alternative is much wiser because the buyer does not pay any interest or finance charges and actually can receive interest on savings accumulated for the purchase.

Credit transactions are often more convenient than cash or check transactions. It is convenient and sometimes necessary to pay by credit card. Purchases made on the Internet and hotel reservations usually require a credit card. Some of these transactions may be possible only with a credit card.

Credit is useful to help meet emergencies. Illness, accidents, and deaths give rise to unexpected expenses, and unemployment eliminates anticipated income. Families with little or no reserve have to rely on credit. After using their savings, they turn to credit lending institutions.

Credit can allow free use of someone else's money. Any credit that is used and paid for before interest is due allows the borrower the free use of someone else's money. An open account at a department store may allow the borrower to use the store's money for a month or more without charge to purchase goods. The time lag between buying on credit and having to pay the bill before interest is charged can be as long as 90 days, and even, in some cases, one year or more.

To obtain protection against faulty or fraudulent transactions. Most credit cards allow consumers to dispute a transaction that is faulty or fraudulent. This protection provides a level of security for the consumer.

To consolidate debts. If the consumer can obtain a reasonable APR, consolidating several small debts onto one credit card makes sense. Lowering the interest paid, as well as assuring that no bill slips through the cracks, can help consumers manage their financial situation.

Switching balances to competing credit card companies can reduce finance charges and may be helpful to those who carry a credit card balance. True or false?

True. Credit card companies often greatly reduce the annual percentage rate on credit cards if a balance is transferred. Dropping the rate from 17.9 percent down to 5.9 percent for a year can considerably cut down on the money you must pay these companies. Be careful, however. Some credit card companies use the lower rate as a "teaser" and then raise the rate for a variety of reasons. Always check the APR, additional fees such as late fees, over limit fees, and transfer fees.

Disadvantages of Using Credit

Using credit also has several potential pitfalls, outlined below.

Overextension of credit. When sellers try to market their goods, their task is not only one of creating desire but also of

Q+A

Making a larger down payment on an automobile loan can reduce substantially the amount of interest you pay over the life of the loan. True or false?

True. Interest on a four-year automobile loan of $20,000 can amount to as much as $5,000 based on a rate of 10 percent. A down payment of $5,000 would reduce the principal balance to $15,000, and the savings in interest would be more than $1,000.

providing the money or credit with which consumers can buy. Before the widespread use of credit, the last defense of consumers against high-pressure selling was their inability to meet the purchase price. Installment selling has broken down this barrier, making it still easier for sellers to dispose of their wares. This development is not altogether undesirable, but when unsuspecting and trusting consumers are enticed to incur too much debt, they can get into trouble. Their financial situations and credit records reflect this difficulty.

Personal bankruptcies. Overextension of credit has led more and more families into bankruptcy. Some employers fire employees who have had more than one **garnishment,** which sometimes forces these individuals into bankruptcy.

Garnishment a legal proceeding whereby the creditor secures a court order directing the debtor's employer to withhold wages for the debtor and to pay the withheld funds to the creditor.

Debt consolidation combining several debts into one loan to reduce monthly payments.

Debt consolidation often is dangerous for consumers. Of all the consumer-credit inventions, the consolidated loan can be the most damaging and is even prohibited in some states. Debt consolidators (or adjusters) take all, or almost all, of a client's disposable income and apportion it among creditors. They are not loan companies. Certain debt-counseling groups perform this service without charge.

Unfortunately, some debt-consolidation operators try to keep their victims in dire straits. The consumer should not select a consolidation loan if the total finance charge or annual percentage rate is higher than that of the original loans. Consumers often use home equity loans to consolidate higher-interest loans. This can be advantageous, but debtors must realize that the home is subject to foreclosure if they do not make payments.

If a debtor has financial problems, various resources are available in most communities. A debtor who belongs to a union or similar organization might consult its financial counselor. Many employers now offer employee assistance programs that include financial counseling. The Consumer Credit Counseling Service (CCCS) has established offices in hundreds of communities in the United States and Canada. It sponsors counseling services that provide free counseling to clients. It may charge nominal fees if debt liquidation is required. Counselors cannot be employed by any creditor of the person or family being counseled. A financial-counseling service can

www.aiccca.org

The website for the Association of Independent Consumer Credit Counseling Agencies (AICCCA) encourages quality credit-counseling services. This membership organization strives to make the consumer financially literate and provides numerous services.

- reduce the risk of personal bankruptcy by providing sound alternative programs
- minimize the garnishment and assignment of wages and salaries
- relieve employers of bothersome and expensive participation in these procedures
- assist individuals and families who are in credit difficulties by recharting their financial program, returning their accounts to current status, and preventing loss of credit standing
- restore self-reliance, confidence, and well-being to individuals and families
- reduce absenteeism and accident risks and generally increase worker efficiency and self-respect
- educate consumers, including the consumers of tomorrow, in the intelligent use of credit

At the same time, these measures strengthen the economic fabric of the community.

Credit life insurance a type of insurance that covers the unpaid balance of a loan in the event of the borrower's death.

Misuse of credit life insurance. Credit life insurance, in itself a valid protective device, has led to abuses such as lender's requiring excessive insurance, overcharging by insurance companies, and nonpayment of claims. Credit unions absorb credit insurance costs. Other lending institutions charge for the insurance.

TIP Do not purchase credit life insurance, as it is typically not cost-effective to do so.

Credit life insurance is big business. Though a creditor usually can legally require consumers to have insurance as security for a debt, to require purchase of the insurance from the creditor or someone named by the creditor is illegal in most states. Consumers have the option of pledging an existing policy or buying coverage elsewhere. If the creditor requires the insurance and it is purchased from the creditor, its cost has to be included in the calculation of the loan's total finance charge and annual percentage rate.

One-sided contracts. One-sided contracts are typical in credit transactions. Sellers who offer installment loans use powerful legal instruments, and the laws and the courts are on the seller's side. A conditional sales contract, or security agreement, is so complicated that few, if any, buyers read or understand it. Buyers who are able to meet their payments regularly have no difficulty, but buyers who are unable to meet payments because of illness or unemployment feel the legal power of the contract they have signed. Even though they may have made all but one payment, if they then default, the merchandise may be repossessed and all previous payments forfeited.

One-sided contract an agreement that favors one of the two parties involved.

The Federal Trade Commission's Credit Practices Rule has dramatically changed the manner in which creditors operate. It prohibited certain provisions in consumer contracts and changed the manner in which co-signers' responsibilities and late fees could be determined. This and similar rules developed by the Federal Reserve Board and the Federal Home Loan Bank Board improved one-sided contracts to place debtors on a more equal footing with creditors.

Debt collection deception. Prior to passage of the Fair Debt Collection Practices Act (FDCPA), **third-party debt collectors** legally used many ruses to obtain information on debts and debtors. Typically, third-party collectors receive 50 percent to 75 percent of the total amount they are able to collect. It was common for collectors to harass debtors at their workplace; humiliate them by contacting friends, relatives, and neighbors; make threatening phone calls; and write intimidating letters.

Third-party debt collector a company or an individual hired as an outside agent (not an employee) to collect a debt.

U.S. shoppers run up bills that total hundreds of billions of dollars a year, and not all of these debts are paid as promised. Therefore, collection agencies obviously are needed. Most are reputable agencies performing an unpleasant but necessary task. The legitimate need for debt collection does not give collectors the right to harass, threaten, or intimidate debtors.

Discrimination in lending. Until the late 1970s, women and minorities were challenged in their attempts to gain economic independence by discrimination on the part of lending institutions. Many people were denied full participation in obtaining credit. The Equal Credit Opportunity Act (ECOA) makes it illegal for banks, retailers, and other lenders to deny or terminate credit on the basis of gender or marital status, age, race, color, religion, or national origin, or because one is on welfare. Although these types of discrimination are illegal, they still exist because acts of discrimination are often left unchallenged. Consumers should know the specifics of this law so that they will not accept discrimination.

If your automatic teller machine (ATM) card is lost or stolen, the most you will lose is $50. True or false?

False. Unless you report the loss within two business days, you could lose much more.

Loan sharking. Creditors are able to take a number of legal actions to assure that they receive amounts they are owed. Although these actions may place the debtor at a disadvantage, creditors who obey the law are not loan sharks. Loan sharking is the act of lending money at rates of interest and under conditions of repayment that are strictly illegal.

The IRS has removed the tax exempt status of several credit counseling services. The IRS found that these companies were preying on vulnerable consumers for the company's own benefit, while allegedly complying with bankruptcy reform legislation that requires consumers to seek credit counseling before pursuing bankruptcy protection.

FYI

All too often the person least able to afford usurious interest rates is the one who, in desperation, borrows from a loan shark. Sometimes the threat of physical violence keeps the debtor from going to the police to expose the illegal activity. Loan sharking is one of the mainstays of the underworld in its illegal operations.

Credit Abuses

Not all buyers are honest. Some people deliberately abuse the use of credit. These include individuals who fail to pay or refuse to repay money or pay for the goods they have received. Some people buy goods on the installment plan, make a minimum down payment, and then fail to pay any more until the goods are repossessed, thereby securing use of the merchandise for what is, in effect, a small rental fee. Although the consumer continues to be liable for the amount owed, plus any expenses, these "deadbeats" presume the creditor will simply forgive the debt. Generally, the debtor is legally obligated for the payment of the debt plus the creditor's attorney's fees, repossession fees, public notification fees, court costs, and so on. Thus, the amount owed can surpass the original obligation—and the debtor will no longer have the product. Losses such as these constitute one of the expenses of the lender, for which all of that lender's customers pay in the form of higher prices.

BANKRUPTCY

Often called "the 10-year mistake" (because it stays on a consumer's credit report for 10 years), bankruptcy is the final step for many in resolving their debt problems. The number of bankruptcy filings has increased to such a level that some bankruptcy courts have to open on Saturdays to handle the overflow. According to U.S. Bankruptcy Court data, nearly one million bankruptcy cases were

CASE STUDY Deceptive Mortgages

Kurt and Vicki Oliver may lose their home to a bank foreclosure, thanks to an unscrupulous mortgage broker. Like many other consumers these days, the Olivers had no idea they were in a "toxic" mortgage until it was too late.

Based on the misleading information given them by a mortgage lender, the Olivers believed they were refinancing their home with a 30-year adjustable rate loan on which they would pay only interest for the first five years, with interest rates of 1 percent for the first year and increasing to 4 percent for subsequent years. Of course, such a plan would lower their payments dramatically.

In actuality, the 1 percent interest period was only for the first 30 days, and when the rate increased to 7.15 percent during the second month, their mortgage payment also significantly increased. The broker had lied to them, but in turn they had signed the papers without fully reading the contract. Victims of predatory lending, the Olivers were forced to pay a prepayment penalty of $7,500, plus fees and other costs, to refinance again with a different and reputable company. Their new fixed-rate loan at 6.5 percent costs them $350 more per month than their original loan, on which the interest rate was 6 percent. They are having difficulty meeting the increased payment and may lose their home.

The Federal Trade Commission has issued a warning to lenders about deceptive mortgage advertisements that give a false impression of true cost of a home loan. Furthermore, the FTC has enforced rules against predatory lenders and has refunded money back to consumers.

QUESTIONS

1. What is the responsibility of the consumers in this example?
2. What do you think should happen to the lender in this example?
3. Do you think the FTC does enough to protect consumers?
4. In your opinion, what will be the long- and short-term effects of the predatory mortgage loan on the consumers?

Source: CNN Money. Retrieved Sept. 17, 2007, from http://money.cnn.com/2007/09/12/real_estate/surprising_face_of_foreclosure_Olivers/index.htm.

filed in the 12 months ending June 30, 2008, up 28 percent from the previous 12 months. Cases are likely to continue to increase with consumers facing new economic challenges, including increasing unemployment and an unpredictable stock market, coupled with greater acceptance of personal debt and increased spending.

www.abiworld.org

This site is sponsored by the American Bankruptcy Institute (ABI), the largest multidisciplinary, nonpartisan organization focused on bankruptcy education, research, and analysis. The site offers current information on bankruptcy issues.

Bankruptcy law has existed since the mid-1500s in England. Seizure and sale of property and distribution of the proceedings to creditors was carried out by a bankruptcy commissioner. In 1604, a law was passed to increase the penalty for noncompliance with the commissioner's orders: the cutting off of the debtor's ear. In a less barbaric move, in the 19th century the United States created debtors' prisons, which existed until approximately 1866. Bankruptcy legislation in the 1920s and 1930s, along with the Bankruptcy Act of 1978, established Chapter 7 and Chapter 13 bankruptcies. A 1984 amendment added several new categories of nondischargeable debts.

In an effort to suppress the rise in bankruptcy filings, President George W. Bush signed the Bankruptcy Abuse Prevention and Consumer Protection Act, which went into effect in October 2005. The major intent of this bankruptcy reform is to require people who can afford to make some payments toward their debt to make these payments, while still affording them the right to have the rest of their debt erased.

One of the most important changes is that the court no longer determines if a consumer can file for Chapter 7 (complete liquidation) bankruptcy. Under the new law, consumers are subject to a two-part means test that uses predefined formulas to determine (1) if 25 percent of the consumer's income can be paid to unsecured debt and (2) if their income is above the state's median. If these two conditions are met, Chapter 7 bankruptcy is not an option. Additional changes include a more stringent restriction on the homestead exemption (protection of home equity); mandatory credit counseling six months prior to applying for bankruptcy; and, before debts are dissolved, mandatory attendance in money management classes at the consumer's expense. Finally, to prevent serial filers, consumers cannot refile bankruptcy for eight years.

*Claims on property can be obtained via **liens** (such as **mechanic's liens**) and **levies**. A levy is more powerful than a lien in that it forces a sale to allow the creditor to collect on the debt. Liens and levies require the creditor to take a series of steps. Consumers should attempt to rectify the situation, if possible, before it progresses to this level.*

FYI

Detractors of bankruptcy reform argue that creditors solicit consumers with excessive offers of credit and thus should absorb the debt they encourage. Proponents of bankruptcy reform feel consumers should take responsibility for their debts; that bankruptcy hurts everyone since creditors who absorb losses then pass these costs on to other consumers. Regardless of your view, it is important to understand the differences between Chapter 7 and Chapter 13 bankruptcies.

Mechanic's lien a claim one person has upon the property of another person, often for unpaid bills due the claimant for work performed.

Lien a notice attached to property (usually a house) creating a record that a creditor claims money is owed. Most liens must be resolved before a property can be sold and the title can be transferred. Liens can be posted for property taxes, IRS payments, and child support.

Levy a judgment creditor's record of attachment on personal property. Levies can be made on bank accounts, safe deposit boxes, and real and personal property. The property is sold, and the creditor is paid out of the proceeds.

Chapter 7 bankruptcy. When people hear the term *bankruptcy,* they typically think of a complete liquidation of property and an immediate dismissal of debts. This is Chapter 7 bankruptcy. Chapter 7 is permitted only under the conditions stated above. Chapter 7 takes about six months to complete and involves filing and administrative fees ranging from $1,000 to $2,000. A bankruptcy trustee is assigned to the case and reviews the filing documents. Nonexempt property is turned over to the trustee and sold, and the creditors are paid off. Exempt property (i.e., allowable equity in a house, the debtor's car, and jewelry) varies by state; most states specify a value of assets that the filer is allowed to retain. Once bankruptcy is filed, creditors must stop collection actions. Consumers cannot refile for Chapter 7 bankruptcy for at least six years.

Chapter 13 bankruptcy. This type of bankruptcy, called the "wage earner plan," involves a reorganization. Debtors wishing to file bankruptcy who do not meet the criteria established for Chapter 7 must instead file under Chapter 13. Like Chapter 7, Chapter 13 stops creditors from proceeding with collection actions (and stops their calls and mail). After filing, a bankruptcy trustee is assigned, and the filing papers are reviewed. Disposable income (money left after reasonable expenses are deducted) is given to the trustee. The trustee makes payments to the creditors and supervises disposable income.

The filer retains his property, but, in exchange, creditors must be paid off over a specified period (usually five years or until debts are paid). Creditors must be paid an amount at least as much as the value of the debtor's nonexempt property. At the end of the specified period, if all required payments have been made, the court dismisses the remaining unpaid debt.

THE DECISION TO BUY ON CREDIT

Whether buying on credit is wise depends on many factors. It depends partially on a person's income. Those whose income is large enough to permit them to buy all necessities and a reasonable number of comforts out of income and savings should pay cash most often. Cash buyers get more merchandise for their money. An individual who has sufficient income and patience to save the purchase price of an item in advance gains in many ways. Consumers who save instead of incurring debt receive interest or capital appreciation on their savings rather than paying interest on debt. For people who lack the income to maintain a cash reserve, purchasing on credit may be the only alternative to doing without.

For the lowest income group, whose weekly income is small, few alternatives are available to the more expensive method of installment buying. For this group, the answer as to whether to buy on credit is most elusive. Installment buying, even though it is expensive, often helps consumers in this group, particularly those who are unable to save in anticipation of a purchase. Installment buying combines immediate satisfaction with a method of "forced" saving.

Membership in a credit union allows borrowing at rates that are competitive with those other lending sources offer. The personal loan departments of commercial banks usually charge rates slightly higher than credit unions and savings-and-loan associations. Consumers should compare the various rates for personal loans to the finance charges on the installment purchase plan they are considering. The Truth-in-Lending Act guarantees consumers the necessary information to decide where they can obtain financing at the lowest interest rate for any credit transaction. Internet shopping can yield lower rates than shopping for loans locally. The prudent consumer will understand fully all costs involved in Internet loans and will verify that the lender is honest and reliable.

TIP When shopping for any type of credit, compare the annual percentage rate (APR) and the total finance charges.

Loan origination fee an amount some creditors charge for offering a loan.

When shopping for a loan, consumers should determine if the lender has any special provisions. For example, some lenders charge prepayment penalties; that is, if the loan is paid in full prior to the full term, a higher rate of interest is charged. Lenders may also charge a **loan origination fee.** This fee can be 1 percent or more of the cost of the loan and is due at the time of signing the loan contract. On mortgage loans, these fees, often called "points," can cost consumers thousands of dollars.

TIP Terms on credit contracts are negotiable, especially if the consumer has an excellent credit rating. Do not accept the idea that charges initiated by banks or other lenders are "standard" and not negotiable.

Rule of 78 a common method of determining amounts to be rebated to debtors who pay off loans early.

Some lenders use a questionable practice known as the **Rule of 78.** During certain economic conditions, this rule is popular among banking institutions. Suppose you purchase an automobile for $22,000. The bank requires you to make a $2,000 down payment;

The Fair Debt Collection Practices Act

The Fair Debt Collection Practices Act prohibits debt collectors from engaging in unfair, deceptive, or abusive practices, including overcharging, harassment, and disclosing consumers' debts to third parties.

Prior to 1978, debt collection practices often included abuse, unnecessary harassment, invasion of privacy, and similar unconscionable actions. Late-night and early-morning telephone calls, requests that neighbors assist with payments due to the creditor, placement of large "payments due" signs on the debtor's home, and other ploys were all too common. These problems continue today but now are illegal as a result of the Fair Debt Collection Practices Act (FDCPA).

The FDCPA applies only to third-party collectors. For example, collection agencies are required to comply, but the creditor itself is not. Most of the flagrant abuses in the past, however, were perpetrated by third parties. Under the law, third-party debt collectors may not:

- use threats of violence to harm anyone or anyone's property or reputation
- publish a list of consumers that specifies delinquent accounts
- use obscene or profane language
- repeatedly use the telephone to annoy anyone
- telephone any person without identifying the caller
- advertise the debt

A debt collector may not make false statements when collecting a debt. For example, the debt collector cannot:

- falsely imply that the debt collector represents the U.S. government or state government
- falsely imply that the debt collector is an attorney
- falsely imply that the debtor has committed a crime
- falsely represent that the debt collector operates or works for a credit bureau
- misrepresent the amount of the debt
- represent that papers being sent are legal forms, such as a summons, when they are not
- represent that papers being sent are not legal forms when they are

A debt collector may not say that:

- the debtor will be arrested or imprisoned if the debt is not paid
- the debt collector will seize, garnish, attach, or sell property or wages, unless the debt collector or the creditor intends to do so and it is legal to do so
- any action will be taken that cannot be taken legally

A debt collector may not:

- give false credit information about the debtor to anyone
- send anything that looks like an official document that any court or agency of the United States, or any state or local government, might send
- use any false name

A debtor has the right to sue a debt collector in a state or federal court within one year from the date the law was violated. The debtor may recover money for the damage suffered as well as court costs and attorney's fees. A group of people may sue in a class action against a debt collector and recover money for damages.

Generally, the Federal Trade Commission enforces this act. Many states also have debt collection laws of their own. Therefore, if you have a complaint, contacting the Attorney General's Office first might be best, to determine your rights under state law. If your state has no collections law, complaints about unfair practices by third-party collectors should be directed to the Federal Trade Commission, Credit Practices Division, 600 Pennsylvania Ave., N.W., Washington, DC 20580.

thus, the total loan is $20,000. Now suppose that you decide to take out a one-year loan with a 7 percent annual percentage rate. Not taking into account the effect of compounding, the total interest charge is therefore $1,400. (Compounding is a common practice by which lenders effectively charge interest on unpaid interest.) The Rule of 78 method is to divide the interest into 78 parts and to allocate between 1 and 12 parts to each month of the loan term: 12 + 11 + 10 + 9 + 8 + 7 + 6 + 5 + 4 + 3 + 2 + 1 = 78. If you repay the loan in month 1, the prepayment charge will be 12/78 of $1,400. This is more than 15 percent

There Oughta Be a Law . . .

Fair Credit Billing Act

The Fair Credit Billing Act establishes procedures for resolving mistakes on credit card accounts.

Prior to 1975, one of the major problems for consumers in using credit cards was that billing errors, often blamed on computers, occurred frequently. Many consumers received bills for merchandise they had not purchased or received or were charged twice for one item they had purchased. When these consumers wrote to the credit card company to correct the mistake, they often received no response, and the incorrect charges, with interest, accumulated month after month.

In 1975 Congress passed the Fair Credit Billing Act (FCBA). Under the law, the following are considered billing errors:

- charges not made or authorized by the account holder
- charges that are incorrectly identified or for which the wrong amount or date is shown
- charges for goods or services not accepted or not delivered as agreed
- computational or similar errors
- failure to properly reflect payments or other credits, such as returns
- not mailing or delivering bills to the consumer's current address
- charges for which the consumer requests an explanation or written proof of purchase

A customer who wishes to dispute an item must send a written notice of billing error to the creditor. The notice must reach the creditor within 60 days after the first bill containing the error was mailed. It should be sent to the address provided on the bill for billing error notices. The following information must be included:

- name and account number
- a statement that the bill contains a billing error and the dollar amount involved
- the reasons why the consumer believes a mistake has been made

The creditor must acknowledge the consumer's letter within 30 days after it is received, unless the problem is resolved within that period. In any case, within two billing cycles (but not more than 90 days), the creditor must resolve the dispute—that is, correct the mistake or explain why the bill is believed to be correct, after having conducted a reasonable investigation. The consumer may withhold payment of the amount in dispute, including the affected portions of minimum payments and finance charges, until the dispute is resolved. Any part of the bill that is not disputed, including finance and other charges on undisputed amounts, must be paid.

While a bill is being disputed, the creditor may not threaten to damage the consumer's credit rating or report the amount as delinquent to anyone. The creditor, however, is permitted to report that the bill is in dispute. If the bill is found to contain a billing error, the creditor must write to the consumer explaining the corrections to be made on the account.

If the creditor investigates and believes the bill is correct, the consumer must be told promptly in writing how much is owed and why. At that point, the disputed amount, plus any finance charges that accumulated while it was disputed, is officially owed. If, however, the consumer continues to disagree, he or she must contact the creditor in writing within 10 days. The creditor may begin collection procedures. If, however, the creditor reports the amount to a credit bureau as delinquent, the amount in dispute also must be reported.

Any creditor who fails to follow the FCBA dispute-settlement procedure may not collect the amount in dispute or any finance charges on it, up to $50, even if the bill turns out to be correct.

---

of the loan—even though only 1/12 (or 8.5 percent) of the debt repayment schedule is over. After the second month, only 1/6 (or 17 percent) of the debt repayment period is over, but you would be obligated to pay nearly 30 percent of the interest if you decided to repay after two months. If possible, avoid this clause by negotiating it out of the contract.

SUMMARY

The total amount of debt in the United States has increased dramatically in the past several decades. Prior to World War II, credit was used by the wealthy as a convenience and by others out of necessity. Since that time, most consumers have

Disputes over the quality of goods or services received are not necessarily billing errors; therefore, the dispute procedure may not apply. If, however, unsatisfactory goods or services are purchased with a credit card, the FCBA allows the consumer to take the same legal actions against the credit card issuer as could be taken under state law against the seller. If state law would permit a consumer to withhold payment to a seller for defective merchandise or to pay and sue for a refund, withholding payment to the credit card issuer (including finance charges) up to the amount owed on the purchase is permitted. The seller, however, must be given an opportunity to remedy the problem. Also, unless the seller is the card issuer (such as a company that issues a gasoline credit card), the item must have been bought in the consumer's home state or within 100 miles of the current mailing address, and the amount charged must have been more than $50.

The FCBA also requires creditors to do the following for their customers:

- give periodic written notices and at other specified times, describing consumer rights to dispute billing errors
- provide a statement for each billing period in which an amount of more than $1 is owed
- mail or deliver bills at least 14 days before the payment is due
- credit all payments to the account as of the date received
- promptly credit or refund overpayments

A creditor who violates any FCBA provision may be sued for damages resulting from the violation, plus twice the amount of any finance charge (not less than $100 or more than $1,000). The court also may order the creditor to pay the consumer's attorney's fees and costs.

In addition to the aforementioned rights, a lesser-known but perhaps more important provision of the FCBA is the cash discount clause, which allows merchants to give customers who pay cash a discount on their purchase. It costs merchants money to let customers use credit. That extra cost is passed along to consumers in the form of higher prices for everyone, just like all other overhead expenses. Supporters of discounts-for-cash programs do not think it is fair to have cash-paying customers bear the extra costs for services used only by charge account customers.

Discounts for cash benefit merchants and consumers alike. Merchants can advertise their policy, when customers pay cash, which might bring in more business. In addition, merchants have immediate cash in return for their goods and services. The principal benefit of consumers' paying cash, however, is that merchants save the fee they otherwise would pay to credit card companies.

Consumers who pay cash have the benefit of the discount and do not have to face the bill at the end of the month. They also may find themselves spending less simply because they must have cash to make their purchases at a discount. Despite all the benefits, however, discounts-for-cash programs are not common.

According to the FCBA, merchants' cash-discount programs must conform to the following guidelines:

- The merchant must post a sign near each public entrance and at all locations where purchases are paid for, stating, "We give discounts for cash," or something similar.
- The merchant must make the discount available to all customers, not just credit card holders.
- The merchant can limit discounts to certain types of products or services or to certain stores in a chain. For example, a gas station operator could decide to give discounts on gas but not on batteries and tires. Whatever the policy, it must be stated on the posted signs.
- The merchant can offer an unlimited discount.

readily accepted credit. Most recently, in the 21st century, credit is used to such an extent that consumer debt it at an all time high. Families are using credit to pay for necessities.

The suggested level of safety for consumer installment debt is 15 percent or less of take-home pay. The average level of installment debt for consumers, however, has exceeded the recommended maximum since the early 1980s, with the result that many families are hopelessly overextended. This overextension, combined with the deep recession in 2008, has caused tremendous strains on the economy.

Formal sources of consumer credit include commercial banks, finance companies, credit unions, consumer finance companies, pawnbrokers, and payday lenders. Internet shopping for all types of loans has become increasingly popular.

One of the most cost-effective loans is a home equity loan. The terms are competitive and the interest is tax deductible up to limits determined by Congress. One caveat: If you fail to make payments as agreed, the lender may foreclose on your house.

FYI

Consumers use credit for a variety of reasons. However, consumers also abuse credit, and creditors also engage in abuses of the system, many of which violate federal or state consumer protection laws. Various federal credit laws are in place, clarifying consumers' rights and responsibilities.

Unfortunately, many consumers become overextended, exhaust all other options, and turn to bankruptcy. Chapter 7 bankruptcy involves a liquidation of assets to pay debts, whereas Chapter 13 bankruptcy entails a reorganization in which payments are made to creditors over a set period of time. In both cases, a bankruptcy stays on the consumer's credit report for 10 years.

Each consumer must decide whether and to what extent to use credit. When consumers do use credit, they should shop around for the best terms, including the lowest annual percentage rate, lowest total finance charges, and most favorable terms, including low prepayment penalties and loan origination fees.

ITEMS FOR REVIEW & DISCUSSION

1. Define the role of consumer credit in the U.S. economy. Delineate some formal sources of consumer credit and their characteristics.
2. Identify some reasons for using and for not using credit.
3. Identify some problems associated with debt-consolidation loans.
4. Discuss some of the abuses of credit by sellers.
5. Identify the services that consumer credit counseling agencies provide. If individuals go too far into debt, what steps might they take to correct the problem?
6. State the purpose of a credit bureau. Describe the provisions under federal law that protect consumers from ruthless creditors.
7. Describe which credit terms consumers should compare when they are shopping for a loan.
8. In earlier years, what was the attitude toward debt in the United States? Why might the United States have developed a "debt syndrome"?
9. Identify the two types of bankruptcy and the differences between them.
10. What are the "5 C's of credit" and why are they important?
11. Discuss how best to prevent identity theft. To what organizations could a victim of identity theft turn for help?

EXPLORING PERSONAL VALUES: PROJECTS

1. Read the following three statements and decide if you agree or disagree with each of them. Explain your answer.
   a. With the possible exception of a house and car, credit should not be used as a means of purchasing goods and services.
   b. Credit should be used frequently because it allows a person to enjoy goods and services while paying for them.
   c. The cost of credit is too high for the service it provides.
2. Interview a creditor and determine the important provisions of credit buying that you should consider. With your fellow classmates, discuss the provisions that the creditor shared with you and discuss the pros and cons of buying on credit. Explain why you feel the way you do about buying on credit.

3. In your journal, trace your personal credit history. Do you plan to continue this way? Why or why not?
4. List all the major purchases you plan to make in the next 5 to 10 years. Plan how you will pay for each major purchase.
5. "Money won't bring you happiness, but neither will poverty." Write your reaction to this statement by Venita Van Caspel.
6. Interview a debt counselor or loan officer to determine the reasons consumers get into trouble with debt.
7. List all the places a person can borrow money in your community, and find out what each lending agency charges for a $1,500 loan for one year to be paid back in monthly installments.
8. Consumers sometimes abuse credit by not paying for goods, using them, and allowing them to be repossessed. Discuss this with several loan officers in your area to determine the remedies available to creditors under repossession proceedings in your state.
9. Research five major credit card companies and compare them from a credit card holder's perspective. Discuss your findings with the class.
10. Choose something you would like to buy through an installment plan (a television, for example). Call around and compare the plans for that item. If you were really going to buy it, where would you buy the product? Also, ask the credit retailers how important selling on credit is to their business.

ADDITIONAL SOURCES OF INFORMATION

Bertola, Giuseppe, Richard Disney, and Charles Grant. *The Economics of Consumer Credit.* Cambridge, MA: The MIT Press, 2008.

Casanova, Karen. *Letting Go of Debt: Growing Richer One Day at a Time.* Center City, MN: Hazelden, 2000.

Detweiler, Gerri. *The Ultimate Credit Handbook: Cut Your Debt and Have a Lifetime of Great Credit.* New York: Plume Books, 2003.

Leonard, Robin, and Deanne Loonin. *Money Troubles: Legal Strategies to Cope with Your Debts.* Berkeley, CA: Nolo, 2003.

Loberg, Kristin. *Identity Theft: How to Protect Your Name, Your Credit and Your Vital Information, and What to Do When Someone Hijacks Any of These.* Los Angeles: Silver Lake Pub., 2004.

Mann, Bruce H. *Republic of Debtors: Bankruptcy in the Age of American Independence.* Cambridge, MA: Harvard University Press, 2003.

Newman, Michael W. *What You Can Do to Conquer Your Credit and Debt Problems.* Scotts Valley, CA: CreateSpace, 2007.

Sommer, Henry J. *Consumer Bankruptcy: The Complete Guide to Chapter 7 and Chapter 13 Personal Bankruptcy.* Hoboken, NJ: John Wiley & Sons, 1994.

Sullivan, Teresa A., Elizabeth Warren, and Jay Lawrence Westbrook. *The Fragile Middle Class: Americans in Debt.* New Haven, CT: Yale University Press, 2001.

Ventura, John, and Mary Reed. *Managing Debt for Dummies.* Hoboken, NJ: John Wiley & Sons, 2007.

> Be it ever so humble, there's no place like home.
>
> **STEPHEN FOSTER,** SONG WRITER

KEY TERMS

adjustable-rate mortgage (ARM)
assumption of mortgage
closing costs
condominium
conventional real estate loan
cooperative apartment (co-op)
FHA loan
fixed-rate mortgage
foreclosure
home equity loan
HOW plan
jumbo loan
margin
mortgage
mortgagee, mortgagor
owner-financing loan
points
prepayment penalty
title insurance
VA loan

The following concepts will be developed in this chapter:

1. It typically requires more than one income source to purchase a house that fulfills a family's needs.
2. Homeowners frequently decide whether to rent or own on the basis of noneconomic issues.
3. Even slight variations in interest rates affect monthly payments and the total interest paid over the life of a mortgage.

After having read this chapter, you should be able to accomplish the following objectives:

1. Cite several reasons why housing is so expensive.
2. Identify and state the meaning of all costs associated with a mortgage loan.
3. Develop a list of questions that a person shopping for a mortgage should ask prospective lenders.
4. Identify a number of advantages and disadvantages of owning and of renting housing.
5. List alternatives to owning a single-family detached dwelling.

THE AMERICAN DREAM

The line quoted above from Stephen Foster's song "Home Sweet Home" captures a basic psychological urge: to own a home. The world over, people value their home and its contents. The concept of "home sweet home" is a very real part of the American dream. People in all age groups have the urge to own their dwellings. Many people want to live in a house rather than an apartment. They want to buy rather than to rent.

In the first decade of the 21st century, home ownership experienced drastic fluctuations, with real estate prices shooting up and then down again. The advent of easy credit and subprime mortgages for potential home buyers had the effect of expanding the pool of home buyers and then shrinking it again as individuals defaulted on mortgages. It is not the purpose of this book to discuss the reasons for or the outcome of the mortgage crisis or the extreme conditions that have prevailed over the housing market during the past decade. Instead, we will discuss home ownership as it works during average times, and hope that readers encounter conditions closer to average than those extreme fluctuations.

Home Ownership

Dream Versus Reality

Many advocates of home ownership suggest that it is an excellent investment. During many decades in the United States' economic history, home ownership has yielded higher rates of returns than stock ownership, certificates of deposit, savings, and many other investments. However, shifts in the economy and factors in specific geographic areas affect whether a home appreciates or depreciates, and there is no guarantee that an investment in a home will be profitable.

The dream and the reality of home ownership often are in conflict. Many homes have defects and require repairs and renovation. During periods of high interest rates, purchasing a home is an unrealistic dream for the average American. In the early 1980s, home mortgage rates surpassed 15 percent and home prices were high. As a result, fewer than 5 percent of Americans could afford to purchase a house. In the first decade of the 21st century, interest rates were at single-digit levels, but home prices remained high. The net result was that many potential homeowners were still unable to purchase a house. The U.S. Department of Housing and Urban Development reports that the national home ownership rate has consistently been around 68 percent since 2000. For minority households, the rate is lower, at approximately 50 percent.

What Can Buyers Afford to Pay?

Regarding the purchase of a home, several rules of thumb may apply. Although many complex factors contributed to the recent mortgage foreclosure crisis, had lenders and borrowers adhered to guidelines such as these many foreclosures might have been avoided.

1. First-time buyers should not pay more than 2.5 times their annual income. For example, if the buyer's income is $60,000, the mortgage should not exceed $150,000.
2. Buyers should not spend more than 28 percent of gross monthly income for total housing expenses. That amount includes mortgage payments, taxes, insurance, repairs, and upkeep.
3. The monthly housing expense should not exceed 28 percent of the buyer's monthly gross income, and the total of mortgage payments, taxes, home insurance, and installment payments on other debts should not exceed 36 percent of the salary.

www.lowermybills.com

The lowermybills.com website assists consumers who are shopping for lower rates on a variety of products or services, including insurance, mortgages, telephone plans, and credit cards, by connecting them to marketplace partners.

www.mbaa.org

The website for the Mortgage Bankers Association of America (MBAA) provides mortgage information to consumers. MBAA is the only mortgage association exclusively devoted to real estate finances.

Home Ownership—More Elusive Than Ever?

In the early 21st century, the median home price for existing homes in the United States was approximately $196,000. A newly constructed home cost about $240,000. Of course, these are only median prices. In some metropolitan areas, for example, San Francisco, Washington, D.C., and other parts of California, the median prices were much higher.

Most families must have at least two incomes to qualify for a mortgage. During the 1990s and even more during the first decade of this century, many lenders relaxed their qualification requirements to allow more consumers to qualify for a mortgage loan. In many cases they ignored the two guidelines that the housing expense should not exceed 28 percent and total debt payments should not exceed 36 percent of monthly income. Some lending institutions increased these percentages to unsafe numbers, loosening their restrictions to accommodate those who would not otherwise have qualified for a mortgage. Subsequently this practice led to disastrous results for many homeowners and for lenders.

Guidelines that take into consideration specific buyers' circumstances may be more helpful than the percentage rules. One, developed by the federal government and still used (see Exhibit 12.1), estimates income available for housing. This form can help a prospective homeowner to identify a reasonable amount to spend on housing.

EXHIBIT 12.1

Estimating income available for housing.

PART ONE

Dependable Monthly Income

Head of family's base pay	$ ________	
Head of family's other earnings	$ ________	
Spouse's base pay	$ ________	
Spouse's other earnings	$ ________	
All other dependable income	$ ________	
TOTAL DEPENDABLE INCOME		$ ________

PART TWO

Monthly Obligations and Salary Deductions

Federal, state, and other income taxes	$ ________	
Personal property taxes (other than real estate and automobiles)	$ ________	
Retirement payments (including Social Security)	$ ________	
Insurance premiums and insurance loan payments		
Life	$ ________	
Policy loan payments	$ ________	
Hospitalization	$ ________	
Household and other insurance (excluding home property and automobile)	$ ________	
TOTAL		$ ________

(continued)

Source: *Handbook for the Home: Yearbook of Agriculture* (Washington, D.C.: U. S. Government Printing Office), p. 101.

EXHIBIT 12.1

Estimating income available for housing, continued.

Automobile and transportation expense

Loan installment payments	$ ______
Insurance	$ ______
Taxes	$ ______
Maintenance and fuel	$ ______
Other job-related transportation (if regularly used)	$ ______
TOTAL	$ ______

Other accounts, notes, and installment payments

______	$ ______
______	$ ______
______	$ ______
TOTAL	$ ______

TOTAL MONTHLY OBLIGATIONS AND SALARY DEDUCTIONS $ ______

Deduct TOTAL MONTHLY OBLIGATIONS AND SALARY DEDUCTIONS from TOTAL DEPENDABLE INCOME. The result will be the amount of income available for HOUSING AND ALL OTHER LIVING COSTS. $ ______

PART THREE

Present Monthly Housing Expense

Rent (or mortgage principal and interest payments if you own your present home)	$ ______
Mortgage insurance premium, if owner	$ ______
Taxes and any special assessments, if owner	$ ______
Hazard insurance, if owner	$ ______
Maintenance, if owner	$ ______
TOTAL PRESENT MONTHLY HOUSING EXPENSE	$ ______

Deduct PRESENT MONTHLY HOUSING EXPENSE from HOUSING AND ALL OTHER LIVING COSTS. The result will be the amount left for ALL OTHER LIVING COSTS on the basis of the PRESENT HOUSING EXPENSE. $ ______

PART FOUR

Proposed Monthly Housing Expense

Principal, interest, and other monthly charges on the proposed financing	$ ______
Taxes and special assessments	$ ______
Hazard insurance	$ ______
Heat and utilities	$ ______
Maintenance	$ ______
TOTAL PROPOSED MONTHLY HOUSING EXPENSE	$ ______

Deduct PROPOSED MONTHLY HOUSING EXPENSE from HOUSING AND ALL OTHER LIVING COSTS in PART TWO. The result will be the amount left for ALL OTHER LIVING COSTS on the basis of the PROPOSED HOUSING EXPENSE. (Compare this figure with the amount left for all living costs under your present housing expense.) $ ______

TIP Elaborate alarm/fire security systems, in addition to the safety they provide, can reduce insurance rates 10 percent or more; thus, a system may pay for itself within a few years.

FINANCING THE PURCHASE OF A HOUSE

Conventional real estate loan a loan obtained at a bank or other lending institution that does not involve federal or state subsidies.

Jumbo loan a loan that has a mortgage amount exceeding maximum mortgage limits set by Fannie Mae and Freddie Mac.

VA loan a type of mortgage that is insured by the Department of Veterans Affairs against losses from default.

FHA loan a loan insured by the Federal Housing Administration against losses from default.

Mortgage a legal instrument that gives the lender conditional title to the property.

Mortgagor a borrower who has agreed to repay a loan under terms dictated by a contract with a mortgagee.

Mortgagee a lender of money under terms dictated by a contract with a mortgagor.

Foreclosure the act by which a lender forces the sale of a property because of default of payment.

Owner-financing loan mortgage in which the seller of the home participates.

Home equity loan a loan that often is a second mortgage, the proceeds of which are used for home improvements or other purposes.

Houses have been sold on the installment plan since the days of Julius Caesar. Most home purchases are financed through a **conventional real estate loan.** However, homes that exceed a certain set value are financed through **jumbo loans.** Other mortgages are financed with a **VA** (Veterans Affairs) **loan,** and still others with an **FHA** (Federal Housing Administration) **loan.** The remaining homes are paid for in cash or financed under some other arrangement. The usual method of financing the purchase of a house is to secure a loan from a lending agency, giving as security a **mortgage** on the property. The mortgage guarantees that if the **mortgagor** fails to pay interest and principal, the **mortgagee** may force the sale of the property, through a process called **foreclosure.**

Equity refers to the amount of a home that the mortgagor has actually paid for. The nominal owner of a $200,000 house who made a down payment of $40,000 started with a 20 percent equity in the property. The term *homeowner* is used loosely to refer to any owner who occupies a house in which the equity ranges from 100 percent to 1 percent. With most mortgages, the monthly payments for the first few years consist almost entirely of interest payments, so equity builds very slowly.

Mortgages are classified as first, second, and third. Although third mortgages are not common, many of the **owner-financing loans** that proliferated in recent years are really second mortgages, as are **home equity loans.** In these types of loans, if a borrower defaults on payments, the holder of the first mortgage may foreclose and has a prior claim over holders of second and third mortgages, meaning the lender for the first mortgage will be paid first out of the proceeds. The 1986 Tax Reform Act eliminated many loopholes, and those that were left became more popular. Home equity loans were continued as a tax shelter in most situations.

The Cost of Mortgage Loans

Although buying on installment has allowed many people who otherwise could not have done so to purchase houses, this method is expensive. For example, on a 30-year mortgage at 10 percent interest, a $120,000 loan would require a monthly payment of $1,053.08, meaning the buyer will have paid over $179,000 interest if the entire loan schedule is paid.

To calculate how much interest a borrower will pay over a period of years we must know the number of years the mortgage runs, the principal amount, and the interest rate. Exhibit 12.2 shows the cost of a $120,000 mortgage loan at varying rates of interest over a 30-year period. Most home mortgages today are for more than $120,000, but this table demonstrates the "unseen" cost of borrowing.

Exhibit 12.3 shows the monthly payments required for interest and principal at different rates of interest for periods of 15, 20, 25, and 30 years. To figure the cost per month of a mortgage, find the appropriate payment period and interest rate and multiply the amount shown by the number of thousands of dollars borrowed. Exhibit 12.4 illustrates the importance of the down payment. The down payment may be considered as the buyer's initial equity in the house. On a $100,000 home, for a 25-year, 10 percent loan, a $10,000 down payment (versus no down payment) decreases the amount of the total monthly principal and interest paid by nearly $30,000. A $20,000 down payment reduces the total amount paid by approximately $55,000.

EXHIBIT 12.2

$120,000 loan at varying interest rates over a 30-year period.

INTEREST RATE (%)	MONTHLY PAYMENT (PRINCIPAL AND INTEREST)	TOTAL PRINCIPAL AND INTEREST OVER 30 YEARS
6	$ 719.46	$ 259,005.60
7	798.36	287,409.60
8	880.51	316,983.60
9	965.54	347,594.40
10	1,053.08	379,108.80
11	1,142.78	411,400.80
12	1,234.33	444,358.80

EXHIBIT 12.3

Monthly payment for each $1,000 borrowed.

INTEREST RATE (%)	PAYMENT PERIOD (YEARS) 15	20	25	30
6	$ 8.43	$ 7.16	$ 6.44	$ 5.99
7	8.98	7.75	7.06	6.65
8	9.65	8.36	7.72	7.34
9	10.14	9.00	8.39	8.05
10	10.75	9.65	9.09	8.78
11	11.37	10.32	9.80	9.52
12	12.00	11.01	10.53	10.29

EXHIBIT 12.4

The effect of down-payment size on the cost of a $100,000 home with interest at 10 percent on a 25-year mortgage.

DOWN PAYMENT	MONTHLY PAYMENTS (PRINCIPAL AND INTEREST)	TOTAL PRINCIPAL AND INTEREST
$ 0	$ 909.00	$ 272,700
5,000	863.55	259,065
10,000	818.10	245,430
15,000	772.65	231,795
20,000	727.20	218,160

The reality is that few homeowners actually live in one home long enough to pay off a mortgage loan and realize the benefits of a large down payment. Trends toward small or no down payments and long-term mortgages have resulted in a rising rate of mortgage foreclosures.

Adjustable-Rate and Other Types of Mortgages

Mortgage instruments are based on such factors as the availability of money and the state of the economy. Depending on the financial and economic environment of the time, different mortgage instruments will be available to consumers. As a result of the mortgage industry collapse in 2008, lenders are more conservative and risk averse in their lending practices. Consumers seek **fixed-rate mortgages** because they offer the security of a fixed payment over a determined period of time. **Adjustable rate mortgages** are less predictable during times of economic upheaval.

Fixed-rate mortgage a mortgage that has a specified rate of interest for a specified number of years.

Adjustable-rate mortgage a mortgage that has rates of interest and perhaps other terms that change after a stated period of months or years.

Margin a percentage amount that a lending institution adds to the index for a loan to cover both the cost of processing the loan and the lender's profit.

The interest rates of adjustable-rate mortgages are tied to an index such as U.S. Treasury bills and also to a specified **margin.** If the index increases, the mortgage loan rate also will increase. ARMs often have caps or limits. This means that the mortgage rate can increase (or decrease) to only a certain upper (or lower) limit, or cap.

Understanding Mortgage Money

Assumption of mortgage a process in which the buyer accepts the terms of the seller's mortgage, usually after negotiating with the lender.

It pays to shop around for a mortgage loan. If the seller has a mortgage on the property, one possibility is to participate in an **assumption of mortgage.** Depending on the economy, the interest rate may be slightly lower than the buyer could obtain for a new loan, and closing costs will be substantially reduced. Most likely, however, the borrower will have to arrange for new financing with one of the usual mortgage lenders.

The conventional lending institutions, which together make the majority of all mortgage loans, typically lend 90 percent of the value of the property, thus requiring a down payment of 10 percent. The usual mortgage term is 15 to 30 years.

WWW

www.zillow.com

Buyers can use this website to locate houses for sale in specific locales. A detailed map shows surrounding locations and street information.

The Department of Veterans Affairs guarantees loans made to eligible veterans by private lenders. VA loans do not require a down payment, but the private lender may ask for a 10 percent down payment. Loan terms run up to 30 years, and interest rates vary with the market.

The Federal Housing Administration (FHA) insures loans made by private lenders up to a specified amount. FHA loans usually can be repaid over 20 to 30 years. In addition to the interest charge, the monthly payment includes a percentage to cover FHA mortgage insurance.

Points charges equal to a stated percentage of the loan.

One way for lenders to increase profits is to charge a one-time fee—often called a premium, or **points.** One point is equal to 1 percent of the loan amount. To illustrate: A two-point charge on a $50,000 loan means that the borrower must pay $1,000 ($50,000 x 2 percent) to the bank to obtain the loan. Points must be paid when the mortgage contract is signed.

Borrowers may also pay points to "buy down" the interest rate. Typically, a lender agrees to reduce the interest rate 1/8 percent for each point paid up front. In other words, a 7 1/4 percent interest rate would be lowered to 7 percent with the payment of two points. Whether it is advisable for a borrower to pay points depends on the specific situation. The advantages and disadvantages of paying points to lower an interest rate vary depending upon factors such as current interest rates, the borrower's credit rating, how long the home will be owned, and so forth.

If you are selling a home, asking your real estate broker to agree to a lower commission can save you a thousand dollars or more. True or false?

True. Assume that a real estate broker charges 6 percent of the sale price when selling a home. On a $180,000 sale, that is $10,800 in commission. If, after negotiating, you get the broker to drop down to 5 percent, the commission is just $9,000, a net savings of $1,800. Alternatively, ask the broker to reduce the commission by a dollar amount if an offer below the asking price is being considered.

When shopping for a mortgage loan, borrowers would do well to ask at least five lenders the same basic questions, pertaining to interest rate, point charges, length of loan, "balloon" clauses, variable-interest clauses, margins, how credit scores are determined, and whether the loan can be repaid early without penalty. By making a table with the responses, borrowers can compare the options readily and choose the one that seems most favorable. This simple strategy may save a consumer many thousands of dollars.

Mortgage-Lending Practices

Prospective buyers should be aware of certain mortgage-lending practices. Many borrowers do not know that when they sign a mortgage contract, they not only pass conditional title to the lender, but they also sign a personal note, usually called a bond. In case of default, the lender can hold the borrower personally liable if the forced sale of the property does not yield enough money to pay the loan. Sometimes mortgage companies require borrowers to purchase insurance coverage at prices higher than market rates.

Another practice is to include a clause denying the borrower the right to pay off the loan faster than the mortgage provides. If a borrower inherits $20,000, it may be to his advantage to apply that sum toward reducing the mortgage and thereby reducing the total interest payments. If a borrower does not inquire in advance and does not read the contract, he or she might find that the lender refuses to let the mortgage be reduced or that a substantial **prepayment penalty** must be paid. This amount is often equal to six months' interest.

Prepayment penalty an amount the buyer pays to the lending institution for the privilege of paying off a mortgage loan before it is due.

Foreclosure losses can be prevented by creating an insurance fund. By paying relatively small premiums, borrowers can build up a fund from which mortgagors can draw interest and principal payments for as long as 36 months.

Mortgage contracts are lengthy documents, drawn in legal language and printed in fine type. An estimated 9 in 10 borrowers do not read the mortgage loan contract. If a borrower defaults, the lender may point to clause after clause in the contract that are to the borrower's disadvantage. If homeowners were to understand the true nature of a mortgage, foreclosures would be fewer and, perhaps, contracts would be changed to be more equitable.

Consumers can protect themselves from predatory lenders by asking Congress to (1) require lenders to qualify consumers only for loans they can afford, both during the introductory rate and after it expires and (2) provide borrowers with the legal means to sue lenders who use deceptive loan conditions. As of 2009, measures to aid families facing foreclosure were being considered.

www.va.gov

The website for the Department of Veterans Affairs (VA) provides information to veterans about benefits, programs, facilities, and medical automation software. Veterans may submit e-mail inquiries to the administration through this website.

WWW

Private Mortgage Insurance

Private mortgage insurance (PMI) is required by lenders if a substantial down payment is not made on the original mortgage. The down payment requirement is usually 20 percent or more. The PMI premium varies with the down payment; the smaller the down payment, the greater is the PMI premium. PMI can be expensive, as much as 2 percent of the mortgage loan amount. PMI must be paid until the unpaid balance of the mortgage loan drops to 80 percent of the home value. If a house is reappraised or refinanced so that the 80 percent requirement is met, PMI payments may also be stopped. Mortgage lenders are required to inform the mortgagor when PMI is no longer required. Nonetheless, the consumer may have to inform the lender that the loan has reached the 80 percent level.

www.fanniemae.com

www.freddiemac.com

Fannie Mae and Freddie Mac are two stockholder-owned government-sponsored enterprises (GSEs) operating under Congressional charter to serve low- and middle-income families by stimulating the flow of mortgage money in the secondary mortgage market. With the mortgage foreclosure crisis that began in 2008, the government stepped in to place both in government conservatorship.

WWW

Title Insurance

Title insurance protects the lender, the new homeowner, or both against the loss of their interest in the property due to legal defects in the title. Title insurance usually covers the amount of a mortgage, with the policy value declining as the mortgage is paid down. This insurance is required by the lender, and the cost, which is typically paid at the loan closing, usually equals approximately 1/2 percent of the mortgage loan amount. Thus, title insurance on a $200,000 mortgage loan would cost approximately $1,000. The homeowner generally pays this premium, but the insurance protects only the lender's interest. The homeowner may consider purchasing a second policy to protect the homeowner's interest in the property. The cost of this optional title coverage is generally less than the required insurance for the lender.

Title insurance an insurance that protects the lender, the new homeowner, or both against loss of their interest in the property due to legal defects in the title.

When pursuing title insurance, consider asking the seller to pay for the coverage. In some states, the lender must pay the premium, but in others the payment may be negotiated. You may also wish to determine whether the title insurance policy issued to the current homeowner may be reissued to you. A reissued policy could result in savings of hundreds of dollars to the new property owner. Finally, shop around for title insurance. In some areas, the cost of title insurance varies by as much as 50 percent among title insurance companies.

THE COSTS OF OWNING VERSUS RENTING

Many potential homeowners have grappled with the question: Is owning or renting more cost effective? No single answer will be correct for everyone at all times. The decision to own or to rent depends on many factors, including individual preference, cost of housing options, and the investment potential of owning a home.

The Real Costs of Ownership

The buyer of a house on the installment plan is responsible for interest and principal payments on the mortgage, as well as for taxes, insurance, depreciation, and repairs and maintenance. For a rented house, the landlord is responsible for these expenses. The amounts involved vary from house to house and from region to region. In addition, owners of homes in undeveloped areas face the possibility of assessments for sewers, water lines, curbing, paving, and sidewalks.

Another cost of ownership is the loss of the opportunity to use the money in other ways. If an owner pays cash for a house, she loses the interest she would have received by investing the money elsewhere. This constitutes an implicit expense of ownership. For example, if the owner pays $100,000 cash for a house and could have received 5 percent interest on that money if it had been invested elsewhere, the house really is costing $5,000 a year, less taxes that would have been paid on the interest.

Suppose the owner finances a house with a first mortgage of 80 percent of the purchase price. On the $80,000 borrowed from a lending agency, suppose he pays 5 percent interest. The $4,000 interest paid the first year is a cost of ownership. Whether the owner borrows the money to buy a house from a lending agency or uses his own funds makes no difference. Either way, a cost is involved. Home mortgage interest, however, is an allowable tax deduction, and this reduces the cost of ownership. In addition, depending on the taxpayer's individual circumstances, other costs (e.g., home office) may be deductible. Finally, the home's appreciation will be a return on investment, often at a higher rate than monies in a bank or other investment will earn.

FYI

A good credit rating often helps the buyer in negotiating the terms of a mortgage. Lenders frequently will reduce interest rates, margin charges, and closing costs for a customer who simply asks for these reductions. Additionally, insurance companies will often give lower rates on a variety of insurance policies to those customers who have an excellent credit rating.

The Cost of Renting

Most people have rented housing at some time. The decision whether to own or to rent is often related to the life cycle. Young married couples may establish their first home in an apartment. As their income increases, the couple may purchase a condo or a small single-family house. The next move might be to larger and more expensive housing to accommodate a growing family. After the children have left home and the parents reach retirement age, many couples buy or rent a smaller single-family house, condominium, or apartment.

TIP

Before you rent an apartment, contact the utility companies to determine the yearly costs of utilities for the specific apartment you are considering. You can also request to pay an average of your yearly bill each month so that you do not have exorbitant bills for air conditioning in the summer or heat in the winter.

In a period of rising prices, renting may be a more viable option than owning. Rents may rise faster and higher than the cost of owning a house, because owners' financing costs often are extended over a 15- to 30-year period and therefore change more slowly than short-run price changes. However, renting may be cheaper than owning if a large supply of houses is available or if the general level of prices is falling. Rents bear little relation to the original cost of a property to the landlord. The renter may pay more or less than is required to cover the landlord's cost. During periods of decline in rents, the renter benefits and during rises, the landlord gains. Beyond these general considerations, comparing the costs of owning a house with renting may not be feasible because too many variables have to be considered. Many experts suggest that the costs of buying a house and renting an apartment are essentially the same in the long run.

Owners who are unable to sell expensive homes also often cannot find renters for the house who are willing to pay enough for the owner to make money. Thus, wise shoppers may be able to rent a $250,000 home for the same rate they might pay for a $150,000 home.

Property owners should consider purchasing insurance against possible loss caused by fire, lightning, explosion, smoke, vandalism, windstorm, flood, earthquake, hail, and other hazards. Some types of insurance may be required by the lender. The owner also needs insurance to cover possible injury to persons on the property, other than residents. Adequate annual coverage will cost from 1/2 percent to 1 percent of the value of the property.

TIP

When buying insurance, purchase replacement cost coverage. The additional premium is small, and the benefits are usually substantial.

Many homeowners do not figure the full actual cost of home ownership. In addition to mortgage payments, taxes, insurance, repairs, and maintenance, extra costs that often are overlooked include:

- supplies and equipment (lawn mower, shovel, etc.)
- appliances (refrigerator, dishwasher, etc.)
- furniture
- moving expenses
- renovation expenses (new carpet, painting walls, etc.)

The landlord shuts off your utilities in an attempt to collect your delinquent rent. This action is legal. True or false?

False. If utilities are cut off without a court's permission, in most states the tenant may have a claim against the landlord for any damages.

"Move-in" expenses such as these can add 10 percent to 20 percent to the cost of the home.

The psychological satisfaction of owning a house is so strong that buyers have a tendency to recognize only the minimum expenses of ownership—a tendency encouraged by those who have houses to sell. To believe that it may cost $12,000 a year or $1,000 a month to own a $150,000 house is a nice thought, but it is not realistic. The real annual cost of owning a house ranges from 10 percent to 20 percent of the home's "price"; thus a $150,000 house may well cost another $3,000 annually and homeowners should allow for that extra $250 per month.

If the Choice Is to Buy . . .

If, after careful consideration of the advantages and disadvantages of owning and renting, a person decides to buy, the first question will be: When? Should the buyer wait for lower prices and lower interest rates? In general, prices tend to become higher rather than lower over time. Even small rises in interest rates have large effects. For a 30-year mortgage, each 1 percent rise in the interest rate increases the monthly payment on principal and interest by approximately 10 percent. Average construction costs have increased every year, and these increases are likely to continue. These facts suggest that buying sooner is often wise, but many factors are involved. Whether to buy now or later is a difficult decision that the buyer alone can make. The right decision, however, could save thousands of dollars.

If you sign a lease and decide to move before it expires, you are legally obligated to pay the landlord the total amount due for the full term of the lease, plus expenses. Be sure to check your lease regarding this possibility before you sign it.

FYI

TIP Before you make an offer on a home, it is a good idea to talk with neighbors to determine whether there are any "external" problems in the area. For example, possible changes in zoning laws, school district boundaries, road access, or numerous other factors may have a devastating effect on the value of the home you are about to purchase. Loud noises from parties, dogs, children, or the firehouse around the corner can affect your enjoyment of the house. These are important factors to discover and consider before you buy.

A co-op or a condominium

Cooperative apartment (co-op) a housing arrangement in which the dweller buys one or more shares in the corporation that owns the building, then leases an individual unit.

Condominium (condo) a housing arrangement in which an individual holds ownership of an apartment in a multi-unit project and a proportionate interest in the common areas outside of the apartment.

If a person decides to buy, what shall it be? A new house? A used house? A cooperative apartment? A condominium? In a **cooperative apartment,** or **co-op,** the owners are shareholders who pay a monthly charge to cover services, maintenance, taxes, and the mortgage on the entire building. A board of directors, elected by the shareholders, determines policies. Each shareholder must agree to accept increases in assessments if someone else fails to meet his or her payments. Shareholders must request permission to remodel, change, or sell their units. Cooperatives have become a viable alternative to renting and other forms of home ownership in some parts of the United States.

Owners of **condominiums** purchase title to the units they occupy, and they share joint ownership of common areas and facilities. Condo owners arrange their own mortgages, pay taxes on their units, and make separate payments for maintenance and services. Each owner is responsible for his or her own unit and for a share of overall operating expenses, which cover all outside work—painting, new roofing, yard care, snow removal, and so forth. A monthly fee is charged to pay these expenses. The owners elect a board. They have the right to refinance or pay off their mortgages, as well as the right to remodel or sell their units.

Historically, condominium buying has the following drawbacks:

1. Maintenance and management fees often are excessive.
2. Neighboring developments of condominiums may not be comparable, making resale difficult.

CASE STUDY Equity Stripping

Gloria and Fred Johnson were homeowners with an adequate income to support their mortgage and other living expenses. However, when an injury forced Gloria to leave her job, the Johnsons were obliged to live on only her disability payments and Fred's salary. This caused them to fall two payments behind on their mortgage.

In an attempt to make things better, Gloria called Home Savers Consulting Corporation, which advertised aid to consumers facing foreclosure. The Johnsons met with the company and agreed to refinance their home at a lower interest rate and more affordable monthly payments. What the Johnsons didn't know was that in the process, they had transferred their deed and the new "buyer" had taken out all the equity and borrowed against the home. Now the Johnsons had a bigger problem on their hands: they were victims of equity stripping, a process whereby home ownership is taken from unsuspecting homeowners, and cash is taken out by the new "owners."

QUESTIONS

1. What do you think should be done at the federal or state level to address this problem?
2. Do you think the consumers in this example had any liability in this matter?
3. What can consumers do to protect themselves from this type of predatory lending?
4. What do you think should happen to the company?

Source: The New York Times, July 7, 2007. Retrieved from www.nytimes.com/2007/07/03/business/03home.html.

3. The condominium owner's right to resell may be restricted.
4. The market for condominiums is much more volatile, and thus more risky, than the more traditional housing market.
5. The sales contract frequently used in selling condominiums is perhaps the biggest problem because it is long and confusing.

Cooperatives and condominiums both may offer some advantages of ownership at a lower cost than that for individual houses. Taxes and mortgage interest for these homes are tax-deductible. Monthly costs usually are less than rental charges for comparable apartments. Many retired people, especially, find one of these forms of ownership desirable.

If real estate investors make repairs and do maintenance on their rental properties, the labor expense is not deductible, but if the same investors hire someone to do the work, the labor is considered an expense and is deductible.

FYI

A house

To guard against shoddy construction, Federal Housing Administration representatives inspect FHA-financed houses to be sure that builders comply with the minimum standards established by the FHA. Even if a buyer does not use FHA financing, she can ask the institution that is financing a newly constructed house to obtain a "conditional commitment" from the FHA. FHA representatives then will review the plans to be sure they meet requirements. In addition, FHA representatives will inspect the building three to five times while it is being constructed. The Department of Veterans Affairs also will appraise a property and supervise construction of a new house, if it is being financed with a VA loan.

When purchasing a house, whether using FHA or VA or conventional mortgage financing, the buyer should have the house inspected by a competent person whom the buyer employs specifically to inspect the property, such as a consultant, a builder, an architect, or an engineer. An expert will examine major structural elements and equipment; enter basements, crawl spaces, and attics; and check the roof, gutters, downspouts, drainage, siding, caulking, and paint. Most real estate purchase contracts allow buyers time to inspect the property with experts and additional time to think about this important economic decision.

Most home buyers, particularly those buying an existing home, will benefit from retaining the services of a real estate salesperson. Although the price of the house may be somewhat inflated to cover a portion or all of the commission, a good salesperson can save a buyer time and money by showing only homes that meet the buyer's requirements and by helping them find reasonable financing. Be aware, however, that in a typical real estate transaction, the salesperson or broker showing homes to a prospective home buyer is legally representing the home seller. This is because the broker and the home seller have established an "agency" relationship, where the broker agrees to be the seller's agent. The broker or salesperson is not necessarily working *for* you just because he is working *with* you. In fact, the broker is legally obligated to disclose information about you to the seller. This may seem difficult to believe when your salesperson seems to have only your interests at heart, but it is a legal reality.

Buyers were misled so frequently in the past that now regulations in most states require brokers and salespersons to "disclose" their agency relationship with the seller. Buyers also are protected by regulations requiring brokers to be honest about defects in a property. Thus, if you think a broker or seller has lied to or misled you, you very likely have legal recourse.

Buyers can arrange for a broker to legally represent them, usually by signing a "buyer brokerage" agreement. Unless you have specifically arranged for the broker to be your agent by signing such an agreement, however, you must assume he or she is the seller's agent. The use of buyers' agents is becoming popular in many areas of the United States.

Identifying a good salesperson or broker can be difficult. Some salespeople consider real estate a part-time job or a way to make a "fast buck." Even though all states

The economic risks of owning a condominium are more substantial than those of owning a single-family house. In most communities, condominiums do not hold their value as well as more conventional housing.

FYI

have basic certification requirements, these standards usually are minimal. The National Association of Realtors requires its members to meet reasonably high standards. If you decide to use the services of a broker, be certain to select one who is well qualified and has sold homes in the community for several years.

Buyers can find excellent deals by shopping for a FSBO, or a house "for sale by owner." Because a private seller may be less aware of full property values, the buyer may be able to buy a house at a price somewhat lower than the market value. In addition, the seller may reduce the asking price by the amount that would have been paid to a commissioned agent.

TIP Be certain that workers such as repairpersons and contractors are bonded or insured before hiring those individuals to perform work on your home.

HOW plan a homeowner's warranty on a newly purchased home against the costs of defects in materials and workmanship.

Warranties on new homes are available in most areas through the National Association of Home Builders Home Owners Warranty. These are called homeowners warranties or **HOW plans.** These plans provide protection against major structural defects on new homes for 10 years; for wiring, plumbing, and duct work for two years; and for defects in material and workmanship for one year. The homeowner pays nothing. Your local builders' association or individual builder can provide information on HOWs.

Warranties on existing homes also are available. For a fee that typically is 1/2 percent of the sale price, homeowners can insure against structural, plumbing, wiring, and other problems. In many cases, the seller purchases the warranty for the new buyer. Local real estate salespeople who participate in warranty programs can provide further details.

Before the purchase of a used home, experts recommend that buyers conduct a thorough inspection. An inspection of the exterior should include a check of the garage, driveways, walks, patios, retaining walls, and outside stairwells, and a complete check on elements of the exterior construction such as roofing, gutters and downspouts, foundations, walls, windows, doors, porches, and stoops. Buyers should check for insect infestation and test for the presence of radon, a hazardous gas. The interior inspection should include walls, floors, and ceilings. The heating, plumbing, cooling, electrical systems, and appliances should be checked, as should signs of leaks in the basement and stains on walls and ceilings.

www.hud.gov

The U.S. Department of Housing and Urban Development's website offers information for buyers, lenders, and builders. Issues such as buying, specific community information, fair housing, and much more are covered.

Differences Among Lenders

Lender requirements, interest rates, and associated costs differ widely. Simply selecting the lowest interest rate available may not assure you the best loan. At a minimum, a prospective buyer should ask the following questions of each lender:

1. What amount (or what percentage of the purchase price) will you lend for the mortgage?
2. What interest rate do you charge?
3. What is the term of years available?
4. Is there a prepayment penalty?
5. What are the total closing costs?
6. How long will loan approval and processing take?
7. What inspections are required?
8. What insurance is required?

The commission that real estate brokers generally charge is often negotiable. Ask for a reduction—if you do not ask, the answer is no!

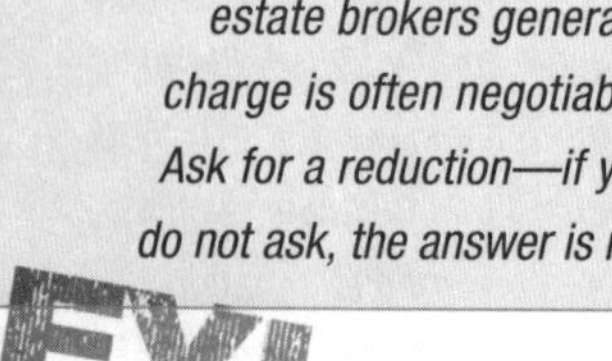

Real Estate Settlement Procedures Act

The Real Estate Settlement Procedures Act requires lending institutions to disclose closing and settlement costs prior to the exchange (sale) of a property.

Prior to 1977, consumers who purchased homes often were shocked to discover they had to pay substantial fees to the mortgage holder, title insurer, attorneys, and others in the form of **closing costs.** Often the amount of closing costs is several times the monthly payment on the mortgage.

In 1977 Congress passed the Real Estate Settlement Procedures Act (RESPA). The law requires the lender to

- provide a good-faith estimate of total settlement or closing costs to the borrower within three days after the home loan application has been received
- provide, for inspection by the borrower, a Uniform Settlement statement itemizing all settlement charges that will be assessed
- allow the borrower to purchase services related to the sale from any person or company and not those selected by the lender

Violations of the Real Estate Settlement Procedures Act should be reported to Housing and Urban Development, Room 5100, Washington, DC 20410 or at http://nhl.gov/offices/hsg/sfh/res/respa_hm.cfm.

Closing costs various expenses, in addition to the sale price of the property, incurred when buying and selling real estate and paid at the closing of the loan.

9. Do I need to escrow the taxes and insurance?
10. Are there other requirements or charges?

If you feel uncomfortable with the process, you may wish to hire an attorney who specializes in real estate to represent you before you sign a contract. The attorney can assist you with the purchase and through closing. An attorney can negotiate out clauses in the contract that may be unfavorable and can advise you as to provisions that should be added to protect your interests. Further, an attorney familiar with closings can help make the potentially hectic day run smoothly. At a minimum, the potential homeowner should have a clause in the contract that allows an attorney to review the contract and further allows the buyer to void the contract if the attorney notices any problem. Fees for these services vary so buyers should ask about them in advance.

Many consumers do not realize that contracts, even "standard" ones, can be modified. Unreasonable provisions in contracts, such as prepayment penalties, can be negotiated out.

FYI

TIP

Homeowners in small development areas should consider having the homeowners' association install fire hydrants. This step will reduce the cost of homeowners' insurance substantially and will pay for itself within a short time, often as little as three to five years.

SUMMARY

The great American dream includes owning a home. Today, however, many consumers cannot take for granted that they will be able to afford a conventional home. Alternative types of housing include cooperatives and condominiums, as well as renting a house or an apartment.

Banks finance most mortgage loans. VA-guaranteed loans and FHA loans are options for those who qualify. Shopping for the best loan arrangement can save the mortgagor many thousands of dollars over the term of the mortgage. The Internet will likely continue to grow as a major source for mortgage information.

The choice of whether to buy or rent housing depends on many factors, which fall into three categories: personal preference, cost, and investment. Each choice has advantages and disadvantages. An individual who wants a house and can afford to buy should purchase it and enjoy it, but not under the illusion that the investment is necessarily a good one.

ITEMS FOR REVIEW & DISCUSSION

1. Explain why housing costs have gone up more rapidly than most other costs. Name some things that can be done to hold down the price of a newly built house. When building or buying a house, to what extent should you consider resale value?
2. List the pros and cons of home ownership.
3. Explain the interest costs in buying a house.
4. Define a second mortgage. Why does it often cost more than a first mortgage?
5. Compare and contrast home ownership versus rental.
6. Define condominium and cooperative and give advantages and disadvantages of ownership in each.
7. Do you favor or oppose the concept of variable-rate mortgages?
8. What kinds of problems may an individual have when purchasing a house? What mistakes do home buyers frequently make?

EXPLORING PERSONAL VALUES: PROJECTS

1. Prepare a list of statements that a person suited to renting might make about herself, and a list of similar statements by a person who would prefer to own a home. Discuss the pairs of statements. For example:

   Being in debt doesn't bother me.

   The thought of long-term debt disturbs me.

   I enjoy puttering around the house.

   I would rather do anything than work around the house or yard.

   I prefer finding a good job and staying with it.

   I prefer the excitement of changing jobs from time to time.
2. In the first decade of 2000, interest rates for mortgages were relatively low. These rates are the same ones that determine how much interest people can earn through money market funds, certificates of deposit, and the like. When rates are low, these investments may earn only 2 percent to 3 percent. Discuss with your classmates the various effects of low interest rates. Note the social as well as the economic effects of low interest rates.
3. Ask 10 students if they hope to own a house of their own eventually or would rather rent. Ask for reasons and compile a list for each alternative.
4. Shop for a mortgage loan. Go to three lending agencies. Tabulate your findings and decide which lender you would recommend. Give reasons for your choice.
5. Debate this statement: "Resolved: It is cheaper to own than to rent a house."
6. Interview a real estate salesperson and find out what is happening to prices of new and used houses in your community.
7. Interview three people who have recently purchased a house or condo and three people who have chosen to continue renting. Are they satisfied with their choices? Report your findings.

8. Interview three people who have owned a house for more than 10 years. Are they satisfied with their choice? What problems have confronted them? Report your findings.
9. Research what is involved in building your own home. Compare building to buying. What are the costs related to buying a home (moving, buying, mortgage, appliances, furniture, and so on)? What are the costs of building?
10. Write a paper about the American dream versus the reality.

ADDITIONAL SOURCES OF INFORMATION

Adamaitis, Joe. *The First-Time Homeowner's Handbook: A Complete Guide and Workbook for the First-Time Home Buyer.* Ocala, FL: Atlantic Publishing, 2006.

Eldred, Gary W. *The 106 Common Mistakes Homebuyers Make (and How to Avoid Them),* 3rd ed. Chichester, UK: Wiley, 2005.

Gadow, Sandy. *The Complete Guide to Your Real Estate Closing: Answers to All Your Questions—From Opening Escrow, to Negotiating Fees, to Signing the Closing Papers.* New York: McGraw-Hill, 2003.

Glink, Ilyce R. *10 Steps to Home Ownership: A Workbook for First-Time Buyers.* New York: Three Rivers Press, 1996.

Irwin, Robert. *How to Buy a Home When You Can't Afford It.* New York: McGraw-Hill Trade, 2002.

Schkeeper, Peter A., Jack P. Friedman, and Jack C. Harris. *The Smart Consumer's Guide to Home Buying.* Hauppauge, NY: Barron's Educational Series, 2008.

Stewart, Marcia, Ralph Warner, Janet Portman, and Ralph E. Warner. *Every Landlord's Legal Guide.* Berkeley, CA: Nolo, 2006.

Tyson, Eric. *Home Buying for Dummies.* Hoboken, NJ: John Wiley & Sons, 2006.

Tyson, Eric. *Mortgages for Dummies.* Hoboken, NJ: John Wiley & Sons, 2004.

United States General Accounting Office. *Multifamily Housing: HUD's Restructuring Office's Actions to Implement the Mark-to-Market Program: Report to Congressional Committees.* Washington, DC: United States General Accounting Office, 2000.

> "Our economy is the result of millions of decisions we all make every day about producing, earning, saving, investing, and spending."
>
> **DWIGHT D. EISENHOWER,** FORMER GENERAL AND U.S. PRESIDENT

KEY TERMS

bond
brokerage fees
callable bonds
capital gain
certificates of deposit
churning
consumer price index (CPI)
convertible bonds
corporate bonds
credit status
debenture
diversification
dollar cost averaging
Dow Jones Industrial Average
equipment trust certificate
hedge
income bonds
Individual Retirement Account (IRA)
investment
Keogh Plan
leverage
liquidity
load funds
marketability
money market funds
mortgage bond
mutual funds
no-load funds
par
penny stocks
proprietor status
serial bonds
Series EE bonds
Series I bonds
sinking-fund bonds
speculation
stocks
Treasury bills
Treasury bonds
Treasury notes
yield
zero-coupon bonds

The following concepts will be developed in this chapter:

1. Although in many families the percentage of household disposable income saved has been declining, in general the consumer has a deep-seated urge to save.
2. People can invest in a great many and varied investment products, some of which are generally better than others for the small investor.
3. The Crash of 1929 brought to light the critical need for government protection of the nation's investors, and this need was confirmed by recent dramatic declines in the stock market. Still, investors' best protection is their own understanding of the types of investments.

After having read this chapter, you should be able to accomplish the following objectives:

1. Differentiate the objectives of spending for investment and spending for other goods and services.
2. Distinguish between investment and speculation.
3. Identify a number of advantages and disadvantages of investing in real estate.
4. Compare and contrast stocks, bonds, mutual funds, and other investment options.

THRIFT OR WASTE?

Saving is a conscious, rational decision to postpone consumption of a portion of one's income. In the United States, saving has been considered a virtue ever since Benjamin Franklin wrote in *Poor Richard's Almanac,* "A penny saved is a penny earned." We could amend Franklin's statement by noting "A penny saved is better than a penny earned, because it's tax free!"

The amount people save is closely related to the size of their income. A small minority of Americans have such large incomes that, notwithstanding their lavish living, they spend less than half of it. At the other extreme is a much larger number whose incomes are so small that they do not save any portion. In between are millions who can and do save.

Many difficulties surround saving and making investment decisions in a pulsating economy in which the market changes. Consumers must take great care in developing a sound investment program, and it must be reevaluated periodically.

Saving and Investing

Why Do People Save?

Regardless of income, many consumers have a strong urge to save. For many people living on a tight budget, life is a series of emergencies—unemployment, accidents, illness, death. These emergencies are called "rainy days," and many people save as much as they can in anticipation of them.

Prudent consumers anticipate large recurring expenses, such as insurance premiums and taxes. Month by month, they budget and save money for these expenditures. They also anticipate large nonrecurring expenditures, including the purchase of furniture, appliances, and household improvements. Increasingly, people are recognizing the importance of saving and investing to supplement their Social Security and company pension payments upon retirement. Teenagers might save to finance a college education, to purchase clothing, or to buy a car.

Some people save for the added income their savings will earn through the magic of compound interest. A simple formula, 72 divided by the interest rate, indicates approximately how long a sum of money will take to double. As examples, at an interest rate of 6 percent compounded annually, savings will double in approximately 12 years; at a 10 percent interest rate, savings will double in about seven years and two months; and a 12 percent rate will double the investment in about six years.

How Do People Save?

A few people hoard. Having saved some of their income, they hide it. The Great Depression in the 1930s made hoarders out of many savers. Many people lost faith in all forms of savings institutions and hoarded cash in safe-deposit boxes. In a depression, as the price levels decline, the purchasing power of the dollar increases, and hoarders gain.

www.AmericaSaves.org

This website offers tips for consumers to save and build wealth. The group was initiated by Consumer Federation of America and involves hundreds of nonprofit, government, and business organizations.

Even today, some observers suggest that consumers should be cautious of placing all of their savings in a bank savings account, stressing the importance of diversification. In any case, for many reasons, the percent of total disposable personal income saved has declined, from 8 percent in the 1970s to less than 1 percent today.

Millions of people place their savings into low- or no-interest–bearing checking accounts. A substantial number of consumers give life insurance companies billions of dollars a year by "investing" in low-interest or no-interest–bearing whole life policies. Some savers prefer to invest their money in antiques, art, jewelry, coins, stamps, stocks, or real estate, hoping for a **capital gain.** The disadvantages of these types of investments are that they cost money to maintain, and the owners can never be sure what their market value will be when they wish to sell them.

Capital gain the difference between the sale price of property and the original cost plus expenses for buying and selling.

How Much and How Should the Prudent Consumer Save?

The American Bankers Association recommends that an individual or a family select a percentage figure for saving. This amount should be put in the budget first, under the heading, "This Is Mine to Keep." The recommended figure is at least 5 percent of net spendable income; 10 percent is preferred if you wish to obtain results in a shorter time.

WWW

www.aba.com

The American Bankers Association (ABA) website represents banks throughout the United States to their customers.

Investment professionals generally agree that the head of a family should not attempt to save for the purpose of future income until the family has purchased adequate insurance protection and a quick-recourse emergency fund equal to half of the family's yearly income. The emergency fund should be convertible into cash on demand or within 30 days, such as in an interest-bearing savings or checking account, certificate of deposit, or money-market funds.

Most stock brokerages and many banks offer "cash management" or similar accounts. Many offer unlimited check-writing services, and the rate of return is often at least double the rates offered by banks for checking accounts. Some restrictions and costs for these accounts do apply, but for many consumers these management accounts are excellent investment vehicles for short-term accounts.

PUTTING SAVINGS TO WORK

Although popular thought differentiates spending as the paying out of income for consumers' goods and saving as depositing money in an institution or spending it for the purchase of securities, a person parting with purchasing power is obviously spending. The difference is in the purpose: spending for products or spending for **investment.**

Investment the purchase of property or claims to property that will yield income, capital gain, or both.

Types of Investments

The two general types of investments are (a) those establishing a **credit status** and (b) those establishing a **proprietor status.** The creditor type of investment is illustrated by savings deposits, the purchase of shares in thrifts (unless an investor buys a paid-up share), and the purchase of bonds or mortgages. In each situation the investor is lending money with the expectation of receiving interest and eventual return of the principal. The greatest risk involved in these transactions is the possibility that the borrower may be unable or unwilling to return the principal. As a safeguard, lending agreements usually include some type of security. Yet, many lending agreements simply pledge the borrower's general credit.

Credit status an investment represented by loans.

Proprietor status an investment represented by ownership.

Investments that establish proprietor status give the investor ownership in something. To illustrate proprietor status, an investor who purchases a restaurant assumes many duties and obligations. He has to spend time managing the business; arranging for deliveries of supplies; paying bills; paying taxes; keeping the property in repair; hiring necessary help; purchasing insurance to cover risks of customers, employees, and property; and arranging for credit at a bank. In payment for these services, the investor receives whatever surplus remains after paying all other bills. Other types of proprietor status investments include stock, real estate, stock in mutual funds, and the like.

Despite consumers' interest in saving, the savings rate in the United States typically is less than half the rate in most other industrialized countries.

FYI

Concerns of the Small Investor

During periods of high inflation, investors often cannot keep pace with rising costs. For example, in the early 1980s, one of the best "safe" investments was a money-market certificate. During a one-year period, these certificates had an average yield of 10.5 percent. During the same period, the inflation rate was about 14 percent. More lucrative "safe" investments may keep up with inflation, but they require substantial amounts of money for the investor to participate. For instance, investment in rental property is considered "safe" in many areas of the United States during most economic periods, but the initial down payment required to secure a real estate loan on investment property may approach 20 percent or more of the purchase price.

www.federalreserve.gov

The Federal Reserve System (FRS) website explains how the central bank of the United States, the Federal Reserve, was founded in 1913 to provide the nation with a more stable and safer monetary system. The Federal Reserve is responsible for conducting national monetary policy, supervising and regulating banking, protecting consumer rights, maintaining stability in the financial system, and providing particular financial services to the government, the public, financial institutions, and foreign institutions.

WWW

To be an aggressive investor necessitates spending a substantial amount of time to study investment possibilities or enough money to hire professional investment counselors. The brief discussion of investment policies and practices in this chapter is not intended for aggressive investors. Defensive investors are those who have smaller amounts to invest and to whom those amounts of money are extremely important. They wish to avoid serious losses. They do not take the time or have the knowledge to study investment possibilities. What are the chief concerns of the small, conservative, defensive investor?

1. *Security of principal.* This is the primary concern. It involves not only the preservation and return of the original sum of money but also the preservation or increase of its original purchasing power. Small investors often must choose between investments that offer security and low yield and investments that offer less security and high yield. In times of inflation, purchasing power is preserved, in the long run, by investing in common stocks, mutual fund shares, or rental real estate ownership. When prices are falling, purchasing power is maintained or increased by investing in bonds or keeping cash in savings deposits.
2. ***Diversification.*** An investor may diversify geographically or by industry, by maturity dates, or by types of securities.
3. *Stability of income.* This is particularly important for people who have retired. Stability of income also involves stability of purchasing power. A steady income of 6 percent is satisfactory if prices are steady or falling, but not when prices are rising. Stability of purchasing power may be achieved through controlling the ratio of fixed-dollar investments to equities in real estate and common stock.
4. *Increasing the capital value of investments.* A person's investments should grow at least as much as the economy grows. In addition, investments should increase in value enough to offset an annual price-level increase.
5. ***Marketability.*** Common stocks listed on a stock exchange can always be sold. They are marketable. In contrast, real estate cannot always be sold when a seller needs cash and, therefore, is not always marketable.
6. *The tax status of an investment.* A low-interest–bearing government bond may be a good investment for some people because the income from it is generally not taxable. Series EE savings bonds are federally taxed unless the dollars are used for tuition and the parents' income is sufficiently low.

Diversification the spreading of money among a variety of investments to achieve security of principal and stability of income.

Marketability the ability to readily exchange an asset for money at whatever price may be attainable.

A solid investment program may yield good results even under adverse conditions. Investment would be easy if a person could assume a continuing economic expansion (although a person can buy the wrong stock or piece of real estate even then). Because investors cannot foresee the future, they can obtain the best results by following others' experience. To select the best investments for their individual situation, they must

Statistically, only one-third of business franchises make money. One-third break even, and the other third lose money.

FYI

consider, among other factors, their age, number of dependents, amount of life insurance, cash reserve, current income, prospective income, and debt and tax status. Then investors must decide how much risk to assume and how much income they need from investments. A young single person can properly assume more risk for the purpose of increasing income; an older married couple is usually more anxious to provide a smaller, secure retirement income.

All investors face the following risks:

1. business risk (a decline in earning power)
2. market risk (market psychology that causes a security to decline in price without reference to a fundamental change in its earning power)
3. purchasing-power risk (a decline in purchasing power as the Consumer Price Index rises)
4. interest-rate risk (a rise in interest rates, depressing the prices of fixed-income securities)
5. political risk (tax increases, price-wage controls, and changes in tariffs or subsidies)

Bonds are more vulnerable to risks 1, 3, 4, and 5. Common stocks are more vulnerable to risks 1, 2, and 5. Nothing is free of risk. Even U.S. government bonds are vulnerable to risks 3, 4, and 5.

Looking backward, we see an investment picture characterized first by a boom from 1962 to 1969. Then the picture becomes one of occasional mild recessions, several major recessions, continuing inflation, sharply rising interest rates, rising taxes, constant war or threat of war followed by some easing of tensions, lower interest rates, higher deficits, and recurring balance-of-payments problems. The mid- to late 1990s saw an extended growth economy, as evidenced by all-time highs in the stock market. The first decade of the 21st century brought upheaval to the stock market, with various market sectors losing one-half or more of their value in less than one year. Many day traders and other market speculators lost fortunes because of their lack of knowledge and their greed.

To evaluate the past is much easier than to peer into the future and predict accurately. Successful investors are the ones who can read the road signs for the future and position themselves accordingly.

The Roth IRA is an alternative way to save. True or false?

True. Provided you meet certain criteria, you can contribute several thousand dollars each year into the Roth IRA. Those contributions are nondeductible, but they can grow tax deferred, and you can withdraw the proceeds tax-free after five years, providing that you are at least 59½ or that you are using the money for qualified reasons, for example a first-time home purchase or college expenses.

Investing or Speculation?

Speculation the investment in property or claims to property whereby the speculator seeks to increase the return by accepting additional risks.

Yield the portion of return produced from dividends, interest payments, rental income, and so on.

To repeat, investing is spending money to accumulate financial assets with safety as an important concern. **Speculation** has a different goal. High income is the goal, even though this can come only at the price of risk. Investors seek a high degree of security and are satisfied with a modest yield. Speculators may receive a comparatively high yield, but at the expense of risking principal.

Although speculators are interested in **yield,** they usually are more interested in the probable market price of a security at a later date. They buy a security or real estate with the hope of being able to sell at a higher price soon. Timing is of the utmost importance to speculators. They prefer to buy the wrong stock at the right time than to own the right stock at the wrong time. For the investor, the stock itself is the most vital concern. Speculation sometimes verges on gambling, which is the creation of an unnecessary risk where none existed before. No social service is performed when speculators assume an unnecessary or artificially created risk. Records of the New York Stock Exchange (NYSE) indicate that the chances of success in speculation are only one in five, and the risk increases with stocks not listed on the Exchange.

Investment and Inflation

Stock market downturns in the first decade of the 21st century forced many people to reevaluate their investment policies. Many stocks did not perform equal to inflation during this period, and their investors lost money. The situation made many investors shy of investing in stocks. However, stocks do historically perform well compared to inflation over the long run. The small investor who is concerned with some protection against inflation still should consider stock investments. Over long periods, in fact, the stock market outperforms virtually all other investment options. Investors should be careful not to allow themselves to be scared out of the stock market in a declining market, but at the same time they should act with caution.

www.bls.gov/cpi

Information about the Consumer Price Index (CPI) can be reached through the Bureau of Labor Statistics website. The CPI is most commonly utilized as an economic indicator of inflation.

WWW

REAL ESTATE INVESTMENTS

Land ownership is a common form of investment. People often prefer to own land because it is tangible, and they can see the sale prices of good property increase decade by decade. When land is converted into building plots, some owners become rich. As the nation's population continues to grow, the demand for land for business, residential, transportation, and recreational purposes increases. Because the supply of land is constant, prices must increase, but not all land rises in price. Local demand and supply vary. Picking land for growth potential may well be as risky as picking stocks. And holding land until prices rise is expensive. Expenses, such as taxes and interest on money borrowed to purchase land, may exceed 20 percent of the original cost of the land, each year.

Some experts suggest that the real estate market in recent years is comparable to the stock market prior to 1929. At that time, a very low percentage (10 percent) of the purchase price of securities was required in cash. The remainder was loaned to investors based on the assets in their account. The lenders felt confident in the security backing the loan. Similarly, real estate is often sold with very little down payment required in cash and an increasing percentage loaned to the buyer. In the booming real estate market, lenders became overly confident in the security of the assets backing the loan. They granted home loans to consumers who were not well qualified, had no down payment, or both. Because housing prices were expected to continue to increase, lenders were not concerned about consumer defaults—they expected to recoup their investment, if necessary, through the resale of the home.

With the downturn of the real estate market, this strategy proved to be unwise. The resulting mortgage and credit crises of 2008 make it difficult to discuss the current status of real estate as an investment. It is likely that real estate will remain a good investment tool for knowledgeable investors.

Small investors are advised to follow the general rule that securities yielding, or promising to yield, more than twice the return available on U.S. Treasury bonds are too risky. Some advisors place the ratio as low as 1½ times.

FYI

Advantages and Disadvantages of Rental Property Investments

The demand for rental housing is increasing in most areas of the United States, partly as a result of high costs of home ownership. This makes investments in rental properties potentially lucrative.

Small investors who have made substantial profits in rental property investment have done so by using **leverage.** Essentially, this strategy calls for investing little and selling often; both parts of this strategy are difficult during a challenging real estate market, but the concept is still an important one to understand. Suppose an investor has $30,000 to invest. She selects a rental property with a selling price of $300,000. The investor keeps in mind that the prime consideration is to invest as little as possible. A lending institution usually requires at least 20 percent down, or $60,000, on this type of mortgage. To make the sale, however, the seller may be willing to lend the investor

Leverage a strategy of investing that involves borrowing to possess a large amount of property.

the $30,000 for the rest of the down payment. If the lending institution agrees to these terms, the investor can purchase the property valued at $300,000 for an investment of only $30,000.

The first part of the strategy—invest little—is now complete. The second part—sell often—is now pursued. In a typical real estate market, the property would be sold after a short time, say, one year. Again in a typical market, assume the property appreciates during the year and is sold for $360,000, a $60,000 profit. (For the sake of simplicity, presume no closing costs to the seller.) The mortgagees are paid off, and the net result is a doubling of the original $30,000 investment in only one year. The process continues, and actually becomes more complex, because the $90,000 now available for down payments can be spread among several properties that may have a combined value of nearly half a million dollars. Within a few years the investor may have properties valued in the millions!

WWW

www.indexfunds.com

Consumers can receive assistance with index investing through the Indexfunds website. The goal is to minimize costs and maximize returns for the investor.

Owning rental property offers many advantages, such as tax deductions for depreciation of personal and real property, maintenance, other taxes, and interest. In addition, the landlord collects rental income. On the other hand, there are also disadvantages of owning rental property, such as vacancies, tenants' nonpayment of rent, and maintenance costs. The above example assumed that the lenders would accept the original terms of the mortgage and a fairly high rate of increase in the property value. This strategy works well when property values are increasing rapidly. When that does not occur, the leverage strategy can cause investors and lending institutions to lose substantial amounts of money.

Should Small Investors Use Leverage and Invest in Rental Property?

Small investors should proceed with caution before becoming involved with leverage and rental-property investment. For the uneducated, leverage strategies in real estate and other investment areas can be risky and time-consuming. They require specific capabilities usually reserved for experienced investors. In the above example, if the investor had erred by investing in a property where values were declining, the $30,000 investment would have been lost. Rental property investment may be risky, is time-consuming, and requires substantial personal responsibility and management capabilities.

BONDS AS AN INVESTMENT

Bond a written promise to pay a certain sum of money on or before a specified date, with interest at an agreed rate.

Bonds are important vehicles of investment for the small investor. **Bonds** give investors a fixed return, low risk, and the return of principal at maturity. The various types of bonds are characterized by certain features.

Type of debtor. The two general types of debtors are government and corporate. The latter includes public-utility corporations subject to public regulation.

Debenture a bond that is unsecured; the only assurance of repayment is the company's earning power.

Mortgage bond a bond that is secured by property.

Equipment trust certificate a provision that secures a bond with assets of substantial and immediate resale value.

Security. Security applies to almost all government bonds and many corporate bonds, often referred to as **debentures.** Many corporate bonds are **mortgage bonds.** In case of default, the secured property becomes the property of the bondholders, which they can sell and use the proceeds from the sale to pay off the bonds. A first-mortgage bond is considered to be stronger security than subsequent property liens, which are of doubtful value in case of forced liquidation.

Mortgage bonds have come under criticism because the property given as a pledge may not be easily converted into cash, or it could be of little market value if it is converted. As a result, **equipment trust certificates** were introduced. These certificates are exemplified by railroad and airline bonds. If the airline, for example, is unable to pay the certificate, its equipment, which is typically of excellent quality, is sold to other airlines. Generally, these bonds have not become significant investment vehicles for the small investor, although these debt instruments tend to have little risk.

Provision for repayment. Although perpetual or long-term bonds are fairly common in Europe, they have not proved popular in the United States. **Sinking-fund bonds** are of interest to small investors. In the case of enterprises such as mining, in which the resource is eventually depleted, sinking funds offer greater assurance to the investor. **Serial bonds** and **callable bonds** also are worthy of note.

Provision for interest payments. Most bonds provide for interest at some fixed percentage. Default on interest payments makes the principal come due and enables the bondholders to foreclose. **Income bonds** are the riskiest bonds a company issues. These usually are issued by weak, reorganized companies whose securities are accepted by holders under compulsion. At best, these are a speculative investment.

Special privileges. Examples of special privileges are that some government bonds carry the privilege of tax exemption and that corporate bonds may be **convertible bonds.** As noted, bonds typically are paid at a fixed rate of interest for a specified period. In part because of high inflation and the volatility of interest rates, however, **zero-coupon bonds** may be issued. With a zero-coupon bond, the investor's funds grow at a designated rate and amount. For example, a zero-coupon bond that sold initially for $385 in 2006 will pay a specific sum when it matures in the year 2016. At that time, the amount paid might have been designated previously to be $1,000. Zero-coupon bonds have variations. Some are taxable and others are not.

In recent years, private companies and the U.S. Treasury have segmented bonds and notes with long-term maturities into their interest and principal components. These are known by a wide variety of acronyms, including STRIPS, CATS, LIONS, and TIGRs. Because of their flexibility, these investment vehicles have been quite popular with small investors.

Sinking-fund bonds a type of bond that provides for earnings to be set aside periodically and applied toward retirement of the bond.

Serial bonds a type of bond that is retired in installments at times indicated on the bond.

Callable bonds a type of bond that the investor must retire prior to maturity.

Income bonds a type of bond that has no stated interest rate, and interest is paid only if the company is profitable.

Convertible bonds a type of bond that may be exchanged for other bonds, stocks, or securities.

Zero-coupon bonds a type of bond that pays no interest and is discounted heavily at the time of sale.

TIP Give strong consideration to purchasing zero-coupon bonds if you know precisely when you will need money in the future (such as to finance a college education).

U.S. Government Bonds

The U.S. government bond is the standard by which all other bonds are judged. These bonds are issued by a sovereign power, their security resting not on a pledge of physical property or on earning power but instead on the government's power to raise money by taxation. The value of government bonds depends on investors' confidence in the government's ability and willingness to repay its debt. In a democratic government, this confidence ultimately is a reflection of the citizens' confidence in themselves as a group, for they constitute and compose the final authority.

The fact that federal bonds are the standard by which all other bonds are judged may be established by another line of reasoning. The nation as a unit is stronger than any individual business enterprise or any of the separate states, counties, or municipalities. It is a matter of record that investors lose confidence in the bonds of some civil and corporate units while they retain full confidence in the bonds of their federal government. If U.S. government bonds were to become worthless, no corporate security would have value.

Some investment experts advise anyone having $5,000 or less to invest to buy U.S. savings bonds for their safety, dependable income, and liquidity. Whereas government bonds often are issued in large denominations of $5,000 or multiples thereof, the

FYI *A person can purchase Treasury securities without paying a commission by contacting the local Federal Reserve Bank directly or visiting www.savingsbonds.gov.*

> **www.savingsbonds.gov**
>
> This government website offers a wealth of information about U.S. Government Bonds and more specifically EE/E and I savings bonds. It is updated frequently as needed. You can purchase, manage, and redeem electronic bonds safely through a personal Treasury Direct account.

government has enabled small investors to purchase bonds in smaller denominations. Investors should be cautious of penalties applied if bonds are cashed in early, and tax and interest penalties if cashed in late (as in the case of Series EE bonds).

Several types of U.S. Bonds are offered by the U.S. Treasury. The two main types of bonds offered are Series EE and Series I bonds.

Series EE bonds U.S. government bonds that are issued at a discount and have a variable rate with a guaranteed minimum rate.

EE/E Savings Bonds. Series EE Bonds are reliable, low-risk government-backed savings products that you can use to finance education, to supplement retirement income, for birthday and graduation gifts, and for other special events. Series EE Bonds purchased after May 1, 2005, earn a fixed rate of return. Paper EE Bonds are still available for purchase through most financial institutions or participating employers' payroll deduction plans. (E Bonds are the predecessor to EE Bonds and are no longer issued by the U.S. Treasury.) You can purchase, manage, and redeem electronic EE Bonds safely through a personal Treasury Direct account online.

Series I bonds U.S. government bonds that are sold in specified amounts at face value.

I Bonds. Series I bonds are U.S. government bonds that are sold in specified amounts at face value. I Bonds were once sold and redeemed solely as a paper security, but now they're also available in electronic form. As a Treasury Direct account holder, you can buy, manage, and redeem I Bonds online.

Treasury bonds long-term U.S. government debts sold in denominations of $100 or more, which pay interest every six months and typically mature in 30 years.

Treasury notes intermediate-term U.S. government debts sold in fairly large denominations, typically maturing in 2, 5, and 10 years.

Treasury bills short-term U.S. government debts, typically sold in large denominations and maturing in a few days to 52 weeks.

Par the stated or face value of a security.

Liquidity the opportunity to quickly, and without loss or penalty, convert an investment to cash.

Treasury securities. In addition to the above are U.S. **Treasury bonds, Treasury notes** (T-notes), and **Treasury bills** (T-bills). Treasury bonds are no longer issued by the U.S. Treasury, but many are in circulation, having not yet reached their maturity date. T-notes and T-bills are issued in units of $1,000. Treasury bonds and notes pay interest semiannually. Treasury bills are issued at a discount and mature at **par.** Banks and brokerage firms sell Treasuries, but they charge a relatively modest commission.

One defect of government securities in general is the lack of security of purchasing power. Although investors are sure of getting their money back, they do not know what it will be worth. If the general level of prices has fallen, the money they receive at maturity will buy more, but if prices have risen—which generally happens—it will buy less. Some investment writers think that government fiscal policies indicate a continued, long-term rise in prices and recommend that investors protect their purchasing power by investing part of their savings in common stocks, the prices of which usually rise with the general price level.

Some experts advise investors to put half their money into government bonds and half into stocks. Others advise defensive investors to divide their holdings between bonds and stocks, in a ratio ranging from 75:25 to 25:75, depending on current economic trends. Still others recommend buying any fixed-income securities with staggered maturity dates. For example, they recommend an investor with $10,000 invest in bonds that mature in 2010, 2012, 2014, and 2016, thus achieving a reasonable yield, limited risk, and higher **liquidity.**

Federal Debt Securities

In addition to the bills and notes the U.S. Treasury Department issues, federal debt securities are issued by the Government National Mortgage Association (GNMA) and the Federal National Mortgage Association (FNMA). Debt securities offered by the GNMA, called "Ginnie Maes," are backed by the full faith and credit of the U.S. government. Typically, the yield on Ginnie Maes is slightly above the Treasury bond yield. Securities offered by the FNMA, called "Fannie Maes," are offered for large-purchase requirements and generally are guaranteed by private corporations.

Municipal Bonds

In discussions on investments, typically no distinctions are made among state, county, and city bonds. All are classified as municipals, or "munis." Municipals include the bonds issued by school districts, irrigation districts, sewer districts, water districts, turnpike authorities, port authorities, and other political subdivisions. We have only one national government but 50 sovereign states, all with authority to issue bonds based on public credit. Investors have varying degrees of confidence in the ability and willingness of the states to repay their obligations. The credit of some states is stronger than that of others, but the disparity is not as great now as it was in the past. In comparing the level of security, investors should consider the fact that a state cannot be sued, even by the holder of a defaulted or repudiated bond.

Financial experts point out that the safety record of municipal bonds is second only to that of federal government bonds. Even so, since 1938, when the Federal Municipal Bankruptcy Act legally allowed cities to go into bankruptcy, hundreds of cities have had to go into default and then work out plans to refinance their debts. Because of these defaults and the increasing potential of future defaults, investors have had to reevaluate municipal bonds as a safe investment. Nonetheless, the track record of munis is outstanding.

The market for municipal bonds is largely institutional. Managers of life insurance companies and pension funds like them because the federal government cannot tax interest on the bonds. In certain cases, the bonds are triple-exempt. For example, when a person who lives in New York City purchases a municipal bond issued by New York City, the interest from this bond is exempt from federal, state, and local taxes.

Because purchasing a single municipal bond is somewhat risky, small investors might consider **mutual funds** that specialize in municipal bonds. With municipal bond mutual funds, the risk is negligible. Prudent investors consider no-load funds superior to load funds. Research repeatedly has indicated that **no-load funds** do as well as **load funds.** When sales and redemption commissions are factored into the equation, no-loads typically provide a better investment return.

Mutual funds portfolios of stocks and bonds in which investors can purchase shares. Investment companies create and manage these funds.

No-load funds a type of mutual fund that does not charge a fee for buying or selling its shares.

Load funds a type of mutual fund that charges a fee to purchase or sell its shares.

Corporate Bonds

Corporate bonds are relatively secure investments. They resemble government bonds but have several differences; chief among them is the security for repayment. Although a corporate bond may be issued on the general credit of a company or on the possibility of its earnings, these bonds frequently are secured by a mortgage on all or a part of the corporate property. They then are designated as first- or second-mortgage bonds.

Corporate bonds bonds backed by a company's promise to pay a stated sum of money on or before a specified date with interest at an agreed rate.

A second difference is that corporate bonds are repaid out of earnings. If earnings are insufficient, the bonds are repaid out of the proceeds of the sale of the property pledged as security. Whether a corporation does or does not earn enough gross income to meet its obligations depends primarily on good management, and it also may hinge on many other factors, some of which are beyond the control of management.

TIP Consider investing in bonds of investment grade (Standard and Poor's ratings of AAA, AA, A, or BBB, and Moody's ratings of Aaa, Aa, A, or Baa), but do not consider Standard and Poor's speculative grades of BB, B, CCC, CC, C, or D or Moody's speculative grades of Ba, B, Caa, Ca, or C.

Depending on the company and its capacity to repay, the average investor may not be wise in purchasing corporate bonds. An investor who lacks experience and expertise in this area may be as helpless as the average consumer trying to buy a home or a used automobile without some expert advice. The bond issues of new, small, or unknown mining and oil companies usually are risky. Some conservative corporate stocks are

www.moodys.com

The website for Moody's Investors Services assists investors in the money market by providing research and risk analysis on fixed-income securities and other credit obligations.

safer investments than certain types of corporate bonds. Securities yielding more than twice the return on U.S. government bonds usually are too risky for the consumer investor. Though a high-yield bond promising an apparently high return might seem attractive, prospective buyers must remember that they are purchasing that larger return at the risk of losing all or part of their principal.

Most consumers are novices in the area of determining the value of a specific bond. Rating services such as Moody's Investors Services and Standard and Poor's Corporation do this. These companies rank thousands of corporate and municipal bond issues from AAA (the highest rating) to D (the lowest rating) by Standard and Poor's, or Aaa (the highest) to C (the lowest) by Moody's.

Certificates of Deposit

Certificates of deposit (CDs) insured investment plans that pay interest at a specified maturity date.

Certificates of deposit (CDs) are popular with conservative investors. CDs are typically available from savings institutions. A CD is similar to a savings account with one major difference: The investor agrees to leave money in the account for a specified period, and the savings institution rewards the investor with a moderate rate of interest. Typically, the longer the commitment, the higher the rate. The interest rate paid on a CD is typically fixed over the term of the CD. During times of high inflation, CDs have paid more than twice the rate of interest than that paid on a passbook savings account. The entire investment (up to $250,000) is guaranteed by federal insurance. CDs are safe, but interest penalties typically apply for early withdrawals.

Money Market Funds

Money market funds investments that typically pay higher rates than passbook savings accounts and in which the investment company uses the proceeds to purchase other securities.

Money market funds are reasonably secure investments. Money market funds are generally offered by brokerage firms, mutual fund companies, banks, and credit unions. They offer yields comparable to CDs. Further, amounts can be withdrawn with no penalty, and check writing against the funds is often allowed, for a limited number of transactions. The rate of interest paid by a money market fund fluctuates with the overall market rate of interest.

CORPORATE STOCKS AS AN INVESTMENT

Stocks certificates showing partial ownership and control in the corporations that issue them.

Dow Jones Industrial Average an average of stock prices of 30 large industrial companies.

Tens of millions of individuals in the United States own **stocks** in corporations or mutual funds. In general, stocks in the 1970s were not good investment vehicles, but, overall, stocks more than tripled in value during the 1980s. The **Dow Jones Industrial Average** nearly quadrupled from the early 1980s through the 1990s. However, late in the first decade of the 2000s, the financial and mortgage industries began to struggle, culminating in dramatic losses in stock prices and other severe economic repercussions. Historically, stocks outperform most other investments for the average investor, but periodic market downturns have resulted in substantial investor losses.

Stock Ownership

So many kinds of stocks are available that generalizing about stock ownership is not possible. Formerly, bond holders were considered creditors with no control in corporate management and no share in corporate profits, and stockholders were owners with voting control and no assured income but with the prospect of a share in net earnings. Many more types of participation are now possible. One investor may own a preferred-share stock that gives him prior claim to participate in net earnings. Another may hold a 6 percent cumulative preferred share, which means that if the 6 percent dividend is not paid one year, other stockholders must forgo any share in net earnings the second year until 12 percent on the investment has been paid. Still another investor may own a share of Class A nonvoting stock, which means that she has incurred all the risks incident to ownership, yet has no voice in control of the company.

The income of a corporation depends on many variables over which corporate management may or may not have control. Individual stockholders in large corporations have no effective control over management. From an investment point of view, they are in the position of having loaned their capital to the corporation without a promise of repayment and without a promise of payment for its use.

www.dowjones.com

The website for Dow Jones & Company offers information on its well-known publications *The Wall Street Journal* and *Barron's* magazine. The company created the Dow Jones Industrial Average.

Tens of thousands of corporate stocks are traded over the counter; that is, sales are handled by brokers without going through the stock exchanges. The stocks of the remaining corporations are rarely traded. Consequently, they are not readily marketable. The stocks of closed corporations are held by individuals or family groups and are not available for investment purchase to the general public. This was the case with stocks of the Ford Motor Company for many years.

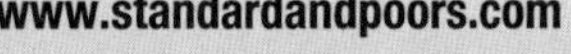

www.standardandpoors.com

The website for Standard and Poor's, Inc., offers financial information and analytical services. Its website provides real-time data, and information about comprehensive services of the company is highlighted.

Advantages and Disadvantages of Common Stock

One of the primary advantages of stock ownership has to do with inflation. Inflation is practically a way of life in the United States. The long-run trend of the price level has always been upward, but people believe this situation is bad. Consumer attitudes toward rising price levels are emotional. They do not think inflation can be justified in peacetime. Millions of Americans have experienced the best years of their lives in times of inflation, yet they think only of higher prices without considering their higher incomes.

A slow, steadily rising price level finances the growth of the U.S. economy. The **consumer price index (CPI)** is often used as a rough guide to inflation. The CPI has its limitations. Those who use it must be aware of and allow for the inability of the CPI to

Consumer price index (CPI) a guide that illustrates price changes in a representative selection of goods and services.

Cheat the Voice Mail Maze

CASE STUDY

The GetHuman™ movement was created in response to millions of consumers who want to be able to reach a human being when they contact a company for customer support. The primary goal of the movement is to convince companies that quality customer service and satisfied customers are ultimately important to the company's well-being and long-term success.

Via their website, GetHuman is helping consumers find their way through the voice mail maze as it attempts to get the human touch back into customer service. Many voice mail systems make reaching a human time consuming if not impossible. GetHuman has created a database of over 1,000 companies, including the company's phone number and the "prompts" needed to bypass the voice mail maze to reach a live person almost immediately. This Interactive Voice Response (IVR) Cheat Sheet is available free of charge at www.GetHuman.com. Consumers are catching on, and the IVR Cheat Sheet is becoming well known.

QUESTIONS

1. In general, what is your opinion of company voice mail response systems?
2. Do you think most companies would be in favor of or against the IVR Cheat Sheet?
3. Would you forgo listening to company messages and use the Cheat Sheet?
4. What outcome, positive or negative, might emerge as a result of widespread use of the Cheat Sheet?

Source: MSN Money and GetHuman. Retrieved April 20, 2009, from http://moneycentral.msn.com/content/Savinganddebt/consumeractionguide/P135866.asp.

account for quality improvements, a higher average living standard, and sale prices below list prices.

The CPI indicates that the dollar in early 2009 is worth about 15¢ when compared with the dollar in the 1960s. To have as much purchasing power as $10,000 had in the 1960s, a person would need approximately $60,000 in 2009. The experts see a continuing decline in the purchasing power of the dollar in the lifetime of the present generation; estimates differ only in the rate of decline. How can a small investor meet that challenge? One answer is to purchase corporate shares of common stock.

Hedge an attempt to offset losses.

The traditional theory that stocks are a **hedge** against inflation requires only that the nominal rate of return be equal to or greater than the rate of inflation. But for a stock to be a complete hedge, its real rate of return must be greater than its normal, required rate of return. For example, if the normal, required rate of return is 8 percent, and the price level rises 4 percent, a stock must yield at least 12 percent if it is to be a real hedge. Fluctuations in stock prices during the past few decades, including sharp declines at the same time the CPI was rising rapidly, are indicators that, in the short term, stock ownership not only may be a poor hedge against inflation but actually may turn out to be a negative investment.

WWW

www.bls.gov/cpi/#data

This site offers an inflation calculator using the consumer price index.

Guidelines for Investing in Stocks

A prudent investor adopts an investment philosophy and stays with it. Good rules to follow in buying stocks include the following:

1. Set goals and stick to them.
2. Investigate before investing.
3. Seek advice from an established and qualified firm.
4. Do not be a one-stock buyer. Diversify.
5. Be prepared psychologically for losses as well as gains.
6. Beware of tipsters; the cheapest thing in the world is unsolicited investment advice from people who are unqualified to give it.
7. Buy quality stocks for long-term investment and commitment.
8. Be cautious regarding new issues of stock, which can be risky.
9. Do not be concerned about daily fluctuations in your investment portfolio.

Of the million-plus active corporations in the United States, the stocks of only a few thousand are listed on the major stock exchanges.

FYI

Fraudulent Practices

The ethics and practices of Wall Street have come under increasing scrutiny due to the financial crisis of recent years. Frauds and manipulations cost investors billions of dollars each year. A common operation is **penny stocks.** Amateur investors are sometimes willing to take a chance by purchasing shares of these stocks, but the downside of the purchase is that the stocks are not scrutinized by the Securities and Exchange Commission (SEC). Therefore, full information about the companies is not available. Furthermore, penny stocks (also called micro-cap stocks) are sometimes offered through spam mail by companies that are either newly formed or approaching bankruptcy; therefore, liquidity is low. These characteristics make penny stocks enticing to fraudulent sellers, both offshore and in the United States, who exaggerate their true worth to potential investors.

Penny stocks stocks usually bought by amateur investors at prices ranging from 1 cent to $5.

Another fraudulent operation is the so-called boiler-room sale of phony stocks by telephone. Some stock salespersons are individuals with no training but with skill in finding gullible and greedy people who hope to make a quick gain. The ones who make the gain are almost invariably the sellers, not the buyers.

www.sec.gov

The Securities and Exchange Commission (SEC) was created as a result of the stock market crash in 1929. The website for the SEC explains its mission of protecting investors and ensuring that the securities market maintains integrity.

Even the so-called ethical brokerage houses have had employees who were indicted in recent years for stock schemes and manipulations that bilked thousands of investors out of billions of dollars. One tactic is **churning.** If you think your broker is involved with this practice, find another broker and lodge a complaint with the brokerage firm and the SEC. Buy stocks only from reputable companies and from reputable stockbrokers who understand the investor's wants and needs. The SEC monitors stock transactions and has issued warnings to the securities industry to stop unfair practices that are not necessarily illegal but may be unethical. Investors are urged to report any apparent improprieties to the brokerage house or the SEC, or both.

Churning a tactic of unscrupulous stockbrokers: telling investors to buy and sell frequently, with the intent to increase commissions for the brokers.

How to Buy Common Stocks

Ways to buy stocks include making direct purchases, investing in mutual funds, buying bond funds, and purchasing money market funds.

Direct purchase

If you decide to purchase growth stocks to hedge against rising prices, how should you proceed? Investment experts are almost unanimous in their recommendations that a small investor should first have an adequate insurance program, a substantial savings account in a bank, and some equity in a house. The investor who starts a stock-purchase plan should buy at regular intervals and hold on to the stock. Frequent buying and selling ("churning" your own account) is not for the inexperienced investor. Starting at about age 30, the small investor should continue to purchase growth stocks through the decades. Even at age 60, the investor should retain these growth stocks because life expectancy still will be 10 or 20 years, during which time inflation may be substantial.

Brokerage fees may be an additional expense associated with the purchase of stocks. One way to save on brokerage fees is to make large, infrequent purchases. For example, consider putting monthly savings into an interest-bearing savings account. After six or 12 months, use the accumulated savings to purchase stock. Alternatively, various brokerage companies offer types of "sharebuilder accounts" that allow periodic savings programs and stock purchases at reduced commission rates.

Brokerage fee the commission paid to a person in the business of securities for bringing about a transaction.

Many experts recommend investing a fixed dollar amount on a regular schedule, regardless of price movements, over a long time. By means of this procedure, known as **dollar cost averaging** (also known as constant dollar plan), the buyer will purchase more shares when prices are low and fewer shares when prices are higher. As a result, the average cost per share will be lower than the average market price. Dollar cost averaging lessens the risk of investing a large amount in a single investment at the wrong time. A dollar-averaging plan may be started at any market level and in any phase of an investment cycle. The investor must be persistent and continue through a multiyear period. Compare brokerage fees. With the advent of Internet discount services (e.g., E*Trade, TD AmeriTrade), competitive fees are readily available.

Dollar cost averaging the practice of regularly investing a fixed dollar amount over a period of time to avoid a one-time fixed large investment.

Specifically which stocks should a small investor buy? This is the real question, which only skilled professionals can answer—and even they sometimes make mistakes. Small, amateur investors who attempt to choose their own stock purchases are like doctors who try to be their own lawyers or lawyers who try to be their own doctors. Investors should choose a reputable and knowledgeable broker. Once they find this person, they should stay with their choice. Investors may find a good broker by asking an investment counselor, a banker, or a lawyer. They should choose a well-known firm that deals on the major exchanges and has offices in or near the place they live. They should ask for samples of the kinds of information that the broker will provide. With the aid of a reputable broker, small investors can diversify their purchases among industries and among companies so as to develop a balanced portfolio.

How much do brokers charge? In 1975, an SEC regulation went into effect that ended the 183-year-old practice of stock exchanges fixing commission rates throughout the country. The SEC's prohibition against fixed rates means that buyers may do comparison shopping among brokerage firms for the lowest commission rates and also may negotiate with brokers for special rates. When selecting a broker, investors should consider the costs of services other than merely executing orders. Many discount brokerage firms have opened during the past several decades. The Internet has further increased competition for both costs and information offered quickly and accurately (e.g., www.morningstar.com). Further, banks and other institutions are now selling stocks, mutual funds, and related services. Commissions of discount brokerages may be up to 70 percent less than those of full-service firms. Commissions often are lower because the discount firms do not offer the advice and the services of a full-service firm.

Advantages of a discount firm are that the client will be charged lower commissions on transactions, and no salesperson will call. These benefits are for individuals who know exactly what they want to do and do not think they need the advice of an investment counselor. On the other hand, a full-service brokerage firm offers a financial consultant rather than an order taker. It provides extensive research, timely advice, and the opportunity to establish a continuing relationship. Whether to choose a discount or full-service brokerage depends on the needs of the individual investor. With all brokers, the investor should negotiate the commission on a stock transaction. Full-service brokers and discount brokers may reduce their commissions to maintain old accounts or to gain new ones.

Mutual funds

Mutual funds are created by investment companies for the purpose of selling shares in the fund to investors, investing the proceeds in the securities of other companies, and managing the investments. The income of mutual funds is derived from dividends and interest received from the operating companies whose shares they own and from capital gains realized from the sale of appreciated securities. Shareholders participate in company income by receiving dividends in proportion to the number of shares owned. Established mutual fund companies number in the thousands.

In principle, the mutual fund is sound. It offers a way for small investors to diversify their investments. A large mutual fund may have in its portfolio stocks and bonds issued by more than a hundred different companies or governmental units. If one security in the mutual fund portfolio declines in price, that decline may be offset by a rise in another security. Similarly, the lower yields of some securities may be offset by higher yields from others. The greater risk of some issues is balanced by the greater security of others.

> WWW
>
> **www.fundalarm.com**
>
> Fundalarm.com informs consumers of mutual funds that are not performing well and are not anticipated to perform well in the future. The website offers individualized services so that the investor can determine if stock holdings are problematic.

In a period of rising prices, holdings of common stocks will yield larger earnings and capital gains. In a declining market, preferred stocks and bonds yield a steady income and maintain principal. The result is that the owner of shares in these funds hopes to have a hedge against inflation and deflation, at least in the long run. During certain periods of the past 30 years, however, many people lost confidence in mutual funds because of the decline in performance of many of these funds.

Four types of mutual funds are available: index funds, stock funds, bond funds, and money market funds. Within each fund group are various subgroups, with differing investment philosophies, risk, volatility, fees, and expenses.

Index funds. These funds invest in companies that mirror the return of market indexes such as the Standard and Poor's 500. These funds achieve their investment objective primarily by investing in the securities of companies in the selected index. Some index funds invest in all companies in an index. Index funds are based on the assumption that in the long term this overall market approach will yield higher returns than most other fund strategies. In addition, index funds have low expense ratios and are tax-efficient because of their low turnover ratios. Index funds are warranted for novice investors.

Stock funds. Among stock funds are many subgroups. Some of the subgroups, along with their investment philosophy, are the following.

- *Growth and income funds* invest in stocks that provide current income through dividends and with the probability of long-term growth.
- *Balanced funds* invest in a variety of stocks and bonds of high-quality companies.
- *Long-term growth funds* invest in companies with an anticipated steady, continual growth potential.
- *Aggressive growth funds* invest in stocks of smaller companies that have great potential; these are risky funds, although the potential for large gains is substantial.
- *International funds* invest in stocks and bonds traded on foreign stock exchanges. Their returns depend, in part, on the strength of the dollar. These funds tend to be somewhat volatile.
- *Sector funds* invest in specific parts of the market (e.g., tech, pharmaceuticals, oil). These funds are speculative because they lack market diversification, but the potential for substantial gain is large.
- *Precious metals funds* invest in stocks of gold mines and similar companies. The types of companies and industries in this grouping make them highly speculative, with a great potential for either gain or loss.
- *Value funds* invest in companies that the market views as underpriced, or low in comparison to their earnings potential. These funds are appropriate for a conservative investor.
- *Blend funds* invest in both high-growth and cheaply priced stocks. The risk factor of these funds is difficult to classify. Blend funds may also be called hybrid funds.

Many stock mutual funds invest in a combination of the above.

TIP

According to *Morningstar, Consumer Reports,* and numerous other reliable sources, consumers should choose mutual funds with low annual expense ratios. These include funds offered by Vanguard, Fidelity, and similar low-cost fund companies that will sell directly to consumers without the need of a financial salesperson middleman.

Bond funds. Mutual bond funds are of many types, some riskier than others. As a group, however, bond funds are more conservative than stock funds. Of course, the probable rate of return is generally lower than with stock-fund offerings. As with stock funds, bond funds invest in different types of bonds, some more risky than others. The safest are those that invest in U.S. Treasuries; these are virtually risk-free. Municipal bond funds issued by municipalities generally are free from state and federal taxes. Finally, corporate bond funds invest in corporations.

Money market funds. Money market funds invest in short-term debt instruments from a variety of sources including the federal government, banks, and large corporations. Virtually no market risk is involved in these funds, but the rate of return on the investment is apt to be only slightly higher than a passbook savings account. Many investors place money in these accounts for a short time when market conditions suggest that waiting to invest in longer-term aggressive investments is prudent. Depending on the debt instruments involved, some money market funds are taxable and others are tax-exempt.

Should Small Investors Use Mutual Funds?

Because small investors are often unable or reluctant to pay for the services of expert investment advisors whose annual fees range in the hundreds or thousands of dollars, many small investors find that mutual funds meet their needs at prices they can afford and are willing to pay. In addition to giving buyers professional management and diversification, mutual funds give them a sense of security. They offer small investors a convenient method of spreading risk at a reasonable cost, and they have raised the average return for many small investors. See Exhibit 13.1 for more information.

If an individual decides to use one or more mutual funds, the next challenge is how to select them. No final answer can be offered, as the situation changes constantly, but among the many factors to consider when choosing a fund are:

1. What type of fund does the investor want—stock, bond, money market, or a combination of any or all three?
2. What is the fund's investment policy?
3. What is its diversification policy?
4. What compensation does management pay itself and its advisors?
5. What is the performance record?
6. Is it a load or a no-load fund?

Questions and Answers Regarding Mutual Funds

What is a mutual fund? A mutual fund is a collection (or portfolio) of stocks and bonds. The manager of a mutual fund buys stock in companies (such as Ford, IBM, DuPont, and General Mills) using money provided by investors. If the manager does a good job picking stocks that increase in value, the mutual fund share price increases—and the mutual fund investor makes a gain.

Are mutual funds all basically the same? No. They vary widely. Some invest only in stocks, and others invest in bonds. Some funds invest in real estate or even in precious metals. Many funds invest in countries outside the United States, and other funds invest in only one country. Hundreds of mutual funds are very conservative because they do not invest in stocks or bonds (called money market mutual funds). They are safe, but they do not offer the potential for the higher returns that stock investments do.

How long have mutual funds been around? They have been in existence for over 100 years; however, the majority of the growth in the number of stock and bond mutual funds has been in the past three decades.

> **TIP** Pay attention to the length of time the mutual fund manager has been "at the helm." If you are comparing mutual funds over a five- or 10-year period, you would want to know how long the current manager had been in charge of the fund. Choosing a fund on the basis of its past performance may be risky if the current manager has been in charge for only a few months.

How does a person invest in a mutual fund? The two most common ways are:

1. You can contact a mutual fund company directly via a toll-free phone number, ask for information and an application form, and after reading the information send a check if you decide to invest.
2. You can purchase shares of a mutual fund through a broker, who normally will charge a sales commission of between 2 percent and 8 percent.

Typically, funds purchased directly from the mutual fund company itself are not subject to a sales commission. These are referred to as no-load funds.

No-load mutual funds. **EXHIBIT 13.1**

("No-Load" indicates that no sales commission is charged when you purchase or redeem shares)

T. Rowe Price funds can be started with a $50 automated monthly investment.
Ariel Funds can be started with a $50 automated monthly investment.
Homestead Funds can be started with a $1 automated monthly investment.

Data as of December 31, 2007

FUND NAME	5-YEAR AVERAGE % RETURN	10-YEAR AVERAGE % RETURN	ANNUAL EXPENSE RATIO (%)	MANAGER TENURE (YRS)	NET ASSETS ($ MIL)	TOTAL NUMBER OF HOLDINGS
LARGE CAP U.S. STOCK FUNDS						
Homestead Value	14.33	7.72	0.71	14.4	703	53
T. Rowe Price Equity Income	13.18	7.73	0.69	22.2	20,664	130
T. Rowe Price Capital Appreciation	13.11	11.00	0.73	1.5	10,339	112
Mid Cap U.S. Stock Funds						
Ariel	11.32	9.46	1.03	11.1	3,436	32
T. ROWE PRICE EXTENDED MARKET INDEX						
(Wilshire 4500 Index)	17.50	—	0.40	5.1	407	2,035
SMALL CAP U.S. STOCK FUNDS						
Homestead Small Company Stock	14.20	—	1.23	9.5	63	38
T. Rowe Price Diversified Small Cap	14.07	4.36	1.26	1.3	88	320
INTERNATIONAL (NON-U.S.) STOCK FUNDS						
T. Rowe Price Intl Growth & Income	22.93	—	0.91	4.9	2,490	170
Homestead Intl Value	20.04	—	0.99	1.6	132	50
BOND FUNDS						
T. Rowe Price Spectrum Income	7.86	6.47	0.80	9.1	5,102	10 other funds
Homestead Short-Term Bond	2.96	4.45	0.80	16.2	228	465

WEB ADDRESS AND PHONE:		
Ariel	www.arielmutualfunds.com	1-800-292-7435
Homestead	www.homesteadfunds.com	1-800-258-3030
T. Rowe Price	www.troweprice.com	1-800-638-5660

OTHER EXCELLENT FUND FAMILIES *(with higher minimums to open an account):*		
Dodge and Cox	www.dodgeandcox.com	1-800-621-3979
Royce	www.roycefunds.com	1-800-221-4268

Source: Craig Israelsen, Brigham Young University, 2008.

Is the money invested in a stock mutual fund guaranteed against loss? No. Savings accounts at a bank or thrift association are insured against loss by the federal government. Mutual funds do not offer the same protection.

What is the most important aspect of investing for the small investor? It is not historical performance. It is much simpler than that: affordability, or the dollar amount required to begin the investment. Generally speaking, most people invest money they have. If they do not have it, they do not invest it. For example, if an investment requires $10,000 and you do not have $10,000 (and do not want to borrow to invest), you cannot invest in that particular investment. To the average on-a-budget individual, what good is a mutual fund with a spectacular performance record if $10,000 is required to open the account?

www.morningstar.com

The website for *Morningstar* magazine offers mutual fund, stock, and variable insurance investment information. An independent company, *Morningstar* does not own, operate, or have holdings in mutual funds, stocks, or insurance products.

Many mutual funds waive the initial investment requirement for investors who start the account with an automatic investment plan (AIP) of at least $50 per month. An AIP consists of authorizing the mutual fund company to withdraw money from your checking or savings account automatically and purchase shares of a mutual fund.

The mutual funds listed in Exhibit 13.1 are "pure no-load"—meaning that the investor pays no sales commission to purchase shares or to sell (redeem) shares. It also means the broker requires no 12b-1 fee (a hidden load of sorts).

Past performance of any investment, again, is no guarantee of future performance. Many of the funds in the exhibit produced unusually high average annual returns during the late 1990s and suffered dramatic losses in several years following 2000.

A few suggestions about investing in mutual funds:

- Investing in stock mutual funds makes sense if you are willing to stay invested for at least three or four years. If you are not willing to commit to the investment for at least three years, you may want to consider investing in money market mutual funds, certificates of deposit (CDs), or a savings account. *The higher the risk of the mutual fund, the longer your investment period should be.* For example, if you decide to invest $50 monthly into the T. Rowe Price Science & Technology fund (a higher risk fund), your investment horizon may have to be at least five or six years. A longer investment period allows an investor time to recover losses in the event the stock market declines. More risky mutual funds may take longer to recover; hence the need for a longer investment period.

- If you are investing for the long term (over 10 years), you might consider selecting several different funds, perhaps one from each risk category. It would make sense for one of the four funds to be a fund that invests internationally or globally. (International funds buy stock in countries outside the United States, whereas global funds purchase stock of companies both in and out of the United States.)

- Once you have chosen funds you feel comfortable with, consider using the automatic monthly investment option to start the accounts. This approach essentially puts your investments on autopilot. Do not check your accounts every day, particularly if the account is for your two-year-old child's college tuition. As one mutual fund manager said, "If you want to take volatility out of your investments, check them less often." Follow up on your long-term investments several times each year. Stick to your plan. If the stock market declines, your automatic monthly investment will purchase more shares of the fund! Do not bail out when stocks (and funds) go on sale. A stock market going down can be a good thing, if you keep investing.

What is the next step for the small investor? Study the funds in Exhibit 13.1, choose a couple of them, and visit their websites. Request an information kit (including an account application) about the specific fund(s) you are interested in. You may request information for a regular account, a Roth IRA, or a traditional IRA (Individual Retirement Account).

An IRA account is designed for retirement savings and is not intended to be withdrawn until the investor is at least 59½ years old. A regular account is designed for additional investment purposes, such as saving for a car or home, and money can be withdrawn from the account at any time.

When you receive the information, find the account application and fill it out either for yourself or your child. If this is to be a custodial account for a minor child (under 18 in most states), use the child's Social Security number.

www.businessweek.com

The website for Business Week magazine offers information on topics ranging from small business to global businesses. Some content is for subscribers only.

WWW

If you decide to invest using the automatic monthly investment, you probably will have to attach a voided check to the application. This allows the mutual fund company to withdraw the monthly investment directly from your checking account. With the application filled out, simply mail it back to the fund company. If you are not using the automatic monthly investment option, attach a check to open the account. For many of the funds in the exhibit, the initial investment is fairly high. For example, a fund may require an initial investment of $5,000; another may require only a $50 initial investment to open a regular account (often lower requirements apply for IRAs). The Homestead Value fund, a below-average risk fund, has a minimum $1 automatic monthly investment.

Affordable funds typically allow investors to open an account with an automatic monthly investment of at least $50 per month, instead of the normal initial investment (often between $500 and $2,500).

FYI

If you have questions that are not answered on the website, call or e-mail the mutual fund companies. They are paid to help you.

Start investing early in life—time is a powerful thing. Consider the power of compound growth as shown in Exhibit 13.2. Plan to start a retirement savings program early in your career; see Exhibit 13.3 for a retirement savings example.

EXHIBIT 13.2

The power of compound growth.

ENDING ACCOUNT VALUE OF MONTHLY INVESTMENTS FOR 15 YEARS					
ANNUAL RETURN	$10	$25	$50	$100	$250
6%	$2,908	$7,270	$14,541	$29,082	$72,705
8%	$3,460	$8,651	$17,302	$34,604	$86,510
10%	$4,145	$10,362	$20,724	$41,447	$103,618

ENDING ACCOUNT VALUE OF MONTHLY INVESTMENTS FOR 30 YEARS					
ANNUAL RETURN	$10	$25	$50	$100	$250
6%	$10,045	$25,113	$50,226	$100,452	$251,129
8%	$14,904	$37,259	$74,518	$149,036	$372,590
10%	$22,605	$56,512	$113,024	$226,049	$565,122

Notice the difference in ending account value after 30 years versus 15 years.

EXHIBIT 13.3

Retirement savings example.

MONTHLY INVESTMENT REQUIRED TO MEET RETIREMENT GOAL OF $375,000*	
CURRENT AGE	ASSUMING A 9% ANNUAL RETURN
25	$80
30	$130
35	$205
40	$335
45	$560
50	$991

*$375,000 in an investment account at age 65 will allow you to receive $25,000 of "real" income (i.e. income that increases at a 5% rate each year) for 20 years. This assumes the investment account can earn an average return of 8% during retirement.

Source: Craig Israelsen, Brigham Young University, 2008.

INDIVIDUAL RETIREMENT ACCOUNTS, KEOGH PLANS, AND OTHER TAX SHELTERS

Individual Retirement Account (IRA) a retirement tax-deferred program designed for employees who have no other eligible tax-deferred program and whose income does not exceed specified limits.

Keogh Plan a retirement tax-deferred program for self-employed individuals.

The **Individual Retirement Account (IRA),** Roth IRA, and the **Keogh Plan** have become very popular in the past two decades, although the Tax Reform Act of 1986 dramatically changed the guidelines for IRAs. Under the old tax law, contributions could be made each year of 100 percent of earned income (maximum of $2,000 annually) to an IRA. If the spouse of a working person was not employed, a total of $2,250 could be contributed to a spousal IRA. Under the law passed in 1986, the total adjusted gross income must be less than $40,000 for a married couple on a joint return, or $25,000 for a single person, if the full deduction is to be allowed. With IRAs, all contributions to be deducted from that year's tax return must be made before participants file their income taxes. No extensions are allowed. All income and gains accumulate tax-exempt while in the account. This money is not taxed until it is withdrawn from the account, usually at retirement.

As of the early 2000s, $6,000 can be contributed to IRAs by a married couple: $3,000 to the wage earner's account, and $3,000 to the spouse's account, whether the spouse is or is not gainfully employed. The Roth IRA is now available to many investors. Exhibit 13.4 compares the traditional IRA with the Roth IRA.

A Keogh Plan is suitable for the self-employed investor. Each year the investor may contribute a certain portion of self-employment income into an investment that is not taxed until later years (usually retirement). Basically, the same types of plans available for IRAs can be initiated for Keoghs. Several retirement plans are available to small business owners and their employees. Basically, the following are available to small businesses and their employees. These include SEP (simplified employee pension) plans, SIMPLE (savings incentive match plan for employees) plans, and Qualified plans (also called H.R. 10 plans or Keogh plans when covering self-employed individuals) and including 401(k) plans. These plans offer employees and employers a tax-favored way to save for retirement. Employers can deduct contributions they make to the plan for their employees as well as the contributions made to the plan for him/herself. Earnings on the contributions are generally tax free until the proceeds are individually distributed from the plan.

FYI

According to the Department of Labor, college graduates earn about one million dollars more than their counterparts who do not attend college. Furthermore, college graduates make about 60 percent more than high school graduates. This is proof that education is worth it!

Various other retirement planning programs have gained interest among some investors. Among those worth consideration are 401(k) plans, 403(b) plans, and annuities.

The 401(k) plan, the 403(b), and the 457(b) plan are similar. The former is a plan for profit-making organizations, the latter two for nonprofits. The employer develops the plan, and the employee designates the amount to be deducted from each paycheck up to an allowable amount set each year by the federal government. Employer plans vary widely regarding the options offered, safety of investments, and so on. The money placed into the account is tax-deferred. Penalties do apply for early withdrawals from these accounts. The 401(k), 403(b), and 457(b) plans are excellent vehicles for most small investors. Many people utilize mutual funds as the underlying investment vehicle for their IRA, 401(k), 403(b), 457(b), and Keogh accounts.

WWW

www.wsj.com

The Wall Street Journal (WSJ) is a newspaper that provides comprehensive market information on a daily basis. Through the WSJ website, consumers may subscribe and read the paper on-line.

Annuities are sold by life insurance companies. They are similar to IRAs, but the maximum limit does not apply. Early withdrawal penalties, however, do apply, as is the case with the other programs noted. The major disadvantages of annuities are the sales commissions and the surrender charges, which, when combined, can exceed 10 percent on all monies invested. Insurance companies often invest these accounts in conservative instruments, and they usually guarantee minimum rates of return.

Saving for Education

Coverdell Education Savings Accounts (ESAs; formerly Education IRAs) are tax-deferred trust or custodial accounts established by a child's parent or guardian. Once set

IRA choices. **EXHIBIT 13.4**

Characteristics	Traditional IRA Rules*	Roth IRA*
Who Is Eligible to Invest?	Individuals under age $70^1/_2$ who have earned income or whose spouses have earned income, regardless of amount.	Individuals (and their spouses) of any age with earned income, whose adjusted gross income is below $116,000 (single) or $169,000 (joint). Individuals age $70^1/_2$ and under may contribute. An individual's participation in an employer-sponsored plan is immaterial to Roth contribution eligibility.
Deductibility of Contribution	Subject to limitation, contributions are deductible. Deductibility depends on income level for individuals who are active participants in an employer-sponsored retirement plan. Full deductions are permitted if taxpayer is not an active participant of an employer-sponsored plan. Partial deduction permitted for active participants of an employer-sponsored plan, who meet the adjusted gross income (AGI) limits ($30,000 to $40,000 for single filers; $50,000 to $60,000 for joint filers).	No deduction permitted for amounts contributed.
Annual Contribution Limits	Individuals (and their spouses) may contribute up to $5,000 annually (or 100% of compensation, if less). *Overall limit for contributions to all IRAs (traditional and Roth combined) is $5,000 annually (or 100% of compensation, if less).*	Individuals (and their spouses) may generally contribute up to $5,000 (or 100% of compensation, if less). Ability to contribute phases out at income levels of $95,000 to $116,000 (individual) and $150,000 to $169,000 (joint). *The allowable contribution is $6,000 per year for those age 50 and older.*
Rollover/ Conversion	Individuals may roll over amounts held in employer-sponsored retirement plans.	Rollovers from other Roth IRAs or traditional IRAs only. An individual whose adjusted gross income is higher than $100,000 is not permitted to roll over a traditional IRA to a Roth IRA. Amounts rolled over (or converted) from traditional IRAs are subject to income tax in the year rolled over or converted.
Tax Advantage	Tax-deferred investment growth.	Tax-free investment growth if account is open for five years or more.
Tax Treatment of Distributions	Total deductible contributions and all earnings taxed as ordinary income in the year of withdrawal. Distributions attributable to nondeductible contributions are considered a (nontaxable) return of capital. Distributions made before age $59^1/_2$ may be subject to a 10% penalty. Early withdrawal can be made penalty-free prior to age $59^1/_2$ upon death, disability, the purchase of first-time home or higher education expenses.	Distributions made after age $59^1/_2$ are tax-free if the Roth IRA has been held for more than five years. Distributions made before age $59^1/_2$ may be subject to a 10% penalty. Early withdrawal can be made penalty-free prior to age $59^1/_2$ if the Roth IRA is held more than five years, upon death, disability, the purchase of first-time home (up to $10,000 lifetime maximum), higher education expenses, medical expenses in excess of 7.5% of AGI, or health insurance premiums (for those unemployed more than 12 weeks). Also, you can withdraw your contributed principal from a Roth IRA without tax or penalty at any time.
Minimum Distribution Requirements	Distributions must start by age 70½.	No requirements to begin withdrawal at age 70½.

Source: Craig Israelsen, Brigham Young University

*Substantive changes in the law in this area frequently occur. Consider the amounts noted as guidelines (examples only).

up, anyone can contribute to the account. The maximum annual contribution from all parties is $2,000.

Not only is the growth of the money in the account tax-deferred, but also the distributions—provided that the money is used to pay for the beneficiary's undergraduate or graduate education expenses at a qualified institution. The money may be applied to the cost of books, room and board, supplies, fees, equipment, and tuition.

In most cases, the money in the IRA must be distributed before the beneficiary reaches age 30. After that time, the money is taxable and penalties will apply. A family may, however, roll the money over to another child in the family prior to the beneficiary's reaching age 30. Should the money not be used for educational expenses at any time during the beneficiary's life, taxes and penalties also apply. Updated information on this program is available at www.irs/gov/publications/p970.

Another plan, the 529 plan (named after its IRS code section number), is a state-sponsored investment program. Two options are available: (1) Prepay tuition at a qualified educational institution at today's tuition rates, or (2) save money in a tax-deferred account (earnings only) to be used to pay for education at future tuition rates. The second option is the most popular. All account earnings are exempt from federal tax when funds are withdrawn (unless funds are used for something other than higher education).

The money in a 529 plan is owned by the account holder, not the child. Anyone can open and contribute to a 529 account, with as little as $25 per month. As with ESAs, the money can go toward tuition, books, room and board, transportation, and computers. Each state offers its own version of the 529 plan, so it is wise to shop around. State programs vary and you are not required to use your state's plan.

www.nyse.com

The website for the New York Stock Exchange (NYSE) is an educational as well as a resource tool for the investor. Stock market data is easily accessible through this website.

SOURCES OF INFORMATION AND SAFEGUARDS

Published Sources of Information

Many amateur investors are naive and demonstrate a surprising lack of precaution when investing. Serious investors, large or small, need to know something about general economic conditions and business prospects, now, in the near future, and in the long run. They need to know how to identify industries having growth potential and how to locate growth companies in growth industries. Security analysis is a highly specialized field in which thousands of analysts function full-time. Even they make misjudgments, but their mistakes typically arise more out of differences in evaluation of information than out of emotion or lack of information.

Basically, an investor should be familiar with financial reports, terminology, and related topics. Both the New York Stock Exchange and the American Stock Exchange publish free materials. Among other main sources of information are Moody's, Standard and Poor's, and Value Line Investment Survey.

TIP Utilize the wealth of free investment information from www.morningstar.com, www.vanguard.com, and other reliable sources.

Moody's Investors Services produces reference materials on corporations, governments, and financial institutions, and a stock guide. Standard and Poor's issues market forecasts and recommendations on specific stocks. Value Line reviews thousands of stocks in nearly 100 industries; it gives an in-depth review of stocks and specific industries on a rotational basis every few weeks. Because these publications and services are quite expensive, however, the small investor might be wise to consult them in libraries, at banks or brokers' offices, or through financial planners.

Some of the most informative newspapers and periodicals are: *The Wall Street Journal, Business Week, Forbes, Barron's Weekly, Money Magazine, Kiplinger's, Consumer Reports, The Financial World, Fortune,* and *Smart Money.*

An investment plan requires keeping accurate records for tax purposes, supervising the account, and storing securities in a safe place. Small investors can do all this themselves, or, for a fee, accountants, attorneys, bankers, brokers, or independent financial planners will do it for them. Fees generally range from 1/3 percent to 1 percent of principal, with a minimum ranging from $500 to $1,000.

Protection for Investors

Amateurs may be victimized both by themselves and by fraudulent sellers of worthless pieces of paper. When a consumer is swindled in the purchase of a product, it is a misfortune, but usually the amount involved is not large. When an investor is swindled, the amount may or may not be large, but it may represent all the investor's savings.

TIP Anyone can legally be identified as a financial planner, so before you hire a financial planner, be certain the individual is certified. Also, recognize that if planners are working for no fee, their fees probably will be made by selling investments for which they will earn commissions. Investment advice given in such situations may be biased.

Until 1933 the prevailing rule in the sale of new securities was, "Let the buyer beware." Heavy losses incurred by investors during the early 1930s resulted in extensive Senate committee investigations. Those inquiries revealed amazing conditions in the securities markets. The testimony and evidence made it clear that under the practices then governing the marketing of securities, prospective investors were fortunate if they avoided losses.

www.amex.com

The website for the American Stock Exchange (AMEX) provides access for investors to various market information. It is the second-largest floor-based exchange, and its vision is to make major advancements in the global securities market.

Federal laws to protect investors

To protect investors, Congress enacted a series of laws, beginning with the Securities Act of 1933. These laws provide that those who issue securities for sale to the public in interstate commerce must file a registration statement containing pertinent information about the issue and the offering. Unless a registration statement is in effect, selling the securities is unlawful. If a registration statement is found to contain misinformation or omissions, the registration may be denied, suspended, or canceled. The fact that a security is registered by the SEC does not constitute a guarantee by the SEC that the facts disclosed are accurate, nor does registration imply SEC approval of the issue. Registration does not insure investors against loss. Its sole purpose is to provide information on the basis of which investors may make informed and realistic evaluations of the securities.

www.fortune.com

The website for *Fortune* magazine allows consumers to access full-text articles about investing, businesses, and other information. Some content is for subscribers only.

Since the original Act, the federal security laws have been amended on various occasions. The Sarbanes-Oxley Act (SOA; also known as the Public Company Accounting Oversight Board or PCAOB) was passed in 2002. Its primary goal is to affect corporate governance, financial disclosure, and the practice of public accounting. Specifically, its new rules are intended "to

Check 21

The Check 21 law (effective October 2004) makes it easier for banks to electronically transfer check images instead of physically transfer paper checks. Check 21 allows for substitute checks that are special paper copies of the front and back of your original check, created to represent the original check. These substitute checks can be transmitted electronically from bank to bank, thus allowing them to be processed more quickly. For example, if Bank A receives a check from you written on Bank B, Bank A wants to receive those funds as soon as possible. Electronic transmission of checks speeds up this process.

If you already receive digital pictures of your canceled checks, this law will not greatly affect you. If you receive paper copies of your canceled checks, you may notice a slightly different format in your monthly statements.

Some important points to remember:

- Your bank may not pay a check unless you authorize it; this is done when you sign it.
- If your bank uses substitute checks, your checks will be processed more quickly.
- The substitute check is a legal copy and proof of payment.
- The law does not require the bank to return the original check to you.
- If there is an error, you may claim a refund (aka expedited recredit) from your bank.
- Your bank and the Federal Reserve have information about this law.

protect investors by improving the accuracy and reliability of corporate disclosures made pursuant to the securities laws."

The SEC administers securities laws to protect the interests of the public and investors against malpractice in the securities and financial markets. This involves surveillance of all persons and companies covered by the several Acts and the prosecution of violators. Anyone may direct a complaint or inquiry to the central office of the SEC or to the appropriate regional office. Registration statements and other public documents are available for public inspection.

State laws to protect investors

Many states have laws to protect investors in securities traded only within the state. As a general rule, state laws are less comprehensive and less effective than federal laws. In spite of federal and state laws, those who are gullible or who hope to parlay a 5-cent share of oil, uranium, or aerospace stock into a fortune will invariably be discovered by slick operators and defrauded.

SUMMARY

Consumers consider investment important in their financial agendas. Small, conservative, defensive investors should be concerned with security of principal, diversification, stability of income, marketability, and tax implications. Real estate, U.S. Treasuries, municipal bonds, corporate bonds, certificates of deposit, mutual funds, and common stocks are some of the investment vehicles that small investors pursue.

The Internet is a substantive information resource for the average investor. Investors should be cautious, however. Before considering investments, the astute consumer will obtain published materials from reliable sources and identify the various federal and state laws that have been enacted to protect investors. This chapter was written with the small investor in mind and with safety as a prime consideration. The best protection is for investors to evaluate their individual needs and to determine tolerable risk, the maximum amount that can be lost, and the primary investment objective; to take the time needed to evaluate options and to build their investment knowledge; and to evaluate the current diversification of assets in their portfolios.

ITEMS FOR REVIEW & DISCUSSION

1. Give some reasons why people save. Identify some ways in which a person can save money. What are the best ways to fund things such as a college education?
2. State the differences between investment and speculation.
3. Define leverage. How does inflation influence investment decisions? Are common stocks a good hedge against inflation?
4. Discuss events affecting the U.S. economy during the 1970s, 1980s, 1990s, and 2000s that made investors reevaluate some investment principles.
5. Classify and evaluate stocks and bonds as investment possibilities. Delineate the hazards of stock ownership and bond ownership.
6. Describe what kind of financial program, or coverage, a person should have before investing in stocks.
7. Compare and contrast buying stocks with buying mutual funds. What are the advantages and disadvantages of each for the small investor?
8. Enumerate the reasons why investors need government protection. Relate ways in which the federal government and your state government attempt to protect investors.
9. Relate some basic concerns of the small investor.
10. Discuss strategies for funding education (tuition).
11. List several advantages and disadvantages of investing in real estate. Should a small investor invest in real estate? Why?

EXPLORING PERSONAL VALUES: PROJECTS

1. Place a check mark next to any item that reflects your attitude:
   - ○ Safety of principal is important to me.
   - ○ I enjoy the thrill of following the stock market.
   - ○ I am sickened by the thought of the market value dropping for any shares of stock I might own.
   - ○ I believe undeveloped real estate represents one of the best investments in today's market.

   Did you notice that the first and third items represent conservative investor attitudes and values, and the second and fourth items represent a willingness to take risk in investments? Selecting a combination points to the development of a highly diversified portfolio.
2. Trace the price and dividend record of three stocks and three bonds over a decade or two. Evaluate them as investments.
3. Find out the various kinds of accounts, interest rates, yields, methods of compounding, and crediting of interest at two credit unions and two commercial banks, and compare.
4. Draw up an investment program for a husband and wife who have two young children and who have inherited $50,000.

5. Find out all you can at a broker's office about one load and one no-load mutual fund.
6. Discuss your parents' (or other relative's) investment program with them.
7. Using the school library and the Internet, research investment information. If you were to receive a gift of $10,000, how would you invest it?
8. Visit your state's securities commission website and determine its roles and responsibilities in protecting consumer interests.

ADDITIONAL SOURCES OF INFORMATION

Bernstein, William J. *The Four Pillars of Investing: Lessons for Building a Winning Portfolio.* Columbus, OH: McGraw-Hill, 2002.

Fischer, Michael. *Saving and Investing: Financial Knowledge and Financial Literacy that Everyone Needs and Deserves to Have!* Bloomington, IN: AuthorHouse, 2007.

Israelsen, Craig L. *The Thrifty Investor: Penny-Wise Strategies for Investors on a Budget.* New York: McGraw Hill, 2001.

Long, Charles. *How to Survive Without a Salary: Learning How to Live the Conserver Lifestyle.* Buffalo, NY: Warwick Publishers, 2003.

Orman, Suze. *The Courage to Be Rich: Creating a Life of Material and Spiritual Abundance.* New York: Riverhead Books, 2002.

Orman, Suze. *The Laws of Money, The Lessons of Life: Keep What You Have and Create What You Deserve.* New York: Free Press, 2003.

Ramsey, Dave, and Sharon Ramsey. *Financial Peace.* New York: Viking Press, 2003.

Tobias, Andrew. *The Only Investment Guide You'll Ever Need.* Orlando, FL: Harvest Books, 2005.

Tyson, Eric. *Investing for Dummies.* Hoboken, NJ: John Wiley & Sons, 2008.

14

> I detest life-insurance agents; they always argue that I shall some day die, which is not so.
>
> **STEPHEN LEACOCK,** CANADIAN ECONOMIST & HUMORIST

KEY TERMS

actuary
beneficiary
chartered life underwriter (CLU)
health maintenance organization (HMO)
indemnity
insurable interest
insured
insurer
life insurance
Medicaid
Medicare
no-fault insurance
preferred provider organization (PPO)
premium
probability
social insurance
term insurance
universal life insurance
variable life insurance
whole life insurance

The following concepts will be developed in this chapter:

1. The purpose of insurance is to protect an individual's financial well-being against the hazards to which it is exposed.
2. Insurance works because it is built on a foundation of sound principles.
3. Social Security should be looked upon as a supplement to one's insurance and retirement program.
4. Property and liability insurances are necessary to protect one's assets.
5. A life insurance program should be designed to fit the unique needs of an individual at any given time.

After having read this chapter, you should be able to accomplish the following objectives:

1. Cite the hazards against which the consumer may wish to be insured.
2. Identify a number of the sound principles upon which the concept of insurance is based.
3. Discuss the contributions of Social Security to U.S. society with respect to life insurance, health insurance, and retirement.
4. Explain the principles and purposes of insurance as they relate specifically to property and liability coverage.
5. Identify the different types of life insurance available, and offer suggestions as to situations in which each would best apply.

WHAT IS INSURANCE?

Approximately 85 percent of Americans are protected by some type of private health insurance, according to the U.S. census. The amount of money spent for insurance contracts increases every year. Over the past 50 years, life insurance purchases increased from a total of approximately $30 billion of coverage a year to more than $1 trillion a year!

Insurance is a mechanism to protect against financial loss. During a lifetime, people face a multiplicity of hazards and risks, many of which can result in temporary or permanent loss of income. The major hazards threatening financial security are premature death (death before normal retirement age), an incapacitating illness or accident, unemployment, and outliving one's

Understanding and Using Insurance

earning power. Added to that are the constant threats of property loss and liability and automobile loss and liability.

Many people trust to luck that they never will have a serious illness or accident; others attempt to accumulate sufficient savings to insure against loss of income or property damage. Both these methods of dealing with the risks of life have serious flaws. The incomes of most people do not allow them to save enough to provide any substantial benefits.

One way people can insure themselves and their families safely against these risks is to cooperate with others who face the same risks. This method substitutes a small, certain loss (the insurance premium) for a larger, uncertain loss. It allows an individual to meet a financial loss if the event insured against occurs, and it also reduces or eliminates the worry caused by uncertainty. This is the insurance method.

Insurance protections include the compulsory payments for Social Security, which provides financial protection to oneself and/or survivors in case of permanent disability or premature death and also provides pension benefits. Other types of insurance include life insurance, health insurance, disability insurance, automobile insurance, and homeowner's insurance. Dental insurance and liability insurance also have become popular in the past decade.

When consumers have responsibility for purchasing something that costs in the tens or hundreds of thousands of dollars, they usually investigate the product or service carefully in advance. How much thought and care should a person put into purchasing financial protection? People have no choice about paying for Social Security, and their employers have no choice about paying premiums for unemployment compensation, but individuals often do have a choice in how to allocate the money spent for almost all of the rest of their financial protection programs. To acquire a reasonable understanding of insurance before purchasing it is prudent.

How Insurance Works

Insurance is a voluntary, cooperative way of sharing risks and minimizing losses. It transfers the risks of many persons to an insurance company by means of a contract between the **insurer** and the **insured.** In the contract, the company promises to pay a

Insurer (insurance company) a profit-making corporation that assumes the risk of financial loss.

Insured (policyholder) the individual or group for whom risk is assumed.

Beneficiary the person or persons named in an insurance policy who are to receive benefits if the event insured against occurs.

Premium periodic payment for insurance coverage.

stated sum of money if and when the event insured against occurs. The money may be paid to the insured or to one or more **beneficiaries.** For example, in a life insurance policy, beneficiaries are the persons who are to receive death benefits after the insured dies. In the contract, the insured—or someone who has an insurable interest—agrees to periodically pay a sum of money, the **premium,** to the insurance company.

To illustrate the way insurance works, assume that the parents of each of 1,000 students in a given college own houses valued at $200,000 each. Assume further that the houses are substantially similar and that the annual fire loss for the group averages 0.5 percent. This amounts to $1,000 per house. For the 1,000 houses, the fire loss would be $1,000,000 each year. Statistically, five of the houses will be destroyed by fire. The uncertainty lies in the fact that no one knows which five. All owners can protect themselves by paying $1,000 apiece into a common fund. These premiums would build a fund of $1,000,000, enough to reimburse the five upon whom the fire loss falls.

What do the 995 property owners whose houses remain intact obtain for their expenditure of $1,000? All receive the assurance that if their houses had been destroyed, their net losses would have been reduced from $200,000 to $1,000. In the same way, every buyer of insurance of any kind has the assurance that if the event insured against occurs, she will be reimbursed out of the payments made by those who are insured. A person who buys sound insurance never loses, because that individual purchases protection, which is delivered day by day, hour by hour.

> WWW
>
> **www.insweb.com**
>
> The InsWeb search engine allows the consumer to find low-cost insurance coverage. Automobile, term life, homeowner's, renter's, and individual health insurance are examples of insurance products listed.

What insurance can do is reimburse the owner for personal loss. The $1,000 that each of the above owners pays provides protection for a limited period, because the total collection is sufficient to meet total claims, including administrative expenses, for just 12 months. The cost is $1,000 for the second year, and so on, indefinitely as long as the policy is in effect. This is **term insurance.**

Term insurance a form of insurance that protects against a stated risk for a specified period of time.

Accumulating a fund of $200 million to reimburse the owner of each of the 1,000 houses is not necessary. As long as the average number of fires remains the same, an annual charge of $1,000 will yield the necessary $1,000,000 to reimburse the five owners on whom the fire loss falls. The premium remains constant year after year. It will not be returned to an owner whose house does not burn, because the owner receives the benefit whether or not his house is destroyed: protection. For $1,000 every 12 months, the owner gets exactly what he buys—protection—at a low price.

> **TIP**
>
> Reevaluate your insurance program periodically with your current agent and with competitors. Often the competition will provide insight as to where your insurance needs could be better met by increasing some coverages and decreasing others.

A contract insuring protection against loss by fire cannot prevent destruction of the property (although the fire-prevention programs of underwriters may reduce the number of fires and the annual loss attributable to them).

The protective function of insurance is illustrated by accident and health coverage. On the basis of accident reports and public health records, it is possible to predict with a high degree of accuracy how many persons in a group of one million will be sick or injured during any year. The **actuaries,** the individuals employed by insurance companies to compute and develop their rates, draw on historical information and mathematical knowledge. Arbitrary **indemnity** can be promised after the actuaries complete their computations.

Actuary an employee of an insurance company who computes risks and then develops premium rates based on those risks.

Indemnity the legal limits of the insurance policy.

An example of the indemnity of disability insurance is $1,200 a month for the rest of the life of the policyholder in the event of total disability. Or the indemnity may take the form of a lump-sum payment, such as $10,000 for loss of the left hand or $50,000 for death if it results from a certain kind of accident. All of this can be promised with almost perfect assurance that the annual premiums will yield a common fund large enough to pay all claims, cover administrative expenses, and yield a profit. Like fire insurance rates, these premiums are constant, annual term charges for protection against the hazards named in the contract. If the insured person lives through the year in good health and without injury, she is happy. The insurance company did not keep the insured person well or safe; nor could the insurance company guarantee that she will escape illness or injury. What the company can do, and does, is to guarantee that if an illness or an accident occurs, the insured person will receive financial reimbursement as provided in the contract. The premium paid goes to reimburse the unfortunate ones who did suffer illness or injury.

FYI

Students graduating in the early years of the 21st century may pay out more than $100,000 by the time of retirement to protect their family from a variety of financial risks!

TIP

Before purchasing insurance from a company, be certain the company is economically sound. Your state insurance commissioner and other independent rating services can assist you.

Health and accident insurance is similar to fire insurance in another respect. Although premiums remain constant in general, as a building grows old, if it deteriorates and becomes a firetrap, the premium may increase. Ultimately, the insurance company may refuse to provide further insurance when the risk becomes so great that the premiums would be greater than the protection would be worth. Although accident and health insurance premiums generally remain constant, some insurance companies refuse to issue contracts to people older than age 65 because the risk that the events insured against will occur is so great that the rate would equal or exceed the contract benefits.

WWW

www.insure.com

The insure.com website offers a wealth of general and specific insurance information for the consumer.

Life insurance policies insure against unexpected death and benefit individuals who depended on the labor or income of the deceased. The unknown variable is not if but when death will occur. Mortality tables show that death is not as likely to occur in a person's early years as in later years, just as health statistics show that ill health is more likely to occur in later years. Although actuaries cannot determine which individuals in a large group will die, they can predict with a high degree of accuracy how many in the group will die within a certain time frame. A year-to-year, term life insurance policy costs very little in a person's early years. In later years, as the likelihood of death increases, the annual premium becomes an increasing portion of the indemnity.

Life insurance a form of insurance that pays the beneficiary a specified sum of money when the insured person dies.

Suppose that 1,000 young people, aged 22, who will graduate from college next June, have each taken out a $1,000 loan from the college. They all expect to repay the loan out of earnings. None of them, of course, anticipates premature death. Nevertheless, mortality statistics show that two of them are likely to die sometime during the next five years. To protect the college against the hazards of premature death during the five-year period, each person pays $6.50 a year to an insurance company. The $6,500 that the insurance company collects is invested to yield interest, which, added to the principal and increased by subsequent premiums, will be sufficient to pay off the deceased students' loans, as well as the expenses of administration. By means of insurance, each of the insured students has substituted a small, certain loss ($6.50 a year) for a larger, uncertain loss (up to $1,000) to the college. This is a simplified example, but it illustrates the principles of life insurance.

Renter's insurance is not a very good buy. True or false?

False. If you are renting an apartment, house, or condo, investing in renter's insurance can relieve a lot of stress and save you money. However, if you are a dependent college student, before you purchase the insurance, check to be certain your parents' homeowner's insurance does not provide adequate coverage for out-of-home college students.

PRINCIPLES OF SOUND INSURANCE

Five insurance principles are explored in the following pages. These apply to all forms of insurance.

Probability

Probability an insurance principle that companies use to calculate the amount of money necessary to reimburse claimants.

Underlying the operation of solid insurance is the concept that the number of people insured must be large enough for the principle of **probability** to apply. This principle is also referred to as the law of large numbers. It is possible to predict what will happen in a group numbering one million with great accuracy. On the basis of mortality statistics for large numbers of people, actuaries may predict with assurance that at age 22 the probability of death is 1.86 per 1,000 lives. Using that information, actuaries can calculate the amount of money necessary to reimburse claimants, pay administrative costs, and produce a profit for the company.

The Insured Must Incur Loss

Insurable interest the requirement that, to obtain insurance, the beneficiary of the contract would suffer a financial loss.

If insurance is to operate on a sound basis, the policyholder must have an **insurable interest.** In accident and health insurance contracts, the insured has an insurable interest because he would suffer a loss if the event insured against should occur. In life insurance contracts, any dependent possesses an insurable interest in the life of the insured. In the case of property insurance, the owner has an insurable interest in the property.

As insurance has developed, the concept of insurable interest has expanded. Not only dependents but also creditors, business partners, and employers may suffer a financial loss if the life or property insured is destroyed. The reason for limiting beneficiaries to persons possessing insurable interest is to prevent the writing of contracts in favor of anyone who would gain more by having the life or property destroyed than by having it preserved.

Indemnity Must Not Exceed Loss

Closely related to the principle that a beneficiary must incur loss is the principle that the amount of indemnity should not exceed the loss caused by the event insured against. Obviously, if a $200,000 house were insured against fire loss for $250,000, the owner would gain if a fire were to occur. In such a case, the gain would be so substantial that the owner might be tempted to start a fire to collect the insurance. Invariably, arson increases in times of business recession when some business firms find themselves in financial straits and the value of the business declines below the level of insurance.

When insuring human lives and writing contracts to cover temporary or permanent loss of health, companies usually limit the indemnity to a percentage of the insured person's earning power. If this were not done, the insured might be tempted to "develop" a chronic illness. Contracts guaranteeing to reimburse the insured for expenses of hospitalization, surgery, and medical care usually stipulate specific amounts.

The federal government has no authority over insurance companies. Insurance laws and regulations are enforced by state, not federal, law.

FYI

The same general rules apply to contracts covering accidents. Sometimes arbitrary amounts are specified for losses of certain parts of the body, such as an eye or a foot. Some contracts combine the loss of, for example, the right eye *and* the left foot. This, of course, is unlikely, and the amounts promised by the insurer are arbitrary. For artists and performers, contracts may be written to cover the hazards of their occupation or the importance of certain parts of the body, such as the fingers of a musician.

In terms of insurance, a person's life is considered to be worth the capitalized net income attributable to that life. An insured person may name almost anyone as a beneficiary and, legally, may insure his or her life for any value. The rule that most companies follow is to limit the amount of insurance on any one life. One company uses a scale that limits the coverage on a single life according to age. A person between ages 20 and 24 may be restricted to $200,000. Another company may have a maximum limit of $500,000. Policies in excess of these limits often are *reinsured* to spread the risk. For example, a $10 million contract on the life of one person may be underwritten by several companies.

The Event Insured Against Must Be Determinable

A fundamental principle in writing insurance contracts is that it must be possible to determine when the event insured against has occurred. For example, before a life insurance company will pay a claim, the beneficiary must present a death certificate issued by a public official. In cases in which an insured person is missing, a seven-year waiting period before the insurance will pay off is common. In cases of accident and health insurance, there may be doubt as to the genuineness and severity of injuries. Malingering, the feigning of illness, is common. To protect themselves, insurance companies depend on physicians' judgment. If a doctor certifies that the insured is ill, injured, or disabled, the insurer usually will pay the claim.

Applying this principle is not usually a problem when those insured present claims under property insurance contracts. Physical destruction or damage is evident and measurable. Automobile accidents, however, present the problem of responsibility. In the early days of insurance, responsibility for an accident had to be determined and would be considered in the calculation of the payout. Currently in many states, however, the fact that an accident did occur is the primary fact, and insurance companies pay claims regardless of responsibility for an accident. This is known as **no-fault insurance.** After paying a claim, however, the legal principle of subrogation permits an insurance company to sue another company, corporation, or person for reimbursement in case the party being sued can be proved to have caused the accident.

No-fault insurance a form of insurance that pays the claims of the injured regardless of who is responsible for the accident.

One reason private companies do not write unemployment insurance contracts is the difficulty in determining when the event insured against has occurred. This type of insurance is written exclusively by government agencies. By requiring those who are collecting unemployment insurance to register at employment offices, malingering can be kept to a minimum.

The Event Insured Against Must Be Uncertain

If a loss is inevitable, risk is not present, and insurance does not apply. Because death is absolutely certain, insurance against death as such is not feasible. Because the time of death is uncertain, however, it is possible to insure against death within a stated period of time. Incapacitating accidents or illnesses are not certain; many people go through life without having an accident or suffering an illness. Unemployment is not certain. Damage to or destruction of property is not certain. Public liability is not a certainty. Because these hazards are possibilities rather than certainties, it is possible to insure against losses resulting from them.

SOCIAL SECURITY

In the midst of the Great Depression in the 1930s, Congress established a **social insurance** plan. The basic difference between private and social insurance is that private insurance is selective whereas social insurance is inclusive. The reason why private insurers are selective is that some individuals are better "risks" than others. Persons who have reason to believe they may die prematurely, incur accident or illness, or suffer unemployment are likely to buy insurance. Private insurers consider them poor risks. The persons who are good risks are more likely to take a chance. Hence, private insurers require thorough physical examinations and investigations of the private lives of applicants for insurance purposes. All undesirable risks are screened and eliminated. Private carriers may refuse to write certain types of insurance coverage, such as unemployment insurance.

Social insurance a type of insurance that requires all members of a society to participate.

Social insurance carries the concept of group insurance to its ultimate. More than 90 percent of people in the United States who are gainfully employed participate in the Social Security system. The only exceptions are some government workers, some clergy, and some individuals working abroad. The compulsory feature of social insurance eliminates the element of adverse selection, where predominantly poor risks are insured. It reduces expenses to a minimum. It pays no commissions. Administrative expenses are relatively low.

Benefits of Social Security

The four different kinds of Social Security benefits are: survivors', disability, retirement, and medical.

Survivors' benefits

If an insured worker dies, survivors may be entitled to receive Social Security benefits up to an amount based on a rate schedule for the specific situation. For example, widows or widowers, children under age 18 (18 to 21 if a student, and any age if disabled), and dependent parents aged 62 and older are eligible for survivors' benefits.

FYI *Eligibility for Medicaid is determined by a recipient's assets—home, bank accounts, and so on. Therefore, before they need assistance, many elderly persons give their homes to their children. If done within the government guidelines, this is a legal way to increase chances of eligibility for Medicaid and should be considered as an option as families plan for medical expenses.*

Disability benefits

Insured workers receive disability benefits for themselves if they are unable to engage in any substantial gainful activity for at least one year. The spouse and children of a disabled worker also receive payments.

Retirement benefits

The typical retirement age for workers has increased. Insured workers born in the 1950s qualify for benefits at age 66. Insured workers born after 1960 qualify for benefits at age 67. Workers also have the option of retiring at age 62, but their monthly benefits are reduced by approximately 30 percent. Family members who qualify for benefits under the insured's work record have the option of selecting reduced benefits at age 62 or full benefits at age 65. (The "full retirement" age will be raised again in coming years.)

From a purely economic standpoint, it is not possible to know which of the above options is more advantageous, because the life expectancy of a specific person is uncertain. Data suggest that if a person lives at least 75 years, retiring at age 65 is more economically advantageous.

Hospital and medical insurance for the elderly

Medicare a federally funded health care insurance program for the elderly and the disabled.

Many Americans are eligible for **Medicare,** a voluntary, federal, hospital and medical insurance program operated under the Social Security system. The hospital insurance program pays most of the costs of services in a hospital or assisted living facility, including rooms, medicines, supplies, general nursing care, and meals. This includes reimbursement for reasonable charges for physicians' services. In addition, the insured are entitled to outpatient hospital services for diagnosis and treatment, and to some home health services. Also included are other medical and health services, such as diagnostic tests, surgical dressings and splints, and rental or purchase of medical equipment. The hospital insurance is financed by payroll contributions, which are a part of the Social Security tax. The medical insurance is financed by monthly premiums paid by the federal government and the insured person.

TIP Be certain your health care facilities, including hospitals, labs, and physicians, are all certified by Medicare before services are provided.

Medicare symbolizes a national commitment to meet, in part, medical needs rationally and effectively. The program has achieved its major aim of freeing the aged from the fear that crushing medical bills will leave them paupers, but the costs have been great. The soaring costs of health care are creating some real problems for Medicare and those who benefit from it. Estimates are that Medicare's trust fund will be depleted by 2019, and "fixes" for the system are being considered.

Medicaid is another part of the Social Security Act. Medicaid is available for certain needy and low-income people—the aged (65 and older), the blind, the disabled, and members of families with dependent children. Medicaid is an assistance program paid for from federal, state, and local taxes. It is a federal–state partnership; the states design their own Medicaid programs within minimum federal guidelines. As a result, Medicaid programs vary substantially from state to state. Medicaid can pay what Medicare does not pay for people who are eligible for both programs.

Medicaid public programs to assist persons, regardless of age, whose financial resources are insufficient to pay for health care.

Evaluation of Social Security

The Social Security tax is a payroll tax. The original Social Security Act was passed in 1935, when economic depression prevailed; minimum taxes and benefits were included in the law. As the economy has grown, higher taxes and larger benefits have become possible. Hospital and medical insurance (Medicare) for the elderly now are included in the program, and coverage is almost universal. In an economy in which the price level continues to rise, Social Security payments are adjusted automatically for changes in the consumer price index.

Much has been written about the precarious future of Social Security. Predictions made by the Social Security Administration (SSA) state that under current operation practices, the Old-Age and Survivors Insurance (OASI) and Disability Insurance (DI) trust fund reserves that partially support retirement and survivor benefits, and disability benefits, respectively, will be depleted by 2041. This means that full benefits will not be made on a regular and timely basis. The primary reason for the depletion of the funds is the burgeoning retirement movement expected between 2010 and 2030 from the baby boom generation (those born between 1946 and 1964). Suggested solutions to problems with the Social Security system include some combination of payroll tax rate increases, benefit decreases, and privatization.

Most families pay more into the Social Security tax system than they do into the federal income tax system.

FYI

How to Meet the Risks of Old Age

When the Social Security system was established in the 1930s, it arose partly out of the idea that older people should be treated as persons, not as derelicts. Instead of being sent to institutions, they should be able to live out their last years in their own homes. They should be freed from dependency on their children and should not have to undergo the humiliation of depending on charity. The Social Security Act of 1935 incorporated the concept of Social Security pensions for the aged. These were to be paid as a matter of right, not as charity.

Although the early Social Security pensions were meager, they represented a fundamental break with the past. As the national income increased, it was hoped that the break from dependence to independence for the aged could be accomplished. The benefits have been liberalized during the intervening years. Nonetheless, few older persons can rely solely on Social Security as their retirement income. According to the Social Security Administration, about 30 percent to 40 percent of retirement income comes from Social Security. The remainder comes from pensions and other company benefits (20 percent to 25 percent), full- or part-time employment (about 20 percent), and the remainder from other assets, such as savings, stock dividends, and public assistance.

www.ssa.gov

This is the official government website for all Social Security matters. It offers a plethora of information about the U.S. Social Security system. Personal Social Security information can be obtained, as well as general announcements, rule changes, instructions for changing your name, and much more.

PROTECTION AGAINST PROPERTY LOSS AND PUBLIC LIABILITY

Young couples contracting to purchase a house for the first time often are unaware of all the hazards they may be facing and liabilities they could incur. All kinds of things might happen, from fire loss to loss caused by windstorms. The more frequent causes of loss or liability have been grouped in various forms of insurance contracts. For specified premiums, property owners may purchase the protection they need.

The homeowner's policy is available in seven forms: basic, broad, comprehensive, special, renters, condominium, and older home. Exhibit 14.1 shows the perils against which properties are insured under these forms. Comprehensive personal liability is included in all seven forms. This coverage protects the insured and all members of the family against liability claims by others resulting from accidents other than automobile accidents that occur on or away from the insured premises. Also included are medical payments up to a specified amount for individuals incurring accidental injury on the insured's premises, or elsewhere if caused by the insured, members of the family, or their pets. Guests on the insured's premises are covered. Liability coverage also includes payments for damage to the property of other people.

WWW

www.iii.org

The website for the Insurance Information Institute (III) offers information about various types of insurance products, including auto, home, and health, to consumers, media, industry, and researchers.

TIP

Consider supplementing a comprehensive homeowner's policy by obtaining coverages for excluded perils (such as flood insurance and earthquake insurance). The cost of the additional coverage is usually quite low, and the risk of substantial losses may be quite high. Unfortunately, participation in these supplemental insurances is typically small (10 percent to 20 percent).

Q+A

You are renting a television set, and it is stolen from your home. You are liable for the loss. True or false?

True. Check your contract. Also, check with your homeowner's or renter's insurance company before you rent, and request a rider on your policy. In some cases, the item will be covered subject to the limits of your coverage.

The homeowner's insurance policy developed for condominium owners (HO-6) has slightly different coverages for personal property and additional living expenses. It has the same coverages for comprehensive personal liability, personal property away from premises, damage to property of others, and medical payments.

A property insurance contract is a formidable document containing hundreds, perhaps thousands, of lines of legal language in small print. It is important to know what perils are not included. The standard form lists 10 exclusions. Individuals may purchase coverage for some of the excluded perils. Most of the perils are possibilities rather than probabilities. Most low-income homeowners cannot afford to buy protection against every possibility. The basic homeowner's contract often provides the necessary protection.

Calculating property insurance premiums is so complicated that no attempt can be made to explain the process in this short discussion. Premiums vary according to the type of house, materials of which it is made, proximity of firefighters and water, and many other variables.

WWW

www.kbb.com

The Kelley Blue Book website can be used as a resource to assess the value of new and pre-owned automobiles.

Several thousand companies in the United States sell property and liability insurance. A good source for insurance information is the Insurance Information Institute.

EXHIBIT 14.1 Perils against which properties are insured under various homeowner's policies.

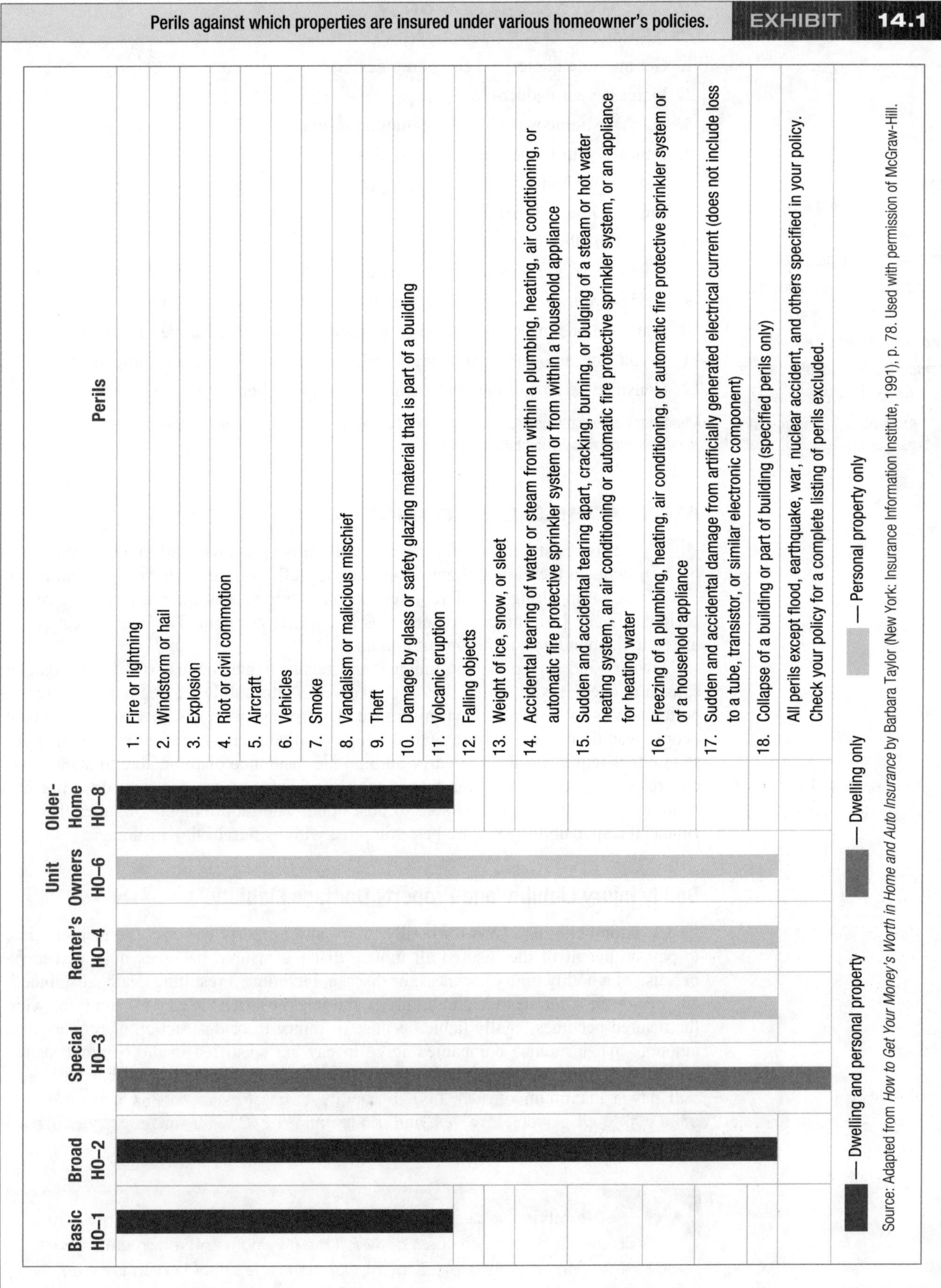

Source: Adapted from *How to Get Your Money's Worth in Home and Auto Insurance* by Barbara Taylor (New York: Insurance Information Institute, 1991), p. 78. Used with permission of McGraw-Hill.

TWELVE WAYS TO SAVE MONEY ON YOUR HOMEOWNER'S INSURANCE

1. Get multiple quotes and compare rates.
2. Increase your deductible.
3. Purchase homeowner's and automobile insurance from the same carrier.
4. Improve your home's resistance to disaster.
5. Insure your home for the rebuilding costs rather than your purchase price.
6. Improve home security.
7. Research other discounts.
8. Check on your eligibility for coverage through a group with which you are affiliated.
9. Review your policy limits and insurance on your possessions annually.
10. Stay with one insurance company to receive long-term customer discounts.
11. If you have a government insurance plan, check rates of private companies.
12. Consider the cost of the homeowner's insurance when buying a home.

Adapted from *Saving Money on Homeowner's Insurance,* Insurance Information Institute, www.iii.org/individuals/homei/hbs/save/.

FYI

Shopping around for homeowner's insurance is well worth the time. The cost of identical policy coverages may vary by as much as 300 percent. By calling five or six agents and comparing Internet offerings, a person might save several hundred dollars each year.

AUTOMOBILE INSURANCE

Over the past half century, several million people have died in automobile accidents in the United States. Automobile traffic on the highway kills and maims at an appalling rate. Every few seconds someone is injured in an automobile accident. Every 10 minutes someone dies in a traffic accident. The overall cost is estimated in the hundreds of billions of dollars.

Owners and drivers of automobiles are legally liable for loss of life and damage caused in accidents in which they are involved. Automobile leasing also requires the policyholders to have their own insurance. The responsibility is so great that sensible people would not dare venture onto the highways without insurance protection. Every state either requires drivers to carry automobile insurance or to be able to show financial responsibility. This means that if the driver is in an accident and does not have insurance, that driver must be able to post bond. The requirements of states that have financial responsibility laws are best complied with by purchasing insurance.

Bodily Injury Liability and Property Damage Liability

Under automobile insurance for bodily injury and property damage, the insurer agrees to pay on behalf of the insured all money that the insured becomes obligated to pay because of a bodily injury, sickness, or disease, including a resulting death, sustained by any person in a car accident. In addition, the insurer agrees to pay all sums for which the insured becomes legally liable because of injury to or destruction of property. The amounts that insurance companies agree to pay are specified in the contract, usually indicated by three numbers, such as 100/300/25. These figures mean that the insurer will pay a maximum of $100,000 for bodily injury to one person, a maximum of $300,000 to all persons involved, and a maximum of $25,000 for property damage in one accident. This level of coverage is common.

TIP

Purchase liability "umbrella" coverage of $1 million or more. The difference in premium costs between the minimum and maximum umbrella coverage is small and therefore the higher coverage should be considered.

Premiums vary according to the area in which the car is driven, the age of the car, the purpose for which it is used, the age and marital status of the driver, and whether a young driver has taken a driver's training course. In addition, some companies have lower rates for individuals who do not drink or smoke and for students who are earning good grades.

Medical Payments or Personal Injury Protection

A medical payments policy pays medical and hospital expenses if the insured is injured in an automobile accident. Additionally, personal injury protection (PIP) coverage allows for medical payments, lost wages, and the cost of replacing services normally performed by an injured person. If the insured dies, these coverages cover part of the funeral expenses. Coverage applies whether the insured is driving his own car, a rented car, or a borrowed car. It also applies if the insured is a passenger or walking. Finally, it protects all members of the insured's family and passengers who are guests in the car.

> **TIP** Be certain that any insurance you purchase does not duplicate coverage you have already (for example, your health insurance policy may cover automobile medical payments for yourself and your guests).

Collision

A collision insurance policy pays for losses incurred if the insured automobile is damaged in a collision. This coverage is expensive, compared with liability coverage. Moreover, if the collision involves another car, the insurance on that automobile may cover the damage. For these reasons, automobile owners should consider carefully the cost of collision insurance compared with the cost of assuming the risk themselves. Most owners would be wise to have collision insurance on new automobiles. If the car is purchased on credit, the lender normally requires collision insurance coverage.

The principle of deductible insurance is used in collision insurance. If the insured agrees to pay the first $100, $250, $500, or $1,000 of damage costs, the premium declines sharply because so many accidents are minor and involve damages of less than those amounts.

> **TIP** Drop collision coverage when an auto's value decreases substantially, typically in the fifth or sixth year. For example, if the book value of the vehicle is $1,500 and the deductible equals $1,000, the maximum insurance benefit is $500.

Comprehensive and Personal Effects

A comprehensive and personal effects policy reimburses the insured person for losses incurred if the automobile is stolen or is damaged or destroyed by fire, hail, hurricane, flood, or other listed perils. Also included are losses of personal effects. Some items, such as expensive sound equipment, are frequently excluded. When comparison shopping, determining exclusions is important. Comprehensive insurance is relatively inexpensive.

Towing and Labor Costs

Under coverage for towing and labor costs, the insurer agrees to pay those costs if the insured automobile is disabled and, with respect to the labor costs, if the labor is performed at the place where the car broke down. The probability of this occurring is minimal. That is why the premium is only a few dollars each year. Automobile clubs usually include this coverage in their membership costs.

> *For many consumers, towing coverage is a better buy than joining an auto club. The cost of the premium is less, and the service typically is more convenient.* **FYI**

Uninsured Motorists

Insurance against uninsured motorists is included in many contracts, and it is required in most states. The insurer agrees to pay the insured for injury by an uninsured or hit-and-run driver. If the insured dies, the insurer pays the amount specified in the contract to a named beneficiary.

Many auto insurance policies automatically cover you when you rent a car. In this case, you will be able to refuse the insurance that is being offered by the rental car company. Be sure to check your coverage for this feature.

FYI

Individual Versus Mass-Marketed Automobile Insurance

Although group accident, health, and life insurance can be purchased under group plans at a lower cost than under individual contracts, property and casualty insurance companies have been slow in developing group plans. Some group plans for auto insurance have rates that are approximately 20 percent below individual rates, but rates still differ among members of the group, according to their accident records, age, marital status, and personal habits. Buyers should compare group plans before buying, because some group policies offer little or no savings from the insurance company's regular price, and others give substantial reductions. Even though states regulate insurance rates, the rates within a state can vary considerably from company to company.

Fault or No-Fault Insurance?

Automobile owners and operators are faced with a dilemma. They must use their cars, and they are legally liable for injury to other persons and for property damage, yet insurance premiums rise faster than the CPI and protection is becoming harder to obtain and keep. Many applicants for insurance are rejected, and many policies are canceled. The fault system of compensation leaves many claimants unpaid or underpaid; all too frequently, it overpays on minor claims to avoid costly litigation. Public dissatisfaction with automobile insurance has risen to such a high level that some state governments have instituted various kinds of no-fault insurance laws.

Under no-fault laws, the victim's insurance company pays medical expenses and income losses. Generally the policyholder does not have the right to sue for "pain and suffering" unless she has serious injuries or relatively high expenses. No-fault laws typically cover only personal injury, leaving property damage to the traditional collision and liability insurance. Provisions of no-fault insurance vary widely from state to state.

When shopping around for insurance, ask for the discounts available. Numerous reductions are offered, and most consumers qualify for one or more of them.

FYI

A nationwide no-fault system of automobile insurance has been proposed several times in Congress; each time it has been defeated. Opponents contend that a national system actually would increase costs. Others suggest that the bill has not passed because powerful attorney groups and insurance groups are opposed to the bill. Attorneys would lose billions of dollars in fees, and insurance companies would be subject to strict federal regulations. In any case, the promise of saving money through no-fault insurance is disappearing as medical costs and losses of earnings continue to increase.

Some property and liability insurance companies have run into serious financial trouble since no-fault laws have gone into effect. Some blame the no-fault laws. Others blame the management of the insurance companies. Insured parties may be partially responsible by padding costs up to the threshold and using the insurance money to hire a lawyer and sue for more.

No-fault laws are here to stay, and eventually they may be in effect in all states, either with or without federal action. Where effective no-fault laws have been passed, the benefits accruing from faster and more equitable compensation for accident victims have been substantial.

INSURANCE TO COVER ACCIDENTS AND ILLNESS

In the 1960s, the right of each citizen to adequate health care was accepted as a national policy goal. In the early 1970s, the challenge was to make that right a reality. Since that time, the issue has been whether it is feasible and economically justifiable for the federal government to assume responsibility for adequate health care. Tremendous increases in health care costs have raised serious questions as to just how the costs should be borne in the future. Elected officials propose plans and changes, but as of this writing no such changes have been implemented.

More than 45 million U.S. citizens do not have health insurance, more than at any other time in our history.

FYI

Costs of Health Care

In 1955, Americans spent approximately $20 billion on health care; by 1965, the figure had risen to approximately $40 billion, which was about 6 percent of GNP. In 2008, health care spending in the United States reached $2.4 trillion, or about 17 percent of GNP. Unless heath care reform is enacted (and succeeds), costs are projected to reach $3.1 trillion in 2012 and $4.3 trillion by 2017, or about 20 percent of projected GDP. Other first-world countries spend a lesser percentage: for example, in 2008 health care spending accounted for 10.9 percent of the GDP in Switzerland, 10.7 percent in Germany, 9.7 percent in Canada, and 9.5 percent in France, according to the Organization for Economic Cooperation and Development.

www.medlineplus.gov

MEDLINEplus provides information from the National Library of Medicine (NLM) at the National Institutes of Health (NIH). Consumers can rely on this website for current medical information.

WWW

It is impossible to discuss in any detail here possible reasons for such increases in health care spending. One factor is an aging baby boomer population, and another may be increases in obesity and other quality of life diseases. The medical community cites the need for increased fees and charges by doctors and hospitals to cover the malpractice insurance premiums, and the costs of additional X-rays and tests ordered to protect themselves against malpractice lawsuits.

As medical costs have gone up, Medicare, the federal government program of health insurance for older persons, is covering a smaller and smaller percentage of the total costs of health care. Meeting higher health care costs has become a critical consumer problem in the 21st century.

How to Pay for Health Care

In addition to HMOs and PPOs, which will be discussed shortly, various other types of health coverage are available. These are:

- *Disability-income insurance.* The oldest form of health insurance, and perhaps the most important protection, it pays cash for loss of income. The recipient may use the money for any purpose. Benefits often provide from one-half to two-thirds of usual income and continue for between 13 and 52 weeks for short-term contracts, and for life on the more expensive, long-term contracts. Social Security benefits include disability coverage for individuals disabled longer than six months.
- *Hospital expense insurance.* This covers room and board. Additional expense insurance covers fees for laboratory, X-rays, operating room, anesthesia, and drugs. Deductibles are typical, with maximum limits for per-day and per-stay coverage.
- *Surgical expense insurance.* This helps to pay the surgeon's fee and typically is purchased with hospital expense insurance. The type of policy usually specifies amounts allowed to surgeons for specific types of surgery.
- *Major medical expense insurance.* This covers catastrophic accidents or illnesses in amounts ranging from $5,000 to $250,000 or more. Deductibles typically range from $100 to $1,000, and the insurance company pays a percentage of the remaining bill (usually 75 percent to 80 percent). The policyholder pays the remainder, up to an annual maximum of a few thousand dollars.
- *Dental expense insurance.* Coverage typically includes full or partial payment for examinations, X-rays, cleanings, fillings, extractions, and other expenses related to dental care.

In addition to these programs, less typical ones have become popular during the past decade. Examples include vision care insurance, contact lens insurance, specified catastrophic disease insurance, and long-term care insurance.

Generally, the coverages noted above and the premiums charged are affected by the insured person's age, gender, physical condition, medical history, occupation, personal habits, moral character, and place of residence. Administrative expenses for group policies are considerably less than for individual contracts. As a result, most Americans who are insured are participants in group plans in which employers pay all or part of the premium. No physical examination is required for group coverage, and the insurer cannot cancel the contracts without canceling the entire group.

Colleges, fraternal societies, consumer cooperatives, and professional associations also make group plans available to their staff and members. Most offer about a 10 percent premium savings. Perhaps the best-known group plan is Blue Cross Blue Shield.

Unlike life insurance, medical insurance should cover every member of the family. In planning a medical insurance program, a family must consider all possible sources of income in case of accident or illness. The most important source of income during illness or disability may well be Social Security payments. The amount of benefits a totally disabled person is eligible for under Social Security depends on a number of variables, including age, amount of previous earnings on which Social Security taxes were paid, and number of dependents. A group health insurance plan at a person's place of employment might cover hospitalization charges for a period of 30 days for short-term illness.

In addition, many employers have sick-leave plans. Some unions also have group medical plans. Most states have workers' compensation laws, under which compensation for hospitalization arising out of accident or illness on the job is fully covered. Veterans of military service may use government military hospitals (VA hospitals) without charge. Most major medical insurance is sold under a group contract. These plans provide protection against catastrophic expenses.

Analysis of the family's needs for medical insurance may show that individual accident and health insurance policies will be needed to fill the gaps. In policies from insurance companies that sell accident and health insurance, disability benefits usually are limited to 50 percent or 75 percent of earnings, with a ceiling. There is no standard contract. Definitions of total disability range from inability to do anything to inability to do the insured person's regular job. The length of time before benefits are paid (called the waiting

CASE STUDY Deadly Life Insurance

Two elderly women, Olga Rutterschmidt and Helen Golay, found a way to make a significant sum of money. They offered to get homeless men off the street in exchange for their signing a life insurance policy, with Olga and Helen as the beneficiaries. The women then used the men's signatures, via rubber stamps, to take out more insurance. The problem was, the only quick way to capitalize on these insurance policies was for the men to die. Olga and Helen arranged this by having the men killed in apparent hit-and-run traffic accidents. Two such accidents are known (in 1999 and in 2007), and authorities believe that there may have been other victims.

This fraud was discovered only coincidentally: two police officers, discussing active cases, determined that their cases were very similar. When they reviewed their paperwork, they found that the same two women were involved. In 2008, the two women were sentenced to life in prison.

QUESTIONS

1. Do you believe the insurance industry has any responsibility in these cases?
2. What do you think could be done to prevent this from happening in the future?
3. Do you think this will affect future insurance policy claims? If so, how?
4. What financial compensation, if any, do you think should be extended to the victims' families?

Source: *The Washington Post,* May 22, 2006.

period) ranges from a few days to several months. The longer the waiting period, the lower the premium. Most contracts exclude certain types of illness, and some are highly restrictive. Some contracts may be canceled by the company at any time; others may not.

Choosing a reputable agent or broker is crucial. Equally important is to choose a reputable company. Substantial premium savings can be attained by selecting high-deductible programs. Many individuals and families can pay for short-term medical expenses out of income. It is the long-term medical care for which insurance is needed. Individual contracts should be noncancelable, and the waiting periods should be the shortest length the family can afford. Potential buyers should read proposed contracts carefully, especially the fine print that lists excluded illnesses.

Some policies insure against a specific disease, such as cancer. The benefits, however, usually are not substantial, and the costs often are disproportionately high. Insurers sometimes use scare tactics to promote this type of coverage. Before buying, the individual should be certain that the benefits offered do not duplicate current coverage, that the coverage is substantial, and that the premium costs are justified.

Managed Care Plans

Managed care plans typically are categorized as either **preferred provider organizations (PPOs)** or **health maintenance organizations (HMOs).**

Preferred provider organizations (PPOs) groups of health care providers that contract with insurance companies to provide health services at a discounted rate.

Health maintenance organizations (HMOs) groups of health care providers that contract with insurance companies to provide health services at a prepaid rate.

Managed care plans did not exist a few decades ago. Today these programs provide health protection for the majority of Americans who have health insurance. An estimated 200 million Americans are currently in managed care programs. Proponents of managed care plans contend that these are more efficient and less costly than other programs and that they promote preventive medicine and health care as well. Opponents suggest that membership is too restrictive, that they offer lower-quality medical care, and that they take shortcuts to keep costs down. Regardless, managed care programs are here to stay and are destined to continue to expand as health care costs increase.

TIP When considering an HMO, be certain that: (a) the HMO's physicians practice at the best hospitals where you reside; (b) at least 80 percent of the physicians are "board-certified"; (c) the HMO is fully accredited; (d) it offers a "report card" from members, consumer groups, and employers; (e) the report card is excellent; and (f) the HMO has an appeals process that is fair and reasonable.

LIFE INSURANCE

Term Insurance

All pure insurance protection is term insurance, meaning that the insured is protected against a stated risk (e.g., death) for a specified period of time. Property protection and liability insurance contracts typically are written for terms of one year. Usually life insurance terms range from one year to the years until a person reaches age 65.

If the event insured against occurs within the specified term, the insured is entitled to the indemnity that the contract specifies. If a person wishes to have maximum low-cost protection against any hazard for a specified time period, term insurance provides that protection.

TIP If you need life insurance, buy term, not permanent insurance, and invest the premium savings in other higher-yield investments.

Decreasing term insurance

Decreasing term insurance is a variation of straight term insurance. The premium is even lower for decreasing term insurance than for straight term insurance. Individuals who purchase decreasing term insurance do so to secure maximum protection for beneficiaries in the early years when savings are low. As the insured's investment program develops and the dollar amounts of the investments increase, the need for insurance protection in case of premature death diminishes. As the need for insurance protection diminishes, the amount of term insurance decreases.

Group term life insurance

Group term insurance is written on a group of lives rather than on individual lives. The cost is minimal because of the yearly renewable term contract. If a group is large enough, an insurance company is safe in forgoing medical examinations of each member of the group. This also reduces expenses. Administrative expenses are reduced further by issuing a master contract instead of individual policies. Payment for the premium is made in one check, thereby eliminating hundreds of thousands of individual bookkeeping entries.

The premium per thousand dollars of insurance varies according to the mortality experience of the group. As group insurance usually is written on employees, the employer pays the variable amount. Employees often pay a fixed premium each year regardless of age, if under age 65, and without medical examination. If a person leaves the employ of the company that provides group insurance, the amount of individual coverage often can be converted to another type of contract without the insured's having to take a physical examination. The person has only to pay the premiums scheduled at the age of conversion.

Group term life insurance accounts for about half of all life insurance in force in the United States. FYI

The amount of group life insurance available to an individual usually is related to the person's annual income. Typically, in case of premature death, the proceeds of a group life insurance policy yield the same amount that the insured would have provided for her family if she had lived another one or two years. In lieu of salary, the proceeds of a group life insurance policy are intended to help beneficiaries make the adjustments necessary in their way of living.

Permanent Life Insurances

Permanent life insurances include whole life, universal life, and variable life insurance. Many people believe or have been told that term insurance may be inexpensive in the early years but premiums increase rapidly as the insured grows older. Actually, term insurance premiums do not increase as sharply as some people suppose. To overcome the objection, however, insurance company actuaries developed the level annual premium, which includes the **whole life insurance** plan. This excess premium charged for whole life policies is invested in a reserve account to meet claims in later years. The investment yields the maximum interest consistent with security of principal.

Whole life insurance a policy on which a lump sum benefit is paid upon the death of the policy holder and which usually offers a low interest-bearing savings program, but at a higher premium than for group term life insurance.

Using a mortality table and an assumed rate of interest, actuaries can calculate with a high degree of accuracy the uniform annual premium that will yield the reserve needed to pay claims in later years. An analogy would be a plan under which a person would pay a doctor more than the actual annual cost of medical care between ages 22 and 48, with assurance from the doctor that the annual charge would not increase from age 48 until death, even though the actual cost would be greater.

This type of contract introduces a new feature into life insurance. No longer is the policyholder buying pure protection at actual cost, except in the long run. The policyholder now is also saving involuntarily. The annual saving creates a fund from which he may borrow in later years or which he may secure by surrendering the policy. Whole life is also called ordinary or straight life.

Universal life insurance

The insurance industry also has developed **universal life insurance** programs. Unlike whole life, universal life pays rather high interest rates on the savings component. Universal plans have as many variations as companies offering the program. For example, annual premiums can change dramatically based on the policyholder's needs and desires; policies may pay different amounts at maturity; and cash withdrawals can be taken as loans.

Universal life insurance a policy that combines death benefits with a savings/investment program.

Universal life plans are better than other life insurance savings programs. Nevertheless, because of high administrative costs and the wide variations in programs, most experts continue to agree that consumers who need insurance should "buy term and invest the difference."

Variable life insurance

With **variable life insurance,** policyholders select the type of investment that best meets their long-term financial planning strategies. For example, instead of the insurance company determining the interest rate, the policyholder determines which investments (e.g., stocks, bonds, money market funds) should be considered. The risk factor often increases as the consumer moves into more speculative areas.

Variable life insurance a policy that combines death benefits with an investment program that is selected by the policyholder.

TIP Be wary of insurance agents who promise high rates of return on your life insurance "investments." Generally, these return amounts are highly inflated and do not include administrative and commission charges that will be assessed.

HOW TO CHOOSE A COMPANY

The big-name company is not necessarily the one that offers the best buys in life insurance, just as the big advertiser is not necessarily a better company than a nonadvertiser. Among the multitude of insurance companies are scores of unknowns whose contracts are good buys. These may be discovered by searching the reputable publications that rate insurance companies. The fact that a company is old does not prove that it is the best. On the other hand, buyers should be cautious in dealing with a new company.

When you are choosing a company, a broker can be helpful in giving advice and printed information, which might include comparative financial reports and statistics. If special hazards exist, extra premiums may be charged, or the coverage may be excluded. The prospective buyer should ascertain which mortality table a company uses and what interest rate it is guaranteeing on its policy reserve. Also, a buyer should compare dividend schedules and net premiums over a 10- or 20-year period.

Credit unions often offer life insurance policies to their members at no cost. **FYI**

When comparing rates, be sure to consider cost indexes. For many years the life insurance industry used the "net cost method." Premiums paid over the years were added together, and then dividends received and the cash surrender value were subtracted. This figure then was divided by the face value of the policy to determine the cost per thousand. The final figure frequently was less than zero, and consumers were led to believe the policy didn't cost anything. Of course, the flaw in this method is that the interest value of the premium money was not considered.

Some insurance agents emphasize that such simple comparisons of an essentially complex product are misleading and that comparative cost indexes are based on arbitrary assumptions not applicable to all cases. Until some better measure is adopted, however, buyers of life insurance should find out what the interest-adjusted cost index is for the policy they are considering.

When in doubt, prospective buyers can consult the insurance commissioner in their home state. This is recommended especially in cases of companies doing business by mail.

Questions and Answers Regarding Life Insurance

Should life insurance be used as a method of saving? Most experts say that a person should save separately. In a typical year, approximately a third of the premiums that purchasers of life insurance pay are paid as death benefits to beneficiaries. More than half of the payments to policyholders are made to insured people who are still living. This means that many people are using life insurance as a method of saving. In some circumstances, life insurance may be a satisfactory method of saving, but for the overwhelming majority of consumers, combination protection-and-saving contracts are more expensive than pure insurance contracts. More important, the combination policies often leave the family underinsured in case of the policyholder's untimely death.

Is life insurance sold or bought? Historically, life insurance has been sold by private firms. Before deciding whether to use a term or whole life contract and whether to use the contract as a method of saving, prospective buyers should consider the objectivity of the advice they have been given. Insurance buyers today are more sophisticated than they used to be. Nevertheless, they still are woefully uninformed. Despite all the information available, consumers have great difficulty understanding how to compare the costs of one life insurance policy with another. Premiums tend to be equated with cost—a mistake that can prove to be expensive. In general, consumers know little about the different types of life insurance available and, in particular, little about the differences between term and cash value policies.

Of families with life insurance, the average coverage per family is far less than the recommended net worth needed, which is at least five times annual salary.

FYI

Millions of households save through life insurance because their information about life insurance usually comes from the insurance agent. Historically, insurance companies, instead of paying salaries, paid their agents a commission to motivate them. The difficulty is in the way the commission schedule is set up. Many companies, for example, pay first-year commissions on whole life policies of about 55 percent to 60 percent of the first year's premium; by comparison, term policy sales commissions average 35 percent to 40 percent. In addition, the premium rate is related directly to the face value of the policy. The premium for whole life policies most often is higher than for term. These factors combine to give agents a strong incentive to sell whole life contracts, regardless of the consumer's needs.

Agents sell life insurance on a full- or part-time basis. Whether they are qualified to advise buyers in planning insurance and investment programs is uncertain. Standards for insurance salespersons are all but nonexistent, although states do require licenses to sell insurance. The chief criterion of an agent's success is often the volume of insurance she writes. A person need not know anything about the intricacies of insurance to secure an agency contract with many companies. A person may have failed in every previous business or professional venture, yet some insurance company will hand him a rate book without question and say "go to it." The result has been the writing of insurance with an eye to the size of commissions rather than to buyers' needs.

Despite all the high-pressure selling, more than 10 percent of American families do not have any life insurance. The average amount of coverage per family is usually inadequate. Because this amount includes life insurance for the entire family, the coverage on the chief breadwinner is even more inadequate. One of the major reasons for underinsurance is that consumers are sold policies that do not meet their needs.

Who should be insured? The original and basic function of life insurance is to provide income for the beneficiaries of the insured if the insured dies prematurely. The person who should be insured, then, is the person or persons who provide the income. Another way to state this is to consider the economic hardship that the loss of a family member would impose on the family. If the economic loss would be little, nothing, or actually an economic windfall, the need for life insurance on that individual is questionable at best.

The primary wage earner and other large contributors to household income need life insurance. In addition, single parents should carry life insurance.

Some insurance agents argue that the services of a homemaker are as valuable as if that person were occupied outside the home. If that is true, the spouse should buy life insurance to yield enough income to replace the homemaker's monetary value if the homemaker should die prematurely. This argument has two flaws:

1. Insurance is expensive, and few families can afford to carry insurance on the wage earner and another person.
2. The argument assumes that all the work the homemaker performs would have to be done by hired help if the homemaker were to die. In most cases, however, the surviving spouse and children assume much of this work.

Should the lives of children be insured? Children rarely should be insured. Parents love their children and are easily persuaded to purchase goods and services for them that will promote their happiness and welfare. Some insurance agents have convinced parents that they should insure the lives of their children. Among the reasons given are:

1. The insurance will cover last-illness and burial expenses.
2. Paying insurance premiums will instill habits of thrift.
3. Life insurance can provide funds for college education, for marriage expenses, or for starting a business.
4. Premiums are low, and the children are guaranteed to be insurable in the future.

Parents must decide for themselves, but here are some points to ponder. Life has many hazards, but the average family's income is not enough to permit the purchase of insurance to cover every contingency. Priorities must be established. Probabilities must be considered. The probability of death from ages 1 through 20 is minimal. Even in cases of death, no loss of income accompanies the death. From a strictly *economic* standpoint, it is usually an economic plus. Most families could pay last-illness and burial expenses out of current income.

The argument that paying insurance premiums instills habits of thrift implies that life insurance is a savings device. This is true also for the arguments that life insurance may provide money for a college education, for marriage, or for starting a business. Children can be taught thrift by putting their savings into savings institutions. Typically they can earn a higher rate of interest if they invest their savings in ways other than in life insurance policies. The purpose of life insurance is to provide protection against loss of income in case of premature death. The insurance function and the saving function are basically different.

Finally, even if the premiums will be lower on children and they can pass the physical examinations, this insurance is not a bargain if the buyer does not need it. Intelligent consumers do not buy goods or services they do not need even though prices may be low.

Should the lives of college students be insured? College students probably should not be insured, especially if they are not married and have no dependents. Returning to the central question—from an *economic* standpoint, what impact will the death of the college student have on the family—the answer is usually very little. Most college students do not provide enough income to parents to justify the need for insurance. Much of what was noted relating to children applies to college students as well.

Of course, students who are married with dependents should consider life insurance. Unfortunately, even when a need is present, students all too often are sold whole life, universal, or endowment policies instead of term insurance. Many are duped into paying low premiums on whole life policies until they graduate, and then the premium rate accelerates, or the insurance companies lend them the money to pay the premiums until they graduate.

Should insurance be bought from a company agent or from a broker? Although most life insurance agents represent a single company, some independent agents represent more than one company, and brokers represent many companies. The basic difference between an agent and a broker is that an agent represents a company, whereas a broker represents the

There Oughta Be a Law . . .

Health Insurance Portability and Accountability Act (HIPAA)

The HIPAA Privacy Rule (2003) creates national standards to protect individuals' medical records and other personal health information. According to the Department of Health and Human Services, the act

- gives patients more control over their health information.
- sets boundaries on the use and release of health records.
- establishes appropriate safeguards that health care providers and others must achieve to protect the privacy of health information.
- holds violators accountable, with civil and criminal penalties if they violate patients' privacy rights.
- strikes a balance when public responsibility supports disclosure of some forms of data—for example, to protect public health.

For patients it means being able to make informed choices when seeking care and reimbursement for care based on how personal health information may be used. The act:

- enables patients to find out how their information may be used, and about certain disclosures of their information that have been made.
- generally limits release of information to the minimum reasonably needed for the purpose of the disclosure.
- generally gives patients the right to examine and obtain a copy of their own health records and request corrections.
- empowers individuals to control certain uses and disclosures of their health information.

For more detailed information about health privacy, visit www.hhs.gov/ocr/hipaa/.

Chartered life underwriter a trained specialist in life insurance who has completed a broad range of college-level subjects and passed rigorous professional examinations administered by the American College of Life Underwriters.

buyer. Both types of sales representatives are paid by the insurance company, but brokers are more likely to help a buyer choose the company that will best serve the buyer's needs.

Whether using an agent or a broker, the buyer should consider choosing a salesperson who is a **chartered life underwriter** (CLU). To obtain the CLU designation, a person must have been an agent for at least three years. Most CLU candidates spend four to five years of part-time instruction to complete the study program.

PLANNING AN INSURANCE PROGRAM

In planning an insurance program, a young husband and wife should work together. Both should understand the purposes of insurance and the protection they are purchasing. After they have learned something about insurance, they should seek the assistance of a competent agent or broker in working out the details of their plan. Impartial advisors substantially agree on the broad recommendations given by the Consumers Union, as discussed above. Additional recommendations are the following:

1. People should buy only what they can afford. If they drop their permanent life policy within the first 10 years, they could lose some of the money paid in, which they might not be able to afford.
2. If people are eligible for group life insurance, they should give it serious thought. It may be the easiest and least costly way to meet their life insurance needs.
3. People should not leave themselves underinsured. During the years when the family has children at home, the insurance needs are generally the greatest. Term insurance gives beneficiaries more protection than permanent insurance for the same premium dollars.
4. Many people think all similar policies cost about the same. They do not. Insurance buyers should shop around. With the advent of the Internet, competitive quotes are much easier to obtain.

5. Buyers should check the rate of return. If they are thinking about using permanent life insurance as a way to save, they should check the average annual rates of return for various policies and compare them with other savings and investments programs.

SUMMARY

Insurance is a voluntary cooperative device for sharing risks and minimizing losses. Insurance can be obtained to protect many assets including property, health, and life. Principles of sound insurance include probability, determination of loss, that the indemnity is not to exceed the loss, that the event insured against must be determinable, and that the event probability must be uncertain. Social Security benefits include survivors', disability, retirement, and medical insurance. Older persons may meet the expenses of old age by depending on supplement retirement payments by employers, income from investments, and part- or full-time jobs, in some combination.

Health care costs have increased dramatically in recent decades. Insurance coverages in the health care area include disability income, hospital expense, surgical expense, major medical expense, and dental insurance. Managed care plans (HMOs and PPOs) have gained popularity and may be attractive and less expensive alternatives to traditional kinds of health insurance.

Life insurance may be either term or permanent insurance. Most experts advise purchasing term life insurance if the insurance is needed. Insurance for children and college students is seldom needed. Before purchasing life insurance, one question the astute consumer should ask is: "If the policyholder dies tomorrow, what economic impact will the loss have on the beneficiaries?" Among additional considerations, buy only what can be afforded; buy group life insurance, if possible; do not be underinsured; shop around; and check the rate of return before purchasing permanent policies.

ITEMS FOR REVIEW & DISCUSSION

1. State the basic purpose of insurance. Delineate the basic principles under which insurance operates. How should you go about determining a family's life insurance needs?
2. Trace the history of social insurance and why Congress passed the Social Security Act. What kinds of benefits could you potentially be eligible for under Social Security during your lifetime? List the strengths and weaknesses of the Social Security system.
3. State the purpose of Medicare and who is eligible for it.
4. Name the various homeowner's policies and how they are different.
5. Differentiate liability, comprehensive, and collision auto insurance.
6. Describe the benefits and drawbacks of no-fault insurance.
7. Name the kinds of health insurance that are available. Explain PPOs and HMOs. Why does health insurance cost so much?
8. Discuss the basic differences between term life insurance and permanent life insurance.
9. What is meant by the expression, "Life insurance is more frequently sold than bought"? What are the implications of the expression, "Buy term and invest the rest"? Should one use life insurance as a method of saving? Why or why not?

EXPLORING PERSONAL VALUES: PROJECTS

1. Respond to the following statements with "agree" or "disagree." Discuss your responses with your classmates.
    a. If a person has no accidents during a given year, the money spent on automobile insurance is wasted.

   b. People who lead cautious, careful lives need not concern themselves with the possibility of an accident.
   c. A person's responsibility for others ends with death.
2. Following are two incidents. Role-play each in your class. After the role-playing activity, identify any aspects that the role-playing participants did not touch upon.
   a. A husband and wife are discussing money problems. One of them, driving as an uninsured motorist (or with minimum liability coverage), struck and permanently disabled a pedestrian. A $500,000 judgment was awarded to the injured party, and a substantial part of the family income was attached to satisfy the judgment.
   b. A husband and wife are discussing money problems. One of them, now confined to a wheelchair, was hit by an uninsured, unemployed motorist against whom a judgment is virtually meaningless.
3. Draw up a list of the various kinds of financial hazards to which you could be subjected and the ways you and your family might cope with them.
4. Interview an older person about Medicare. Does he or she like it? Why or why not?
5. Interview a life insurance agent, a banker, and a stockbroker about buying term insurance and investing the difference versus buying cash-value insurance.
6. Participate in a class debate on cash-value life insurance versus term insurance with the difference invested.
7. Discuss with your family the various options available to the beneficiary of a life insurance policy. Write a brief paper on the choice your family made and why.
8. Ask a life insurance agent and an automobile insurance agent how many people come to them to buy insurance and how many people they solicit to sell insurance.
9. Draw up a complete insurance plan for a person from age 22 to age 65, who marries, has two children, and owns a house and an automobile.
10. Read one of the reference entries in this chapter or obtain similar information from your library or the Internet, and write a report on it.

ADDITIONAL SOURCES OF INFORMATION

Baldwin, Ben G. *The Complete Book of Insurance: The Consumer's Guide to Insuring Your Life, Health, Property, and Income.* Scarborough, Ontario, Canada: Irwin Professional Publishing, 1996.

Baldwin, Ben. *New Life Insurance Investment Advisor.* New York: McGraw-Hill, 2002.

Epstein, Lita. *The Complete Idiot's Guide to Social Security and Medicare.* New York: Alpha Books, 2006.

Gilbert, Jersey, and Ellen Schultz. *Consumer Reports Life Insurance Handbook: How to Buy the Right Policy from the Right Company at the Right Price.* Yonkers, NY: Consumer Reports Books, 1994.

Heins, D. *How to Buy Insurance and Save Money.* Charleston, SC: BookSurge Publishing, 2007.

Hungelmann, Jack. *Insurance for Dummies.* New York: Wiley, 2001.

Mulligan, Elizabeth A., and Gene Stone. *Accounting and Financial Reporting in Life and Health Insurance Companies.* Atlanta: Life Management Institute, LOMA, 1997.

Nader, Ralph. *Winning the Insurance Game: The Complete Consumer's Guide to Saving Money.* New York: Main Street Books, 1993.

Rowell, Jo Ann C. *Understanding Health Insurance: A Guide to Professional Billing.* Albany, NY: DelMar Thomson Learning, 2004.

Vaughan, Emmett J., and Therese M. Vaughan. *Fundamentals of Risk and Insurance.* New York: Wiley, 2003.

PART FOUR

Help Is on the Way

ASSISTANCE FOR CONSUMERS

Ask for a discount. If you don't ask, you'll never get one.

SCOTT BENDER, PRESIDENT AND CEO, AMBITIOUS ADVENTURES, INC.

KEY TERMS

back date
code dating
expiration date
freshness date
goodwill
irregulars
one-price system
open dating
pull date
push money (PM)
seconds
shopping bots
SPIF
unit pricing

The following concepts will be developed in this chapter:

1. The marketplace is one of ongoing confrontation between the amateur consumer exercising the principles of buymanship and the expert seller exercising the principles of salesmanship.
2. Consumers can improve their position in the marketplace relative to sellers by accumulating as much buying knowledge as they can about specific products.
3. Careful shoppers follow some specific "rules" to get more value for the dollar than careless shoppers.

After having read this chapter, you should be able to accomplish the following objectives:

1. Define and explain the terms *buymanship* and *salesmanship.*
2. Give a number of reasons why the seller has the advantage in the marketplace.
3. Identify and evaluate several sources of preshopping information.
4. Describe a number of techniques the intelligent buyer customarily practices, citing the contribution of each to wise buymanship.

SPENDING MONEY

Money is necessary in our capitalistic marketplace. Most people enjoy exchanging their money for the goods and services that will give them satisfaction and pleasure. In the act of exchanging money for goods and services, consumers are converting their money income to *real income*—the quantity of goods and services that one's money (income) will buy. The term *psychic income* refers to the satisfaction gained in consuming the goods and services purchased with one's income; it also refers to income in a form other than monetary, such as power, prestige, job satisfaction, and so on. Psychic income may be temporary, as in consuming food, or it may be long term, as in consuming (enjoying) one's home.

Most people love a bargain. There is an added satisfaction when a consumer gets a high-quality item at a low price. "Bargain hunters" are consumers who are constantly on the search for good buys.

Spending is a form of escape rather than enjoyment for some people. They refuse to face the reality that their incomes are limited. Even though they do not have enough money, they spend as if they had a lot. Spendthrifts use their credit to the limit. When they reach the limit, they

Savvy Buying

face the real possibility of bankruptcy. Reasonable spending is a normal part of everyday life, but compulsive spending, much like compulsive drinking or gambling, is a disease. Psychologists report that people spend money to offset frustrations or to create the illusion that they can control their own destinies.

BUYERSHIP VERSUS SELLERSHIP

The literature on advertising and sales is filled with suggestions to sellers, telling them how they can break down sales resistance. In reality, however, sales resistance is slight. Consumers need and want goods and services. The better buyers substitute rational for emotional consumer responses, and they develop resistance to high-pressure selling methods.

Buyers want to obtain the most they can for their money, just as much as sellers want to obtain prices as high as they can for their goods and services. The consumer, however, is the amateur, and the seller is the professional. Better buying practices will help make the contest more fair.

CONSUMER DECISION MAKING

Consumers make decisions constantly. These decisions may be small (where to eat lunch, what brand of cereal to buy), or they may be big (whether to buy a car, and if so, new or resale? What model?) Informed decision making is a process, in contrast to buying on a whim, or making a snap judgment about a purchase. If we can identify the steps of this process and understand their purpose, we are more likely to make good, informed decisions. Here is one consumer decision-making model, outlining the process a consumer may follow (adapted from Malhotra, 1982):

- *Decide the issue.* Determine the many alternatives available to you. This can involve the purchase of goods or services, and may lead to the decision to forgo purchase.
- *Determine the resources.* You will use resources to purchase or barter for the goods or services. What do you want to pay for the item and what resources will it cost you? What costs are associated with using those resources?
- *Weigh alternatives.* Weigh all of your alternatives, considering the costs and benefits of each alternative.

www.benefits.gov

This site offers access to government benefits and assistance programs. It is sponsored by the U.S. government and is not affiliated with for-profit organizations.

- *Visualize the alternatives in action.* Envision each alternative purchase playing out in real life.
- *Decide on the action and execute.* Once the aforementioned steps are completed, pick the single best alternative.
- *Review your decision and the results.* After acting upon the decision, evaluate the outcome of the decision.

In today's economic environment, prudent consumers have more reason than ever to carefully weigh their purchasing decisions. Moving through these steps will help you slow down the buying process and thus buy less compulsively and with more forethought. Consumers who make careful decisions will be more in the tune with their needs, wants, and desires in relation to their pocketbooks.

BECOMING INFORMED

To develop better buying techniques, consumers first have to arm themselves with information. Rational buyers should obtain as much information as they can, within reason, about the products they need. In addition to product information, they can acquire knowledge about devices for measuring or ascertaining quantity and quality characteristics. With this information at their disposal, they can ask salespeople the right questions and judge whether a salesperson is qualified to give helpful answers. The amount of information needed often depends on the situation. The consumer should be aware that too much information may lead to "information overload" and confusion.

Consumer Reports

The Consumers Union (CU) was chartered in February 1936, as a nonprofit corporation. Its purpose is to test products, inform the public, and protect consumers regarding a wide variety of products and services. All income for Consumers Union is generated from the sale of *Consumer Reports* magazine and other publications.

Consumer Reports is CU's primary publication, with a subscription base of over 4 million. From January through November of each year, it publishes 11 regular issues. December brings an enlarged issue, the *Buying Guide.* The *Guide* summarizes the results of tests made in that year and previous years and also gives buying advice that is not included in the other issues. CU's publications contain reports of laboratory tests and controlled-use tests, expert opinion and experience reports, or a combination of these. No test products are accepted as gifts or loans from manufacturers; all are purchased in retail stores by CU's shoppers, who do not identify their CU affiliation.

Product ratings usually are based on estimated overall quality without regard to price. "Best Buy" ratings are accorded to products that not only are rated high in overall quality but also are priced relatively low. Thus, they should provide more quality per dollar than the products rated "Acceptable" in that set of ratings. CU also has a "Not Acceptable" rating, usually reserved for a product that is a very poor buy or has a safety problem, or both.

Consumers Union, publisher of Consumer Reports, *does not accept advertising. Indeed, CU has a policy that it will initiate litigation against any company using the name of* Consumer Reports *in its advertising, marketing, or sales presentations.*

Consumer Reports contains much useful information. In addition to general articles, each report on a specific product is prefaced with a statement telling consumers what they need to know about that specific product when shopping. CU has become famous for its reports on new and used automobiles. In addition to point-by-point technical comparisons of makes, readers learn much about how automobile companies operate, what goes into their products, and what buyers should know about an automobile. Additional publications and services from CU are related to personal and leisure topics, money, automobiles, and the home. The *Consumer Reports* website is www.consumerreports.org. Over the years,

CU has published books on a multitude of topics, including health care, funerals, new and used cars, energy, classical music, economics, life insurance, learning disabilities, and online shopping. CU has developed educational materials for elementary, secondary, and university students and instructors.

Consumers Union is well respected by its readers and by consumer professionals alike. Its information is highly reliable, the technical competence is exemplary, and the integrity of the organization is above reproach. Further evidence of CU's competence and impartiality is that a study of its ratings over the years reveals that one company's product may receive a low rating one year and an "Accepted" rating in another year. These changes in rating indicate significant improvements in the product. In some product lines, one company's product may be consistently check-rated or in the runner-up category.

www.consumerreview.com

Consumers can research products they use on consumerreview.com, which allows consumers to share hobbies or recreational interests with others.

CU's success depends on brands and trademarks. Nationally advertised and available brands have an advantage over local brands and unbranded products because favorable ratings may lead readers to purchase the national brands even though regionally produced products may be as good or better.

One of the most significant voices for consumers in the United States, CU took the lead in organizing the International Organization of Consumers Unions (IOCU), which is now Consumers International (CI). U.S. organizations initiated with CU assistance include the Consumer Federation of America, a national consumer organization, and the American Council on Consumer Interests, a national, professional, consumer education organization.

Specialty Magazines

Many specialty magazines evaluate products, but their objectivity in general is questionable. These publications, which rely on the industries they cover for advertising revenue, are prone to emphasize positive developments in their fields. Consumers should be cautious in using these sources of information because their tendency is to state the advantages of products and not to note deficiencies.

U.S. Government Materials

The federal government publishes a vast amount of free and low-cost consumer information materials. Most federal agencies offer materials regarding the services and legislation for which each is responsible. The following offices provide general information of consumer interest. Several specific federal agencies are discussed further in the chapter on federal government.

USA.gov

Perhaps the most dramatic addition to the federal government's information dissemination program is the development of a single U.S. government website, www.usa.gov. This one-stop Internet site consolidates thousands of government sites and tens of millions of web pages into one site.

Federal Consumer Information Center

The Federal Consumer Information Center (FCIC) was established as a result of the merger of the Consumer Information Center (CIC) and the Federal Information Center (FIC). The merger combined the CIC website www.pueblo.gsa.gov, the *Consumer Information* catalog, and the Pueblo publication distribution program with the FIC nationwide toll-free telephone assistance center. FCIC is a one-stop source for information

www.pueblo.gsa.gov

The Federal Consumer Information Center (FCIC) was created in February 2000 as a result of the merger of the Consumer Information Center (CIC) and the Federal Information Center (FIC). The FCIC website answers consumer inquiries about consumer problems and government services.

www.gpoaccess.gov

This website offers a plethora of information about federal publications and resources, from all three branches of government. In addition, consumers can obtain answers to questions about the GPO and buy books that it prints.

about federal agencies, programs, and services. Additional information may be obtained by calling 800-688-9889.

U.S. Government Printing Office

The Government Printing Office (GPO) operates bookstores in U.S. cities. Its purpose is to print and sell the more popular federal publications. It offers thousands of titles, including hundreds of subscriptions.

Extension Service

The Extension Service, a division of the U.S. Department of Agriculture (USDA), serves as the national office for the U.S. Cooperative Extension Service. The Cooperative Extension Service is a three-way partnership encompassing the state land-grant universities, the USDA, and county governments. In addition to consulting services, many extension divisions offer consumer information and education programs focusing on family-related concerns such as food and nutrition, auto insurance, health insurance, housing, budgeting, and use of credit. Information regarding the services offered in a given state is available from county or state extension offices. The government listings in your local telephone directory will list the office nearest you.

www.consumeraction.gov

This website lists consumer protection offices in each state. Mailing addresses, phone numbers, and websites are provided, as well as other valuable information.

State Government Guides

Most state governments publish information guides covering a wide variety of topics. Examples include prevention of fraud, wise buying techniques, insurance, and explanations of state consumer laws and regulations. Materials usually are provided free. Sources of consumer information include, but are not limited to: office of the attorney general, governor's office, consumer affairs office, office on aging, state banking authority, insurance office, state utility commissions, and state weights and measures office.

Other Buying Aids

CBBB booklets

The Council of Better Business Bureaus (4200 Wilson Blvd., Suite 800, Arlington, VA 22203-1838) publishes hundreds of quality consumer-oriented materials, including tip sheets, fact books, and information pamphlets. Sample booklets are available for a minimal charge. A complete list of the CBBB's titles is available free from the Council.

Consumers who live in or near a metropolitan area should utilize the services extended by their local Better Business Bureau. Some bureaus publish monthly bulletins containing preshopping information and warnings against misleading advertising and fraudulent selling practices. Contact your local Better Business Bureaus (via telephone, mail, or the Internet at www.bbb.org) for reports on complaints concerning specific businesses.

FYI

One reason the Better Business Bureaus were initiated in 1912 was to stave off development of an anticipated plethora of consumer legislation.

Kiplinger's Personal Finance Magazine

Kiplinger's Personal Finance Magazine, for middle- and upper-middle–income consumers, carries articles on topics such as stocks and bonds, income taxes, life insurance, housing, retirement income, and investing in real estate. In 1980, *Kiplinger's* began accepting advertising. This change apparently has not affected the publication's credibility, although about 40 percent of the pages are devoted to advertising.

www.kiplinger.com

The website for *Kiplinger's* magazine allows investors to search for financial information. Information regarding investing, managing, and spending can be found here. Some content is for subscribers only.

Money

Money is published by Time, Inc., for upper-middle and upper-income consumers. Information on investments, tax shelters, travel, housing, and careers predominates.

ACCI

A good way to keep informed about items of interest to consumers is to read the information published by the American Council on Consumer Interests (ACCI), an international educational professional organization (see website information below). Note that ACCI stresses that they are a research organization and not a consumer advocacy group.

WWW

www.money.cnn.com

Investors may search www.money.cnn.com for information on money market investments, real estate, insurance, autos, and retirement. Some content is for subscribers of *Money* magazine only.

www.consumerinterests.org

The website for American Council on Consumer Interests (ACCI) provides information about consumer issues and family economics.

TIP

Devote an hour each week to reading practical, money-saving magazines like those described in this chapter. Your economic life will improve dramatically, and your overall quality of life will be enhanced at the same time.

HOW TO SHOP EFFECTIVELY

Savvy shoppers are serious about the job of purchasing. They endeavor to buy intelligently to obtain the most value for their money. The following techniques are characteristic of careful shopping, whether the purchase is for goods or services.

Use Advertising Wisely

Grocery stores and retail stores commonly use local newspapers to advertise special prices on certain items. Armed with factual information that allows some comparison of quality, the wise buyer will save many steps and considerable time by comparing the newspaper advertisements of competing stores. Comparing prices by reading advertisements is much easier than going from store to store. By comparing prices in mail-order catalogs, the catalogs of discount sellers, and Internet websites, careful buyers can find the best prices or learn to judge the prices they see in stores.

TIP

Generally, mail-order and Internet shopping prices are lower than the prices of identical merchandise available locally. When comparison shopping, though, remember to add shipping and handling charges and sales tax, if any, to assess the differences accurately. Website "shopping bots" such as www.pricescan.com are especially useful.

Internet Shopping

Shopping on the Internet has become commonplace. Many "brick and mortar" businesses have expanded to "brick to click," adding an Internet sales component. Consumers should be certain that the sites they patronize are trustworthy.

Privacy and security on-line have emerged as important aspects of on-line sellers' service. Protection of consumers' valuable personal and financial information is critical in combating fraud. Consumers should check that a privacy mechanism is in place when they send sensitive information over the Internet.

Another way that consumers can protect themselves when buying on-line is to use an escrow service. The escrow service provides a third party that holds the payment until the buyer confirms her receipt of satisfaction of the goods. Additionally, consumers can receive protections by using their credit cards to make purchases on-line.

Shopping bots websites with software tools that allow a consumer to shop at several sites while visiting only one.

To find the best deals on-line, consumers may turn to **shopping bots.** An Internet search for "shopping bot" will reveal a multitude of bots. Two examples include www.pricescan.com and www.shopping.com.

Watch for Lures and Traps

Retail stores in the United States used bait advertising so widely in the past that federal and state legislation rendered it illegal. A merchant cannot offer low-priced specials that are either unavailable or depreciated by the seller in order to sell higher-priced merchandise. These practices continue, however, and consumers must be on their guard against them. Government officials advise consumers to compare prices in one store with those in other stores before buying and to report misleading ads to their state attorney general's office or the FTC.

When an advertised special is not available, savvy shoppers ask for a substitute or a rain check, and they take the newspaper ads along when shopping to make sure they are not being charged more than the advertised price. Careful shoppers check to ensure against mispricing and mislabeling, improper weighing, and inaccurate marking of measurements on packages.

www.publiccitizen.org

This national, nonprofit group was founded in 1971 by Ralph Nader. Its purpose is to serve as a watchdog over Congress and to represent the consumer on a wide variety of social and economic issues.

Shoppers also must be alert as they pass through the supermarket maze of displays designed to entice them to buy. Savvy retailers have substantial control over their customers' purchasing, by means of shelf-position, stack-outs in aisles, special displays, and tie-ins. Chain grocery store sales increase greatly as a result of using aisle-end displays, shelf-extenders, dump racks, tower displays, island displays, and snack racks. The average store has more than 20 special display areas where traffic is 15 times greater than in other parts of a store. Merchandise displays of high-profit items at the checkout counters catch many an impulse buyer. A basket or card display of inexpensive items near the checkout area may give the shopper an impression that he is visiting a low-price store.

Does a shopper want merchandise or merchandise plus atmosphere? The latter is available in luxury stores that may charge higher prices simply to create an image. At the other extreme are supermarkets, warehouses, factory outlets, discount-type stores, and e-commerce sites where shoppers can purchase merchandise at lower prices with no frills. Between these extremes are many kinds of retail stores.

Push money (PM) also known as "spifs," an amount offered above the regular payment to a commissioned salesperson for selling a specific brand or product.

SPIF sales promotion incentive fund, additional incentive money provided to salespeople working on commission (also written as spiff).

Wise shoppers do not rely exclusively on a salesperson for product information and evaluation. Consumers should be aware that salespeople are often offered special incentives for selling certain items. The product manufacturer or retailer may offer a special incentive, often known as **PM,** for **push money,** or a **SPIF,** to salespeople on commission. Or the salesperson may assume that Product A is better than B, and recommend it, because it is higher in price or has more gadgetry. *Consumer Reports* repeatedly refutes the higher-price, higher-quality theory.

Avoid Impulse Buying

Experts in retail merchandising say that the profitability of a store depends on its success in stimulating impulse buying. To do this, managers place impulse items at the foot of the down escalators in department stores to catch the eyes of captive shoppers. Managers of grocery stores with checkout counters place a variety of profitable small items where shoppers cannot miss them. While waiting to be checked out, consumers are likely to pick up candy, gum, or magazines. The aroma of baked goods vented out to the street sets up physical and psychological reactions that impel shoppers to consume bakery items. Many auction sites on the Internet create, by design, a hurried atmosphere to develop an impulse buying need in the unsophisticated buyer. The intent is often to convince "bidders" that they must buy now.

> **TIP** Develop a food shopping list before entering the supermarket, and do not deviate from that list. Remember that hungry shoppers buy more food, so it is a good idea to eat before grocery shopping.

The average consumer buys on impulse quite often. Experts report that about one-half of all purchases are made on impulse. And, unfortunately, many shoppers exert little effort to seek information. Impulse buying seems to be increasing, perhaps because of time constraints and enticing packaging, and because shoppers depend on in-store shelf displays as reminders. Some general tips to help you avoid impulse buying are:

1. Buy only what is on your shopping list.
2. Determine if the item you are considering purchasing is actually a need, or simply a want.
3. Put the item on hold for 24 to 48 hours, then make the decision.
4. Leave your form of payment at home.
5. Realistically consider the purchase in relation to your budget.
6. Make fewer trips to the store (fewer visits means fewer purchases).

Watch for Sales

The best weapon to use against impulse buying is the shopping list, especially for recurring purchases such as food and household items. Many consumers have adequate storage space; therefore, they can purchase items on sale and store them until needed. The result is fewer trips to the store and hence fewer purchases.

Many foods are seasonal. When they are in season, supplies are abundant and prices tend to be lower. Conversely, when these foods are out of season, supplies are limited and prices are relatively high. A family can save up to 20 percent of its food expenditures by purchasing foods in season.

Clothing buyers can save money by planning ahead and purchasing when needed items are on sale. Sales volume declines in January, so, as a traditional trade practice, retailers mark down prices at least 20 percent after the first day of each year. Stores mark down their merchandise anywhere from 10 percent to 75 percent, according to its type and the length of time it has been in the store. These bargain prices often are advertised as pre-inventory and storewide clearance sales.

> **TIP** The Internet offers hundreds of excellent travel websites for the cost-conscious consumer. Some examples are www.orbitz.com, www.frommers.com, www.fodors.com, www.sidestep.com, www.expedia.com, and www.travelocity.com.

Season-end clearances usually are offered in late January and early February. These often are advertised as anniversary sales, storewide clearances, and Presidents' birthday sales. Buyers will find substantial price reductions on winter clothing, tires, and furniture. By late March and early April, spring stocks of merchandise are ready for the peak Easter season. Pre-Easter sales offer significant savings on boys' and menswear. Also, pre-Easter sales feature washers, dryers, luggage, china, silver, and gift items. Volume sales of spring merchandise continue through May. By June, some clearance sales are advertised, but the best time to buy spring and summer goods is immediately after July 4.

By August, stores are stocked with fall and winter merchandise, which consumers buy actively through October and November. From the store manager's point of view, December is the peak month. Approximately a third of all retail annual sales are made in December. After Christmas, sales decline, and the annual cycle begins again when store managers offer clearance sales in January and February. Price-conscious consumers who plan their purchases do most of their buying in January–February and June–July.

In addition to seasonal sales, store managers and e-commerce sites offer private sales, special-purchase sales, anniversary sales, closeouts, and one-day sales. Private sales usually are held a few days before the public announcement of a sale. Regular customers are notified privately in advance. For these sales, buyers for stores often purchase goods from manufacturers or wholesalers at reduced prices. Some special-purchase goods are of standard quality; others are substandard or imperfect items. For this reason, the shopper should look at the merchandise carefully. Good stores mark substandard merchandise as **seconds.** Some **irregulars** actually are first-quality items marked for quick sale to reduce inventory. Both of these often are good buys.

Seconds products that have major flaws.

Irregulars products that have minor flaws.

While some going-out-of-business sales are legitimate, others are gimmicks. Some stores are forever "going out of business," although this practice is illegal. Buyers must be cautious of such claims.

Comparison Shop

Buyers who never shop around end up spending more. Surveys in many different markets have consistently shown the possibility of saving 20 percent by comparing prices in three or more stores. Shopping around yields savings in the purchase of all types of consumer goods, from automobiles to apparel. People who are loyal to one store form the basis of what merchants call **goodwill,** which larger stores may value at millions of dollars. It refers to the probability that patrons will continue to make all their purchases at the same store. Consumers who instead shop around, comparing quantity, quality, and price, are the ones who promote real competition.

Goodwill the advantage in the way of custom that a business has acquired beyond the value of what it sells.

CASE STUDY Medicare Fraud

In 2006, Medicare began offering voluntary coverage for prescription drugs. The coverage is more popularly known as Medicare Part D. This is an optional plan in which users pay the premiums, copayments, and deductibles. A list of approved prescription drug plans is available through www.medicare.gov. Companies offering the plans must meet specific federal standards and be approved by the Centers for Medicare and Medicaid Services (U.S. Department of Health and Human Services). Unfortunately, con artists are trying to cash in on this new opportunity by offering phony Medicare prescription drug plans. Often, these "companies" offer modest prizes or gifts to promote their plans, which is illegal.

Many consumers have fallen victim to promises made by these companies, and have had their personal information and money stolen. The National Fraud Information Center suggests that consumers be on the lookout for anyone posing as a Social Security Administration (SSA) employee asking for personal financial information. Note that because the companies offering this new service are private firms, any representative claiming to work for the government is likely fraudulent.

QUESTIONS

1. What do you think could be done to stop unscrupulous companies from duping consumers?
2. Do you think consumers have any responsibility in this fraud?
3. What would you tell consumers about how to prevent falling victim to this fraud?
4. Have you or someone you know been affected by this or a similar fraud?

Source: www.fraud.org. Retrieved June 12, 2008.

Bargain for Lower Prices

In the United States, the **one-price system** is standard. Bargaining, though, is practiced in some situations. For example, if an item appears damaged or substandard the consumer might ask a manager for a lower price. In some situations, such as at flea markets and swap meets, bargaining is not only commonplace, but is expected.

One-price system a method of pricing whereby the seller determines the price for a good or service, and that price is not negotiable.

The one-price system

Most sellers in the United States profess to follow the one-price system, reputedly introduced by the founder of Tiffany's, a prestigious jewelry store founded in New York City. Under this system, retailers add a markup to their wholesale cost to determine the price at which they are willing to sell an item. The buyer then may decide whether to buy at that price. Proponents of the one-price system argue that bargaining takes so much time that it slows the marketing process. The kind of mass selling found in supermarkets would certainly not be possible without the one-price system.

Lower-income buyers are less likely than middle- and upper-income buyers to shop in more than one store. FYI

The assumption underlying the one-price system is that if buyers think prices are too high, they will purchase elsewhere. If large numbers of consumers purchase elsewhere, the high-price retailer is forced to lower prices. In practice, some sellers stress quality and service as a justification for maintaining higher prices.

Bargaining in the United States

Some buyers attempt bargaining despite the prevalence of the one-price system. Rather than lose the business of these buyers, retailers often bargain in one way or another. As a consequence, the one-price policy has often been modified, even by more conservative stores. The prices of automobiles and houses, in particular, are simply the starting price in the bargaining process. Only uninitiated and naive buyers pay the asking price in these and certain other product areas.

Studies indicate that the vast majority of owners of small businesses by policy allow negotiations for their products and services. The consumer simply has to make an offer. FYI

Buyers may obtain price reductions in several ways. One is to secure a reduction in the *list* price. This is not as difficult to do as many buyers believe. They simply have to use the same competitive weapons that business people do. Normally, buyers need have no compunction about using such tactics, for sellers will not cut their prices to a point that is too low to cover costs. By learning about margins and markup, prospective buyers will be able to estimate how much reduction a seller can give and still make a profit.

The growth of discount stores, membership clubs, mail ordering, and Internet shopping has led increasing numbers of stores to engage in bargaining. Many retail stores have a policy meeting or beating competitors' prices. Usually the consumer must bring in proof of the lower price (an Internet printout, newspaper advertisement, etc.). In some cases, the store will not only meet the competitor's price but also take an additional percentage, such as 10 percent, off the price.

Consumers may secure price reductions indirectly by bargaining for a larger allowance when trading in a used article. In selling things such as appliances and automobiles, dealers allow a considerable margin for trade-ins. Only a part of this allowance will be given to careless or naive buyers, while shrewd buyers will bargain until they secure the full amount.

Another way to secure an indirect price reduction is by prevailing on the seller for certain extra items or services that usually are not included. For example, the buyer of an automobile may obtain extra equipment, and the purchaser of a household appliance may receive free installation.

www.salvagesale.com

The salvagesale.com auction website assists sellers in recovering their costs of goods. Generally, sellers have the products that they sell on this site because the goods have been repossessed, returned, or damaged. The items listed on this website all have market value; the winning bidders determine that value. WWW

Discounts might also be obtained through business, professional, or friendly connections. Often, wholesale buying is extended to consumers in these categories. For example, many businesses offer a AAA discount to anyone who simply shows the membership card. A work affiliation may also qualify the buyer for discounts.

When buying a car, you can save money by knowing which companies are offering "incentives." True or false?

True. Magazines such as Automotive News and websites such as www.edmunds.com disclose dealer incentives. Incentives are similar to manufacturer rebates. However, rebates are offered to consumers, whereas incentives are offered to dealers and are not disclosed to the customer.

Many consumers—such as older persons, students, government employees, and members of the military—belong to groups that qualify them for special discounts. Students should always ask for discounts, for example at movie theaters and for travel. In most cases, identification is required.

Hotel chains have different definitions of those who qualify for discounts. One chain may define a government employee as a federal, state, or local government employee; another company may consider only federal employees. One chain may include faculty members or students who work part-time for a state university as government employees; another may not. In any event, people who seek the best discounts will receive the best rates.

Experienced travelers know that they can bargain for lower prices for hotel and motel rooms even if they do not qualify for a discount. Managers of hotels and motels would like to follow the one-price system. Some of them may tell a prospective bargainer that they never bargain, but managers of motels and hotels are faced with the same dilemma of excess capacity that confronts managers of many other enterprises. Their prices may be based on a 60 percent occupancy rate. A substantial portion of their expenses continues whether the rooms are occupied or not. From the manager's point of view, is it better to insist on a price of $100 and let a room remain unused or to be realistic and accept an offer of $65? Many managers are realistic and readily accept $65 from a traveler who knows the economic facts of pricing.

TIP When telephone shopping for a hotel room, clearly indicate that price is your main concern and that you are shopping around for the best rates. Ask for the lowest price available, and state any discounts for which you qualify (e.g., government, student, AAA, commercial, weekend, or promotional).

The owner of a house who has decided to have it painted should bargain with three or more reputable painters before settling for a price. The same is true for most other services. When bargaining for services, one has to be certain that the quality of materials and workmanship that will be provided by each candidate is comparable. A contract that clearly indicates specific materials to be used, the warranty terms, and so on is mandatory.

Instead of buying a brand-new automobile, buying a used car that is two to three years old is often a wise decision. True or false?

True. The depreciation on new cars is substantial during the first few years. Thus, if you buy a used car, the cost may be only 50 to 60 percent of a new car. Always have a mechanic evaluate a used car before you purchase it.

Even though the United States nominally has a one-price economy, in practice it has a bargaining economy. Readers who are not convinced of the validity of this statement may experiment. Thousands of students have done so, and invariably the results of the experiments have been positive. Not only do bargainers often obtain lower prices, but they also often enjoy the "game" of bargaining. Bargaining is easiest during slack times, when sellers have trouble selling their products and services.

In the U.S. economic system, in which free enterprise and competition play the major roles, sellers have the right to ask whatever prices they want, and buyers have the right to offer whatever prices they wish. A transaction can take place only when the buyer and the seller reach a price that is mutually satisfactory.

Read Labels and Understand Freshness Codes

Federal law requires that most foods sold in interstate commerce be labeled to show the ingredients and that the ingredients be labeled properly. A blend of cane and maple syrup may not be labeled "Vermont maple syrup." A can labeled "tuna with noodles" must contain more tuna than noodles. The law now requires that extensive nutritional information be included on most food product labels. Consumers should read these labels carefully and regularly. The information can help shoppers make more intelligent choices.

Shoppers may wonder how long a food has been on the store shelf or may suspect it might be stale. Store management has typically known this information through **code dating** on the merchandise. The shopper, however, had no way of interpreting the code-dating systems that processors used. Code dating raised questions, such as: Why did food processors believe this information should be kept from consumers? Today, **open dating** is more widely used. Open dating specifies the month, day, and year in a comprehensible format, whereas code dating uses numbers that consumers cannot interpret. Even with open dating, the consumer needs to know whether the date given is the **pull date,** the **freshness date,** the **expiration date,** the **back date,** or another date or code developed by the manufacturer. As more and more processors, particularly processors of dairy and bakery products, open date their products, many are also indicating on the package what the date means. Several states and localities now require open dating on some perishable products. Prudent shoppers ask merchants to help them understand date codes.

Code dating a statement on a package indicating to the merchant the last day the product should be sold.

Open dating a statement on a package indicating clearly, in a format understandable to consumers, a pertinent date pertaining to freshness or expiration.

Pull date the date after which a product should not be offered for sale.

Freshness date the date after which a product will not be of optimum quality.

Expiration date the date after which a product should not be used.

Back date the date on which the product was manufactured, processed, or packaged.

Check the Quantity

The National Bureau of Standards and state weights and measures officials advise buyers to check the weights and measurements of their purchases. Savvy shoppers do not buy unless the weighing and measuring devices that are available for their use, such as scales and gasoline pumps, have a seal indicating that they have been inspected and approved by state measurement officials.

Devices that compute prices by measurement are helpful and time-saving for sellers. Computing devices, however, are not infallible; even if they are accurate, they may be misread. Therefore, buyers themselves should calculate the prices of the purchases that sales clerks weigh for them.

> **TIP** Do not be fooled by the size of a container. Manufacturers often decrease the quantity of ingredients in a package and keep the size of the container the same.

Check Prices and Totals

For items priced on the basis of fractional weights and prices, most people cannot make the necessary calculations mentally. Even if they use a calculator, they must be adept at using fractions. Which is the better buy, a 7 5/8-ounce package at 39 cents or a 12 7/8-ounce package at 53 cents? Only by reducing these figures to a comparative basis can a buyer compare prices per ounce. The answer is that the 7 5/8-ounce package is a slightly better buy at 5 cents per ounce than the 12 7/8-ounce package at 6 cents per ounce.

> *If the label of a food product states "low cholesterol" or "no cholesterol," it still may contain large amounts of fat. Peanut butter is one example.* **FYI**

> **TIP** Often the easiest way to determine if a bulk item is a good buy is to read the unit pricing comparisons noted on the shelf.

It is important for consumers to calculate the true price of items they purchase. Buying in bulk is not always the best decision. In addition to considering storage space needed, consumers must determine if they are actually getting a deal by buying in larger quantity. Most grocery stores now provide **unit pricing** on the shelves near the product, which is an easy way to become a better informed shopper.

Unit pricing providing prices of products in standard measures so consumers can compare the prices of a variety of similar products.

No matter how good a reputation a store may have, shoppers should verify charges. Mistakes happen. Good shoppers are just as quick to call attention to mistakes in their favor as they are to insist on correcting mistakes in favor of the seller. From the time the purchasing department of a firm places an order until the accounting department approves the invoice, the seller checks and rechecks the quality, price, and amount. If these practices are good for business firms, they are equally good for individuals.

Consider Cash or Credit

Credit costs money. Consumers may pay for credit directly or indirectly, but they always pay. As a general rule, good shoppers pay cash, or, if they use credit cards, they pay the amount due in full to avoid paying interest. A family that manages its finances well pays cash for recurring expenditures. By budgeting its expenditures, the family can also pay cash for larger, nonrecurring purchases. When good shoppers must use credit, they shop around for the lowest annual percentage rate (APR).

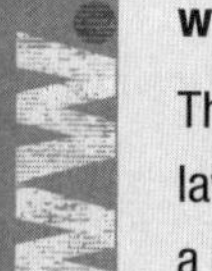

www.clpblog.org

This website has blogs from consumer lawyers and law professors. It is sponsored by Public Citizen and is a great way to protest, learn, and share about products.

In some circumstances, open-account credit may be a convenience that costs no more than if the buyer were to pay cash. Some stores allow buyers 30 days, 90 days, or even one or more years' credit without charge. However, the buyer must read the agreement carefully. Some creditors apply back interest if the balance is not paid in full at the end of the specified period. As long as they meet all the requirements, however, the price of the merchandise is not more than if the buyer paid cash. If prices in these stores are competitive with those in cash-and-carry stores, buyers might as well take advantage of the opportunity to defer payment. In fact, consumers paying cash should ask for a cash discount. This is particularly true for large purchases, such as for furniture or appliances. Many sellers will agree to a 10 percent to 20 percent discount for buyers who pay cash.

Keep Records and Receipts

A transaction does not necessarily end after the purchase is made. The buyer may discover that the product is defective, the wrong size or color, or not suitable for the purpose for which it was intended. Intelligent shoppers retain sales slips, warranty information, instruction booklets, and all other records they might need in the future. Some stores require a sales receipt to make adjustments or give refunds. A good filing system can help you ensure that records are available in case of a problem. Other information that you should note includes delivery dates that have been promised and the names of salespersons and other personnel with whom you have corresponded.

By determining the merchant's refund policy *before* you make a purchase, you can reduce or eliminate problems with returned merchandise. This is particularly important when you shop by mail or the Internet. In these cases, restocking and shipping fees for returned merchandise may be prohibitive.

TIP Always ask for a receipt for work covered under a warranty. A federal warranty law requires that a warranty be extended if the same problem occurs during the warranty period and again after the warranty period has ended. For the extension, you may need proof of your claim.

Know When and How to Protest

Consumers have the right and the responsibility to protest. Yet, many buyers never exercise that right. Some consumers exercise their protest function negatively by refusing to make additional purchases in an offending store. If enough consumers were to stop buying there, store managers would know something was wrong, but they would not know what. In the absence of a concerted group boycott, the refusal of a few consumers to patronize a store will have little effect.

Wise shoppers exercise their right of protest positively. They know prices for comparable merchandise in competing stores. If prices in a store are too high, they not only refuse to buy, but they also tell the store manager why. If a warranted item is defective, they report it to the seller, who then has an opportunity to make an adjustment. If the seller does not make a satisfactory adjustment, good shoppers do not stop with the local manager but instead report their dissatisfaction to the owner.

If the purchase is from a local dealer of a large corporation, the consumer should express any dissatisfaction to a top official. A letter to a corporate official should indicate that copies will be sent to appropriate government agencies (such as the Food and Drug Administration, Federal Trade Commission, or state consumer protection office) if the official does not respond satisfactorily. A copy of the letter should be sent to the Better Business Bureau in the city where the company is headquartered. Keep copies of letters, faxes, and e-mail messages that you send, as well as all related documents. Keep a record of people you have talked with or have corresponded with. Exhibit 15.1 shows a sample complaint letter.

Studies have indicated that the typical disgruntled consumer will tell at least seven others about a negative shopping experience with a specific company. A wise merchant will recognize this and attempt to satisfy all reasonable, and some unreasonable, consumer requests.

FYI

EXHIBIT 15.1

Sample complaint letter.

John Adams

13579 West 90th Avenue
Los Angeles, CA 90200

(213) 555-1234, *fax* (213) 555-5678
e-mail: johnadams@mymail.com

[Date]

[Name of Contact Person, if available]
[Title, if available]
[Company Name]
Consumer Complaint Division [If you have no specific contact]
[Street Address]
[City, State, ZIP Code]

Dear [Contact Person]:

Re: [account number, if applicable]

On [date], I [bought, leased, rented, or had repaired] a [name of the product, with serial or model number or service performed] at [location, date and other important details of the transaction].

Unfortunately, your product [or service] has not performed well [or the service was inadequate] because [state the problem thoroughly but briefly]. I am disappointed because [explain the problem: for example, the product does not work properly, the service was not performed correctly, I was billed the wrong amount, something was not disclosed clearly or was misrepresented, etc.].

To resolve the problem, I would appreciate your [state the specific action you want: money back, charge card credit, repair, exchange, etc.]. Enclosed are copies [do not send originals] of my records [include receipts, guarantees, warranties, canceled checks, contracts, model and serial numbers, and any other documents].

I look forward to your reply and a resolution to my problem, and will wait until [set a time limit] before seeking help from a consumer protection agency [list appropriate organization]. Please contact me at the above mailing address, phone number, or e-mail address. Thank you for your swift resolution to this matter.

Sincerely,

John Adams

Enclosure(s) [as appropriate]

Adapted from the Consumer Action website, www.consumeraction.gov.

WEBSITES FOR CONSUMERS

Thousands of websites have been developed to assist consumers. The following is a sample of some of the more popular ones. Visit this book's website (http://ce.hh-pub.com) for links to many of these sites.

AARP **www.aarp.org**

Ad Busters **www.adbusters.org**

Ad Council Organization **www.adcouncil.org**

Amazon Books and Merchandise **www.amazon.com**

American Arbitration Association **www.adr.org**

American Association of Retired Persons **www.aarp.org**

American Bankers Association **www.aba.com**

American Bar Association **www.abanet.org**

American Council on Consumer Interests **www.consumerinterests.org**

American Council on Science & Health **www.acsh.org**

American Express Company **www.americanexpress.com**

American Institute for Cancer Research **www.aicr.org**

American Medical Association (AMA) **www.ama-assn.org**

American Society of Travel Agents **www.astanet.com**

American Stock Exchange **www.amex.com**

Association of Independent Consumer Credit **www.aiccca.org**

Autobytel Car Information **www.autobytel.com**

Automobile Buying **www.cartalk.com**

Banking Online **www.bankamerica.com**

Barnes and Noble Books and Merchandise **www.barnesandnoble.com**

Best Fares Magazine **www.bestfares.com**

Bureau of Labor Statistics **www.bls.gov**

Business Week magazine **www.businessweek.com**

Cars **www.cars.com**

Center for Science in the Public Interest **www.cspinet.org**

Centers for Disease Control **www.cdc.gov**

Commodity Futures Trading Commission **www.cftc.gov**

Consumer Federation of America **www.consumerfed.org**

Consumer Lab Testing **www.consumerlab.com**

Consumer Law Page **www.consumerlawpage.com**

Consumer Market Analysis & Forecast **www.simbanet.com**

Consumer Price Index Information **www.bls.gov/cpi/home.htm**

Consumer Protection **www.agnr.umd.edu/nnfr/econ/conprot.htm**

Consumer Reports magazine **www.consumerreports.org**

Consumer Review **www.consumerreview.com**

Consumer World **www.consumerworld.org**

Consumers International **www.consumersinternational.org**

Consumers Union **www.consumersunion.org**

Cool Savings Coupons **www.coolsavings.com**

Council of Better Business Bureaus **www.bbb.org**

Counseling Agencies (AICCCA) **www.aiccca.org**

Countrywide Mortgage Loans **www.countrywide.com**

Dealtime Shopping Search Engine **www.dealtime.com**

Department of Veterans Affairs **www.va.gov**

Direct Marketing Association **www.the-dma.org**

Direct Selling Education Foundation **www.dsa.org**

Dow Jones & Company **www.dowjones.com**

Edmunds **www.edmunds.com**

E-Loan Mortgage Loans **www.e-loan.com**

Environmental Defense **www.edf.org**

Environmental Protection Agency **www.epa.gov**

Esmarts **www.esmarts.com/coupons.html**

Expedia Travel Search Engine **www.expedia.com**

Federal Aviation Administration **www.faa.gov**

Federal Communications Commission **www.fcc.gov**

Federal Consumer Information Center **www.pueblo.gsa.gov**

Federal Deposit Insurance Corporation **www.fdic.gov**

Federal National Mortgage Association **www.fanniemae.com**

Federal Reserve System **www.federalreserve.gov**

Federal Trade Commission **www.ftc.gov**

Financial Aid **www.finaid.org**

Fodor's Travel **www.fodors.com**

Fortune magazine **www.fortune.com**

Frommer's Budget Travel **www.frommers.com**

Fundalarm **www.fundalarm.com**

Gateway Computers **www.gateway.com**

Government National Mortgage Association **www.ginniemae.gov**

Government Printing Office **www.gpo.gov**

WEBSITES FOR CONSUMERS

Hotwire Travel Services **www.hotwire.com**

Index Investing **www.indexfunds.com**

Insurance Guide **www.insure.com**

Insurance Information Institute **www.iii.org**

Insurance Institute for Highway Safety **www.hwysafety.org**

Insurance Search Engine **www.insweb.com**

Internal Revenue Service **www.irs.gov**

International Chamber of Commerce **www.iccwbo.org**

International Data Corporation **www.idc.com**

Investment Strategies **www.datek.com**

JumpStart Coalition **www.jumpstart.org**

Kelley Blue Book **www.kbb.com**

Kiplinger's magazine **www.kiplinger.com**

Lending Tree Mortgage Loans **www.lendingtree.com**

Lower My Bills **www.lowermybills.com**

Mapquest **www.mapquest.com**

MasterCard **www.mastercard.com**

MedicAlert Organization **www.medicalert.org**

MEDLINE **www.medlineplus.gov**

Money magazine **www.money.com**

Moody's Investors Service **www.moodys.com**

Morningstar magazine **www.morningstar.com**

Mortgage Bankers Association of America **www.mbaa.org**

Motley Fool **www.fool.com**

Motorist Assurance Program **www.motorist.org**

My Simon **www.mysimon.com**

National Audubon Society **www.audubon.org**

National Consumers League **www.nationalconsumersleague.org**

National Council Against Health Fraud **www.ncahf.org**

National Endowment for Financial Education **www.nefe.org**

National Fire Protection Association **www.nfpa.org**

National Foundation for Credit Counseling **www.nfcc.org**

National Fraud Information Center **www.fraud.org**

National Funeral Directors Association **www.nfda.org**

National Highway Traffic Safety Administration **www.nhtsa.dot.gov**

National Institute for Automotive Service Excellence **www.asecert.org**

National Resources Defense Council **www.nrdc.org**

New York Stock Exchange **www.nyse.com**

Nuclear Regulatory Commission **www.nrc.gov**

Occupational Safety and Health Administration **www.osha.gov**

Planet Feedback **www.planetfeedback.com**

Privacy Rights Clearinghouse **www.privacyrights.org**

Public Interest Research Group (PIRG) **www.pirg.org/consumer**

Quack Watch Consumer Advocacy **www.quackwatch.org**

Salvagesale **www.salvagesale.com**

Securities & Exchange Commission **www.sec.gov**

Sierra Club **www.sierraclub.org**

Standard and Poor's **www.standardandpoors.com**

The Wall Street Journal **www.wsj.com**

Travelocity **www.travelocity.com**

U.S. Attorney General's Office **www.usdoj.gov**

U.S. Consumer Gateway **www.consumer.gov**

U.S. Consumer Product Safety Commission **www.cpsc.gov**

U.S. Department of Agriculture **www.usda.gov**

U.S. Department of Education **www.ed.gov**

U.S. Department of Energy **www.doe.gov**

U.S. Department of Health and Human Services **www.dhhs.gov**

U.S. Department of Housing and Urban Development **www.hud.gov**

U.S. Department of Interior **www.doi.gov**

U.S. Department of Justice **www.usdoj.gov**

U.S. Department of Labor **www.dol.gov**

U.S. Food & Drug Administration **www.fda.gov**

U.S. Government Information **www.usa.gov**

U.S. Postal Service **www.usps.gov**

Unclaimed Baggage **www.unclaimedbaggage.com**

Vanguard Financial Information **www.vanguard.com**

Wal-Mart **www.walmart.com**

Weather Channel **www.weather.com**

Weddings On-Line **www.weddings-online.com**

World Currency Exchange **www.rubicon.com/passport/currency/currency.htm**

There Oughta Be a Law . . .

Consumer Leasing Act

The Consumer Leasing Act requires lessors to give consumers specific information on lease costs and terms.

Many consumers find that leasing provides a viable option to outright purchasing of various goods. A federal law, the Consumer Leasing Act (CLA), assists consumers in this domain. The intent of the law is to allow for better comparison shopping by consumers.

The CLA applies to personal property and individual leases for more than four months for personal, family, or household use. It covers long-term rentals of cars, furniture, appliances, and other personal property. It does not cover:

- daily car rentals or month-to-month rentals that can be canceled without penalty at the end of the month
- leases for apartments, houses, or furniture that comes with a rented apartment
- property leased to companies or to individuals for business use

The law requires the lease to have a statement of its cost and terms including:

- the kind of insurance needed
- any express warranty on the property
- who is responsible for maintaining and servicing the property
- any penalty for default or late payment
- how the customer or the leasing company may cancel the lease, and the charges for doing so
- whether the property can or cannot be bought and at what price

The FTC enforces the Consumer Leasing Act for almost all leasing companies other than banks. Although the FTC does not resolve individual consumer complaints, comments and complaints can be registered at www.ftc.org, and the site gives phone numbers and other contact information.

Although complaints are not always resolved satisfactorily, many consumers who complain to top officials are both pleased and surprised by the attention their complaints receive. Executives know that a prompt and positive effort to satisfy a buyer is good business practice in the long run and that a disgruntled buyer can be converted to a satisfied buyer by speedy and fair handling of a complaint.

SUMMARY

A first step in developing better buying techniques is to obtain information about products and services available in the marketplace. Historically, the publication *Consumer Reports* has provided vital services to consumers in the area of product testing.

The U.S. government publishes a wealth of free and low-cost consumer information materials through agencies such as the Federal Consumer Information Center, the Government Printing Office, and the USDA's Extension Service. The website www.usa.gov consolidates 20,000 government websites into one and is a good place to start looking for government resources. Private agencies, such as the Council of Better Business Bureaus, also offer quality consumer information materials.

Careful shoppers make good use of advertising; are on the alert for lures and traps; avoid impulse buying; watch for sales; shop around; bargain for lower prices; buy in bulk when feasible; read labels, warranties, and freshness codes; check quantities, prices, and totals; pay cash when feasible; keep records and receipts; and know when and how to protest effectively.

ITEMS FOR REVIEW & DISCUSSION

1. "The buyer is the amateur and the seller is the professional." Discuss the implications of this statement.
2. Explain the differences between money income, real income, and psychic income, and give examples.
3. Discuss the implications of buymanship versus salesmanship.
4. More sales are held in January, February, June, and July than in other months. Why do you suppose sales are concentrated in those months?
5. Besides a reduction in price, what else may a shopper bargain for?
6. Is bargaining compatible with the U.S. economic system? How do you feel about bargaining for lower prices? Have you ever bargained for something?
7. Why do you think some food processors date their products in codes?
8. Name some techniques of wise shoppers.
9. What records of your purchases should you keep? Why?
10. What are several consumer-oriented magazines? What contributions do each of them make to consumer education?
11. What is the function of the Better Business Bureau? How might you use its services?

EXPLORING PERSONAL VALUES: PROJECTS

1. Good buymanship implies that the consumer deals fairly and honestly in the marketplace. With that in mind, respond to the following:
   a. If you are given too much change at the checkout counter, do you call the error to the cashier's attention?
   b. When you are particularly happy with a product or service you have purchased, do you let the seller know of your satisfaction?
   c. If you were to witness what is clearly an act of shoplifting, would you report it to the management of the store?
2. Refer to the techniques of careful shoppers listed in this chapter and respond to each with one of the following statements:
   a. I always use this technique.
   b. I sometimes use this technique.
   c. I rarely use this technique.
   d. I never use this technique.

   Compare your responses with those of your classmates, and determine which are the most used and least used techniques.
3. In your journal, write down all of your impulse buys for a week. Reflect on this information. How will you combat impulse buying in the future? Next, write down the times you remember bargaining. What happened? How did you feel? Finally, list sources of information for consumers. Why don't more people know about or use these sources?
4. Interview a few readers of *Consumer Reports,* as well as some people who do not use it. What are their opinions about the publication? Find out about any valuable buying guides or information not mentioned in this chapter.

5. Order a publication from the Council of Better Business Bureaus and evaluate its helpfulness to you as a consumer.
6. Make a price comparison study of the same product in several stores. Are the prices different enough to justify shopping around?
7. Study the advertising of local supermarkets, either in printed material or in the store, and compare the ads. Report your findings.
8. Visit a supermarket and notice how the products are dated. How many of the products are open-dated?
9. Watch sales at a department store closely. Write a report about whether so-called sales are really good buys.
10. Go to a grocery store, a department store, and a retail store. At each place, use bargaining to attempt to get a lower price on a product. Report the results.
11. Interview five people who have had a complaint about a purchase in a store. Why were they upset? What did they do about it?

ADDITIONAL SOURCES OF INFORMATION

Cline, Elizabeth, and Tricia Cline (Eds.). *The Bargain Buyers Guide 2004: The Consumer's Bible to Big Savings Online and by Mail.* Bearsville, NY: Print Project, 2004.

Consumer Reports. Buying Guide 2008. Yonkers, NY: Consumer Reports Books, 2008.

Howard, Philip K. *The Collapse of the Common Good: How America's Lawsuit Culture Undermines Our Freedom.* New York: Ballantine Books, 2002.

Jones, Ellis. *The Better World Shopping Guide: Every Dollar Makes a Difference.* Gabriola Island, BC, Canada: New Society Publishers, 2008.

Kanner, Bernice. *The 100 Best TV Commercials—And Why They Worked.* New York: Times Business, 2000.

Karp, Gregory. *Living Rich by Spending Smart: How to Get More of What You Really Want.* Upper Saddle River, NJ: FT Press, 2008.

Lindquist, Jay, and Joe Sirgy. *Shopper, Buyer, and Consumer Behavior.* Mason, OH: Atomic Dog Publishing, 2005.

Malhotra, N. K. Multi-stage information processing behavior: An experimental investigation. *Journal of the Academy of Marketing Science, 10* (1), 54–71, 1982.

Murray, Alan. *The Wealth of Choices: The Guide to Protecting Your Money Through Savvy Buying and Smart Investing in a World Turned Upside Down.* New York: Three Rivers Press, 2001.

Shell, G. Richard. *Bargaining for Advantage: Negotiation Strategies for Reasonable People.* New York: Penguin USA, 2001.

Smith, Vernon L. *Bargaining and Market Behavior: Essays in Experimental Economics.* New York: Cambridge University Press, 2000.

> Retailers should be buying agents for consumers, not selling agents for producers.
>
> JAMES TURNER

KEY TERMS

arbitration panel
brand
express warranty
implied warranty
information overload
mediation panel
trademark
Underwriters Laboratories (UL)
warranty (guarantee)

The following concepts will be developed in this chapter:

1. Sellers are in business to make a profit, and the help they offer to consumers, whether valuable or not, results in higher prices for the consumer.
2. Certain seemingly helpful consumer aids, such as some warranties, may protect the seller more than the consumer.
3. Efforts such as consumer action panels and mediation groups provide valuable services, but such aids are few in number.

After having read this chapter, you should be able to accomplish the following objectives:

1. Define and explain the following terms: brands and trademarks, testing laboratory, label, trade association, warranty.
2. Recognize assistance available through consumer product testing services and consumer reporting.

DO CONSUMERS NEED HELP?

The proliferation of products and their increasing complexity complicate the task of being an intelligent consumer. A typical retail store may carry 20,000 different products. An Internet shopping site may carry 10 times that number! Computers, for example, are complicated machines with so many different characteristics that consumers may be inclined to buy them without investigating fully. How well equipped are buyers to make the necessary decisions when they enter the labyrinth of the marketplace? What ability do consumers have to judge quality, quantity, and price? What abilities are necessary to be a good consumer? Individuals should ask themselves these questions when they are approaching buying decisions, whether they are entering a supermarket, a department store, or an appliance store, whether they are buying home furnishings, an automobile, or a house, and whether they are shopping in person, by mail order, or on the Internet.

Consumers want to purchase goods and services with the best combination of price, quantity, quality, and service to meet their specific needs. The difficulties of finding the best combination often may seem overwhelming. The variety of items to choose from increases every day. The barrage of advertising and marketing ploys that extol the virtues of products adds to the complexity of the marketplace.

Sellers' Efforts to Help Consumers

What are the sellers doing to assist consumers through this marketplace maze? Business executives know that most consumers are not good judges of the quality of the things they buy. Classified according to their reaction to this situation, sellers generally fall into three groups:

1. A few try to capitalize on consumer ignorance by misrepresenting what they have to sell.
2. A second, larger group also seeks to profit from consumer ignorance. These sellers use brands, trademarks, and advertising to try to make consumers think that their products are superior. Producers spend enormous sums on advertising and marketing techniques to create goodwill and to develop consumer buying habits that will profit them.
3. Realizing that consumers are unable to compare the quality of numerous brands of merchandise, the third group of sellers attempts to provide special assurance that their products are as good as they are claimed to be.

WHEN CONSUMERS NEED HELP

Consumers typically need assistance at any one or all of three points in their buying decision. First, consumers may seek information before a purchase. This is known as the information-gathering period. With the Internet, valuable information is available about virtually any product or service. Other sources of information include magazines and word-of-mouth. The plethora of information, however, can result in **information overload.**

Information overload having too much information to make a decision about a topic; difficulty identifying what information is relevant to the decision.

A second point when consumers may seek information is at the time of purchase. At this point, the consumer might read literature provided by a manufacturer or learn more through conversations with a salesperson. The accuracy and quality of this information varies depending on the knowledge of the salesperson.

The final time when consumers may need help is after the purchase. This is typically when a consumer either has a question about the operation of a product or is dissatisfied with a product or service. To resolve the question or complaint, the consumer must take action. This chapter suggests sources of help and information that may assist a consumer's search before, during, or after making a purchase.

COMMON TYPES OF HELP FROM SELLERS

onsumer help includes brands and trademarks, labels, warranties, and consumer affair managers. These are discussed in the following pages.

Brands and Trademarks

Trademark a legal term for a name, symbol, design, device or any combination thereof, adopted and used by a manufacturer or merchant to identify its goods and distinguish them from those manufactured or sold by others. The trademark can be registered and become an exclusive legal right for its owner.

Brand the dimension of the trademark that represents the *associations* a consumer affiliates with the trademark.

Research suggests a correlation between the amount of education consumers have and the extent to which they depend on brand names. The higher the education level attained, the less dependence on brand names.

FYI

Those of us reared in a world of **trademarks** and **brands** have difficulty imagining an economy in which the market is not filled with brand-name commodities. Why do brand names play such an important role in our marketplace? They are an outgrowth of the process of the mass production of goods. By using brand names and trademarks, sellers attempt to differentiate their products from competing products and to convince consumers of a real difference, even if there is none.

The use of machinery and large factories entails substantial fixed expenses. By marking their products and advertising them under brands and trademarks, manufacturers hope to lessen the impact of price competition. If these efforts are successful, sales increase and stabilize, the fixed expenses can be spread over a greater volume, and the per-unit expense decreases.

At one time, trademarked merchandise may have saved consumers time when they shopped. After making purchases of a specific trademarked product and finding the items satisfactory, they could choose to purchase that brand again and avoid shopping around or risking purchasing an unsatisfactory product of another brand. Today, buyers are confronted with scores of brands of similar products that often are nearly identical.

An argument in favor of trademarked merchandise is that once buyers have made a satisfactory purchase, they can be assured of the same quality in the future. But who is to give this assurance, other than the manufacturer? The quality of products from a single brand can and does vary considerably. A brand or trademark does not preclude inconsistent quality or prevent manufacturers from changing the quality of the product if they desire.

Do brands and trademarks increase or diminish competition? If they were used only to indicate the sources or origins of products, they could stimulate competition. When they are used in conjunction with advertising, however, they can contribute to monopolistic power.

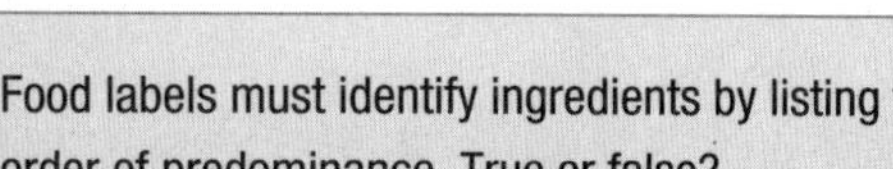

Food labels must identify ingredients by listing them in order of predominance. True or false?

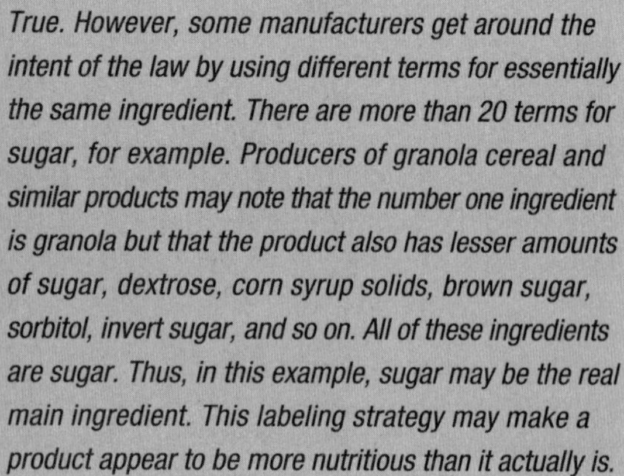

True. However, some manufacturers get around the intent of the law by using different terms for essentially the same ingredient. There are more than 20 terms for sugar, for example. Producers of granola cereal and similar products may note that the number one ingredient is granola but that the product also has lesser amounts of sugar, dextrose, corn syrup solids, brown sugar, sorbitol, invert sugar, and so on. All of these ingredients are sugar. Thus, in this example, sugar may be the real main ingredient. This labeling strategy may make a product appear to be more nutritious than it actually is.

Labels

Labels are closely associated with trademarks. Prior to enactment of the Labeling Law discussed in Chapter 3, labels and trademarks were not much different. A label frequently was nothing more than a device for applying a trademark to a product.

Today, labels impart a considerable variety of information. They usually include the name of the product, the manufacturer, and the manufacturer's address. Commonly, labels carry directions for use of the product, claims for what the product will do, and statements of quality. Some labels tell buyers when the merchandise was packed or the time frame within which it should be used. In many cases, the law requires that the quantity of product contained in the package be indicated on the label. And most food products now carry the nutrient information discussed in Chapter 3. All labels on foods, drugs, cosmetics, woolen and fur goods, hazardous products, and textile products entering interstate commerce require specific information. In addition, energy information is required on major home appliances such as furnaces, refrigerators, and room air conditioners.

It may be argued that many consumers do not read labels, so providing informative labels is useless. Certainly some consumers do not read labels, but the fact remains that consumers have a right to know the information that labels provide. As more consumers realize that labels give adequate and helpful information, they will come to understand the value of reading labels carefully.

Food labels are required to list potential food allergens. True or false?

True. Food and Drug Administration updates to the food label law require food labels to identify foods that may cause an allergic reaction. Eight foods account for 90 percent of all allergies; they are milk, eggs, peanuts, tree nuts, fish, shellfish, soy, and wheat. When these ingredients are present, manufacturers are required to indicate this on the food label in simple terms, either in the ingredient list, after the list, or next to the list.

Warranties

A **warranty** (guarantee) is a type of disclosure that should affect a consumer's purchase of a product. A warranty usually carries a promise of reimbursement if the product fails to meet specifications. Most often it is a written guarantee of the integrity of a product and of the maker's responsibility for repairing or replacing defective parts. In common parlance, the terms *warranty* and *guarantee* are used interchangeably. The Federal Trade Commission made no distinction between the two terms until the Magnuson-Moss Warranty Act in 1977, which told manufacturers to drop the word guarantee in representations to consumers about the performance of their products and to substitute the word warranty.

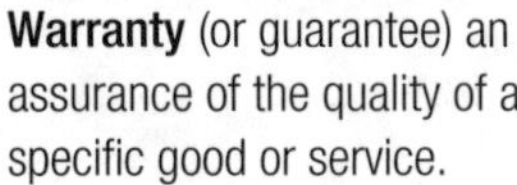

Warranty (or guarantee) an assurance of the quality of a specific good or service.

The warranty is an outgrowth of the law of caveat emptor, "Let the buyer beware." The buyer is therefore responsible for determining quality, and wise buyers disregard sellers' claims of quality as mere puffery. In response, producers developed the warranty to assure prospective buyers that they could rely on the seller's statements. The warranty was intended to give the warrantor (seller) a competitive advantage. Unscrupulous sellers soon adopted the warranty but refused to honor it. Legal action led to a body of laws that rendered the warranty comparatively useless.

Warranties may take several forms.

Customer Service Hall of Fame

CASE STUDY

Mike, a subscriber to Disney's online *Toontown,* decided to cancel two of the four accounts his children had set up. The two were not being used and were thus unnecessary. Mike works as Operations Manager for a call center, so he is fully aware of the games some phone representatives play. Although he prepared himself for a verbal struggle with the customer service representative; Mike was pleasantly surprised by the service he received.

The Disney operator who handled Mike's call was polite, did not attempt to prevent him from canceling, and even arranged for a refund without his asking. When Mike asked to cancel the accounts, she asked why. After Mike explained they were not being used, she indicated Disney would refund the current month's payment and thanked him for calling. That was the end of it. Quick, simple, pleasant, and productive.

QUESTIONS

1. Customer service lines often are not so helpful. What did Disney do differently?
2. Do you think that customers should have to provide a reason for canceling or should they just be able to say "cancel it"?
3. Many companies will mail a survey or do a phone survey to see if the customer was satisfied with the representative's service. Do you think asking customers if the company's service was good is useful or not? In what way?
4. What do you think are the long- and short-term implications of effective customer service?

Source: www.consumerist.com, March 10, 2007. Retrieved April 20, 2009, from http://consumerist.com/consumer/disney/above-and-beyond-disney-makes-canceling-easy-and-fun-243029.php.

Express warranties

Express warranty a written promise that a product will perform in a specified manner.

An **express warranty** is a specific statement of fact or a promise that the goods being offered will perform as the warranty states. A seller usually creates an express warranty in writing, such as through an advertisement, although express warranties may be offered orally as well.

Implied warranties

Implied warranty a promise that a product is of average salable quality.

When a merchant sells a product, the law requires that certain automatic guarantees are made to the buyer of the product. For example, we assume that merchandise sold to us is fully owned by the seller. This is called "warranty of title" and "warranty against encumbrances." Thus, you cannot sell your friend's automobile and keep the money for your own purposes, because you do not own the automobile. If you were to participate in such a transaction, you would be violating a part of the state's implied warranty law. Even though an **implied warranty** may seem to be obvious, it is legally enforceable only because the government has intervened and passed laws to assist consumers and honest businesspeople in marketplace transactions.

Less obvious but equally important consumer protections are fitness of purpose warranties and warranties of merchantability.

Implied warranties of fitness and merchantability

The *implied warranty of fitness for a particular purpose* means the seller guarantees that the item will be suitable for the purpose for which it is bought. The implied warranty of fitness applies where the seller has reason to know, at the time of the purchase, the purpose for which the buyer intends to use the product. Thus, if you order a specific model number of toner for your copy machine, and the merchant indicates that the toner she recommends will work in your copier, she has offered you a warranty of fitness for a particular purpose. If the toner does not work in your machine, you have a legal right to a refund.

TIP If you purchase a used auto, avoid a "50/50" warranty and obtain a 100 percent warranty instead. A 50/50 warranty indicates that if a repair is made, the dealership will pay 50 percent and the consumer will pay the remaining 50 percent. Often, the dealership inflates the repair charges, rendering the "warranty" worthless.

The *implied warranty of merchantability* is less restrictive than the implied warranty of fitness. The implied warranty of merchantability indicates only that the product works under ordinary uses. Thus, an auto manufacturer must provide an automobile that operates normally, but the manufacturer is not obligated, under the implied warranty of merchantability, to have the auto perform extraordinarily—for example, to accelerate to 70 mph in five seconds.

The value of warranties to sellers depends largely on the extent to which the sellers honor them. If buyers find that a seller not only makes but also honors its warranties, they may pay higher prices and purchase more from that seller.

TIP If your new auto is a lemon, hire an attorney who specializes in these cases before submitting to arbitration. If a competent attorney is involved, most auto manufacturers try to settle the claim quickly because they realize that litigation, including court action, may cost them a thousand dollars or more per day.

Many department stores, e-commerce sites, and mail-order stores have developed reputations as reliable warrantors. They try to satisfy customers as completely as possible, even though this may entail recognizing some invalid claims. Customers who use a charge account with a retail store or a credit card issued by a bank are in a stronger bargaining position, which frequently assures them a more satisfactory adjustment in case of a problem than if they had paid cash.

Although warranties are related to the use of trademarks and labels, buyers probably do not rely much on them. Experience has shown that warranties are easily made but hard to enforce. As a result of buyers' and legitimate sellers' increasing irritation with abuses of the warranty device, the FTC has developed a five-point guide for sellers. The FTC says advertising of warranties must include information about:

1. what parts of the product or what types of problems the warranty covers (and, if necessary for clarity, what parts or problems it does not cover)
2. the period of coverage
3. what the warrantor will do to correct problems (and, if necessary for clarity, what it will *not* do)
4. how the customer can get warranty service
5. how state law may affect certain provisions of the warranty

Tires and batteries on a new vehicle are warranted not by the auto manufacturer but instead by the tire manufacturer and the battery manufacturer, respectively. These warranties tend to be much more limited than the vehicle warranty.

FYI

The Major Appliance Consumer Action Panel (MACAP) suggests that consumers ask the following questions about warranties:

1. Does the warranty cover the entire product? Only certain parts? Is labor included?
2. Who is responsible for repairing the product? The dealer? A service agency? The manufacturer?
3. Who pays for repairs? Parts? Labor? Shipping charges?
4. How long does the warranty last on the entire product? On individual parts or assemblies?
5. If the product is out of use because of a service problem or if it has to be removed from the home for repair, will a substitute product or service be provided? By whom?

In addition to reading and understanding the operating instructions, buyers should make sure they find and understand the answers to these questions about warranties.

Q+A

You fail to mail in your warranty registration card for your new cellular phone. You know that you have a one-year warranty on the phone, but it is not working properly after only eight months. Do you have any recourse?

Yes! Even if you do not mail in the warranty registration card, your warranty is still valid. Your receipt for the purchase is proof of your purchase date. Be sure to keep your receipts in case you need them at a later date.

TIP

Shop only at retail stores (including e-commerce sites) that have favorable return policies, and understand all return policies fully before you make a purchase.

Consumer Affairs Managers

During the past several decades the number of consumer-relations departments in corporations has increased. Only a few companies had these departments prior to the rise of the consumer movement in the 1960s. Today, thousands of companies have them. In addition, a professional organization has been established for those working in the consumer area of business. The Society of Consumer Affairs Professionals in Business (SOCAP), founded in 1973, has members from business, government, and consumer organizations. Its purpose

You have a nonrefundable airline ticket. You need to change your plans because of a medical problem, but the airline refuses. You are out of luck. True or False?

False. Many times, with proper documentation, airlines will refund your money in emergency situations.

is to "foster the integrity of business in its dealings with consumers; promote harmonious relationships between business and government and consumers; and advance the consumer affairs profession."

The benefits to consumers of consumer affairs departments have been mixed. In some companies, these departments are mere window dressing. In other companies, they have successfully lessened the tensions between producers and consumers.

SELLERS' JOINT EFFORTS

Sellers have instituted some joint efforts to help consumers. These include Better Business Bureaus, industry and trade associations, arbitration and mediation panels, and customer service departments.

Better Business Bureaus

Joint efforts of sellers include activities designed not so much to aid consumers as to protect the more scrupulous business people from those who are less scrupulous. Success in these efforts benefits buyers as well as ethical sellers.

Better Business Bureaus developed out of efforts to secure truth in advertising. As far back as 1912, the Associated Advertising Clubs of the World undertook a campaign to reduce misrepresentation and fraudulence in advertising. For more information about Better Business Bureaus, see Chapter 8.

It is important to request a receipt for a product repair performed free under a warranty. True or false?

True. If a product is repaired under a warranty and the same problem recurs within a reasonable amount of time after the warranty expires, the manufacturer must repair the product again at no charge. The receipt documents the problem and the initial repair.

Industry and Trade Associations

Establishment of the Major Appliance Consumer Action Panel was a step forward by the Association of Home Appliance Manufacturers, the Gas Appliance Manufacturers Association, and the American Retail Federation. This consumer panel, chosen from educators and consumer affairs counselors, was established to advise the industry on its relations with consumers, and it provides an effective procedure for handling complaints. In addition, MACAP makes recommendations to consumers to help them purchase and secure maximum benefit from appliances and takes positions on public issues concerning consumers.

Arbitration and Mediation Panels

Arbitration panel a group whose function is to attempt to resolve complaints between buyer and seller; decisions usually are binding on one or both parties.

In part because of the threat of government regulation, industries have developed **arbitration panels** to review and rule on consumer complaints. The panel often consists of three to five members, the majority of whom represent the consumer interest.

Arbitration panels in the automobile industry are especially noteworthy. These were created as a direct result of passage of "lemon laws" in each state. Virtually all lemon laws allow third-party panels to rule on complaints resulting from purchase of a new automobile. Most lemon laws specifically designate the manner in which the appeal process must be conducted, but automobile manufacturers sometimes violate these provisions. As a result of problems with auto arbitration panels, some states have instituted government-sponsored panels to oversee functioning of the arbitration panels!

Mediation panel a group whose function is to attempt to resolve complaints between a buyer and seller but whose decision carries no force of law and thus is nonbinding.

Other industries do not offer formal resolution of complaints by third parties. They do, however, offer mediation of complaints through **mediation panels.**

Consumer action panels (CAPs) and mediation groups provide a valuable service to consumers. Complaints tend to be handled fairly, quickly, and with minimal cost to the consumer. Unfortunately, few industries have committed funds and time to these efforts.

The Magnuson-Moss Warranty Act

The Magnuson-Moss Warranty Act requires that warranty information be made available to consumers before they make a purchase. If a warranty is offered, it must be either a full or limited warranty, and it must be clearly stated.

In the past, warranties and guarantees were classic examples of "big print giveth and small print taketh away." The bold type of the warranty might note that the product is fully guaranteed, whereas the small type would include a major retraction such as an extremely high charge for handling. Further, many warranties were written in legal language that only attorneys could understand.

As a result of abuses like these, the Magnuson-Moss Warranty Act became law in 1977. The Act treats guarantees and warranties as the same. It does not require a manufacturer to give a warranty, but if a warranty is given, it must be either a full or a limited warranty. A *full* warranty promises that:

- A defective product will be repaired or replaced free, including removal and reinstallation when necessary.
- The product will be repaired within a reasonable time period after the consumer has informed the company.
- The consumer will not have to do anything unreasonable to get warranty service.
- The warranty is valid for anyone who owns the product during the warranty period.
- If the product has not been repaired after a reasonable number of tries, a replacement or a refund will be provided (known as the "anti-lemon" provision).
- The consumer does not have to return a warranty card for a product with a full warranty (but a company may give a registration card and suggest that it be returned, as long as it is clear that the return of the card is voluntary).
- Implied warranties cannot be disclaimed or denied or limited to any specific length of time.

The title "full" does *not* mean the following:

- It does *not* mean that the warranty covers the entire product.
- It does *not* mean that the warranty has to last for one year or any other specific length of time.
- It does *not* mean that the company must pay for "consequential or incidental damages" (such as towing, car rental, or food spoilage).
- It does *not* mean that the product is warranted in all geographic areas.

A *limited* warranty lets the consumer know that the warranty gives less than the full warranty gives. For example, the consumer

- may have to pay for labor, reinstallation, or other charges.
- may be required to bring a heavy product back to the store for service or do something else that may be difficult.
- may be promised a pro-rata refund or credit.
- should realize that the anti-lemon provision does not apply to limited warranties.

The title "limited" does *not* mean the following:

- It does *not* mean that the product is inferior or will not work as promised.
- It does *not* mean that only part of the product is covered (a limited warranty may cover the entire product).
- It does *not* mean that the warranty covers only the cost of repair parts (a limited warranty can include labor, too).
- It does *not* mean that the warranty will last for any specific length of time.
- It does *not* mean that warranty service may be done in only a few locations.

A product can carry more than one written warranty. For example, an automatic washer can have a full warranty on the entire product for one year and a limited four-year warranty on the gear assembly. To avoid problems, the consumer should

- keep sales slips.
- do any maintenance required by the company for warranty coverage.
- use the product according to the manufacturer's instructions (abuse or misuse is not covered by any warranty).
- realize that a warranty is only as good as the company that stands behind it.

Violations of the Magnuson-Moss Warranty Act should be reported to the Federal Trade Commission, Marketing Practices Division, 6th and Pennsylvania, N.W., Washington, DC 20580.

Customer Service Departments

Many companies now have customer service departments. Definitions of "good customer service" vary, but availability of these service departments is a step in the right direction. Customer service for some companies means genuinely caring for the consumer and his or her needs; in these cases the company builds a positive reputation. Often the customer wants only a replacement or to know that the company cares enough to remedy a problem.

Companies may employ a follow-up call, letter, or email, asking customers to rate the quality of service their representative provided. This tactic may be overused, even to the point of annoyance. Customers want tangible results, not to be bothered by surveys that seem unconnected to results.

OTHER TYPES OF HELP

Additional assistance to consumers is available through testing laboratories and consumer reporting.

Testing Laboratories

Underwriters Laboratories (UL) a nonprofit organization established to investigate materials, devices, products, equipment, construction methods, and systems with respect to hazards affecting life and property.

The **UL** mark is found on many electrical products. It refers to **Underwriters Laboratories,** Inc., founded in 1894. A product may carry a listing mark (the letters UL in a circle), when UL is satisfied that the product conforms to established safety requirements. Use of the phrase "UL Approved" is technically incorrect because "approved" has legal implications that do not apply to UL's listing system. In addition to looking for the UL mark on electrical appliances, buyers should make sure that the mark is for the entire electrical appliance, not for just one part of it. A UL listing indicates that the product has been tested and is safe, not necessarily that the product is of high quality.

www.quackwatch.org

Quackwatch, Inc., is a nonprofit organization and a member of the Consumer Federation of America (CFA). The Quackwatch website focuses on exposing health-related frauds, myths, fads, and fallacies.

Consumer Reporting

During much of the United States' history, consumer journalism has revealed the excesses of both government and business. Much of the "consumer reporting" in the past decade, however, has become noncombative and noncontroversial. Much of it tends to focus on personal finance, appearing on the business pages. Some feel that the politically conservative 1980s and/or the boom economy of the 1990s may have worked to dilute consumer journalism. Others believe that it remains an important vehicle for informing consumers of flagrant violations. These advocates point to the numerous television news "magazines," such as *Dateline,* that continue to expose fraud, government waste, and other forms of consumer exploitation.

IS HELP PROVIDED BY SELLERS RELIABLE?

Although producers' judgment may be biased by their primary purpose—to make more profit—many sellers do sincerely wish to help their customers. Still, the number of sellers who are sufficiently concerned with their customers' welfare to exert special effort to assure them of quality and fair prices is too small.

Further, buyers are skeptical about whether these efforts will really benefit them. This skepticism is well founded. Businesspeople constantly remind the public that they are in business to make money. Taking them at their own word, consumers are right in concluding that a consumer-aid program will be maintained only as long as it pays measurable profits. Consumers have a right to ask who pays for special services such as testing laboratories and guarantees.

In one way or another, the costs of consumer services are paid by consumers themselves, in the form of higher prices. The higher prices may be justified by the assurance that the merchandise will prove satisfactory. Because consumers are paying for these services, however, considerable duplication may be avoided and greater reliability assured if the laboratory testing and reporting services are performed by a nonprofit association owned, operated, and financed by consumers.

You purchase an item from a store that advertises "Satisfaction guaranteed or your money back." You are not satisfied with the product but the store refuses to refund your money. There is nothing you can do. True or false?

False. Report the store to your state attorney general's office. If a store represents that it has a return policy, it must comply with that policy or it is violating the law.

SUMMARY

Sellers provide various types of assistance to consumers. These include brands, trademarks, labels, and warranties. Brands and trademarks allow some assurance of uniform quality, but trademarks offer no pricing information and can create monopolistic power. Labels give considerable information; they often carry directions for use, claims of what the products will do, and statements of quality. Some labels, however, are deceptive or omit information consumers need in order to make intelligent selections. Warranties can assure quality, service, and, often, the duration of expected use. The value of warranties depends on the seller's reliability.

Other efforts by sellers to assist consumers include consumer affairs associations, Better Business Bureaus, industry and trade associations, and testing laboratories. Ultimately, the value of the information that sellers provide depends on whether the sellers' efforts are conceived sincerely and executed honestly.

ITEMS FOR REVIEW & DISCUSSION

1. Based on the information in this chapter and in Chapter 3, state the information that, by law, has to be included on a food label.
2. State the advantages and disadvantages of brand names to consumers. Why does a correlation seem to exist between the amount of education a consumer has and the extent to which he or she depends on brand names?
3. State the major difference between a mediation panel and an arbitration panel.
4. Differentiate implied and expressed warranties. How might warranties be made more meaningful to consumers?
5. State the questions the FTC says the advertising of warranties should answer.
6. Enumerate five ways you can tell whether sellers' efforts are honest. Do you think consumers need help from sellers? Why?
7. What might happen in the marketplace if brand names and trademarks were removed from all products?
8. Why do you think consumer action panels have not become more popular?
9. Do you think the sellers' aids discussed in this chapter are reliable?

EXPLORING PERSONAL VALUES: PROJECTS

1. Do you believe that brand names are worthwhile or that brand names are worthless? Discuss your position with your classmates. Compare your opinions, citing reasons for your view.

2. Find the warranty for a product that was purchased recently in your household. Review the warranty and determine what type of warranty coverage you have.
3. In your journal, write your reactions to this chapter. Do you feel that buying is a complicated process? Do you diligently buy the same trademarks? Record your thoughts regarding labels and warranties. Did you learn anything new about them from this chapter? If so, will this new knowledge change how you shop? If so, how?
4. Collect labels from 10 products and evaluate the labels as to their usefulness to the consumer. Then collect warranties for five different products, including an automobile, and evaluate them.
5. Write to a trade association or a consumer action panel for information about its activities. Write a report on your findings.
6. Have a class debate on the statement: "Resolved: Better Business Bureaus are interested in serving the needs of businesses over the needs of consumers."
7. Brainstorm suggestions for ways consumers can be more informed and better protected.
8. Research a consumer-relations department in a large company. Report your findings to the class.
9. What are the three largest retail stores in your area? As a class, compare and contrast the services each store offers to consumers.

ADDITIONAL SOURCES OF INFORMATION

Cross, Gary S. *An All-Consuming Century: Why Commercialism Won in Modern America.* New York: Columbia University Press, 2002.

Howells, Geraint G., and Stephen Weatherill. *Consumer Protection Law (Markets and the Law).* Burlington, VT: Ashgate Publishing Ltd., 2005.

McEwen, William J. *Married to the Brand: Why Consumers Bond with Some Brands For Life.* New York: Gallup Press, 2005.

Moore, Geoffrey A. *Crossing the Chasm.* New York: HarperBusiness, 2002.

O'Guinn, Thomas, Chris Allen, and Richard J. Semenik. *Advertising and Integrated Brand Promotion.* Boston: South-Western College Publishing, 2008.

Ries, Al, and Laura Ries. *The 22 Immutable Laws of Branding: How to Build a Product or Service Into a World-Class Brand.* New York: Harper Business, 2002.

Roberts, Kevin, and A. G. Lafley. *Lovemarks: The Future Beyond Brands.* New York: Powerhouse Books, 2005.

Rogers, Everett M. *Diffusion of Innovations.* New York: Free Press, 2003.

Twigg-Flesner, Christian. *Consumer Product Guarantees.* Burlington, VT: Ashgate Publishing, 2003.

Law is the highest reason implanted in Nature, which commands what ought to be done and forbids the opposite.

MARCUS TULLIUS CICERO, ROMAN ORATOR, PHILOSOPHER, STATESMAN

KEY TERMS

arbitration
civil case
common law
consideration
constitutional law
consumer law
contract
criminal case
defendant
licensing boards
mediation
ordinance
parol evidence rule
plaintiff
precedent
reasonable person
regulatory law
small-claims court
statutory law
Uniform Commercial Code (UCC)

The following concepts will be developed in this chapter:

1. Consumers are not necessarily protected by consumer laws just because many laws have been enacted.
2. Consumer laws are enforceable and may be classified in several ways.
3. Reading and understanding contracts is essential in the marketplace.
4. Alternative dispute resolution is a viable option in today's litigious society.

After having read this chapter, you should be able to accomplish the following objectives:

1. Identify the three elements necessary for adequate consumer protection.
2. Explain the differences in classifications of consumer law.
3. List and understand the elements necessary to have a legally binding contract.
4. Understand the similarities and differences between arbitration and mediation.
5. Give at least three advantages and disadvantages of using small-claims court.

CONSUMER LAWS: QUANTITY AND QUALITY

Hundreds of federal consumer laws and regulations have been enacted to protect consumers. Further, each state has consumer-protection laws that include a general fraud law. Each state also has a small-claims court law to protect its citizens. Most states have a plethora of additional safeguards in the form of laws and regulations. Many municipalities also have their own local ordinances to protect consumers. With all these laws and regulations, why do we continue to see so much fraud, deception, and unethical behavior on the part of sellers in the marketplace?

People have differing views as to why consumers need better protection in the marketplace. Essentially, these views can be divided into three schools. There are "legislation critics," "regulation critics," and "consumer education critics."

1. *Legislation critics* generally believe that the existing laws that have been developed to assist consumers are sufficient in number but that too many consumer laws have loopholes that allow sellers to circumvent the intent of the laws easily. Therefore, legislation critics contend, consumer statutes are of little value.

2. *Regulation critics* contend that the regulatory agencies with the responsibility to enforce consumer laws and regulations are not doing their jobs. These agencies lack the necessary financial support, and many enforcement agencies lack the motivation to enforce legislative mandates strictly. It is easier not to "rock the boat" of powerful, well-organized business interests than to pursue violators aggressively on behalf of consumers.
3. *Consumer education critics* contend that the laws and regulations and their enforcement are adequate and that an educated citizenry is all that is needed. This group notes that few consumers are aware of the multitude of protections in the marketplace, which makes them either unwilling or unable to defend themselves against seller abuses. Consumer education critics generally believe that the consumers are responsible for learning about laws and regulations that can assist them.

All three of these groups probably are correct to some extent. Without adequate laws, enforcement of those laws, and educated consumers, the marketplace never will be as effective and as efficient as it should be in protecting the interests of all consumers.

WHAT IS CONSUMER LAW?

Society's distaste for fraud, deception, and unethical practices is reflected in the requirements that public agencies enforce on sellers to prohibit marketplace misrepresentations. These requirements form **consumer law**—a type of law that is as varied as the goods and services we consume. Consumer law usually deals with exchanges involving modest sums of money. Home buying, personal investing, and automobile purchasing often are considered part of consumer law, although these activities frequently involve thousands (or hundreds of thousands) of dollars. Consumer law includes statutory law, regulatory law, constitutional law, and common law. These classifications of laws are all fully enforceable. The significant difference among them is the manner by which they were developed originally.

Consumer law the law of everyday contracts and transactions involving consumers and sellers.

Statutory Law

Statutory law law enacted by the legislative branch of government.

Ordinance a local law adopted by a municipality or other local government entity.

Regulatory law laws (rules/regulations) promulgated by agencies of the federal or state government.

Statutory law encompasses laws that are developed and passed by Congress or by elected officials at the state level. An **ordinance** is similar to a statutory law except that ordinances are passed by elected officials at the local government level.

Regulatory Law

Most consumer laws are statutory in origin, but many consumer defenses also are developed by federal and state agencies. These agencies came into being through federal or state legislation that empowered them to develop and enforce regulation. Agencies' regulations provide the framework of **regulatory law,** also known as *administrative law.*

> **TIP** When you need legal assistance, it is a good idea to hire an attorney who specializes in the area of law in which you need help. You will be better represented, and the total fees (especially if you are paying by the hour) will likely be lower than if you hire an attorney who has to take additional time to research your case.

Most regulatory laws are enforced by the chief protector of consumers at the governmental level, which is the Federal Trade Commission. Other agencies, such as the Food and Drug Administration and the Department of Agriculture, also have rule-making authority. State regulations are typically enforced by the state attorney general's office or by other consumer-related agencies. New rules may be issued when administrative personnel find evidence of unfair or deceptive practices in an entire industry. Before these rules become law, public hearings and public comments are solicited.

More than 100 federal regulatory laws have been enacted to protect consumers. These cover a wide range of goods and services from food packaging to airline travel and safety.

Licensing boards

Licensing boards committees formed to discipline members of specific professional or occupational groups who deceive or mistreat consumers.

Much state activity in the field of consumer protection takes the form of administrative regulation of occupational and professional groups. Typically, **licensing boards** oversee these specific groups.

Licensing boards are under the jurisdiction of state authorities, although licensing board members tend to be professionals in the discipline that they oversee. Many boards include consumer representatives who are laypersons, in an effort to balance the views presented at committee meetings. These boards often have considerable sovereignty. For example, many are empowered to issue and revoke professional and occupational licenses. Professions and occupations represented by licensing boards include, among others, physicians, attorneys, chiropractors, funeral directors, and prizefighters.

> **TIP** If you feel the fees that an attorney is charging you are too high, contact the attorney and try to negotiate a reduction in fees. Most attorneys are willing to reduce fees if asked to do so.

Critics of licensing boards contend that these boards "police their own" and, thus, render decisions that are biased in favor of the professional. In rebuttal, defenders of these boards contend that decisions regarding these professions are complex and that a board without strong internal representation would not be qualified to render informed judgments.

Constitutional Law

A government's constitution sets forth its fundamental principles, aims, and laws. The laws set forth in the constitution form the basis of **constitutional law.** The U.S. Constitution, written in 1787, is the "master plan" of the land. Constitutions are designed to last forever, but if they become obsolete, there is a way to alter them. In the United States this is done by constitutional amendment. The amendment procedure is, by design, cumbersome. In the history of the United States, there have been only about 30 amendments to the U.S. Constitution.

Constitutional law the law enacted when a nation or state becomes a separate entity; its fundamental principles are enumerated in its constitution.

Common Law

Common law was brought to the United States by colonists who had been governed by this type of law in England. Essentially, common law is based on judicial rulings. For instance, if a British judge ruled that it was illegal for a merchant to overcharge a consumer, that ruling became part of the common law. Later, when a similar case was tried, the second judge used the first judge's ruling in deciding the case. The first judge's ruling would be a **precedent.** As a result, common law is termed *precedent law.*

Common law (precedent law) unwritten law whose source is the recorded decisions of judges.

Precedent a judge's ruling that becomes an example for subsequent rulings involving similar circumstances.

THE UNIFORM COMMERCIAL CODE

The Uniform Commercial Code (UCC) is an important part of consumer law. Its major purpose is to set a standard by which merchants who operate in more than one state can comply with each state's laws. The Code is a set of rules governing consumer transactions that was adopted by each state to make consumer laws throughout the United States consistent.

Until the UCC became part of state laws, merchants had to know and comply with different laws in as many states as they had businesses. The problem was complicated in that the laws of one state often conflicted with those of another. Even in circumstances where two states' laws were similar, they may have differed from those imposed by the federal government. The result was costly, burdensome, and inefficient use of business resources. The UCC was designed to remedy this problem. It applies to sales of goods as opposed to services.

Uniform Commercial Code (UCC) a statute that has been adopted, at least in part, in all states, which regulates most sales of goods and many other consumer transactions.

CONTRACTS

Most legal instruments that are covered by consumer law are in the form of contracts. A **contract** consists of a voluntary promise, enforceable by the law, between competent parties to do, or not to do, something. To have a legally binding contract, the law states that the following five elements must be present: mutual agreement, competent participants, legal subject matter, consideration, and legal form.

Contract a legally enforceable agreement between two or more competent parties; it may be written, oral, or implied.

Mutual Agreement

A contract requires a clear offer and a clear acceptance by the party to whom the offer was made. Suppose you just graduated and you offer your friend, Andy, $100 to help you move your furniture to your new apartment. Andy declines, but another friend, Ben, overhears your offer and says, "I'll do it." Is this a contract? The answer is no, because the offer was made to Andy, not Ben. If, however, you agree to have Ben help you move, you now have accepted Ben's offer, and a contract is in force.

www.usconstitution.net

This website provides the text of the U.S. Constitution on-line. The site also includes history, amendments, amendment procedures, failed amendments, and proposed amendments.

TIP

Be suspicious if your attorney wants to play "hard ball" with the opposition. Often this posture forces the other side to act in a like manner. The end result may be that a lot of your time and money are wasted. A fairer, more equitable solution might be obtained by a more reasonable approach to litigation.

Competent Participants

A contract negotiated in one language but presented in writing in another language may be voided in some states.

FYI

To have a contract, the participants to the contract must be competent in the legal sense. For example, they must be of age. Generally, the minimum legal age to enter into contracts is 18 years. Exceptions include contracts that involve necessities of life. These contracts typically are binding even on minors. Further, the parties must be mentally competent; otherwise, the law stipulates that the contract is unconscionable, or obviously unfair, and is, thus, not binding. Persons who are intoxicated also are deemed incompetent; thus, they cannot enter into a binding contract. Ultimately the courts decide the competency test if a contract is challenged on those grounds.

Legal Subject Matter

Any contract that includes terms that are illegal is most likely unenforceable. Examples of illegal contracts include violations of state usury laws (laws prohibiting excessive interest charges on credit contracts), agreements that violate antitrust laws, and contracts to provide services by a person who is not licensed to do so.

When part of a contract is illegal but the rest of it is not, is that contract enforceable? Most contracts include a provision (clause) stating that if part of the contract is deemed illegal, all other parts remain in force. Courts generally have ruled that the "legal" part of the contract is enforceable.

Consideration

Consideration whatever the promisor demands and receives as the price for a promise.

For a contract to be legal, it must include value for both parties. This is called **consideration.** A promise without consideration is not legally binding. For instance, if your friend Kirstie promises to room with you next year and then reneges on that promise, you could not force her to comply unless you could prove that you had provided some consideration to her. Generally, consideration is in the form of goods, services, or money.

Legal Form

To be legally enforceable, certain contracts must be in writing and in a particular form, depending on the state in which they are made. Such contracts include agreements that cannot be completed in less than a year, real estate contracts, agreements that involve a large sum of money, and wills. The specifics of the legal form requirements differ markedly from state to state. As noted earlier, not all contracts are written. A contract may be oral (known as a verbal contract), or a contract may even be only hinted at. This contract is known as an implied contract.

www.ftc.gov

The website for the Federal Trade Commission (FTC) offers information on federal antitrust and consumer protection laws. The FTC is responsible for enforcement of those laws, and it promotes activities that aid consumers in making informed choices.

Written contracts

In consumer law, most significant agreements are in writing. Written contracts reduce the risk of misunderstandings that can lead to legal actions. The importance of reading and understanding a contract is obvious, as failure to do so is not a valid legal defense. You do not have to hire an attorney for every contract you sign, nor do you need a lawyer to form a contract. Nevertheless, depending on the amounts of money involved and the expertise of the parties, you may benefit from legal representation to assist with interpreting the provisions in the contract. Chapter 6 gives advice on how to select an attorney.

When you enter into a contract, you are bound by it in almost all situations. Read and understand any contract *before* you sign it.

Standard contracts can be, and often are, changed. The typical requirement is that both parties agree to the changes. Consumers often are surprised to find that merchants are willing to modify a contract to make the sale!

FYI

Oral and implied contracts

All states recognize and enforce oral contracts. Under the common law, an oral agreement is as binding as a written agreement prepared by lawyers. Nonetheless, prudent consumers and sellers will insist that substantial agreements be in writing. A contract that is written fairly protects both sides and reduces the risk of misunderstandings. Unfortunately, many contracts that consumers sign are one-sided, and these documents usually favor the seller.

All states also recognize implied contracts. A good example is when you are at a baseball game and the vendor yells, "Who will have peanuts here? Only $3." Your response may be to simply raise your hand with $3 in it. The vendor may throw you the peanuts and you, in turn, may hand the $3 to other fans, who eventually will pass it on to the vendor. No written or oral dialogue occurred, and yet you entered into a contract when you accepted the peanuts. This is an implied contract.

Consumers have three business days after signing a contract during which they can rescind it. This is known as the "three-day cooling-off period." True or false?

False. Unless otherwise stipulated in the contract, or unless federal or state law mandates otherwise, the terms are enforceable as soon as the contract is fully executed (signed by all parties involved). The "three-business-day cooling-off period" applies only to specific types of contracts.

Parol evidence rule

Most consumer contracts are in writing. Frequently in consumer contracts, the salesperson may make promises that conflict directly with the written agreement you sign later. Which agreement is the one that is in effect? Generally the written agreement will take precedence over any oral agreement. This is known as the **parol evidence rule.** If litigation arises because of a dispute over verbal versus written agreements, courts typically look only to uncontested testimony for the facts of the case.

Parol evidence rule a rule of law stipulating that written agreements take precedence over oral agreements.

Identity Theft Danger

CASE STUDY

The Identify Theft Resource Center has warned about Social Security numbers and other sensitive information being bought and sold to "data brokers." Unfortunately, this practice is legal. Data brokers capture personal information such as Social Security numbers, drivers' license information, and home addresses. Brokers such as ChoicePoint and LexisNexis build files on individuals and sell this information to employers, banks, landlords, debt collectors, and so on. Sadly, many compiled databases are not secure, and thieves have accessed and stolen information from data brokers. In addition, the data brokers may be misled about the companies to which they sell data; for example, recently ChoicePoint sold data for more than 140,000 individuals to a company posing as a legitimate business. Unfortunately, this "business" was an identity theft group.

QUESTIONS

1. If you were in the legislature, what might you do to address this issue?
2. Have you, or has someone close to you, experienced identity theft?
3. In your opinion, what level of responsibility should be placed on data broker companies?
4. What would you recommend to a person whose identity has been stolen?

Source: Identity Theft Resource Center. Retrieved Nov. 19, 2008 http://consumertipsheet.com/identitytheft.html.

ALTERNATIVE DISPUTE RESOLUTION

Courts in the United States have become backlogged with cases, many of which are civil in nature and include consumer disputes. As a result, many consumers and sellers have opted for alternative dispute resolution methods, such as arbitration and mediation.

Arbitration

Arbitration the settlement of a disagreement between parties by one or more adjudicators (arbitrators) by whose decision the parties agree to be bound.

Arbitration has been popular in labor disputes for many decades. The use of **arbitration** to settle consumer–seller disputes, however, is a relatively new phenomenon. Arbitration usually is less formal, less complex, and, therefore, less costly than court proceedings. In arbitration, both sides present evidence and witnesses to the arbitrator. After all evidence has been submitted, the arbitrator reviews the evidence and makes a final decision. The arbitrator usually has wide latitude in reaching a decision. The ruling may favor one party or the other, or a compromise solution may be rendered.

Arbitrators' decisions are considered final, although appeals to the courts are provided by the law. Nonetheless, courts generally affirm the arbitrators' decision because both parties agreed to adhere to the decision beforehand.

> **TIP** Never sign an agreement with an insurance company in which you waive future litigation rights until you have consulted with a competent attorney.

Arbitration has become a popular force in settling disputes. In fact, in some areas, such as stock brokerage disputes, arbitration is the only means to settle claims against a broker or the broker's firm. Before customers purchase stock, they must agree to settle any disputes through arbitration, not formal litigation.

Mediation

Mediation a form of alternative dispute resolution whereby the parties bring their dispute to a neutral third party who assists the disputants in reaching a voluntary negotiated settlement.

Mediation has become quite popular in recent decades. It differs from arbitration in numerous ways. Whereas the arbitrator's main function is to issue a final ruling, the mediator's function is generally not to issue any ruling but simply to help the parties work out a settlement that both parties agree is equitable. The mediator will try to frame the dispute so the parties better recognize the issues at hand.

Although mediation usually is voluntary, it often results in a signed agreement. Mediation is less formal than arbitration, and usually witnesses are not needed or encouraged. Arbitration typically is less expensive than a legal proceeding; nonetheless, the cost typically is in the hundreds (or thousands) of dollars. Mediation costs, on the other hand, are minimal, and mediation often is free. Frequently mediation is provided as a public service by a local law school or other nonprofit organization. The mediators usually receive some training, but it is not as extensive as arbitration training. Arbitrators receive substantial amounts of money for their services, whereas mediators receive little, if any, compensation. Quite often mediation precedes arbitration. If the dispute cannot be settled through mediation, the parties may agree to have their case heard by an arbitrator.

SMALL-CLAIMS COURT: THE CONSUMER COURT

Small-claims court is a simplified civil court, typically administered by a county court. Small-claims courts exist in every state. The purpose of these courts is to resolve disputes that involve modest amounts of money. The monetary amount is set by state law, with a typical limit being $3,000 to $10,000. The small-claims court is designed for the individual consumer to represent himself in the proceedings. In most

Gramm-Leach-Bliley Privacy Act

Prior to 2001, banks, brokerage houses, credit card companies, and insurance enterprises were able freely to disseminate personal data about their customers to other companies. These companies would purchase information and then market their products to consumers in certain targeted groups. However, because of the Federal Trade Commission rule called the Gramm-Leach-Bliley Act, which became fully operational in 2001, financial institutions are limited as to information dissemination.

The Act sets forth three requirements. First, a financial institution must provide to its customers a notice about its privacy policies and practices. That notice must be clear, conspicuous, and accurate and must describe the conditions under which a financial institution may disclose nonpublic personal information to nonaffiliated third parties and their affiliates. Second, a financial institution must provide its customers with annual notices of its privacy policies and practices. Like the initial notice, the annual notice must be clear, conspicuous, and accurate. Third, a financial institution must provide consumers with a reasonable opportunity to "opt out" of disclosures of their nonpublic personal information to nonaffiliated third parties and must also provide a reasonable means by which to opt out. Consumers may exercise the right to opt out at any time. The rule limits the disclosure by those financial institutions of "nonpublic personal information" about individuals to whom they provide financial products or services for personal, family, or household purposes. The rule does not cover affiliates or subsidiaries of the financial institution.

states, anyone 18 years of age or older may file a complaint in small-claims court. As in any court, there is a **plaintiff** and a **defendant.** Both the consumer and the merchant have the right to initiate a lawsuit. Although attorneys usually are allowed to represent the seller or the consumer, they are not required to represent either interest.

Plaintiff the initiator of a lawsuit.

Defendant the person required to answer a lawsuit.

The procedure for filing suits in the small-claims system is simple. Most actions begin by the plaintiff paying a small filing fee and completing a complaint form that sets forth the litigants' names and addresses, as well as the grievance. Cases generally are put on the court docket within a few weeks.

www.nationalconsumersleague.org

The website for the National Consumers League (NCL) explains the NCL's commitment to protect, represent, and advance social and economic interests of the public. The site provides information for all types of economic enterprises on topics such as child labor, food safety, and privacy.

Small-claims hearings have few rules and are informal. A judge exercises broad powers in this court. For example, hearsay evidence usually is accepted. The judge decides the case, and there is no jury. The judge's rulings may be appealed to a higher court.

Despite the apparent advantages of the small-claims court, it has the following distinct problems:

1. Because businesses are entitled to file suits, courts can, and often do, become collection agencies for the businesses. Most states have remedied this problem by setting a maximum number of filings that an individual or a corporation can bring before the court in any given year.
2. Generally, states allow attorneys to represent the defendant or the plaintiff or both. This often puts the person who cannot afford legal assistance at an unfair disadvantage. It also tends to defeat the purpose of the court because the proceeding is no longer inexpensive or informal when attorneys are involved.
3. If a small-claims decision is appealed, the case becomes more complicated and often requires a formal appellate hearing. Those persons who have lost decisions in small-claims court may appeal with the hope that the previously successful party will terminate the claim because the appeal will be more costly, more time consuming, and more formal than a small claims hearing.

If you visit your state's official website, you will find information about specific laws in your state. In addition, many state websites provide useful information about small claims court procedures.

FYI

4. Even if a plaintiff is successful, there is no guarantee that the defendant will pay. Few small-claims courts are required to collect a judgment after rendering a decision.

Despite these potential problems, small-claims courts continue to be an important remedy for consumers with complaints that cannot be resolved through direct negotiation between the buyer and the seller. Information regarding small-claims courts in any state may be obtained by writing to the county court or the state attorney general's office.

REASONABLE PERSON

Reasonable person a hypothetical person who exercises rational qualities of attention, knowledge, intelligence, and judgment for the protection of his or her own interest.

Because the law cannot provide for every possibility, the standard of the **reasonable person** has evolved to furnish some uniform standards and guidance to the courts. Through the concept of the reasonable person, the law creates a standard that a judge or jury may apply to each set of circumstances. Thus, a court might decide whether an oral contract exists by asking whether a reasonable person would conclude that one did exist. Many judges have defined "reasonable" to denote what an average responsible adult would consider appropriate in the circumstances at hand.

CRIMINAL ACTION AND CIVIL ACTION

Criminal case a violation of law that relates to an injustice against the government or society.

Civil case a violation of law that relates to an injustice against a private citizen.

Criminal cases involve the upholding of public or official codes of behavior that society believes are necessary to protect its citizens or society itself. In a criminal case, the government brings charges against a person (or business) who supposedly committed a crime. The result is that the perpetrator of the crime, if found guilty, is punished with incarceration (prison).

Civil cases mostly involve the settlement of private conflicts between people or institutions such as businesses. Many civil cases involve consumer-related issues such as contract disputes and landlord–tenant disagreements. The end result of civil cases is that the perpetrator of the wrongdoing, if found guilty, usually is required to pay a monetary amount to the aggrieved individual. Some adverse behavior involving consumer transactions can be so egregious that the courts may deem the act to be criminal, and the person who committed the wrongdoing may be subjected to a large fine or imprisonment.

SUMMARY

Three elements are needed for a competitive marketplace to be effective and efficient in protecting consumers' interests: adequate laws, enforcement of those laws, and an educated citizenry. Public agencies enforce consumer law—including statutory, regulatory, and common law—to prohibit fraud, deception, and unethical practices. The UCC was formed to regulate business practices nationwide in a fair and consistent manner. Contracts, which can be written, verbal, or implied, are the legal instruments in consumer law. The parol evidence rule stipulates that written agreements take precedence over verbal ones.

Alternative means exist to resolve disputes; they include mediation and arbitration. Small-claims court is the consumer court. In criminal cases, the government brings charges against a person or business; civil cases settle private conflicts.

www.mlaw.org

This website is supported by a nonpartisan, grassroots organization based in Michigan, whose purpose is to oversee the court system. "Wacky Warning Labels" and "Loony Lawsuits" are two of the sections of the website.

CONSUMER LAW TERMINOLOGY

The intent of this chapter is not to make you an expert in consumer law. It is to give you a better understanding of the law as it relates to your rights and responsibilities. The average consumer may not use or need much "legalese." Nonetheless, consumers should be able to identify certain terms that are commonly used in discussions of consumer law. The following is an alphabetical listing of terms that a consumer may encounter.

action The lawsuit contested in a court.

adversary proceeding The legal procedure used in the United States and numerous other countries that features a plaintiff and a defendant.

adversary system The trial methods used in the United States and some other countries. This system is based on the belief that truth can be determined best by giving opposing parties full opportunity to present and establish their evidence, and to test by cross-examination the evidence presented by their adversaries. All this is done under established rules of procedure before an impartial judge or jury.

answer A defendant's response to a plaintiff's claims as stated in a complaint.

breach of contract A legally inexcusable failure to perform a contractual obligation.

class action A lawsuit brought by one or more persons on behalf of a larger group.

complainant The person who files the lawsuit; also named the plaintiff.

complaint The legal document that usually begins a civil lawsuit. It states the facts and identifies the remedy requested.

default A failure to respond to a lawsuit within a specified time. When a defendant does not respond in a timely fashion or does not appear at the trial, a default judgment is entered against the defendant.

deposition The testimony of a witness taken under oath in preparation for a trial.

discovery The pretrial process by which one party ascertains the evidence that the opposing party will rely upon in the trial.

dismissal A means by which a court may end a lawsuit. The court may dismiss the case without prejudice, which permits the suit to be filed again. A dismissal with prejudice, however, prevents the lawsuit from ever being filed again.

enjoin To require a person to do or to refrain from some specific act. This is done by means of an injunction.

fiduciary A person having a legal relationship of trust to another and having a duty to act primarily for the other's benefit. Examples include an executor of a will, a guardian for a minor, and a trustee for a trust fund.

fraud Intentional deception to deprive another person of his or her assets.

garnishment A legal proceeding in which the court requires that the debtor's money (often a portion of the debtor's paycheck) be applied to the debts. The court distributes these monies to creditors.

injunction A proceeding in which the court orders a party to terminate a particular act. A preliminary injunction is a short-term demand that the court orders until a full hearing can be held to determine if the injunction should be permanent.

interrogatories Written questions asked, prior to the court date, by one party of an opposing party, for which written responses must be given.

joint and several liability An understanding that makes each of the parties responsible for all the damages awarded in a lawsuit if the other parties responsible cannot or will not pay their "share."

joint tenancy A form of legal co-ownership of property (also known as survivorship). At the death of one co-owner, the surviving co-owner becomes sole owner of the property. Tenancy by the entirety is a special form of joint tenancy between a husband and wife.

judgment The final deposition of a lawsuit. The several types of judgment include default judgment, rendered because of the defendant's failure to appear in court, and summary judgment, given on the basis of written documents that have been accepted by the court. With a summary judgment the court determines that there is no need for a trial because there is no dispute as to the facts of the case. A consent judgment occurs when the plaintiff and the defendant agree to the terms of the judgment, and the court sanctions their agreement.

liable Legally responsible.

lien A legal claim against another person's property. This allows the lienholder a right to have a debt satisfied out of the proceeds of the property sale if the debt is not settled prior.

litigant A party to a lawsuit.

negligence Failure to apply the degree of care that a reasonable person would exercise under the same circumstances.

notice Formal notification to a party that a lawsuit has been filed against him or her.

permanent injunction A court order requiring that a party take some action or refrain from taking some action. It differs from forms of temporary relief such as a temporary restraining order or a preliminary injunction.

rebuttal Evidence given in an attempt to refute other evidence given previously by the adversary in a lawsuit.

settlement An agreement between the parties that terminates a lawsuit.

subpoena A court order compelling a witness to appear.

summons A notice to a defendant that he or she has been sued and is required to appear in court.

verdict The conclusion of a lawsuit that forms the basis for the court's judgment.

ITEMS FOR REVIEW & DISCUSSION

1. Who really decides if consumer protection is sufficient? Do consumers have representation in the legislature when laws are being developed? Give some suggestions to improve consumer protection in the marketplace. Specifically, how can consumers become more involved?
2. Explain what consumer law means. In your opinion, do consumer laws protect consumers adequately?
3. State the differences among statutory law, regulatory law, constitutional law, and common law.
4. State the purpose of a contract. Name the five elements that must be present to have a legally binding contract. What are the advantages and disadvantages of written and oral contracts? What are some of the mistakes that consumers make when forming a contract? Identify precautions that should be followed when forming a contract.
5. Explain the need for the Uniform Commercial Code (UCC).
6. Explain the difference between arbitration and mediation. Give the advantages and disadvantages of using alternative dispute resolution. Do you believe alternative dispute resolution methods are beneficial to consumers? Why or why not? Will alternative dispute resolution become more or less popular in the future? Why or why not?
7. Some people assert that there are enough consumer laws to protect consumers adequately. What is your response?
8. Do you believe that licensing boards regulate effectively, or should all regulation be the sole authority of the government?
9. Why is small-claims court also called the consumer court? Is small-claims court easy enough for consumers to understand and use? Explain. Is it the best legal remedy for the average consumer? Why or why not?
10. What are some ways by which consumers can be more educated about the laws that protect them and the options available to them?

EXPLORING PERSONAL VALUES: PROJECTS

1. Visit a small-claims court session in your state. Discuss with your classmates the circumstances under which you would file an action under small claims. Give specific examples that apply to your life. Consider the time involved, overall costs, and the limitations of small-claims court.
2. In your journal, write your opinion of the following statement: "Many judges have defined 'reasonable' as what an average responsible person would consider appropriate in the circumstances at hand."
3. It has been suggested that consumers should have three business days to rescind any contract. Do you agree? Do you think three business days is enough time to consider fully every contract you will have to sign (contracts for renting videos, getting an e-mail service, subscribing to cable television, buying a car, renting an apartment, buying a condo)? List some situations for which three days would be enough time. List some for which this would not be enough time.
4. Identify and report on several consumer laws in your state that you believe are worthwhile. Also identify several laws that do not seem to be in the consumer's best interest.
5. Draw up a proposal for a model consumer protection program at the state level.

6. Does your community have any consumer protection agencies? If so, determine how these agencies are helpful to consumers.
7. Contact your state attorney general's office and request consumer protection literature available to consumers. From the material you receive, report your findings to the class.
8. Obtain various sample contracts and discuss with your classmates the provisions in each contract that assist or hinder the consumer. Also, research warranties for different products (e.g., automobile, DVD player). Report your finding to the class.
9. Interview several people about their experiences with various kinds of contracts. Report your findings to the class.
10. Set up a role play with two sides in a dispute and a mediator.

ADDITIONAL SOURCES OF INFORMATION

Irving, Shae. *Nolo's Encyclopedia of Everyday Law: Answers to Your Most Frequently Asked Legal Questions.* Berkeley, CA: Nolo Press, 2008.

Irving, Shae, Kathleen A. Michon, and Beth McKenna. *Nolo's Encyclopedia of Everyday Law: Answers to Your Most Frequently Asked Legal Questions.* Berkeley, CA: Nolo Press, 2005.

Jasper, Margaret. *Consumer Rights and the Law.* New York: Oxford University Press, 2007.

Kramon, James M. *You Don't Need a Lawyer.* New York: Workman Publishing Company, 2002.

Miller, Frederick H., and John D. Lackey. *The ABCs of the UCC.* Chicago: ABA Publishing, 2004.

Warner, Ralph E. *Everybody's Guide to Small Claims Court.* Berkeley, CA: Nolo Press, 2008.

Warner, Ralph E., and Robin Leonard. *101 Law Forms for Personal Use.* Berkeley, CA: Nolo Press, 2007.

White, James J., and Robert S. Summers. *Uniform Commercial Code.* St. Paul, MN: West Publishing Company, 2000.

> Government is the great fiction, through which everybody endeavors to live at the expense of everybody else.
>
> **FREDERIC BASTIAT,** FRENCH POLITICAL ECONOMIST

KEY TERMS

act
amendment
bill
binding arbitration
civil penalty
class action
conference committee
interstate commerce
intrastate commerce
markup
private action
quorum
ranking member
regulatory agency
report
restitution
veto

The following concepts will be developed in this chapter:

1. Consumers do have a voice in policy, and their efforts influence public policy.
2. The nature of intrastate commerce necessitates adequate consumer protection at state and local levels.

After having read this chapter, you should be able to accomplish the following objectives:

1. Identify processes to affect the development of public policy.
2. Discuss the role of several consumer protection services offered by state and local governments.
3. Specify the types of consumer protection activities best suited for action by state governments and those best suited for action by local governments.

GOVERNMENT AND THE CONSUMER

One of the functions of government is to see that the rules of the marketplace are fair for consumers and sellers alike. Governments can take at least three approaches to foster the economic welfare of consumers:

1. To educate consumers so they will be more aware of their options and be able to act more effectively in their individual interests.
2. To regulate sellers to discourage or ban undesirable practices.
3. To change the legal relationship between the seller and the buyer so fraud will become unprofitable and the seller and the creditor will bear greater responsibility for success of the transaction.

Dual Control

The government of the United States encompasses the federal government and the governments of 50 states, the District of Columbia, Puerto Rico, the Virgin Islands, and thousands of counties and cities. Which of these agencies shall regulate economic activities in those areas? Federal and state constitutions divide authority, creating jurisdictional problems. The federal government is unable to regulate commercial activities confined to a single state, and states are powerless to regulate interstate commerce. The failure of any

State and Local Government Efforts to Assist Consumers

jurisdiction to act may create legislative vacuums. Also, many states fear that too stringent regulation may antagonize business, discourage new business, and perhaps encourage established firms to move to other states.

Usually a dozen or more agencies in state governments are involved with consumer concerns. These may include agencies dealing with agriculture, banking, commerce, conservation, education, health, insurance, pharmacy, public utilities, universities, and the attorney general's office.

Overseeing the marketplace is the responsibility of governments at federal, state, and local levels. Passage of legislation that protects consumers is initiated by U.S. Congress or state legislature. The federal government regulates **interstate commerce,** and each state government regulates **intrastate commerce.**

The increasing prevalence of mass-produced goods that are nationally advertised and nationally marketed means that commerce tends to become interstate and therefore subject to federal control. There is minimal cooperation and interaction between federal and state agencies. Much more interaction occurs among state consumer protection agencies. In part, this involvement is a direct result of a professional association, the National Association of Attorneys General (NAAG). Members of this association frequently exchange information via a communication network, referrals of consumer complaints to members in other states, publications, and conferences. Unfortunately, an organization representing both state and federal governments has not been initiated. Some laws (e.g., the Federal Bankruptcy Act) have provisions allowing state law to take precedence over federal law as long as the federal law allows this.

Interstate commerce business activities that involve commercial trade across state borders.

Intrastate commerce business activities that involve commercial trade within state borders only.

Policing Business for Consumers

The interests of the consumer and business are not the same. The rational consumer is concerned with obtaining the best combination of good quality, good service, and low price in a product or service to meet a specific need. The primary interest of business is to maximize profit. Thus, the consumer wants to buy as much for as little money as possible, and business wants to give as little as possible for as high a price as possible. This adversarial relationship is essential in the U.S. economic system. If the economic

> **www.naag.org**
>
> This is the official site of the National Association of Attorneys General. It provides general consumer protection information and legislation.

system is functioning properly, with many consumers and producers, both parties to a business transaction will benefit from competition. The consumer will be able to secure a satisfactory product at a reasonable price, and the seller will be able to sell products at prices adequate to cover costs and return a profit that will enable the business to continue operating. Even though the objectives of the consumer and business are not the same, neither can prosper without the other.

Every state constitution grants broad police power to the legislative body to enact laws to protect public health, morals, and welfare. The scope of this legislation is broader than most people realize. For example, laws govern sanitary conditions under which goods and services are produced, such as those requiring sanitary inspection of dairies and restaurants. Laws compel special treatment of products to make them safer, such as requiring all milk offered for sale to be pasteurized and all hair and feathers used in mattresses to be sterilized. State and local laws forbid adulteration of food and drugs and commonly forbid the sale of food that is unfit for human consumption. Most cities have sanitary regulations covering restaurants, bakeries, and meat shops. Barbershops and beauty salons operate under more or less rigid sanitary regulations. Housing regulations have become stricter; most cities fix minimum standards of lighting, air, and sanitary facilities in all buildings leased for residential purposes.

> **www.dol.gov**
>
> The United States Department of Labor (DOL) is responsible for administering and enforcing more than 180 federal statutes that are concerned with workplace issues.

Because approximately one-third of all foods, drugs, and cosmetics move in intrastate commerce only, and because conditions vary among states and cities, state and local laws enforced by state and local agencies are needed to supplement federal control. The failure of some states to pass or enforce minimal legislation indicates a high degree of business influence on the lawmakers.

Regulatory Agencies

Regulations typically are developed by administrative agencies (e.g., the Federal Trade Commission at the federal level, the attorney general's office at the state level). Authority for an administrative agency to develop regulations is granted by Congress or the state

CASE STUDY Too much customer service?

Liz Pulliam Weston had a problem with her e-mail service. Efforts by three companies over several days were required to fix it. After the problem was resolved, a surprising thing happened: each of the three companies confronted her with phone calls and e-mail surveys to investigate their level of customer service. Microsoft alone called three times and e-mailed two surveys asking her to rate their customer service. Although Weston was pleased with the service she received from all three companies, she was not pleased with level of probing about customer service after the fact.

Many consumers have reported similar incidents of being barraged with eager customer service representatives. Customer service is important, and rating it is also important; however, there is a limit to the number of times consumers want to report on the service received.

QUESTIONS

1. Have you had any personal experience with follow up calls about customer service received?
2. What do you think is the impact of such persistent measures of customer service by companies?
3. Do you think consumers should be more patient and grateful that companies are interested in their feedback?
4. What, if any, regulations do you think could apply in this example?

Source: Adapted from MSNMoney.com, "Hounded by Customer Service." Retrieved April 20, 2009, from http://articles.moneycentral.msn.com/SavingandDebt/ConsumerActionGuide/HoundedByCustomerService.aspx.

legislature. Once an agency is created, it often has the authority to promulgate or develop rules and regulations that have full force of law. Federal and state legislatures typically maintain oversight functions. They can, and often do, increase or decrease the agency's authority by changing its mandate or by increasing or decreasing the agency's funding.

www.consumeraction.gov/state.shtml

This site features an alphabetical list of state consumer protection offices, as well as information for county and city jurisdictions where applicable.

Regulations are important to consumers because these can be developed over a relatively short time and often do not have the loopholes inherent in many consumer legislative mandates. This is particularly true of "informal rule making," a process which requires that a notice of the proposed rule be posted, that a comment period be established, and that notice of the final rule be published. "Formal rule making" requires more extensive processes before a rule becomes law.

In addition to developing regulations, **regulating agencies** have the responsibility of enforcing their policies. In part because of staff and budgetary constraints, each agency must determine which laws and regulations should be priorities to be enforced. An agency may be given broad powers to charge and prosecute a business if that agency believes that laws or regulations have been violated.

Regulatory agencies government organizations that enforce various laws and rules.

Regulatory agencies sometimes fail in their responsibility to consumers. They are caught between the pressures of the industries they regulate and the interests of the consumers for whose benefit they have been established, and in the worst cases they may become the tools of the utilities they are supposed to regulate.

STATE LEGISLATIVE ACTIVITY

The Federal Trade Commission has urged all states to enact consumer protection legislation. Stopping undesirable practices locally before they grow into problems of interstate proportions minimizes the need for federal action. Local legislation also allows the people affected most directly by unfair or deceptive practices to determine the laws that should address them.

In fact, every state and the District of Columbia have enacted consumer protection laws in one form or another. The laws often are similar to the Federal Trade Commission Act to prevent deceptive and unfair trade practices. However, the number of consumer-oriented state laws passed since 1980 has not approached the number passed in the early to mid-1970s. In reality, many of the consumer protection laws enacted during the 1970s have been modified to the consumer's disadvantage or have been eliminated since the early 1980s.

The Federal Trade Commission indicates that every state has enacted some form of a "little FTC act," modeled after the federal law. Although each is worded differently, the acts generally prohibit and declare illegal any "unfair or deceptive acts and practices," comparable to those declared illegal under the federal statute.

The FTC also notes that most of the states authorize the administering or enforcement official to conduct investigations through use of subpoenas and to issue a cease-and-desist order or obtain a court injunction to halt the use of anticompetitive, unconscionable, deceptive, or unfair trade practices. Cease-and-desist orders, issued by an enforcement agency, require the seller to discontinue a specific action that may be in violation of law. An injunction is a court order requiring the performance or restraint of performance by the wrongdoer.

The consumer protection laws in most states include clarifications of the laws. These usually pertain to restitution, civil penalties, class actions, private actions, and the promulgation of trade rules and regulations. **Restitution** may be obtained in nearly all states. **Civil penalties** may be assessed in more than half of the states. **Class actions** are available in more than one-third of the states. **Private actions** are available in virtually all states. Finally, nearly two-thirds of the states allow enforcement agencies (usually the attorney general's office) the right to establish rules and regulations that have the full force of law.

Restitution court-ordered restoration of both parties to where each was prior to initiation of a contract.

Civil penalties court proceedings that allow private individuals or groups to recover money.

Class actions court proceedings that allow similarly aggrieved consumers to act as one.

Private actions court proceedings that allow a consumer to file a lawsuit for a violation of consumer protection laws.

Government-Owned Sellers of Consumer Services

In a lifetime, a consumer spends a considerable amount of money for goods and services provided by legally sanctioned monopolies. These public utilities provide electricity, water, gas, telephone, and public transportation. Some are involved in interstate commerce and are regulated by federal agencies. Others are involved only in intrastate commerce and are regulated by state agencies. A few, primarily water companies, are regulated locally, and many of them are municipally owned.

Water companies are not the only sellers of consumer services that government owns. Local and state government bodies own and operate many services. Their costs are paid out of tax revenues or from fees charged to the users. Local governments may provide "free" police and fire protection to those needing these services, with the cost met out of tax revenues. Local governments also frequently own and operate water companies, hospitals, and local transportation systems, which charge fees for their use. Most park systems are government owned and operated, with the costs met both by user fees and from tax revenues. Most school systems are government owned and operated, with the cost met by taxes.

If you sign a lease for an apartment and you decide to back out of the lease before you move in, the most you will lose is your security deposit. True or false?

False. In most states the tenant could owe the total amount of the lease and any additional charges as outlined in the lease.

Legislatures and citizens continue to debate which government services should be financed entirely by taxes, entirely by user fees, or by a combination of the two. Similarly, there is no consensus as to what consumer services the government should or should not provide. Some services, though, such as police and fire protection, clearly do not lend themselves to private ownership or operation.

Small-Claims Court—The Consumer Court

Every state has a legal mechanism to solve problems that involve small sums of money—the small-claims court. In most states, anyone 18 years of age or older may file a complaint in small-claims court. Refer to Chapter 17 for more information.

State Lemon Laws for Automobiles

All states have their own version of a lemon law for automobiles. While these laws have differences (e.g., coverage of used vehicles or motorcycles), some basic guidelines are shared. Coverage in each state usually includes the following:

1. A definition of what a lemon car is and a requirement that the manufacturer (not the dealer), repair the defects. The traditional definition of a lemon is a car on which a number of attempts have been made to repair a defect that significantly impairs its use, value, or safety, and that continues to have this defect.
2. A delineation of a warranty rights period (usually 12 to 24 months or 12,000 to 24,000 miles) in which the defect must occur.
3. Specific guidelines regarding what constitutes a sufficient number of attempts to repair, and whether these attempts entitle the consumer to a refund or replacement. For example, the consumer may be given the right to request repurchase or replacement of the vehicle if any one of the following conditions are met:
    a. The defect is a serious safety defect involving brakes and/or steering. The manufacturer is granted one attempt to repair.
    b. There is a safety defect that is not considered a serious safety defect. The manufacturer has two attempts to repair.
    c. Any other defect exists. The manufacturer is usually given three or four chances to repair the same defect.

   d. The vehicle is in the shop for a cumulative total of 30 days in a one-year period, with at least one of those days occurring during the first 12,000 miles.
4. A reduction in the consumer's purchase price, relating to the number of miles and wear and tear on the car. A formula such as (miles at time of refund x purchase price) ÷ 100,000 may be employed.
5. A provision allowing the consumer to recover attorney's fees from the manufacturer.

If you think you have a lemon, research the details of your state's lemon law and seek state assistance according to its provisions. Also consider contacting an attorney who specializes in lemon law litigation.

WHAT STATE GOVERNMENTS COULD DO

Action by state government in the consumer's interest is essential to protect consumers' rights. No consensus has been reached, however, as to what direction this action should take, how the desirable goals should be attained, or what type of government organizational structure should be established. In addition, many consumer advocates believe that consumer complaints can be handled best at the local level. This would be true only if the local authorities were to have adequate enforcement powers, either through jurisdictional authority or through **binding arbitration.**

Although binding arbitration often carries no legal obligation to accept the decision, nearly all courts have maintained that once both parties agree to binding arbitration, the decision rendered should stand. This is true especially when the complaint is between a local buyer and seller. The sheer size of the country and the population make effective handling of all complaints impossible at the federal level. Even at the state level, complaints can easily bog the courts down. In many respects, the efficient and quick handling of consumer complaints at the local level might be one of the most vital services the local government can offer the consumer. Some coordination at the state or national level is necessary, however, to obtain effective action against businesses operating statewide or nationally. Effective consumer protection is possible only when it is a responsibility of all levels of government—local, state, and national.

Binding arbitration informal proceedings in which an impartial third party is given evidence concerning a complaint and then renders a decision based on the information given. Generally, both the plaintiff and the defendant agree to accept any decision rendered in this process.

HOW A BILL BECOMES STATE LAW

Any member of the state legislature may introduce, or "sponsor," a **bill.** However, in most states, bills are introduced by House and Senate leaders, often the Speaker of the House or president of the Senate. Generally bills may be filed during the legislative session, until a predetermined date, according to state law. Many states allow members to "prefile" bills—to file before the legislature is in session. In some states these individuals have substantial latitude and may decide not to introduce a bill, thereby "killing it" for future consideration.

Once a bill is filed, it goes to a specific committee for review. The full committee or a subcommittee then "marks up" the pending legislation. After the **markup** is completed, the House or Senate issues a **report.**

Committee input is probably the most important part of the law-making process, because this is where the substance of the review occurs. Testimony by individuals interested in the merits and demerits of the proposed legislation is accepted. Often the committee chair, in consultation with the **ranking member,** makes the final determination as to whether the bill should proceed to the next step—a debate by the entire House.

State laws differ widely on the procedures, or rules, that must be followed when the bill proceeds to the entire House for "floor consideration." One state, for example, may require a **quorum** before accepting a vote. Others may have different mandates regarding quorums and various other rules. What is consistent, however, is that if a bill is

Bill a proposed law.

Markup the procedure whereby a committee or subcommittee reviews and often rewrites legislation to prepare it for consideration by the full House or Senate.

Report the written summary of a committee's views, which also includes the bill, as amended.

Ranking member the majority member on a committee, having authority second to the chair.

Quorum a majority of members that must be present before a legislative body is authorized to conduct business.

rejected in one house, it no longer is considered during that legislative session. If a bill is accepted by the first chamber, it proceeds to the next chamber, where it usually proceeds through a process similar to that of the first.

Amendment a modification attached to a proposed bill.

Conference committee members from the House and Senate who are selected by their leaders to help resolve differences between the two versions of a bill.

Act a bill that has passed both the House and the Senate.

Veto at the state level, a governor's refusal to sign legislation passed by the House and Senate.

If the act has an **amendment** attached to it, it usually is forwarded to a **conference committee.** The objective of the conference committee, which has members from each chamber, is to remedy differences. Once a bill is acceptable to both houses, it becomes an **act** and is sent to the governor.

When an act is sent to the governor for signature, he or she may sign it, **veto** it, or allow it to become law without his or her signature. Most state laws mandate that a bill becomes law if it is not signed or vetoed within a stated number of days.

If a governor rejects proposed legislation, the veto can be overturned if both houses vote to "override" the veto. Usually this requires a two-thirds majority in both houses. If a governor vetos a bill, it usually is dead because a two-thirds majority is nearly impossible to obtain in most states. In some states, where unsigned legislation does not become law, the governor may veto a bill by not signing it and thus not be vulnerable to an override of a veto. This may occur if the legislature adjourns before the time the governor is required to sign the bill. This tactic is called the "pocket veto."

HOW TO INFLUENCE STATE REPRESENTATIVES

State legislatures write the laws that guide and protect consumers in the marketplace. Policy makers in government have a substantial impact on consumers' lives, yet few of us are willing or able to help develop the laws that guide and protect us. Regardless of the widely accepted notion that various corporations, industries, and labor groups have inordinate influence on the development of public policy, individual consumers can have an impact on the political process. Individual letters, telephone calls, faxes, and e-mail are recorded by legislative staff, and these can help a representative decide which way to vote on a consumer-related issue.

Legislators pay more attention to certain types of contact than to others, simply because of the approach the constituent takes. By following a few basic suggestions, you can increase the chances of a legislator paying attention to your concerns.

FYI

Consumer agencies often are able to bring both civil and criminal cases before the courts. Civil cases are easier to prosecute, and obtaining restitution is more likely.

1. Become knowledgeable about the legislator before you make contact. Determine the committees on which the representative sits. Legislators have more influence on legislation brought before the committees on which they serve.
2. Initiate contact early in the session. Determine which issues are important as early as possible in the legislative process. You can influence a legislator more readily before he makes commitments to other constituents or colleagues.
3. Determine the method of communication. Generally, people who are effective letter writers should write letters. Those who are more effective speakers may be more effective with a direct telephone call.

   Regardless of the method of communication, follow these guidelines:

- Indicate the issue of interest to you. Bring up only one issue at a time, and be clear and concise.
- Be professional and positive in your approach. Your goal is to influence, not alienate.
- State why the issue is important to you and the majority of constituents in the politician's district.
- If you are part of a special-interest group, do not disclose that fact. A communication that does not seem to be part of a "campaign" usually has more influence. Even if there is a group effort to influence a given piece of legislation, communicate your feelings with minimal guidance from others in your group.

There Oughta Be a Law . . .

The Telemarketing and Consumer Fraud and Abuse Prevention Act of 1996

The Telemarketing and Consumer Fraud and Abuse Prevention Act, which was fully implemented in January of 1996, is one of the most important federal consumer protection laws passed in recent years. Some of the more important provisions are the following:

- Telemarketers must disclose that the call is for sales purposes and must identify the product or service and the company selling the product or service.
- State law enforcement agencies may prosecute telemarketers who operate across state lines and may sue for nationwide injunctions in federal court.
- Calls are prohibited to consumers who do not want to be solicited.
- Calls made before 8:00 A.M. or after 9:00 P.M. local time are prohibited.
- If a prize is involved, it must be made explicit that no purchase is necessary.
- Material facts pertaining to the goods or services offered for sale must be disclosed clearly and conspicuously to potential customers.
- Telemarketers are prohibited from withdrawing money from a customer's checking account without verifiable consent to do so.

This law, enforced by the FTC, allows penalties of up to $10,000 per violation. Individual consumers are allowed to file lawsuits. Although the law offers important assistance to consumers against telemarketing schemes, various substantive protections were removed from the final bill. Thus, consumers still must exercise caution when doing business with sellers in this industry.

SUMMARY

State legislation wends its way through a long process before it is signed by the governor and becomes law. Various groups may obtain inordinate influence over lawmakers. Individual consumers need to develop simple but effective techniques to influence the development of public policy.

Every state government has laws and agencies whose purposes include consumer protection similar to the Federal Trade Commission Act. Most laws give the enforcing officials power to issue subpoenas and cease-and-desist orders; provide for injunction rights, restitution, civil penalties, class actions, and private actions; and permit the promulgation of trade rules and regulations. States also offer lemon laws for automobiles.

Perhaps the best legal remedy for the average consumer is to be found in small-claims court. This court enables consumers to resolve their complaints informally, inexpensively, and quickly.

ITEMS FOR REVIEW & DISCUSSION

1. Explain how a bill becomes a law.
2. Explain the ways by which you can influence your state legislature.
3. Explain the difference between a law and a rule.
4. Describe the responsibility and some of the weaknesses of a state consumer protection office.
5. Explain some basic similarities in state lemon laws.
6. State the advantages and disadvantages of small-claims courts.

7. Should the various levels of government increase or decrease their activities as sellers of consumer services? Why?
8. What consumer services might and should a local government provide?
9. Why do governments have to police business for consumers?
10. Make a list of issues that interest or concern you about consumer protection. Write a letter to a state representative about one of these issues.

EXPLORING PERSONAL VALUES: PROJECTS

1. Small-claims courts sometimes are referred to as consumer courts. Discuss with your classmates the circumstances under which you would file an action under small claims. When you are dissatisfied with a good or service and cannot get satisfaction from the provider, would you file a small claim against the seller if
   a. the amount were less than $50?
   b. the amount were more than the maximum allowed in your state?
   c. the provider was unsympathetic and seemed to lack principle?
   d. you previously have had trouble with this seller?

   Center your discussion on the dollar limit for small claims in your state, the cost, and the time involved.
2. The conservative view is to get the federal government "off people's backs." Applied to consumer protection, this means that state and local governments would pick up responsibility in this area. Discuss with several classmates the idea of whether the federal government should leave consumer protection to state and local governments. Identify four or five positions on this question and write a paragraph on each one.
3. How do you feel about government policing business for consumers? Write your response in your journal. Identify and report on government programs in your community that you believe are a waste of taxpayers' money.
4. The process of a bill becoming law varies from state to state. Investigate the process in your state and report your findings to the class. In addition, draw up a proposal for a model consumer protection program at the state level.
5. Find out what kinds of consumer legislation your state government has passed in the past five years and summarize them for the class.
6. Write a report on consumer protection in your state. Note specifically the type of law your state has and your perception of the effectiveness of the agency or agencies responsible for consumer protection.
7. Interview an officer of a public utility concerning problems the utility has with the regulatory agency and with consumers.
8. Find out if your local community or county has a consumer protection office. If an office is established, find out how it serves consumers. Interview the local district attorney to find out if he or she renders any consumer protection services and, if so, in what areas and to what extent.
9. Investigate local and state legislation to see whether any legislation has been passed under the banner of consumer protection that is not actually in consumers' best interest.
10. Write a report on how small-claims court works in your locality.
11. Research your state lemon law. Do you think it is one of the stronger or weaker ones, compared to other states'?

ADDITIONAL SOURCES OF INFORMATION

Donovan, Sandy. *Making Laws: A Look at How a Bill Becomes a Law (How Government Works).* Minneapolis, MN: Lerner Publishing Group, 2003.

Feinman, Jay M. *Law 101: Everything You Need to Know About the American Legal System.* New York: Oxford University Press, 2006.

Issacharoff, Samuel, Pamela S. Karlan, and Richard H. Pildes. *The Law of Democracy: Legal Structure of the Political Process.* New York: Foundation Press, 2005.

Richards, Eric L. *Personal Law.* Mason, OH: Thomson Custom Pub., 2003.

Safir, Howard, and Ellis Whitman. *Security: Policing Your Homeland, Your City, Yourself.* New York: Thomas Dunne Books, 2003.

Shaffrey, Mary M., and Melanie Fonder. *The Complete Idiot's Guide to American Government.* New York: Alpha Books, 2005.

United States House of Representatives. *Item Veto Constitutional Amendment: Hearing Before the Subcommittee on the Constitution of the Committee on the Judiciary, House of Representatives, One Hundred Sixth Congress, Second Session, on H.J. Res. 9, March 23, 2000.* Washington, DC: U.S.G.P.O., 2000.

Warner, Ralph. *Everybody's Guide to Small Claims Court.* Berkeley, CA: Nolo Press, 2008.

> We cannot rest content until the consumer is in the front row—not displacing the interest of the producer—yet gaining equal rank and representation with that interest.
>
> **LYNDON B. JOHNSON,** FORMER U.S. PRESIDENT

KEY TERMS

antitrust violation
Consumer Product Safety Commission (CPSC)
Department of Justice
Federal Consumer Information Center
Federal Trade Commission (FTC)
Food and Drug Administration (FDA)
lobbying
National Highway Traffic Safety Administration (NHTSA)
political action committee (PAC)
special-interest group
trade regulations
U.S. Department of Agriculture (USDA)

The following concepts will be developed in this chapter:

1. The complex nature of the marketplace compels the federal government to provide U.S. citizens with protection and service wherever these are required.
2. Generally speaking, the federal government has responded with consumer legislation or trade regulations when its attention was called to an existing need, and upon receiving enough complaints.

After having read this chapter, you should be able to accomplish the following objectives:

1. Discuss the political process in implementing consumer protection.
2. List the services and responsibilities of the following federal agencies: Consumer Product Safety Commission, Department of Transportation, Federal Trade Commission, Food and Drug Administration, Department of Justice, U.S. Department of Agriculture.

COMPLEXITIES OF THE MARKETPLACE

The U.S. marketplace has changed dramatically since 1776. At one time, consumers produced most of the goods they consumed. Today, products reach retailers through middlemen and are consumed by millions of people who are thousands of miles from where the products were produced. Every day each of us consumes products that are vital to our health and life, produced by people we never have seen and never will see.

Although changes in technology have enabled today's consumers to have products and services that our grandparents never knew, these advances also have created dilemmas. When a family produced its own goods, it had control over purity and quality. Now consumers are more dependent on others as producers, with the result that consumers need assistance in the marketplace because it has become more specialized and impersonal. Government must do for us what we cannot do for ourselves. That is why a century ago, the U.S. Congress passed the first consumer protection legislation, the Pure Food and Drug Act and the Meat Inspection Act, and why Congress has continued to pass consumer protection legislation over the years.

Federal Government Efforts to Assist Consumers

EVOLUTION OF FEDERAL LEGISLATION

President John F. Kennedy indicated that all U.S. citizens have four basic rights in the marketplace: the right to safety, the right to information, the right to choose, and the right to be heard. The right to be heard suggests that consumers have the right to have their interests advocated when government policy decisions are being formulated. Kennedy and many others believed consumers were underrepresented when legislation was being considered and regulations were being developed at the federal level.

Consumers were quite well represented in Washington during the Kennedy years. That adequate representation continued through much of the 1960s and 1970s, when consumers' demands for greater protection and services in the marketplace produced the greatest involvement by the federal government in consumer protection in history. More than 50 laws were passed, approximately 100 federal programs were established, and every federal department implemented procedures to protect or advance the consumer's interest. The consumer's welfare was a politically attractive issue, and legislatures and government agencies responded in varying ways in attempting to meet consumer needs and demands.

Since 1980, many analysts have suggested that the status of consumers has not improved vis à vis government policy making. Others believe the consumer voice has actually declined during the past 30 years. During the administrations of Presidents Ronald Reagan, George H. W. Bush, Bill Clinton, and George W. Bush, many consumer protection efforts at the federal level have been curtailed or eliminated. In fact, very few substantive federal consumer protection laws and regulations have been passed since 1980.

Agency budgets were cut dramatically under the Reagan administration, with some increases during the first Bush and the Clinton administrations. The consumer advocates who held high-level positions in the Carter administration were replaced, for the most part, by people who were more favorable to the business sector. In addition, the number of laws passed by Congress and rules promulgated by federal agencies decreased sharply. The philosophy seemed to be that the marketplace is the best protector of the consumer interest.

New questions about the ability of the marketplace to govern itself arose late in the first decade of this century, as the government poured billions of dollars into bailouts in an attempt to save insolvent companies and stimulate the economy. The term *corporate socialism* surfaced to refer to companies that privatize profits and socialize risks. New regulations and procedures for Wall Street and other firms were being considered as the decade drew to a close, and the impact on market processes had yet to be determined.

POLITICAL INFLUENCES

Special-interest group a unit of two or more persons who have a common interest and who attempt to influence government.

Lobbying representing a special interest with the goal of influencing government policy.

Political action committee (PAC) any group that solicits funds to support and influence a specific candidate and political party.

Many criticisms have been advanced regarding **special-interest groups, lobbying,** and **political action committees (PACs).** Lobbying techniques may be direct or indirect. Approaching a policy maker (usually a member of the legislature) and attempting to influence that person is considered the direct approach. The indirect method involves initially garnering support from other citizens so that the larger group support will result in a better outcome. Most trained lobbyists use a combination of the direct and indirect approaches to obtain their objectives.

Prior to the late 1970s, the most powerful political action committees in Washington, DC, and in most state capitals were those aligned with labor interests. Some pundits suggest that the ability of labor to command special treatment made it necessary for businesses to counteract the labor initiatives and to develop their own PACs. In the past several decades, corporate America has substantially increased its funding to political parties and to individual candidates. Although federal and state laws limit the amount of money that a group can give to a specific political party or legislator, technicalities of the laws result in millions of dollars being raised and then given to government leaders. These leaders too often return the favor by sponsoring legislation that supports the PAC position but that is not necessarily in the best interest of consumers.

www.consumer.gov

This is the official site of consumer protection information at the federal government level. Related links and information abound on this site.

Effective lobbying often retains programs long past their time of value simply because the lobbying voice is louder and more knowledgeable than the consumer voice. Periodically, this imbalance is brought to the fore, with much rhetoric to curtail or eliminate it. Often the program continues regardless.

FEDERAL GOVERNMENT AGENCIES

The following pages briefly describe the agencies that are most involved with protecting consumer interest: the Federal Trade Commission (FTC), the Food and Drug Administration (FDA), the U.S. Department of Agriculture (USDA), the Consumer Product Safety Commission (CPSC), the Department of Transportation, and the Department of Justice.

Federal Trade Commission

Federal Trade Commission (FTC) a federal agency whose basic responsibility is to enforce consumer protection laws against any illegal acts that are deemed unfair methods of competition or unfair or deceptive trade practices (www.ftc.gov).

Among the earliest consumer protection laws was the Federal Trade Commission Act, passed in 1914. The Act established the **Federal Trade Commission (FTC).** The original FTC Act has been amended several times. In 1938, the Wheeler Lea Amendments were passed to clarify the FTC's role by including "unfair or deceptive acts or practices" among those to be supervised by the FTC. Thus, deceptive advertising was made a violation of federal law.

The Magnuson-Moss Warranty Act of 1977 included FTC improvement provisions. Essentially, this Act strengthened the FTC's power to deal with consumer problems by reaffirming its authority to promulgate trade regulation rules, and it provided funds to allow for public participation in FTC hearings.

The Act also authorized the FTC to enforce its rulings (previously enforcement could be achieved only by requesting that the Department of Justice intervene). Finally, the Act enabled the FTC to seek consumer redress and civil penalties for rule violations in the courts. Congress has diluted some of the FTC's authority in recent years, specifically in the area of rule making. Further, any FTC rule may be challenged in court.

The effectiveness of the FTC has been debated over the years. In the late 1970s, some believed that it had become too aggressive in its quest to protect consumers. More recently, others have suggested that the FTC has become a puppet for business interests. As with other agencies, the benefits that accrue to consumers seem to be determined primarily by the level of funding provided by Congress and by the orientation of the agency's top leadership.

More than 100 federal laws have specific objectives of protecting consumers.

FYI

The work of the Federal Trade Commission is directed by five commissioners appointed by the president and confirmed by the Senate for terms of seven years. The FTC perceives among its major responsibilities reviewing complaint letters, conducting investigations, taking court action, educating consumers, and promulgating trade regulation rules.

Complaint letters from consumers are often the first indication of a marketplace injustice. The FTC does not act on individual complaints. It acts when a pattern of abuse becomes clear. Consumers provide the pattern plus the evidence necessary to begin an investigation.

Investigations can begin in many different ways. Complaint letters, scholarly articles on consumer or economic subjects, or congressional requests may give rise to an investigation. Investigations are either "public" or "nonpublic." Public announcements generally signify investigation of the practices of an entire industry, whereas investigation of an individual company most often is nonpublic.

Cases arise when, after investigating, the FTC finds reason to believe that a business has violated the law. Then the FTC often seeks a consent order requiring the merchant to stop a specific action. The FTC also might issue a "complaint." After that, and if no settlement is reached, a formal hearing is held before an administrative law judge. Members of the public can participate at this point if, for example, they have evidence relating to the case. The administrative law judge issues a decision, which may be appealed to the FTC commissioners. The commissioners' decision may be appealed to a U.S. Court of Appeals and ultimately to the U.S. Supreme Court.

Trade regulations or rules, when implemented, are perhaps the FTC's most effective method of protecting consumers and ethical businesses. These regulations may apply to industries across the country, or they may be limited to specific areas. The rules have the full force of law, and violation of a rule is equivalent to violation of any other law. The rules have substantial value because all businesses in the industry must follow a rule, and, thus, a single action addresses a broad consumer problem. An FTC rule may be challenged in any U.S. Court of Appeals. Many of the rules that the FTC has promulgated are discussed later in this chapter.

Trade regulations rules developed by state and federal agencies defining and prohibiting various industry activities.

Food and Drug Administration

The **Food and Drug Administration (FDA)** and the FTC are the most influential federal agencies designed to protect consumers. As technological changes through the 1800s brought new health hazards, the need for federal laws became evident. With growing evidence of a great variety of abuses, the public demanded federal government protection. Between 1879 and 1906, more than 100 food and drug bills were introduced in Congress. On June 30, 1906, President Theodore Roosevelt signed into law the first federal Pure Food and Drug Act, which established the Pure Food and Drug Administration. The act was popularly called the Wiley Act for the crusading Dr. Harvey W. Wiley, who led the battle for its passage. On the same day, the president also signed the Meat Inspection Act.

Food and Drug Administration (FDA) a federal agency whose basic responsibility is to assure the safety and efficacy of food, drugs, and cosmetics (www.fda.gov).

The Federal Trade Commission has seven regional offices to assist in resolving consumer problems. For the address of the nearest office, visit www.ftc.gov.

FYI

From 1906 to the present, many efforts have been directed to strengthening the food and drug law. Most important was passage of the federal Food, Drug, and Cosmetic Act of 1938, which replaced the outmoded Wiley Act. Even though it contained many compromises, it was far stronger than the original Act. Among many changes, it covered, for the first time, cosmetics and therapeutic devices, authorized food standards, and made it a penal offense to refuse inspection.

Many amendments followed over the years, to deal with specific problems. A Pesticide Chemicals Amendment, passed in 1954, set up a system of enforceable residue tolerances. The Delaney Amendment (1958), known as the Food Additives Amendment, requires that the safety of additives be established before they are marketed, and it prohibits the approval of food additives if these are found to induce cancer when ingested by humans or animals.

In 1960 two amendments were passed. The Color Additive Amendment allowed the FDA to set safe limits on the amounts of coloring that may be used in foods, drugs, and cosmetics, and required manufacturers to retest previously listed certifiable colors. A separate law, the Federal Hazardous Substances Labeling Act, required prominent warning labels on household chemical products. Beginning with this law, the FDA developed the extensive product safety program now administered by the Consumer Product Safety Commission.

One of the most significant amendments to the Food and Drug Act was the Kefauver-Harris Drug Amendment, passed in 1962, requiring premarketing proof of drug effectiveness, to assure a greater degree of safety and reliability in prescription drugs, and strengthening new drug clearance procedures that allow drugs to be introduced into the market at an accelerated rate.

The Fair Packaging and Labeling Act, enacted in 1966, attempted to detail how consumer products in interstate commerce must be labeled. Many food manufacturers found ways to circumvent the intent of this law. As a result, and because of the public's interest in better dietary labeling, the Nutrition Labeling and Education Act was passed in 1990. Provisions of this act were fully in force in 1998.

Functions of the Food and Drug Administration include the following:

- Enforcement of laws that relate to food, drugs, cosmetics, and therapeutic devices
- Premarket approval of safety and effectiveness of food additives, color additives, antibiotic drugs, and most prescription drugs
- Licensing of the production of vaccines, serums, and other biological drugs
- Enforcement of safety standards for radiation-intensive products such as televisions, X-ray equipment, sunlamps, and microwave ovens
- Promulgation of rules

All states have laws requiring lobbyists to register, although the definition of "lobbyist" differs with each state.

FYI

The FDA has six centers, each of which is responsible for a specific area. These centers are the Center for Food Safety and Applied Nutrition, the Center for Drug Evaluation and Research, the Center for Veterinary Medicine, the Center for Devices and Radiological Health, the National Center for Toxicological Research, and the Center for Biologics Evaluation and Research. Additional offices and centers are also in place; these are less directly related to the consumer.

U.S. Department of Agriculture

U.S. Department of Agriculture (USDA) a federal agency, one of whose major responsibilities is to assure consumers that food is safe, clean, nutritious, and attractive (www.usda.gov).

The **U.S. Department of Agriculture (USDA)** is another federal agency that is important to consumers. One of the oldest American laws pertaining to food safety is the Meat Inspection Act, passed in 1906. The Act forbids the interstate shipment of meat and meat products that have not been inspected and that are not stamped with the familiar purple mark, "U.S. Inspected and Passed."

Standards have been established for many processed meat products, including luncheon meats, meat pies, and soups. These standards establish the minimum amounts of meat in the product. Inspection of meat and meat products is different from grading. The inspection mark tells the buyer that the meat is wholesome. A grade mark tells the buyer the quality of the meat. A product may be inspected but not graded, but every graded product has been inspected. Inspection is required, while grading is not.

Labeling must be informative and may not be false or deceptive. To enforce this part of the law, the FDA examines all labels in advance, and the labels must be approved before use. Generally, the first word in a food product's name on a label must identify the ingredient present in the largest amount. Certain exceptions are allowed, such as *Pork and Beans, Chicken Noodle Dinner,* and *Turkey and Rice with Vegetables.* The industry won the argument that the public knew that beans, noodles, and rice were the chief ingredients in these products and relabeling was not necessary. Labeling regulations also require that statements of ingredients on products list the ingredients in order of predominance.

Upton Sinclair's 1906 exposé about unsanitary conditions in Chicago meatpacking plants, The Jungle, *spurred the first wave of consumerism. This book also assisted in initiation and passage of the Pure Food and Drug Act of 1906.*

FYI

The 1990 Nutrition Labeling and Education Act, noted earlier, pertained only to food products under the jurisdiction of the FDA. Although this included the vast majority of foods, many products were not included because these foods were subject to USDA jurisdiction. The USDA, in cooperation with the FDA and the Department of Health and Human Services, worked to develop regulations to conform to the 1990 law, and final guidelines were approved by the FDA and USDA in late 1992. During 1993 and early 1994 almost all food products became subject to the food labeling law passed in 1990.

The USDA was one of the early movers in the field of consumer services. Almost every county in the United States has a USDA Extension Home Economist. The work of USDA Extension Home Economists is to help consumers improve their nutrition, money management, use of credit, budgeting, and family relations, and to assist with home improvement and problems of community concern. Extension economists are affiliated with the land grant colleges.

Consumer Product Safety Commission

The **Consumer Product Safety Commission (CPSC)** was created in 1972 in response to a 1970 report by the National Commission on Product Safety predicting that each year the country could expect millions of serious injuries associated with consumer products and billions of dollars' worth of economic loss to the nation.

Consumer Product Safety Commission (CPSC) a federal agency with the basic responsibility for protecting consumers against injuries associated with consumer products (www.cpsc.gov).

The purposes of the CPSC are:

- to protect the public against injuries associated with consumer products
- to assist consumers in evaluating the comparative safety of products
- to develop uniform standards for consumer products
- to minimize conflicts in state and local regulations
- to promote research and investigations into the causes and the prevention of product-related deaths, illness, and injuries

To preserve existing product-safety regulations, developed over the previous several decades, Congress transferred to CPSC the authority to enforce the Flammable Fabrics Act, the Poison Prevention Packaging Act, the Federal Hazardous Substances Act, and the Refrigerator Safety Act.

CPSC has jurisdiction over thousands of different types of products, hundreds of thousands of manufacturing plants, and millions of retail establishments. The only consumer products over which it does not have jurisdiction are foods, drugs, cosmetics, medical devices, alcohol, tobacco, motor vehicles, firearms, boats, pesticides, and aircraft—all of which are regulated to some extent under other laws by other agencies.

The agency is involved in monitoring the injuries and deaths caused by consumer products, issuing recall notices for unsafe products, setting standards for specific products, and educating consumers in the safe use of products. The law requires retailers and manufacturers to inform CPSC about hazardous products and to provide full refunds, with the manufacturer ultimately bearing the financial burden. Recalls and refund procedures have been mandated for many toy products, as well as for household thermostats, day-and-night activators, and coffeemakers.

Although CPSC has the authority to establish mandatory safety standards and regulations, it has offered only minimal protection to consumers in this area. Its accomplishments include developing standards and regulations for a variety of products, including lawn mowers, chain saws, baby cribs, baby rattles, and mattresses. The commission has recalled or eliminated the production of various unsafe products including three-wheel, all-terrain vehicles and lawn darts.

TIP The CPSC recommends that parents use "choke tubes" to test toys and small items for safety near small children. A substitute for a choke tube is a toilet paper roll. If a toy fits inside, it should not be given to a child under age 3.

Department of Transportation

National Highway Traffic Safety Administration (NHTSA) a federal agency, part of the Department of Transportation, that works to reduce highway deaths, injuries, and property losses (www.nhtsa.dot.gov).

The Department of Transportation (DOT) has become involved in consumer activities through its **National Highway Traffic Safety Administration (NHTSA).** NHTSA develops minimum performance standards and enforces safety standards on motor vehicles. It has jurisdiction over automobiles, trucks, buses, recreational vehicles, motorcycles, bicycles, mopeds, and all accessories for these vehicles. In recent years, the agency has required lap and shoulder safety belts in forward-facing rear seats and also has required new light trucks, vans, and buses to have head restraints on driver and passenger seats. NHTSA also investigates safety-related defects and may require recall and free repair of these defects.

The NHTSA's recall campaigns have not been completely successful. Fewer than half of the vehicles recalled are actually brought in for inspection and correction. Consumers can check to determine whether a vehicle is subject to recall by contacting NHTSA.

Department of Justice

Department of Justice a federal agency whose responsibility is to enforce antitrust laws and assure compliance in the marketplace (www.usdoj.gov)

Antitrust violation a practice that involves unlawful restraint of trade.

The **Department of Justice** is another federal agency that protects the broad-based interests of consumers. The record justifies the assertion that, even though the business community lauds the concept of competition, many business firms try to stifle competition. Even as you read these words, it is likely that, somewhere, business representatives are meeting secretly to allocate markets, establish quotas, and set prices.

Consumers should watch for telltale signs of price-fixing. An **antitrust violation** may be taking place if there are large price changes involving more than one seller of a similar product, particularly if the price changes are of equal amounts and occur at the same time, if competing sellers price identical or similar products the same, if prices among competing sellers seem to move in the same direction at the same time, or if a seller tells a consumer, "No, we don't sell in that area; so-and-so is the only firm that sells in that area, according to our agreement."

These signs are not conclusive evidence of antitrust violations. Investigation by trained lawyers and economists is required to prove a violation. Suspected antitrust violations should be reported to your state attorney general's office and to the Department of Justice's Antitrust Division.

Other Federal Agencies

Other agencies of the federal government can also assist consumers, although to a lesser extent than those noted on the previous pages. The following is a partial listing of these agencies, with a brief summary of their roles and responsibilities.

Bureau of Alcohol, Tobacco, and Firearms (ATF). Within the Treasury Department, the ATF mandates labeling of ingredients for alcohol and information for safe storage of explosives. It maintains jurisdiction over alcohol, alcohol containers, tobacco, firearms, and explosives; www.atf.treas.gov.

Commodity Futures Trading Commission (CFTC). The CFTC is an independent government agency involved in regulating commodity futures, options, leverage, and deferred deliveries. Its main concern is protecting customers who buy and sell contracts, and it works to prevent market manipulation. It accepts claims against brokers and sales people through its reparations procedures; www.cftc.gov.

Department of Education. The Department of Education is charged with developing and maintaining federal educational programs and equal opportunity in education; www.ed.gov.

Department of Energy. The Department of Energy works to set federal energy policies regarding energy conservation, consumption, prices, and imports; www.doe.gov.

Department of Health and Human Services (HHS). The main efforts of the Department of Health and Human Services are directed toward health research; regulation of products relating to health; disease prevention, through the Centers for Disease Control; medical care; maintenance of national health records; and prevention of drug and alcohol abuse; www.dhhs.gov.

Department of Homeland Security (DHS). Created in 2002 under the National Strategy for Homeland Security and the Homeland Security Act, the mission of DHS is to provide a "unifying core" for the organizations and institutions involved in preserving the United States' national security. Strategic goals include awareness, prevention, protection, response, recovery, service, and organizational excellence; www.dhs.gov.

Department of Housing and Urban Development (HUD). HUD is responsible primarily for problems relating to quality and availability of all types of housing. Its responsibilities include setting standards for the safe construction of mobile homes; www.hud.gov.

Department of the Interior. The Department of the Interior has jurisdiction over government-owned land and natural resources. Its responsibilities include protection of wildlife and natural resources, preservation of national parks and historical places, ensuring appropriate use of land and water resources, and assessment of energy and mineral resources for the nation's best interests. In addition, it administers state grants for outdoor recreation; www.doi.gov.

Environmental Protection Agency (EPA). The Environmental Protection Agency (EPA) sets standards for air, water, and noise pollution, as well as for toxic substances. It also recommends federal and state environmental policies that affect factories, automobiles, hazardous wastes, and solid-waste disposal. The EPA regulates the manufacture and use of pesticides in the United States; www.epa.gov.

Federal Aviation Administration (FAA). The FAA, part of the Department of Transportation, sets standards for aircraft safety, including aircraft construction and flammability of interior finishes. It also handles complaints about carry-on baggage, airport security, child safety seats, and airplane noise; www.faa.gov.

Federal Communications Commission (FCC). This agency monitors radio and TV programming. The FCC also sets standards for cable TV use and licenses radio stations, TV stations, and communications satellites; www.fcc.gov.

Federal Deposit Insurance Corporation (FDIC). The FDIC provides insurance of bank deposits and handling of complaints about FDIC-insured banks that are not part of the Federal Reserve System; www.fdic.gov.

Federal Emergency Management Agency (FEMA). FEMA's mission is to manage emergency response to any and all national incidents (hurricanes, earthquakes, fires, etc.). In addition, it manages the National Flood Insurance Program and the U.S. Fire Administration. As of 2003, FEMA is part of the U.S. Department of Homeland Security; www.fema.gov.

Federal Reserve System (the "Fed"). The Board of Governors of the Fed handles consumer complaints about state banks and trust companies that are members of the Federal Reserve; www.federalreserve.gov.

Internal Revenue Service (IRS). The IRS is responsible primarily for tax information, tax credits, and tax publications. Most areas have local offices; www.irs.gov.

Nuclear Regulatory Commission (NRC). The Nuclear Regulatory Commission inspects, licenses, and regulates all nuclear energy facilities, thereby ensuring the safety of the use of radioactive materials in the United States; www.nrc.gov.

Occupational Safety and Health Administration (OSHA). This agency is charged with maintaining safety and health in work areas. Workplaces with one or more employees in the private sector must meet OSHA standards. Exceptions include state and municipal employment areas and workplaces covered by other laws (such as mining, atomic energy, railroads); www.osha.gov.

Securities and Exchange Commission (SEC). As an independent agency, the SEC regulates investment companies; oversees the operations of stock exchanges, investment advisors, brokers, and dealers; and sets up regulations preventing fraud in the securities markets. It requires information such as registration statements, annual reports, and proxy-soliciting material from publicly held companies to protect the public and investors from dishonest management, malpractice, and unfair practices. Investors may make complaints to the SEC, which the SEC in turn investigates. It also makes available to the public the information filed by corporations required by its mandate; www.sec.gov.

U.S. Customs and Border Protection (CBP). The primary mission of this agency, now under the Department of Homeland Security, is to protect U.S. borders against terrorism; www.cbp.gov.

U.S. Postal Service. As an independent federal establishment, the U.S. Postal Service is responsible primarily for mail delivery. Local postmasters handle complaints and mail fraud allegations. If the local postmaster is unable to act, the Consumers Advocate of the U.S. Postal Service handles those complaints; www.usps.gov.

Information Dissemination Activities

As was noted in Chapter 15, numerous government information dissemination activities were merged and refined in the early years of the 21st century. The information offered in Chapter 15 is worth repeating here.

usa.gov. Perhaps the most dramatic addition to the federal government's information dissemination program is the development of a single U.S. government website, www.usa.gov. This one-stop Internet site, developed in the year 2000, consolidates thousands of government websites and tens of millions of Web pages into one site.

Econsumer.gov. This site is an international "cross-border" complaint site for consumers who have been defrauded outside of their own country. All participating organizations are members of the International Consumer Protection Enforcement Network.

mymoney.gov. This is a federal government–sponsored site to help consumers better understand money management.

Federal Consumer Information Center (FCIC) a one-stop source for information about federal agencies, programs, and services.

Federal Consumer Information Center. The **Federal Consumer Information Center (FCIC)** was established early in the 21st century as a result of the merger of the Consumer Information Center (CIC) and the Federal Information Center (FIC). The merger combined the CIC website (www.pueblo.gsa.gov), the Consumer Information catalog, and the Pueblo publication distribution program with the FIC nationwide toll-free telephone assistance center. FCIC is a one-stop source for federal agencies, programs, and services.

CONSUMER ACTIVITIES AT THE WHITE HOUSE LEVEL

From 1970 through 1977, legislation was introduced in Congress to establish an independent consumer agency. The agency would have represented consumer interests before all other agencies and in the courts. The rationale for the agency was that special-interest groups from business and labor, through well-financed associations and lobbying groups, were able to promote causes in which they had vested interests. Consumers, however, were not organized and did not have this forceful representation within government or outside it.

Throughout the early and mid-1970s, passage of the legislation was hindered because of lack of support by Presidents Richard Nixon and Gerald Ford. Ford threatened to veto any such legislation. By 1975, pressures were building to limit the expansion of federal bureaucracy, and the consumer agency bill became a main target of this decentralization of government. Members of Congress who had supported the legislation previously now had second thoughts. Business interests, including the U.S. Chamber of Commerce, the National Association of Manufacturers, and the Business Roundtable, worked diligently to defeat the measure. Their efforts were successful. Despite President Jimmy Carter's strong support for it, the House defeated the bill by a five to four margin.

Termination of Office of Consumer Affairs

The Office of Consumer Affairs (OCA) was a federal consumer agency, established in the 1960s, that sponsored National Consumers Week, offered a toll-free helpline for consumers, and provided various other types of assistance to consumers. It was eliminated in 1998. Presumably the OCA efforts have been merged with other federal agencies. Many skeptics, however, believe closure of the OCA represents further silencing of the consumer voice in Washington.

Toxic Toys

CASE STUDY

Shelby Esses knew that her 20-month-old son Jacob was in trouble when he went into a coma. Doctors could not explain the coma, but Shelby was determined to find a cause. Earlier the same day, Jacob had swallowed some Aqua Dots beads. Convinced there was a link, Shelby asked relatives to look on store shelves for Aqua Dots to determine the ingredients on the package. The toy was indeed toxic, with ingredients that, when ingested, metabolized into GHB (also known as the date rape drug).

Esses' actions led to a recall of over 4.2 million sets of Aqua Dots beads. Esses also lobbied Congress to enact tougher safety rules for children's products. She lobbied for stricter testing on toys by independent labs, the posting of phone numbers and websites for parents, among other things. Congress is working on legislation to address these toy safety issues.

QUESTIONS

1. What do you think should be done in this case? Should the mother seek damages from the toy manufacturer?
2. Do you think enough is done to guarantee toy safety in the United States?
3. What might you add to the legislation under consideration?
4. Have you heard of similar issues regarding toy safety in the United States or in other countries?

Source: Based on "Shelby Esses: A mother's intuition exposes a toy hazard," www.consumerreports.org, April 22, 2008. Retrieved April 21, 2009, from http://blogs.consumerreports.org/safety/2008/04/shelby-esses.html.

OTHER LEGISLATION THAT BENEFITS CONSUMERS

The following is a chronological sampling of various consumer protection and related laws passed since 1906 along with a brief summary of their provisions.

Mail Fraud Act (1872). Defrauding consumers through the mails became a federal crime.

Sherman Antitrust Act (1890). This act stated that any contract that restrained interstate trade was in violation of federal law.

Clayton Act (1914). Corporate mergers, interlocking directorates, exclusive contracts, and other devices that lessen competition were deemed illegal.

Communications Act (1934). This act consolidated regulatory control of all media in the Federal Communications Commission and specified that the media must be competitive and must operate primarily for the public's benefit.

Fur Products Labeling Act (1939). Under this law, all fur products sold must state the type of animals from which each was produced.

Wool Products Labeling Act (1939). This act provided that wool products must be labeled clearly by type and by percentage of wool content.

Lanham Trade Mark Act (1946). This act allows the FTC to terminate a trademark if the certification has become a common descriptive name, has been abandoned, or has been used for fraudulent or deceptive purposes.

Flammable Fabrics Act (1953). The law prohibits interstate shipment of fabric products that do not contain flame retardants.

Automobile Information Disclosure Act (1958). Automobile manufacturers are required to post retail prices of all passenger vehicles.

Textile Products Identification Act (1959). All textile products sold must be labeled clearly with their contents.

Federal Hazardous Substance Labeling Act (1960). Any hazardous household chemical must have a warning label.

Wholesome Meat Act (1967). States are required to develop inspection programs for meat products and to eliminate unsanitary conditions in processing plants.

Wholesome Poultry Products Act (1968). States are required to develop inspection programs that meet federal standards for poultry products.

National Environmental Policy Act (1969). A Council on Environmental Quality was established, and the Secretary of the Interior was empowered to conduct investigations relative to the nation's ecological system.

Public Health Cigarette Smoking Act (1969). This act, strengthened by more recent amendments, requires that cigarette labels specifically warn of the danger in cigarette smoking.

Poison Prevention Packaging Act (1970). This law established the need for minimum standards for child-resistant packaging of hazardous products.

McCarran-Ferguson Act (1970). This act provides that activities of insurance companies are subject to federal law if no state law exists in the regulation or taxation of insurance businesses.

Interstate Land Sales Disclosure Act (1979). Land developers are required to file a detailed statement of record with the Department of Housing and Urban Development, and each purchaser of land is required to receive a detailed report on the property to be purchased.

Credit Card Fraud Act (1984). The law increases penalties for unauthorized use of credit cards and similar devices.

Drug Price Competition and Patent Term Restoration Act (1984). This act makes it easier for consumers to obtain inexpensive prescribed drugs and allows drug companies greater patent protection.

Toy Safety Act (1984). This act gives the Consumer Product Safety Commission more authority to recall dangerous toys.

Trademark Counterfeiting Act (1984). The sale or distribution of counterfeit products is a criminal offense under this law.

Veterans Compensation and Program Improvements Amendment (1984). This legislation provides that financing for Veterans Administration (VA) loans must be made available on the same basis as those for other housing.

Amended Wool Products Labeling and Textile Fiber Products Identification Act (1986). This act requires all wool and textile items, domestic and imported, to be labeled with the country of origin.

Hobby Protection Act (1986). Imitation coins, medals, and other monetary items must be marked "copy," and imitation political items must be marked with the year of manufacture.

Smokeless Tobacco Law (1986). Chewing tobacco and other smokeless products must bear health warnings that the product causes mouth cancer and is not a safe alternative to cigarettes.

Textile Wool and Fur Acts (1986). This act protects consumers against mislabeling, false advertising, and false invoicing of textile, wool, and fur products.

Appliance Energy Standards Act (1987). This law requires that most major home appliances adhere to energy conservation standards and disclosures.

Expedited Funds Availability Act (1988). Banks, savings-and-loan companies, and credit unions must make funds available from check deposits within one to five days, depending on the check guideline.

Fair Housing Amendments Act (1988). This act prohibits discrimination in the rental or sale of housing on the basis of physical disability.

Odometer Tampering Law (1988). Automobile odometer tampering now is a felony rather than a misdemeanor. Civil penalties are $2,000, and criminal penalties are three years' imprisonment.

OTHER LEGISLATION THAT BENEFITS CONSUMERS

Omnibus Trade Act (1988). Through this act, the metric system is designated as the preferred system of weights and measurements for U.S. trade and commerce.

Canadian–American Free Trade Agreement (1989). According to this agreement, all tariffs between Canada and the United States must be phased out by 1999.

Credit Card Disclosure Act (1989). This act requires credit card–issuing companies to give specified information regarding the provisions of a credit card contract before the consumer applies for the credit card.

Financial Institutions Reform, Recovery, and Enforcement Act (1989). The act establishes two insurance funds under FDIC purview.

Home Equity Act (1989). This law requires specified disclosures on home equity mortgages and disallows changes in the repayment schedule once an agreement has been completed.

Omnibus Drug Law (1989). All containers of beer, wine, wine coolers, and liquor must contain specified warning labels.

Clean Air Act (1990). This act, completely revising the 1977 law, was intended to reduce smog, reduce toxic chemical use, reduce acid rain, and better protect the ozone layer. The law phased in requirements through the year 2000.

Smoking Ban Act (1990). Smoking is banned on domestic flights of six hours or less.

Telephone Consumer Protection Act (1991). This act bans unsolicited advertising by fax, restricts random machine-generated sales calls, and directs the FCC to develop rules limiting unsolicited calls to consumers who wish to reduce or eliminate them.

Americans with Disabilities Act (1992). This law bans discrimination against the 43 million consumers with disabilities and guarantees equal access to goods and services of all types.

Medicare and Medicap Improvements Act (1992). All states must comply with standards for Medicap Insurance. Specified sales practices are banned, the number of plans that may be offered is limited to 10, and these plans must be standardized.

Truth in Savings Act (1993). This act requires that banking institutions disclose the uniform annual percentage yield (APY) for savings accounts, which allows consumers more easily to compare savings rates offered by various institutions.

Communications Decency Act (1996). This law penalizes persons and providers of any telecommunications facility who transmit indecent or offensive materials to minors.

Telecommunications Act (1996). This act increases competition of cable television, radio, and local and long-distance telephone services. Most cable rates were deregulated by the year 2000.

Federal Food and Drug Administration Act (1997). This legislation offers gravely ill patients easier access to experimental drugs, cuts the time for approval of new drugs substantially, and continues funding for 600 new FDA staff employees.

Deceptive Mail Prevention and Enforcement Act (1999). This act gives the U.S. Post Office new powers to penalize marketers who fail to follow specific guidelines for sweepstakes and "skill" contest mailings.

U.S. Electronic Signatures in Global and National Commerce Act (2000). This act specifies that no contract, signature, or record shall be denied legally binding status just because it is in electronic form.

Patriot Act (2001). This act expands the surveillance and investigative powers of law enforcement agencies in the United States, in the name of anti-terrorism efforts. The Act expands jurisdiction in the areas of personal financial information, student files, credit use, Internet information, wire tapping, and other areas.

Dot Kids Implementation and Efficiency Act (2002). This legislation facilitated the creation of a new Internet domain within the United States country code domain that will be a safe haven on the Internet for material that promotes positive experiences for children and families.

Notification and Federal Employee Antidiscrimination and Retaliation Act (2002). This act reaffirms the existing commitment to assure that federal employees are comfortable reporting incidents of discrimination, wrongdoing, or misconduct.

National Consumer Credit Reporting System Improvement Act (2003). This act requires the FTC to provide a summary of rights for victims of identity theft or fraud and for those disputing information in their credit reports. It also seeks to streamline the reporting of fraud and identity theft among the three major credit reporting agencies.

Fair and Accurate Credit Transactions Act (2003). This act protects both the merchant and the consumer by requiring the truncation of credit card numbers on computer-generated receipts. It also gives consumers the right to a free credit report each year. The law also includes additional anti-fraud protections.

Identity Theft Penalty Enhancement Act (2004). This law established stricter penalties for persons convicted of aggravated identity theft, including a mandatory two-year prison term. If the case is related to terrorism, the prison term is extended.

Notification and Federal Employee Antidiscrimination and Retaliation Act (No FEAR) (2004). This act requires Federal agencies to provide information on discrimination and whistleblowing, offer training to employees and discipline employees who engage in misconduct.

Food Allergen Labeling and Consumer Protection Act (2004). This law requires manufacturers to label foods that contain recognized food allergens.

Cameron Gulbransen Kids Transportation Safety Act (2007). This act directs the USDOT to issue new safety standards to lead to the installation of safety features to prevent deaths and injuries (such as cameras in cars for better vision when backing up).

Children's Gasoline Burn Prevention Act (2008). This act closes a loophole that exempted gas cans from stricter child-resistant packaging for dangerous household materials and products. Previously, gas cans were exempted because they were sold empty (i.e., without gasoline).

Fair Credit Reporting Act

The Fair Credit Reporting Act (FCRA) gives consumers the right to know what information consumer reporting agencies are reporting about them to creditors, insurance companies, and employers.

Ever since World War II, with the exception of a few brief periods, the use of consumer credit has increased. To qualify for credit, most creditors require information about the applicant's history. This information is often obtained from a credit bureau—an agency whose purpose is to accumulate this information and provide it to creditors. Prior to 1970, the consumer's credit file was open only to creditors. Misstatements could appear in the file, and consumers had no way to challenge its accuracy. Many consumers were denied credit as a result of incorrect information.

The Fair Credit Reporting Act of 1970 offers consumers certain remedies. Specifically, the law requires that consumers:

- be told the name and address of the consumer reporting agency responsible for preparing a consumer report that was used to deny them credit, insurance, or employment, or to increase the cost of credit or insurance
- be told the nature, substance, and sources (except medical data) that a consumer reporting agency collects about them
- be able to take anyone with them to the credit bureau to review the file
- obtain this credit information free of charge when the consumer has been denied credit, insurance, or employment, within 30 days of the denial (otherwise, the reporting agency is permitted to charge a reasonable fee for making the disclosure, usually $5 to $10)
- be told who has received a consumer report within the preceding six months (or within the preceding two years if the report was furnished for employment purposes)
- have incomplete or incorrect information reinvestigated and, if the information is found to be inaccurate or cannot be verified, to have the information removed from the file
- have the consumer's version of the dispute placed in the file and included in subsequent consumer reports when a dispute between the consumer and the reporting agency cannot be resolved
- request the agency to send the consumer's version of the dispute to businesses that received the report previously
- have a consumer report withheld from anyone who under the law does not have a legitimate business need for the information
- sue a company for damages if it willfully or negligently violates the law and, if successful, to collect attorney's fees and court costs
- have most adverse information not reported after seven years (one major exception is bankruptcy, which may be reported for 10 years)
- be notified that a company is seeking information that would constitute an "investigative consumer report"
- request from a company that ordered an investigative report further information as to the nature and scope of the investigation
- discover the nature and substance (but not the sources) of the information that was collected for an investigative consumer report; that is, one that notes character, reputation, or mode of living

Amendments to the Fair Credit Reporting Act

In October 1997, major amendments to the Fair Credit Reporting Act became law. The amendments require credit bureaus and other credit reporting agencies to investigate disputed items quickly and thoroughly (within 30 days). These agencies must disclose corrections to the consumer within five days after the investigation.

Credit agencies no longer are allowed to reinsert deleted adverse information, unless the creditor has certified the accuracy of the adverse information and the consumer has been notified of the reinsertion. The credit bureau then must allow the consumer to add an explanatory statement.

Credit reports that consumers request are free to the consumers in numerous specified cases, and a minimal charge is allowed in other cases. Employers now must get written permission from the employee before information is gathered as part of the employment process. The Act increases monetary penalties against creditors who violate the law.

It is in consumers' interest to review the contents of their file periodically to find and correct inaccuracies that might cause problems. The fee usually is less than $20 and may be waived in many cases. Violations of the Fair Credit Reporting Act should be reported to a regional FTC office or to the Federal Trade Commission, Credit Practices Division, Washington, DC 20580.

Other Important Rules

In addition to the rules already noted in this text, others, perhaps of lesser significance, have been passed in recent years. The following is a sample, along with a brief summary of their provisions.

Credit bureau files contain only accurate information. True or false?

False. Unfortunately, your credit report may contain incorrect or obsolete information (it may even include information that reflects someone else's credit and not yours!). You have a right to correct your credit file every year, but credit agencies are not always as responsive as they need to be. Check your credit report every year to prevent long-standing problems.

Octane Posting and Certification Rule (1980). Requires the posting of octane ratings on gasoline dispensers.

R-Value Rule (1980). Requires sellers to disclose the thermal efficiency of home insulation.

Appliance Labeling Rule (1984). Requires the disclosure of energy costs of home appliances.

Negative Option Rule (1985). Requires sellers who use negative option purchase plans, such as book and record clubs, to give members at least 10 days to reject the monthly selection.

Used Car Rule (1986). Requires dealers to post on each used car a "Buyers Guide" that gives information about warranty coverage, explains the meaning of an "as is" sale, and suggests that consumers ask about getting an independent inspection before buying a car.

C.O.D. Rule (1987). Allows consumers the option to pay for C.O.D. packages with a personal check made out to the mailer.

Games of Chance in the Food Retailing and Gasoline Industries Rule (1988). Requires disclosure of the odds of winning prizes, random distribution of winning prize pieces, and publication of winners' names.

Retail Food Advertising and Marketing Practices Rule (1988). Allows grocers to offer rain checks or substitutes for advertised items and, alternatively, permits grocers to issue disclaimers indicating that a specific advertised item is available only in limited quantities.

Odometer Fraud Rule (1989). Requires that states issue automobile titles that are more resistant to counterfeiting and that vehicle mileage be disclosed before an auto is sold.

Optometrists Commercial Practices Rule (1989). Prohibits states from restricting certain activities of optometrists, including limiting the number of branch offices an optometrist may have.

Omnibus Drug Rule (1990). Requires that all containers of beer, wine, wine coolers, and hard liquor contain specified-language warning labels regarding dangers to unborn babies and the hazards of operating motor vehicles while under the influence of alcohol.

Escrow Rules (1995). Requires lenders to disclose escrow account activity for the past year. They must further disclose projected activity for the year ahead. Surplus amounts in accounts in excess of $50 must be sent to the borrower.

Lost Baggage Rules (1995). Increases the penalties for lost baggage from $1,250 to $1,850. Also clarifies record keeping by airlines, as required by DOT, so consumers are better able to compare airline's "on-time" records.

Savings Bonds Rules (1995). Terminated the U.S. Savings Bond interest rate guarantee. Prior to 1995, U.S. Savings Bonds offered a guaranteed minimum of 4 percent interest. Now, market-based rates are in effect. Long-term bonds, those that are held at least five years, now pay 85 percent of the average yield of Treasury securities.

Meat and Poultry Rules (1996). Initiated the first changes in meat inspection regulations in 90 years. Inspectors now are able to use microscopes to detect *E. coli* and salmonella bacteria. Previously, the visual, touch, and smell inspections that were in effect could not detect these deadly organisms.

Banking Rules (1997). Allows banks for the first time to change their out-of-state auxiliary operations to branch offices. This allows banks to expand their operations more easily.

Financial Planning Rules (1997). Gives state agencies the principal authority to oversee financial planners whose assets are less than $25 million. Thus, most planners now are under the scrutiny of state law. Many observers believe state governments will do a better job of oversight than the Securities and Exchange Commission. The SEC, however, continues to regulate financial planners with assets in excess of $25 million.

Auto Leasing Rule (1998). Automobile leasing companies must disclose clearly and unequivocally such provisions in contracts as fees, taxes, and insurance.

Milk Products Rule (1998). Such terms as "fat free," "low fat," and "reduced fat" may not be used interchangeably. Fat free, for example, may only be used to designate skim milk; low fat, 1 percent milk; and reduced fat, 2 percent milk.

The Children's On-line Privacy Protection Rule (2000). Operators of commercial websites that collect personal information from children under 13 years old must follow certain disclosure requirements, including obtaining "verifiable consent" forms from parents before the information is collected.

The Slamming Rule (2000). This rule indicates that if a telephone company switches consumer services without the customer's consent (a practice known as slamming), that company is not entitled to payment for the telephone services rendered.

Telemarketing Sales Rule (2003). This rule amended the 1995 rule of the same name. Specifically, the 2003 rule expanded consumer rights of disclosure on sales calls and made it illegal to call a consumer whose name is on the national do-not-call registry.

Local Number Portability (LNP) (2003). This FCC rule allows customers to switch telephone service providers and keep an existing phone number.

Adult Labeling Rule (2004). This rule makes it illegal for any company to send sexually explicit spam e-mail.

Electronic Stability Control Systems Rule (2007). This rule provides for a comprehensive plan to reduce the risk of death and injury from rollover crashes. An ESC system will be required as a standard feature by 2012.

Energy Independence and Security Act (2007). This act's stated purpose is "to move the United States toward greater *energy independence* and *security;* to increase the production of clean renewable fuels; to protect consumers; to increase the *efficiency* of products, buildings, and vehicles; to promote research on and deploy greenhouse gas capture and storage options; and to improve the energy performance of the federal government." Provisions call for more efficient lightbulbs, funding for alternative fuel research, increased CAFE standards for automobiles, and many others.

Insurer Reporting Requirements (2007). This rule amends a previous rule. Insurers are required to file reports on their motor vehicle theft loss experiences.

SUMMARY

The U.S. marketplace has changed dramatically over the past 230-plus years. This is why Congress has passed, and will continue to pass, consumer protection legislation. Special interest groups try, through lobbying, to influence the decisions of the government regarding consumer protection legislation.

A variety of government agencies have been set up to help protect consumers. Some of the most relevant ones are the Federal Trade Commission, the Food and Drug Administration, the U.S. Department of Agriculture, the Consumer Product Safety Commission, the Department of Transportation, and the Department of Justice.

Many laws and rules have been enacted to protect consumers' best interests. Among the most recent of these address the emerging communications and telecommunications industries.

ITEMS FOR REVIEW & DISCUSSION

1. State how the Federal Trade Commission, Food and Drug Administration, USDA, Consumer Product Safety Commission, and NHTSA protect consumers.
2. Select one of the consumer protection laws noted in this text. State how it could be strengthened to better protect consumer interests.
3. Select one of the rules mentioned in this text and state how it could be strengthened to better protect consumer interests.
4. List the salient features of the Fair Credit Reporting Act.
5. Outline the evolution of federal legislation regarding consumer protection. Do you think federal government involvement with consumer protection will have increased or decreased by the year 2016? Why?
6. Do you think PACs should be eliminated? Why or why not?
7. What are the cost–benefit aspects of federal protection for consumers?
8. What is your opinion of lobbying? Discuss it with your classmates.
9. How do you feel about the fact that consumers must place so much trust in others (in the USDA, for example, that the meat they buy is safe)?
10. Do you think the Food and Drug Administration, the USDA, and other federal agencies are doing a good job of protecting you? Why or why not?

EXPLORING PERSONAL VALUES: PROJECTS

1. Choose a piece of consumer legislation, rule, or federal agency aiding the consumer, and discuss with your classmates the topic of overregulation versus underregulation. Think about things such as the cost of regulation borne by the consumer and the abuses that existed prior to regulation.
2. Do you agree or disagree with the following statements? Discuss your responses with your classmates.
   a. The consumer needs protecting.
   b. The U.S. marketplace can regulate itself.
   c. Even without legislation, business would not discriminate against any group of consumers because it simply is not good business.
3. Interview your local credit bureau manager and determine what problems, if any, the bureau has in complying with the Fair Credit Reporting Act.
4. Write an in-depth report about one of the federal agencies serving consumers.
5. Discuss the role of the FDA with a pharmacist or a food processor, or both, and report the results.
6. Write to one federal agency discussed in this chapter and request material relating to consumer protection and welfare. Also, call the USDA hotline and ask for the

same type of information. Write a report evaluating the materials and information you receive.

7. Interview a retail owner concerning his or her opinion of federal government regulations related to his or her business. Write an analysis of the interview.
8. Write a letter to your senator or representative and try to ascertain what consumer legislation is being considered by Congress, as well as the senator or representative's position on the legislation.
9. Read Upton Sinclair's *The Jungle.* Write a report about it and give a report to the class.
10. Reread your journal. Then trade journals with a classmate and read each other's notes. Come up with a list of "Top 10 Guidelines" that you will use to be a more intelligent consumer. Discuss in small groups the most important things you have learned from this course.

ADDITIONAL SOURCES OF INFORMATION

Felcher, E. Marla. *It's No Accident: How Corporations Sell Dangerous Baby Products.* Monroe, ME: Common Courage Press, 2001.

Hawthorne, Fran. *Inside the FDA: The Business and Politics Behind the Drugs We Take and the Food We Eat.* Hoboken, NJ: John Wiley & Sons, 2005.

Henderson, Gerard Carl. *The Federal Trade Commission: A Study in Administrative Law and Procedure.* Clark, NJ: Lawbook Exchange, 2003.

Hilts, Philip J. *Protecting America's Health: The FDA, Business, and the One Hundred Years of Regulation.* Chapel Hill, NC: University of North Carolina Press, 2004.

Labaree, Robert V. *The Federal Trade Commission: A Guide to Sources.* New York: Garland Publishing, 2000.

National Research Council. *The National Highway Traffic and Safety Administration's Rating System for Rollover Resistance: An Assessment.* Washington, DC: National Academy Press, 2002.

Sinclair, Upton. *The Jungle.* New York: Doubleday, 1906.

Smith, Mark A. *American Business and Political Power: Public Opinion, Elections, and Democracy.* Chicago: University of Chicago Press, 2000.

Glossary

Acid rain The combination of toxic chemicals harmful to living beings and plant life created by various forms of industrial air pollution.

Actuary An employee of an insurance company who specializes in computing risks and developing premium rates based on those risks.

Adjustable-rate mortgage (ARM) A loan offered by a lending institution, with rates of interest and perhaps other terms that often change after a stated period of months or years.

Advertising Any paid form of nonpersonal presentation and promotion of ideas, goods, or services by an identified sponsor.

Advertising Council A private, nonprofit organization supported by business and advertising firms whose purpose is to conduct advertising campaigns on non-controversial programs in national problem areas.

Affluenza An unfulfilled feeling that results from efforts to keep up with the rest of society; an epidemic of stress, overwork, waste, and indebtedness caused by consumers' pursuit of the American dream.

Annuity Investment in which a person gives a company, an investment firm, or a college or charitable organization a sum of money and receives in return a regular income for a specified time (usually life).

Anticipated expenditures The total amount of financial obligations an individual or family expects to incur within a specified period.

Anticipated income The total amount of financial resources an individual or family expects to obtain within a specified period.

Antitrust Laws and regulations to protect trade and commerce from unlawful restraints.

Antitrust violations Practices that involve unlawful restraint of trade.

Arbitration panel A group whose function is to attempt to resolve complaints between buyer and seller, and whose decisions usually are binding on one or both parties.

Assets The value of owned items, stated in dollars.

Assimilation The process whereby an immigrant group gradually adopts the characteristics of the new culture.

Assumption of mortgage A process in which the buyer accepts the terms of the seller's mortgage, usually after negotiation with the lender.

Back date The date on which the product was manufactured, processed, or packaged.

Bait-and-switch A tactic whereby a product or service is advertised at a low price (bait), but when the consumer offers to buy, the merchant deprecates the product or service and recommends a higher-priced product or service (switch).

Bargaining Negotiating the terms of a contract, agreement, or purchase.

Basal metabolic rate (BMR) The amount of energy needed to maintain the continuing processes of life.

Beneficiary A person named in an insurance policy who is to receive death benefits.

Bequest An individual's request in his or her will to leave to certain survivors the assets remaining in the estate.

Binding arbitration Informal proceedings in which an impartial third party receives evidence concerning a complaint and then renders a decision based on the information given.

Biodegradable Property of a material that results in decomposition naturally by biological processes.

Blend Mortgage combining an existing loan with a new loan.

Bond A written promise to pay a certain sum of money on or before a specified date, with interest at an agreed rate.

Boom A period of rapid business growth.

Brand the dimension of the trademark that represents the associations a consumer affiliates with the trademark.

Brokerage fee The commission paid to a person in the business of securities for bringing about transactions.

Budgeting Planning for the coordination of income and expenditures.

Built-in obsolescence Deliberate underengineering of a product to give it an unnecessarily short life span so as to require premature replacement.

Bushing A deceptive sales practice whereby the salesperson adds unordered products or services to the final price.

Buy-down A process used to reduce the overall interest rate of a mortgage; usually the amount of the difference is paid by a builder of a new home or owner of an existing home.

Callable bond A type of bond that must be retired by the investor when called for by the issuer.

Calorie The amount of heat required to raise the temperature of a gram of water one degree centigrade.

Capital gain The difference between the sale price of property and the original cost plus expenses for buying and selling.

Carbon footprint The total greenhouse gases directly and indirectly produced by an entity.

Caveat emptor Literally, "let the buyer beware"; a principle in commerce making the buyer responsible for determining quality.

Caveat venditor Literally, "let the seller beware"; a principle in commerce implying that consumers are on alert and will not tolerate poor quality.

Cease-and-desist An order by an enforcement agency requiring the seller to discontinue a specific action that may be in violation of law.

Ceremony A formal series of acts prescribed by ritual, protocol, or convention.

Certificate of Deposit An insured investment plan that pays interest at a specified maturity date.

Chartered life underwriter (CLU) A specialist trained in life insurance who has completed a broad range of college-level subjects and passed rigorous professional examinations administered by the American College of Life Underwriters.

Chattel mortgage The type of debt for which the creditor holds the title of the goods or home until the debt is paid.

Chlorofluorocarbons (CFCs) Synthetic chemical substances consisting of chlorine, fluorine, and carbon with various household applications.

Churning A tactic used by unscrupulous stockbrokers whereby investors are told to buy and sell frequently; the intent is to increase commissions for the brokers.

Civil penalties Court proceeding that allows private individuals or groups to recover money to enforce a law or to prevent a wrongdoing.

Class actions Court proceeding that allows similarly aggrieved consumers to act as one.

Closed-end investment company Mutual fund company that does not issue new shares in the company until the original issue has been sold.

Closing costs Various expenses, in addition to the sale price of the property, incurred when buying and selling real estate.

Code dating A statement on a package indicating to the merchant the last day the product should be sold.

Collective consumption Expenditures for public needs such as education, highways, and police.

Commercial bank A state or federally licensed organization that makes fairly competitive loans for a variety of consumer goods.

Commission-only financial planner Specialist who offers free services to clients and is paid through the commission earned on investments recommended.

Competitive consumption Consumers' irrational desire to compete with one another to prove financial superiority by paying higher prices.

Condominium A housing situation in which an individual holds ownership of an apartment in a multiunit project and a proportionate interest in the common areas outside of the apartment.

Consent order An agreement between an enforcement agency and a merchant requiring the merchant to stop a specific action.

Conspicuous consumption Spending and consuming on a lavish scale.

Consumer credit The money or purchasing power that lending institutions grant to individuals.

Consumer finance company A state-licensed company that makes installment cash loans to customers.

Consumer Fraud Act A state law that pertains to all forms of fraudulent, deceptive, and sometimes unfair acts and practices in trade and commerce.

Consumer Leasing Act (CLA) An act requiring lessors to give consumers specific information on lease costs and terms.

Consumer life cycle Stages in the average person's life that present varying sets of conditions affecting the person's needs and ability to meet those needs.

Consumer Product Safety Commission (CPSC) A federal agency whose basic responsibility is to protect consumers against injuries associated with many consumer products.

Consumer sovereignty Literally, "the consumer is king"; the idea that satisfying the consumer's need is the only important function of an economy.

Consumption The use of a good or service.

Consumption pattern The extent to which goods and services are used up.

Contingency fee A legal fee determined on a percentage basis. The attorney receives a predetermined portion of the amount of money awarded to the client. If the client receives no award, the attorney also receives no payment for his or her services. The client must still pay expenses, filing fees, and so on.

Continuous market A market with sufficient activity that a normal-size sale can be made at any time without affecting the current market price.

Conventional real estate loan A loan obtained at a bank or other lending institution that does not involve federal or state subsidies.

Convertible bond A bond that may be exchanged for other bonds, stocks, or other securities.

Cooperative apartment A housing situation in which the dweller buys a share in a corporation that owns the building, and then leases an individual unit.

Corporate average fuel economy (CAFE) The average miles per gallon the federal government allows for all of a specific manufacturer's fleet of automobiles.

Corporate bond A promise by a company to pay a stated sum of money on or before a specified date with interest at an agreed rate.

Credence good A good or service whose quality characteristics consumers cannot assess before, during, or even after the purchase.

Credit life insurance Insurance that covers the unpaid balance of a loan in the event of the borrower's death.

Credit Practices Rule Provision prohibiting certain security interests and collection remedies in consumer credit contracts.

Credit status An investment represented by loans.

Credit union A cooperative agency organized by consumers for the purpose of saving and borrowing at competitive rates.

Cremation Reduction of a dead body to ashes by fire.

Culture Learned patterns of behavior and symbolism passed on in a society from one generation to another.

Custodial care Services generally including room and board but minimal assistance for personal living and health needs.

Custom The tendency on the part of a group to consume according to a fixed pattern.

Debenture A bond that is unsecured; the only assurance of repayment is the company's earning power.

Debt consolidation Combining several debts into one loan to reduce monthly payments.

Deception Perversion of truth, most often—but not necessarily—intentional, whereby a person, having been misled, parts with something of value for something of little or no value.

Deceptive Trade Practices Act A consumer protection state law itemizing deceptive practices, usually with a catch-all clause to reach other forms of deception.

Defendant The person required to answer a lawsuit.

Demand The amount of a product or service that will be purchased at a specific price.

Demand schedule A series of amounts of a product or service that will be purchased at a series of prices at a given time in a given market.

Department of Justice A federal agency with the authority to enforce antitrust laws and assure compliance in the marketplace.

Diminishing marginal utility A concept signifying that as more of a given product is consumed, per-unit satisfaction of the product declines.

Discretionary income That portion of disposable income remaining after paying basic necessities.

Disposable personal income The amount of income left after deducting personal taxes from personal income.

Diversification Spreading one's money among a variety of investments to gain security of principal and stability of income.

Dollar-cost averaging The practice of regularly investing a fixed dollar amount over a period of time to avoid a one-time fixed large investment.

Double-dipping A legal but questionable sales tactic whereby the buyer, with little or no down payment, is required to acquire two loans—one from a bank at a reasonable interest rate and one from a loan company at a high interest rate.

Dow Jones Industrial Average Average of stock prices of 30 representative industrial companies.

Dunning Another term for debt collection. The act of seeking to collect a debt; a request for payment.

Duopoly A market situation in which two sellers dominate a specific market industry.

Durable goods Items that are consumed over a long period of time, usually at least one year.

Economic adult A rational and informed consumer, regardless of age.

Economic freedom The implied right of consumers to choose the goods and services they want.

Economic minor An irrational and uninformed consumer, regardless of age.

Elasticity of demand A rise in demand for a product or service in proportion to reduction in its price, leading to a rise in total sales revenues.

Endowment insurance Insurance that pays the insured's beneficiaries if the insured dies prematurely and also the insured if he or she lives beyond the term of the contract.

Equal Credit Opportunity Act Legislation prohibiting any creditor from denying credit to a consumer on the basis of gender, marital status, color, race, religion, national origin, age, or receipt of public assistance.

Equipment trust certificate A provision securing a bond with assets of substantial and immediate resale value.

Exchange transaction A transaction in which the buyer sells money and buys merchandise and the seller sells merchandise and buys money.

Expiration date The date after which a product should not be used.

Express warranty A written promise that a product will perform in a specified manner.

Eyeglass Rule A government provision requiring eye doctors to make available to patients their eyeglass prescriptions, at no extra cost, immediately after an eye exam.

Fad The accepted manner in which a group of people behaves for a brief time period.

Fair Credit Billing Act Legislation establishing procedures for resolving mistakes in credit card accounts.

Fair Credit Reporting Act Legislation giving consumers the right to know what information consumer reporting agencies are reporting about them to creditors, insurance companies, and employers.

Fair Debt Collection Practices Act (FDCPA) Legislation prohibiting debt collectors from engaging in unfair, deceptive, or abusive practices, including overcharging, harassment, and disclosing consumers' debts to third parties.

Fair Packaging and Labeling Act (FPLA) Legislation requiring that consumer commodities be accurately labeled to describe the product's identity and net quantity.

Fair Trade Laws Legislation allowing manufacturers legally to fix prices by requiring retailers to charge a specified price for products supplied.

Fashion The accepted manner in which a group of people behaves at a given time.

Federal Bankruptcy Act Legislation allowing the debtor to eliminate responsibility for most debts and to protect specified assets.

Federal Consumer Information Center A one-stop source for information about federal agencies, programs, and services. A combination of the former Consumer Information Center and the Federal Information Center.

Federal Trade Commission (FTC) An agency whose basic responsibility is to help consumers find needed information or locate the appropriate agency to assist them with their problems.

Fee-and-commission financial planners Those who charge the client a fee and also are paid commissions on the investments they recommend.

Fee-only financial planners Those who charge the client a fee for recommending an investment plan.

Fee splitting A payment made from one physician to another for referral of a patient.

FHA loan A type of mortgage that is insured by the Federal Housing Administration against losses from default.

FICO score A score (a number between 300 and 850) that helps lenders predict, based on an individual's credit history, the type of borrower he or she will be.

Finance company A state-licensed institution that makes high-interest installment loans to customers for a variety of goods.

Financial counselor A professional whose main function is to attempt to reduce a client's debt.

Financial planner A professional whose main objective is to manage a client's assets.

Fiscal policy One of the tools government uses to achieve economic goals through its power to tax and spend.

Fixed-rate mortgage A mortgage offered by a lending institution, with a specified rate of interest for a specified number of years.

Flat-rate book A publication listing the suggested time that a specific auto repair should take; the mechanic simply multiplies that time by the hourly wage to determine the total cost of the repair.

Food and Drug Administration (FDA) A federal agency whose basic responsibility is to assure the safety and efficacy of food, drugs, and cosmetics.

Foreclosure The act by which a lender may force the sale of a property for reason of default of payment.

Fraud Intentional perversion of truth in order to induce another person to part with something of value.

Free entry (or the freedom to enter or supply) The implied right of any individual to enter a business or profession and to choose or to reject a job.

Freshness date The time after which a product will not be of optimum quality.

Full information The implied right of any individual to obtain essential data in order to make intelligent choices in the market.

Full warranty A guarantee that a product will perform in a specific manner, and if not, the consumer is entitled to have it repaired, generally without charge.

Garnishment A legal proceeding whereby a creditor secures a court order directing the debtor's employer to withhold wages for the debtor-employee, and to pay the withheld funds to the creditor.

Global warming Increase in the average temperature of the earth's atmosphere.

Goodwill The advantage in the way of custom that a business has acquired beyond the value of what it sells.

Greenhouse effect The belief that polluting gases are trapping solar heat in the lower atmosphere and thereby increasing the earth's temperature.

Gross domestic product (GDP) The total value of goods and services produced for consumers within the borders of the United States.

Gross national product (GNP) The total value of goods and services an economy produces in a given year.

Habit An individual's tendency to consume in a fixed pattern.

Harmonious consumption The tendency to purchase combinations of things, such as matching clothes and accessories.

Health maintenance organization (HMO) A group that provides comprehensive health care services for its members for a fixed fee.

Hedge An attempt to offset losses by selecting investments whose values are expected to keep pace with inflation.

High-balling A deceptive sales practice whereby the salesperson offers a high trade-in price in order to sell an artificially high-priced product or service.

Home equity loan A loan, often a second mortgage, the proceeds of which are used for home improvements or other purposes.

Home Owners Warranty (HOW) A plan that offers a guarantee of a newly purchased home against the costs of defects in materials and workmanship.

Hourly fee Fees calculated based on the actual amount of time expended.

Iceberg research Studies on specific products that reveal only the results that are favorable to the advertiser.

Identity theft The use of an individual's personal information, without his or her knowledge, to commit fraud or other crimes.

Ignorant consumer standard A guideline based on the assumption that even consumers who are ignorant, careless, and wasteful should be protected by law.

Illth Goods and services that harm the consumer.

Implied warranty A promise that a product is of average salable quality.

Incentives Money, bonuses, or special consideration during performance reviews received by dealership personnel for selling additional products such as service contracts.

Income bond A type of bond with an unstated interest rate that is paid only if the company is profitable.

Indemnity The legal limits of an insurance policy.

Individual retirement account (IRA) A tax-deferred program designed for employees who have no other eligible tax-deferred program and whose income does not exceed specified limits.

Indoor air pollution Any manmade or natural contamination that adversely affects the health of living organisms.

Inelasticity of demand An insufficient rise in demand for a product or service in relation to a reduction in its price, leading to a decline in total sales revenues.

Information overload Having too much information to make a decision about a topic or difficulty identifying what information is relevant to the decision.

Informational advertising A type of advertising that offers valuable data about products or services to be sold.

Injunction A court order requiring the performance or restraint of performance by the wrongdoer.

Installment buying The purchasing of a good or service in which the debt is paid in specified amounts over a specified period.

Insurable interest The requirement that in order to obtain insurance the beneficiary of the contract must suffer a financial loss.

Insurance A mechanism used to protect against financial loss.

Insured (also called the policyholder) The individual or group for whom risk is assumed.

Insurer (also called the insurance company) The profit-making corporation that assumes the risk of financial loss.

Intermediate care Services that generally include room and board and more extensive but rather minimal personal living and health care services.

Investment The purchase of property or claims to property that will yield income, capital gain, or both.

Irregulars Products that have minor flaws.

Jumbo loan A loan that has a mortgage amount exceeding maximum mortgage limits set by Government Sponsored Enterprises (Fannie Mae and Freddie Mac). Interest rates on jumbo mortgages are typically between 1/4 percent and 5/8 percent higher than those on conforming mortgages.

Keogh Plan A retirement tax-deferred program for self-employed individuals.

Large-scale fraud Practices by businesses and industries that extract billions of dollars from consumers for questionable return.

Law of diminishing returns The principle holding that after a given time, increasing labor and capital combined with a fixed amount of land will produce progressively smaller yields.

Level of living The actual quality and quantity of goods and services experienced by individuals and society.

Leverage A strategy of investing that involves borrowing in order to possess a large amount of property.

Levy A judgment creditor's record of attachment on personal property. Levies can be made on bank accounts, safe deposit boxes, and real and personal property. The creditor is paid from proceeds of the sale of the property.

Liabilities The financial obligations (or debts) for which an individual or a family is responsible.

Lien A notice attached to property (usually a house) creating a record that a creditor claims money is owed. Most liens need to be resolved before the property can be sold and the title can be transferred. Liens can be posted for property taxes, IRS payments, and child support.

Life insurance policy Insurance that pays the beneficiary a specified sum of money when the insured dies.

Limited warranty A promise that a product is of a specified quality and will perform satisfactorily for what is considered the life of the product.

Liquid assets Resources that can be converted quickly to cash.

Liquidity The ability to quickly, and without loss or penalty, convert an investment to cash.

Little FTC Act A consumer protection state law declaring that unfair methods of competition and unfair or deceptive acts or practices in trade or commerce are illegal.

Load fund A mutual fund that charges a fee to purchase its shares.

Loan origination fee An amount a lender charges for locating and processing a mortgage.

Loss leader pricing The practice of pricing some products so low that the store makes no profit on those items.

Low-balling A deceptive sales practice whereby the salesperson offers an unrealistic price for a good or service that will not be honored when the customer returns.

Magnuson-Moss Warranty Act Legislation requiring that warranty information be made available to consumers before they make a purchase, and that if a warranty is offered, it must be either a full or a limited warranty, and it must be clearly stated.

Margin A percentage amount that a lending institution adds to the index to cover the cost of processing the loan and the profits.

Marginal tax bracket That percentage of taxes paid on the top dollar's worth of taxable income.

Market The place where the forces representing demand and supply meet.

Marketability The ability to dispose of an asset for money at whatever price may be attainable.

Marketing The process of moving goods and services from producer to consumer by influencing sales through changing stimulus conditions.

Market segmentation A marketing practice in which sellers attempt to modify their products so they will appeal to a specified group.

Material measure A synonym for standard of living.

Mechanic's lien A claim that one person has upon the property of another, often for unpaid bills due the claimant for work performed.

Mediation panel A group whose function is to attempt to resolve complaints between buyer and seller but whose decision carries no force of law and thus is nonbinding.

Medicaid State public assistance programs to persons, regardless of age, whose financial resources are insufficient to pay for health care.

Medicaid residents Older persons who qualify for Medicaid assistance in assisted living facilities because their total assets do not exceed state minimums.

Medicare A federally funded health care insurance program for older persons and persons with disabilities.

Memorial societies Cooperative programs providing simple, dignified funerals at low cost.

Monetary policy Measures to achieve economic goals by regulating the supply of money and credit through the Federal Reserve System.

Money income The amount of pay one receives.

Money management The prudent handling of income and expenditures.

Money market funds Uninsured investments that typically pay higher rates than passbook savings accounts and in which the investment company uses the proceeds to purchase other securities.

Monopolistic competition A situation in which there are numerous sellers of similar or identical products and services.

Monopoly A situation in which one seller controls the supply of a product or service.

Mortgage A legal instrument that gives a lender conditional title to a property.

Mortgage bond A bond that is secured by property.

Mortgagee The lender of money under terms dictated by a contract with a mortgagor.

Mortgagor The borrower who has agreed to repay a loan under terms dictated by a contract with a mortgagee.

Mutual funds Investments organized by promoters for the purpose of selling shares to investors, investing in securities, and then managing the funds.

National Advertising Review Board (NARB) An industry-sponsored organization that attempts through mediation to attain high standards for national advertising.

National Highway Traffic and Safety Administration (NHTSA) A federal agency, part of the Department of Transportation, working to reduce highway deaths, injuries, and property losses.

National income The net national product minus indirect business taxes.

Natural monopoly A situation in which government edict creates one seller because competition would be wasteful as a result of duplication of resources.

Nealth Goods and services that have a neutral effect, neither helping nor harming the consumer.

Negative economic freedom of choice Lack of the purchasing power to implement the right to consume anything an individual wishes.

Net national product The gross national product minus depreciation.

Net worth The difference between one's total assets and total liabilities.

No-fault insurance A type of auto insurance that pays the claims of the injured regardless of who is responsible for the accident.

No-load fund A mutual fund that does not charge a fee for buying or selling its shares.

Nonliquid assets Resources that cannot be converted to cash quickly.

Objective exchange value The power of a product or service to command other products or services in return.

Obsolescence of quality A substantial improvement in a product that causes prior versions to be obsolete.

Oligopoly A situation in which few sellers (usually four or fewer) control the majority of a supply or service produced.

One-price system A system of pricing whereby once a price is determined for a good or service, that price will not be negotiable.

One-sided contract An agreement that obviously favors one of the two parties involved.

Open dating A statement on a package indicating the last date on which the product should be sold or used.

Open-end investment companies Mutual fund companies that guarantee to repurchase shares at any time at their net asset price.

Ophthalmologists Physicians who specialize in diagnosing and treating eye diseases; they prescribe drugs, perform examinations and eye surgery, and also may provide eyeglasses and contact lenses.

Opticians Eye care professionals who take measurements and design, verify, and deliver vision aids upon prescriptions written by ophthalmologists or optometrists.

Optometrists Eye care professionals who are not physicians but have doctor of optometry degrees in eye care.

Outsourcing Paying another company to provide services that a company might otherwise have employed its own staff to perform.

Owner financing loan A mortgage in which the seller of the home participates.

Ozone layer A thin gas in the upper atmosphere; it screens the sun's ultraviolet rays.

Packing Adding extra charges, such as exorbitant preparation fees, to the price of an automobile in order to raise the price paid.

Par The stated or face value of a security.

Paralegal A person trained in law who can legally perform specific tasks under the direction of a practicing attorney; allowable tasks are diverse and dependent upon individual state mandates.

Pawnbroker A group or an individual who lends money at high interest rates in return for a pledge to offer goods as collateral.

Pecuniary power Monetary and financial well-being.

Penny stocks Stocks usually bought by amateur investors at prices ranging from 1 cent to $1.

Per capita disposable income Total disposable personal income divided by current total population figures.

Perfect competition A market situation containing so many knowledgeable sellers and so many knowledgeable buyers that the action or inaction of one or a few cannot have any noticeable effect on market price.

Personal income The total of wages, rent, interest, dividends, transfer payments, and unincorporated net income.

Phishing Obtaining, by unscrupulous means, sensitive information about a person by posing as someone trustworthy with a true need for the information.

Plaintiff The initiator of a lawsuit.

Planned obsolescence The superficial redesign of a product for sales purposes only.

Points Charges equal to a stated percentage of a loan.

Portfolio All the securities and related assets an investor owns.

Positive economic freedom of choice The right to consume anything one wishes along with the purchasing power necessary to implement that right.

Premium The payment for insurance coverage.

Pre-need contract An agreement between a consumer and a funeral director in which a specified amount is set in advance for the consumer's own funeral.

Prepayment penalty An amount the buyer pays to a lending institution for the privilege of paying off a mortgage loan before it is due.

Price-fixing When businesses conspire to set prices higher than they would be if normal competition were at play.

Principle of diminishing utility A concept holding that as consumption increases for a specific product or service, the per-unit power of the product to satisfy a human want decreases.

Principle of probability Information insurance companies use to calculate the amount of money necessary to yield the amount needed to reimburse claimants.

Principle of variety in consumption The suggestion that consumers prefer to spread their purchases over a wide range of products to increase the satisfactions they gain.

Printer's Ink A model law—drafted in 1911 by an advertising trade journal of the same name—that made false advertising a serious offense.

Private action A court proceeding that allows the consumer to file a lawsuit for violation of consumer protection laws.

Private-pay resident A consumer who does not need government assistance to help pay for assisted living expenses.

Progressive tax A tax that requires a larger fraction of income as that income increases.

Promulgation of trade rules and regulations Agency establishment of legal guidelines that carry the full force of law.

Proportional tax A tax that requires the same fraction of income from taxpayers of all income levels; some income taxes at the state level require a specific percentage to be paid by all.

Proprietor status An investment represented by ownership.

Psychic income The satisfaction gained in consuming the goods and services purchased with one's income.

Puffery A claim that is so obviously false that the advertiser does not expect consumers to believe it but uses it with the hope that they will buy the product anyway.

Pull date The date after which a product should not be offered for sale.

Push money (P.M.) Also known as "spiff," the amount offered to a commissioned salesperson above the regular payment for selling a specific brand or product.

Pyramid franchising scheme The granting, on the condition that an investment be made, of a license or right to recruit for additional investment one or more additional persons who also are granted this license to recruit others.

Quackery Making a lot of noise about nothing. For example, blatant self-promotion of a "miracle cure."

Quota A limitation on the number of products permitted to be imported.

Radon A colorless, odorless gas emitted naturally through the earth, which increases the likelihood of cancer and other diseases in humans.

Real Estate Settlement Procedures Act (RESPA) Legislation requiring that lending institutions disclose closing and settlement costs prior to the exchange (sale) of a property.

Real income Monetary intake determined by the amount of goods and services one's income will buy.

Reasonable consumer standard A guideline based on the assumption that government should protect consumers but also that consumers have the responsibility to be informed and rational.

Recession A period of general decline in business.

Reference group A group that influences an individual's attitudes or behavior.

Referral selling An attempt, often illegal, by a sales person to get the consumer to buy a product by offering an incentive for every person the consumer recommends to buy the product too.

Regressive tax A tax requiring a smaller fraction of income as that income increases; a sales tax is an example of a regressive tax, when the tax is measured against what is spent.

Regulatory agencies Government organizations that enforce various laws and rules.

Resistance lane A high-pressure sales tactic many funeral directors use to persuade a buyer to purchase a higher-priced funeral.

Restitution Restoration by the court of both parties to where each was prior to the initiation of a contract.

Rip-offs Goods and services that are not in the best interests of consumers.

Rule of 78 The most common method in determining amounts to be rebated to debtors if they repay loans early.

R-value The "resistance" measure or capacity of insulation to resist the flow of heat from a warm room to the cold outside.

Satiety A principle of consumption denoting the desire to obtain an unlimited amount of goods and services.

Seconds Products that have major flaws.

Self-regulation An industry's minimum standards of conduct for itself.

Serial Bond A type of bond that is retired in installments at times indicated on the bond.

Series EE Bond A U. S. bond that is issued at a discount and has a variable rate with a guaranteed minimum rate.

Series HH Bond A U. S. bond that is sold at a specified amount at a specified interest rate.

Series I Bond A U. S. bond that is sold in specified amounts at face value.

Service The offering of intangible assistance that a consumer requires.

Shopping bots Software programs that find the cheapest prices for products offered on the Internet.

Sinking-fund bond A bond providing that periodically amounts of earnings be set aside and applied toward the bond's retirement.

Skilled nursing care Services that generally include room-and-board and extensive personal living and health care.

Small-claims court A legal mechanism available in all states to solve legal problems involving small sums of money, usually $2,000 or less.

Social insurance Insurance that requires all the members of a group to participate (e.g., Social Security).

Spamming Sending unsolicited e-mail in bulk.

Specific job fee (or "flat fee") A legal fee of a predetermined amount, usually involving a simple legal service.

Speculation Investment in property or claims to property whereby the speculator seeks to increase the return by accepting additional risks.

SPIF (sales promotion incentive fund) Additional incentive money provided to salespersons working on commission; also written *spiff.*

Standard of living The quality or quantity of goods and services consumed or aspired to by individuals or societies.

Stocks Certificates representing partial ownership and control of the corporations that issue them.

Style A permanent, distinctive expression in some field of human endeavor, such as matching clothes and accessories.

Tariff A tax assessed on imported goods.

Taste The ability to discern and appreciate that which is appropriate.

Tax expenditures Deductions and expenditures that lower actual taxes due; also called tax loopholes.

Telemarketing scheme Use of the telephone to deceptively sell a wide range of products and services.

Television code A code voluntarily subscribed to, enumerating specific minimum standards in programming and advertising.

Term insurance policy Insurance against a stated risk for a specified time (e.g., one year).

Testimonial advertising Endorsement of a product or service by a recognized person, such as a television star.

Third-party debt collector A company or individual hired as an outside agent (not an employee) to collect a debt.

Title insurance Insurance that protects a lender, a new home owner, or both against loss of their interest in the property due to legal defects in the title.

Trade (or industry) association An organization developed by businesses whose members agree to abide by established standards or practices and codes of ethics.

Trademark a legal term for a name, symbol, design, device or any combination thereof, adopted and used by a manufacturer or merchant to identify its goods and distinguish them from those manufactured or sold by others. The trademark can be registered and become an exclusive legal right for its owner.

Trade regulations Rules developed by state and federal agencies that define and prohibit various industry activities.

Treasury bills Short-term U. S. government debts that are typically sold in large denominations and mature within three months to one year.

Treasury bonds Long-term U. S. government debts that are sold in denominations of $1,000 or more and typically mature in 10 years or more (no longer available).

Treasury notes Intermediate-term U. S. government debts that are sold in fairly large denominations and typically mature in one to 10 years.

Truth-in-Lending Act Legislation requiring creditors to disclose in writing certain cost information, such as the annual percentage rate (APR), before consumers enter into credit transactions.

Underwriters Laboratories (UL) A nonprofit organization established to investigate materials, devices, products, equipment, construction methods, and systems with respect to hazards affecting life and property.

Uniform Consumer Sales Practices Act A consumer protection state law that is similar to the Deceptive Trade Practices Act but extends to unconscionable consumer sales practices.

Unit pricing Setting prices of given items by the pound, ounce, quart, or other standard measure.

Universal life insurance Life insurance that combines death benefits with a savings/investment program.

U. S. Department of Agriculture (USDA) A federal agency, one of whose major responsibilities is to assure consumers that food will be safe, clean, nutritious, and attractive.

Usury laws Mandates, usually set by state law, limiting the rates of interest lenders may charge on loans.

Utility The power of an economic product or service to satisfy a human want.

VA loan A type of mortgage insured by the Department of Veterans Affairs against losses from default.

Values Individual or collective beliefs and ideas about what is desirable.

Variable interest bond A typically long-term bond yielding interest rates that vary with changes in short-term rates.

Variable life insurance A policy that combines death benefits with an investment program that is selected by the policyholder.

Variable pricing Marking down the prices of some items and raising the prices of other items.

Variety A principle of consumption describing the desire to accumulate different kinds of goods.

Warrantor The manufacturer or retailer who assures the quality of a specific good or service.

Warranty (or guarantee) An assurance of the quality of a specific good or service.

Wealth Goods and services that promote the well-being of consumers.

Whole life insurance Insurance on which a lump sum benefit is paid upon the death of the policyholder and which usually offers a low-interest–bearing savings program but at a higher premium than for group term life insurance.

Word-of-mouth advertising The type of advertising in which consumers talk among themselves regarding the merits of a specific product.

Yield The actual rate of return earned by an investment.

Zero-coupon bond A bond that pays no interest and is heavily discounted at the time of sale.

Index